China's Future
Nuclear Submarine Force

China's Future Nuclear Submarine Force

Edited by Andrew S. Erickson, Lyle J. Goldstein,
William S. Murray, and Andrew R. Wilson

PUBLISHED IN COOPERATION WITH
THE CHINA MARITIME STUDIES INSTITUTE

NAVAL INSTITUTE PRESS
Annapolis, Maryland

Note: The views represented in this book are those of the authors themselves and do not represent the official policies or assessments of the U.S. Navy or any other U.S. government agency.

Naval Institute Press
291 Wood Road
Annapolis, MD 21402

LIBRARY OF CONGRESS CATALOGING-IN-PUBLICATION DATA
China's future nuclear submarine force / edited by Andrew S. Erickson . . . [et al.].
    p. cm.
  Includes bibliographical references and index.
  ISBN-13: 978-1-59114-326-0 (alk. paper)
  ISBN-10: 1-59114-326-8 (alk. paper)
  1. Nuclear submarines—China.   2. Sea-power—China.   3. China—Military policy—21st century.   I. Erickson, Andrew S.
V859.C6C55 2007
359.9'30951—dc22

                                                          2006039757

Printed in the United States of America on acid-free paper ∞

14   13   12   11   10   09   08   07   9   8   7   6   5   4   3   2
First printing

This volume is dedicated to the memory of Capt. Robert G. Lowenthal, USN (Ret.), a wonderful gentleman, respected submariner, esteemed colleague, and valued friend.

Contents

Andrew S. Erickson, Lyle J. Goldstein,
William S. Murray, and Andrew R. Wilson

Introduction

AS THE FIRST DECADE OF THE TWENTY-FIRST CENTURY draws to a close, it has become increasingly clear that the emergence of China is not a passing fad, and that China is not merely a regional power completely pre-occupied with internal problems. Instead, China's growing confidence and influence around the globe, from Kazakhstan to Canada to Brazil to Zimbabwe, becomes ever more apparent. China's emergence as a global power need not be interpreted as an inherently destabilizing factor in the future international security environment, not least because of its extensive role in trading with developing states around the world. But there is an increasing need for sober assessments of China's developing military capabilities. Such objective analyses will enable responses to Beijing's new posture that are measured and deliberate, rather than reflexive and frenetic—and thus potentially wasteful or even provocative.

It is natural that China's naval modernization has been of acute interest to defense analysts recently. What makes the accelerating pace of Chinese development so fascinating is that China has not been a first-rate naval power since the fifteenth century. Indeed, during the intervening six hundred years China has witnessed more than its share of spectacular naval failures (particularly in the nineteenth century), and even more acutely, military debacles caused in part by China's fundamental weakness on its maritime flank. China's turn to the sea is not only consistent with firm intellectual foundations put in place by Deng Xiaoping's insistence that China open up to the world, but also represents a fundamentally new and unprecedented development in modern world politics.

It is now widely recognized that submarines are the centerpiece of China's current naval strategy. Though this could change in future decades, this approach contrasts markedly with the power-projection navies, most notably the United States Navy but also the Indian navy, which are organized above all around aircraft carriers. To grasp the energy that China is now committing to undersea warfare, consider that during 2002–04 China's navy launched thirteen submarines,[1] while simultaneously undertaking the purchase of submarines from Russia on an unprecedented scale.[2] Indeed, China commissioned thirty-one new submarines between 1995 and 2005.[3] When confronted with the facts of this obviously rapid buildup, one Chinese strategist responded with characteristic bluntness: "Please ask [President] Chen Shuibian [of Taiwan]."[4] Indeed, diesel submarines are ideal coercive and anti-access instruments for coping with the Taiwan problem. The undersea dimension of various Taiwan scenarios is a vital component of the military balance and is rightly of intense interest to the defense analytical community in the United States and all around the Pacific. But this book is not specifically concerned with that particular scenario.

Instead, this edited volume is both more specific and simultaneously broader in its conception. It is more specific in that it focuses on a narrow and neglected sector of China's undersea force, the relatively small proportion of China's submarines that use nuclear propulsion. The last complete treatment of Chinese nuclear propulsion was published in 1993 by John Lewis and Xue Litai. Thus, the papers in this volume break considerable fresh ground regarding China's newest undersea arsenal. It should be noted, however, that this volume contains substantial new analysis and data concerning the Chinese submarine force and Chinese navy as a whole, and therefore is appropriate for readers who are not necessarily focused on Chinese nuclear propulsion. Indeed, this volume will appeal to students of Chinese grand strategy as well, because it is widely held that the trajectory of Chinese nuclear propulsion may be one of the best single indicators of whether or not China has ambitions to become a genuine global military power. With no need to surface in order to recharge batteries or any requirement for refueling, not to mention unparalleled survivability, nuclear submarines remain ideal platforms for persistent operations in far-flung sea areas. They will form an efficient means for China to project power should it choose to do so. Therefore, the direction of China's nuclear submarine fleet bears watching by a larger community of strategists outside of naval circles, and obviously nuclear strategists as well.

China's Strategic Seapower, published over a decade ago, was a stunning research accomplishment by John Lewis and Xue Litai, and more broadly for the field of studies in Chinese military and technological development. That and other studies by these accomplished scholars remain the highest empirical standard in the field. And yet the conclusion that the successful 1988 launch of a JL-1 submarine-launched ballistic missile (SLBM) from China's first nuclear ballistic-missile submarine (SSBN) 092 signaled that "China had acquired a sea-based retaliatory capability" was premature. These authors, it seems, may have underestimated the training, doctrinal, and maintenance challenges associated with a genuinely operational nuclear submarine fleet. For example, the 092 submarine is believed to have never made a single deterrent patrol into the central Pacific.[5] Moreover, they downplay the survivability issues that would arise if China was confronted by the antisubmarine (ASW) prowess of such modern fleets as those of Japan or the United States. If Lewis and Xue were somewhat premature in their conclusions, they did seemingly accurately predict that Chinese high command would "give sustained impetus to the development of strategic forces at sea for the long term."[6] The present volume aspires to serve as a successor to that distinguished study.

With the launching of China's second generation of nuclear submarines—the type 093 nuclear attack submarine (SSN) in 2002 and the type 094 SSBN in 2004—a new era in China's military development has arrived. In October 2005, a conference on "China's New Nuclear Submarine Force" was convened at the U.S. Naval War College (NWC) in Newport, Rhode Island. NWC is a recognized center of excellence at the nexus of academic and policy worlds. It has been identified as a logical center for open-source analysis of Chinese naval development, because of its unique mix of regional and naval warfare specialists. In order to harness these capabilities, Rear Adm. Jacob Shuford, president of NWC, formally created the China Maritime Studies Institute (CMSI) in October 2006. The 2005 nuclear submarine conference was the first in a series of yearly conferences that will evaluate different aspects of Chinese maritime development. CMSI is particularly pleased to partner with the Naval Institute Press to publish the proceedings of these important conferences.

The 2005 conference participants, which included representatives from Fleet ASW Command, Naval Undersea Warfare Command, Navy Warfare Development Command, Third Fleet, Seventh Fleet, Submarine School, and Sandia National Laboratories, probed several areas of agreement and also wide disagreement regarding the developing Chinese nuclear submarine force. There was broad consensus that Chinese naval modernization had accelerated with submarines as the focal point. There was additional agreement the new Chinese SSN (Type 093) significantly extended the strategic reach of the Chinese Navy. A final major area of agreement was that the 093 SSN could serve as an important indicator of China's ultimate naval ambitions, insofar as continued focus on the diesel submarine program would tend to indicate a naval strategy geared primarily for a Taiwan scenario or operations in the East Asian littoral, as opposed to expanded operations in the global oceans.

There was serious disagreement concerning the nature of the SSBN program. Many participants were dismissive of the 094 program, characterizing it as merely a "symbol" of China's great power status, with little actual strategic significance. Other participants viewed the new Chinese SSBN as a vital component of China's improving nuclear force posture. It was even suggested that Beijing might design its future naval strategy at least partially around protecting these assets in a manner similar to the Soviet "bastions" from the late Cold War era. Another important area of disagreement among participants concerned the overall trajectory of nuclear propulsion within China's navy. Some argued that these new nuclear vessels would have increasing importance, while others maintained that diesel submarines would remain the focus of the People's Liberation Army Navy (PLAN) for the foreseeable future. This book does not come to any fundamental conclusions on these important debates. Rather, it seeks to present a variety of perspectives that readers themselves are free to evaluate, so as to make their own judgments. In this regard, we believe it is noteworthy that five of the chapters draw substantially on original Chinese sources, in order to better acquaint the reader with the growing amount of military analysis that the Chinese are producing themselves.

This book has five parts: 1) the wider context for Chinese nuclear submarine development, 2) the dimensions of the new submarine capabilities, 3) a discussion of current and future PRC nuclear submarine operations, 4) an assessment of Cold War lessons for understanding the development of the PRC nuclear submarine force, and finally 5) a discussion of the implications for U.S. national security, and for the U.S. Navy in particular.

The first chapter by Rear Adm. Eric McVadon (USN, ret.) provides a detailed summary of current developments in the Chinese navy, as well as highlighting critical synergies with other new Chinese military capabilities. McVadon's analysis demonstrates the truly broad and deep nature of China's anti-access maritime strategy. He concludes that a young Chinese naval officer "must today see the prospect, at least, of a promising career ahead as a nuclear submariner" with "esteem comparable to that of an American counterpart. That in itself is a remarkable and telling change from a few years ago." Bernard D. Cole's authoritative volume *The Great Wall at Sea* (Naval Institute Press, 2001) broadens the context further by establishing the PLAN's developmental stages and surveying its present and future goals and challenges. In his contribution to this volume, Cole concludes that "[PRC former commander Admiral] Liu Huaqing's reported strategy—to control China's adjacent seas out to the 'first island chain'—is reasonable and currently within reach. . . ." The third chapter, by long-time People's Liberation Army (PLA) watcher Paul Godwin, sets current developments firmly within reigning PLA doctrinal principles of "offshore defense" and also "active defense" within "local wars under high-tech conditions." According to Godwin, "China's new SSN fits well with the PLAN's offshore defense strategy . . . it would not be excessive for Beijing to be thinking of an SSN force in the range of twenty 093 platforms."

A second section analyzes available data concerning the capabilities of China's new nuclear submarine fleet. A submariner qualified to command nuclear submarines, NWC professor William Murray provides a comprehensive overview of PLAN submarine development. He discusses possible trade-offs between diesel and nuclear submarines, concluding that "with [air-independent propulsion] and a continuously fully charged battery, even a diesel submarine can act like a nuclear vessel, if only for a couple of hours. An AIP submarine can . . . sprint . . . to intercept and attack . . . [while retaining enough power to] creep away." Another submariner and a recent graduate of NWC with experience aboard SSBNs, Chris McConnaughy, traces the rather arduous historical development of China's SSBN program, arguing that the first generations of PRC nuclear submarines should be viewed as an interim investment rather than a failure. Suggesting a looming challenge for the U.S. Navy, he observes: "If China elected to threaten a nuclear response to U.S. interference in what it considers an internal issue, U.S. commanders would presumably be forced to shift assets from defense of carriers to strategic ASW, thereby increasing the risk to [the] carriers."

Another product of student research at NWC is the paper by Shawn Cappellano-Sarver, yet another submariner with expertise in nuclear propulsion systems. Recognizing the extremely opaque nature of China's naval nuclear propulsion program, Cappellano-Sarver employs an indirect methodology of examining China's civilian nuclear program to learn about possible developments in Chinese naval nuclear propulsion. He notes,

"Various PRC articles state that the 093 has an advanced high-temperature high-efficiency reactor plant. The use of the technology gained by the civilian nuclear industry has the potential to greatly improve submarines designed and built in China." Richard D. Fisher, Jr., has long pioneered research into PLA development. His chapter offers an excellent summary of new PLAN capabilities, with an emphasis on technology transfers from Russia and other parts of the world. Fisher states that "new technologies offer enhanced capabilities, which in turn could also justify fewer submarines" for the PLAN. "But technology [e.g., land-attack cruise missiles, or LACMs] may also justify larger numbers [of SSNs, for example]."

A third section of the book delves into current and future operations by PLAN nuclear submarines. NWC Professor Peter A. Dutton, an expert on Chinese maritime legal perspectives, examines the legal and strategic implications of the November 2004 "Han incident," in which Japanese ASW forces vigorously pursued a Chinese nuclear submarine alleged to have penetrated Japanese territorial waters. Dutton credits Japan with a strategic victory in this incident and also notes "In response to the Japanese demands for a Chinese apology for the presence of the Han submarine, the PRC officially 'regretted' the intrusion, rather than moving its stance toward a broader right of transit passage." NWC professors Andrew S. Erickson and Lyle J. Goldstein evaluate Chinese writings concerning these new PLAN submarine capabilities, attempting to reveal the operational objectives of the Chinese SSN and SSBN programs. Among other findings, their research reveals that "[According to PRC writings,] . . . if [Chinese] nuclear submarines can 'break through the island chain blockade' they can conduct long-distance operations without hindrance from the enemy's airborne ASW." In the next chapter, China analysts Garth Hekler, Ed Francis, and James Mulvenon of the Defense Group, Inc., provide a path-breaking study of Chinese submarine command and control. Their overall conclusion is that "while the PLAN may recognize the effectiveness of decentralized [command, control, and communications, or] C3 for certain types of submarine missions, it appears to be seeking to create a more tightly centralized submarine C3 system by developing command automation, network centric warfare strategies, and advanced communications technologies." NWC professors Andrew S. Erickson and Andrew R. Wilson broaden the context for considering Chinese nuclear submarine operations by raising the aircraft carrier issue, asking in particular whether these capabilities are in competition for the same resources. According to Erickson and Wilson, "In fact, while submarines seem to be ascendant, the Chinese are still actively engaged with [the deck aviation] question and are reframing the terms of the debate, [which] has been reinvigorated by recent events [e.g., the 2004 tsunami]."

A fourth section of the book probes the Cold War era for possible insights for understanding the development of China's nuclear submarine force. James Patton, retired commanding office of a nuclear attack submarine, offers a compelling history of this dynamic weapons platform. In reflecting on China's naval trajectory, he offers, "A . . . certain conclusion to be drawn from a nation acquiring an SSN fleet is [that it is seeking] to obtain a significant degree of global maritime influence." Robert Loewenthal, former commanding officer of a U.S. Navy ballistic-missile submarine, discusses the complicated challenge of building and training an SSBN force. His assessment is that "Beijing has the resources, the access to technology, and seemingly, the will to continue to create a viable SSBN force, [but it will require] . . . a lot of experience at sea to make that force a legitimate SSBN weapons system to support a deterrent strategy." In one of the most creative contributions to this volume, naval strategist Peter Swartz of the Center for Naval Analyses looks at similarities and differences between the prospective rivalry with China and the approach of President Ronald Reagan's Maritime Strategy in dealing with the Soviet naval challenge. Among the most illuminating findings of Swartz's paper is the observation that, in contrast to consensus during the 1980s, "the cacophony of contemporary competing strategic visions will affect the nation and the U.S. Navy's approach to the PRC, the PLAN, and the emerging PLAN nuclear submarine force."

Continuing on this theme, the final three chapters all discuss implications for the U.S. Navy of China's new generation of nuclear submarines. NWC professor Toshi Yoshihara discusses possible linkages between U.S. ballistic-missile defense and the Chinese SSBN program. He argues that "for at least the next two decades, missile defense . . . will have no answer to a capable SSBN patrolling the open ocean. . . . This asymmetry in capability suggests that . . . the only effective response to a capable Chinese SSBN is the employment of traditional antisubmarine warfare assets, particularly hunter-killer nuclear attack submarines." Rear Adm. Michael McDevitt (ret.) of the Center for Naval Analyses evaluates the overall trajectory of Chinese naval strategy, concluding that it is a variant of the Soviet sea denial concept. With respect to the PLAN nuclear submarine force, his assessment is that "[The PLAN is now focused] on modern conventional submarines, [but] . . . over the long term, it is reasonable to expect the PLAN to try to master modern quieting techniques, since the vast distances in the Pacific combined with the logistic limitations of conventional submarines make nuclear powered submarines a better weapons system." In the final chapter, NWC professor Tom Mahnken takes note of the other imperatives confronting the U.S. Navy (especially the global war on terror) and also draws attention to the rapid development of the Japanese Imperial Navy between the world wars as a possibly useful analogy when considering the Chinese naval challenge. Though he notes that PLAN submarine proficiency is difficult to gauge, he cautions: "Extrapolations from the past are, if anything, likely to understate the pace of improvement of the Chinese submarine force."

It is imperative to note that the opinions expressed in this volume are those of the authors and editors themselves and do not reflect the official policies or assessments of the U.S. Navy or any other agency of the U.S. Government. The editors wish to thank each of the respective authors for their outstanding research contributions. We are particularly proud of the two student paper contributions, as both count among the most thoughtful essays in this collection. In addition, we wish to thank the NWC leadership for its support of this endeavor, and Capt. J. R. Mathis and Amy Grubb for superb efforts to ensure the success of the 2005 conference. Finally, we appreciate the hard work of the editorial team at Naval Institute Press. As we go about developing the China Maritime Studies Institute (CMSI), we look forward to future joint efforts with Naval Institute that serve the national interest, as we grapple with the complex issues associated with China's rapid emergence as a maritime power.

May 2006

Notes

1. Jim Yardley and Thom Shanker, "Chinese Navy Buildup Gives Pentagon New Worries," *New York Times*, 8 April 2005, http://www.nytimes.com/2005/04/08/international/asia/08china.html?ex=1270612800&en=c76dc1da37f15f20&ei=5090&partner=rssuserland.

2. China received eight new Kilo-class diesel submarines from Russia during 2005–06.

3. Ronald O'Rourke, "China's Naval Modernization: Implications for U.S. Navy Capabilities—Background and Issues for Congress," Congressional Research Service Report for Congress, updated 29 August 2006, Order Code RL 33153: 8, www.crs.gov.

4. Interview, Shanghai, December 2005.

5. John Lewis and Xue Litai, *China's Strategic Seapower* (Stanford, Calif.: Stanford University Press, 1993), 205.

6. Ibid., 230.

China's Future
Nuclear Submarine Force

Rear Adm. Eric A. McVadon, U.S. Navy (Ret.)

China's Maturing Navy

THE EAST ASIAN SECURITY ENVIRONMENT in which China is emerging demands that the matter of a maturing Chinese navy be put in a political context. Tension across the Taiwan Strait has recently relaxed. In Beijing, the leaders of economically successful and internationally active China do not want to jeopardize their nation's prospects for a bright future by initiating military conflict with Taiwan and the United States—quite the contrary. In Taipei, despite profound disagreement with Beijing and a major stir in domestic politics, a more cautious posture in relations with Beijing now prevails. So, remarkably, amid deep, persistent, and mutual distrust, the current prospects for avoiding conflict across the Taiwan Strait are good. Well-informed Chinese officials and prestigious Americans who have had exchanges with senior Chinese leaders confirm the relaxed circumstances and express the conviction that Beijing is confident about the situation as Chinese leaders see it developing and that Taiwan, again content with the status quo, will remain measured in its actions. War across the Taiwan Strait is not looming.

Nevertheless, by modernizing its military, Beijing is ensuring that things will not go awry with respect to Taiwan, that its policy of intimidation continues to work. The indisputable reality is that this military, the People's Liberation Army (PLA), and particularly its naval and missile components, the PLA Navy (PLAN) and the 2nd Artillery Corps, are growing greatly in capability; further, this is a growing concern to defense and naval leaders in Washington, D.C., and other capitals, including Tokyo and Taipei. In a time of American preoccupation with the global war on terrorism, it is appropriate to draw attention to the crucial features of this modernization of components of the PLA. Beijing, if the "Taiwan problem" were to suffer a dramatic reversal, would have available an impressive force acquired for this purpose. If that force were properly trained and employed it would be sufficient in terms of hardware to undertake a two-pronged, PLA Navy–led campaign, with a significant maritime component, against Taiwan and U.S. forces in a fashion that could be termed "jointness with Chinese characteristics."

A Military to Defend and Deter

When pressed on the subject, Chinese officials began in 2005 to deliver both publicly and privately (to the author and undoubtedly many others) the consistent message that the military budget is not excessive, manpower is shrinking, and the newly modernized PLA is not a threat.[1] Chinese characterize the PLA instead as a deterrent force—as were U.S. forces during the Cold War, they are quick to remind. When pressed further, they accept unabashedly the retort that the modernization surge is, so far, narrowly focused on the Taiwan contingency. It is directed to deterring Taiwan's movement toward independence, which they consider the top "threat to Chinese sovereignty," and to curbing the ability of the United States to intervene rapidly and effectively were China compelled, as Beijing perceives it, to use military force against Taiwan.[2]

So the concern is that hard-liners in Beijing, obsessed by the "Taiwan problem," might not allow prudence to prevail in decision-making in a crisis and, consequently, could order the use of military force because of what they perceive as intolerable "splittist" conduct by Taipei. In evaluating the risks of an imprudent decision by Beijing, it might be asked rhetorically whether the current Chinese Communist Party is capable of as bad a choice in a future Taiwan crisis as most observers think the Party made with the Great Leap Forward, the Cultural Revolution, and the actions in 1989 now referred to simply as "Tiananmen." Some observers increasingly find reason to be optimistic, but it is hard to offer unqualified assurance that Beijing could not again make a very bad decision.

It is the result of decisions obviously made several years ago that a new, modern, and much more capable PLA Navy has, along with the air force and

2nd Artillery Corps (the ballistic and long-range cruise-missile force), been acquired and deployed. A stunning modernization effort continues. Regardless of how Beijing's intentions are viewed, the surge in PLA modernization has radically changed the military situation for Taiwan. Taipei is more than ever forced to look to Washington to cope with this more advanced, capable PLA, with the strategic depth of huge China behind it.

Moreover, the PLA now hopes to genuinely realize concepts its strategists have written about, such as how an inferior force can prevail against a superior opponent—that is, China versus the United States. Specifically, the critical aspects of a new navy and the highly significant synergies that may develop between it and the missile and air forces warrant full attention, because they are directed specifically to deterring, delaying, or complicating timely and effective American access and intervention. U.S. forces must be able, should the Taiwan pot boil over, to turn the tables and deter Beijing from using its proclaimed deterrent forces—or to ensure a favorable outcome if mutual deterrence fails. The ultimate American goal, however, should be to make the chances of conflict even less than they are. Understanding the important developments described here seems a necessary step toward that goal.

Starting with Questions

The following questions and answers may be an unusual way to begin probing the specific naval aspects of the issue, but they focus on an often neglected, but arguably the most surprising, single PLAN acquisition program: its bold move to quickly build a modern nuclear submarine force despite its troubled past in this arena. These incisive questions—posed to the author in 2005 by experts on the Chinese submarine force—are especially useful in that they take the PLA's Taiwan obsession fully into account but also look beyond. They reveal the layers of complexity and uncertainty inherent in the very rapid and impressive modernization of the PLA Navy—a navy that, it is worth emphasizing, is arguably the only one in today's world that the U.S. Navy must deter or be able to defeat, but also a navy that under different circumstances could become a high-seas partner.

How "mature" is China's navy? Does the PLAN have the requisite human capital, organizational practices, and exercise regimen to become a world-class fleet? The PLAN is most nearly mature with respect to platforms and weapons but, approximately in the order listed, progressively less so in human capital, organizational practices, and exercise regimen. It is working to become better in each of these areas.

Are nuclear submarines a good fit for China's emerging naval strategy? Will the balance of forces (i.e., nuclear versus diesel submarines) change in the future? The currently emerging balance is a good fit, especially vis-à-vis China's current set of potential adversaries. If the Taiwan problem were eliminated somehow, a shift toward nuclear submarines to protect more distant sea-lanes would be a logical option. This makes the PLAN nuclear submarine program a possible bellwether for future naval policy more generally.

What are the trends in undersea warfare and antisubmarine warfare (ASW) in the western Pacific region? The superiority of the U.S. nuclear submarine force will continue; however, the Chinese are apparently developing ballistic missiles with maneuvering warheads and terminal seekers to hit ships at sea. This capability to lob numerous accurate ballistic missile warheads high over the heads of all defenders could effectively circumvent the anticipated quiet and capable U.S. nuclear attack submarines that the PLAN has previously seen as all but impossible to penetrate with its own submarines (or surface ships) in order to reach the carriers and cruisers it wants to disable.

Despite the PLAN's ineptitude at antisubmarine warfare, short of a plausible major breakthrough, the trend in submarine/ASW competition is going China's way: the PLAN's submarine numbers and diversity trump, or at least could saturate, likely ASW opposition for the foreseeable future, especially in case of the short war Beijing contemplates. With respect to Taiwan's ASW capability (almost an oxymoron now), the Republic of China (ROC) navy would still have to learn to use its P-3C antisubmarine patrol aircraft after getting them; its prospective new submarine force of eight diesel submarines, if approved for acquisition (as currently remains uncertain), would be a decade or more from operational status and even then inadequate for antisubmarine warfare against what would by then have become a remarkably numerous, diverse, and advanced PLAN submarine force.

What strategic dilemmas might Washington encounter as a result of China's new nuclear submarine force? Beijing's smug confidence that Washington must always keep in mind China's status as a nuclear power will be reinforced if the PLAN is successful with its ongoing program to build several modern Jin-class (Project 094) nuclear-powered ballistic-missile submarines (SSBNs). Its sequential construction of at least two Shang-class (Project

093) nuclear-powered attack submarines (SSNs) adds the component of reach (range and speed) to the existing qualities of numbers of its nuclear and conventional submarines, as well as quietness for a growing portion of that force and potency of weapons for a similar portion—especially for the new Kilo-class diesel submarines from Russia, with their long-range, supersonic, sea-skimming antiship cruise missiles (ASCMs). A "new PLAN" with these new nuclear-powered submarines and stunning array of other new and modern platforms and weapons is highly likely to view itself in a different strategic light, as yet unrevealed, than has the "old PLAN."

A Maturing but Still Adolescent Navy

Harking back to the title of this article, the PLA Navy might best be described as an adolescent rather than mature navy, with the caution that adolescents can exhibit qualities across the range from juvenile to adult, often commit crimes that warrant treatment as adults, and mature unpredictably. To extend the adolescence analogy a bit more, the PLAN is growing remarkably in size and strength, even "bulking up" (in the American vernacular); all observers remark how it has grown since the last time they saw it.[3]

Simply fielding more modern units does not make the PLAN a truly modern operational force. The limits (described below) on how China's and the navy's leaders are able to employ their new capabilities represent significant shortcomings, and success in the effort to overcome them is far from assured. Put another way, the PLAN has matured remarkably insofar as acquiring platforms and equipment (ships, submarines, aircraft, radars, and so on) and weapons (antiship cruise missiles, air defense missiles, torpedoes, and the like) is concerned, but this "new PLA Navy" has not matured fully in exercising its forces and developing the command and control capabilities, coordination means, and intelligence and targeting support needed to make that force fully operational—especially in comparison with its most important and most capable potential adversary, the U.S. Navy.[4]

Better officers are on the way up—if they make it. The PLAN recognizes that to conduct complex joint operations, exercise greatly enhanced command and control, and effectively employ modern weapons it needs a better-educated, more worldly officer corps, and it is striving to do that, or so it says.[5] PLAN officers are taking more prominent positions in institutions that do strategic thinking; for example, in two recent firsts for naval officers, former PLAN commander Admiral Zhang Dingfa previously headed the Academy of Military Science, and Rear Admiral Yang Yi is still director of the Institute of Strategic Studies at the National Defense University in Beijing. The PLA Navy seeks officers educated in first-rate civilian universities.[6] The emphasis, however, appears to be on specific technical and scientific educations;[7] this approach neglects, it seems, the parallel need for specialists in operations, security issues, strategic studies, and international affairs.[8]

Details aside, an important and yet unanswered question is whether the PLA Navy wants officers better educated or considers them better "Red." That is, will competent, forward-thinking officers be selected for flag rank, or will party loyalty and personal connections continue to prevail as the paramount selection criteria?[9] This author has lectured and conferred at the National Defense University and other PLA institutions on several occasions at which junior officers asked all the questions and did all the talking while flag and general officers who were students remained silent—at least in part, it appeared, for fear of being outshone in these lively and insightful discussions. It would seem that at some point the demands of a modern PLA will force the promotion of more of the officers who have all the intelligent questions and original thoughts.

Organization is improving, but maybe not yet enough. The PLA Navy structure has been streamlined: naval aviation no longer stands alone as though an almost separate service, closer ties have been established with the PLAN's marine corps, and there are fewer layers in the chain of command.[10] Nevertheless, the author has observed and been told, there is still much dead wood at the top: individuals in green uniforms with two or more stars on their shoulders (PLA ground-force generals) who persist in treating the PLAN as mostly an adjunct to the army, and senior officers who, through lack of vision, fail to move decisively toward true joint operations. These generals represent obstacles at a time when real coordination by the PLAN with the 2nd Artillery Corps and the PLA Air Force would lead to enormous advances in the ability to coerce Taiwan, threaten American intervention capabilities, and keep Japan off balance.

China's navy is still failing to conduct exercises needed to develop its potential capability. It continues to steam in the littoral for the most part. However, the PLAN aspires, and is erratically striving, to conduct training and exercises in more distant waters; to make its training more like combat; to challenge itself in exercises with active, maneuvering opposition forces; and otherwise to add realism to its training and exercise activity. It has even been so bold as to engage, in August 2005, in a major multiphased exercise with the Russian navy, a notable advance beyond the minor, very basic exercises it has conducted with the French, British, Australian, Pakistani, and Indian navies in recent years.[11] Rudimentary exercises were conducted with the U.S. Navy in September 2006. A few years ago the PLAN would not have participated in such exercises at all, fearing not only prying (as well as spying) but embarrassment, that its shortcomings and backwardness would be revealed. Chinese naval leaders now seem sufficiently confident in their crews to seek international partners for exercises. It seems that several unflattering post-exercise Russian media reports did not rejuvenate concerns that bilateral exercises lead to ridicule and embarrassment.[12]

Still, the import of the Russian-Chinese exercise should not be overstated. It was initially described by many as preparation for countering U.S. forces in the region. As later and more accurately described, however, it primarily demonstrated that Sino-Russian bilateral relations are strong, especially military-to-military relations and arms sales. The exercise itself, held in waters just off the Shandong Peninsula, was hardly a simulation of access-denial against approaching U.S. forces. Its significance in that respect would seem to be less direct. The fact that it was held at all suggests that the Russians are more likely than we might have surmised to provide logistic and possibly intelligence support—specifically, to offer to resupply missiles and spare parts for the key Russian weapon systems that China would employ in combat with Taiwan and the United States.[13]

If it would be exaggeration, then, to assess this exercise as a sign of emergence as a fully mature force, the PLAN is nevertheless creeping toward real blue-water exercises with composite task forces including surface combatants, submarines, and aviation. So far, only in occasional and isolated distant submarine transits does it approximate the task of confronting an enemy—the U.S. Navy—that it might need to keep at arm's length, many hundreds of miles from the Chinese coast.[14] In short, the PLAN is not visibly conducting exercises, alone or with other services, that rehearse confrontation with approaching U.S. Navy forces. The United States should be alert to such a development with this new force, a force designed to have the capabilities that could make such operations feasible.

Attacks from Several Axes

A new aspect of budding maturity, what could facetiously be termed "socialization," is looming and demands attention—the prospect that the PLAN and the 2nd Artillery Corps could join hands to bolster the nation's capability to attack Taiwan and pose a significantly greater and more diverse threat to the ability of the United States to intervene in the region. The greatly increased number and highly improved accuracy of China's medium- and short-range ballistic missiles (MRBMs and SRBMs) plus strategic and technical writings suggest strongly that senior Chinese military leaders have recognized the enhancement of naval capabilities that would result from support by ballistic and land-attack cruise missiles. China's MRBMs (the DF-21C) and SRBMs (DF-15 and -11), with conventional warheads, have capabilities well beyond the psychological intimidation of Taiwan.[15] Prospective synergies stem from the ability of these potent missile arsenals to suppress Taiwan's offensive and defensive air power, support amphibious and airborne assaults on the island, strike American bases in the region, and possibly damage heavily Taiwanese naval forces before they could leave port.

However, arguably the most important aspect of the increasing ballistic-missile threat is the prospect that within a few years China may be able to seriously threaten not only American land bases but also carrier strike groups, with maneuvering reentry vehicles (MaRVs).[16] MaRVed missiles, with conventional warheads, would maneuver both to enhance warhead survival (defeat missile defenses) and home on mobile (or stationary) targets.[17] The implications for the PLAN of this prospective 2nd Artillery capability are, of course, profound; they include the ability to degrade U.S. air and missile defenses (including the Aegis systems and carrier flight decks). That would allow follow-on attacks by layered, diverse, and appropriately redundant PLAN submarine, air, and surface forces firing large numbers of very modern and capable ASCMs, torpedoes, and even their guns if the earlier attacks suppress most defenses.[18] This and what follows are in clear outline the sort of the threat the PLA and PLA Navy wish to pose to U.S. Navy forces. The precisely focused force the Chinese have built and what they have written about its use leave no doubt about the concept—although there are grave doubts about their ability to execute it.

Whether, or how soon, the ballistic-missile threat becomes a factor in the ability of the PLAN to deter, confuse, and delay or, alternatively, confront approaching U.S. Navy forces, the ability to launch lethal antiship cruise missile attacks is an area where the PLAN is already near or at maturity—even if the targeting of American forces at which to launch them has not reached a mature state. The PLAN early on became a cruise-missile navy, as a way of overcoming other deficiencies. Now it must be described as a modern cruise-missile navy, at least with respect to the platforms and lethal, evasive missiles it is deploying.[19] The PLAN's four newest classes of submarines, armed with potent ASCMs, fall just below MaRVed ballistic missiles in the hierarchy of potential or emerging threats to U.S. forces.

At the top of the submarine component of the overall threat are the eight new Kilo-class diesel-electric submarines from Russia that are now being successively delivered to China. These submarines threaten carrier strike groups through their ability to launch, while submerged over a hundred miles away, the SS-N-27B/Sizzler antiship cruise missile.[20] After a subsonic flight to the target area, the SS-N-27B makes a supersonic, sea-skimming, evasive attack.[21] It is described by its marketers and others as part of the best family of cruise missiles in the world and, in the opinion of some, as able to defeat the U.S. Aegis air and missile defense system that is central to the defense of carrier strike groups.[22]

Shang-class (Type 093) SSNs are possible partners for the new Kilos. The surprisingly rapid construction of a second unit in this new class of nuclear-powered attack submarine implies special utility in a Taiwan contingency. The Shangs could, if they prove sufficiently quiet and fast, and are properly equipped with sensors, be part of the net by which the PLAN locates and identifies approaching U.S. carrier strike groups.[23] If used this way, they could be part of a matrix composed of such detection and reporting means as satellites, merchant ships, and even fishing boats with satellite phones.

Having served as part of the matrix that detects targets for the ballistic missiles and Kilos, the Shangs could then join with the Song- and Yuan-class nonnuclear submarines (SSs) in attacks against selected U.S. forces that have, as expected in the sequenced PLA attack concept, suffered by that point significant degradation of their air and missile defenses.[24] These three classes of submarines could carry out, from several attack axes, submerged launches of large salvoes of subsonic, but still very capable, ASCMs. Of course, further follow-on attacks by torpedoes cannot be discounted if they appear to be needed.

China's other new nuclear-powered submarine program, the Jin-class (Project 094) ballistic-missile submarine, is primarily a part of China's strategic deterrent, but it will necessarily play a role as backdrop for this Taiwan scenario.[25] As with China's modernized and augmented land-based intercontinental ballistic missiles, Beijing can act more confidently in bold undertakings vis-à-vis the United States when its strategic forces are more secure. Beijing is, with the Jins, adding a layer of insurance that American missile defenses could be saturated—and that Washington would know it. Washington, of course, would have to take into account the fact that it is dealing with a capable nuclear power whose missiles have become very mobile and difficult to detect.

A Daunting ASW Challenge

The success of the described PLAN submarine attacks using submerged-launched antiship cruise missiles depends to some degree on thwarting or coping with U.S. antisubmarine warfare capabilities, primarily aircraft (P-3Cs and to a lesser extent shipborne helicopters) and SSNs. One method by which the Chinese might complicate the ASW picture for the Americans is to use large numbers of submarines, including the twenty or more older submarines—Han-class SSNs and Romeo- and Ming-class SSs—which may be noisy but cannot be ignored. In round numbers, the PLAN might, in a campaign where it has chosen the time to ready the crews and initiate operations, be able to deploy more than twenty modern SSNs and SSs and roughly the same number of older submarines.[26] The long range of the ASCMs carried by the new Kilos means that those submarines need not come within a hundred miles of the target ships, if targeting information can be obtained remotely—greatly expanding the areas that American SSNs and P-3Cs would have to search. The speed and practically unlimited underwater endurance of the new Shang SSNs could allow them to close targets promptly to launch their shorter-range ASCMs after the initial attacks by longer-range missiles have degraded defenses.

The role of Taiwan in antisubmarine warfare deserves some attention. Taiwan's current ASW capability is minimal. That capability might improve in the foreseeable future were Taiwan to obtain from the United States the much-discussed P-3Cs, but that will depend on how seriously the ROC Navy pursues the demanding task of learning how to perform antisubmarine warfare with that aircraft. If it does that well, Taiwan's P-3Cs might offer a measure of help in the big ASW problem that the PLAN could create in the East China Sea and beyond.[27] The Japanese Maritime Self-Defense Force would offer another measure of assistance, if Tokyo were to make a political decision to involve its forces in that way. All this said, China's growing and improving submarine fleet has outpaced United States, Japan, and Taiwan ASW in the difficult littoral waters of the region, which generally favor submarines seeking to escape detection.[28] Open-ocean areas may be a slightly riskier proposition for the PLAN's submarines, unless they actually achieve the elusive new levels of stealth to which China aspires.

The previously described antisurface-warfare roles seem the most likely ones for the PLAN's new Shangs. It does not seem likely that the PLAN, inexperienced compared to the U.S. Navy in undersea warfare, would use its few new SSNs—precious to the Chinese but almost certainly not comparable to American SSNs in capability and stealth—in an effort to strip the carrier groups of their submarine protection. So far, China has conceded that aspect of the game to the United States and chosen to avoid dueling with the superior American submarines. By electing to develop a land-based ballistic-missile threat against ships at sea, China is pursuing a path that could keep U.S. submarines from blocking a critical initial attack on carrier strike groups. If in the event the ballistic-missile concept is not usable or fails in execution, the new Kilos with the SS-N-27B, the many other submarines with ASCMs, and the increasingly capable PLA naval air force B-6s, FB-7s, and Su-30MK2s (to be mentioned in more detail later) provide other alternatives that largely avoid American underwater-warfare superiority. The point is that, as the Shangs are introduced into the fleet, it seems unlikely that they would be expected to take on American SSNs directly.

Enough to Make Washington Pause?

The intensity and persistence of PLAN attacks on U.S. Navy forces could well be affected by Beijing's perception of the fragility of a government on Taiwan subjected to a major assault from everything from ballistic missiles to aircraft, to special forces—and much more. It should be remembered that the primary purpose of denying or delaying access by U.S. forces would be to convince Taipei that waiting for help is futile, that capitulation and negotiation—on Beijing's terms—are the only reasonable option. Success against U.S. forces is, therefore, important largely for its effect on Taipei's will to fight on. Success in such conflict would be sweetest for the PLA if the United States had never become actively involved—concern about the capabilities of a modernized Chinese force having led American leaders to delay or withhold carrier strike groups.

Returning from strategic considerations to the fight itself, were one to occur, the Chinese can be expected next to deliver air-launched antiship cruise missiles once the air defenses of the U.S. strike groups, and possibly regional bases as well, are degraded. So this "layer" in the assault might be the PLA Navy Air Force, attacking several hundred miles out to sea from China (in some cases possibly much farther) with potent new air-launched ASCMs fired from new aircraft from Russia (the Su-30MK2) and indigenous long-range B-6s (a new version with new missiles) and FB-7 maritime interdiction aircraft, also new versions with new ASCMs.[29] (Note how many times the word *new* appeared, correctly, in that sentence.) Some PLA Air Force aircraft have similar capabilities. At a minimum, the U.S. Navy would have to be concerned about vulnerability to such an attack and, if it had, indeed, sustained damage, might feel it had to retreat. Beijing would make sure that such a development was not lost on Taipei—and we are seeking here to understand more fully how Beijing envisions a conflict with its modernized forces, not necessarily the actual reality.

Surface combatants would be a final layer if a supposedly casualty-averse Washington and teetering Taipei have not yet taken the point. Cleanup attacks might in such a case be intended with very capable ASCMs from the several new or upgraded classes of destroyers and frigates. These warships are led, with respect to lethal firepower, by the Russian *Sovremennys* (soon to increase from two to four) with supersonic, very evasive SS-N-22/Sunburns.[30] China has built or is building enough new and modernized destroyers and frigates to form several modern surface action groups, each capable of long-range attacks with almost equally lethal, although subsonic, ASCMs. Also—and here it is finally beginning to overcome a long-standing shortcoming—the PLA Navy is on the way to acquiring good fleet air defenses using surface-to-air missile systems.[31]

To capture succinctly the scope of the modernization of the surface combatant force, it can be said that the Chinese are now building and dramatically upgrading more *classes* of modern destroyers and frigates (these combatants clearly outmatch those of Taiwan) than previous rates suggested they might acquire *ships* in this decade.[32]

The question that cannot now be answered with respect to this PLAN surface fleet is whether such a visible and slow-moving force, even with dramatically improved air defense, could actually engage even a damaged U.S. force and not be subject to devastating attack by other American strike forces. There are, however, broader uncertainties for the PLAN. As noted, the concepts outlined above emerge from the force Beijing is building and from PLA doctrinal and other writing. Beijing has made hard decisions and executed expensive programs in the ongoing surge in modernization of the PLA, with great emphasis on naval, air, and missile forces for such operations as described. But surveillance and targeting support will be needed if this force is to deter or confront American intervention efforts. To that end, it appears that China is making significant efforts to gain a varied capability from space, land, sea (including undersea), and air to locate, identify, track, and target naval forces.[33] China is lagging in this arena—real success in the intelligence, surveillance, and reconnaissance (ISR) arena could take a decade—but one might make a guess that some rudimentary, if not reliable and consistent, capability could be cobbled together within a couple of years.

In other words, there is impending danger that U.S. ships could be detected and effectively targeted. At least equally important is whether China will be able to coordinate, command, and control such operations—that is, what of the command, control, communications, and computers (C4) to go with the ISR? The PLAN, although now more realistic and somewhat bolder in its training and exercises, as mentioned above, has not, for example, touted or otherwise given evidence of rehearsals of encounters with simulated carrier strike groups hundreds of miles east of China, as it might do as part of a deterrence scheme.

There is, as described, no doubt about the acquisition of modern platforms and threatening weapons, but there remains uncertainty as to whether and how promptly the PLA Navy and the other crucial components of the PLA will make all this capability truly operational. There is, nevertheless, an additional serious corollary as to whether Beijing would feel compelled in some circumstance to initiate hostilities against Taiwan and to confront U.S. forces even if preparations were short of optimal. It is hard to relax with respect to Beijing and Taiwan, even if we think Chinese command and control is not up to the task.

This all adds up to a complex planning and execution challenge for an inexperienced PLA. In the scenario depicted above, it would be conducting two major campaigns simultaneously: one to subdue Taiwan and the other to delay effective American intervention. The campaign against Taiwan would likely include initial ballistic-missile and land-attack, cruise-missile attacks; special forces actions, fifth-column sabotage, information operations, major air attacks, and amphibious and airborne assaults to secure lodgments to allow occupation and control of Taiwan. The campaign against the United States, in addition to being preceded by extensive efforts temporarily to cripple American command, control, communications, computers, intelligence, surveillance, and reconnaissance (C4ISR), would, it should be remembered, consist of the described ballistic- and cruise-missile attacks on carrier strike groups and possibly regional U.S. bases, submarine attacks using various forms of antiship cruise missiles, and then selections from such follow-on options as ASCMs from air or surface forces. This would be an extraordinarily demanding undertaking against a daunting foe for a PLA leadership that has no experience in such combat.

The author's guess is that the PLA would quickly succeed against Taiwan but would probably falter against U.S. forces, against which it would encounter surprises, countermeasures, and other capabilities that would likely cause severe reversals. It must also be remembered, however, both that China's best strategic and military minds are working on these problems and that Beijing may feel it has to act against Taiwan regardless of how challenging the prospect may appear. Moreover, it is unlikely that the leaders of today's modernized PLA would tell the civilian leadership that their military is not ready. On the contrary, Beijing and the military have reason to believe that their forces are of such a nature as to avoid American strengths, like SSNs and advanced C4ISR, and to make the most of China's strengths, such as its ballistic and cruise missiles and new conventional- and nuclear-submarine forces. The United States has the task not only to deter this modern military that could embolden Chinese leaders but also, irresistibly yet subtly, to lead those leaders to the conviction that a decision to attack Taiwan is not in China's interests and would not likely result in reunification.

Beyond "The Taiwan Problem"

The PLA, and especially the PLAN, now seems almost wholly, even obsessively, focused on the Taiwan problem. Two other factors should be taken into account, however, and already seem to be intruding into Chinese strategic thinking. First, an emerging China wants to build a military appropriate to the country that it is becoming. Second, China's all-important national economic growth, which keeps the Communist Party in power, is dependent on ocean commerce. As the PLA Navy tries to look beyond Taiwan or to decide what, even now, it should be thinking about besides that, it sees a long-term capability to secure sea and land routes for the flow of oil and natural gas, as well as other commodities, as a leading priority for China.

Will we see an organic air capability and a shift to more nuclear submarines? A PLA Navy able to carry out that mission would almost certainly have some form of organic air, so that it could effectively operate beyond the range of land-based aircraft—far south in the South China Sea, the Strait of Malacca, even to the Indian Ocean. Current shipyard work on the incomplete aircraft carrier *Varyag* may be the start of a move in that direction, unlike so many Chinese aircraft-carrier rumors of past decades.[34] Another consideration could be a leaning toward submarines with greater range, speed, and independence from land bases. This could mean that nuclear-powered attack submarines, despite the added cost, might be preferred over diesel-electric or even air-independent-propulsion submarines.

SSNs are a possible bellwether of PLAN strategic thinking. China is now building and buying three classes of nonnuclear submarines, the Kilos, the Songs, and the Yuans (some speculate about the exact character of the

Yuan propulsion system). These submarines, along with the older Mings and remaining Romeos, represent a major investment and will almost certainly constitute a majority of the submarine fleet for the next fifteen years or more. It will, nevertheless, be worthwhile to keep an eye on China's success with the Shang attack class to ascertain whether it will feel the need suggested above for a faster, more independent force to protect distant sea lanes, and whether an emerging China will follow the American example and diversify its SSN fleet to include land-attack cruise- and ballistic-missile capabilities and the ability to insert special forces—or possibly other, novel capabilities needed in emerging missions for an emerged China.

China's navy has developed in many remarkable ways, but perhaps the biggest test of maturity is the bold attempt to leap to a new status in the prestigious and unforgiving domain of nuclear submarines—where it had previously faltered. To a significant degree, the success or failure of its new nuclear-powered submarines, the Jin-class ballistic-missile class as well as the Shangs, is likely to determine future decisions for the Chinese submarine force. The American example in diversifying its nuclear submarines may also become a factor. The outcome for the nuclear submarine force could set the tone for a navy that either comes to feel that it ranks with the best or, having "tried out for the pros," finds that once more it has faltered.

In any case, it is instructive to imagine a particularly intelligent and competent young Chinese naval officer just beginning his service. That junior officer must today see the prospect, at least, of a promising career ahead as a nuclear submariner in a globally capable "real navy"—the prospect of professional challenge and esteem comparable to that of an American counterpart. That in itself is a remarkable and telling change from a few years ago, when serving on troubled Chinese nuclear submarines was thought by some to be as much a joke as a job. Such success as the Chinese submarine force attains would tend to be infectious and to bolster the professionalism of other components of the modern PLAN, where newfound pride is thriving as well. The PLA Navy is not fully mature, but it has established its potential for that status in the air, on the sea, and, conspicuously, under the sea.

Notes

1. Previously, the author had been told privately that the PLA was surging in capability because it finally had the funds from Beijing, the technologies and assistance from Moscow, and the realization that Washington was not going to accept Beijing's position on Taiwan. Prominent in the recent public exchange was the Chinese response to three events: first, Secretary of Defense Rumsfeld's complaints about

the large PLA budget made at a conference sponsored by the International Institute for Strategic Studies in Singapore on 4 June 2005; second, his similar comments in Beijing in October 2005; and third, the 2005 annual Department of Defense report to the Congress on PRC military power. Typical of the strongly stated disagreement were the widely noted immediate objection expressed by Cui Tiankai, top Chinese representative at the Singapore conference, and the sharp retort of Vice Foreign Minister Yang Jiechi, the former Chinese ambassador in Washington, as quoted in the *Washington Post* on 21 July 2005, A24. He chastised the United States for "improper comments about China's defensive national defense policy and measures" and called the buildup "normal national defense building." Yang asserted that most of the new spending went for improving living conditions for troops, noting, rather disingenuously, that the military also "updated some weapons equipment."

2. On 4 December 2005, while preparing this article, the author met with two long-time Chinese colleagues, a diplomat (senior foreign service officer) and a senior PLA Navy officer, both of them well informed and well connected. They agreed with each other (and unknowingly with American observers) that conflict with Taiwan and the U.S. was unlikely and that cross-Strait relations were relaxed. The diplomat said that Beijing's relaxed attitude stemmed in part from recently enhanced confidence with respect to political developments in Taipei favorable to Beijing and prospects for eventual peaceful resolution. They offered no apology or explanation for the fact that PLA modernization is focused on the Taiwan issue; both seemed to consider the unprecedented military buildup as simply appropriately responsive to the task of deterring and being able to cope with China's most important contingency—the Taiwan-U.S. "threat."

3. For a description of this PLA Navy, Air Force, and 2nd Artillery modernization surge, see the author's testimony on Capitol Hill on 15 September 2005 before the U.S.-China Economic and Security Review Commission, available at www.uscc.org or at www.ifpa.org/pdf/mcvadon.pdf. For an exhaustive but illuminating description by a non-American source of the PLAN program, see Mikhail Barabanov, "Contemporary Military Shipbuilding in China," *Eksport Vooruzheniy,* 1 FBIS CEP20050811949014, August 2005. This piece (perhaps unexpectedly) is a remarkably accurate and uniquely comprehensive open-source reference on the recent stunning surge in modernization of the PLAN.

4. U.S. Defense Dept., *FY04 Report to Congress on PRC Military Power* (available at www.defenselink.mil/pubs/d20040528PRC.pdf), states on page 6: "China has continued to improve its potential for joint operations via development of an integrated command and control network, a new command structure, and improved C4ISR platforms. As in previous years, China's leaders realize that most of the PLA's C4ISR equipment lags generations behind that of the West and are encouraging a new generation of researchers, engineers, and officers to find ways to adapt to the demands of the modern battlefield. The acquisition of advanced C4ISR technology is one of the principal objectives of PRC collection activities."

5. David Shambaugh, *Modernizing China's Military: Progress, Problems, and Prospects* (Berkeley: University of California Press, 2002), 32, 46–47. "The PLA is still the

party's army, all officers above the rank of senior colonel are party members, and the CCP still institutionally penetrates the military apparatus." "The rules of the game . . . have changed as a result of several developments: [among Shambaugh's listed developments]—Increased professionalism in the senior officer corps and a concomitant decline in the promotion of officers with backgrounds as political commissars."

6. Paul H. B. Godwin, "China's Defense Establishment: The Hard Lessons of Incomplete Modernization," in *The Lessons of History: The Chinese People's Liberation Army at 75*, ed. Laurie Burkitt, Andrew Scobell, and Larry M. Wortzel (Carlisle, Pa.: U.S. Army War College, Strategic Studies Institute, July 2003), 33. Godwin states: "Officer recruitment has been changed to an emphasis on college graduates rather than selecting from the ranks of serving enlisted men and women, and advancement in rank now requires attendance at the appropriate PME schools."

7. Bernard D. Cole, "The Organization of the People's Liberation Army Navy (PLAN)," in *The People's Liberation Army as Organization: Reference Volume v1.0*, ed. James C. Mulvenon and Andrew N. D. Yang (Santa Monica, Calif.: RAND, 2002), 476. "The PLAN is emulating the U.S. reserve officer-training corps (ROTC) programs for producing well-educated, technically oriented candidate officers."

8. Beijing *Xinhua*, 17 August 1999, translated in FBIS-CHI-99-0817: "The Chinese navy plans to recruit about 1,000 officers from non-military universities and colleges yearly beginning this autumn in an effort to meet its need for command and technical talent . . . [these officers] will account for 40 percent of all naval officers by the year 2010." This was originally cited in Cole, "The Organization of the People's Liberation Army Navy (PLAN)," 477.

9. Elizabeth Hague, "PLA Leadership in China's Military Regions," in *Civil-Military Change in China: Elites, Institutes, and Ideas after the 16th Party Congress*, ed. Andrew Scobell and Larry Wortzel (Carlisle, Pa.: U.S. Army War College, Strategic Studies Institute, September 2004), 247, 250. Two extracts from this chapter illustrate that party loyalty, *guanxi* (connections), and a reputation for not rocking the boat remain important in promotion decisions: "Several military region commanders have been promoted . . . to the national level. . . . In all cases they involve a candidate . . . valuable for a national-level position—*even when other factors, such as connections, were a strong factor in a promotion*" [emphasis original]. Further, "Military leaders reflect PLA priorities, even in some cases when what the leader has to offer is continuity rather than new ideas or techniques."

10. The author and another longtime American specialist on the PLAN were separately told of these organizational changes by knowledgeable PLAN officers.

11. These exercises with foreign navies consisted of search-and-rescue drills, communications exercises, and even replenishment alongside in at least one case; however, conspicuously absent were tactical operations. The author has been told authoritatively that planned or proposed exercises with Thailand and other ASEAN countries also will have the goal of fostering bilateral relations, not of achieving operational capability.

12. Nikolay Petrov, "Moscow and Beijing Did Not Mention Their Loses That They Incurred during the Joint Maneuvers," *Moscow Kommersant,* FBIS CEP20051013330001, 8 September 2005. The following FBIS reports contain left-handed compliments and question PLA competence: "Chinese Army's 'Iron Discipline' Impresses Russian Defense Minister," Moscow RIA-Novosti, CEP20050825002002, 25 August 2005; "Russia: Results of Joint Military Exercise with China Assessed," Moscow Rossiya television, CEP20050927027016, 24 September 2005; "Russian TV Looks at Military Cooperation with China Post-Exercise," Moscow Zvezda television, CEP20050919027182, 19 September 2005.

13. "China-Russia: PRC Media on Sino-Russian Military Exercises Project Image of Converging Interests in Asia," FBIS Feature, FEA20050831007588, 31 August 2005. This analysis of the August 2005 Russian-Chinese exercise quotes the principal Chinese and Russian generals involved as saying the exercise represented "a major strategic decision of the Russian and Chinese leaders" aimed at deepening "strategic cooperative partnership"—a phrase described by the FBIS analyst as normally used to describe bilateral relations.

14. Richard Halloran, "Chinese Sub Highlights Underseas Rivalries," *Japan Times,* 30 November 2004, available at search.japantimes.co.jp/print/opinion/eo2004/eo20041130a1.htm.

15. U.S. Department of Defense, *Annual Report to Congress: The Military Power of the People's Republic of China 2005,* July 2005, 12–13; available at www.defenselink .mil/news/Jul2005/d20050719china.pdf. On MRBMs, see Mark A. Stokes, "Chinese Ballistic Missile Forces in the Age of Global Missile Defense: Challenges and Responses," in *China's Growing Military Power: Perspectives on Security, Ballistic Missiles, and Conventional Capabilities,* ed. Andrew Scobell and Larry M. Wortzel (Carlisle, Pa.: U.S. Army War College, Strategic Studies Institute, September 2002), 113, available at www.strategicstudiesinstitute.army.mil/pdffiles/PUB59.pdf. The DF-21 family is also called the CSS-5. On SRBMs, see ibid., 116. The DF-15 and DF-11 families are also called the CSS-6 and CSS-7, respectively.

16. Stokes, "Chinese Ballistic Missile Forces in the Age of Global Missile Defense," 150 n. 12.

17. See Eric A. McVadon, *Recent Trends in China's Military Modernization,* written statement prepared for testimony before the U.S.-China Economic and Security Review Commission, 15 September 2005, available at www.ifpa.org/pdf/mcvadon .pdf. The information was derived from many translated Chinese articles during recent years; sources can be identified for serious researchers.

18. Lowell E. Jacoby, Director, Defense Intelligence Agency, *Current and Projected National Security Threats to the United States,* statement (excerpted) to the Senate Select Committee on Intelligence, 24 February 2004, available at www.ransac .org/Official%20Documents/U.S.%20Government/Intelligence%20Community/492004113202AM.html.

19. See Barabanov, "Contemporary Military Shipbuilding in China," for an open-source catalogue of PLAN modernization efforts.

20. John R. Benedict, "The Unraveling and Revitalization of U.S. Navy Antisubmarine Warfare," *Naval War College Review* 58, no. 2 (Spring 2005): 102. "The recent sale [to China] of eight additional Project 636 Kilos equipped with wake-homing anti-ship torpedoes and submerged-launch 3M54E Klub-S [the SS-N-27B] anti-ship cruise missiles is indicative of the transformation of this submarine force. The Project 636 Kilo 'is one of the quietest diesel submarines in the world' [quoting the Office of Naval Intelligence]; . . . the Klub-S missile has a 220-kilometer maximum range . . . and a terminal speed of up to Mach 3. Such a capability represents a very formidable threat to American and allied surface units."

21. "Klub (SS-N-27) ASCM," *Barat Rakshak: The Consortium of Indian Military Websites,* 12 September 2004, www.bharat-rakshak.com/NAVY/Klub.html. This and several of the following citations from public sources serve usefully to describe Chinese acquisitions and deployments; the varied character of these sources also illustrates that reasonably accurate descriptions of the ongoing PLA modernization are publicly available. The problem can be culling inaccurate reports; the author is often able to do so by asking knowledgeable PLA officers and through active exchanges with other diligent specialists.

22. "Russia to Deliver SS-N-27 to China," *Chinese Defence Today,* 29 April 2005, available at www.sinodefence.com/news/2005/news29-04-05.asp.

23. On quietness and sensors, see Zachary Moss, "Nuclear Submarines Worldwide: Current Force Structure and Future Developments," *Bellona Nuclear Naval Vessels,* 13 May 2004, www.bellona.no/en/international/russia/navy/northern_fleet/vessels/34070.html. On employment, see www.globalsecurity.org/military/library/report/2005/d20050719china.pdf. The U.S. Defense Department, in its 2005 *Annual Report to the Congress: The Military Power of the People's Republic of China,* 33, states: "China is developing capabilities to achieve local sea denial, including . . . developing the Type-093 nuclear attack submarine for missions requiring greater at-sea endurance."

24. "Yuan Class Diesel-Electric Submarine," *Chinese Defence Today,* available at www.sinodefence.com/navy/sub/yuan.asp. For the Song class, "Type 039 Song Class Diesel-Electric Submarine," ibid., www.sinodefence.com/navy/sub/039.asp.

25. Jing-Dong Yuan, "Chinese Responses to U.S. Missile Defenses: Implications for Arms Control and Regional Security," *Nonproliferation Review* (Spring 2003), available at cns.miis.edu/pubs/npr/vol10/101/101yuan.pdf, 89.

26. This is an estimate based on the author's acquaintance over fifteen years with the PLAN submarine force and discussions in recent years with others who have extensive experience concerning that force.

27. With respect to Taiwan's ASW capability and potential, the author drew on numerous exchanges with ROC naval officers and think-tankers over many years, including numerous visits to Taiwan. For judgments on other aspects of the ASW environment, the author relied on his three decades of ASW experience flying P-2 and P-3 aircraft, the major portion of which was gained with the U.S. Seventh Fleet in western Pacific waters.

28. Benedict, "The Unraveling and Revitalization of U.S. Navy Antisubmarine Warfare," 97 fig. 2, where the ASW situation for 2003 is described as "Few new ASW sensor & weapon capabilities fielded to counter diesel subs in littorals." Also, on 99–100, the U.S. Navy vice admiral commanding Atlantic submarine and ASW forces is quoted as saying, "Our ASW capabilities can best be described as poor or weak," and the Pacific Fleet commander as warning, "We will need greater ASW capability than we have today. . . . Future technologies are essential to counter the growing submarine threat."

29. For the Su-30, Charles R. Smith, "New Chinese Jets Superior, Eagle Loses to Flanker," NewsMax.com, 26 May 2004, at www.newsmax.com/archives/articles/2004/5/26/154053.shtml. This article illustrates that open sources were reporting this PLA naval air force acquisition and its antiship role soon after its purchase from Russia was consummated: "China is about to receive 24 advanced Sukhoi Su-30MK2 Flanker fighters from Russia. . . . The new Chinese fighters are reportedly equipped with enhanced anti-ship strike capabilities including the Kh-31 Krypton supersonic anti-ship missile. . . . The PLA Naval Air Corps will deploy the latest batch of Su-30MK2 fighters." For the B-6, Robert S. Norris and Hans M. Kristensen, "Chinese Nuclear Forces, 2003," *2003 Bulletin of the Atomic Scientists* 59, no. 6 (November/December 2003): 77–80, available at www.thebulletin.org/article_nn.php?art_ofn=ndo3norris. Using the Chinese designation for B-6—that is, H-6—this article states: "Although increasingly obsolete as a modern strike bomber, the H-6 may gain new life as a platform for China's emerging cruise missile capability. The naval air force has used the H-6 to carry the C-601/Kraken anti-ship cruise missile for more than 10 years, and *Flight International* reported in 2000 that up to 25 H-6s would be modified to carry four new YJ-63 land-attack cruise missiles." For the FB-7, see "JH-7 [Jianhong Fighter-Bomber] [FB-7] / FBC-1," Globalsecurity.org, 27 April 2005, www.globalsecurity.org/military/world/china/jh-7.htm: "China reportedly is developing an improved version of the FB-7. The twin-engine FB-7 is an all-weather, supersonic, medium-range fighter-bomber with an anti-ship mission. Improvements to the FB-7 likely will include a better radar, night attack avionics, and weapons." For ASCMs, see Nuclear Threat Initiative (NTI), *China's Cruise Missile Designations and Characteristics,* 26 March 2003, www.nti.org/db/china/mimport.htm. This material is produced independently for NTI by the Center for Nonproliferation Studies at the Monterey Institute of International Studies.

30. "Naval Forces," *Strategy Page,* 20 March 2005, www.strategypage.com/htmw/htsurf/articles/20050320.aspx. This source states: "The primary weapon of the *Sovremenny* is the SS-N-22 *Sunburn,* a high-speed sea-skimming missile with a huge 660-pound warhead. The *Sunburn* is probably the best anti-ship missile in the world." This article is cited primarily to illustrate the widespread reputation of the Sunburn missile as extremely lethal and evasive.

31. "Type 052c (*Lanzhou* Class) Air Defence Missile Destroyer," *Chinese Defence Today,* 27 August 2005, available at www.sinodefence.com/navy/surface/052c.asp: "Jiangnan Shipyard started to build two Type 052C destroyers . . . with more advanced weapon systems and sensors specifically for fleet air defence role. . . . The most

notable feature is the four-array multifunction phased array radar (PAR) similar to the U.S. AN/SPY-1 Aegis system. Additionally, the destroyers are also fitted with the vertical launch system (VLS) for the indigenous HQ-9 long-range air defence missile system."

32. The U.S.-China Economic and Security Review Commission annual report for 2005, chap. 3, sec. 1, based on testimony of expert witnesses, available at www .uscc.gov/annual_report/2005/chapter3_sec1.pdf, states: "The PLA Navy (PLAN) is engaged in an unprecedented level of construction and acquisition of major surface combatant ships. It currently is deploying seven new major ship classes at one time, building up to two new ships in each class per year. These include the Project 956 *Sovremenny*-class guided-missile destroyer (DDG); the Type 52B DDG; the Type 52C, Aegis-like DDG; the Type 54 guided-missile frigate."

33. U.S. Defense Department, *FY04 Report to Congress on PRC Military Power*, 43–44, states: "Acquisition of modern ISR systems remains a critical aspect of Beijing's military modernization. China is developing its ISR capabilities based on domestic components, supplemented by foreign technology acquisition and procurement of complete foreign systems. PLA procurement of new space systems, AEW [air early warning] aircraft, long-range UAVs [unmanned aerial vehicles], and over-the-horizon radar will enhance its ability to detect, monitor, and target naval activity in the western Pacific Ocean. It appears, from writings on PLA exercises, that this system currently lacks integration and that a fused, efficient ISR capability will not be achieved for many years." See also Richard A. Bitzinger, "Come the Revolution: Transforming the Asia-Pacific's Militaries," *Naval War College Review* 58, no. 4 (Autumn 2005): 42–43, 46.

34. For the saga of China and aircraft carrier acquisition, see Ian Storey and You Ji, "China's Aircraft Carrier Ambitions: Seeking Truth from Rumors, *Naval War College Review* 57, no. 1 (Winter 2004).

Bernard D. Cole

China's Maritime Strategy

"The Chinese nation was one of the first in the world to develop [and] utilize marine resources [in the eighth century B.C.]. . . . Establishing a Chinese maritime strategy has become a task of top importance [as we look] to the seas for our future survival space."

> —Yan Youqiang and Chen Rongxing, "On Maritime Strategy and the Marine Environment," Beijing Zhongguo Junshi Kexue [*China Military Science*] 2 (20 May 1997): 81–92, in FBIS-CHI-97-19.

Introduction

IN DEVELOPING THE NECESSARY CONTEXT for a discussion of China's future nuclear submarine force, this chapter addresses the current state of development of a maritime strategy in China, a strategy that draws on Chinese, Russian, and other Western concepts of sea power. China's record as a naval power during the long period of empire and republic focused on continental rather than maritime concerns. It suffered disastrously from its lack of naval power during the "One Hundred Years of Humiliation" in the nineteenth and twentieth centuries.

Great Britain, the United States, and Japan dominated much of revolutionary China with relatively small military forces, by using sea and river transport to penetrate China's vast interior, moving troops rapidly from one crisis area to another.[1] The pre-1949 Republic of China government had no effective maritime strategy, since its security threats came from the Chinese Communist Party (CCP) and internal warlords.

The Early Years: 1949–1954

The new CCP government in 1949 believed its coastline and island territories were threatened by both the United States and the Kuomintang (KMT) regime on Taiwan. Mao Zedong obtained Soviet military assistance during his 1949–50 visit to Moscow, including naval equipment and advisers.

The Russian advisers may not have consciously applied a maritime strategic theory to their task in 1950, but their background would have been the Soviet "Young School," focusing on coastal defense by a navy of small surface craft and submarines. The Young School of maritime strategy had developed in the Soviet Union shortly after World War I, based on the conditions in post-revolutionary Russia:

1. a new regime under military and political attack by several capitalist countries, with still unsuppressed domestic fighting;

2. a regime that *expected* to be besieged and attacked by capitalist nations, including amphibious attack, especially from "the ultimate bastion of imperialism, the United States";[2]

3. a navy in disarray and manned by captured/defecting enemy personnel;

4. severe budgetary shortages;

5. lack of an industrial infrastructure to produce modern naval armaments; and

6. a maritime frontier hemmed in by adversarial fleets and bases.

These conditions seemed also to apply to 1949 China, as did an absence of a modern maritime tradition.

The initial group of approximately five hundred Soviet naval advisors grew to between fifteen hundred and two thousand by 1953, and was assigned throughout the Chinese chain-of-command from Beijing headquarters to individual ships and squadrons. Furthermore, "large numbers" of Chinese officers, including the new head of the PLAN, were sent to study in the Soviet Union.[3]

Although its maritime strategy in the early 1950s was defensive, Beijing worked to develop the capability needed to recover the many offshore islands still occupied by the KMT, as part of a campaign designed to culminate in the August 1950 invasion of Taiwan.[4] This plan was frustrated by the beginning of the Korean War and President Truman's dispatch of the Seventh Fleet to the Taiwan Strait in June.

1955–1959

The mixed lessons of the Korean War did nothing to change Beijing's belief that an amphibious invasion remained a threat and would best be countered by short-range defensive sea forces; no ocean-going navy was planned during the 1950s. Mao Zedong cited the need for "a strong navy for the purposes of fighting against imperialist aggression" when the Korean War ended, and in December 1953 assigned the People's Liberation Army Navy (PLAN) three missions: (1) eliminate Guomindang (GMD) naval interference and ensure safe navigation; (2) prepare to recover Taiwan; and (3) oppose aggression from the sea.[5] China also began planning for a sea-based nuclear deterrent during the latter part of the decade, although PLAN modernization was limited by continued Maoist belief in "people's war," constrained resources, and a planning horizon defined by a brown-water defensive strategy.

A New Situation: 1960–1976

The 1960s were marked by major foreign and domestic events that further limited Chinese interest in developing a seagoing navy. Most important was the 1960 split with the Soviet Union, when Khrushchev withdrew Soviet advisors (and their plans) from China.

Mao's concept of People's War remained the guidance for the navy during this decade and a half, modified by some significant naval developments. The operational implications of the strategic situation—with the Soviet Union posing a maritime threat—contributed to a national commitment of resources to the development of nuclear-powered attack and ballistic-missile submarines.[6]

As the 1970s progressed, PLAN missions seemed still to reflect Young School thinking: assistance to the army; offshore patrol against criminal activities such as smuggling, piracy, and illegal immigration; and lifesaving and safety of navigation.

Meanwhile, the Soviet navy in the 1960s and 1970s underwent dramatic changes under the leadership of Admiral Sergei Gorshkov, partly as a result of the Cuban Missile Crisis's glaring demonstration of Soviet maritime weakness. Under Gorshkov's guidance, the Soviets built a large fleet with ambitious wartime missions:

1. defend offshore areas;

2. counter an adversary's strategic strike systems;

3. control sea in fleet ballistic-missile (FBM) submarine operating areas;

4. launch strategic nuclear strike;

5. disrupt an adversary's sea lines of communications (SLOCs); and

6. protect friendly SLOCs.

Gorshkov's maritime strategy also included specific peacetime tasks:

1. show the flag;

2. gain international respect;

3. support economic interests;

4. manage crises;

5. limit an adversary's options;

6. exercise local sea control; and

7. use in local wars.[7]

Gorshkov's vision and strategic plans may well be influencing China's current naval modernization.

A Modern PLAN Emerges

A revolution similar in kind if not in scale to that in the post-1962 Soviet Union has been taking place in China since the mid-1990s, with the U.S. naval intervention in the 1996 Taiwan Strait Crisis analogous to the Cuban Missile Crisis. Maritime strategic thought has been reinvigorated, as PLAN planners are now extending naval power beyond China's coastal arena.

Beijing's revitalized maritime strategy is also based on the coastal concentration of China's burgeoning economy and many military facilities, and is marked by significant growth above and beyond the basic mission of coastal defense as the navy's strategy. Significantly, the resources necessary for modernizing the PLAN have become available with China's dramatic economic development and increasing wealth.

An important influence on China's current maritime strategy is General Liu Huaqing, commander of the PLAN from 1982 to 1987 and then Vice-Chairman of the Central Military Commission until 1997. Liu observed that "the strategic position of the Pacific is becoming more important [and] as China is gradually expanding the scale of its maritime development, the Chinese Navy will have to shoulder more and heavier tasks in both peacetime and war."[8] He argued that "the scope of sea warfare operations has extended from the limited space of air, the surface, the water, and coasts, to all space from under the sea to outer space and from the sea inland. . . . In order to safeguard China's coast, resist possible foreign invasion, and defend our maritime rights and interests, it is only right and proper that China should attach great importance to developing its own navy, including 'emphatic' development of its submarine force."[9]

Liu directed the PLAN's Naval Research College in 1982 to develop a strategy of "offshore defense."[10] The definition of "offshore" in this construct is imprecise, with estimates ranging from two hundred kilometers to two hundred–six hundred nautical miles, but he probably meant the area from China's coast seaward to the "First Island Chain," defined by the Kurile Islands, Japan, the Ryukyu Islands, Taiwan, the Philippines, Borneo, and Natuna Besar.[11] This area includes the Yellow Sea, facing Korea and Japan; the western East China Sea, including Taiwan; and the South China Sea (SCS).[12]

This strategy stipulated: (1) stubborn defense near the shore; (2) mobile warfare at sea; and (3) surprise guerrilla-like attacks at sea.[13] Executing these missions would require significant national resources for naval forces, especially since Liu's maritime ambitions envisioned a PLAN composed of multiship task groups supported by integral logistics forces.

Liu's definition of maritime strategic theaters by fixed geographic boundaries reveals a strong continentalist perspective, and is contrary to the argument of Western maritime strategists that while the soldier thinks of terrain and theaters, the sailor of necessity thinks in wider terms, outside immediate physical limits—there is no "terrain" at sea.[14] His framework should not be dismissed out-of-hand, however, although it may reflect his early Soviet training and the continuing influence of Russian naval strategy.

By the mid-1980s, Soviet naval strategy included a division of Russian waters out to about two thousand nautical miles from the coast into defense zones. The Soviet's innermost zone was called the "area of sea control"; the second was the "area of sea denial"; the third was a broad region for long-range reconnaissance and submarine interdiction. Liu Huaqing's delineation of island chains almost certainly owes its origin to these "zones," the first and second of which extended seaward two thousand kilometers, closely matching Liu's lines, the second of which lies eighteen hundred to two thousand kilometers from China's coast. In addition to championing a national maritime strategy, Liu reorganized the navy, gave new life to the marine corps, upgraded bases and research and development facilities, and restructured the navy's school system.[15]

Most significantly, Liu's strategy provided rationale and direction for continued PLAN modernization. It described control of vast oceanic expanses as a vital national interest; an ambition perhaps unattainable in the face of continued U.S. and Japanese naval presence, but effective within the PLA in obtaining significantly greater resources for naval modernization and securing national command authority belief in the value of strong maritime power.

Liu emphasized naval missions well to seaward of the coastal zone that had formed the basis for past PRC maritime thinking.[16] PLAN modernization depends on a well-articulated offshore mission, envisioning China's capability as the strongest maritime power in East Asia. A direct line may be drawn from Sergei Gorshkov to Liu Huaqing: indeed, the former was an instructor at the Voroshilov Naval Academy in Leningrad when the latter was a student at the school.[17]

The PLAN in 2005 has not been tasked with all of the 1970s Soviet maritime strategic objectives. It has no "FBM operating areas" to control, for instance, and its "strategic nuclear strike" capability is almost nonexistent— but both of these missions will be applicable with the deploying of new (Type 094) ballistic-missile submarines. It has already adopted peacetime strategic missions almost identical to those outlined by Gorshkov—who cited the American threat as his basic justification for a strong navy. Writing in 1975, he accused the United States of following an "oceanic strategy" of aggression against the Soviet Union;[18] Chinese strategists today use similar words.

Strategy, Politics, and Geography

Current PLAN modernization follows the "sea change" in national strategic thinking that occurred in 1985, when Beijing's expectations of global nuclear war or large-scale conflict with the Soviet Union gave way to a focus on small, local wars on China's periphery. The local, limited wars envisioned include (1) small-scale conflicts in disputed border areas; (2) conflicts over disputed islands or ocean areas; (3) surprise air attacks; (4) deliberate incursions into China; and (5) counterattacks by China against an aggressor or "to uphold justice and dispel threats."[19]

This poses an important shift for Chinese maritime strategic thought. First, the PLAN has moved from a general strategy of coastal defense to one of offshore defense. Second, it has moved the navy from army acolyte to lead service in certain operational scenarios, including challenges over sovereignty claims and maritime interests from Taiwan, Japan, the United States, India, and Southeast Asian nations.

The Western Influence

The classic maritime strategic concept in Western thought is "command of the sea," most simply defined as the ability to use the sea while denying its use to an adversary. "Sea control" is a lesser but nonetheless powerful concept, defined as a nation's ability to control the events over a discrete ocean area; i.e., both friendly and opposing forces are able to operate, but within bounds favorable to one's own side. Finally, "sea denial" refers to denying an opponent the use of a discrete ocean area for a period of time necessary to achieve a specific strategic goal.

Achieving any of these objectives requires strong naval surface forces, but may also be achieved through mastery of the air-space continuum and/ or the subsurface space relative to the maritime area in issue. Sea denial in littoral waters is a particularly attractive and inexpensive option for even a small naval power, if it has access to mines, missiles, submarines, and shore-based aircraft in sufficient numbers and capability—as does China.[20]

The PLAN is continuing to acquire modern, capable platforms on, above, and under the ocean surface, but several other advances contribute even more significantly to Beijing's accrual of maritime power during the past decade. These include:

1. the complete overhaul of training and education programs, one result of which is improved professionalization of the officer corps and an improving noncommissioned officer corps;

2. the accession of modern naval systems and platforms costs, capabilities, and sustainability;

3. the expansion of a national scientific and industrial infrastructure for research, development, and production of naval warfare technology and systems, including increasing tie-ins to civilian enterprises;

4. a focus on developing and exercising doctrine and tactics for specific strategic objectives;

5. the ability to administer, operate, and command and control tactical units beyond individual ships;

6. improved C4ISR, with an emphasis on state-of-the-art technology and the utilization of space;

7. recognition at senior civilian and military leadership levels of the advantages to be gained from maritime power.[21]

Maritime Strategic Interests

In the October 1992 Fourteenth Party Congress political report, General Secretary Jiang Zemin described the PLA's mission as defending "the unity, territorial integrity, and maritime rights and interests of the homeland." He later instructed the PLAN "to safeguard the sovereignty of China's territorial waters, uphold the country's unity and social stability and create a safe and stable environment for the nation's economic development."[22] The navy's first priority is defense of China's long sea frontier stretching from Korea to the Indochinese Peninsula, a great maritime sweep marked by major offshore island chains from Japan to the Malacca Strait.

The PLAN aspires to play a central national security role, as described by PLAN vice-chief, Vice Admiral Cheng Mingshang, who argued in 1991 that the navy is "the tool of the state's foreign policy . . . an international navy can project its presence far away from home. It can even appear at the sea close to the coastal lines of the target countries. . . . This has made the navy the most active strategic force in peacetime, a pillar for the country's foreign policy and the embodiment of the country's will and power."[23] Economic justification for a strong Chinese navy rests on the concentration of modern economic interests and growth in the special development zones clustered along China's seaboard.[24] Seabed minerals are also important, especially potential petroleum deposits in the ECS and SCS.[25]

Jiang Zemin in 1995 described China as "a continental power, and a coastal power as well." He emphasized the coastal region's "dense population, with its scientific, technological, and economic levels," noting that "the ocean as a natural protective screen covers this region of strategic significance. . . . We can be sure that the development and utilization of the ocean will be of increasingly greater significance to China's long range development . . . we must see the ocean from a strategic plane, and . . . set out new and higher requirements on navy building. We must . . . step up the pace of navy modernization to meet the requirements of future wars."[26]

Territorial Claims

East China Sea

China's maritime petroleum disputes with Japan have drawn more media attention, but fisheries disputes are an equally troublesome issue with both that country and with South Korea. Negotiations so far have established only temporary measures for resolving fisheries disputes and none for disputed petroleum deposits.[27]

Japan

China claims the Diaoyu, also claimed by Japan as the Senkaku Islands.[28] These five small islands and three rocky outcroppings lie 90 nautical miles northeast of Taiwan and 220 nautical miles west-southwest of Okinawa. They were considered to be Chinese, based on a fourteenth-century claim, until acquired by Japan under the Treaty of Shimonoseki following its victorious war with China in 1895. The Senkakus remained with Japan when the allied powers returned Taiwan to China in 1945.

The islands are uninhabited and have no intrinsic value, except as a symbol of national pride. They lie on China's continental shelf, but the United Nations Convention on the Law of the Sea (UNCLOS) parameters do not support that necessarily as determining ownership. In fact, a 1968 UN study suggesting the presence of petroleum reserves stimulated the present dispute.[29] Tokyo argues that the two nations' overlapping exclusive economic zones (EEZs) should be divided midway between Japan and China, while Beijing's position is that any mineral deposits on China's continental shelf are Chinese.

PLAN ships continue steaming in the disputed area around the Senkakus; in September 2005, a Chinese task force of five ships loitered in the area.[30] This is probably part of a deliberate Beijing policy similar to the American Freedom of Navigation (FON) program, under which U.S. ships deliberately transit seas claimed as sovereign by nations whose claims the United States disputes. The Chinese incursions are increasing and the potential for confrontation is increasing between one of Beijing's incursions and a Japanese ship or aircraft, which routinely respond to them.[31]

The South China Sea

This relatively small body of water holds important economic, political, and nationalistic strategic implications. These include rich fisheries; possible large petroleum, natural gas, and manganese deposits; vital sea lines of communication (SLOCs); and the issue of national pride.[32]

China, Taiwan, and Vietnam claim all of the Paracel and the Spratly Islands, while Malaysia and the Philippines claim several of the islands. Brunei in 1984 established an "exclusive fishing zone" that includes Louisa Reef in the southern Spratlys, but has not officially claimed that bit of land. Indonesia does not claim any of the Spratlys, but the rich oil and natural-gas fields surrounding its Natuna Islands extend into the area of the South China Sea (SCS) claimed by China; hence, it is a very concerned participant in the region's territorial disputes.

The National People's Congress passed the Law of the Territorial Sea and Contiguous Zones in February 1992, which implies that the entire SCS is sovereign Chinese territory, water as well as land areas.[33]

The PLAN has limited resources for projecting sustained power throughout the South China Sea and China will likely continue its present, dual strategic approach in the area. First, it is pursuing discussions to resolve conflicting claims.[34] In the 2001 Code of Conduct signed by the claimant countries, Beijing agreed to peaceful efforts to exploit South China Sea resources. Then, in January 2005, China and the Philippines signed an agreement, soon joined by Vietnam, in which they agreed to pursue joint exploration of possible petroleum reserves.

Second, however, Beijing has established a military presence on disputed islands and other land features by building facilities ranging from navigation markers to structures capable of housing personnel and berthing small ships.[35] Despite its diplomatic moves, Beijing consistently phrases its maritime claims in categorical terms.[36] Additionally, China uses "straight baselines" to demarcate its claims along its coastline and the Paracels, a method contrary to the 1982 UNCLOS.[37]

The South China Sea is the route for more than one-half of the world's total merchant shipping; over three times as many ships pass through the Malacca Strait as pass through the Suez Canal, and more than five times as many as pass through the Panama Canal.

This traffic, half of which passes near the Spratly Islands, is dominated by raw materials, particularly petroleum products. Nearly two-thirds of the tonnage transiting the Malacca Strait and half of that passing near the Spratlys is crude oil from the Middle East. Two-thirds of the world's total liquefied natural gas (LNG) shipments pass through the South China Sea.[38]

Taiwan

Taiwan is the primary focus of Beijing's offshore strategic concerns, and despite possible U.S. intervention China refuses to renounce the use of military force to ensure the island's reunification. Beijing must count on the PLAN for policy options ranging from intimidation to outright invasion.[39] Chinese planners are almost certainly concentrating their efforts on devising a strategic paradigm under which the navy would be able to secure its objectives despite or before the United States could intervene. Such plans probably include a full range of operational options, from full-scale amphibious assault to decapitating Taiwan's leadership, but seem to be focusing on a deployed submarine force in the East China Sea, both to isolate Taiwan and to slow American naval intervention until Taipei yields to Beijing's pressure.

Additionally, China is already using the threat of short- and medium-range ballistic missiles to restrict Taipei's policy options and deter Taiwan's leaders.

Beyond the China Seas

Sea Lines of Communication (SLOCs)

Ships carry between 85 and 90 percent of China's trade. Continued development of China's economy into the twenty-first century depends on reliable sources of electrical power from fossil fuel. The nation currently imports up to 40 percent of its annual petroleum requirements, an amount sure to grow.[40] This imported petroleum, most from the Middle East, arrives over sea lanes that pass through the Indian Ocean, as well as the South and East China Seas. These routes include several geographic "choke points," including the Luzon and Taiwan Straits, the Strait of Malacca, and the Straits of Hormuz and Bab el-Mandeb.

China can project almost no naval control over these choke points, except for the Taiwan narrows, and Beijing is very concerned with their potential as strategic buttons the United States might push in the event of a conflict. President Hu Jintao has specifically discussed "China's Malacca dilemma" in this respect,[41] and we must assume that PLAN leaders have improved SLOC defense capabilities high on their priority list. Beijing believes a strong

PLAN is vital to resolving all these (and many other) issues of national security concern.

India

Chinese strategic concern about India includes that nation's propinquity to the Indian Ocean SLOCs over which so much of China's imported petroleum flows. Beijing must also be concerned about India's campaign for an increased economic and naval presence east of Malacca, with an increased role in decisions affecting the South China Sea.[42]

China appears to be establishing a maritime security presence in Burma and nearby waters. The two nations have announced a "framework of future bilateral relations and cooperation," and economic and military relations are expanding. A rationale for a PLAN presence in these areas would position Beijing to influence the vital SLOCs through the Malacca Straits and into the Indian Ocean. China and Burma have during the past decade and a half established a close relationship. This includes military cooperation, trade and Chinese investment programs, and Beijing's political support for the isolated Rangoon regime. Indeed, despite Burma's rather tenuous membership in the Association of Southeast Asian Nations (ASEAN), China is that country's only significant friend.

India finds this presence very disquieting, despite recent joint statements to "resolve to maintain peace along [their] borders."[43] Even more disturbing to New Delhi is China's close relationship with Pakistan. Beijing makes no secret of its military and economic support for India's most obdurate enemy, support that includes China's major role in expanding the Pakistani harbor at Gwadar into a major port facility.

Achieving the reputed completion of Liu Huaqing's strategic paradigm—global maritime power—would require China's leaders to alter allocation of national resources to build a very large navy during the next fifty years. This maritime strategic objective, if distant in accomplishment, or even chimerical, may still serve the PLAN in domestic budget battles.[44]

The PLAN does seem to be pursuing objectives described by its 1999 commander, Admiral Shi Yunsheng:

1. an "'offshore defense' strategy";
2. "making the navy strong with science and technology, narrowing the gap between it and other military powers";[45]

3. "more advanced weapons," including "warships, submarines, fighters, missiles, torpedoes, guns, and electronic equipment"; and

4. trained personnel and "more qualified people."[46]

Although this construct omits logistics or the ability to keep a fleet at sea for the extended period of time necessary to power projection,[47] significant advances are being made in improving the shore- and sea-based infrastructure necessary to support PLAN operations. China's booming economy has allowed the national government to devote increased resources to military modernization, and the PLAN continues to benefit from this development.

Composition of the nascent Chinese navy seems still gauged to East Asian security concerns, but it would not be wise to conclude that Beijing will not allocate the resources necessary to deploy an inter-regional navy once the Taiwan issue is resolved in its favor. Immediate indicators of expanded strategic missions for the PLAN include significant increases in distant logistics support capability, the development of air-capable ships (beyond the current two-helicopter-per-ship limit), or the expanded use of nuclear power for submarines and perhaps for surface combatants. Current fleet composition and expansion efforts include an increase in such power plants—the Types 093 and 094 submarines—but appear to form a small part of China's fleet ambitions.

Conclusion

China faces five major maritime security situations in Asia: Taiwan, Japan, the South China Sea, India, and its SLOCs. The American naval presence overlies all of these. Maritime strategists in Beijing are reminded of their navy's shortcomings every day the U.S. Navy deploys across East Asia—a fact that helps fuel the current campaign to modernize the PLAN.

China's naval strategy long reflected influence from the Soviet "Young School." Since the mid-1990s however, Beijing has realized the inadequacy of this paradigm for a PLAN offering China's leaders a flexible, ready instrument of national security. Instead, the emerging maritime strategy reflects elements of Julian Corbett and Alfred Thayer Mahan's theories. The former's emphasis on using naval power to support achieving continental objectives seems to apply to Chinese concerns about island sovereignty issues, as does his concept of "sea control," which is more limited than Mahan's "command of the sea." But the latter's vision of naval power as a primary instrument of national security strategy is increasingly applicable to Beijing's security concerns. This also subsumes Mahan's characterization of seaborne trade as an important part of national power, a category in which China excels.

China's maritime strategy is codified as "offshore defense," which has clear offensive implications. Beijing is moving its strategic line seaward from the coast, demonstrating that the navy has an increasingly visible role in China's twenty-first-century national-security goals. Insofar as the PLAN is concerned, a strategy of offshore defense includes:

1. preparing for operations against Taiwan;

2. defending Chinese claims in the East and South China Seas;

3. maintaining a strategic deterrent force against the United States (and possibly India and Russia);

4. protecting vital SLOCs—some lying a great distance from China;[48] and

5. serving as a diplomatic force.[49]

Beijing's naval development seeks to take advantage of both modern technology and Maoist doctrine, as in "the use of strategy can reverse the balance of combat strength."[50] In Beijing's view, the ideal maritime strategy must overcome shortcomings in doctrine, equipment, and training.[51]

The PLAN remains a long way from achieving naval dominance in East Asia, even apart from the U.S. maritime presence. The Japanese Maritime Self-Defense Force (JMSDF) is certainly superior to the PLAN, and the Republic of Korea Navy (ROKN) would be a very difficult opponent. Even the Taiwan navy would not be a pushover for the PLAN. Clearly, a wise maritime strategist in Beijing would not, in the event of conflict, pose the PLAN "one-on-one" against any of these modern naval forces.

China's navy would require a more thoughtful strategy if opposed by any of these navies, especially the USN. One likely strategic step in a maritime conflict would be to gain the initiative through preemption. This might involve a "bolt from the blue,"[52] but also might be achieved by launching operations when an adversary's naval forces are weak, due to out-of-area commitments.

Chinese strategists have described the seas as "a protective screen," but also as "a marine invasion route," and have emphasized the "priority . . . of maritime strategic competition":

Military control of the seas means achieving and defending national unification, defending national maritime territorial sovereignty and maritime rights and interests, protecting legitimate maritime economic activities and scientific research, and ensuring a peaceful and stable climate for national reform, opening, and coastal economic development, by dealing with possible maritime incidents, armed conflicts, and local wars . . . our Navy has an inescapable mission. . . . The 21st century is going to a maritime one . . . we will have to make our maritime strategy a key part.[53]

The PLAN must be able to utilize East Asian seas if Beijing's strategic aims are to be secured in that region; however, China faces significant hurdles in the technological and industrial infrastructure and resource availability needed to deploy a regionally dominant navy. Beijing's maritime strategy for the new century includes:

1. establishing a genuine maritime nuclear deterrent force at sea;

2. maintaining a naval presence throughout East Asia;

3. joint capability for specific objectives, including credible power-projection capability with the amphibious and logistics support to take and hold disputed territory in the East and South China Seas;

4. SLOC defense at least to the Tsushima Strait in the north, the Malacca Strait in the south, and the Marianas in the east; and

5. prevailing in Taiwan scenarios (which will dominate maritime strategic planning).

In the near term, Beijing is building a navy capable of decisively influencing the operational aspects of the Taiwan and South China Sea situations, should diplomacy and other instruments of statecraft fail. The first phase of Liu Huaqing's reported strategy—to control China's adjacent seas out to the first island chain, is reasonable and currently within reach, as Beijing continues allocating the national resources necessary to build a modern maritime force.

Sea denial is the term in the maritime strategic lexicography that most closely describes Beijing's ambition for a navy sufficient to ensure the success of regional strategic plans, despite possible interference by the United States. Further maturation of the PLAN as an important instrument of national security will depend on how naval power and maritime economic interests are viewed by China's strategists. The value to the nation of its rich offshore mineral and biological resources, and its dependence on seaborne trade and transportation, are clearly understood in Beijing. Countering the present emphasis on building a strong navy is China's historic record as primarily a continental power, with periodic maritime power acquired only for specific strategic objectives for relatively brief periods. PLAN strategists are also looking beyond the Taiwan conundrum, with a view to SLOC defense over the great distances through the Indian Ocean.

China's widening maritime interests and increased budget resources are fostering a strong, modernizing navy. The new force is already capable of projecting power throughout China's littoral, from Honshu to Sumatra, including the waters surrounding Taiwan. Continuing growth and modernization of the PLAN will almost certainly lead to the belief by Chinese maritime strategists in Beijing's ability to include within its strategic maritime goals those areas considered vital to its national security—all of East Asia.

Notes

Note on sources: FBIS reports remain an important source of information about the PLAN, but since approximately 2003, items addressing Chinese maritime strategy have been significantly reduced from the level of the previous ten years. This is apparently not due to FBIS management, but may reflect a decision by the PLA to stop publicizing discussions about maritime strategy; the reduction also seems to have coincided with the removal from office of former PLAN commander Admiral Shi Yunsheng.

1. The United States, for instance, used just two navy transports and a commercial passenger liner to move Marine and Army regiments from the United States to the Far East, between the Philippines and China, and between north and south China, as crises waxed and waned.

2. Vladimir Lenin, cited in Bruce W. Watson, "The Evolution of Soviet Naval Strategy," in Bruce W. Watson and Peter M. Dunn, eds., *The Future of the Soviet Navy: An Assessment to the Year 2000* (Boulder, Colo.: Westview Press, 1986), 115.

3. Watson, 15.

4. David G. Muller, Jr., *China's Emergence As a Maritime Power* (Boulder, Colo.: Westview Press, 1983), 16.

5. Quoted in Srikanth Kondapalli, "China's Naval Strategy," *Strategic Analysis*, 23 (March 2000): 20–38.

6. China's Xia-class fleet ballistic missile submarine, patterned on the U.S. *George Washington*-class/Soviet Hotel-class, successfully launched a missile in 1988, but may have never made any patrols at sea. See Richard Sharpe, ed., *Jane's Fighting Ships: 1995–1996* (London: Butler and Tanner Ltd., 1996), 114.

7. Kenneth R. McGruther, *The Evolving Soviet Navy* (Newport, R.I.: Naval War College Press, 1978), 47–48, 66–67.

8. Quoted in Bradley Hahn, "PRC Policy in Maritime Asia," *Journal of Defense and Diplomacy* 4, no. 6 (June 1986): 20.

9. Quoted in Bradley Hahn, "China: Third Ranking Maritime Power—and Growing," *Pacific Defense Reporter* (October 1988): 47.

10. See Harlan Jencks, "The PRC's Military and Security Policy in the Post-Cold War Era," *Issues & Studies* 30, no. 11 (November 1994): 74, about a 1989 study ordered by Liu, *Balanced Development of the Navy in the Year 2000*, which called for a strategy of "active offshore defense."

11. Jing-dong Yuan, "China's Defense Modernization: Implications for Asia-Pacific Security," *Contemporary Southeast Asia* 17, no. 1 (June 1995): 70, cites the first distance; Alexander Huang, "Chinese Maritime Modernization and its Security Implications: The Deng Xiaoping Era and Beyond" (Ph.D. diss., The George Washington University, 1994), 13, gives the latter range.

12. See John Downing, "China's Evolving Maritime Strategy," *Jane's Intelligence Review* (1 March 1996), 1; and Huang, 230

13. See Huang, 225ff. for this discussion.

14. J. C. Wylie, *Military Strategy* (Westport, Conn.: Greenwood Press, 1967; reprint 1980), 49, is a classic work on modern naval strategy. Also see Winnefeld, 66: "The soldier shapes and exploits his environment; the sailor must adjust to it."

15. Liu's accomplishments are summed up in Alfred D. Wilhelm, Jr., *China and Security in the Asian Pacific Region Through 2010*, CNA Research Memorandum 95-226 (Alexandria, Va.: Center for Naval Analysis, 1996), 43.

16. Ibid., 191.

17. This point is discussed by John Downing, "China's Maritime Strategy, Part 2: The Future," *Jane's Intelligence Review* 8, no. 4 (April 1996): 188.

18. Quoted in Watson, 120.

19. Paul H. B. Godwin, "Force Projection and China's Military Strategy" (paper presented at the Sixth Annual Conference on the PLA, Coolfont, Va., June 1995), 4. Also see Godwin, "Changing Concepts of Doctrine, Strategy, and Operations in the People's Liberation Army 1978–1987," *China Quarterly* 112 (December 1987): 573–90.

20. Although, as J. R. Hill, *Maritime Strategy for Medium Powers* (Annapolis, Md.: U.S. Naval Institute Press, 1986), 85, points out, if China were to employ this strategy, say in the case of Taiwan, "the penalties for getting it wrong may be quite severe." Ibid., 229, Hill also delineates five indicators of "sea dependence," all of which apply to China: seagoing trade, fish catches, size of Merchant Marine, ship building and repairing, and the offshore zone.

21. This list is a variation on the seventeen points delineated by David Alan Rosenberg, "Process: The Realities of Formulating Modern Naval Strategy" (paper presented at the Corbett-Richmond Conference, Newport, R.I.: U.S. Naval War College, September 1992), 6–20.

22. Cited in Huang, 99.

23. Quoted in You Ji, "A Test Case for China's Defense and Foreign Policies," *Contemporary Southeast Asia* 16, no. 4 (March 1995): 379.

24. Liu Huaqing has used this argument, stating that "the Chinese navy must live up to the historical responsibility to grow rapidly up into a major power in the Pacific area

in order to secure the smooth progress of China's economic modernization." Quoted in Jun Zhan, "China Goes to the Blue Waters: The Navy, Seapower Mentality and the South China Sea," *The Journal of Strategic Studies* 17, no. 3 (September 1994): 191.

25. See Hong Kong *Ping Kuo Jih Pao* (7 March 1997), A20, in FBIS-CHI-1997-114, for the State Oceanography Bureau's estimate of China's maritime wealth as "three million square kilometers of sea areas rich in fishing, petroleum, and mineral resources." Beijing *Xinhua* (23 June 1999), in FBIS-CHI-1999-0623, Fujian Province reported in 1998 that "more than 900 deep-sea trawlers had been dispatched [around the world], bringing home a total catch of 600,000 tons" of fish—which was considered unsatisfactory.

26. Quoted in Huang Caihong, "Witnessing Maritime Exercise of the Chinese Navy," *Liaowang* 45 (6 November 1995), in FBIS-CHI-95-235.

27. Most recently, see "ROK, China Resume Fishing Talks in Beijing," *The Korea Times* (8 March 2000), in FBIS-KPP20000308000078: "Korea and China initialed a draft fisheries agreement in November 1998" which agreed on temporary EEZ boundaries; but also "ROKG to Intensify Watch Against PRC Boats Violating EEZ," Seoul *Yonhap* (1 June 2000), in FBIS-KPP20000601000093, which quotes Maritime Affairs and Fisheries Minister Lee Hang-kyu stating "he expects an increase in the number of Chinese fishing boats illegally operating in the [Korean] EEZ," as "the China-Japan fisheries treaty went into effect." Also see "Japan, China Plan Talks on New Fishery Pact," Tokyo *Jiji Press* (5 April 2000), in FBIS-JPP20000405000014, announced the beginning of the latest in a series of discussions to activate "a new bilateral fishery accord," based on "a provisional zone created as a result of a territorial dispute over the Senkaku Islands."

28. Physical description of these "islands" is from Richard Chapman, "Senkaku-Diaoyu Island Dispute," USCINCPAC "VIC" (Honolulu, 29 February 2000), 1.

29. The UNCLOS, Article 83, states that "the delimitation of the continental shelf between States with opposite or adjacent coasts shall be effected by agreement on the basis of international law, . . . If no agreement can be reached within a reasonable period of time, the States concerned shall resort to the procedures provided [herein]," which include submitting the dispute to "conciliation" (Annex V), the International Tribunal for the Law of the Sea, the International Court of Justice, or a special arbitral tribunal.

30. "Chinese Warships Make Show of Force at Protested Gas Rig," *Japan Times* (10 September 2005, www.japantimes.co.jp/cgi-bin/getarticle.pl5?nn20050910a1.htm).

31. See, for instance, "Isle Issue, Taiwan Threaten Ties Between Tokyo, Beijing," *Yomiuri Shimbun* (8 August 1999), for a report that "PRC ocean research ships have conducted 25 surveys in the territorial waters and exclusive economic zone near the Senkaku Islands."

32. The most optimistic estimate of SCS petroleum reserves, 55 billion tons, is in *Xinhua* (5 September 1994), in FBIS-CHI-1994-172.

33. Taiwan also passed a "Territorial Sea and Contiguous Zone Law" in 1993, in which it claims sovereignty over the same U-shaped line in the South China Sea as does Beijing in its 1992 legislation, and issued a "White Paper on Maritime Policy,"

Taiwan Central News Agency (22 June 99), in FBIS-CHI-1999-0622, which "stresses the ROC's jurisdiction over the disputed Spratly Islands in the south China Sea" but notes that it is "willing to jointly develop the region's natural resources with neighboring countries. . . ." In fact, Taiwan has not played a constructive role in settling the South China Sea territorial disputes, but has preferred to ride Beijing's rigid coattails: as a former senior naval intelligence officer in Taiwan told the author, "What do we have to lose?"

34. See *Xinhua* (23 July 1996), in FBIS-CHI-1996-144, for Foreign Secretary Qian Qichen's conciliatory statement at the ASEAN Regional Forum that the situation in the Spratlys was "stable."

35. Mischief Reef (*Huanyidao* in Chinese), located well within the Philippines' two-hundred-nautical-mile economic zone (EEZ), is the prime example of this encroachment. Whether the facilities will last past the first significant typhoon to blow through is another question. The United Nations Convention on the Law of the Sea (UNCLOS) specifies that to be considered to have an "exclusive economic zone or continental shelf," land must be able to "sustain human habitation or economic life of their own" (Art. 121). Hence, the efforts by various claimants to SCS rocks and reefs to construct facilities capable of "sustaining human habitation."

36. See, for instance, Chinese Foreign Ministry spokesman Sun Yuxi, "Hong Kong *Zhongguo Tongxun She* (16 January 1999), in FBIS-CHI-99-025: "China has indisputable sovereignty over the Nansha Islands and the contiguous maritime area." Also, Defense Minister Chi Haotian, "Chi Haotian Reiterates PRC Stand on South China Sea Issue," *Xinhua* (15 September 1999), in FBIS-CHI-99-0915: "the South China Sea has been China's territory from ancient times and . . . China has had indisputable sovereignty over the Nansha Islands and their adjacent sea areas."

37. C. M. LeGrand, "Memorandum for Undersecretary of Defense (Policy) and Director for Strategic Plans and Policy, 'Chinese Straight Baseline Declaration'" (Washington, D.C.: Department of Defense Representative for Ocean Policy Affairs, 21 May 1996), 1: "all of the straight baselines within the Chinese declaration are excessive and not in accordance with international law." Beijing applies "straight baselines" for its mainland and offshore islands, but has not stated that they apply to the Spratlys.

38. "South China Sea Region," *eia*, 4. John H. Noer, with David Gregory, *Chokepoints: Maritime Economic Concerns in Southeast Asia* (Washington, D.C.: National Defense University Press in cooperation with the Center for Naval Analysis, 1996), provides a thorough breakdown of the merchant traffic through the South China Sea, by cargo and by ship ownership, and estimates costs for alternate routes in the event the Malacca or other straits are closed.

39. Zhu Rongji reiterated this during his visit to Washington, D.C., in April 1998. See "Stratfor's Global Intelligence Update," *alert@stratfor.com* (14 April 1999): 2.

40. Daniel Yergin, Dennis Eklof, and Jefferson Edwards, "Fueling Asia's Recovery," *Foreign Affairs*, 77:2 (March–April 1998): 42, estimate China will import "as much as 3 million" barrels of oil per day by 2010. Also see Hugar, 22ff., for a discussion of Chinese oil imports.

41. Quoted in David Zweig and Bi Jianhai, "China's Global Hunt for Energy," *Foreign Affairs* 84, no. 5 (September/October 2005): 34.

42. India's increasing presence is suggested by New Delhi's agreement with Hanoi for mutual naval training events. See Ben Barber, "Indian Navy Exercises Seen Apt to Irk Beijing," *The Washington Times* (8 May 2000): 1. "Intelligence," *Far Eastern Economic Review* 163 (20 April 2000): 4, reports that the Vietnamese navy's deputy chief, Do Xuan Co, was exploring the possibility of repairing or even building ships in Indian shipyards.

43. "India, China Reiterate Resolve to Maintain Border Peace," New Delhi *Hindustan Times* (5 April 2000). See Tan Hongwei, " China Strives to Build a Fine Peripheral Environment," Beijing *Zhengguo Xinwen She* (5 September 1999), in FBIS-CHI-99-1023, for Singh's statement that India "does not regard China as a threat," a statement that must be regarded with some skepticism.

44. One recent U.S. Naval Attaché to Beijing described PLAN strategists and planners as "completely focused on the Taiwan mission."

45. See, for instance, Si Yanwne and Chen Wanjun, "Navy to Develop More High-Tech Equipment," *Jiefangjun Bao* (9 June 1999) in FBIS-CHI-1999-0611, citing General Cao Gangchuan, director of the General Armaments Department that "it is necessary to put [navy] armament development in a prominent position of army building . . . increase armaments' scientific and technological contents; and improve the quality and speed of armament development"; and Beijing *Xinhua* (10 June 1999), in FBIS-CHI-1999-0609, citing Cao that "the navy's rapid reaction capacity, emergency field repair ability and defense readiness must also be improved."

46. Quoted in Beijing *Xinhua* (21 April 1999), in FBIS-CHI-1999-0421.

47. Geoffrey Till, "Maritime Strategy in the Twenty-First Century," in Geoffrey Till, ed., *Seapower: Theory and Practice* (Portland, Ore.: Frank Cass, 1994), 193, notes that the United States was able to maintain a task force off the coast of West Africa for *seven months* in 1990–91, before finally evacuating civilians from strife-torn Liberia.

48. China ratified the UNCLOS in 1996, and some strategists use this pact as rationale for including "military control of the seas [as] legitimate maritime economic activities." Li Jie and Xu Shiming, "The UN Law of the Sea Treaty and the New Naval Mission," Beijing *Hsien-Tai Chun-Shih* (February 1997), quoted in Hugar, 73.

49. See Lu Ning, *The Dynamics of Foreign-Policy Decisionmaking in China* (Boulder, Colo.: Westview Press, 1997), 126ff., for an interesting description of the 1988 naval conflict with Vietnam when, according to the author, PLAN forces exceeded their instructions and drove national strategy.

50. The question of "red vs. expert" may remain a facet of civil-military relations in China, but drawing too sharp a dichotomy between army loyalty (to state, government, or party) and professionalism should be avoided. See works on this topic by Harlan Jencks, *From Muskets to Missiles: Politics and Professionalism in the Chinese Army, 1945–1981* (Boulder, Colo.: Westview Press, 1982); Ellis Joffe, *The Chinese Army After Mao* (Cambridge, Mass.: Harvard University Press, 1987); David

Shambaugh, *Modernizing China's Military: Progress, Problems, and Prospects* (Berkeley, Calif.: University of California Press, 2002); and Michael Swaine, *The Role of the Chinese Military in National Security Policymaking* (Santa Monica, Calif.: Rand Corporation, 1998).

51. Sr. Col. Huang Xing and Sr. Col. Zuo Quandian, "Holding the Initiative in Our Hands in Conducting Operations, Giving Full Play to Our Own Advantages To Defeat Our Enemy—A Study of the Core Idea of the Operational Doctrine of the PLA," Beijing *Zhaongquo Junshi Kexue* [China Military Science] 4 (20 November 1996): 49–56, in FBIS-CHI-1997. See ibid., 8, where the authors, who serve at the Academy of Military Science, clearly identify the United States as "our enemy," and also display an imperfect knowledge of American weapons systems.

52. "Bolt from the blue" was first used in modern maritime strategy in the early twentieth century to describe a possible surprise German naval attack on Great Britain. See Arthur M. Marder, *From the Dreadnought to Scapa Flow: The Royal Navy in the Fisher Era*, vol. 1, *The Road to War, 1904–1914* (London: Oxford University Press, 1961), 144, for discussion of this concept.

53. Yan Youqiang, "Director of a Naval Headquarters Research Institute," and Chen Rongxing, "On Maritime Strategy and the Marine Environment," *Beijing Zhongguo Junshi Kexue* 2 (20 May 1997), 81–92, in FBIS-CHI-97-197. This may be a good description of China's maritime strategic thought.

Paul H. B. Godwin

China's Emerging Military Doctrine

A Role for Nuclear Submarines?

Introduction

WITH THE INTRODUCTION OF TWO NEW CLASSES of nuclear-powered submarines—the 093 SSN and the 094 SSBN—China has built combatants undoubtedly far superior to their aging predecessors in the attributes that make SSN and SSBN such important components of the leading navies. These virtues are stealth, speed, endurance, autonomy, mobility, and especially in the case of an SSBN, lethality. The new SSBN's missile has an estimated range of some 5,000 miles—more than four times that of its 1,000-mile-range predecessor. These new nuclear-powered classes are accompanied by the continued acquisition of Kilo-class diesel-electric submarines (SSK) from Russia and China's indigenous development and production of advanced SSKs. This chapter will assess China's maritime and nuclear doctrine to suggest how these new and extremely capable submarines may be employed.

In the mid-1980s, China's maritime doctrine and strategy began a transition from coastal defense (*jinan fangyu;* 近岸防御) to offshore defense (*jinhai fangyu;* 近海防御). As that transition has taken place, China's basic military doctrine and national military strategy have undergone dramatic changes. The most significant revisions reflect more than a response to the technological advances that have so transformed the conduct of military operations. The most critical change results from Beijing's perception of the United States. Beijing's defense White Papers make it quite evident that the potential adversary now most feared by China is actually the United States.[1] Albeit currently improbable, the most likely Sino-American military confrontation is over Taiwan. Beyond Taiwan, however, there is the looming question of how Beijing sees China's role in Asia's future security environment. Will China continue to accept the dominant position in the western Pacific now occupied by the United States, or will it choose to offset U.S. regional maritime dominance by building a navy with the capability to counter this dominance? A substantial SSN force would serve this purpose well. In terms of doctrine for nuclear forces, does the new SSBN class signal Beijing's intent to reinforce China's strategic deterrent with a potent sea-based component to complement its new family of solid-fueled, mobile land-based systems?

Whereas Beijing's primary concern is the United States, China does have additional security concerns influencing its naval programs. These include maritime territorial claims in the East and South China Seas and defense of increasingly important sea lines of communications (SLOC). With China's growing dependence on Middle East oil, these SLOCs conceptually include the Indian Ocean. When joined with Beijing's perception of the potential threat from the United States and preventing Taiwan's de jure independence, these are major demands on a navy that has only recently begun to enter the modern era. This is especially so for a navy that has so little experience with naval and air operations beyond coastal defense. While recognizing the broader maritime security interests influencing China's naval developments, this chapter will focus on the central role played by the United States in establishing Beijing's defense modernization priorities.

The United States as Primary Potential Adversary[2]

The United States' role in the priorities established for China's military modernization programs is evident even if indirectly stated. Beijing's defense White Paper released in December 2004 asserts that the global military imbalance is widening and that military strength now plays an increasingly important role in preserving national security. Although not directly charged with creating this imbalance, the logic employed by the White Paper to explain the increasing importance of military power and the global military imbalance is manifestly centered on the United States.

First, the metric employed to describe the developments in military capabilities so radically changing the conduct of war is clearly drawn from the technological advances and doctrinal changes found in the U.S. armed forces. What the White Paper refers to as the effects of the "World Wide Revolution in Military Affairs (RMA)" on the conduct of war can only refer to the United States. U.S. armed forces are the leaders in incorporating advanced technologies into military operations and have applied these operations in war. Second, the White Paper states that the PLA's[3] modernization is dedicated to "building an informationalized force and winning an informationalized war."[4] The principal adversary the PLA will potentially confront in an "informationalized" war is the United States. Third is the rationale provided for granting the PLA's naval, air, and strategic forces priority in China's defense modernization programs. The White Paper states that this priority is required "in order to strengthen the capabilities for winning both command of the sea and command of the air, and conducting strategic counterstrikes."[5] A military confrontation with the United States over Taiwan is the only probable near-term scenario requiring this particular combination of military capabilities.

The PLA Navy's Status, Mission, and Modernization

The precedence granted the PLA Navy (PLAN) in China's defense-modernization priorities in the 2004 White Paper is significant. Traditionally, PLA ground forces have held pride of place over the navy and air force. In earlier White Papers, the protocol order was army, navy, and air force, with the 2nd Artillery Corps listed last as an "independent arm" of the PLA responsible for ground-to-ground nuclear and conventional-armed missiles. Placing the navy first in modernization priorities is a major change from past practice. The navy's enhanced status in 2004 was joined by the air force and 2nd Artillery Corps. For the first time, all three of their commanders have been appointed to the highest policy-making body for the armed forces: the Chinese Communist Party's (CCP) Central Military Commission (CMC) chaired by Hu Jintao, the CCP General-Secretary.

The navy's new status did not change the PLAN's mission as defined by the defense White Papers. It remains, ensuring China's maritime security and maintaining the sovereignty of its territorial waters. Nor did the PLAN's modernization objectives change. They are directed at extending the reach of the PLAN's offshore defense operations. This goal is being achieved by developing new combat ships, updating weapons and equipment, improving long-

range precision strike capabilities, and acquiring "special purpose aircraft."
Naval modernization is accompanied by exercises designed to improve the
PLAN's joint operations capabilities.

Although China's defense White Papers assign a nuclear counterattack
mission to the PLAN,[6] Western analysts do not believe China's single *Xia*
(夏)-class SSBN is operational. The boat entered service in 1983, but did not
complete a successful submerged missile launch until 1988 and is not known
to conduct regular patrols, let alone extended deterrence patrols. Interestingly, the wording of the counterattack mission in the 2004 White Paper
changed from the 2002 edition. The 2002 White Paper said "the nuclear-
powered submarine force, which assumes the strategic nuclear counterattack
mission, is under the direct command of the CMC."[7] It further stated that a
counterattack could be conducted either independently by the 2nd Artillery
Corps or "jointly with the strategic nuclear forces of other services, at the
order of the supreme command."[8] This distinction suggested that the PLAN
has the mission of performing an independent strategic counterattack.
Nonetheless, in the discussion of strengthening the Navy to better perform
its missions, the 2004 White Paper says only that the PLAN's "capability of
nuclear counterattacks is also enhanced."[9] There is no specific discussion of a
PLAN strategic nuclear mission.

The Doctrine Dilemma

Despite its common use among Western observers of China's armed
forces, the Chinese lexicon of military terms does not contain a word for
"doctrine."[10] When referring to U.S. military doctrine, for example, Chinese sources translate "doctrine" as *lilun* (理论) or *xueshuo* (学说), which
are best translated into English as "theory." This therefore raises the issue of
what to assess as China's emerging military doctrine? It makes more sense
to ask what function doctrine provides to those militaries that do employ
the word and then ask if there is a functional equivalent in Chinese documents. The U.S. Department of Defense defines doctrine as: "Fundamental
principles by which military forces or elements thereof guide their actions
in support of national objectives. It is authoritative but requires judgment in
application."[11] The essential concepts in this definition are that doctrine is an
officially endorsed statement of *fundamental principle*s that *guide* the application of military force. As guidance, these principles require *judgment* when
applied and are therefore not to be understood as Holy Writ. There are many
terms employed by Chinese documents that do fulfill the guidance require-

ment. These include *junshi fangzhen* (军事方针), which can be translated as "military guiding principles." Another is *junshi yuanze* (军事原则), perhaps best translated as "principles of military operations."

A hierarchy of authoritative documents does exist to guide the PLA as it develops strategy and concepts of operations for future military conflicts. Unfortunately, the substance of these documents is not known. Akin to the U.S. National Military Strategy, the current overarching authoritative source for the PLA's roles and missions is the "National Military Strategic Guidelines for the New Period" (*xin shiqi guojia junshi zhanlue fangzhen;* 新时期国家军事战略方针). Promulgated in 1993 by Jiang Zemin as the CCP General Secretary and CMC Chairman, this source is clearly authoritative. The new guidelines replaced those issued in 1985 that moved PLA war preparations (*zhanbei;* 战备) from "people's war under modern conditions" to "limited local war" (*jubu zhanzheng;* 局部战争). The 1993 guidelines stemmed from a detailed assessment of the military implications of the 1991 Gulf War, which resulted in modifying PLA war preparations from local war to "local war under high-tech conditions" (*gao jishu tiaojian xia jubu zhanzheng;* 高技术条件下局部战争).[12] Beijing has not publicly declared what its national military strategy is beyond stating that "China adheres to the military strategy of active defense" (*jiji fangyu;* 积极防御)[13]—to be discussed below.

In 1999, six years after the new national military strategic guidelines were issued, Jiang Zemin ordered the "New Generation Operations Regulations" (*xin yidai zuozhan tiaoling;* 新一代作战条令) to be issued, replacing those published in the mid-1980s.[14] This was followed by a series of six manuals setting out the "essentials" of joint campaigns, ground force campaigns, air force campaigns, naval campaigns, 2nd Artillery campaigns, and campaign logistics.[15] In this use, "essentials" is a translation of *gangyao* (纲要). As a concept, *gangyao* also contains the meaning of "outline" and "compendium." Nor is the term limited to military use. The CCP and the Chinese government also use this term for documents establishing authoritative guidance. As Finkelstein has noted, it is useful to think of the PLA *gangyao* as similar to U.S. military field manuals or the Pentagon Joint Staff's publications on joint operations. In its own publications, the PLA refers to these U.S. manuals as *gangyao.*[16] Nevertheless, references to the new *gangyao* found in the official English translations of the defense White Papers issued in 2000, 2002, and 2004 translate the term as *doctrine.* These White Papers also note that the PLA is developing operational *doctrine* as guidance for operational training.[17]

Thus, although there is no Chinese word for "doctrine" as this term is used in the United States and other defense establishments, authoritative guidance provided the PLA serves as doctrine. This is especially noticeable at the operational level of war. The U.S. armed forces and those of China have a common understanding of this level. For the United States, it is: "The level of war at which campaigns and major operations are planned, conducted and sustained to accomplish strategic objectives within theaters or areas of operations."[18] For the PLA, it is *zhanyi* (战役)—campaigns/operations. For convenience, this chapter will employ the concept of "doctrine" to refer to the authoritative guidance the PLAN receives at any level of war.

Two of the six 1999 operational *gangyao* promulgated in 1999 directly effect the PLAN. "The Essentials of Joint Campaigns of the Chinese People's Liberation Army (*zhongguo renmin jiefangjun lianhe zhanyi gangyao;* 中国人民解放军联合战役纲要) provide authoritative guidance for the PLA's move toward joint operations. "The Essentials of Campaigns of the Chinese People's Liberation Army Navy" (*zhongguo renmin jiefangjun haijun zhanyi gangyao;* 中国人民解放军海军战役纲要) no doubt includes guidance on how to conduct independent campaigns in addition to joint operations. Although the substance of these manuals is not available for assessment, there is sufficient reliable information about China's maritime strategy to make a reasonable although speculative assessment of the roles and missions of the PLAN's nuclear submarines within a mixed submarine force.

China's Changing Maritime Strategy[19]

In the two decades since the PLAN's first conceptual steps toward off-shore defense were taken in the mid-1980s, China's perceived security environment has dramatically changed. Russia as the USSR's successor has been transformed from a potential threat to become China's principal arms supplier and a diplomatic ally. Moscow has granted the PLA access to modern weaponry and military technology that it had not had since the Sino-Soviet split in the late-1950s. In contrast to U.S. constraint following diplomatic recognition of the People's Republic of China in 1979, Russia apparently places only limited restraint on what it will sell China. Russia's willingness to sell advanced platforms, weaponry, components, and technologies together with licensed production agreements was made even more significant by the post-Tiananmen embargoes applied by the United States and the European Union in 1989.

Over these same decades, China's relations with the United States underwent a complex transition from quasi-allies against the USSR to possible adversaries. Each now views the other with apprehension and both follow a policy of pragmatic engagement. For good reason, Washington and Beijing believe their national interests are best served by avoiding confrontation and cooperating in all realms where this is possible. It is within this context that Beijing's 2000, 2002, and 2004 defense White Papers clearly identified the United States as China's most important potential foe.[20] In doing so, Beijing believes it must prepare for a possible military conflict with the world's most technologically advanced and powerful military. With the U.S. strategy in the western Pacific rooted in maritime force projection, China's shift toward offshore defense in the 1980s has taken on a new significance.

First, however, it is necessary to determine what "offshore defense" means to the PLAN. It is now two decades since the first and second island chains were used to define the limits of offshore defense.[21] They are rarely employed officially today as defining the outer limits of the PLAN's offshore defense. It seems probable that offshore defense is now a strategic *concept* with no defined geographical limit and serves the PLAN primarily by declaring that it is no longer a purely coastal defense force.[22] The conceptual offshore defense strategy could also be employed in part as a tool the PLAN can manipulate in the PLA budget process to argue for more capable weapons and supporting systems.

The long-standing limitation on the offshore operational range of the Chinese navy has been its weak antiair warfare (AAW) capabilities, making surface combatants dependent on land-based aircraft for air defense. Over the last few years, however, the PLAN has made definite progress in the area air defense capabilities of its new ships.[23] It is yet too early to determine the effectiveness of these new air defense enhancements, but it is evident that the navy is focused on overcoming this critical deficiency. Nonetheless, until the PLAN has effective area AAW to protect more than one or two surface action groups (SAG), or acquires aircraft carriers, the range of its offshore operations for surface ships will be constrained.

To some extent, submarines avoid the constraints provided by the combat range of China's land-based air power, but they are subject to the airborne, surface, and subsurface antisubmarine warfare (ASW) capabilities of an adversary. This is especially true of the capabilities organic to U.S. aircraft carrier strike groups (CSG). These include not only the SSNs that form part of a CSG, but also the airborne ASW of the carrier itself and the defending escort ships. Unless equipped with air-independent propulsion (AIP), diesel-electric submarines are required to snorkel on a regular basis, making them particularly susceptible to a CSG's ASW despite their normal acoustic quietness. Thus far, China is not known to have acquired or developed AIP SSKs. SSNs are less susceptible because they are not required to snorkel. The increasing range of submerged-launch antiship cruise missiles (ASCM), however, will provide SSNs and SSKs some relief from a CSG's organic ASW capabilities. The Klub ASCM, for example, deployed on the Kilos acquired from Russia, has a range of some 120 nautical miles and supersonic terminal homing.[24] The range of these weapons allows the submarine to attack some distance from a CSG, greatly expanding the search area for U.S. ASW. The PLAN nonetheless recognizes the hazards involved in attacking U.S. carrier strike groups.[25]

Speculations Concerning Emerging Doctrine and Nuclear Submarines

The SSBN

As Beijing works through the doctrinal issues required to guide the future of its nuclear submarine force in an offshore defense strategy, it continues to confront the dilemma faced by Mao Zedong in the civil war with the Kuomintang and the war with Japan. Mao had to develop doctrine, strategy, and concepts operations to defeat an adversary that was superior in the technology of war.[26] The core guiding principle developed by Mao and that continues as the heart of the PLA's doctrinal evolution is "active defense" (*jijifangyu*; 积极防御), which Mao defined as "offensive defense, or defense through decisive engagements."[27] At the operational level of war, this doctrinal principle directed his forces to seize the battlefield initiative through offensive operations. China's doctrine for nuclear deterrence, however, has stayed close to Mao's principle for the strategic level of war—strike only after the enemy has struck (*hou fa zhi ren*; 后发制人).

China's longstanding public doctrine for its nuclear forces is one of "No First Use" (NFU). The consensus among observers is that China's twenty or so inaccurate, slow-responding, liquid-fueled intercontinental-range ballistic missiles (ICBMs) with their huge three–four megaton warheads suggest that Beijing intends to respond to a nuclear attack with a punitive countervalue strike. Beijing evidently believes the potential destruction inflicted by a countervalue strike conducted by even two or three surviving weapons would be so great as to deter any adversary, including a superpower. Western analysts have dubbed this strategy "minimal deterrence."

The problem Beijing faces is ensuring that China's deterrent is perceived as credible. To be credible within an NFU doctrine, two issues are involved. First, some of China's retaliatory force must be seen as possibly surviving a disarming first strike. Second, the adversary must believe that Beijing would launch the remaining missiles. Given the overwhelming number of strategic nuclear weapons in the United States' inventory, a retaliatory punitive strike from what few Chinese weapons survived could result in China's destruction. Consequently, a nuclear deterrent composed of a few silo-based ICBMs may lack the required credibility. When ballistic-missile defenses (BMD) become effective, the credibility of this small deterrent will erode even further. In the late 1980s, an internal debate began in China because some analysts doubted the deterrent credibility of a single punitive retaliatory strike. Some advocated a doctrinal transition to a nuclear war fighting capability.[28] Thus far, there has been no outward indication that Beijing is changing its nuclear doctrine.

Beijing is, however, fully aware of the credibility problem it confronts. Over the past five decades, China has devoted considerable resources to developing sea-based and mobile land-based weapons. Mobile land-based systems joined with the stealth and endurance found in SSBNs will enhance the survivability of China's strategic deterrent. However, enhancing the survivability of a second-strike force does not resolve the question of how many weapons must be deployed to counter BMD. The credibility of a small strategic deterrent can be improved by deploying multiple warheads. These can be simple multiple reentry vehicles (MRV) or the far more technologically challenging multiple independently targeted reentry vehicles (MIRV). Increasing the number of weapons carried by a single launcher enhances the capabilities of a small strategic force. If China can develop the smaller warheads required for MRVs and MIRVs, it could plan to penetrate BMD with the aid of decoys. It could also consider developing maneuvering reentry vehicles (MaRV) to cope with missile defenses.

Such enhancements can be applied to both land-based and sea-based weapons. Nevertheless, SSBNs are expensive to build and maintain, and perhaps redundant with the deployment of mobile land-based systems. China's internal debates on precisely this issue more than a decade ago delayed the development of the 094 SSBN.[29] More recently, as Avery Goldstein has reported, Chinese analysts were impressed by the survivability of the mobile Scud missiles during the 1991 Persian Gulf War. The allies had great difficulty in finding and destroying these relatively crude weapons, suggesting that pouring resources into SSBNs and their missiles was not necessarily a good decision.[30]

The fact that the 094 and its missile program, although delayed, were sustained despite these criticisms suggests that Beijing has decided to put more of its strategic deterrent to sea. What percentage of the deterrent should be seabased remains a difficult problem for the Chinese leadership to resolve. At issue is the survivability of an SSBN in an environment where ASW capabilities will likely improve. This would be especially true if the 094 proves to be acoustically noisy enough to be an easy ASW target. One 094 SSBN will carry twelve Julang-2 (JL-Big Wave) missiles. If the number of land-based ICBMs were doubled to around forty by retaining the silo-based *Dongfeng* (东风)-5A (DF-East Wind) and deploying twenty DF-31A mobile missiles, losing one 094 to ASW would mean losing a large percentage of China's second-strike force. This suggests that China may consider placing its SSBNs in safe havens similar to the USSR's bastion strategy. Nevertheless, where would they be based? Perhaps the Yellow Sea with its maximum depth of five hundred feet would prove to be attractive.[31] Alternatively, China could build six 094s to ensure that two are always on patrol. Richard D. Fisher suggests that the PLAN base at Yulin on Hainan Island could host SSBNs. If based in Yulin, the SSBNs with their five-thousand-nautical-mile-range ballistic missiles would have quick access to deep waters for deterrent patrols.[32] Either choice obviously invites the United States to invest significant resources in keeping a constant watch on China's SSBNs, especially if Beijing decided to join a bastion strategy with deterrent patrols. Nonetheless, even if China's leadership decides to increase its strategic deterrent to one hundred or more weapons, determining the most effective distribution between sea-based and mobile land-based missiles will not be easy.

The SSN

It is important to recognize that despite the overriding principle of "active defense" in China's basic military doctrine, Chinese sources do not define PLAN strategy as "active offshore defense." Chinese documents refer only to "offshore defense." Yet, it must be assumed that "active defense" with its connotation of offensive operations designed to gain battle space initiative in the opening phase of a campaign is at the core of PLAN operational doctrine. Active defense is at the heart of PLA doctrinal tradition, and the PLAN draws on this tradition.

Over the past decade and more, China's military journals and research centers such as the PLA's Academy of Military Science (AMS) and National Defense University (NDU) have assessed the requirements for defeating an adversary that is superior in the technology of war.[33] Because this is a long-standing PLA problem extending back to the 1930s, the results are not too surprising. The doctrinal conclusion is that Chinese forces must take offensive operations, striking first at elements of the opposing forces that will degrade their overall combat effectiveness. The concept introduced calls for attacking "critical points" or "key points" in the enemy's "combat system." These include command, control, communications, and intelligence (C3I) nodes, battlefield surveillance, and electronic warfare systems. These are seen as degrading the adversary's ability to conduct high-technology combat operations. Also to be targeted are the adversary's major offensive weapons, including "large seaborne combat platforms," which have to be aircraft carriers.[34] Indeed, now, as a decade ago, much of PLA strategy and operational doctrine is clearly devised with the U.S. armed forces as the potential adversary.

When joined with China's commitment to offshore defense and the resources required to acquire a large force of extremely capable diesel-electric and nuclear-powered submarines,[35] the principle of key-point attack seems to make the SSN's probable mission abundantly clear. If one interprets offshore defense as reflecting an anti-access and sea-denial strategy with a Taiwan scenario currently at its center, then the division of missions between SSKs and SSNs appears to be self-evident. Key point attacks would be focused on defeating or degrading the offensive capabilities of U.S. battle groups. The SSKs would attempt to implement a sea-denial strategy in the Taiwan area of operations (TAO) where Chinese land-based aircraft would threaten U.S. airborne ASW. The SSNs would exploit their endurance, speed, and stealth, seeking targets much farther out to sea in order to implement an anti-access strategy. Assuming the SSN commanders have the confidence of their navy, it should not be beyond their skills to deploy SSNs in areas that would threaten the U.S. Navy far distant from the TAO. The approaches to Yokosuka naval base, homeport to the single forward-deployed U.S. CSG, is one obvious operating area. Another would be the approaches to Guam. Similarly, the PLAN will remember that in March 1996, when the PLA conducted threatening exercises in the area of the Taiwan Strait, the *Nimitz* CSG was dispatched to the TAO from the Persian Gulf. SSNs could well be employed far from Taiwan to cover the approaches from the Persian Gulf. One possible location is the northern exit from the South China Sea.

Consequently, in a Taiwan scenario, PLAN SSNs would have two military objectives. First, to disable U.S. aircraft carriers, thereby limiting the air power the United States could use for the defense of Taiwan.[36] If this were not possible, the second objective would derive from the simple presence of SSNs in the ocean area. Beijing would hope that the mere threat of SSNs with torpedoes and submerged-launch ASCMs would hinder and thereby slow the entrance of U.S. CSGs into the battle for Taiwan.

How many 093 SSNs China will build to buttress the PLAN's offshore defense mission is not a function of capabilities. Series production of advanced indigenous SSKs is underway, so the ability of China's shipyards to construct submarines is not a question. It is probable that China has received Russian assistance in SSN construction, which will assist China's yards in undertaking series production of nuclear-powered submarines. The single most significant limit is the resources Beijing is willing to commit to building an SSN fleet. With five of the original and problematic 091 Han (汉)-class SSNs that first entered service in the water in 1974, it would not be excessive for Beijing to be thinking of an SSN force in the range of twenty 093 platforms.

Whereas it is conceptually plausible for SSNs operating at the outer edge of an undefined offshore defense realm to contest the U.S. Navy, when the PLAN will have sufficient submarines and have developed the operational capabilities required to implement the strategy is unknown. A number of questions remain unanswered. PLAN SSNs will have to confront the ASW capabilities of the carrier and its escorts, including the SSNs. If the PLAN were to try to interdict a CSG in the approaches to Yokosuka or any other base, it would be confronted with the capabilities of land-based airborne ASW. If the SSNs patrol far out to sea to avoid land-based aircraft, locating a CSG in what is a very large ocean will be difficult until China has wide-area intelligence, surveillance, and reconnaissance (ISR) capability together with the capacity to communicate the strike group's location in real time. Although the submerged-launch long-range ASCM is deadly, the weapon's target must be located, and it will be over the horizon. Communicating target location to a submerged submarine in real time is essential even with the ASCM's advanced terminal guidance. One has to conclude that the PLAN is a decade away from developing the operational capabilities demanded by its emerging doctrine.

Conclusions

Although the specific doctrinal guidance provided the PLAN to implement China's evolving offshore defense strategy is not available in open sources, there is sufficient evidence to suggest what this guidance entails.

Identifying the United States as driving the priorities for China's current defense modernization programs provides an important insight. Beijing does have other security concerns that will influence these programs, but the United States is central to the established priorities. Granting the PLAN precedence, together with the People's Liberation Army Air Force (PLAAF) and the 2nd Artillery Corps, is a definite indicator that U.S. naval, air, and strategic forces are Beijing's major concern. China's new SSBN and SSN appear to have critical roles to perform in offsetting what are recognized as superior U.S. military capabilities.

The SSBN mission as a component of the counterattack strategy established by Beijing's NFU doctrine has been stated in China's defense White Papers. Nonetheless, because an SSBN's survivability advantage is eroded by China's development of mobile land-based systems, whether Beijing will ultimately decide to put a major component of its strategic retaliatory force to sea is unknown. Given the expense involved in building and maintaining SSBNs, it is likely the fleet will remain small. Much will depend on how many Beijing wishes to keep on patrol and/or place in safe havens such as the Yellow Sea. This number will depend on how Beijing views the credibility of its strategic deterrent in a BMD environment. Six SSBNs would allow two to be on patrol at any time. Given the costs involved, this may well be the maximum number built, but the final order of battle could be less. The crucial debate in Beijing will be focused on two issues. One is the size of the total force required to survive a disarming first strike and overcome BMD. The second is how to ensure the credibility of China's deterrent. The development of mobile land-based ICBMs suggests that the SSBN will play a greater role in the latter issue than the first.

China's new SSN fits well with the PLAN's offshore defense strategy and the evident focus on a Taiwan scenario where it is assumed the United States will intervene with aircraft carrier strike groups. At the operational level of war, the strategy applied will be active defense using key-point attacks directing the PLA to seize and maintain battle-space initiative using offensive actions as early as possible in a campaign. Employing SSNs to attack U.S. CSGs far from Taiwan at the earliest opportunity would fulfill this doctrinal principle.

An interesting development is derived from applying this doctrine. The PLAN will not be attacking a soft spot in U.S. Navy defenses but one of the hardest operational targets in the world. The U.S. Navy has had more than sixty years to refine the defense of a CSG against air, surface, and submarine attack. Penetrating this defense is an incredibly difficult task. PLAN focus on acquiring and developing long-range submerged-launched ASCMs and wake-homing torpedoes for its submarines, however, suggests Chinese tacticians believe they have found weaknesses in this traditionally hard defense. Undoubtedly, the PLAN recognizes that executing active defense doctrine against the formidable capabilities of the U.S. Navy remains a dangerous mission. Nevertheless, with active defense at the heart of PLA operational doctrine, joined with concept of key-point strikes conducted by increasingly capable weapons, the aircraft carrier strike group may now be more vulnerable than in even the recent past.

Notes

1. China has published defense White Papers since 1995. The 1995 White Paper was titled *China: Arms Control and Disarmament* but was functionally a defense White Paper. Beginning in 1998, defense White Papers have been published in alternate years. The most recent is *China's National Defense in 2004* (Beijing: State Council Information Office, December 27, 2004).

2. This discussion draws from *China's National Defense in 2004*, 1–3.

3. The services and branches of China's armed forces are collectively named the Chinese People's Liberation Army.

4. Ibid., 5–12.

5. Ibid., 6.

6. Ibid., 7.

7. *China's National Defense in 2002* (Beijing: State Council Information Office, December 9, 2002), 7.

8. Ibid.

9. *China's National Defense in 2004*, 7.

10. The following discussion draws on David Shambaugh, *Modernizing China's Military: Progress, Problems, and Prospects* (Berkeley: University of California Press, 2002), 56–60; and Dr. David M. Finkelstein, "Thinking About the PLA's 'Revolution' in Doctrinal Affairs," in James Mulvenon and David Finkelstein, eds., *Thinking About the PLA's Revolution in Military Affairs: Emerging Trends in the Operational Art of the Chinese People's Liberation Army* (Washington, D.C.: Beaver Press, 2005), 1–27.

11. Joint Publication 1-02, "DOD Dictionary of Military and Associated Terms" (As amended through 31 August 2005), www.ditc.mil/doctrine/jel/doddict/.

12. Lieutenant General Chen Bingde, "Intensify Study of Military Theory to Ensure Quality Army Building; Learn From Thought and Practice of the Core of the Three Generations of Party Leadership in Studying Military Theory," *Zhongguo Junshi Kexue* (中国军事科学; *China's Military Science*), March 6, 1998; in *Foreign Broadcast Information Service, China* (hereafter *FBIS-China*), March 10, 1998.

13. *China's National Defense in 2004*, Chapter 2, "National Defense Policy," 3.

14. "Basic Guidelines for Our Army's Combat Drill in the New Period—Written on the Promulgation of Operational Ordinance of a New Generation," Beijing, *Jiefangjun Bao* (解放军报; *Liberation Army Daily*), January 25, 1999; *in FBIS-China, January 25, 1999.*

15. Finkelstein, "Thinking About the PLA's 'Revolution,'" 13.

16. Ibid.

17. See, for example, *China's National Defense in 2004*, 9.

18. Joint Publication 1-02.

19. For a succinct discussion of the changes in China's maritime strategy, see John W. Lewis and Xue Litai, *China's Strategic Seapower: The Politics of Force Modernization in the Nuclear Age* (Stanford, Calif.: Stanford University Press, 1994), 219–30. For an assessment of China's changing national military strategy and the PLAN's role in this strategy, see Paul H. B. Godwin, "From Continent to Periphery: PLA Doctrine, Strategy and Capabilities Towards 2000," in David Shambaugh and Richard Yang, eds., *China's Military in Transition* (Oxford: Oxford University Press, 1997), 200–223.

20. See David M. Finkelstein, "The United States, China, and Taiwan: Some Key Issues and Personal Thoughts" (Alexandria, Va.: CNA Corporation, June 2002) for an assessment of China's apprehensions beyond that seen in the defense White Papers.

21. For a discussion of the first and second island chains, see Alexander Huang, "The Chinese Navy's Offshore Active Defense Strategy: Conceptualization and Implications," *Naval War College Review* 47, no. 3 (Summer 1994): 16ff.

22. Kenneth W. Allen, Conference report, *PLA Navy Building at the Start of a New Century* (Alexandria, Va.: CNA Corporation, July 2001), 4.

23. For details see, Lyle Goldstein and William Murray, "China Emerges as a Maritime Power," *Jane's Intelligence Review* (October 2004): 36.

24. Lyle Goldstein and William Murray, "Under Sea Dragons: China's Maturing Submarine Force," *International Security* 28, no. 4 (Spring 2004): 166.

25. See, for example, Feng Changsong, Xu Jiafeng, and Wang Guosheng, "Six Aircraft Carrier 'Busters,'" *Zhongguo Guofang Bao* (中国国防报; *China's National Defense News*), March 5, 2002; in *FBIS-China*, March 28, 2002.

26. For an assessment of how China's operational doctrine has evolved since the 1930s, see Paul H. B. Godwin, "Change and Continuity in Chinese Military Doctrine," in Mark A. Ryan, David M. Finkelstein, and Michael A. McDevitt, eds., *Chinese Warfighting: The PLA Experience since 1949* (New York: M. E. Sharpe, 2003), 23–55.

27. Mao Tse-tung, "Strategy in China's Revolutionary War," *Selected Military Writings of Mao Tse-tung* (Peking: Foreign Languages Press, 1972), 105.

28. See Alastair Iain Johnston, "China's New 'Old Thinking': The Concept of Limited Deterrence," *International Security* (Winter 1995–1996): 5–42, for a detailed assessment of this debate.

29. Chinese debates over this issue are discussed in Lewis and Xue, *China's Strategic Seapower*, 235–36.

30. Avery Goldstein, *Deterrence and Security in the 21st Century: China, Britain, France and the Enduring Legacy of the Nuclear Revolution* (Stanford, Calif.: Stanford University Press, 2000), 244 n. 66.

31. Depth taken from *North Pacific Ocean Theme Page* accessed through www.pmel .noaa.gov/np/pages/seas/yellowsea.html.

32. Richard D. Fisher, Jr., "Trouble below: China's submarines pose regional, strategic challenges," *Armed Forces Journal*, March 8, 2006.

33. Assessments of the core products from these PLA research and teaching institutions are found in Mulvenon and Finkelstein, eds., *Thinking About the PLA's Revolution in Military Affairs*.

34. This approach to defeating a superior adversary was outlined a decade ago by Colonel Yu Guohua of the PLA NDU's Campaign Research and Teaching Department. See his "On Turning Strong Forces Into Weak and Vice Versa In a High-Tech Local War," *Zhongguo Junshi Kexue* (*China's Military Science*), May 20, 1996; in *FBIS-China*, January 3, 1997. For a valuable assessment of "key point attacks" in PLA operational doctrine, see M. Taylor Fravel, "The Evolution of China's Military Strategy: Comparing the 1987 and 1999 Editions of *Zhanluexue*," in Mulvenon and Finkelstein, eds., *Thinking About the PLA's Revolution in Military Affairs*, especially 93–95.

35. See Goldstein and Murray, "Undersea Dragons," for an assessment of China's growing submarine force.

36. Disabling U.S. aircraft carriers has been a constant theme of articles in Chinese military journals and the public press for a decade. In addition to note 25, see Ying Nan, "The Defects of Aircraft Carriers and Anti-Aircraft Carrier Operations, *Conmilit* (Hong Kong) no. 252 (January 11, 1998): 13–15; in *FBIS-China*, March 13, 1998.

William S. Murray

An Overview of the PLAN Submarine Force

OF ALL THE NAVIES THAT OPERATE SUBMARINES, only Russia and China build and employ both nuclear and diesel submarines as fighting ships. This peculiarity is rather easily explained. Russia's submarine fleet is little more than a Cold War artifact, built to help defend the Soviet SSBN bastions. Speaking simplistically, diesel submarines would patrol and defend the approaches relatively close to the motherland, whereas the nuclear ballistic-missile submarines would conduct deterrent patrols in bastions such as the Barents Sea and the Sea of Okhotsk. SSNs would conduct operations against adversary SSNs, SSBNs, and carrier battle groups at greater distances from Russia. The Soviet Union saw separate roles, and hence strategic requirements, for each type of vessel.

Similarly, the composition of China's submarine force stems from strategic demands. Deployed in the adjacent, shallow waters of the Yellow and South China Seas, Beijing's large fleet of diesel submarines was reasonably well suited to the role of opposing foreign invasion. These aging, unsophisticated, Soviet-designed vessels were inexpensive, and could be built with relatively unskilled labor. Much more expensive, but somewhat more capable, are China's handful of first-generation nuclear submarines. Though limited in capability against modern forces, they have served China as symbols of national prestige. This legacy fleet suited the China of the 1960s through the 1990s well, but was inadequate for responding to Taiwan contingencies in the contemporary strategic environment.

Consequently, China's submarine force has undergone a remarkable metamorphosis in the last decade. Domestic and imported modern diesel submarines are replacing older vessels, and China's solitary nuclear shipyard is building two new classes of nuclear submarines. All of these vessels are far more modern and capable than were the vessels they are replacing. This aggressive program of modernization mirrors similar changes occurring within the PLAN surface fleet, within the 2nd Artillery rocket forces, and within the People's Liberation Army Naval Air Force (PLANAF) and People's Liberation Army Air Force (PLAAF). It is a time of great change for the PLAN, constituting a tremendous technological leap forward for the Chinese submarine force. This chapter establishes a full context for our understanding of Chinese nuclear submarine development by surveying both diesel and the nuclear components of the PLAN submarine force, focusing on the developing relationship and also on the critical trade-offs between these respective parts of China's growing undersea warfare capabilities.

China's submarine force has long been characterized by a reliance on antiquated submarine designs. Emblematic of this are the PLAN's large number of Romeo- and Ming-class submarines. China built over eighty of the Soviet designed Romeos from 1962 to 1984, and continues to operate somewhere between twenty and thirty of them to this day.[1] Numerous and noisy, they are nearing the end of their service lives. China also operates nearly twenty Ming-class diesel-electric submarines, which were all built between 1971 and 2001. Derived from the Romeos, they too suffer from antiquated design and relatively high noise levels, though some of the newer versions of the class feature such advanced features as flank sonar arrays and noise-absorbing anechoic rubber tiles.[2]

These older ships are being replaced by much-improved and significantly more modern submarines. Two classes of vessels, known as the Song, an indigenous model, and the Kilo, imported from Russia, make up the vast majority of these replacements. The first Song was launched in 1994 and entered service in 1999. Most sources describe the Song as a modern vessel, and include its advanced seven-blade skewed propeller, its French-origin digital sonar (as compared to the older and less-capable analog systems on preceding classes of Chinese submarines), anechoic tiles, and German diesel engines as its defining characteristics.[3] The Song reportedly carries the twenty-two-nautical-mile-ranged C-801 antiship cruise missiles (ASCM), which can be launched while submerged—a first for the PLAN—as well as torpedoes and mines.[4] It is likely that the Song is the rough equivalent of a mid-1980s Western diesel submarine, which makes it a formidable, quiet submarine that will be very difficult to detect and locate, at least when the vessel operates on its batteries. Photographs available on the Internet chronicle the development of three different models of the Song, and demonstrate that there are now at least ten of these vessels. Most sources agree that eight Song-class submarines were built in Wuhan shipyard, and that starting in 2004, Jiangnan shipyard in Shanghai built and launched the other pair.[5]

Adding to the PLAN's stable of modern diesel submarines are the twelve Kilo-class submarines that China has purchased from Russia. Kilos enjoy a reputation for being extremely quiet, and have been noted as being as stealthy when operating on their batteries, as are U.S. *Los Angeles*-class submarines.[6] China has two variants of Kilos, having first imported two export-Model 877 class vessels in 1994, and another two of the formerly only-for-Russian-use Model 636 in 1996. In 2002 China signaled satisfaction with these four ships by signing a contract for an additional eight model 636 Kilo submarines, with final delivery due in 2005.[7] These eight Kilos are especially noteworthy since they are being sold with the Klub fire control system and the one-hundred-and-twenty-nautical-mile-range, supersonic homing SS-N-27 ASCM. As of October 2006, all eight Kilos had been delivered.

The first of what is probably Beijing's newest class of diesel submarine, known in the West as the Yuan, was launched in May 2004 from Wuhan shipyard. Similar in appearance to the Song and the Kilo, the Yuan might best be described as either "a Kilo with Chinese characteristics," or a "Song with Russian characteristics." Like the Kilo, the Yuan has a two-over-four torpedo tube arrangement, and the pronounced hump along its back. Like the Song, it has fairwater planes (horizontal control surfaces) on its sail, and a dorsal rudder. The Kilo has neither fairwater planes nor a dorsal rudder, and photos from the Yuan's launching show that it has a planar array along its circular hull, unlike either the Song or Kilo. These characteristics suggest the Yuan might be well suited to perform ASW, but this is a tentative conclusion. What appears likely is that the Yuan is a new class of submarine that incorporates certain design elements from both Russian and previous Chinese diesel submarines. Hence, the Yuan is probably especially quiet, and like the Song and newer Kilos, almost certainly incorporates a seven-blade screw, modern periscopes, digital sonar, and is capable of launching sophisticated torpedoes, antiship cruise missiles, and mines. Some claim the Yuan has air-independent propulsion (AIP), but there is no information available to confirm or deny such speculation.

A common and sensible practice for a country contemplating incorporating AIP in its submarines is to first build a prototype that can be tested at sea. This usually involves developing a suitable technology, placing the appropriate machinery in a section of submarine hull, and inserting that section into an existing submarine, which is then tested at sea. The Swedish navy did this in 1988 by inserting an eight-meter addition containing a Stirling engine and associated tanks and machinery in the submarine *Näcken*. The German and Dutch navies also experimented with AIP by adding sections to the ex-German navy Type 205 submarine U1.[8] France sold an AIP system to Pakistan that is being inserted into an Agosta-class submarine currently under construction in Karachi. This will increase the vessel's length by roughly nine meters.[9]

Based on the above, one could conclude that AIP submarines tend to be much longer—by about nine meters—than those without AIP, but such is not really the case. The examples above involved modifying existing vessels to serve as test beds or "after-market" conversions. As Table 1 indicates, submarines' physical dimensions do not reveal whether or not they posses AIP. The two smallest submarines listed in the table, the *Gotland* and the Type 212A, have AIP, whereas the *Collins* and the Kilo, which are the largest, do not. Size alone does not indicate whether or not the Yuan has AIP.

The newspaper *PLA Daily* recently released a series of reports describing the successful sea trials of the Yuan,[10] but little other official information about this vessel is available. The absence of official Chinese news releases or authoritative naval journal articles leaves analysts guessing as to whether any more of this class are under construction. It seems that the PLAN has two choices in this regard. It could delay Yuan serial production some years as it did with that of the Song, or it could assume that the Yuan is well designed and proceed immediately into serial production. Either course seems feasible, and each is consistent with various Chinese historical precedents.

The four-and-a-half-year interval between the launching of the first and second Song submarines suggests significant "teething problems" with that class, and similar difficulties could be expected with the Yuan. Since the Song's somewhat troubled beginning, however, at least ten vessels of that submarine class have been built, in three ever-refined versions. This suggests a PLAN submarine philosophy of building a prototype, testing it thoroughly, fixing design and systems integration issues, and then, when confident of the

Table 1. AIP and Conventionally Powered Submarine Dimensions

Submarine	Length (meters)	Beam (meters)	Displacement (tons)
Gotland[1] (AIP)	60	6.2	1,500
Collins[2]	77.8	7.8	3,350
Type 212A[3] (AIP)	56	7 and 5.6	1,450
Type 209[4]	62	6.2	1,450
Yuan[5]	72	8.4	unknown
Kilo[6]	73.8	9.9	3,076

Notes
1. "The Gotland Class Submarine," http://www.kockums.se/Submarines/gotland.html.
2. "Collins Class Submarine (SSG)," http://www.navy.gov.au/fleet/submarine.html.
3. "Submarines—Type 212A," https://www.hdw.de/index_en.php?level=3&CatID=1.140 .240&inhalt_id=1116.
4. Submarines—Type 209/1400 mod, https://www.hdw.de/index_en.php?level=3&CatID =1.140.240&inhalt_id=1115. The *Gotland* and the Type 212A are AIP submarines, the *Collins* and Type 209 are conventional diesel-electric submarines. The *Gotland* and *Collins* were designed in Sweden, the Type 209 and 212A are German creations.
5. "Yuan Class (Type 041) (SSK)," *Jane's Fighting Ships*, August 23, 2005, http://www.janes .com.
6. "Kilo Class," *Jane's Underwater Warfare Systems*, April 14 2005, http://www.janes.com.

quality of design, embarking on serial production. This pattern, however, has seemingly been abandoned by the PLAN surface and submarine force. As will be discussed shortly in greater detail, two 093 nuclear fast-attack submarines are currently under simultaneous construction.[11] Similarly, since 2000 the PLAN simultaneously built two of each of the 052C (pennant numbers 171 and 170), 052B (168 and 169), and 051C (115 and 116) classes of guided missile destroyers as well as a pair of the 054 (525 and 526) frigates. Typifying this apparent newfound confidence in design and systems integration is the immediate serial production of the PLAN's fast-attack 2208 missile catamaran, of which at least twelve have appeared since photos of the first were published on the Internet in April 2004.[12]

All of these examples suggest that in recent years the PLAN has become sufficiently confident of its design processes, systems engineering maturity, and manufacturing quality to forego lengthy prototype testing before embarking on serial production. Hence, it is likely that more Yuan-class submarines are already being built. If so, construction of sister ships of the first of the class could conceivably be occurring at both Jiangnan and Wuhan shipyards. Conversely, both manufacturing facilities could be building additional Song-class submarines, or both shipyards could be building both classes. Regardless of which class might be under construction at either shipyard, the 2004 launching of two submarines at each location strongly suggests that China is quite capable of producing four indigenous diesel-electric submarines per year.[13] Beijing is also simultaneously building two new classes of nuclear submarines.

China has long devoted significant national will to building and operating nuclear submarines. Its first efforts—the Han SSN and Xia SSBN classes—had numerous technical failings, and are now widely regarded as quite primitive.[14] China built five Hans, with the first one going to sea in 1974. The fifth Han was commissioned in 1990. The solitary Xia entered service in 1983, and still goes to sea, albeit very occasionally, and has never made a credible deterrent patrol. Aging, noisy, and obsolete, these early Chinese nukes require replacement and modernization if China's nuclear submarines are to be at all effective for any purpose other than serving as demonstrations of national prestige. Toward this end the PLAN is building two new classes of nuclear submarines. The first 093 SSN, known in the West as the Jin-class, was launched in December 2002; the second in 2003.[15] The second class is the 094 SSBN, known as the Shang-class, and will carry the JL-2 SLBM. This 8,000–10,000-kilometer-range missile was successfully test-launched from underwater in June 2005.[16]

Nuclear versus Conventional Propulsion

The fundamental advantage that nuclear submarines have over their diesel-electric counterparts is an ability to harness the tremendous energy resident in their nuclear reactors. This energy can be used to maintain high speeds over prolonged periods of time, to attempt to outrun torpedoes, to keep up with or overtake high-speed targets, or to operate equipment that requires large amounts of power, such as water purifiers, oxygen generators, or air conditioners. The singular feature of this nearly boundless energy is that it is available at all times, under all weather conditions, at any depth. Therefore, it provides nuclear submarines unparalleled tactical flexibility.

Diesel submarines, conversely, store their energy in large banks of batteries. This very limited amount of power must be jealously husbanded, and decisions regarding its expenditure are carefully made. Hence, diesel submarines typically operate at very slow speeds, and can only operate at high speeds for short periods of time.[17] When the state of charge of their batteries is low, diesel submarines must approach the surface of the ocean and operate their diesel engines, which are connected to generators that create electricity, which in turn charges the batteries. Snorkeling (or snorting), as this is called, is a very noisy operation, which greatly compromises a diesel submarine's stealth, and consequently dramatically raises its vulnerability. Snorkeling also requires raising a snorkel mast—essentially a large pipe—above the waves. This provides a supply of oxygen to the diesel engines, but the raised snorkel mast is highly vulnerable to being sighted or detected by specialized radars. Diesel submarines typically have to snorkel several hours a day to maintain their batteries at a desired state of charge, though they can operate for two or three days without snorkeling, if they are willing to nearly fully deplete their batteries.

On the other hand, when operating on the battery, diesel submarines are extraordinarily quiet, and hence proportionally more difficult for opposing forces to detect. As mentioned earlier, modern diesel submarines are as quiet as or even quieter than some of the world's most capable nuclear vessels. They are also much cheaper to acquire, operate, and maintain; require far less supporting infrastructure; are physically much smaller than their nuclear counterparts; and require smaller crews.[18] The weapons they can fire are every bit as lethal as those carried by nuclear submarines.

Most submariners would agree that their vessel's greatest attribute, regardless of its propulsion mechanism, is stealth. Essentially, a submarine's stealth allows it to exert an influence over a very wide area in which it is operating, even if it can only deliver its weapons over a relatively small portion of that expanse of ocean.[19] Since naval forces do not know the location of patrolling enemy submarines, they must assume that these hidden menaces could be nearly anywhere, and that any submerged artifacts, echoes, or other detected phenomena should be assumed to be a submarine, until proven otherwise.

Frequently, the only conclusive way, or at least the one with the least possibility of catastrophic failure in wartime, is for opposing forces to investigate submerged contacts by shooting live ordnance.[20] During the 1982–83 Falklands campaign, Britain's deployed surface fleet expended nearly its entire inventory of ASW weapons on false submarine contacts.[21] The solitary patrolling Argentine submarine remained unscathed. Properly operated, a submarine can maintain its stealth during all phases of an approach and attack, even after it shoots its weapons. Generally, however, once a submarine's stealth is lost, the advantage rapidly shifts to those hunting the submarine, which can use the speed and endurance of surface and airborne systems to amass enough sensors and weapons to hunt down and kill their quarry.[22] This vulnerability certainly applies for diesel submarines, which have limited power available with which they can conduct high speed evasions. Instead, diesel submarine commanders have to rely on cunning and guile—poor but respectable alternatives against modern sensors and weapons.

Herein lies another advantage of nuclear submarines. Once detected, SSNs have the brute power to disengage from unfavorable tactical situations at high speed for prolonged periods of time. The immediate availability of essentially unlimited energy gives the SSN unparalleled flexibility and freedom, but comes with large acquisition and ownership costs. Nuclear submarines require expensive shore infrastructure, and their crews require extensive, specialized training. Most SSNs are also physically large, a feature mandated by the oversized nuclear and propulsion machinery,[23] the shielding necessary to protect the crew from the reactor's radiation, the requirement to use extensive sound-absorbing devices to prevent machinery noises from being transmitted to the ocean, and the need to house the large crews required to operate and maintain these complex machines. This is not to say that diesel submarines are simple machines that are cheap to acquire or easy to operate. They are, nonetheless, less costly to own and operate, and are less complex, than nuclear submarines. Diesel submarines are also readily available on the international marketplace, whereas nuclear submarines are not.[24] Adding to the obstacles involved in acquiring nuclear submarines are the irreducible problems associated with developing and integrating the necessary technologies, including the nuclear reactor. Solving these issues requires large investments in time, technology, and infrastructure. Certainly China's semisuccessful efforts in designing and building the Han and Xia, though admirable—especially given the domestic tumult and international isolation of China during that period—underline the very substantial difficulties involved in fielding submarines that can be expected to fare well in battle (which the Han and Xia most certainly cannot). These are not problems restricted to China, either. India has been trying to develop an indigenous nuclear submarine for years, thus far apparently without success.[25]

Essentially then, setting aside the vexing and important issue of crew proficiency, countries desiring submarines must make a series of trade-offs revolving around relative costs as compared to performance. On the one hand, they can quickly purchase quiet, capable diesel submarines from abroad.[26] On the other, they can devote decades and immense resources to indigenously developing nuclear submarines. In the past few years, however, a third option of air-independent propulsion has become available.[27]

Air-Independent Propulsion

Several air-independent propulsion (AIP) schemes offer the potential to revolutionize non-nuclear submarines, and the military missions they are capable of undertaking. AIP gives non-nuclear submarines much greater submerged endurance at speed, and greatly increases the vessels' operational flexibility.[28] Although the mechanisms pursued differ, the net effect of AIP, as it currently exists in German-, Swedish-, and French-built vessels, allows the ships to travel submerged without snorkeling for, it is estimated, up to two weeks, all the while maintaining fully charged batteries.[29] This is a revolutionary development, and it can be fairly said that AIP represents a poor man's nuclear submarine.

The common diesel submarine's lack of mobility has long led to it being derided by others as a mobile minefield, the implication being that a successful engagement for a diesel submarine was essentially a matter of chance, and that there was little the submarine could control or affect once it had selected its limited patrol area. Conventional wisdom also held that even if a diesel submarine made a successful attack, it would be a suicide mission. But with AIP and a continuously fully charged battery, even a diesel submarine can act like a nuclear vessel, if only for a couple of hours. An AIP submarine can, for example, sprint at high speed to intercept and attack with a wake-homing torpedo a carrier battle group transiting at high speed to a war zone. This gives an AIP submarine an effective combat radius much greater than a non-AIP vessel. Once in position after a high-speed approach, the AIP submarine, even with a flat battery, could still operate at slow speeds by powering its motors and electronics with the electricity generated from its AIP system, and after attacking, could creep away using the same, limited power. A conventional diesel submarine, conversely, would have little choice but to surface and surrender, or stay submerged and suffocate, unless the ASW forces abandoned their prosecution before its air ran out. Consequently, many countries either already operate, or have signed contracts, to obtain AIP diesel submarines.[30]

Employing Diesel-Electric Submarines

China's large diesel-submarine force matches the nation's geographic conditions. If, as most analysts tend to agree, China is building its navy and submarine force as a potential means to coerce Taiwan, then China's continued acquisition and employment of diesel submarines certainly supports that goal. Taiwan is only about one hundred nautical miles from the China coast, after all, and the PLAN's diesel submarines could arrive in likely patrol areas outside Taiwan's ports or in the Philippine Sea in just four or five days, if traveling submerged at four knots from their East Sea Fleet ports, or even in as little as a day and a half if traveling on the surface at fifteen knots. Once in place, these submarines could perform intelligence and reconnaissance, lay mines, enforce declared exclusion zones or a blockade, target specific merchant ships, sink Taiwan's naval ships, and threaten or sink naval ships from intervening countries. Simultaneously, the large number of conventional submarines in China's inventory would allow some vessels to remain near critical mainland ports in a defensive posture, or to patrol the entrances to the Yellow Sea and Bohai Gulf, if those areas ever become "bastions" for strategic forces.

Although most analysts conclude that a battle designed to create a collapse of Taiwan (presumably before the U.S. could effectively intervene), will—and could—end quickly, such a speedy outcome cannot be assumed by any side. In the event of a prolonged crisis, the close distance between logical PLAN submarine patrol areas and the vessel's home ports would allow fairly rapid cycling between war patrol and refurbishment and replenishment.

As mentioned earlier, one of the greatest weaknesses of diesel submarines occurs when they are snorkeling. This vulnerability stems primarily from airborne radars, most notably those carried by ASW aircraft such as P3C Orions or Taiwan's S-2 Trackers. The effective use of these maritime patrol aircraft (MPA), however, is predicated on maintaining air superiority. China's new area air defense surface destroyers, such as the two 052Cs and the pair of 051Cs, could seriously challenge Taiwan/U.S. air superiority. Another potent threat to MPA may be the PRC's growing fleet of imported SU-30 MKK air superiority fighters. Making this potential threat more effective will be Beijing's Airborne Warning and Control System (AWACs)-like battle management aircraft, which are apparently now being developed and tested.

Even with the ability to rapidly deploy submarines into the area of concern, China is still faced with notable limitations. Presumably, the United States has means available to determine whether or not China's submarines are tied to their piers. Barring some sort of mass exodus from port, China's submarine fleet remains a fleet in being, and merely a potential threat.[31] Further limiting China's ability to effectively employ its submarines is the likely lack of proficient, professional crews and officers. Certainly, China is making great efforts to change this limitation, but available evidence suggests they have some distance to go before they can be confident of their abilities, especially when subjected to wartime conditions. There is little evidence, furthermore, to suggest that China regularly deploys its submarines to the waters around Taiwan, denying to the PLAN the familiarity with acoustic and hydrographic conditions there that they presumably enjoy in the Yellow Sea and other areas near their submarine ports. Although occasional press reports describe the deployment of Chinese submarines, such forays still seem to be unusual occurrences.[32] All of this combines into what is probably an overall lack of experience, which would most likely translate into a lack of decisive battlefield success. Still, warfare is defined partly by chance and partly by preparation, and even marginally skillful submarine commanders can be expected to achieve some successes.

Employing Nuclear Submarines

Jane's estimates that the PLAN has three 093-class submarines in various states of completion, and is expected to build an additional three.[33] The U.S. Department of Defense reports that the first 093 should enter service in 2005.[34] This imminent incorporation of the first of what might be a relatively large class of submarines begs the question of how large such a fleet could turn out to be, and how the professionalism of such a fleet should be evaluated.

Mao famously said that China would build a nuclear submarine "if it took 10,000 years." Judging by the 093/094 programs, Mao's determination still reverberates in PRC leadership circles. As compared to the limitations of Mao's era, much more money is available with which to purchase these expensive ships, and modern China's manufacturing capacity could probably support a more robust building program. But even if China wanted to create a large nuclear submarine force, it would run up against some difficult obstacles in its effort to achieve such a goal. As the United States has well learned and as the Russian Federation is painfully aware, modern, state-of-the-art nuclear submarines are exorbitantly expensive. At its peak, the U.S. Polaris program represented 14 percent of the U.S. Navy budget.[35] Twelve *Franklin*-class SSBNs were ordered in fiscal year 1963 alone.[36] Similar resource decisions are probably within China's ability to make, but several conditions argue strongly against such explosive growth in its undersea nuclear force. First, unlike the symmetric Soviet/U.S. nuclear rivalry in the early 1960s, China does not as yet appear to regard any country as an imminent strategic threat. The PRC does not rely on large numbers of nuclear weapons, preferring instead to rely on a minimal deterrent. China also currently has just one shipyard, at Huludao, that has any experience in building nuclear submarines.[37] Further, competing fiscal demands will tend to dampen any Chinese desires to greatly expand its nuclear submarine force. China is making significant expenditures on other high-priority military systems, including most notably its burgeoning force of solid-fuel missiles, its modernizing air forces, and its increasing numbers of capital surface ships. Furthermore, China has competing domestic budgetary pressures that would also tend to work against large nuclear submarine fleets.

On the other side of this argument is the possibility that China could determine that a large underwater nuclear fleet is a matter of necessity and a national priority. It would be foolhardy to discount China's ability to build and maintain such a fleet, but it would also be a mistake to simply assert that since the United States and the Soviet Union did, China will as well. Absent a compelling, unifying strategic rationale, and given other, more-pressing demands, it is much more likely that China will continue to maintain a modest-sized nuclear fleet.

Accurately assessing the professionalism of any size Chinese submarine fleet is an important but difficult matter. Reliable, relevant information is sparse, with Beijing carefully controlling what little information is released. For instance, despite the 093's imminent incorporation into the fleet, there is only one picture of the 094 SSBN, and no confirmed pictures of the 093 SSN available on the Internet, in contrast to hundreds of pictures of its diesel submarine fleet.[38] Still, reasonable estimates can be inferred from analysis of available information. At some level, mirror imaging can be useful. In 2001, Adm. F. L. Bowman, the head of the U.S. Navy's nuclear reactor program, stated that eight features define a successful nuclear submarine program.[39]

1. Select, then train, the best people to operate the equipment.

2. Establish high standards of continuous training and qualification.

3. Demand the highest possible quality and reliability of submarine components and equipment.

4. Establish centralized control of submarine systems and components.

5. Learn from experience—adopt an honest acceptance that mistakes will occur and set up a well-defined system for critique, feedback, and corrective action.

6. Require redundancy in critical systems.

7. Design a layered defense for safety.

8. Face the facts. Do not let factors such as costs or schedules lead to accepting questionable actions or to short-cutting established policies.

There is anecdotal evidence to suggest that China has implemented some of these standards. For example, a recent series of stories published by *PLA Daily* related how an inspector at Wuhan shipyard insisted, despite great pressure from the shipyard, that a slightly out-of-specification piece of submarine machinery be replaced. He stuck to his convictions, the part was replaced, and he is now cited as a model worker.[40] The article also discussed the painstaking efforts of other naval inspectors to ensure that shaft seals and piping in bilges perform as required in a new class of Chinese submarine. Signs of Chinese desires (if not commitment) to some of the other of the eight standards, such as training, are evident in other releases and articles.

Regarding the training that PLAN submariners undergo, some information is available, but details are lacking. For example, a November 2004 *PLA Daily* report describes a submarine performing a "confrontation exercise in rough sea."[41] An August 2005 report shows cadets training on how to escape from a damaged submarine via a torpedo tube.[42] Occasionally a report will surface that provides genuine insight into PLAN efforts to improve professionalism, such as occurred in a 2002 article that described the overhauling of the curriculum at Qingdao Submarine Academy,[43] but for the most part, analysts are left to carefully review the trends reported in innocuous official press releases. Bilateral exercise and military-to-military contacts could be valuable sources of supporting information.

The PLAN submarine force is in the midst of a fundamental transition. For decades it has been a coastal patrol force, hindered by obsolete technology, poor training, and indifferent construction and material standards. Consequently, it has had more than its share of deadly accidents, of which the April 2003 Ming 361 disaster, in which seventy-one sailors suffocated, is emblematic. Despite this humble past, there are many signs that China is rapidly improving its force through aggressive foreign purchases and indigenous submarine construction programs, enhanced weaponry, and renewed efforts to improve the quality and training of the personnel who take those submarines to sea.

Properly operated, modern, quiet submarines are very difficult (for even the most sophisticated and well-trained opponents) to detect and attack. Simultaneously, such submarines, equipped with modern, easy-to-use weapons, are a potentially deadly nemesis for surface naval forces, which are significantly easier for submarines to detect and attack. This imbalance arises not from misplaced training priorities, unrealistic exercises, inadequate funding, or other forms of bureaucratic neglect (though all those causes can exacerbate the problem), but instead, from physics. Physical laws and limitations, akin to gravity and just as difficult to overcome, are what make antisubmarine warfare exceptionally difficult. The PRC recognizes this reality, realizes it can manipulate it to their advantage, and is doing just that. Observers should therefore expect to see a sustained Chinese determination to continue to replace its obsolete submarines and weapons with much more modern equipment.

The U.S. Navy will doubtless find the ascension of China's submarine force a perplexing, long-term issue.

Notes

1. Type 033 (Romeo-class) Diesel-Electric Submarine, at http://sinodefence.com/navy/sub/033.asp.

2. The flank-array sonar can be clearly seen below the sail on Ming hull numbers 360 and 361. See "Ming class type 035 Thread," and "PLAN subs, an Identification Guide," http://www.china-defense.com/forum/index.php?showtopic=9559, and at http://www.china-defense.com/forum/index.php?showtopic=6614, respectively. The hull tiles are visible in a photo in *Jinchuan Zhishi* 285 (June 2003): 6.

3. The source for this consensus opinion is probably the 2002 *Annual Report on the Military Power of the People's Republic of China, Report to Congress Pursuant to the FY 2000 National Defense Authorization Act*, http://www.defenselink.mil/news/Jul2002/d20020712china.pdf, 21. A multitude of photos of the Song on websites such as the "PLAN Thread (Pics, news, speculations . . . everything)," http://forum.keypublishing.co.uk/showthread.php?t=37296 confirm the presence of the anechoic tiles.

4. See "Song class (Type 039/039G) (SSG)," *Jane's Fighting Ships*, February 3, 2006. http://www.janes.com.

5. Ibid.

6. Shirley Kan, Christopher Bolcom, and Ronald O'Rourke, "China's Foreign Conventional Arms Acquisition: Background and Analysis," *CRS Reports for Congress*, October 10, 2000, http://www.fas.org/man/crs/RL30700.pdf, 60–61. Kan, Bolcom, and O'Rourke base this assessment on graphs from United States Office of Naval Intelligence, *Worldwide Submarine Challenges, 1996* (United States Government Printing Office, February, 1996), 11. These graphs indicate that the broadband noise of the 877 Kilo, of which China has two, is roughly as quiet as a first-flight *Los Angeles*, and the broadband signature of the 636 (China's remaining ten Kilos) is as quiet as that of an improved *Los Angeles* submarine.

7. See "Russian Shipyard Begins Building Submarines for Chinese Navy," *Agenstvo Voyennykh Novostey* (Interfax-AVN), January 15, 2003, FBIS Document No. CEP20030115000216; and "Two diesel subs built for China to be set afloat in April–May," *Kazakh Information Agency*, January 20, 2005, http://www.inform.kz/txt/showarticle.php?lang=eng&id=108240.

8. Swedish AIP experiments are discussed in "The Stirling Engine: An Engine for the Future," http://www.kockums.se/Products/products.html. Similar German efforts involving fuel cells are summarized in Peter Hauschildt and Albert Hammerschmidt, "PEM Fuel Cell Systems—An Attractive Energy Source for Submarines," http://www.industry.siemens.de/data/presse/docs/m1-isfb07033403e.pdf. Dutch experiments with closed-cycle diesel AIP are summarized in "Air Independent Propulsion Systems," http://www.thyssen-nordseewerke.de/e/prod/fe_aip_ccd.html.

9. See "SSK Agosta 90B Class Attack Submarine, France," http://www.naval-technology.com/projects/agosta/.

10. These two Chinese news releases are available at http://www.chinamil.com.cn/site1/xwpdxw/2005-08/20/content_277327.htm, and http://www.chinamil.com.cn/site1/xwpdxw/2005-08/19/content_277122.htm.

11. "Shang class (Type 093) (SSN)," *Jane's Fighting Ships*, February 3, 2006, http://www.janes.com.

12. "New PLAN stealthy fast missile crafts? Catamaran hull, pump-jet propulsion," *China Defense.com*, http://www.china-defense.com/forum/index.php?showtopic=6725&st=0.

13. In 2004 Wuhan shipyard launched the Yuan and Song, as indicated by photos at "PLAN New 'Yuan' Class Diesel Sub Thread," http://www.china-defense.com/forum/index.php?showtopic=7256&st=0. Jiangnan shipyard in Shanghai launched two Songs that year, one in September, and the other in November. See "039 SSK, Diesel-Sub thread, some pics of improved Song," http://www.china-defense.com/forum/index.php?showtopic=2046&st=400.

14. These were both first-generation submarines. The United States and the Soviets both also built relatively primitive first-generation submarines (the *Nautilus* and *Seawolf*, for instance and the Hotel, Echo, and November-classes) that were roughly equivalent to the Xia and Han. China, however, continues to operate its first-generation submarines nearly two decades after the United States and Soviet Union stopped sending theirs to sea.

15. Jane's claims that two 093s have been launched. See Commodore Stephen Saunders, TYPE 093 (SSN), *Jane's Fighting Ships*, March 14 2005. www.janes.com. Bill Gertz reports that two 093s are under construction, as is one 094. See Bill Gertz, "Beijing Building Deep-Sea Naval Might," *The Washington Times*, June 26, 2005, at http://washingtontimes.com/specialreport/20050626-113506-6621r.htm.

16. Bill Gertz, "China Advances Missile Program," *The Washington Times*, June 22, 2005. http://www.washingtontimes.com/national/20050621-102521-5027r.htm.

17. Rubin, the bureau that designed Kilo submarines, advertises that the most modern of the class can reach speeds of twenty knots. It is unlikely that this speed can be

maintained for more than a very few hours before the ship's batteries are depleted and must be recharged. A catalogue for the submarine can be viewed online at http://www.china-defense.com/forum/index.php?showtopic=3228&st=75.

18. A U.S. *Virginia*-class SSN costs approximately $2.5 billion dollars, displaces 7,800 tons, and requires a crew of 134 personnel. Russia sold China Model 636 Kilo class submarines for approximately $200 million each. Kilos displace 2,350 tons, and require a crew of 52. See United States Navy Fact File, "*Virginia*-Class," http://www .chinfo.navy.mil/navpalib/factfile/ships/ship-ssn.html, and the Rubin Kilo brochure, posted August 20, 2005, on page four of the "8 New Kilos for China" thread of China Defense.com website, at http://www.china-defense.com/forum/index.php ?showtopic=3228&st=75.

19. Most modern torpedoes have an effective range against surface ships of less than ten nautical miles. Chinese Song submarines' C-801 (YJ-1) antisurface cruise missiles have a range of approximately twenty-two nautical miles. See CSS-N-4 Sardine (YJ-1/-12/-82 and C-801) and CSSC-8 Saccade (YJ-2/-21/-22/-83 and C-802/803), *Jane's Strategic Weapon Systems*, June 8, 2005, http://www.janes.com. The eight new Kilo submarines being delivered to China will include the Russian-built, 120-nautical-mile-range 3M-54E antiship cruise missile. See "China's Navy," *Jane's Sentinel Security Assessment—China And Northeast Asia*, June 13 2005, http://www.janes.com.

20. This is known as "classifying with ordnance."

21. Harry D. Train, "An Analysis of the Falkland/Malvinas Islands Campaign," *Naval War College Review* 51, no. 1 (Winter 1988): 40. It is important to also state that the Argentine submarine did not successfully attack any British ships, suggesting that both antisurface and antisubmarine warfare are difficult enterprises.

22. This was especially true during World War II, when, generally speaking, the allies succeeded in using radar to detect and attack German U-boats via airplanes.

23. These factors are described in detail in Shawn Cappellano-Sarver's contribution to this volume.

24. To date, with one temporary exception, no country has exported a nuclear submarine to another. The exception occurred in 1988, when for three years India leased from Russia a Charlie-class nuclear-powered guided-missile-carrying submarine. See "Submarines," in the Indian Nuclear Forces pages of Federation of American Scientists, at http://www.fas.org/nuke/guide/india/sub/.

25. Ibid.

26. Currently, Russia, Germany, France, Sweden, and Spain are the countries that offer diesel submarines for export. Greece, Italy, and South Korea are all building U212 and U214 submarines of German design, presumably with extensive help from HDW, the German-based conglomerate that designed the vessels. See "U212 / U214 Attack Submarines, Germany," http://www.naval-technology.com/projects/ type_212/. DCN, a combined French and Spanish consortium, designed and builds the Scorpene-class, which is being purchased by the Chilean, Indian, and Malaysian navies. See "SSK Scorpene Attack Submarine, Chile," http://www.naval -technology.com/projects/scorpene. Kockums, the Swedish submarine manufacturer of the *Gotland* class, is now a part of HDW. Russia offers the Kilo and, more

recently, the Amur series of submarines for export. All the submarines listed in this footnote are offered with AIP technology.

27. For an excellent primer on AIP see Edward C. Whitman, "AIP Technology Creates a New Undersea Threat," *Undersea Warfare* 4, no. 1 (Fall 2001): 12–15, 31. http://www.chinfo.navy.mil/navpalib/cno/n87/usw/issue_13/propulsion.htm.

28. This appraisal is based on the author's interviews with commanding officers of foreign diesel submarines, including those who have commanded AIP vessels.

29. Kockums offers the Stirling engine. Sweden's three *Gotland*-class submarines have been in service now for a decade, with the first commissioned in 1996. See "SSK Gotland Class (Type A19) Attack Submarine," Sweden, http://www.naval-technology.com/projects/gotland/, and "The Gotland Class Submarine," http://www.kockums.se/Submarines/gotland.html. HDW offers fuel-cell technology. DCN offers the MESMA system for its submarines, and Russia offers fuel cell AIP with its exports. See Don Walsh, "The AIP Alternative," *Navy League of the United States*, http://www.navyleague.org/seapower/aip_alternative.htm, and page nine of the Kilo sales brochure, posted August 20, 2005 on page four of the "8 New Kilos for China" thread, http://www.china-defense.com/forum/index.php?showtopic=3228&st=75.

30. Germany and Sweden already operate AIP submarines. Greece, South Korea, Portugal, and Italy have contracts to acquire German technology AIP vessels. Japan has operated the Swedish AIP system for several years on its training submarine, and recently signed a contract to purchase the system for its fleet. Pakistan is installing a French AIP system in one of its Agosta-class vessels. See "Breakthrough in Japan for Stirling AIP," *Kockums News*, July 11, 2005, http://www.kockums.se/News/latest-news.html, and "Germany Export Behavior," *Center for Non-Proliferation Studies*, http://cns.miis.edu/research/submarines/germany/export.htm.

31. "In naval warfare, a fleet in being is a naval force that extends a controlling influence without ever leaving port. Were the fleet to leave port and face the enemy, it might lose in battle and no longer influence the enemy's actions, but by simply remaining safely in port the enemy is forced to continually deploy forces to guard against it." From "Fleet in Being," Wikipedia, http://en.wikipedia.org/wiki/Fleet_in_being.

32. The Han submarine that was detected near the Japan's Ishigaki Jima in November 2004 was an exception to the rule that Chinese submarines rarely are detected outside their home waters. A November 2003 incident in which a Ming submarine was detected on the surface southwest of Kyushu is another notable exception.

33. See "China's Navy," *Jane's Sentinel Security Assessment—China And Northeast Asia*, June 13, 2005, http://www.janes.com.

34. 2005 *Annual Report to Congress on the Military Power of the People's Republic of China*, http://www.defenselink.mil/news/Jul2005/d20050719china.pdf, 5.

35. Harvey Sapolsky, "The POLARIS System Development" (Cambridge, Mass.: Harvard University Press, 1972), 169, 172.

36. "SSBN-640 Benjamin Franklin-Class FBM Submarines," http://www.fas.org/nuke/guide/usa/slbm/ssbn-640.htm.

37. In comparison, the United States built its *Lafayette-* (SSBN-616) class submarines at Electric Boat Shipyard in Groton, Connecticut; at Mare Island Naval Shipyard in California; at Portsmouth Naval Shipyard in Kittery, Maine; and at Newport News Shipbuilding in Newport News, Virginia. The United States also built nuclear submarines at Ingalls Shipyard in Pascagoula, Mississippi; and at New York Shipbuilding in Camden, New Jersey.

38. One grainy photo of a submarine sail exists that is probably that of the 093 SSN.

39. The points in the text are abbreviated due to space limitations. The full text contains important nuance that directly affect the intent of the standards. For example, item one reads in its entirety: "First, select the best people available. Then train them to operate the equipment under the worst possible conditions,—and educate them to know everything and to do everything necessary, without question, to bring the submarine and her crew home safely—before they step foot aboard their first boat." "Admiral Bowman, Remarks at Undersea Defense Technology Conference Hawaii 2001," *The Submarine Review* (January 2002): 6–11.

40. http://www.chinamil.com.cn/site1/xwpdxw/2005-08/19/content_277122.htm.

41. Zhang Luocan and Liang Jianhua, "Submarine Flotilla of South China Sea Fleet Carries Out Confrontation Exercise In Rough Sea," *PLA Daily*, July 21 2004, http://english.chinamil.com.cn/site2/militarydatabase/2004-09/14/content_13726.htm.

42. Qiao Tianfu, "Submarine Cadets in Training," *PLA Daily*, August 3 2005, http://english.chinamil.com.cn/site2/militarydatabase/2005-08/03/content_265084.htm.

43. The article related how the previous curriculum was completely overhauled, with relevant training replacing dogma, and skills required for safely operating submarines taking the place of political theory indoctrination. See Fan Ping, Liu Ping, and Wang Yongsheng, "Blue Whales Dive Deep to Train Skills of Fighting, Winning—True Account of In-Depth Teaching Reform Under Water at the PLA Naval Submarine Academy," *Jiefangjun Bao* (*Liberation Army Daily*), October 21, 2002, FBIS CPP20021021000066.

Christopher McConnaughy

China's Undersea Nuclear Deterrent

Will the U.S. Navy Be Ready?

We will have to build nuclear submarines even if it takes us 10,000 years!
—Mao Zedong, 1959

THERE IS A GENERAL CONSENSUS THAT CHINA is rapidly modernizing its military. However, there is no clear consensus on what this modernization means to the United States.[1] While some analysts argue that focusing
on specific Chinese nuclear capabilities without looking at the nuclear strategy debate behind those capabilities is too narrow, at some point capabilities
must be reviewed to assess potential threats in order to provide a solid foundation for future force structure planning.[2] China's newest nuclear-powered
ballistic-missile submarine, known as the Type 094, is no exception. The rev-
elation in the open press during late fall 2004 that the first prototype had
been launched in July of that year underlines the imperative for such analyses, although the boat is not yet operational;[3] that is especially true given that
"the advent of truly reliable SSBNs capable of regular long patrols . . . would
revolutionize [China's] second strike nuclear capabilities."[4]

There are no absolutes in the world of international relations and politics. It is, therefore, prudent to ask whether the United States will be prepared to counter given weapon systems. Defense planners cannot sit on

the sidelines and wait for the resolution of a debate over a potential adversary's intentions.

Under many circumstances, the deterrence provided by SSBNs is a significant and credible strategic threat. From a purely military perspective, they have the capacity, quite literally, to change the world, by exacting severe destruction on whole societies. From a geopolitical perspective, the threat of a strike from an SSBN can force another state to deal with their adversary on a level playing field, however backward the opposing economy and ideology may seem. In other words, a credible SSBN force could translate directly into political leverage in a United States-China crisis. For China's navy, "the development of nuclear-powered submarines [has been] the chief objective of [the twentieth] century."[5] All indications are that this priority on nuclear submarines will continue and even accelerate in the twenty-first century.

The United States advertises its ballistic-missile submarine fleet as the most survivable component of its nuclear arsenal, and for good reason. Nuclear power enables ballistic-missile submarines to stay submerged for weeks and even months, the only limiting factor being food for the crew. The submerged endurance of an SSBN allows it to patrol quietly in locations known only to its commanders, greatly complicating the tracking problem for those interested in knowing where they operate.

In principal, there are two methods for neutralizing the threat from a submarine-launched ballistic missile.[6] The first is to employ a nuclear-powered attack submarine (SSN) to destroy the SSBN before it can launch its nuclear weapons. In the unlikely event of an unexpected missile launch, the SSN would immediately eliminate the SSBN to prevent further launches. This method requires having available a sufficient number of SSNs (in terms of the number of the enemy's SSBNs) to devote to such an undersea warfare campaign. The second method of countering SLBMs would be to establish a ballistic-missile-defense system to destroy any missiles after their launch. Significant advantages that the SSN enjoys over a ballistic-missile-defense system in this scenario include the facts that the SSN is proven technology and does not have to contend with decoys deployed by the ballistic missile.[7]

However, only a few nations, since the demise of the Soviet Union, possess the capability to hunt an SSBN in blue water, and as yet no nation can guarantee the destruction of intercontinental ballistic missiles in flight.[8] SSBNs, accordingly, when properly operated and supported, provide a very robust, highly assured second-strike—or even preemptive nuclear strike—capability. For any state that seeks to have its voice heard in the world and does not want to be subjected to nuclear coercion, SSBNs are prized commodities—albeit so expensive that they are feasible only for the most determined and advanced aspirants.

Much has been written within the last decade on China's defense modernization, as if it had only recently begun. To the contrary, while China's defense modernization has not progressed equally within all areas, and its pace has been inconsistent—with a more rapid pace seen in the last decade, due to a newly opened intellectual climate and increased economic capacity—China has been modernizing and improving its strategic nuclear forces since their inception over four decades ago. The editors of a recent publication on the People's Liberation Army observe, "The Chinese military is anything but stagnant."[9]

China is only now reaching the point in the development of its nuclear arsenal that it can strike globally. The present articulation of the U.S. triad recognizes that today's conventional capability—through better technology—may be able to accomplish what would have previously required a nuclear strike.[10] However, the United States cannot lose sight of the fact that nations like China lack the awesome, global, conventional strike capability that the U.S. military enjoys and so still place significant emphasis on their strategic nuclear forces. China recently achieved a limited capability to threaten the continental United States from deep in the central Pacific. Now a more capable SSBN, with a new SLBM of far greater range and accuracy, will be able to strike the United States from the relative safety and security of proximate waters.

Still, it is easy to discount Chinese efforts at SSBN development and the threat that they may pose.[11] Currently, the Xia (Type 092)—which has recently emerged from an extended overhaul—is the only operational Chinese SSBN; the 094 is expected to become operational in the next few years—contingent on the successful development of the JL-2 (Great Wave) SLBM.[12] Nevertheless, China's defense modernization must be viewed in terms of contemporary China, not the backward political and economic practices of the past; the China of today is not that of yesteryear. China is enjoying a relatively stable social and political environment; its economy is thriving.[13] In contrast with the period when China built its first generation of nuclear submarines, today its defense modernization is receiving a substantial amount of assistance from Russia. Naturally, China is trying to play catch-up. The U.S. Navy already had a strong conventional submarine program when it made the decision to build nuclear-powered submarines, and only when it had a firm footing in nuclear propulsion did it embark on submarine-launched ballistic missiles. China tried to do it all at the same time; now, however, it has emerged from those dark days.

There has been little written on China and its ballistic-missile submarine program, which is not surprising, given the program's slow progress and how little information there is upon which analysts can draw. In *China's Strategic Seapower,* however, John Wilson Lewis and Xue Litai provide a remarkably detailed and insightful analysis into the extreme challenges that China's nuclear-powered submarine (both SSN and SSBN) and SLBM projects faced. Lewis and Xue's work is a neglected resource that deserves the careful attention of American naval strategists. It makes the divergence between the China of the past and that of the future acutely clear. China's capabilities are changing—from its aggressive and widely watched, overarching, defense modernization efforts to the recent introduction of its newest nuclear-powered fast-attack submarine, to China's first manned space flight, to a more mobile, more secure, and more lethal nuclear-strike capability. The China of tomorrow will be radically different.

China is seeking a secure nuclear-strike capability through both road-mobile intercontinental ballistic missiles (ICBMs) and SSBNs. In 1997, General Liu Huaqing of China's Central Military Commission stated, "Fewer than 10 percent of China's land-based missiles would survive a large-scale nuclear first strike; the less vulnerable SLBMs would preserve our nuclear counterattack capabilities."[14] China is displaying a patient and steady determination to produce a modern military with a viable and credible land-mobile and undersea nuclear deterrent that is worthy of focused study.

This chapter is written in two basic sections that reflect the distinct dichotomy between the struggling China of the past and the emerging powerhouse. The first part examines the development of China's nuclear-powered submarine program and, more specifically, the development of its first SSBN, the Xia. Relying heavily on the path-breaking research of Lewis and Xue, it offers technical detail to illustrate the tremendous difficulties China experienced in the production of its first submarines. Some would argue that it was an exhibition of gross incompetence in the Chinese defense industry; it would be more accurate to say that these were the first faltering steps of amateurs, not outright ineptitude. It is a safe and logical bet that Chinese technology will only continue to improve. The Xia experience was neither a great success nor a total failure. Above all, it was a down payment on China's robust nuclear future. Although the Xia has, for the most part, remained alongside the pier, China is now in a position to capitalize on the investment; it has an indigenous capability to design and construct SSBNs and their SLBMs. China's future in submarines looks bright.

The second part of the chapter is a look at what the future may bring if a Sino-U.S. maritime and nuclear rivalry becomes more intense. Accordingly, it asks whether the U.S. Navy will be prepared to resume a more aggressive strategic ASW posture in the event that China does deploy a substantial SSBN force, as has been projected. Future advances in Chinese attack submarines, improvements in the education and training of the People's Liberation Army Navy, the number of Chinese submarines that already exist today, the geographic constraints of the Asia-Pacific region, the decline of the U.S. Navy's antisubmarine warfare (ASW) capability, and the expected reduction in the number of American SSNs are all variables here. This chapter reaches the preliminary conclusion that the U.S. Navy will be ill prepared to execute strategic ASW against China in the coming decades unless the atrophy of its ASW assets is not only stopped but reversed.

> I felt that the Bureau of Ships had in the past been so restricted in their design studies by contradictory instructions concerning characteristics that it was impossible for them to produce the best submarines. . . . First, they designed a hull and then every person in the Department began to stuff it from both ends. In the old days, design became a four ring [*sic*] circus. The Bureaus of Ordnance, Engineering, Navigation and Construction and Repair all vied with one another to get their own pet projects included.[15]

Rear Adm. Charles B. Momsen made this statement in 1948, during the design of the USS *Albacore,* the U.S. Navy's first submarine with a teardrop-shaped hull. His observation reflects how bureaucratic organizations can unnecessarily complicate what should, ideally, be a purely scientific endeavor. China's first experiences in submarine design were different only in the extremes to which the domestic and organizational politics interfered.

The pace of the Chinese SSBN and SLBM programs has been excruciatingly slow by Western standards. On the other hand, when viewed within the context of a developing nation that at the beginning of its quest possessed only a rudimentary indigenous defense industry and no capacity for nuclear-reactor, submarine, or ballistic-missile production, the performance is rather remarkable. China has built—from square one—a formidable, albeit still incomplete, military-industrial base in less than half the time that the United States and other Western powers developed theirs.

Great Leap Forward, Cultural Revolution, and Third Front

The Chinese defense industry can trace its existence to the SSBN and strategic weapons programs.[16] In July 1958, a nuclear-powered ballistic-missile submarine project (Project 09) and submarine-launched ballistic-missile project (the JL-1, Project 05) were authorized, though China did not possess the military, industrial, or scientific capacity for such ambitious undertakings.[17] If the lack of both intellectual and physical resources were not enough, from 1958 to 1960 China endured Chairman Mao Zedong's misguided Great Leap Forward, in which Mao set aside all rationality in an attempt to exceed British industrial production levels within fifteen years. The social turmoil just before and during the Great Leap severely impacted the SSBN and SLBM projects, to the point that their "defense scientists and engineers were devoting less than half the day to professional work."[18]

On the heels of the failed Great Leap, from 1966 to 1976, came Mao's Cultural Revolution. Supported by Mao, "radicalized technicians and workers in the research organs under the [Defense Science and Technology] commission berated, persecuted, and then sundered the relations between senior scientists and leadership cadres, between the technical community and the policy makers."[19] Political upheaval, social unrest, and cuts in spending were not the limits of the damage done by the Cultural Revolution. Mao, in an effort to purify the Chinese Communist Party, demanded that "reactionary leading academic figures" be tracked down.[20] The violence resulted in numerous casualties in the submarine and ballistic-missile research communities, including the director of Institute 703, Yao Tongbin, who was responsible for JL-1–materials testing.[21] Mao's Cultural Revolution was to blame for the killing and suicide of personnel involved in the strategic weapons programs, lack of funding for equipment and facilities, poor working conditions and diet, destruction of equipment, distrust in political leaders, poor quality in materials and workmanship, and outright warfare among technicians.[22] In 1966, defending the premises of the Cultural Revolution, Lin Biao, Vice Chairman of the Central Committee, stated, "It stands to reason that a cultural revolution should accelerate production, and this has been borne out by the facts."[23] Quite to the contrary, China's Cultural Revolution, in addition to the enforced geographic separation of various organizations involved (as will be seen below), resulted in a ten-year stagnation of the JL-1 project.[24] Mao's belief "that men equipped with correct political ideas were more important in war than weapons" turned the Chinese defense industry on its head and cost China dearly.[25]

As if political, social, and economic turmoil were not enough, the research and development phases of the SSBN and SLBM projects were fraught with inefficiency and contradiction. Mao ordered the creation of a "Third Front," by which virtually the entire Chinese defense industry was moved to the interior, far from the coasts, to guard against attack.[26] This effort began in earnest in 1965; ultimately 483 factories and 92 research academies were constructed on the Third Front, and 1.6 million workers were transferred to China's interior from the coastal areas.[27] The economic costs and the delays resulting from the Third Front effort were staggering.

Marshal Nie Rongzhen, in overall charge of the strategic submarine and missile programs, appears to have severely underestimated their magnitude and complexity. The talent and expertise required to design and produce an SSBN is not abundant in the most technologically advanced societies today, let alone the relatively backward China of the 1960s. Nevertheless, Nie chose to pursue a competitive strategy, assigning two separate organizations to perform research and development. This diluted the small pool of scientists and engineers, as well as material resources.[28]

From 1958 until the first successful submerged test launch of the JL-1 SLBM in 1988, the various organizations involved went through countless restructurings.[29] Yet the reorganizations were often ineffective: they failed to get to the root cause of the problem and did not produce the desired progress: "The logic of the times was to destroy the system in order to save it."[30]

If China has been persistent in its efforts to produce both nuclear-powered attack and ballistic-missile submarines, that desire has wavered at times. When it was recognized that design and production were not going to be speedy, some demanded that the projects be discontinued. General Luo Ruiqing, the director of the National Defense Industry Office (NDIO), wanted to see Project 09 terminated, arguing in a remarkable moment of candor that China could not produce a diesel-powered submarine, let alone a nuclear-powered one. Opposing Luo, the Chinese foreign minister, Chen Yi, argued that for the sake of national security the effort should continue, regardless of the time it required.[31] Project 09 research continued but was downsized substantially in August 1962. Unrestricted design and production did not resume until August 1965.[32]

Research and Development

Considering that China was creating its technological and industrial base from scratch, and on the back of the strategic-weapons program, it is not difficult to see why the learning process was painfully long.[33] This section addresses the numerous challenges associated with various aspects of China's early submarine development.

Nuclear Power

Aside from the political climate, Project 09 engineers faced daunting obstacles in the design and development of the first submarine nuclear reactor plants. The work was as problematic as one might expect an initial foray into nuclear-reactor design and construction to be. The first reactor design was completed in 1960 and then went through numerous iterations.[34] The two organizations tasked by Nie for reactor plant design, the Qinghua University Institute of Nuclear Energy Technology and the Reactor Engineering and Technology Institute (Institute 194), gathered what information they could on foreign designs and made separate proposals. Qinghua University promoted a design based on a German nuclear-powered ship, the *Otto Hahn;* Institute 194 favored a design based on the Soviet icebreaker *Lenin.*[35] The decision between the two proposals was based not on their merits and suitability for submarine operations but on the political clout of the two agencies. Institute 194 had more, and in 1965 the *Lenin* design was selected.[36]

The Institute 194 designers were to encounter difficulties with, among other things, control-rod drive mechanisms, nuclear instruments, reactor instrumentation, and the steam generator.[37] The physics calculations were completed by hand, which required an extraordinary amount of time; they had to be repeated with each successive modification to the plant design.[38] The uranium-235 fuel concentration for the reactor plant was enriched to only 3 percent, meaning that the Chinese submarine would require more frequent refueling than American submarines.[39]

The initial stages of the reactor development, under Institute 194's Reactor Engineering Research Section, were difficult at best. Working conditions were poor; worse, "young and inexperienced technical personnel . . . [were] left . . . to their own devices, without any data, experimental equipment or computers."[40] Counting on Soviet assistance, China had placed little emphasis on the development of indigenous support capability for nuclear research and manufacturing. When Soviet assistance was withdrawn in 1960, the Chinese were no longer able to focus exclusively on production and instead had to step back and try to fill the void left by the departed Soviets.

Successful operation of a prototype reactor, to verify the validity of the design, was a prerequisite to the installation of a submarine unit.[41] The sense of urgency in Project 09 to get the first attack submarine to sea is amply evident in the fact that China opted to design and build prototype and submarine reactor plants simultaneously.[42] From an engineering perspective, failure to evaluate a design properly prior to the manufacture and operation of the final product is an invitation to disaster. This is especially true in the world of nuclear engineering, as the Chinese apparently learned the hard way.[43]

The exact dates are unclear, but sometime around 1970 the prototype reactor was tested at its full rated power.[44] The engineers experienced difficulties with test instrumentation, pulse tube leaks, and secondary valves. Further design problems were encountered with the reactor safety set-points, which apparently caused several unwarranted automatic shutdowns.[45] The design, construction, and testing of China's first prototype nuclear reactor was to take twelve years.

China also had, from the beginning, major difficulties with the submarine reactor plant. Initial criticality of the SSN reactor plant and the maiden voyage of the attack submarine on which it was fitted, the Han, occurred in 1971. During sea trials (which were not completed until 1974) and thereafter, "severe problems" were encountered with the reactor plant.[46] These included high radiation exposure to the crew; leakage in the steam generator from the primary water circuit to the secondary, with the result that radiation was detected in the secondary system drains; primary system valve leakage; and steam line ruptures. These persistent problems—as well as corrosion, steam leaks from the steam generators, and defective pumps, main condensers, and main reduction gears—demonstrated that the Project 09 engineers had much to learn about materials and precision design and construction.[47] The PLAN accepted the Han—designated hull number 401—in August 1974, but it could hardly be considered fully operational. China incorporated design modifications in the second Han-class unit, hull number 402, commissioned in 1977, but many of the original problems persisted.[48]

The Submarine: Hull and Interior Arrangement

The design and construction of the submarine itself was no less difficult. China decided to complete its first nuclear-powered submarines as attack boats, due to the time required to develop the JL-1 missile and an SSBN launcher system.[49] When the Soviet Union terminated its assistance in submarine design and construction, the Chinese, unlike in the reactor project, turned to other external sources to fill the void. Huang Xuhua, the chief designer for Project 09, summed up their attitude: "To derive nourishment from others' experiences . . . you can get twice the result with half the effort if you know how to pick others' brains." (Some argue that this practice continues to this day, as is consistent with a Chinese proverb, "Stones from the other hills may serve to polish the jade of this one—advice from others may help one overcome one's shortcomings.")[50] Accordingly, Chinese engineers adopted the teardrop hull shape of American and Soviet nuclear submarines and chose to construct a double hull similar to those of Soviet boats.[51]

High-quality welding, to conjoin hull plates and attach interior and exterior equipment and fittings to the hull, is absolutely critical to the survival of a submarine. Chinese engineers and shipyard welders had serious difficulties; numerous weld failures on the hull resulted from improper welding techniques and equipment. The engineers might have been expected to determine the causes of the defective welds and provide solution to the welders, but they did not; the welders were left to conduct experiments on their own and devise a method for heat-treating steel hull plates.[52] China's first submarine hull, accordingly, was not a product of exceptional Chinese engineering or first-rate ship construction; instead, China's first nuclear submarine hull was a product of trial and error.[53]

In keeping with the trial-and-error principle, engineers at the Bohai Shipyard (Plant 431) did not have a sound plan to fit out the submarine. In fact, construction of the hull commenced before the layout of interior subsystems had been completed. The risk was not to the basic hull shape but to the configuration of compartments, hull openings, bulkhead penetrations, and interior supporting structures. Although limited use was made of a wooden scale model, pipefitting was completed and subsystems were installed by the best guess method. Not surprisingly, in view of the inevitable numerous rearrangements, the builders encountered a great degree of difficulty in calculating the boat's center of gravity and center of buoyancy.[54] In general, the manner in which the Chinese constructed their first nuclear-powered attack submarine suggests a deep urgency in the minds of China's leaders, who continued to push forward regardless of unresolved technical issues.

The Submarine: Sound Silencing and Combat Systems

The stealthiness of a submarine—its ability to stay hidden from an adversary—depends a great deal on the noise it emits. The engineering, manufacture, and operation of the submarine determine how much or how little noise it will radiate into its environment. The Project 09 engineers recognized the need for silencing and took measures to limit the noise level of their submarines, such as mounting equipment on pedestals and covering the equipment with sound-absorbent material.[55] Other factors considered were the number of hull openings, flow noise through internal piping and over the hull, and screw cavitation.[56]

Ideally, weapons systems are designed to meet particular needs, specified prior to construction. This was not the case in China's SSN and SSBN development. For the SSN, it was not until 1966, eight years after the decision to build the nuclear submarine, that China's Defense Science and Technology Commission identified the type's desired functions. Neither was the SSBN the product of a rational strategic debate. Mao saw in the unlimited Soviet assistance then available simply an opportunity to acquire a weapons system that might prevent other states from taking further advantage of China.[57] Failure to identify specific capabilities required of the submarines proved detrimental to their development.

One area in which this failure manifested itself was in combat systems. The principal mission of an attack submarine is attack, and to carry out an attack, it requires torpedoes.[58] China's torpedo development, however, lacked focus. Gas-powered torpedoes, electric-powered torpedoes, rocket-assisted aerial torpedoes, torpedoes with passive acoustic homing, torpedoes with active and passive acoustic homing, torpedoes for surface targets, and torpedoes for deep-water submerged targets—all were given consideration at one point or another from the early 1960s until 1989, when China believed it had finally fielded a weapon comparable to Western torpedoes, the Yu-3.[59] As a further example, the director of China's Seventh Academy (and subsequently commander of the PLAN, 1982–88), Liu Huaqing, instructed his engineers "to copy a Soviet model torpedo for missions against surface targets. Although Liu's experts understood that the principal prey for the torpedoes of the future would be submarines, not surface ships, they accepted the assignment and made it one of their top priorities."[60] The consequence of this haphazard approach to the torpedo—the sine qua non of the SSN—was that the Han did not have a capable torpedo until 1989, fifteen years after its commissioning.[61]

The Ballistic-Missile Submarine and the JL-1

A preliminary design for the SSBN was completed in 1967, with the intention of launching a boat in 1973.[62] The major difference between the attack submarine and the ballistic-missile submarine, of course, was the addition of the missile compartment. For that reason, China's first SSBN encountered many of the same problems with the reactor plant and combat systems that the attack submarine endured, in addition to those of the launching system and the SLBM itself.

By March 1964, when the JL-1 project was initiated, China had been working on missile technology for nearly eight years.[63] In 1967 China, perceiving the vulnerability of its fixed land-based strategic-missile systems to satellite reconnaissance, decided to focus more of its efforts on road-mobile missiles and SLBMs.[64] Today, China's basic missile technology seems fairly robust and at least moderately successful.[65] At the time, however, the crucial differences between an SLBM and a land-based missile created technological hurdles that the PLAN could not easily or quickly overcome. Like the U.S. Navy, China explored liquid fuel for its first SLBM.[66] When the Soviets withdrew, China, noting the progress of the U.S. Polaris Missile Program, decided to pursue solid-propellant technology for the JL-1. Solid rocket propellant, therefore, was one of the first obstacles the program encountered.[67]

Unlike a land-based missile, an SLBM must be ejected from the missile tube underwater to a point above the surface, from a depth that can vary with each launch. Moreover, if a ballistic missile is to strike a target, its guidance system must be given the precise location from which it is being launched. For a land-based missile this is for the most part a static problem; even with a road-mobile system, technicians can determine the launch location with relative ease. In contrast, the SLBM requires dynamic information; its position is continuously changing up to the moment of launch.[68] Lastly, once the missile is above the surface, its motor must ignite. At that point, as for its land-based counterpart, guidance and flight control systems must put the missile on target with an accuracy inversely proportional to the yield of its warhead.[69]

China's initial work on solid rocket propellant began in 1956; the designs for the JL-1, including the motor, were finalized in 1967.[70] As for the SSBN, the work on the JL-1 proceeded by trial and error, and it was not until 1980 that the Chinese engineers developed a satisfactory motor.[71] Chinese engineers working on the project moved through a series of stages, starting with a 65mm-diameter design and then trying 300mm and 654mm approaches before settling upon the 1,400mm design ultimately utilized in the first- and second-stage motors of the JL-1.[72] The designers had to overcome challenges presented by the motor's chemical composition, the star-shaped hollow core needed for even burning, case-bonding of the propellant to the motor casing, plastics, high-strength steel, heat shields, adhesives, nozzles, and thrust-vector control—to name only a few problem areas.[73]

Chinese engineers chose "to copy foreign models as best they could" for the JL-1's guidance system, finally adapting the guidance system of the JL-1's land-based DF variant. The guidance system, which used inertial navigation, was capable of in-flight course corrections only in the boost phase, not in the missile's ballistic phase.[74] China's choice to shoot the SLBM from a moving (as opposed to a hovering, static) submarine created additional problems.[75] The flow of water over the hull during a launch sequence subjects an SLBM to forces perpendicular to the desired direction of travel. The designers apparently found that the missile could be pushed as far as sixty degrees from the vertical; they had to ensure that the launcher and the missile's flight controls could compensate for the induced error.[76] The functional gyros this required were not completed until 1976, and an adequate altitude-control system was not available until 1980.[77] Two years later, the JL-1 was successfully launched from a surfaced Golf-class submarine.[78]

The End Result

As a result of such technological challenges, as well as of political and organizational upheavals, China did not conduct a successful submerged launch of the JL-1 from the Xia until 1988—a full thirty years after the decision to build China's first SSBN, and fifteen years after the intended launch date of the Xia.[79] The question remains of China's ability to effectively operate such a complex piece of machinery—especially in the face of advanced ASW forces. It is believed that the Xia has had very little time at sea and that its operational readiness is highly questionable.[80] It seems that the years of struggle to provide China with a more-secure nuclear-strike capability produced in the end a submarine of marginal value, an SSBN that has been brushed off as a nonthreat.[81]

The Xia itself, as a weapons platform, is much less significant than the process by which China built it, developing a physical and intellectual infrastructure that has enabled the state to continue its forward progress. The launch in December 2002 of the Type 093 attack submarine, the successor of the Han class, and in July 2004 of the Type 094, China's first follow-on to the Xia, are telling indicators of how far China's technology has advanced—though the boats' true capabilities are likely to remain a mystery for some time.

Strategic ASW and the U.S. Navy Today

One would like to destroy these missiles or the means of launching them before they are launched, if possible, and if so launched we would like to destroy the missiles immediately and then get those that have not been launched. In other words, missile destruction is considered as associated with the antisubmarine warfare program.

—Admiral Hooper, Director of ASW Research and Development, 1965

Strategic ASW

During the Cold War, American and Soviet submarines engaged in a high-stakes underwater contest. The wartime mission of the SSNs, in the event of hostilities between the United States and the Soviet Union, was to destroy the SSBNs—preferably before any SLBMs were launched. Owen R. Coté, Jr., labels the period of time between 1945 and 1990 the "Third Battle" of undersea forces, one in which both the United States and USSR invested heavily in undersea technology, each side trying to maintain qualitative or quantitative advantages.[82] Coté describes the little-studied topic of *strategic* antisubmarine warfare—ASW directed specifically at submerged strategic weapons carrying platforms, the SSBNs. Generally, ASW involves, as the term suggests, the detection, location, and destruction of submarines; it has been pursued in a variety of ways since the introduction of the submarine. Strategic ASW, however, is a product of the nuclear age.

Were hostilities to break out between two countries in possession of SSBNs, the goal of their respective attack submarines would be to eliminate the other's SSBNs—that is, the SSNs would conduct strategic ASW. Conversely, the goal of the SSBNs would be to remain undetected and able to launch their SLBMs if so ordered. Strategic ASW requires SSNs to shadow SSBNs, to track them continuously, utilizing cues from such sources as satellite imagery, antisubmarine aircraft, and fixed, passive underwater acoustic arrays.[83] Since the demise of the Soviet Union, the U.S. Navy has not had to face a peer competitor underwater, and consequently its ASW skills and capabilities have atrophied.[84] They have also declined, in part, due a reduction in funding as increased emphasis is given other mission areas, such as power projection ashore.[85] Today the U.S. Navy is forcing a greater emphasis on antisubmarine warfare by the creation of a new Fleet ASW Command, but funding remains a critical issue. For example, the Navy recently announced that it will reduce the size of its P-3C Orion maritime patrol aircraft fleet by one-third, due to funding shortfalls, airframe fatigue, and the need to fund the next-generation ASW aircraft—the Multimission Maritime Aircraft (MMA).[86] In the words of Owen Coté, "Geopolitics and technology are conspiring to pull the Navy ashore from the sea, without eliminating the traditional and *irreducible* need for a navy that is capable of controlling the sea."[87]

Scholars, analysts, and government officials all seem to believe that the years 2005–10 will see the emergence of China's newest SSBNs. It is time to reenergize antisubmarine warfare, to ensure that the United States has an adequate number of submarines and other ASW assets in the coming decades to ensure its security. Once the new Chinese Type 094 SSBNs become operational, world events could oblige the United States to hold them at risk of immediate destruction, as was once done against the Soviet Union, when strategic ASW was a national mission of extreme importance.[88] In those years, sizeable resources were sunk into developing and deploying attack submarines, maritime patrol aircraft, surface-ship ASW capability, and undersea sound monitoring. For much of the Cold War, these resources were employed (as will be seen in more detail below) in an effort to create a barrier that would prevent Soviet SSBNs from coming close enough to the continental United States to launch a nuclear strike that would arrive on short notice. American strategic ASW capability evolved through improved technology and better operational practices that optimized all components that could be brought to bear—air, surface, and subsurface. The American civilian leadership and the Navy recognized the nature and seriousness of the threat and, accordingly, gave a high priority to strategic ASW. Today there is a danger that U.S. strategic ASW capabilities, so formidable a few decades ago, will not be up to the task if called upon again.[89]

China's Advance

China is gradually emerging as a serious undersea power. As U.S. ASW capability has withered, Chinese diesel submarines are becoming extremely difficult to detect and, consequently, more lethal. In the world of nuclear-powered submarines, China's technology is also improving. Unlike the notoriously noisy Han class, the Type 093 is estimated to be acoustically comparable to the Soviet Victor III.[90] Certainly, the 094 will benefit from the improvements in the 093.[91] "The Victor III, introduced in the mid-1980s, was the first Soviet submarine that surprised the Navy with its acoustic stealth, and its deployment was a harbinger of worse to come."[92] The Soviet Victor III was the forerunner of the Akula, "the first Soviet submarine that approached or achieved acoustic parity with its American contemporaries."[93]

Granted, that was two decades ago; the U.S. Navy has continued since then to upgrade its own submarine technology while China is trying to catch up. Nonetheless, it is likely that the second generation of Chinese nuclear submarines will represent a "great leap forward."

China's purchase of advanced Russian-built Kilo-class diesel submarines (SSK) represents much more than a mere increase in its number of attack submarines; it has afforded China the opportunity to improve the silencing and combat systems of the indigenous Song-class diesel boats and, surely, its new nuclear-powered boats as well.[94] Unlike its first foray in nuclear submarine design and construction, China is now receiving assistance from Russia—a great deal of it—and its SSBNs will certainly benefit.[95] Even without Russian assistance, however, advanced computer technology is widely available today. The last two decades' exponential improvement in microprocessor performance allows designers rapidly to shrink margins in performance. According to the Defense Department's 2003 annual report to Congress on the PRC, "China will continue purchasing foreign technology to improve quieting, propulsion, and submarine design. China also will benefit from the maturation of its domestic submarine research and development infrastructure to achieve a capability to design and manufacture modern submarines domestically."[96] The Chinese defense industry that is building the 094 SSBN is without a doubt far more capable than the one that struggled with the Xia.

What We Know and What We Don't Know

Regarding intelligence estimates, Michael I. Handel asks, "How can anyone know, in a world of secrecy, deception, and subjective perceptions, that his estimates of the enemy's strength are correct?"[97] Not surprisingly, estimates concerning China's future SSBNs vary considerably, but they are all in agreement that China will have an improved undersea nuclear strike capability in the very near future.[98] Nonetheless, Handel's point is well taken, in the sense that the consequences of not being prepared to hold a future Chinese SSBN fleet at risk make it prudent to hedge one's bets.

Although China's early SSBN and SLBM programs reflected the politi-

CHINA'S UNDERSEA NUCLEAR DETERRENT   93

cal and social upheaval and a lack of physical and intellectual infrastructure, such is not the case today. China enjoys political and social stability, its economy is blossoming, and the costs of the necessary infrastructure have been paid. China is making parallel improvements in both its officer and enlisted training.[99] Also, notably, a submariner, Admiral Zhang Dingfa, until recently led the PLAN, which suggests the greater emphasis placed on the submarine force. In the fall of 2004 Admiral Zhang was given a seat on the Central Military Commission; this gave a submariner a voice in China's most important national security decision-making body.

The U.S. Defense Department reported in 2003 that "training and exercise activity [of the PLAN] in 2002 was robust"; exercises were conducted in the South China Sea utilizing air, surface, and subsurface assets. Close observers of China's submarine force have stated that the PLAN is in fact undergoing a training revolution—joining the rest of the PLA in moving from rote, scripted exercises to "confrontational training" that encourages innovation and on-the-spot decision making.[100] To become effective and potent, the PLAN submarine force needs to make regular use of instrumented ranges for weapon shots at sea, and its crews—both of attack and ballistic-missile boats—need, when not deployed, regular sessions in attack training centers in realistic simulated environments.[101] This would be especially important for China's SSBN crews, who have had little, if any, time at sea. Indeed, China has established training centers where PLAN personnel, including submariners, can train ashore in their respective warfare areas.[102]

Should We Be Concerned?

The increased emphasis within the U.S. submarine force on strike, special operations, and intelligence, surveillance, and reconnaissance raise the question of whether the U.S. Navy will be able to perform the strategic ASW role adequately in the future. Given enough time, however, it is easier to train than acquire an adequate force structure; therefore, the U.S. Navy's ASW forces are the real question mark. It cannot be said with any certainty what the future holds for Sino-U.S. relations. The United States might, however, someday have to confront a China that seeks a much more prominent position on the world stage and is unwilling to bend to Washington's wishes. Indeed, initiatives by the pro-independence movement in Taiwan during the winter of 2003–04 led China once again to make very public and deliberate statements that it is willing to go to war to prevent Taiwanese independence, even if that means suffering a setback in its economy and sacrificing the 2008 Beijing Olympics. This seeming willingness to bear such costs is contrary to what some analysts have argued.[103]

It is widely agreed that a war between Taiwan and China could involve the United States, although it is entirely possible that the United States and China will never come to blows—and, yes, China's economic growth and integration into the world could lead to peaceful and prosperous coexistence between the United States and China.[104] Still, the cost of preparedness for strategic ASW would be minuscule compared to the catastrophic costs of being surprised by a potent new Chinese SSBN capability—especially in the midst of a crisis.

A Worthy Opponent?

There is a certain apparent reluctance in the West to take the Chinese submarine force seriously. Regarding the current and future capabilities of the American submarine force vis-à-vis China, one U.S. submarine captain wrote, "You can buy the very best submarines, you can study the lessons learned by others and utilize the training methods of the very best, but still it will take *many* years of internal growth to produce an effective submarine force."[105] With respect to a conflict between the United States and China over Taiwan, he writes, "China could put its entire [submarine] force to sea around Taiwan and the U.S. will still be at risk to lose one or two platforms (if only to bad luck). However, our [the U.S.] submarine force alone would *easily* be able to go in and destroy the Chinese submarine force." He believes that China will not, within the next ten years, have a submarine force capable of competing with the U.S. submarine force as a peer competitor, although "the [submarine] force they are building will *increase* the risk of U.S. losses . . . in the future."[106] Referring to a possible conflict over Taiwan and to the recent purchase of eight Kilo-class submarines, he states, "If the political will of the U.S. holds and there is a willingness to accept the loss of a few ships or submarines, then the outcome of the battle is not in question—[the United States would triumph]. But if U.S. [leaders] are not willing to have even one U.S. submarine or ship [sunk] then we have already lost the battle and they [the Chinese] might as well stop at four Kilos [versus] eight."[107]

The latter point, concerning losses, is an important one that deserves careful consideration in light of the possible deployment of a larger, more capable Chinese SSBN fleet. It implies that were a conflict between the United States and China over Taiwan to erupt when China possesses more capable attack submarines than before, American SSNs and other antisubmarine assets might not be able to guarantee the safety of high-value forces, such as aircraft carriers. If the SSNs could not protect aircraft carriers, it is likely that they could not perform strategic ASW either. For that reason, although confidence in the capabilities of the U.S. submarine force is not unwarranted—it is undeniably the strongest submarine force in the world today—a note of caution is prudent and necessary.

There is reason, however, to examine opposing viewpoints. Simply in terms of numbers alone, the entire Chinese submarine fleet—currently numbering approximately sixty-nine—could severely challenge the U.S. submarine force.[108] Other significant complications would be knowledge of the local acoustic operating environment, the shallow water of the Chinese littorals, a hostile merchant and fishing fleet, and mines. The experience of the Royal Navy during the Falklands War provides ample evidence of the difficulty diesel-electric submarines represent for antisubmarine forces.

In 1982, Argentina possessed four submarines of varying capability. Only one, the *San Luis,* could conduct offensive operations against the British task force. Facing that single submarine were elements of NATO's North Atlantic ASW force, Antisubmarine Group 2, arguably one of the most experienced in the world at the time. Nonetheless, the Argentine submarine was able to conduct two attacks on the British task force (both of which failed, but only due to weapon malfunctions). Local acoustic conditions rendered British forces helpless; they released over 150 weapons but scored no hits. According to the captain of the *San Luis,* "There was no effective counter attack. I don't think that they knew we were there until they heard our torpedoes running." The implication is that every weapon expended in the British ASW effort was fired at false targets.[109]

The Royal Navy was fortunate in that the weapons of the lone Argentine submarine failed. In a face-off with China, odds are that not every weapon on every PLAN submarine would do so. The U.S. submarine force would be further stretched to its limits if Chinese SSBNs were involved. The United States would undoubtedly prevail, albeit at some cost, in a series of submarine-on-submarine engagements. If, however, China chose to threaten the United States with nuclear weapons—even if as a bluff—the U.S. Navy could have difficulty, with the number of attack submarines it is projected to have, in holding even a small Chinese SSBN force at risk.

The United States cannot afford to become overconfident in its ability to cope with China. Prominent analysts like David Shambaugh believe that China will be hard pressed to catch up to the technology of the West;[110] certainly, China's submarine force would pose a greater threat to the U.S. Navy were its capabilities equal. However, because of the nature of undersea warfare, with its complexities and variables, and of SSBN operations in particular, China does not have to catch up with the West to be a serious threat to the United States in a conflict.

Is Ballistic-Missile Defense the Answer?

It will be many years before U.S. ballistic-missile defense (BMD) will be capable of providing the level of protection required to counter the Chinese nuclear forces of today, let alone those of ten or twenty years from now. The JL-2 SLBM, as well as other mobile land-based Chinese ICBMs, will have (or already have) multiple independently targeted reentry vehicles (MIRVs).[111] Multiple warheads on each missile and the dozens of ballistic missiles that China is already capable of launching could deliver an attack that any BMD system would find exceedingly difficult to counter with 100 percent accuracy.[112] Even were a future ballistic-missile defense system thought capable of intercepting all attacking ballistic missiles, with their multiple warheads and decoys, it would be folly to rely on that technology alone—the United States would be putting all of its eggs in the BMD basket. Perhaps when U.S. BMD becomes a reality, American SSNs could increase its effectiveness in a conflict by containing the Chinese submarine force within a geographic area, such as the Yellow Sea, enabling the defenses to focus on that single vector. But until that time, it is incumbent upon U.S. planners to ensure that the defense against ballistic missiles is a layered one, in which strategic ASW is the first line. In the words of President John F. Kennedy, "Until technology permits the deployment of an effective defense against submarine-launched ballistic missiles, the principal measures of protection should be provided by the capability to attack prior to launch."[113] Kennedy advocated the ability to hold Soviet SSBNs at risk of destruction through a stronger ASW capability, and his words still have relevance today.

Will the U.S. Navy Be Ready?

A former commander of naval submarine forces, Vice Adm. John J. Grossenbacher, has stated that if at least two *Virginia*-class boats are not built per year, the U.S. Navy's fleet of SSNs will decline to thirty submarines.[114] He argues that American SSNs would then no longer be able to meet the demands placed on them. In the defense arena, a significant amount of time is needed to make ideas reality. The time to begin construction of a larger, more robust fleet of nuclear-powered attack submarines has already arrived.

If relations between the United States and China deteriorate, will there be enough SSNs to maintain continuous contact with a growing fleet of Chinese SSBNs? Many factors must be considered. How many SSBNs would China be able to keep deployed simultaneously? How long would they stay deployed? Would each SSBN have two crews, like the U.S. SSBNs, and so be able to sortie more frequently? Where would they operate from, and where would they patrol? Would the United States have assets other than SSNs that could assist in tracking them? How robust would Chinese SSBN defenses—protection by diesel or nuclear attack boats—be?

If maintenance support for its SSBN was robust and each boat had two crews, it is conceivable that China could keep four of six SSBNs deployed continuously, the remaining two undergoing maintenance between deployments. To maintain close contact with the four deployed SSBNs, up to twenty SSNs would be required—nearly half of the current inventory.[115] Even that rough estimate illustrates that a substantial commitment would be required of a submarine community that is already turning missions away due to a lack of resources. Even if the PLAN does not make such a significant transition (from a single SSBN that rarely goes to sea to a fleet of six that stay deployed 60 percent of the time) and only one or two SSBNs were on patrol, the U.S. Navy would still require five to ten SSNs to hold them at risk.[116]

China may choose to use the Yellow Sea as a bastion, in order to provide better protection for its SSBNs; that could significantly complicate matters. The Yellow Sea is, relatively speaking, extremely shallow. Shallow water and high traffic density places substantial restrictions on submarine maneuverability, and its poor acoustic environment degrades ASW. China would have the advantage of greater familiarity with the underwater environment. China can employ a barrier strategy, as the United States did during the Cold War. Existing shore-based defenses on the Yellow Sea would be to China's advantage; its aircraft would enjoy short transit times and, accordingly, longer periods on station than would U.S. aircraft, if without nearby shore bases of their own. If China were to use the Yellow Sea as a bastion, therefore, a U.S. ability to stage naval and air ASW operations from South Korea, the Philippines, and Guam would be essential.[117]

Venturing out into the Pacific or other oceans, however, would require Chinese SSBNs to be sufficiently quiet to avoid U.S. Navy ASW assets that could form a barrier along the "first island chain" (an arc from the Kuriles through Japan, the Ryukyus, Taiwan, and the Philippines to the Indonesian archipelago).[118]

China has reportedly begun construction on a submarine base on Hainan Island from which its SSBNs could operate in the South China Sea. It would provide China's SSBNs with immediate access to the South China Sea and put them much closer to the Indian Ocean. For political reasons, basing SSBNs on Hainan Island, in its South Sea Fleet area of operations, makes sense for China, because the United States is not China's only concern in the Asia-Pacific region. Additionally, if Chinese SSBNs were to operate from two bases about sixteen hundred nautical miles apart, U.S. ASW assets would be denied the opportunity to concentrate in a particular area.[119] Furthermore, an additional base would afford China more pier space. Whether or not China would actually launch JL-2 SLBMs from the Indian Ocean, its SSBNs might operate there, and elsewhere, simply to complicate U.S. ballistic-missile defense and tie up more antisubmarine assets.[120]

During the first three decades of the Cold War, prior to introduction of the Soviet Delta SSBN, the U.S. Navy relied on a barrier strategy to detect Soviet SSBNs. Pre-Delta Soviet SSBNs were forced to pass through geographic choke points, such as the "Greenland-Iceland-U.K. Gap," in order for their SLBMs to be able to reach the United States. The barrier strategy took advantage of this weakness; fixed passive acoustic arrays, submarines, and land-based ASW aircraft made it quite successful.[121] The Delta SSBN, when introduced in 1972, however, could threaten the continental United States from Soviet territorial waters. This effectively negated the U.S. barrier strategy, since the Deltas could strike the United States without having to cross the barriers—the Deltas used bastions.[122] In light of the eventual deployment of possibly up to six Chinese SSBNs, the American response to the Soviet Deltas is worthy of consideration.

Then-Chief of Naval Operations, Adm. Elmo Zumwalt, favored an emphasis on sea control to ensure the ability to reinforce Western Europe.[123] Focusing on the defense of Western Europe, Zumwalt argued, would avoid a potentially costly diversion of naval assets to Soviet SSBN patrol areas, which could escalate a conflict between the United States and the Soviet Union from a strictly conventional to a nuclear level. The alternative viewpoint was that "an explicit attempt should be made to go forward and hold Soviet SSBNs at risk."[124] The argument was that the destruction of Soviet SSBNs would change the strategic nuclear balance and therefore possibly decrease the will of the Soviets to escalate in the event of a stalemate. Furthermore, holding the Soviet SSBNs at risk in their bastions was held to be beneficial to the U.S.

mission of sea control, in that it would force the Soviet Navy to divert assets in an attempt to deny access to American SSNs—a strategy that worked during the Cold War.[125]

The same logic could be applied to a conflict between China and the United States over Taiwan, but only if the United States has available sufficient strategic ASW assets to hold Chinese SSBNs at risk—which it will not. If the numbers were sufficient, however, and assuming China's SSBNs left port, knowledge that U.S. SSNs and other ASW assets were hunting them would force China to withdraw its best submarines to protect its SSBNs. Due to the geography of a Taiwan conflict, the U.S. Army and Air Force would be hard pressed to join in a fight over Taiwan. Consequently, every asset that the U.S. Navy could muster to the region would be vital to success. Coté alludes to such a challenging scenario in his concluding remarks: "The most challenging scenario for the Navy is one where U.S. access to overseas bases is greatly reduced, and where the proliferation of relatively low cost and easy to use access denial weapons—such as modern diesel-electric submarines, antiship and antiaircraft missiles, and naval mines—continues to grow. This is a world in which the Navy will have to provide a larger portion of national power projection capabilities, while also placing much more emphasis on sea control than it does now."[126]

In a war over Taiwan, United States ASW forces would likely be completely occupied protecting its battle fleet by finding and destroying the numerous Chinese submarines—including even the low-technology platforms that the PLAN still operates. During a major conflict over Taiwan the United States would likely locate one or more carrier battle groups within operational range of Taiwan. One can imagine the "one-way conversation" that would occur when the local ASW commander told the battle-group commander that it could take weeks to eliminate the subsurface threat to his ships, due to the large number of Chinese submarines, not to mention the submarine-laid mines that China could employ.[127] If China elected to threaten a nuclear response to U.S. interference in what it considers an internal issue, U.S. commanders would presumably be forced to shift assets from defense of carriers to strategic ASW, thereby increasing the risk to carriers engaged in the defense of Taiwan while reducing the strategic threat to the United States.

Such dire scenarios can be mitigated if the right force-structure planning decisions are made today. To prepare for the future and all of its conceivable threats, the U.S. Navy needs a fleet of close to seventy SSNs and enough air and surface ASW capability to support not only the missions the submarine force is already tasked with but also strategic ASW, if China does in fact build a significant undersea nuclear deterrent.[128] In testimony before the House Armed Services Committee in June 2000, the Commander Submarine Forces U.S. Pacific Fleet, Rear Adm. Albert H. Konetzni, testified that the United States needs a minimum of sixty-eight SSNs to meet current and future requirements.[129] If, after China begins deployment of the first of its new SSBNs, it is evident that they will adhere to the habits of the past—remain pierside, employ single crews, or stay within a defined geographic area—the American strategic ASW force structure can be adjusted as necessary. It would be much easier to cut funding and halt construction than it would be to respond suddenly to a threat, having been caught unprepared.[130]

The U.S. Navy cannot always rely on being "saved by the bell, as it has in the past."[131] Recent and upcoming advancements like the Multimission Maritime Aircraft, the Advanced Deployable System, the new Fleet ASW Command, and the Littoral Combat Ship, to name only a few—represent significant present day and future ASW achievements but they are not the complete solution.[132] Force-structure planning involves identification of threats in the near, middle, and long terms; the United States has the opportunity to "get a jump" on a threat now on the horizon by modernizing and rejuvenating its antisubmarine prowess. Ensuring the U.S. Navy has the right number of SSNs and air and surface ASW assets—more than it has today—is vital to the security of the United States.

Conclusion

The development of the Chinese defense establishment over the past five decades has been excruciatingly slow and turbulent, and so was the development of China's first SSBN. Having invested in a physical and intellectual infrastructure to create its early strategic weapons programs, China is now reaping the benefits. China has a solid capability to design and construct SSBNs and SLBMs that are much more advanced than their predecessors.

The debate regarding China's true intentions will continue, but the strategic implications of a more numerous and capable Chinese SSBN fleet are already clear. China seeks an assured nuclear-strike capability, and SSBNs are well suited to the job. Such a force would raise the risks of confronting China in a crisis, unless it can be effectively neutralized, and may even decrease American leverage in a given crisis.

China has already a limited ability to threaten the continental United States, but the introduction of new, more capable submerged strategic systems with far greater range and accuracy would enable it to strike the United States from the relative safety of its own or adjacent waters. The rationale behind the decision to hold Soviet SSBNs at risk are applicable today. By the time China's new SSBNs are deployed, it is unlikely that the United States will have developed a totally reliable ballistic-missile defense system—especially against sophisticated countermeasures. Therefore, as in the Cold War, it is incumbent upon the U.S. Navy to equip and train itself for strategic ASW.

Will the U.S. Navy be able to resume a more aggressive strategic ASW posture in response to a new and improved fleet of Chinese SSBNs? As a result of the future advances in Chinese attack submarines, improvements in the PLAN education and training, the numerous Chinese submarines in existence today, Asian-Pacific geography, and American ASW capability that is likely to decline, the U.S. Navy could be ill prepared to do so.

It is quite conceivable that strategic ASW will once again rise to the highest national importance. The period remaining before China deploys a larger number of SSBNs—within the next five years—affords the United States and its navy a vital opportunity. The United States should act aggressively to improve U.S. strategic ASW capability, by halting the decline in the number of SSNs, increasing SSN end-strength to at least seventy, and build up air and surface ASW capability. After all, nuclear-powered submarines, aircraft, and surface ships are cheap—compared to the cost of replacing the city of Los Angeles.[133]

Notes

1. For example, at a recent conference on "China's Nuclear Future," many of the nation's leading China military analysts had widely divergent views on the significance of recent developments within the People's Liberation Army. "China's Nuclear Future" conference, Boulder, Colorado, U.S. Air Force Institute for National Security Studies, U.S. Air Force Academy, 30–31 July 2003.

2. Michael S. Chase and Evan S. Medeiros, "China's Evolving Nuclear Calculus: Modernization and the Doctrinal Debate" (unpublished research paper, RAND Corporation, Washington, D.C.: 2002), 1.

3. Bill Gertz, "China Tests Ballistic Missile Submarine," *Washington Times,* 3 December 2004, available at washingtontimes.com/national/20041202-115302-2338r.htm.

4. Richard D. Fisher, "Navy Systems" in *The Impact of Foreign Weapons and Technology on the Modernization of China's People's Liberation Army,* A Report for the U.S.-China Economic and Security Review Commission, January 2004, 3, http://www.globalsecurity.org/military/library/report/2004/04fisher/8navysystems.htm.

5. Admiral Zhang Lianzhong, former commander of the PLA Navy (1988–96), quoted in Office of Naval Intelligence, *Worldwide Submarine Challenges* (Washington, D.C.: U.S. Navy Department, 1997), 18.

6. An argument could be made that there are more than two methods to neutralize an SLBM, in that air and surface antisubmarine assets possess an offensive antisubmarine capability. However, the assumption is that the aircraft or surface ship would have to be in the immediate vicinity of the SSBN at the time of launch and be able to detect preparations for launch. It is possible but not likely that an SSBN would launch its ballistic missiles in the immediate vicinity of a surface ship or aircraft. To do so would be to jeopardize the accomplishment of its mission— that of remaining as covert as possible to continue its launch sequence. It is more likely that a U.S. SSN could remain undetected in an SSBN's baffles, enabling it to be present immediately prior to or immediately after, than it is for a hostile (to the SSBN) surface ship or aircraft to remain undetected by the SSBN and not prompt it to go elsewhere.

7. Of course, if the ballistic-missile-defense system was capable of destroying the missile prior to the deployment of its warheads and decoys, that is to say in the boost phase, any employed decoys would be rendered useless.

8. From 1985 to 2002, Congress appropriated nearly $65.7 billion dollars for ballistic missile defense and will be deploying a system with only limited capability in 2004. See "Historical Funding for BMD FY85–02," *Missile Defense Agency MDAlink,* "Budget and Legislative Guidance," www.acq.osd.mil/bmdo/bmdolink/html/guide .html.

9. "The Lessons of History: The Chinese People's Liberation Army at 75," *Strategic Studies Institute,* "Regional Studies: Asia/Pacific," www.carlisle.army.mil/ssi/ pubs/region.html#asia.

10. See excerpts at GlobalSecurity.org, "Nuclear Posture Review," www.globalsecurity .org/wmd/library/policy/dod/npr.htm.

11. This appeared to be the outlook of most analysts at the "China's Nuclear Future" conference.

12. The 094 project may have experienced a considerable setback during the summer of 2004 when a JL-2 suffered a testing failure. Bill Gertz, "China Tests Ballistic Missile Submarine," *Washington Times,* 3 December 2004, available at www .washingtontimes.com/national/20041202-115302-2338r.htm. According to Jane's, the Type 094 SSBN may be operational by 2008, with four to six boats to be built. They will carry eight to eighteen missiles with a range of eight thousand kilometers and one warhead, or three to eight MIRVs with decoys and penetration aids. The exact timeline may be constrained by the development of the JL-2 SLBM. See "JL-2(CSS-NX-5)," *Jane's Strategic Weapon Systems,* 3 June 2003, www.janes. com; also *Jane's Fighting Ships,* "China/Submarines: Strategic Missile Submarines/ Introduction," 20 March 2003, www.janes.com. The *2003 Annual Report on the Military Power of the People's Republic of China* is vague. It states that the JL-2 is expected to be deployed sometime within the next decade but is not specific about

the 094. U.S. Defense Department, *Annual Report on the Military Power of the People's Republic of China* (Washington, D.C.: 2003), 27.

13. "China's Economy Is No 'House of Cards,'" *Business Week Online*, 16 January 2003, www.businessweek.com.

14. General Liu Huaqing, quoted in Office of Naval Intelligence, *Worldwide Submarine Challenges* (Washington, D.C.: U.S. Navy Department, 1997), 1.

15. Charles B. Momsen, quoted in Richard E. Winslow III, *Portsmouth-Built Submarines of the Portsmouth Naval Shipyard* (Portsmouth, N.H.: Peter E. Randall, 1985), 138.

16. John Wilson Lewis and Xue Litai, *China's Strategic Seapower* (Stanford, Calif.: Stanford University Press, 1994), 20.

17. Ibid., 4.

18. To illustrate further, Marshal Nie Rongzhen, who was responsible for weapons research and development of the SSBN and SLBM projects, relocated the Metal Physics Research Section of China's Institute of Atomic Energy (IAE) from Shenyang and Beijing to the Gobi Desert in Inner Mongolia to shield its workings from the effects of the Great Leap. Nie was forced to walk both sides of the fence by appearing to support the party line while at the same time insulating his workers from the impact. See Lewis and Xue, *China's Strategic Seapower,* 26, 34.

19. Financial resources were heavily impacted as well. There are examples too numerous to be recounted here of the impact of the economic devastation that resulted from the Great Leap and the Cultural Revolution on the SSBN and SLBM programs. Nevertheless, a brief illustration of what the defense establishment had to endure occurred in 1966 during the development of the JL-1 solid propellant engine. The Fourth Academy, under the Seventh Ministry, which was responsible for development of the JL-1 solid propellant engine, had to halt construction of engine test facilities in 1968 due to spending cuts that resulted in a substantial modification of the testing schedule and a two-year delay. See Lewis and Xue, *China's Strategic Seapower,* 144–46.

20. Ibid., 146.

21. Ibid., 147.

22. Ibid., 138, 144–45, 147–49, 162, 163.

23. Lin Biao quoted in Michael Schoenhals, ed., *China's Cultural Revolution, 1966–1969* (Armonk, N.Y.: M. E. Sharpe, 1996), 11.

24. Lewis and Xue, *China's Strategic Seapower,* 149.

25. "The Lessons of History: The Chinese People's Liberation Army at 75," *Strategic Studies Institute,* "Regional Studies: Asia/Pacific," www.carlisle.army.mil/ssi/pubs/region.html#asia, 7 September 2003, 409.

26. Lewis and Xue, *China's Strategic Seapower,* 88–89.

27. Massive amounts of scarce financial resources were thrown at the Third Line and after the effort was largely completed, a partial reversal occurred from 1986 to 1989,

in which "121 of the 2,000 large and medium-sized enterprises in remote mountain areas were removed to the coastal provinces" to curtail the defection of isolated and disgruntled workers from the Third Line. See David Shambaugh, *Modernizing China's Military* (Berkeley: University of California Press, 2002), 227.

28. Lewis and Xue, *China's Strategic Seapower,* 26. Under the right circumstances competition can be a positive force for developing capable, high-quality, and low-cost weapons systems. For example, the U.S. Department of Defense tasks multiple defense contractors to develop competing designs for a single weapon system. However, China simply did not have the financial strength or scientists and engineers educated in submarine and ballistic-missile design to pursue a competitive strategy in its state-run defense industry.

29. Lewis and Xue, *China's Strategic Seapower,* 138–40, 162, 183, 186, 203.

30. Ibid., 162.

31. Gen. Luo Ruiqing was the director of NDIO from 1961 to 1966. He was also the chief of the General Staff and secretary general of the Central Military Commission from 1959 to 1966, a member of the Central Secretariat, and the office director of the Fifteen Member Special Commission from 1962 to 1966. He was toppled during the Cultural Revolution, because he stood for a more professional and less ideological PLA. Others were involved in the debate as well, such as He Long, the director of the National Defense Industrial Commission (NDIC), and Premier Zhou Enlai. See Lewis and Xue, *China's Strategic Seapower,* 28–29, 246.

32. Lewis and Xue, *China's Strategic Seapower,* 29, 32.

33. As a point of comparison, the U.S. SLBM effort also suffered many growing pains in its initial stages. In the 1950s, the U.S. Navy was unable to articulate a cohesive position on ballistic missiles and, consequently, was forced to pursue a joint endeavor with the U.S. Army on the Jupiter Program as a cost-saving measure. For one year the Navy worked with the Army on the liquid-fueled *Jupiter,* until it recognized the need to pursue a solid-fueled option and was able to convince the Department of Defense of the rationale for pursuing a solid-fueled ballistic missile. Additionally, the Special Projects Office within the Department of the Navy, responsible for the development of the Fleet Ballistic Missile (FBM) submarine force, was considered the model of managerial success, when in fact it was not. It should be noted, however, that even though the U.S. Navy went through some growing pains with the FBM program, it was still one of the most successful weapons development programs in the history of the United States; only five years elapsed from the establishment of the Special Projects Office until the first successful submerged test launch of a Polaris in 1960. Even after the U.S. Navy had the experience of constructing its first SSBNs—the "Forty-one for Freedom"—the follow-on *Ohio*-class SSBNs were not without their own governmental, defense contractor, and funding problems. Overall, however, the delays in the U.S. Navy's strategic weapons programs have been minuscule in comparison to those of China. See Harvey M. Sapolsky, *The Polaris System Development* (Cambridge, Mass.: Harvard University Press, 1972). For an interesting overview of the Polaris and Fleet Ballistic Missile (FBM) submarine programs see Bureau of Naval Weapons Special Projects Office, *Polaris Fleet*

Ballistic Missile Weapon System Fact Sheet (Washington, D.C.: U.S. Navy Department, 1 June 1966). For an overview of the Trident program see D. Douglas Dalgleish and Larry Schweikart, *Trident* (Carbondale: Southern Illinois University Press, 1984).

34. Lewis and Xue, *China's Strategic Seapower,* 25.

35. Ibid., 30–31.

36. It is interesting and somewhat ironic to note that the *Lenin* reportedly suffered in 1966 or 1967 a major reactor-plant casualty—possibly a reactor meltdown—that may have killed up to thirty of its crew. More than a year after the accident, the three original reactor plants on the *Lenin* were replaced by two of a different design. It is impossible to say what the exact cause of the casualty was. Even if the casualty was due to operator error, the root cause of such a major reactor accident could still be traced to plant design, since the reactor-plant safety features were apparently inadequate. At the time of the accident on the *Lenin,* Sino-Soviet relations were at a low point; it is possible that the Chinese designers were unaware of flaws. It is also possible that any flaws in the *Lenin* design were completely irrelevant, since the Chinese may have used the design as a general guide rather than a specific template. China's choice was an ominous one nonetheless. (See Lewis and Xue, *China's Strategic Seapower,* 31.) According to *Jane's Defence Weekly,* CBS News obtained CIA documents that provided details on the *Lenin* accident. See "Soviet Submarine Accidents: New Details," *Jane's Defence Weekly,* 19 January 1985, 85.

37. Lewis and Xue, *China's Strategic Seapower,* 24, 27. Control-rod drive mechanisms enable an operator to remotely insert or withdraw the control rods within the reactor core to start up the reactor, maintain criticality, or shut it down. The Chinese utilized hafnium (Hf) control rods.

38. Lewis and Xue, *China's Strategic Seapower,* 27.

39. According to one source, U.S. submarines use a uranium enrichment of 93 percent. Lewis and Xue, *China's Strategic Seapower,* 23, 259 n. 1.

40. Ibid., 7.

41. Deng Liqun, Ma Hong, and Wu Heng, eds., *China Today: Defence Science and Technology* (in English) (Beijing: National Defence Industry Press, 1993), 318.

42. Lewis and Xue, *China's Strategic Seapower,* 27.

43. For a basic introduction to submarine reactor design, see "Nuclear Propulsion," Federation of American Scientists, www.fas.org/man/dod-101/sys/ship/eng/reactor.html. The Chinese reactor was a pressurized-water reactor with separate primary and secondary systems. Primary plant pressure was 140–150 atmospheres (2,057–2,204 psi), and the fuel cells (which Lewis and Xue call "fuel rods") were clad with zirconium alloy. The rated reactor power for the prototype plant was forty-eight megawatts; it was reportedly capable of twelve thousand shaft horsepower. Chinese designers evidently had some serious difficulties with the primary-to-secondary heat exchanger—the steam generator. They discussed the imperative to maintain the integrity of both the primary and secondary systems to ensure that the radioactive primary coolant does not enter the secondary system, but the only

detail provided is that "the Chinese had serious problems devising a safe exchange system between the two loops. Early on they felt the iron fist of Murphy's Law." This suggests that in their initial reactor plant design efforts, the Chinese most likely suffered a primary-to-secondary reactor coolant leak. See Lewis and Xue, *China's Strategic Seapower,* 24; and Deng, Ma, and Wu, eds., *China Today,* 321–31. The prototype reactor remained in operation for nine years, from July 1970 to December 1979, for full testing to be completed. Ibid., 328.

44. According to Lewis and Xue, construction apparently began on the plant and facilities in early 1968, more than a year before the complete design of the prototype reactor was finalized in 1969. *China Today* states that construction began in 1965 but was delayed by the Cultural Revolution until 1968. Construction of the prototype reactor plant was said to have been completed in April 1970, with test operations beginning in May 1970; however, according to Lewis and Xue, manufacture of the fuel cells for the prototype was not begun until the summer of 1970. The fuel cells most likely were completed well before May 1970. *China Today* also lists May 1970 as the first operation of the prototype reactor. Lewis and Xue, *China's Strategic Seapower,* 45; and Deng, Ma, and Wu, eds., *China Today,* 318, 324–26.

45. Lewis and Xue, *China's Strategic Seapower,* 43, 45.

46. Ibid., 106, 108, 109.

47. Ibid., 109, 110.

48. Ibid., 68, 110.

49. Deng, Ma Hong, and Wu, eds., *China Today,* 314. At the beginning of Project 09, a group of designers studied and took notes on a toy model of a U.S. Polaris SSBN, which provides some insight into how little knowledge the Project 09 engineers had on submarine design and the "somewhat unreal world in which [they] operated." Lewis and Xue, *China's Strategic Seapower,* 50.

50. Huang Xuhua, quoted in Lewis and Xue, *China's Strategic Seapower,* 65; and Chinese proverb quoted by David Lai, "Learning from the Stones: A Weiqi Approach to Mastering Sun Tzu and the Chinese Way of War and Diplomacy," Asia-Pacific Studies Group Research Seminar, Naval War College, 3 November 2003.

51. China conducted scale-model tests in a large indoor wave tank and arrived at the meaningless conclusion that "the scale-model experiments repeatedly verified the overall superiority of the more revolutionary water-drop shape, but the tests left unresolved several questions about the maneuverability and stability of a submerged submarine so configured." That the engineers could conclude that the teardrop-shaped hull was superior without resolving the critical factors of maneuverability and stability illustrates the primitive nature of Chinese submarine design at that time. See Lewis and Xue, *China's Strategic Seapower,* 51–53, 56. The USS *Albacore* was an experimental U.S. submarine built by the Portsmouth Naval Shipyard to test, among other things, the concept of a teardrop-shaped hull. The design subordinated the performance of the surfaced submarine to that of the submerged submarine. Extensive testing resulted in greater submerged control and underwater speed records. See Winslow, *Portsmouth-Built Submarines of the Portsmouth*

Naval Shipyard, 143, and "USS Albacore," *American Society of Mechanical Engineers,* "ASME Roster of Landmarks, Sites and Collections," www.asme.org/history/roster_a.html.

52. China had to develop nondestructive inspection techniques to verify the quality of each weld and had difficulty implementing the quality control necessary to eliminate the defects resulting from the inexperienced shipyard workers. For more specific information on welding difficulties on China's submarines, see Lewis and Xue, *China's Strategic Seapower,* 52, 104–6, 286–87 nn. 9–16.

53. Coincidentally, but not surprisingly, China's first submarine hull was completed in 1970 on Mao's birthday, 26 December. Lewis and Xue, *China's Strategic Seapower,* 105.

54. Engineers were told to go to the factories where the various components for the subsystems were being built in order to weigh them and determine individual component centers of gravity. Foreshadowing the quality of the product they were to eventually complete, they resorted to "educated guesses" to determine the stability of the submarine and a practice of "designing while manufacturing." This paragraph summarizes Lewis and Xue, *China's Strategic Seapower,* 65–66, 106.

55. The effectiveness of the pedestals depends on the type of mounts used and their ability to prevent the transmission of the equipment vibration to the hull. Covering of the equipment in sound-absorbent material is of limited value, since the air between the covered equipment and the hull is a poor transmission medium for sound relative to the direct path between the equipment mounts and the hull.

56. Cavitation results from the movement of the screw (propeller) through the water, which in turn creates areas of extremely low pressure. The low pressure causes local boiling of the water, which can cause cracking, pitting, and corrosion of the screw blades, further increasing cavitation. The design, machining, speed, and cleanliness of the screw as well as the ambient water pressure (which is proportional to depth) all contribute to screw cavitation. With respect to the speed of the screw through the water, the lower the shaft RPM (SRPM), the less likely it is that cavitation will occur. The SRPM of China's first nuclear submarine was 125 to 200, even after the engineers had already been forced to lower it due to excessive cavitation. Lewis and Xue, *China's Strategic Seapower,* 53, 109.

57. Ibid., 4, 67.

58. The capabilities of a torpedo are dependent on the environment and the target. The depth of the water in which the torpedo will be fired and whether or not it is intended to strike a submerged or surface target are critical variables for which designers must account.

59. Lewis and Xue state that the Yu-3 is the Chinese Sturgeon 2. According to *Jane's Naval Weapon Systems,* the Yu-3 is equivalent to the Soviet SET-53 acoustic homing torpedo. *Jane's Fighting Ships* states that the Yu-3 is equivalent to the Soviet SET-65E wake homing torpedo. China's earlier torpedoes, the Yu-1, the Yu-2, the Yu-4A, and the Yu-4B were all deemed inadequate by China. See "Underwater Weapons/Russian Federation/Type 53/SAET/SET (Test-71/Test-96) TE/YU 1/YU 3/

YU 4 Heavyweight Torpedoes," *Jane's Naval Weapon Systems*, 29 November 2002, www.janes.com; "Xia Class (Type 092) (SSBN)" *Jane's Fighting Ships*, 20 March 2003, www.janes.com; Lewis and Xue, *China's Strategic Seapower*, 66–67.

60. Lewis and Xue, *China's Strategic Seapower*, 66–67.

61. Similarly, it was not until the mid-1980s that the Han was outfitted "with acceptable [navigation and communication] subsystems." Ibid., 66–67, 110.

62. Ibid., 68.

63. In 1956, Mao Zedong initiated the research on missiles capable of carrying nuclear warheads. At the time of the JL-1–project initiation the missile designation, JL-1, meant Great Dragon No. 1 *(julong yihao)*. In 1972, the meaning of the designation was changed to Great Wave *(julang)* for political reasons. Lewis and Xue, *China's Strategic Seapower*, 130, 137.

64. Ibid., 143.

65. National Intelligence Council, *Foreign Missile Developments and the Ballistic Missile Threat through 2015* (Washington, D.C.: 2001), 9.

66. In 1959, the Soviet Union sold China the designs and necessary equipment to produce its own version of the liquid-fueled Soviet SLBM, the R-11FM. However, China decided to focus first on the production of a land-based strategic weapon, to produce a nuclear strategic deterrent in less time than it would take to produce a functional SSBN. See Lewis and Xue, *China's Strategic Seapower*, 131–32.

67. Lewis and Xue, *China's Strategic Seapower*, 132–33.

68. Sapolsky, *The Polaris System Development*, 136.

69. For an SLBM, missile ignition does not occur immediately, as it does for a land-based missile, but after the missile is above the surface of the water. Ignition would be triggered, most likely, as a result of the negative acceleration rate sensed by the missile flight control system. As the missile reaches its highest point following missile ejection it momentarily falls back toward the surface; the missile flight control system senses this and triggers engine ignition.

70. Lewis and Xue, *China's Strategic Seapower*, 133, 143–44. See Lewis and Xue, chapter 6, for a more detailed analysis of China's solid rocket propellant development.

71. The price paid for the trial-and-error method was at times high. In 1962, a technician was killed while working with the composite propellant at Plant 845 (part of the Solid Rocket Motor institute under the Fifth Academy) in Xian, and in 1974 there were several mishaps involving the grain casting plant, the worst killing the deputy head of the plant. Lewis and Xue, *China's Strategic Seapower*, 136–37, 151–52, 153.

72. Ibid., 136–37, 139, 141, 144, 151.

73. Ibid., 139, 143, 153.

74. Ibid., 158, 159.

75. The other option would have been to launch the SLBMs while the SSBN hovered in place. To facilitate a hovering SSBN, the ship must have a ship control system capable of making rapid adjustments in ballast by either bringing water on board

or driving water into and out of variable ballast tanks. Hovering, therefore, requires technology that can automatically detect changes in ship's depth and rapidly compensate by utilizing a system of pumps and valves capable of moving massive amounts of water in a very short time. The Chinese designers developed a launch-assistance system that incorporated rails within the missile tube to compensate for the perpendicular force of the water (relative to the direction of the ejected missile); it is likely that they believed this system would be less complicated than designing a hovering system for the submarine. Lewis and Xue, *China's Strategic Seapower*, 71, 174.

76. Ibid., 155.

77. Ibid., 171, 175.

78. China built a Golf-class diesel-electric submarine under license from the Soviet Union. The Golf was modified to be a test platform for JL-1 missile launches; it is believed to have continued service as a test platform for the new JL-2 SLBM. See Lewis and Xue, *China's Strategic Seapower*, 69, 111–15, 186, 197–200. Beyond the challenges particular to an SLBM, China had to develop the telemetry systems for testing and tracking, as well as the tracking ships necessary to monitor the performance of the JL-1 during its flight tests. Lewis and Xue, *China's Strategic Seapower*, 73, 171, 191–96. For a more in depth overview of the JL-1's guidance and flight control systems, function, and performance, see ibid., chapter 7.

79. In 1967, when the initial design for the Xia was completed, Nie Rongzhen and the Defense Science and Technology Commission set the target launch date for the Project 092 submarine as 1973. Lewis and Xue, *China's Strategic Seapower*, 68, 204.

80. Bernard D. Cole, *The Great Wall at Sea* (Annapolis, Md.: Naval Institute Press, 2001), 93; Shambaugh, *Modernizing China's Military*, 271; "NRDC Nuclear Notebook," *Bulletin of the Atomic Scientists*, "Nuclear Notebook," www.thebulletin.org/issues/nukenotes/nukenote.html.

81. At the "China's Nuclear Future" conference, several questions were posed to leading experts on the PLA about the Xia in one-on-one exchanges and in open forum. The general consensus was that the Xia did not represent a threat.

82. See Owen R. Coté, Jr., *The Third Battle: Innovations in the U.S. Navy's Silent Cold War Struggle with Soviet Submarines* (Newport, R.I.: Naval War College, 2003), paper no. 16. Coté defines the First and Second Battles as World Wars I and II, respectively.

83. On the U.S. Navy's fixed underwater passive acoustic Sound Surveillance System (SOSUS) initiative during the Cold War, see Coté, chapter 4.

84. John Morgan, "Anti-Submarine Warfare: A Phoenix for the Future," *Undersea Warfare* (Fall 1998): 18 (Morgan was the Director, Anti-Submarine Warfare Division [N84] in the Office of the Chief of Naval Operations); James E. Pillsbury, Naval War College, interview by author, 22 August 2003, Newport, R.I.; Coté, *The Third Battle*, 84.

85. "Antisubmarine Warfare after the Cold War," *MIT Security Studies Program*, "Publications, Conferences, & Symposia Page," web.mit.edu/ssp/Publications/pubs.html.

86. See "Navy to Downsize P-3 Fleet after Tests Revealed Structural Fatigue," InsideDefense.com, 20 November 2003, www.insidedefense.com.

87. Coté, *The Third Battle*, 84 [emphasis original].

88. Ibid., 20.

89. In order to ensure the SSN fleet does not continue to decline in numbers, the Navy must begin in the near future to build at least two new submarines per year. Congress recently rejected a plan to build seven *Virginia*-class submarines in a five-year period. See Dale Eisman, "Congress Gives $2 Billion for Navy Shipbuilding Plan," *Virginian Pilot*, 30 September 2003.

90. *Worldwide Submarine Challenges, 1997,* 21.

91. U.S. Defense Department, *Annual Report on the Military Power of the People's Republic of China* (Washington, D.C.: 2003): 8, 28.

92. Coté, *The Third Battle*, 66–67.

93. Ibid., 69.

94. U.S. Defense Department, *Annual Report on the Military Power of the People's Republic of China* (Washington, D.C.: 2003): 8, 27.

95. In the 1990s, China spent nearly $7 billion on advanced Russian weapons systems and its purchases have continued. The contract with Russia to purchase eight Project 636 Kilo-class submarines as well as other weapons systems will provide China with formidable weaponry that could, if properly utilized, present a serious challenge to the U.S. Navy. See Shambaugh, *Modernizing China's Military,* 218.

96. U.S. Defense Department, *Annual Report on the Military Power of the People's Republic of China* (Washington, D.C.: 2003): 27.

97. Michael I. Handel, *Masters of War* (London: Frank Cass, 2001), 237.

98. As noted previously, credible reports suggest the 094 prototype was launched in July 2004. However, estimates on its initial operating capability vary considerably (see note 11 above). In addition, Bernard Cole states that the first 094 will not be in service until 2010 and that the JL-2 will have a range of twelve thousand kilometers. See Bernard D. Cole, *The Great Wall at Sea* (Annapolis, Md.: Naval Institute Press, 2001), 185. David Shambaugh says that the 094 will be in service possibly within a decade and that it will carry sixteen JL-2 SLBMs each carrying six warheads and will have a range of eight thousand kilometers. See Shambaugh, *Modernizing China's Military,* 272. A monthly Hong Kong magazine article states that there are or will be three variants of the JL-2: the JL-2 with an 8,600-km range with four to five warheads, the JL-2A with a 12,500-km range with seven to eight warheads, and the JL-2B with a range of 14,000 km and ten warheads. See Ch'ing T'ung, "China's First- and Second-Generation Nuclear-Powered Submarines," *Hong Kong Kuang Chiao Ching,* 16 June 2003, FBIS CPP20030620000084. A less credible article in the *Chinese Military Update* published by the Royal United Services Institute states that three 094 SSBNs have already been commissioned and that they may already have six 094s. See Sheng Lijun, "PLA Modernization: Tactical and Strategic Weapons for the Taiwan Strait," *Chinese Military Update* 1, no. 3 (June 2003): 6. There does seem to be some convergence in that the 094 will likely

carry sixteen JL-2 SLBMs, that they will have a range between eight and twelve thousand kilometers, and that they will have MIRV.

99. For a more detailed look at the improvements China has made training its officer and enlisted personnel, see Cole, *The Great Wall at Sea,* chapter 6.

100. Lyle Goldstein and William Murray, "Undersea Dragons: China's Maturing Submarine Force," *International Security* 28, no. 4 (Spring 2004): 175–76.

101. Pillsbury interview with author, 22 August 2003.

102. Cole, *The Great Wall at Sea,* 70–71.

103. Joseph Kahn, "Chinese Officers Warn That Taiwan Referendum Could Lead to War," *New York Times on the Web,* 3 December 2003, www.nytimes.com/2003/12/03/international/asia/03CND-Chin.html?ex=1071678576&ei=1&en=b38e0023e2b245d8. A 2003 report from the *Council on Foreign Relations* states, "China's hosting of the 2008 Olympics creates an even greater need [for China] to avoid additional external tensions." See "Chinese Military Power," *Council on Foreign Relations,* www.cfr.org/content/publications/attachments/china_TF.pdf, p. 37.

104. Visiting the United States, the Chinese premier, Wen Jiabao, and President George W. Bush were fairly united in their response to Taiwan's recent push to conduct a referendum. David Stout, "Bush Tells China's Leader He Opposes Taiwan's Referendum," *New York Times on the Web,* 9 December 2003, www.nytimes.com/2003/12/09/international/asia/09CND-Bush.html?ex=1072000124&ei=1&en=f134bf550961d0c4.

105. The commentary, quoted with permission, was provided to the author as a review of an unpublished draft on China's submarine force written by a colleague of the author. The U.S. submarine captain has extensive experience in both fast-attack and ballistic-missile submarines and wished to remain anonymous (emphasis original).

106. Anonymous U.S. submarine captain (all emphases original).

107. Ibid.

108. This number is derived from Christopher Langton, ed., *The Military Balance 2003–2004* (Glasgow, U.K.: Oxford University Press, 2003), 153.

109. "Submarines and Peacekeeping," *Journal of Military and Strategic Studies* (Spring 2000), available at www.jmss.org/2000/article3.html. An account in the U.S. Navy's *Undersea Warfare* magazine argues, "The *San Luis* operated in the vicinity of the British task force for more than a month and was a constant concern to Royal Navy commanders. Despite the deployment of five nuclear attack submarines, 24-hour per day airborne ASW operations, and expenditures of precious time, energy, and ordnance, the British never once detected the Argentine submarine." John Morgan, "Anti-Submarine Warfare: A Phoenix for the Future," *Undersea Warfare* 1, no. 1 (Fall 1990), available at www.chinfo.navy.mil/navpalib/cno/n87/vsw/autumn98/index.htm.

110. Shambaugh, *Modernizing China's Military,* 283.

111. National Intelligence Council, *Foreign Missile Developments and the Ballistic Missile Threat through 2015* (Washington, D.C.: 2001), 8.

112. For more detailed information on U.S. Ballistic Missile Defense efforts, see the Missile Defense Agency at www.acq.osd.mil/bmdo/. At the July 2003 "China's Nuclear Future" conference, Michael McDevitt of the Center for Naval Analyses stated that he believes China is building to a "substantial force" of 250–300 road-mobile ICBMs.

113. John F. Kennedy quoted in Coté, *The Third Battle*, 20.

114. Robert A. Hamilton, "Lack of Subs Could Slow Pace of Technology, Admiral Warns," *New London Day*, 30 September 2003, A1, A3.

115. The estimate of twenty SSNs assumes that the U.S. submarines would be easily able to locate and maintain contact with an SSBN. The estimate is based on a forty-day maintenance period, a seventy-day patrol, and two-crew manning for each SSBN, allowing four to six SSBNs to be at sea at any given time. The SSNs would be deployed for six months, with twenty days of transit or training time on either end of the deployment, and twelve months between deployments. The estimate assumes that five SSNs would normally be in-theater for four deployed SSBNs; it does not take into account nonavailability for such reasons as technical problems or medical emergencies.

116. The number of SSNs is based on similar assumptions as the previous estimate with the change being that a lower number of SSBNs are on patrol. If the U.S. Navy were to develop armed, unmanned undersea vehicles, it is possible that the number of SSNs required in such a scenario could be reduced, but such technology could take at least two decades to mature.

117. There could be drawbacks to the use of the Yellow Sea as a bastion. It would negate one of the principal advantages of the SSBN—the ability to exploit the expansive Indian and Pacific Oceans, or at the very least the South China Sea. Additionally, unlike the Cold War, when Soviet SSBNs made use of bastions to avoid SOSUS barriers and stay within the protective envelope of the Soviet Navy, in today's world, with ballistic-missile defense systems looming on the horizon, the use of bastions may not be feasible. Maintaining SSBNs in the Yellow Sea would reduce the uncertainty for a future theater ballistic-missile defense system. For a more detailed discussion of U.S. and Soviet use of barrier strategies as well as the use of bastions, see Coté, *The Third Battle*.

118. For the Chinese perception of "island chains," see Chris Rahman, "Defending Taiwan, and Why It Matters," *Naval War College Review* 54, no. 4 (Autumn 2001): esp. 73.

119. Thanks to William Murray from the War Gaming Department of the Naval War College for this insight, as well as for many others.

120. Chinese SSBN operations in the Indian Ocean would preclude launch against the United States, due to the range. However, China may choose to demonstrate its nuclear deterrent to India. To do this, its submarines would have to transit some of the busiest shipping lanes in the world.

121. For a more detailed discussion on the barrier strategy, see Coté, *The Third Battle*.

122. Ibid., 63–64.

123. Ibid., 64.

124. Ibid.

125. The ASW debate that occurred as a result of the Soviet deployment of its Delta SSBNs is covered in ibid., 64–65.

126. Ibid., 86.

127. Ibid., 82.

128. Brad Roberts of the Institute for Defense Analyses sees China's nuclear future as more mobile, more penetrable, more accurate, and capable of surprise ("China's Nuclear Future" conference). A more robust fleet of Chinese SSBNs and the JL-2 SLBM are consistent with all of these. China wants an assured second-strike capability that is less vulnerable to U.S. precision conventional strike and nuclear attack. For this reason, an investment in a larger fleet of SSBNs is highly plausible, and there is little reason to doubt it.

129. "Statement of Albert H. Konetzni, U.S. Navy Commander, Submarine Force United States Pacific Fleet before the House Armed Services Committee Procurement Subcommittee Submarine Force Structure and Modernization Plans Hearing 27 June 2000," *Federation of American Scientists*, "Military Affairs in Congress: 2000," www.fas.org/man/congress/2000/index.html. From the U.S. Navy's *Undersea Warfare* magazine: "The new challenge is becoming clearer, and it is time to shift gears. . . . [T]he Defense Planning Guidance (DPG) and the Navy's Long-Range Planning Objectives—also call for a robust ASW capability that links warfare requirements to the real dangers and vulnerabilities introduced by the proliferation of next-generation submarines." Morgan, "Anti-Submarine Warfare," 20.

130. Thanks to Dan Farson of the Navy Warfare Development Command (NWDC) for his thoughtful critique and suggestions.

131. Coté characterizes the ability of the Navy to keep pace with ASW development during the first, second, and third battles as having been "saved by the bell." See Coté, *The Third Battle*, 2, 78.

132. While these advancements are positive, there remain many negatives for U.S. ASW capability. The MMA aircraft, if it remains on schedule, will not be available until 2013 at the earliest. Additionally, S-3 Vikings that in the past were devoted almost exclusively to ASW now function as aerial refueling aircraft. The SOSUS system capability has been severely downgraded, and the number of ASW-capable surface combatants is being drastically reduced. Without an easily identifiable threat to the United States, the tendency in force planning is to build weapons systems capable of performing multiple missions—the Littoral Combat Ship and the SSGN are good examples. The disadvantage to this approach is that crews that operate these weapons platforms are not afforded the opportunity to specialize and excel at specific mission areas, such as ASW. For a more complete discussion on U.S. ASW capability, see Goldstein and Murray, "Undersea Dragons."

133. This is a reference to remarks, sometimes regarded as a nuclear threat, by Gen. Xiong Guangkai offered to former State and Defense Department official Charles W. Freeman, Jr., in December 1995. On this event, see James Mann, *About Face: A History of America's Curious Relationship with China, from Nixon to Clinton* (New York: Vintage Books, 2000), 334.

Shawn Cappellano-Sarver

Naval Implications of China's Nuclear Power Development

Introduction

CHINA'S SUBMARINE FORCE DEVELOPMENT has been much in the news of late. Most of this attention has focused on the new indigenous diesel boats emerging at a swift pace from yards at Shanghai and Wuhan, as well as the large batch of eight advanced Kilos that has arrived in China from Russia during 2006. But China's simultaneous development of two new classes of nuclear-powered submarines, the 093 and 094, suggests a new imperative to focus analytical attention on Chinese naval nuclear propulsion.

Since China's earlier Han-class (091) is considered by most to be inferior to all other modern submarines, it is important to determine if China has now developed the skills and obtained the technology necessary to support a formidable nuclear undersea fleet. Several Chinese publications imply that China has not only obtained these skills and technology but could perhaps even have developed a completely new generation of submarine propulsion plants. One Chinese source states that the 093 may use a high temperature/high efficiency reactor plant.[1] These reports may not be credible, but after a close look at the progress that China's nuclear power industry has made over the last two decades it is evident that naval planners must take this possibility seriously.

China plans to build 2GWe (2,000MW electrical) of nuclear power capability per year to address its growing energy needs.[2] Western companies are rushing to sell nuclear power plants and technology to China. The drive to get a portion of the estimated $40 billion investment in China's nuclear power industry has encouraged companies to offer their most advanced designs. Western companies, with the support of their home governments, are involved in upgrading and modernizing the entire Chinese nuclear industry from fuel production to building complete plants. While this is lucrative for the companies, the effects that this has on China's ability to build advanced weapons systems such as nuclear submarines have not been adequately considered.

There is a close connection between the civilian and military nuclear power programs in nearly all countries that have built nuclear-powered warships. Westinghouse Electric Corporation is one of the nuclear-power industry's leading companies in the United States; it was also one of the original contractors for the U.S. Navy's nuclear propulsion program. AREVA Group of France owns both Framatome, which builds civilian nuclear power plants, and Technicatome, which designs the French navy's nuclear propulsion plants. This close connection, while helpful in building a knowledge and technical base for both programs, means that technology from one program will invariably be present in the other. The building of the plants in China will not only provide technology that will help build better propulsion plants but will also train Chinese engineers to design even more advanced reactors in the future.

The development of a nuclear industrial base with a flow of advanced technology from various countries and a robust research and development program will allow China to develop advanced nuclear propulsion plants for submarines. This process could include improving current pressurized water reactor designs or development of plants based on revolutionary technology such as high-temperature gas-cooled reactors (HTGR), in keeping with China's desire, to leap generations of weapons systems, in order to produce cutting-edge systems.

The Organization of China's Nuclear Industry

The Chinese nuclear industry dates back to January 15, 1955, when Chairman Mao Zedong and the Central Secretariat decided to develop atomic weapons.[3] The resulting imperative to develop the technical and scientific knowledge required to build bombs laid the technology base for building nuclear-powered submarines and eventually a civilian nuclear-power industry.

The Second Ministry of Machine Building was formed in 1958. It was tasked with the development of nuclear weapons, the nuclear submarine propulsion plant, and all associated industries. The Second Ministry controlled the nuclear industry from prospecting, mining, and processing uranium; processing fuel; constructing nuclear facilities; to developing and producing all instruments and control (I&C) equipment.[4] In 1982 its name was changed to the Ministry of Nuclear Industry (MNI), and in 1988 it was reorganized into the China National Nuclear Corporation (CNNC). Like the Second Ministry, the CNNC oversees all aspects of China's civilian and military nuclear programs.[5] CNNC consists of over one hundred subsidiary companies and institutions and still controls the vast majority of the civilian and military nuclear programs.[6]

The China Institute of Atomic Energy (CIAE) is the main research and development organization of CNNC. It was created in the early 1950s and directly supervised the development of the first submarine nuclear-power plant as part of the 09 submarine project. In 1958 the CIAE created the Reactor Engineering Research Section,[7] renamed the Reactor Engineering Institute in 1964.[8] The Reactor Engineering Institute (Code 194) did the initial design studies for the 09 submarine project,[9] and today is still the primary design institute for submarine propulsion plants.[10]

China's effort to develop nuclear power has not been restricted to the CNNC, however. Several universities have made contributions, most notably Qinghua University, which is often described as China's MIT. Qinghua's Institute of Nuclear Energy Technology (INET) was established in 1960. One of its first initiatives was the study of maritime nuclear propulsion. INET actually submitted a design for the 09 propulsion plant in 1965. The design was not accepted,[11] but INET contributed to the 09 submarine project by providing technical support.[12] INET has continued researching advanced nuclear technologies, including one of the world's most advanced high-temperature gas-cooled reactors.[13]

Initial Steps in Chinese Naval Nuclear Propulsion

The development of Chinese naval nuclear power followed a slow and painful process. The lack of trained technical personnel, a weak industrial base, and the political upheavals of the late 1950s and 1960s slowed the submarine and its propulsion plant's development. The final product was marginal by international standards, being both noisy and apparently plagued with significant technical problems. It is nevertheless impressive that a country so politically chaotic and industrially backward could produce one of the most complex machines on earth.

The Chinese naval nuclear power program started in July 1958 when Mao and the Central Military Commission approved the 09 submarine project.[14] The Institute of Atomic Energy (IAE, known today as the China Institute of Atomic Energy, or CIAE) studied U.S. and Soviet submarines and selected a pressurized water reactor (PWR) based on the Russian icebreaker *Lenin's* propulsion plant. A land-based prototype was built first for testing and training. The IAE created the Reactor Research Section (RRS) and within a few months had recruited over two hundred engineers and technicians to design the plant.

RRS personnel scrutinized foreign textbooks, reports, and any other resources available to determine the plant's specifications. The design was completed and approved by mid-1960. The Second Ministry of Machine Building was placed under Marshal Nie Rongzhen,[15] and between 1961 and 1963 was given control of dozens of factories that were capable of producing the specialized instruments, controls, and major components required for a nuclear propulsion plant.[16]

The project was greatly affected by the Great Leap Forward (1958–61), the Cultural Revolution (1965–75), and the Third Front movement. These three movements halted the program several times. Despite funding cuts and losses of talented engineers, the land-based prototype design was completed by 1967 and construction started in March 1968. The PLA was required to participate in the construction effort in July 1968 to compensate for the disruptions caused by the Cultural Revolution, and the prototype was completed in April 1970. The plant conducted full power operations in July 1970. The prototype was a success, and the plant's basic design proved adequate.[17] The infrastructure built up around Jiajiang, named the Southwest Reactor Engineering Research and Design Academy, or First Academy, became China's largest nuclear power industrial complex.

At the same time, the submarine design progressed along with the development of the reactor plant. The layout of the submarine and its subsystems was determined by the use of a full-size wood and steel model used to test fit all the components. This slowed the construction but avoided costly reworks in the actual hull. The reactor was in place by early 1971. The submarine was able to get underway for the first time on August 23, 1971. Not surprisingly, many technical abnormalities occurred during the cruise. It was not until 1974 that the submarine was deemed ready to join the fleet.

The development of China's first nuclear submarine paralleled that of the Chinese nuclear industry and catalyzed many aspects of China's industrial system. The technology that was developed by Chinese scientists and engineers on the 09 submarine project and other strategic weapons systems helped to build the confidence of a hitherto undeveloped nation. Surmounting manifold technical challenges amidst the political chaos of the 1960s shows an extraordinary determination by the Chinese to complete the project and their potential to accomplish other high-technology projects.

The Chinese Civilian Nuclear Power Industry

Due to the structure of the PRC's heavy industry, the Chinese civilian nuclear power industry is closely related to the military program. CNNC has responsibility for many aspects of both programs. However, the civilian industry is not merely a cover for military programs. It is a viable industry that is rapidly growing to provide power to China's booming economy.

China's use of nuclear power for peaceful purposes officially began in 1955 when the Soviet Union agreed to provide other socialist countries, China in particular, with help to "promote the peaceful utilization of atomic energy."[18] This was actually a cover for the nuclear weapons program; however, it did help to create the industrial base discussed above that would develop into the civilian industry. The actual beginning occurred in 1970 when Zhou Enlai delivered a speech emphasizing the development of nuclear power plants to supply electricity.[19] This set in motion several reorganizations in the Second Ministry, including the creation of Shanghai Nuclear Engineering, Research, & Design Institute (SNERDI) in 1970 to design civilian nuclear power plants.[20]

Construction on the first plant was started in 1985 at Haiyan, in Zhejiang Province. This project, known as Qinshan 1, was a pressurized water reactor designed by SNERDI that used mostly Chinese-made components, though the main pressure vessel was purchased from Mitsubishi of Japan. This 300MWe (capable of producing 300,000kW of electricity) reactor was first connected to the electrical grid in 1991. The plant did not start producing at full power until 1994 and was shut down for a year in 1998 for major repairs.[21] The design for this plant was used to build the Chasnupp 1 plant in Pakistan that came online in June of 2000. Though the Qinshan 1 plant has had problems, it has operated safely for over ten years. It has also been used to train many of the technicians that operate other nuclear power plants in China.

The next plants built include the Daya Bay 1 and 2 complexes in Guangdong Province, near Hong Kong. These, unlike Qinshan, were built by the French company Framatone, with assistance from Chinese engineers. Started in 1987 and completed in 1994, each of these reactors is capable of producing 900MWe.[22] These plants also marked the end of the first phase of nuclear power plant construction. In the mid-1990s China began to plan a second phase of construction that started in the late 1990s. This phase relied heavily on foreign technology and designs, with China pursuing a more self-sufficient nuclear industry by obtaining new skills and technology.

The second phase of nuclear construction started in 1997 with four major projects. China used a variety of foreign companies to build the new plants. Qinshan 2 has two PWRs similar to Qinshan 1 but larger, each producing 600 MWe. The plants rely on Chinese designs but use more Japanese and French technology. Qinshan 3 consists of two Canada Deuterium Uranium (CANDU) 665MWe heavy PWRs, designed and built by Atomic Energy of Canada (AECL). Two huge, imported, French-designed 950MWe plants make up Ling Ao complex located a mile from Daya Bay. All of these plants were supplying commercial power by 2004. Tianwan, in Jiangsu Province, consists of two Russian 1,000MWe PWRs (also known as VVERs), expected to come on line in 2005 and 2006.[23] This construction phase has increased China's nuclear power capacity by 75 percent.

In 2004 China solicited bids for four more reactors, two in Guangdong and two in Zhejiang. Beijing also approved two completely indigenous reactors at Ling Ao and Qinshan. Sixteen other provinces and municipalities have announced intentions to build nuclear power plants within the next decade. Plant construction reveals the following general trends in the Chinese nuclear power industry: (1) PWRs will be the major type of plant; (2) domestic manufacturing of plants and equipment is being maximized; (3) foreign plants will be bought but significant technology transfer and Chinese involvement in all phases of construction will be required.

Beijing seeks to steadily increase domestic nuclear-power generating capacity by about two GWe per year for the next fifteen years or so, while developing a comprehensive, self-sustaining domestic industry.[24] The first phase consists of domestically manufacturing fuel assemblies. China has made considerable progress, producing fuel assemblies at Yibin Fuel Plant (FYP) in Sichuan Province[25] and Baotou Nuclear Fuel Component Plant in

Inner Mongolia.[26] FYP produces fuel assemblies for the Qinshan 1 and 2, Daya Bay, and Ling Ao generating complexes. Framatome helped upgrade FYP to produce the fuel for Daya Bay and Ling Ao.[27] FYP is reportedly being upgraded with assistance from Russia to produce fuel for the Tianwan reactors. In addition, Baotou Nuclear Fuel Component Plant will supply the fuel for the Qinshan 3 CANDU reactors.[28] China's growth will require enlarging the capacity of these plants or building new ones, but China is well on its way to meeting its goal of being self-sufficient in its fuel supply.

China's nuclear industry has become more sophisticated over the last two decades. It has developed a regulatory system, albeit a weak one, to ensure safety.[29] The National Nuclear Safety Administration (NNSA), established in 1984, set up a Nuclear Safety Center in 1989 to provide analysis to the NNSA. Both staffs have been steadily growing and their technical knowledge is increasing. The largest challenge facing these organizations is the diverse technology that is being used in the nuclear power plants.[30] The Chinese are following the International Atomic Energy Agency (IAEA) guidelines for such things as emergency preparedness plans and inspections. China has been a member of the IAEA since 1984 and CNNC is a member of several international organizations, such as the World Association of Nuclear Operators, that promote the sharing of operational experience and safety.[31]

Current Research and Development

China's drive to make its nuclear power industry capable of indigenously designing and producing reactor plants has resulted in an impressively robust nuclear R&D system. The Chinese have dozens of institutes working on different components ranging from instrumentation to complete advanced reactor plants. These institutes currently operate at least fifteen test reactors of various types, some of which are considered the most advanced of their type in the world.

The goal of designing and building a commercially viable 1,000-MWe (AC-1000) plant for domestic use and for possible export has been a top priority. The Southwest Reactor Research and Design Academy and SNERDI are both heavily involved in this project. Some design features are unclear, but it appears to be a PWR similar to either Framatome or Westinghouse designs. The design is supposed to reduce construction time and cost while increasing safety.[32] The success of this plant will greatly reduce Chinese dependence on foreign companies to build the estimated two power plants per year planned for the next fifteen years.

INET is conducting China's most advanced research yet on an HTGR. This type of reactor has been in existence since the 1950s but only in the last decade have the technical issues been resolved sufficiently to allow it to be considered for commercial use. One of the HTGR's advantages is its great efficiency. Normally, a PWR can achieve an efficiency of 18–23 percent, while a HTGR is 36–50 percent efficient. This allows a much smaller core to generate the same electrical power. INET has built a successful HTGR called the HTR 10.[33] HTR 10 is not only highly efficient, but has also proven to be very safe to operate.[34]

The HTR 10 design is being used to design a series of small (200MWe) power plants that can have their major components manufactured in a factory and then assembled at the site. The increased safety of these plants will allow them to be built at industrial sites and close to population centers where the need for power is greatest. The high operating temperatures of these plants will also allow a more economical source of heat for industrial uses such as hydrogen production and heavy oil recovery. The design of this type of reactor plant appears to be scalable, allowing a customized reactor to be built for a specific use.[35]

The basic operation of the HTGR reactor differs from that of its PWR counterpart in several ways. The first involves the way in which fuel is loaded. Instead of fuel loaded in rods clad in metal, it is formed into ceramic balls. This method for fuel loading is one of the reasons the reactor is safer. Even during the worst accident, the temperature of the fuel does not exceed the design temperature of the ceramic and thus it cannot melt down and release the fission products. This inherent safety will allow this type of reactor to be built much closer to energy consumers.[36]

The next difference is the much higher temperatures at which the plant can operate. The imperative of maintaining very high pressure to keep the water from boiling limits a PWR's operating temperature. By contrast, the HTGR is cooled by helium, a gas. This allows operating temperatures as high as 950 degrees Celsius but at a much lower pressure. This high temperature allows for greater plant efficiency and versatility.

Several combinations of generators can create electrical power from the heat produced by the reactor. The most efficient is a gas turbine driven by helium in the primary loop. This configuration would be close to 50 percent efficient but due to maintenance issues it is not currently seen as the most cost effective. One of the limiting factors on this design has been the lubrication of the bearings for the gas turbine and blower. Since conventional oil or water lubrication systems risk contamination of the helium, a new system must be developed. INET has been researching magnetic bearings to eliminate the need for an external lubricant.[37]

The second system is an external gas turbine system in which nitrogen is heated by the helium in a heat exchanger and then used to turn a gas turbine. This system would simplify the secondary plant since it could use more conventional types of gas turbines; however, the efficiency of the plant would be reduced to 40–45 percent. A steam cycle, similar to the ones used in PWR could also be used, but the efficiency would drop to around 34 percent. The HTR 10 will initially be equipped with a steam cycle; an external gas turbine system will be added later. This combination will allow testing of the most efficient and cost effective combination. China's ultimate goal is to design a plant with a closed-loop gas turbine driven by the primary helium.

Foreign Involvement in China's Civilian Nuclear Program

The international nuclear industry has become more integrated over the last two decades. It must balance the imperatives of thwarting military proliferation and spreading technology to make nuclear power both safer and more economical. In several countries, the nuclear industry is also tied closely to the development of nuclear power plants for use in naval nuclear power. It is hard to differentiate between technology used in civilian power plants and that used in naval nuclear power plants. The safety features that are developed for a submarine plant often have applicability to civilian plants and vice versa. This makes it difficult for companies that export civilian nuclear power components and plants not to also export technology that can be directly used to improve naval nuclear power plants.

China has always insisted that any large purchase of nuclear plants or components involve the transfer of technology.[38] This has included assistance to retool factories in order to produce more components in China and has clearly been seen in the fuel production area discussed above. Since it is impossible to give a detailed description of every type of technology transfer that has occurred in the nuclear industry, this section will summarize the major companies that have transferred technology and the types of assistance they have provided to China. This is only a small sample of the foreign enterprises involved; the U.S. Embassy in Beijing estimates that over "300 enterprises [are] engaged in the development and production of nuclear technology in China."[39]

United States

Washington did not allow direct transfer of nuclear technology until 1998. This did not prevent American companies from legally transferring non-nuclear technology to China, however. The American company Westinghouse Nuclear (recently purchased from British Nuclear Fuels LTD by Toshiba of Japan) is the leading American company involved in the Chinese nuclear industry. Its connection to CNNC and its subsidiaries goes back to the early 1980s, when it assisted the Shanghai Steam Turbine Co. in developing 300- and 600MWe steam turbine generators for use in nuclear power plants. The Qinshan 1 power plant uses one of these turbines.[40]

The first major joint effort that dealt directly with nuclear technology was a 1994–96 limited technology partnership with Nuclear Power Institute of China to integrate the design features of Westinghouse's AP-600 with the Chinese AC-600 power plant to produce the CAP-600.[41] SNERDI is also listed on the Westinghouse web site as part of the design team for the AP-600. The AP-600 and the AP-1000 (a larger version of the AP-600) are Westinghouse's most advanced commercial reactors.[42]

Westinghouse was also involved in the manufacture of the steam generators (SG) for the Qinshan 2 project. Westinghouse's Spanish subsidiary Equipos Nucleares (Ensa) manufactured two of the SGs, and the Shanghai Boiler Works (with Westinghouse's technical assistance) manufactured the other two.[43] Westinghouse signed two contracts in 2003 to become more involved with Chinese nuclear fuel production. The first is with Shanghai Gaotai Rare and Precious Metals Company to provide engineering services and zirconium-alloy for use as cladding in nuclear fuel cell manufacture. The second contract is with SNERDI to provide technology and engineering services for the design of reactor cores and associated fields. Mike Saunders, senior vice president of Westinghouse Nuclear Fuels, says, "This will ensure that the Chinese have access to the most experienced and widest range of products, technology and services."[44]

Westinghouse is currently bidding for the first time to build complete nuclear power plants in China: two in Guangdong and two in Zhejiang. This is a major contract since it could lead to additional projects as China tries to standardize its industry. The projects could be worth up to $6 billion. French, Canadian, and Russian companies are also bidding for the projects. The high value of these projects has drawn the attention of American political leaders, including Vice President Richard Cheney, who on a trip in 2004 reportedly encouraged the Chinese to buy the Westinghouse plants.[45] This would result in additional new technology being available to the Chinese.

Canada

The Canadian company Atomic Energy of Canada Limited, design authority for the CANDU reactors, was also design authority for the Qinshan 3 project. It consists of two pressurized heavy-water reactors (PHWR) that became operational in 2003. The contract also included training operators and engineers in Canada on the operation and maintenance of the plants. The plants were constructed with close cooperation between AECL and SNERDI engineers. Computer aided drafting and design systems (CADDS) were extensively used during the building of the plants. This appears to be one of the first large-scale projects in China to use this advanced software.[46] The building of these plants also involved the upgrade of the Baotou fuel factory to supply the follow-on fuel loading.[47]

AECL signed a strategic alliance with SNERDI in January 2005. This partnership is to include the establishment of a CANDU Engineering Center at SNERDI to provide technical support to Qinshan 3 and assist AECL in designing the next generation of reactor plants. It specifically calls for joint refining and application of advanced engineering tools used by AECL in design, construction, and operations.[48]

France and Germany

AREVA is the major company in France involved in nuclear power. It owns 66 percent of Framatome ANP (Siemens of Germany owns the rest). Framatome has been involved in the construction of or supplying components for eight of China's nuclear power plants and is also involved in its fuel production. AREVA is also the owner of Techicatome, which designed France's naval nuclear power plants for submarines and aircraft carriers.

Framatome was the first foreign company to build a nuclear power plant in China. It designed and built the Daya Bay reactors. The contract was signed in 1988; the plants came on line in 1994. The company transferred all the technology for building the plants to the Chinese in 1992. This was also the design the Chinese used for building the Qinshan 2 reactors.[49]

The French were contracted to build the Ling Ao plants in 1995. These plants were to use more domestically produced components. Framatome assisted the Donofang Boiler Company in the manufacture of the heavy components of reactor islands (vessels), and Shanghai No. 1 Machine and Tool Works in the production of the first reactor cores for the plants. This technology transfer also included full access to all design technology for the newest French reactors operating in Chooz and Civaux, France.[50]

Framatome is also heavily involved in Chinese fuel cell production. In 1991 it assisted CNNC's Yibin Fuel Plant in upgrading its technology to provide the fuel cells for the Daya Bay and the Qinshan 2 plants. The plant was upgraded again in 1998 by Framatome to provide more advanced fuel cells that have a longer life. It now also produces fuel cells for the Ling Ao plant.[51]

Siemens of Germany, in addition to being part owner of Framatome, also has supplied components to the Russian-built Tianwan nuclear power plant.[52] The company reports that it has supplied Tianwan with its latest digital instrumentation and safety control system.[53] This would make Tianwan one of the most advanced civilian reactor plants in the world.

Russia

The involvement of Russia in China's nuclear power industry is the most difficult to trace due to the endemic secrecy of both countries. It is known that the Soviet Union provided China with its first test reactor in the 1950s and trained many of its early engineers and scientists.[54] This aid ceased after the Sino-Soviet split in the early 1960s. Since the early 1990s, however, the relationship between the two countries has rapidly improved.

The largest project in which Russia is known to be involved is the construction of the Tianwan 1, which will consist of two Russian VVERs (Russian PWRs). The construction started in 1999 and the first plant came on line in early 2005. The second plant is expected to be operational in late 2005.[55] This joint project will include technology transfer and personnel training. The Yibin Fuel Plant is being back-fitted to produce the fuel for the Tianwan plants under a production license from the Russian Atomic Energy Ministry.[56]

Russia has also assisted China in upgrading its Lanzhou uranium enrichment plant in Gansu Province that was originally built in the 1950s with Soviet assistance.[57] In addition, the Russian Institute of Atomic Reactors and the China Institute of Atomic Energy have collaborated on a sodium-cooled experimental fast breeder reactor, also located at the Lanzhou site.

The technical support that Russia has provided to China is also estimated to be substantial. The Type 093 nuclear submarine is thought to closely resemble a Russian Victor III submarine and the Russian Rubin

Design Bureau might have provided technical assistance.[58] This submarine has also been discussed in Chinese articles in which Russian technical assistance is mentioned.[59] This suggests the possibility that some level of Russian assistance has been provided directly to China's submarine nuclear power program.

Government and Institutional Cooperation

China is also heavily involved in international cooperation and collaboration on research and development in the nuclear field. The International Thermonuclear Experimental Reactor (ITER) is a project to research fusion power started by the United States and Japan in the late 1980s. China joined the project in 2003 and has been an active member. The actual ITER will be built in France, with China contributing 10 percent of the cost.

The HTR 10 at INET, part of Qinghua University, has drawn international attention. Massachusetts Institute of Technology (MIT) has been researching similar HTGR technology in a program funded by the Department of Energy. The two institutes signed a collaborative agreement in 2003 to share research and technology on the development of a commercially viable HTGR.[60]

Naval Implications

The above section demonstrates the extent of foreign nuclear-technology transfer to China. The Chinese civilian nuclear power industry, as discussed above, is closely related to China's military program. The technology sold to Chinese companies is in fact being sold to CNNC, a state-owned enterprise. It is reasonable to assume that any technology that is brought into China will eventually be transferred to the military.

The basis for any country's naval nuclear power industry is a strong civilian program that allows for technology to be developed and the cost shared between the two programs. This is certainly the case for the United States and France. The development of a strong civil industrial base in both countries since the 1950s has produced experienced personnel who bring new ideas from one program to the other. This makes both programs advance faster and become more efficient. Every nuclear project that has been built in China has had extensive involvement by Chinese engineers. It is not unusual for a country to require a foreign vender to use domestic engineers and local construction assets; however, it must be acknowledged that since the mid-

1980s Western companies have trained a large cadre of Chinese engineers in all aspects of the nuclear industry. This will allow them to vastly improve their ability to develop advanced reactor plants for submarines that are more efficient and reliable than in the past.

China's ability to produce large, complex structures for use in nuclear power plants has been vastly improved by the technology and training from Western companies. The Qinshan 1 plant, though reportedly produced domestically, had many of its major components imported, including the vessel (Japan) and Main Cooling Pumps (Germany).[61] Today, China produces many of these large components domestically. The skills and technology needed to produce components such as turbines, steam generators, and pressure vessels for civilian power plants are essential for producing these components for submarines.

China now uses the most advanced computer software for plant design. The Qinshan 3 project extensively used CADDS provided by AECL.[62] This will significantly improve China's ability to produce complex machinery such as submarines and ships. The use of these types of programs has been integral to the development of the most advanced class of U.S. submarines.[63] The agreements that CNNC has signed with AECL and AREVA indicate that this type of software will be used extensively in future design projects, giving the Chinese even more experience with it.

Instrumentation and Control equipment is the most complex part of designing a nuclear reactor. The I&C systems that the Chinese have received from companies such as Siemens, AECL, and AREVA are the most advanced in the world. These can be duplicated and used for many other applications, including propulsion plants of submarines and other ships. The availability of an I&C system that incorporates the latest technology will significantly increase the submarines' reliability.

China's Prospective Nuclear Submarine Fleet

The development of China's type 093 submarine started sometime in the 1980s or before. The first unit was started in 1994 and was not launched until 2002. It is speculated to be similar to a Russian Victor III using two PWRs and other Russian technology.[64] Various articles state that the 093 has an advanced high-temperature high-efficiency reactor plant.[65] The use of the technology gained by the civilian nuclear industry has the potential to greatly improve submarines designed and built in China.

The transfer of technology has most likely played a part in providing the

093 and future submarines with advanced I&C equipment, a better-designed reactor fuel cell, and higher quality construction of the reactor plant. This is the minimum that China would be able to get from the technology that they had obtained by the mid-1990s, when the 093 was started. The delays on the ship could have been caused by the attempt to continuously update the design as construction progressed. The 093 was laid down in 1994,[66] but construction began on Qinshan 2 in 1996 (domestic with French assistance), Qinshan 3 in 1998[67] (Canadian), and Ling Ao in 1995 (French). The Yibin Fuel Plant was upgraded by the French in 1994,[68] and from 1994 to 1996, Westinghouse made the plans for the AP600 available for the Chinese to study.[69] Thus, the technology flowing into China during the period from 1994 to 2002 was very substantial by any measure. The Chinese may very well have made the decision early on to delay the 093 in order to incorporate the maximum amount of foreign nuclear technology possible.

The most extreme possibility is that China has already developed a submarine-compatible HTGR. This possibility is worth considering for several reasons. The first is that, if successful, a HTGR would allow for a much lighter power plant. A HTGR is twice as efficient as a PWR, so it would require a substantially smaller core for the same power output. It is also cooled by helium at a relatively low pressure instead of by high-pressure water. This reduces the weight not only of the coolant but also of the piping. The reduced weight would potentially allow the submarine to be faster and smaller.

The second reason is that the Chinese have been discussing that their goal in designing weapons is to use the latest technology to leap ahead. This would support development of a unique reactor system. The research on HTGR in China started in the 1970s,[70] before a substantial amount of development in the civilian nuclear power industry began; this may indicate that some type of military use was envisioned. This would also help to explain why it is taking so long to build the 093. The current wisdom that the 093 is similar to a Victor III design, and that the Russians are assisting in its construction would indicate that it would proceed along quickly. This, however, is reportedly not the case, suggesting at least the possibility that there is something significantly different about this submarine.

The technical difficulties that would have to be overcome with the blowers (the need for magnetic bearings) and the fuel-loading system to make an HTGR compatible with a submarine are formidable. This makes the probability of the 093 being equipped with an HTGR small. However, it should be taken into consideration that if not the 093, then a future submarine may have a reactor of this type. This could take a form that is significantly different from current nuclear submarines that are designed for open-ocean, long-endurance operations.

China's strategy for the next several decades appears to be focused on pushing its defenses out to the first island chain, which includes Japan, Taiwan, and the Philippines. This will require more shallow-water access-denial platforms, instead of long-range open-ocean submarines. A small submarine similar to a diesel electric—save for a small HTGR to recharge its batteries—would be an ideal sea-denial platform. It could stay submerged for extended periods of time while laying in wait for a passing ship. This submarine could have technology currently available from the recently purchased Kilo-class submarines for the batteries and propulsion, while using a reactor on the scale of the HTR 10 (2500 kW generator). An HTGR equipped with an integral gas turbine/blower outfitted with magnetic bearings could be designed to be very quiet.

Conclusion

We would be foolish to underestimate China's ability to develop complex weaponry. The 091 submarine is often used as an example of Chinese engineering incompetence, since the submarine is viewed as one of the worst in the world. But when considered in context of when it was built and the state of the Chinese economy and political system at the time, it is actually impressive that the submarine was ever finished. No one denies that China's economy and industrial base have made extraordinary strides since that time, and the level of technical expertise in China has risen dramatically. Combine this with the advanced technology currently available to China and it should seem evident that the 093 submarine is unlikely to be a simple copy of a 1970s vintage Russian design, but rather something significantly more advanced.

The use of nuclear power is vital to China's economy and to reducing its dependence on coal and imported oil, while also decreasing its greenhouse gas emissions.[71] The United States confronts the same issues and is likewise returning to nuclear power. A major concern is how much technology should be transferred to China to make its industry safer. The United States does not want China to have a Three Mile Island- or Chernobyl-type accident, of course, so it is in Washington's interest to ensure that China has the most advanced technology to operate its nuclear power plants safely. Moreover, there are obviously strong commercial incentives to feed China's appetite for nuclear power technology. Of course, this same dilemma is present in all technology transfers but few other industries have such direct links between the civil and military programs. U.S. naval analysts should be concerned, lest such transfers aid China in developing a robust nuclear submarine fleet that could unhinge the delicate balance of security and stability in the Asia-Pacific region.

Notes

1. 简杰 [Jian Jie] "神话中德双子座" ["The Legend of the Virtuous Twins"], 22–23. See also 林长盛 [Lin Changsheng], "我国核潜艇的战力" ["The Combat Power of China's Nuclear Submarines"], 世界航空航天博览 [*World Aerospace Digest*], no. 103 (September 2004): 28.

2. Oxford Analytica, "China: Expansion to End Power Shortage," *OxResearch,* 29 March 2004 [online journal]; available at http://proquest.umi.com/pqdweb?did= 592085241&sid=9&Fmt=3&clientld=18762&RQT=309&VName=PQD.

3. John Wilson Lewis and Xue Litai, *China Builds the Bomb* (Stanford, Calif.: Stanford University Press, 1988), 38.

4. Ibid., 55–59.

5. Nuclear Threat Initiative, "China National Nuclear Corporation," available at http://www.nti.org/db/china/cnnc.htm.

6. Ministry of Foreign Affairs of the People's Republic of China, "General Manager Kang Rixan of China National Nuclear Corporation (CNNC) elaborates on the Development Status of China's Nuclear Power and the Exchanges and Cooperation with International Counter parts." Available at http://www.fmprc.gov.cn/eng/xwfw/wgjzxwzx/ipccfw/t199253.htm.

7. John Wilson Lewis and Xue Litai, *China's Strategic Sea Power: The Politics of Force Modernization in the Nuclear Age* (Stanford, Calif.: Stanford University Press, 1994), 24.

8. Nuclear Threat Initiative, "Nuclear Facilities and Organizations," available at http://www.nti.org/db/china/nucorg.htm.

9. Lewis and Xue, *China's Strategic Sea Power,* 25.

10. Nuclear Threat Initiative, *Nuclear Facilities and Organizations.*

11. Lewis and Xue, *China's Strategic Sea Power,* 30–31.

12. Ibid., 265–66.

13. Xu Yuanhui, "Power Plant Design: HTGR Advances in China," *Nuclear Engineering International* (16 March 2005), 22. Available at http://web.lexis-nexis.com/universe/printdoc.

14. Lewis and Xue, *China's Strategic Sea Power,* 7–8.

15. Marshal Nie Rongzhen was an army marshal and veteran of the Long March. He was placed in charge of the strategic weapons (atomic bomb) program in 1955 and

it was he who convinced Mao that China should develop nuclear-powered subma-rines. Nie was a protégée of Zhou Enlai, who provided political protection for the programs during the Cultural Revolution.

16. Lewis and Xue, *China's Strategic Sea Power*, 24–28.

17. Ibid., 45–46.

18. Lewis and Xue, *China Builds the Bomb,* 105.

19. Energy Information Administration, US Department of Energy, "Timeline of the Chinese Nuclear Industry, 1970 to 2020," available at http://www.eia.doe.gov/cneaf/ nuclear/page/nuc_reactors/china/timeline.html.

20. Shanghai Nuclear Engineering Research and Design Institute, "Introduction," available at http://www.snerdi.com.cn/en-introduction.htm.

21. World Nuclear Association, *Nuclear Power in China, June 2005,* Available at http:// www.world-nuclear.org/info/printable_information_papers/inf63print.htm. .

22. Ibid.

23. Energy Information Administration, U.S. Department of Energy, "Reactor Summaries," available at http://www.eia.doe.gov/cneaf/nuclaer/page/nuc_reactors/ china/reactors.html.

24. World Nuclear Association, *Nuclear Power in China, June 2005.*

25. Nuclear Threat Initiative, *Yibin Fuel Plant (YFP),* available at http://www.nti .org/db/china/yibin.htm.

26. Nuclear Threat Initiative, *Baotou Nuclear Fuel Component Plant,* available at http://www.nti.org/db/china/baotou.htm.

27. AREVA, *AREVA in China,* Available at http://www.framatome-anp.com/servlet/B lobServer?blobcol=url&blobheader=application/pdf&blobkey=id&blobtable=pres skit&blobwhere=1082483458312.

28. Nuclear Threat Initiative, *Baotou Nuclear Fuel Component Plant.*

29. Nuclear Threat Initiative, *National Nuclear Safety Administration (NNSA),* available at http://www.nti.org/db/china/nnsa.htm.

30. Richard P. Suttmeier, "China Goes Nuclear," *The China Business Review* 23, no. 5 (September/October 1996): 19, available at http://proquest.umi.com/pqdweb? did=10279722&sid&Fmt=3&clientld=18762&RQT&VName=PQD.

31. Suttmier, 19.

32. Ryan, "China Will Insist on Technology along with Any Nuclear Imports," *Nucle-onics Week* 39, no. 20 (14 May 1998): 1, available at http://web.lexis-nexis.com/ universe/printdoc.

33. For further information on China's HTGR development, particularly Qinghua University's HTR 10, see 吴宗鑫 [Wu Congxin] 先进核能系统和高温气冷堆 [*An Advanced Nuclear Reactor System: The High Temperature Gas Cooled Reac-tor*] (Beijing: Qinghua University Press, 2004), 204–6. For further information on Chinese research and development in the area of nuclear power, see 朱齐荣 [Zhu Qirong], 核动力机械 [*Nuclear Propulsion*] (Changsha: National University of

Defense Technology Press, 2003); 马栩泉 [Ma Xuquan], ed., 核能开发与应用 [*Nuclear Energy Development and Application*] (Beijing: Chemistry Industry Press, 2004); 孙中宁 [Sun Zhongning], 核动力设备 [*Nuclear Energy Equipment*] (Harbin: Harbin Engineering University, 2003); 张建民 [Zhang Jianmin], 核反应堆控制 [*Control of Nuclear Reactors*] (Xian: Xian Communications College Press, 2002).

34. International Atomic Energy Agency, "HTTR and HTR-10 Test Reactors," *IAEA-TECDOC—1198: Current Satus and Future Development of Modular High Temperature Gas Cooled Reactor Technology*, 130. Available at http://www.iaea.org/inis/aws/htgr/fulltext/gcr_review_05.pdf. Accessed on 5 August 2005.

35. World Nuclear Association, *Nuclear Power in China, June 2005.*

36. International Atomic-20 Energy-20Agency,-20"HTTR-20and HTR-10 Test Reactors," 130.

37. Yang Goujun, Geng Wenji, Li Hongwei, and Yu Suyuan, "Study on the Relationship about Magnetic Bearings Rotor Structure and Natural Frequency for 10 MW High Temperature Gas-Cooled Reactor," *Gaojishu Tongxun* [*High Technology Newsletter*], no. 4 (Beijing: Tsinghua University and Institute of Nuclear Energy Technology, 2003), 72–76.

38. Ryan, 1.

39. Energy Information Administration, U.S. Department of Energy, "Future of the Chinese Nuclear Industry," available at http://www.eia.doe.gov/cneaf/nuclaer/page/nuc_reactors/china/outlook.html. Accessed on 18 July 2005.

40. Shanghai Steam Turbine Co., "Introduction," available at www.nuclear.cetin.net.cn/cnic/hzn/032.htm.

41. Ryan, 1.

42. Westinghouse Electric Company, "Design team," *AP600 website*, available at http://www.ap600.westinghousenuclaer.com/D1.asp.

43. Westinghouse Electric Company, "Westinghouse Steam Generators Shipped to Qinshan II Nuclear Station," Westinghouse news release 24 March 1999, available at http://www.prnewswire.com/cgi-bin/micro_stories.pl?ACCT=127481&TICK=WE&STORY=/www/story/07-09-1999/0000978482&EDATE=Mar+24,+1999.

44. Westinghouse Electric Company, "Westinghouse Wins Two Fuel-Related Contracts in China," Westinghouse news release 19 August 2003, available at http://www.prnewswire.com/cgi-bin/micro_stories.pl?ACCT=127481&TICK=WE&STORY=/www/story/08-19-2003/0002003475&EDATE=Aug+19,+2003.

45. H. Josef Hebert, "Cheney to Promote American-Made Nuclear Reactors to China," *Detroit News Business,* 10 April 2004, available at http://www.detnews.com/2004/business/0404/11/business-118468.htm.

46. Peigen Yu, "Qinshan NPP, Long-Term Plans for Nuclear Power in China," *Inside WANO* 9, no. 2 (2001): 6.

47. Nuclear Threat Initiative, *Qinshan Nuclear Reactors,* available at http://www.nti.org/db/china/qinshan.htm.

48. Atomic Energy of Canada Limited, "AECL Signs Strategic Alliance" AECL news release 18 January 2005, available at http://www.aecl.ca/index.asp?latid=55&csid=168&csidi=120&menuid-48.

49. AREVA, *AREVA in China,* Available at http://www.framatome-anp.com/servlet/BlobServer?blobcol=url&blobheader=application/pdf&blobkey=id&blobtable=presskit&blobwhere=1082483458312.

50. AREVA, *AREVA in China,* Available at http://www.framatome-anp.com/servlet/BlobServer?blobcol=url&blobheader=application/pdf&blobkey=id&blobtable=presskit&blobwhere=1082483458312.

51. AREVA, *AREVA in China,* available at http://www.framatome-anp.com/servlet/BlobServer?blobcol=url&blobheader=application/pdf&blobkey=id&blobtable=presskit&blobwhere=1082483458312.

52. Nuclear Threat Initiative, *Tianwan-1 & 2,* available at http://www.nti.org/db/china/jiangsu.htm.

53. Energy Information Administration, U.S. Department of Energy, "Reactor Summaries," Available at http://www.eia.doe.gov/cneaf/nuclaer/page/nuc_reactors/china/reactors.html.

54. Lewis and Xue, *China Builds the Bomb,* 105–6.

55. Energy Information Administration, U.S. Department of Energy, "VVER Reactors," available at http://www.eia.doe.gov/cneaf/nuclaer/page/nuc_reactors/china/vver.html.

56. Nuclear Threat Initiative, *Tianwan-1 & 2.*

57. World Nuclear Association, *Nuclear Power in China, June 2005.*

58. Jane's Underwater Warfare Systems, "Type 093" *Submarines: Submarines and Submersible Designs* [online] posted 01 March 2005, available at http://www4.janes.com/K2/doc.jsp?t=A&K2DocKey=/content1/janesdata/yb/juws/juws1722.htm@current&QueryText=%3CAND%3E%28%3COR%3E%28type+%3CAND%3E+093+%29%29&Prod_Name=JUWS&.

59. Chinese Military Aviation, "Submarines," available at http://mil.jschina.com.cn/huitong/han_xia_kilo_song.htm.

60. Elizabeth Thomson, "MIT, Tsinghua Collaborate on Development of Pebble-Bed Nuclear Reactor," MIT press release 22 October 2003, available at http://web.mit.edu/newsoffice/2003/pebble.html.

61. Energy Information Administration, U.S. Department of Energy, "Future of the Chinese Nuclear Industry," available at http://www.eia.doe.gov/cneaf/nuclaer/page/nuc_reactors/china/outlook.html.

62. Peigen Yu, "Qinshan NPP, Long-Term Plans for Nuclear Power in China," *Inside WANO* 9, no. 2 (2001): 8.

63. Computer Sciences Corporation, "CSC Works With General Dynamics to Build Digital Design Solution," *Aerospace and Defense Case Study,* available at http://www.csc.com/industries/aerospacedefense/casestudies/1266.shtml.

64. Jane's Underwater Warfare Systems, "Type 093" *Submarines: Submarines and Submersible Designs* [online] posted 01 March 2005, available at http://www4.janes .com/K2/doc.jsp?t=A&K2DocKey=/content1/janesdata/yb/juws/juws1722.htm@cu rrent&QueryText=%3CAND%3E%28%3COR%3E%28type+%3CAND%3E+093+% 29%29&Prod_Name=JUWS&.

65. See, for example, Chinese Military Aviation webpage, "Submarines," available at http://mil.jschina.com.cn/huitong/han_xia_kilo_song.htm.

66. Jane's Underwater Warfare Systems, "Type 093" *Submarines: Submarines and Submersible Design.*

67. Peigen Yu, "Qinshan NPP, Long-Term Plans for Nuclear Power in China," *Inside WANO* 9, no. 2 (2001): 6.

68. AREVA, *AREVA in China,* Available at http://www.framatome-anp.com/ servlet/BlobServer?blobcol=url&blobheader=application/pdf&blobkey=id&blobta ble=presskit&blobwhere=1082483458312.

69. Ryan, 1.

70. Xu Yuanhui, "Power Plant Design; HTGR Advances in China," *Nuclear Engineering International* (16 March 2005): 22, available at http://web.lexis-nexis.com/ universe/printdoc.

71. 吴宗鑫吴宗鑫 [Wu Congxin] 先进核能系统和高温气冷堆 [*An Advanced Nuclear Reactor System: The High Temperature Gas Cooled Reactor*] (Beijing: Qinghua University Press, 2004), 1–6.

Richard D. Fisher, Jr.

The Impact of Foreign Technology on China's Submarine Force and Operations

Introduction

AS WITH MOST OTHER ELEMENTS of China's ongoing military modernization, the People's Liberation Army Navy (PLAN) has exploited foreign technology to achieve rapid capability enhancement, both by outright weapon systems purchase and by acquiring select foreign technologies to improve its capacity to build modern indigenous submarines and supporting surface combatants. The PLAN has demonstrated its capacity for copying Russian submarine designs, for incorporating Russian and European technology into recent designs, and for building new designs based largely on Russian technology.[1] Since the early 1990s, China has embarked on a new stage of gathering foreign inputs. These include Russian Kilo conventional attack submarines (SSKs) and their modern weapons, as well as Russian nuclear submarine technology and design expertise. In addition, Russian technology is also facilitating a "revolutionary" advance in PLAN nuclear attack and ballistic-missile submarines. Russian surface combatants, naval weapons, and naval aircraft are enabling the PLAN to better support its submarines and defend against an adversary's air and naval forces. The PLAN is also interested in acquiring greater European submarine and naval combatant technologies, a prospect that will grow should the European Union lift its 1989 arms embargo.

Factors That May Drive PLAN Submarine Growth

China is developing a large and modern fleet of nuclear- and conventional-powered submarines as part of a more comprehensive military modernization designed to advance strategic goals in Asia and beyond.[2] While new conventional and nuclear-powered submarines (SSNs) are viewed as anti-carrier/surface combatant platforms, for potential conflicts over Taiwan crises or maritime resources, both China's increasingly global interests and emerging technology may push th e PLAN into more complex submarine missions. The advent of China's second generation SSBN may lead to the dedication of more attack submarines to Gorshkov-style "bastion" missions, while the development of land attack cruise missiles and aircraft carriers for the PLAN could see Beijing's SSNs devoted to future power-projection missions. Such factors might lead China's leadership to support construction of more and better submarines.

In late July 2005, retired U.S. Adm. Al Konetzni stated that by 2020 the PLAN could have twice the number of submarines as the U.S. Navy, and three times by 2025.[3] Konetzni's reported comments did not explain his estimates, but they certainly reflect planned U.S. SSN inventory reduction.[4] Unfortunately, China does not publish any open official data that might allow confirmation of its submarine modernization or construction plans. Nevertheless, reasonable estimates can be made from a variety of open sources, as seen in Table 1.

Table 1 projects that the PLAN submarine inventory will remain nearly constant, at approximately seventy vessels until 2010. It is important to note, however, that during that period the number of modern, capable submarines will sharply increase, from six in 2000 to an estimated forty in 2010. This percentage of modern vessels will be less if series production of the Yuan-, Shang-, and Jin-class submarines become delayed by development obstacles. On the other hand, it may underestimate both the size and capability of the order of battle if accelerated indigenous submarine production is matched by additional orders for Russian submarines. Estimates of PLAN submarine forces beyond 2010 are especially speculative. Several factors, nonetheless, affect the direction and rate of that growth.

Table 1. Estimated Chinese Submarine Order of Battle

	PLAN Submarine Growth Estimates		
	2000	2005	2010 (est.)
Type 094 JIN SSBN	0	1	3–4
Type 092 Xia SSBN	1	1	1
Golf SSB	1	1	1
Type 093 Shang SSN	0	2	≈5
Type 091 Han SSN	5	4	3
Type 041 Yuan SSK	0	2	≈7
Type 039/039A Song SSK	2	12–14	≈25
Type 035 Ming SSK	19	17	≈17
Type 033 Romeo SS	≈35	≈20	0
Project 887 Kilo SSK	2	2	2
Project 636 Kilo SSK	2	2	2
Project 636M Kilo SSK	0	≈3	8
TOTALS	≈68	≈74	≈74

Note: Table derived from: *Jane's Fighting Ships*; International Institute for Strategic Studies; www.sinodefense.com; press reports; author interview data. Numbers count launched not commissioned submarines. Kilo numbers for ships already in China. Song projection assumes two–three annual production. 2010 estimates are author speculation. Chart is intended to be illustrative, not definitive.

Drive for Modernization

One critical factor affecting PLA submarine investment is the desire to build a modern fleet. It appears that the Type 093 Shang SSN will complement the existing four Type 091 Han SSNs. But Han force levels are likely to reduce to three—the number of vessels that received midlife upgrades between 1998 and 2002. Should the PLA opt for multiple squadrons of SSNs, it could continue to replace Hans with 093s, or perhaps even introduce a more advanced SSN design early in the next decade. Similarly, it is possible that 1960s vintage Type 033 Romeo submarines are being rapidly replaced by Kilo, Song, and Yuan SSKs. Type 035 Mings built in the 1980s and 1990s still have years of useful life and may be assigned to reserve units for coastal defense, barrier patrol, mining or training missions. Key factors affecting force levels include further Kilo or Lada/Amur purchases from Russia. Also unknown is whether Song and Yuan production will continue simultaneously, or if advanced versions of the latter will, perhaps with air-independent propulsion (AIP), succeed the Song.

Nuclear Deterrent/Warfighting Mission Configuration

Another factor affecting submarine force levels might come from a Chinese leadership decision to invest a substantial proportion of its nuclear missile forces in SSBNs, and whether the PLAN would then be charged with building Soviet-style SSBN bastions. Former PLAN chief and Vice Chairman of the Central Military Commission (CMC) Admiral Liu Huaqing, who studied in the Soviet Union, has been noted for his admiration of Gorshkov, and his bastion strategy.[5] The Bohai Gulf could become one such bastion. Supporting this possibility is a report of an "underwater" submarine base under construction in Huludao.[6] The JL-2 SLBM's estimated 5,400NM range would allow for substantial coverage of the continental United States and all of India from these waters.[7]

The Bohai Gulf has an average depth of approximately one hundred fifty feet, which would make interdiction by U.S. SSNs difficult, but the PLAN cannot ignore the possibility that U.S. unmanned underwater vehicles (UUVs) could turn the constricted gulf into an SSBN trap.[8] In addition, a potential deepening of U.S.-Japanese missile defense cooperation might allow eventual boost-phase targeting of Bohai-launched SLBMs.[9] As such, it is possible that the PLAN is preparing for access to safer deep-water patrol areas for its SSBNs. This could explain why the PLAN is building a nuclear submarine facility due East of Yulin Base on Hainan Island.[10] One Asian military source expects this base to become operational in 2006.[11] Located on Hainan's south coast, this base will afford access to deeper patrol areas in the South China Sea, but PLAN SSBNs may have to sail between Taiwan and the Philippines to reach launch areas that would allow JL-2 SLBMs to reach the United States. Such a requirement could strengthen PLA determination to conquer Taiwan, since Hualien and Su Ao, for example, have immediate access to deep water patrol areas.[12] Such a dispersal of SSBN operating areas could be accompanied by an increase in PLAN SSNs in anticipation of potential United States, Japanese, and Indian ASW opposition. The PLA might also invest in more long-range-bomber, surface-ship, and even aircraft-carrier elements consistent with a Soviet-style bastion strategy.

Both SSN and SSBN numbers could increase should the PLAN be given counter-SSBN and space-related defensive missions. There has been some debate within the PLA over which service should control military space,[13] with recent reporting suggesting the future formation of a new and independent Space Force subordinate to the CMC.[14] Inasmuch as the DF-21 and -31 land-based missiles are being modified for mobile space-launch vehicles (SLVs)[15] that could carry future antisatellite payloads, it is possible that PLAN SSBNs could also be configured for space warfare missions. Since the JL-2 is said to be based on the DF-31, it may be large enough to boost payloads into low earth orbit if launched near or south of Hainan Island's 20° latitude. In early 2004 one Dalian Naval Academy author noted, "By deploying just a few antisatellite nuclear submarines in the ocean, one can seriously threaten the entire military space system of the enemy. In addition to anti-satellite operations, these nuclear submarines can also be used for launching low-orbit tactical micro-satellites to serve as powerful real-time battlefield intelligence support."[16]

Technology and Logistical Drivers

As compared with previous decades, new technologies offer enhanced capabilities, which in turn could also justify fewer submarines. For example, it is not likely that production for the new Song or Yuan classes will match the 80–160 of the now-ancient Romeo. But technology may also justify larger numbers (e.g., with SSNs). For example, Asian sources note that China is developing two families of long-range land attack cruise missiles (LACMs), one for the 2nd Artillery, and another that will be used by the PLA Air Force and the PLAN.[17] These, plus the expected deployment by 2005 of a new constellation of PLA navigation, data-relay, and radar and electro-optical surveillance satellites,[18] could turn the new generation of PLA LACMs into a global power-projection tool—if deployed by sufficient numbers of Type 093 SSNs. The production of further Shang or successor SSNs would allow China's leadership to intervene abroad to defend economic and political interests. A Chinese decision to build aircraft carriers might also serve to justify the construction of larger numbers of SSNs.[19]

The modernization and possible expansion of the PLAN submarine fleet will also require improvements to the PLAN's logistics, training, and submarine design/production capabilities. While open reporting on these subjects is not extensive, there is some evidence the PLAN understands these requirements. Asian sources, including one from the PLA, have noted that the PLAN intends to build or expand five submarine bases.[20] The recent acquisition of eight new Kilo submarines suggests that the PLAN has overcome its publicized training shortfall for these new vessels. It is significant that in 2004 Song production was expanded to a second shipyard in Shanghai, which may indicate that SSK production capacity has doubled. It is probable that improved design and production techniques and technologies have also been passed to the submarine sector from China's burgeoning, modernizing commercial shipyards. This would help to explain the dramatic improvements of the Song and Yuan over previous submarine classes. Modern modular construction techniques, suggested in ample Internet photos of Song-class submarines in Shanghai, were also likely facilitated by the absorption of advanced Western computer-aided design technologies.[21] Modular techniques are very likely also used in the construction of Yuan SSK and Type 093 and 094 nuclear submarines.[22]

Major Technology Sources

PLAN leaders have always relied on foreign technology and have placed a high priority on purchasing needed submarine systems. In coordination with various PLA and PRC state intelligence services, China has also placed a consistent high priority on exploiting all manner of open-source information on submarines from North America, Europe, Israel, and Russia.[23] China also relies on espionage to gather information on all submarines, with recent incidents reported in Japan,[24] and one in which Russia stopped China from buying some derelict subs from its Pacific Fleet.[25] In addition, on October 28, 2005, U.S. authorities arrested four ethnic Chinese accused of compromising sensitive information concerning quiet electric drive technology for U.S. ships and submarines, electronic defenses for U.S. aircraft carriers, and electromagnetic pulse weapons.[26]

Russia

Following the collapse of the Soviet Union, the Russian Federation emerged as the PLAN's most important source of both conventional and nuclear submarine technology. For both Russia and China, the submarine technology relationship is perhaps one of the most important, if lesser known, dimensions of their growing bilateral "strategic partnership." For Russia the commercial aspects are critical as submarine and related technology sales support domestic design and production capacity. In 2005, Russian naval weapons exports were projected to eclipse previously dominant aviation exports, comprising roughly $3 billion out of $5 billion in anticipated exports. Of the $3 billion in naval exports, half are expected to comprise submarines and related products, for which the PLAN is the largest customer.[27]

While Russian Kilo SSK sales are visible manifestations of this relationship, much less is known about the degree and depth of Sino-Russian cooperation in SSN and SSBN design and construction. Since the mid-1990s there have been reports about Russian assistance to China's Type 093 SSN and 094 SSBN. In 1997 Jane's reported that Russia's Rubin submarine-design bureau began assisting China's SSN development in 1995.[28] In 1997 the U.S. Office of Naval Intelligence (ONI) estimated that the 093 would be similar in capability to the Soviet Victor III SSN,[29] the last of which entered the Russian navy in 1992. Furthermore, in 2003 the Pentagon stated, "The Type 093-class will compare to the technology of the Russian Victor III SSN and will carry wire-guided and wake-homing torpedoes, as well as cruise missiles."[30] What is not clear from these sources is whether Russia is providing the PLA with Victor III (Project 671)– or the advanced Victor III (Project 671RTM)–level technology. In 2004 ONI reported that the Type 094 "benefits from substantial Russian technical assistance,"[31] but did not elaborate. In 2003 the CIA noted in a report to Congress, "Russia continued to be the main supplier of technology and equipment to India's and China's naval nuclear propulsion programs."[32]

One might therefore assume that not only Rubin, but also a larger swath of Russia's submarine sector, is interacting with China. Rubin was not the lead bureau for Russia's second–third generation Project 671RTM Victor III, but it is the lead bureau for the design of the next fourth generation SSBN, Russia's Project 955 Borei.[33] If indeed Rubin is currently the main interlocutor with China's SSN/SSBN design sector, it may be possible that Russian SSBN-related systems have been adopted for both Type 093 and 094. Other possibilities include either direct Chinese interaction with the Malachite Bureau, which is now leading the design of the fourth generation Project 885 Yasen/Severodvinsk SSN,[34] and was also involved in the Project 671 family, or potentially subcontracting elements of this bureau to Rubin to assist Chinese SSN development.

While producing an SSN with the capabilities of the Project 671RTM would represent a remarkable advance for the PLAN, it might also be expected that China would press hard for Russia's latest fourth generation SSN and SSBN technologies, and use its clout as Russia's largest military customer to secure them. It is curious that the latest ONI artist projection for the Type 094, and most drawings and models of the Project 955, show both carrying twelve SLBMs in slightly separated groups of six.[35] However, this projection is contradicted by what appeared to be the first Chinese Internet source photo of the Type 094 that emerged in mid-2006. If legitimate, this photo suggests the new Chinese SSBN to be more of an evolution from the Type 092, lacking even the acoustic advantages of a smooth hull.

This, however, does not dismiss the possibility that some Russian fourth-generation submarine technologies may have been sold to support this program. Russia previously sought to limit the sophistication of military technology sold to China, and there are powerful incentives for Russia to keep China just below its future submarine capabilities. But such restrictions have eroded in recent years as Russia has sought to boost sales and to ward off potential European competition.[36] Russian weapons manufacturers' faith in being able to make the next generation system apparently serves to justify their willingness to sell very capable current generation systems.[37]

Submarine Purchases

Over the last decade, Russia has promoted progressively advanced SSKs and related technology for sale to China. In 1993 the PLA ordered four Kilo conventional submarines—two Project 877EKMs and two Project 636s—all delivered by 1999. In 2003 the PLA ordered eight more improved 636M SSKs, to be delivered by 2006 or 2007. These are the most advanced Kilos in any navy and their sale made China the largest foreign Kilo customer. In late 2003 there were reports that Russia was considering allowing Chinese co-production of its submarines in order to preempt possible European submarine exports.[38] More recently there have been suggestions of Chinese interest in the latest Project 677 Lada SSK[39] (also known by the export designation Amur), the first of which was launched in April 2004. There have been periodic suggestions, especially in the Russian press, of Chinese interest in buying advanced Project 971 Akula SSNs and Project 949 Oscar-class nuclear-powered cruise missile submarines (SSGNs).[40] China may well decline to match India's potential purchase of one or more Akulas, and instead absorb as much Russian technology as possible to further its own advanced nuclear submarines. The fact that China has not opted for Russian Akulas may also mean that it is pleased with the Russian components that may be making the Type 093 and 094 into formidable submarines.

Design Philosophy

There is some evidence that China is perhaps moving to adopt a critical Russian practice: design competition. The Yuan's Russian-style attributes may emphasize combat survivability, which contrasts to some degree with the design of the Song SSK. This suggests the possibility that China may be adopting some degree of design competition. Movement in this direction would be consistent with the PLA's General Armament Department and logistic reforms of 1998, but there was little such evidence in the submarine sector until the Yuan's emergence. Russia, however, has ample experience with sustaining multiple design bureaus for the purpose of obtaining better designs through competition. If China moves to adopt similar design competition, one might expect greater innovation its submarine designs and related technologies.

Technology

Since the mid-1990s China has pressured Russia to reduce its sales of weapons systems in favor of increased components and technology. This trend is visible concerning air force weapons and surface warships, and likely is true for submarines as well.[41] Regarding SSKs, there are enough outward similarities between the 677 Lada and the PLAN's new Yuan to suggest it has benefited from some level of Russian technology transfer. Russia would have much to offer, as the Chinese are well aware from their experience with the Kilo. It is likely that China has been well briefed on the new engine, quieting, anechoic tiling, automation, and combat control systems developed for the Lada. Russia has also been developing fuel-cell- and chemical-based AIP systems, and has offered them for sale or for refitting to Kilo SSKs.[42]

China would have an interest in practically all nuclear-related submarine technologies that Russia would have to offer, regardless of whether they were made available. There is one report that China obtained sophisticated automatic welding technology, potentially from Russia,[43] which is critical for submarine hull construction. China would also be interested in Russian advances in submarine metal and material technology. China would have particular interest in the newer Russian OK-650 series nuclear reactors, which use natural cooling circulation at low speeds to remove radiated noise from cooling pumps. China would also be interested in all manner of passive and active Russian noise-reduction technologies, from advanced anechoic tiles, to platform and machinery isolation, to hull-flow dynamics, and active noise-canceling systems. Inasmuch as India manufactures Russian-designed anechoic tiles for its Kilo submarines, it is reasonable to assume this technology has also been transferred to China. In addition, China would also seek the latest Russian submarine sonar systems, both fixed and towed arrays, and advanced computer programs to process data. Russian advances in non-acoustic detection technologies that measure wake and radiation parameters would also be of interest to China.

Weapons

With the acquisition of Kilos, *Sovremenny* DDGs, and Kamov Ka-28 ASW helicopters, the PLAN has also had access to a wide array of submarine and antisubmarine weapons. It can be assumed that with the Kilo the PLAN also acquired a package of modern Russian wire-guided and wake-homing torpedoes, mobile mines, torpedo decoys, and perhaps even antitorpedoes. China has also reporedly purchased the VA-111 Skhvale-E rocket-powered supercavitating torpedo.[44] However, it is not clear that it is being used as a weapon, while other sources have noted that the PLA seeks to develop indigenous supercavitating weapons.[45] In 2004 it is likely the PLAN also contracted to purchase the entire Novator Klub-S system of antiship, land-attack, and antisubmarine torpedo-carrying missiles.[46]

Training

In the late 1990s there were reports that the PLAN's early difficulties with its new Kilos resulted from failure to purchase adequate crew training from Russia. In recent years there has been no open commentary pointing to persistence of this problem. In 2005, however, Russian submarine exports to China entered a new phase, the transfer of doctrine and tactics, or "software." Submarines from both countries participated in blockade, antiship, and antisubmarine warfare exercises as part of the August 18–25 "Peace Mission 2005" combined arms exercises. This is most likely the first time that PLAN submarines have ever exercised with naval forces, much less other submarines, from a peer-level power.

This new phase holds the potential to accelerate improvement of PLAN submarine operations, particularly as subsequent bilateral exercises increase in size and sophistication. Since the 1960s, the Soviet navy has sought to perfect the coordination of naval missile strikes from submarine, ship, and air platforms, and even by ballistic missiles. This was a tremendous effort for the former Soviet Union, prompting advances in multiple weapons platforms, space surveillance, satellite communication, and command and control. Despite its current financial distress, the Russian navy retains smaller numbers of modernized SSNs, SSGNs, Tu-22M3 Backfire and Tu-142 Bear bombers, and even one aircraft carrier, to sustain its missile-strike–based doctrine. As the PLA purchases more of these systems, and Moscow continues to view large-scale military exercises as strategically and commercially advantageous, the PLAN may gain experience with advanced Russian naval doctrine and tactics.

Europe and Israel

Substantial European submarine or related technology sales may become an option for the PLAN after the European Union ends its 1989 post-Tiananmen arms embargo. As the EU started to do so in late 2003, the Bush administration began an intense political campaign to block the initiative, and achieved such a stay by May 2005. However, the principle proponents of lifting the embargo, France and Germany, may revive efforts to do so. In early September 2005, EU foreign policy director Javier Salona told the Chinese that it was still the EU's long-term objective to lift the embargo.[47] While some may argue that much-threatened American retaliation would follow the sale to China of a weapon as potent as a modern submarine, it is worth noting that the United States does little submarine business with continental Europe, and some companies, particularly French, may not be deterred from seeking PLA sales. It is significant that Europeans have been deterred by Chinese threats of retaliation if they sell submarine designs to the United States to facilitate new submarine sales to Taiwan.

It must be emphasized, moreover, that the EU embargo has not prevented submarine technologies from going to the PLA. For example, Germany argues that its sale of MTU 16V 396SE marine diesels involves dual-use technology, though they power both the Song SSKs, and possibly the Yuan as well. This is not a simple component purchase: it requires great knowledge of the submarine. As a German corporate official explained, the Song experienced trouble during the 1990s because Israeli consultants could not meld the disparate technologies then being employed. He implied that the Germans could and perhaps did.[48] There is substantial cooperation on fuel cell technology between the Dalian Institute, Germany,[49] and with other countries. PEM fuel cells, with an output of 30–40 kW on Germany's new Type 212 submarine, allow it to cruise for 420 NM at eight knots speed, or a longer range at a slower speed. Other sources suggest that this may confer the ability to remain underwater for fifteen–seventeen days,[50] significantly increasing the submarine's tactical flexibility. Germany's newer Type 214 submarine is slated to use more powerful PEM fuel cells with 120 kW output. French DUUX-series sonar sold during the 1980s is used on the Type 035, and likely influenced the Song's flank array sonar.

Looking toward a post-embargo period, there is much that Europe could offer the PLAN's submarine sector. Britain, France, Germany, Norway, and Sweden are all working on UUV concepts to fulfill a range of military missions.[51] Germany's Type 212 and 214 SSKs are perhaps the world's most advanced, using new fuel-cell based AIP systems, and the latest combat system technologies.[52] More recently, Germany is developing antitorpedo defenses, towed satellite communication buoys, and even miniature unmanned aerial vehicles (UAVs) launched from tubes in the sail, to aid submarine surveillance.[53] France, whose Agosta SSK appears to have influenced the Song's shape, could also offer its Mesma AIP system along with other advanced submarine weapons and systems. France also has long experience with SSBNs and makes the smaller Rubis SSN. Its nuclear submarine technology sector may eventually be allowed to sell similar systems to China. Spain, Italy, and the Netherlands likewise produce SSKs and may be tempted by commercial opportunities in a post-embargo world. Britain also has a significant domestic nuclear-submarine sector capable of producing modern SSNs, SSBNs, and their related weapons and systems.

United States

Beyond the sale of ASW torpedoes to the PLAN in the 1980s, it is not known if the United States has sold or given the PLA substantive submarine related technologies. However, the late 2005 exposure of the alleged Chi Mak spy ring suggests that China may have gained substantial insights into advanced U.S. submarine designs and capabilities. One U.S. official offered a chilling assessment to the *Washington Times*: "China now will be able to track U.S. submarines, a compromise that potentially could be devastating if the United States enters a conflict with China in defending Taiwan."[54] In addition, one has to consider that there may have been an indirect transfer of U.S. technology if Russia has chosen to sell the PLA knowledge obtained from the Walker-Whitworth spy ring. Such sharing might include knowledge of U.S. war planning procedure, SSBN operations, and the capabilities of Sound Surveillance System (SOSUS) arrays.[55] While such data would be dated today, when combined with purchased information on how the Soviets used the data to their advantage, Beijing might gain numerous insights into U.S. SSN, SSBN, and ASW practice. This might be of some use to China in developing future offensive tactics against U.S. SSBNs.

Perhaps the more profound U.S. impact on China's submarine program has been the influence of the U.S. example as it gained and then maintained world leadership in nuclear submarine technologies. Even at the beginning of the Cultural Revolution, when some engineers were afraid to do so, the U.S.-influenced teardrop hull form was chosen for the Type 091 Han-class SSN.[56] It is likely that Chinese submarine designers remain keenly focused on U.S. technological advances[57] and debates, and will continued to be influenced by U.S. Navy choices. As the U.S. Navy moves to investigate future submarine designs that stress modularity, novel electric drives, and laser and other energy weapons, it can be expected that China will also consider such capabilities for its future submarines.[58]

Foreign Technological Impact on Major PLAN Submarines

Type 093 Shang SSN

The PLA's long-standing ambition to deploy a second-generation SSN was realized in December 2002 with Russian assistance.[59] Asian sources revealed that the second Type 093 was launched in late 2003.[60] A third is expected to be launched in 2006.[61] In 2003, the Pentagon reported that there could be four 093s launched by 2010.[62] Other sources report that eventual production could reach six to eight units.[63] The first unit was reported to have commenced construction in 1999[64] and was expected by the Pentagon to enter service in 2005.

Rubin Bureau assistance for Chinese nuclear submarines is reported to include new hull coatings to reduce radiated noise.[65] However, Rubin or other Russian submarine concerns potentially would have been able to offer a range of technologies, including overall hull design, engine and machinery quieting, combat system design, as well as weapon systems and countermeasures outfitting. If the 093 is in fact similar to Russia's Victor III, then Russian contributions based on this design would have been eased considering that this SSN was built in the Komsomolsk shipyard near Vladivostok, and thus proximate to China.

To date there are no known open-source complete photographs of the Type 093 that would allow an assessment of its degree of Russian influence. However, in April 2004 an Internet picture of a purported Type 093 sail appeared. The photo does show enough similarities with the Han sail to lend credibility, but also shows that the PLAN has chosen a sharp-tall vertical sail design over the low, long, and sometimes thick Russian SSN sail preference. In 1997 ONI artists projected that the 093 would feature a teardrop hull similar to the U.S. *Skipjack*-class, but the projection does not match the sail of the 2004 photo. A PRC artist's projection from a 2001 issue of the mainland Chinese magazine *Modern Ships* showed the 093 with a bow structure that resembles that of the Russian Victor- or Akula-class nuclear attack submarines.[66] This would tend to support U.S. expectations for the Type 093. However, this may also be disinformation, and it may suggest that the Type 093 has a large spherical-bow sonar array and side-mounted torpedo tubes consistent with some Russian descriptions and models of the Project 885 Yasen.[67] The PRC artist's projection also shows six flank sonar arrays on the 093 for passive sonar detection. It illustrated the 093 launching a cruise missile from a torpedo tube.

If the 093 succeeds in matching or exceeding the Victor III's performance, then it would represent a significant advance in PLAN SSN technology over its first-generation Project 091 Han class. Russia's Victor III is rated nearly as quiet as early models of the U.S. SSN-688 *Los Angeles* class.[68] However, it should be expected that the PLA would seek further Russian-developed quieting advances that help make the Project 885 nearly as quiet as the *Sea Wolf* (SSN-21).[69] In the early 1990s Russia experimented with propulsor technology on a Kilo.[70] Some illustrations of the Project 885 Yasen show that it uses a propulsor. Furthermore, the Victor III uses a sophisticated sonar system, which includes bow, flank-mounted, and towed sonar arrays. The Type 093 can be expected to incorporate either Russian- or PLA-designed sonar of each type. In addition, inasmuch as the Victor III's maximum dive depth is said to exceed four hundred meters,[71] perhaps up to six hundred meters, it is possible that the Type 093 may also be able to reach these depths. This would exceed the reported maximum depth for the 688-class SSN, and complicate detection in deep-ocean areas.

Regarding weapons, comparison with the Victor III and Chinese sources[72] suggest that the Type 093 will be armed with both regular 533mm width and the exceptional Russian 650mm torpedo tubes. The latter would allow the Type 093 to use Russia's unique class of heavy torpedoes, including the TT-5. Twice the weight of the largest Russian 533mm torpedoes, these are designed for long-range strikes against large combat ships such as aircraft carriers. In addition, it can be expected that the Type 093 will carry a range of other Russian and indigenous designed weapons. These might include the Russian Shkval rocket-propelled supercavitating torpedo or a new PLA-designed version of this weapon, and Novator Klub-S long-range antiship missiles. It is also likely that by the end of the decade that the Type 093 SSNs will be equipped with new PLA-designed LACMs.

As the United States considers truncating the planned thirty-ship production run for the SSN-774 *Virginia* in favor of more advanced SSNs,[73] it is necessary to consider that the PLAN may be developing advanced versions of the Type 093 or perhaps a new class of SSN for the early or middle part of the next decade. Russian success with Project 885 might allow a more rapid transfer of early versions of the advanced technologies developed for this class, if they have not been already sold to China. This possibility is also suggested by reports in early 2006 that Russia plans a new five-thousand- to six-thousand-ton SSN to counter the SSN 774.[74] PLA interest in UUVs and advanced cruise missiles may lead to their incorporation into subsequent SSNs.

Type 094 Jin SSBN

In 1997 ONI estimated that the first Type 094 SSBN would be ready by 2005,[75] while the Pentagon expected a launch "by the end of the decade."[76] The PLAN, however, exceeded these projections by launching the first Type 094 in July 2004.[77] In 1997 ONI estimated that three 094s would be completed by 2010, while other reports suggest that the PLA may build a total of three to four 094s.[78] Jane's expects the second Type 094 to be launched in 2006.[79]

Following the example of the relationship between the 091 SSN and the 092 Xia SSBN, it is expected that the 094 SSBN will be based on the new 093 SSN. As such, the 094 will also incorporate Russian design assistance from the 093. In 1997 ONI projected that the 094 would be equipped with sixteen tubes to carry the new JL-2 SLBM. But in 2004 ONI changed this projection to twelve JL-2 SLBMs, a number also reported by Jane's.[80] If the 2006 Internet-source photo of the Type 094 is correct, this may be the main projection for which ONI was correct. This photo shows the Jin to be an evolution of the Xia, but with a higher post-fin housing for the larger JL-2 SLBM. This photo, however, does not show the missiles farm to feature a slight separation as in the 2004 ONI projection. A Chinese source notes that the 094 may be quieter than Russia's most advanced SSBN, the Typhoon.[81] This projection, however, is contradicted by the 2006 photo, which shows the Jin to contain numerous water ports, which would tend to generate noise, especially at higher speeds.

While it does remain possible that the Jin has benefited from Russian internal quieting, propulsion, sonar, and combat systems, that cannot be ascertained from the 2006 photo. It must be considered, however, that China has attempted to gain access to some Russian fourth-generation submarine technologies to improve the Type 094. An advanced development of the Delta-IV SSBN, the Project 955 reportedly displaces fourteen thousand tons surfaced and may be capable of a maximum 450-meter dive depth. According to one report it does not use a new large spherical bow sonar array, but rather a version of the SKAT sonar array with 2 x 650mm and 4 x 533mm torpedo tubes placed above. Some illustrations of the Project 955 show that it employs two propeller screws, a feature that may enhance its combat survivability.[82]

Possible Purchase of Russian Oscar and Akula Submarines

While a possible sale of advanced Russian SSNs or SSGNs to China may be seen as a declining possibility as the PLAN succeeds in perfecting the Type 093 SSN, there are reasons to continue to search for relevant indications. As Russia has relaxed previous limits on selling strategic systems such as the Backfire bomber to China, it is possible that it may also consider selling whole SSNs or SSGNs, especially if that might aid Russia's submarine development by providing otherwise unavailable funds. Indications of the PLA's interest in this ship include reports that a PLA officer perished on the Russian Oscar II SSGN *Kursk* when it sank in August 2000 following an onboard explosion.[83]

A possible sale of the Akula II SSN to the PLAN is made more realistic by India's apparent decision to purchase two of these SSNs. Were that to occur, sale of the latest Akula II would provide an immediate boost to the PLAN's antisubmarine and antisurface capabilities. Currently the most modern SSN in Russian service, it is also among the most capable and effective SSNs in use today. The Akula II SSN's design is thought to have radiated noise levels lower than those of the U.S. SSN-688I class.[84] It incorporates active noise-reduction technology and is credited with a maximum operational dive depth of six hundred meters,[85] which is reported to be matched in the West only by the new SSN-21.[86] For emergency operations, however, the Akula II may be able to dive as deep as eight hundred meters.[87]

Russian Kilo 636/636M SSK

After buying two export-model Project 877EKM Kilo SSKs, the PLAN acquired two more advanced Project 636 Kilos, delivered in 1998 and 1999. The 636I incorporates significant improvements in quieting. These include elastic drive shaft couplings, a slower RPM skew-back seven-bladed propeller, and new sonar designed to monitor hull and propeller-generated noise.[88] The 636 is said to be almost as quiet as the U.S. 688-class SSN.[89] This version is also slightly larger, faster, and has a greater range than its predecessor.

A contract to purchase at least eight more Kilos was signed in May 2002.[90] To ensure their delivery by 2005–06, this batch of 636 Kilos were built in three Russian yards: five were to be built at the Admiralty Shipyards in St. Petersburg, one at Krasnoye Sormovo shipyard in Nizhny Novgorod, and two in Severodvinsk. In mid-2002 the decision to shift two Kilos from the Komsomolsk-na-Amur to Severdovinsk was criticized because the latter had not built diesel-electric submarines for forty years.[91] But by mid-2003, Kilo construction was underway at Severdovinsk.[92] Two from St. Petersburg were delivered to China by August 2005. All eight Kilos were delivered in 2006.

This new batch of Kilos likely consists of an improved model that could include most of the improvements slated for the 636M Kilo.[93] Expected improvements in the 636M may include increased missile stowage, an integrated weapon and machinery control system, an ability to launch larger missile salvos, upgraded digital sonar with mine-detection capabilities, improved target classification, non-hull-penetrating periscope and radar, better batteries, and eventually, perhaps, new fuel cells.[94]

This batch of eight 636M Kilos will be armed with the Klub-S antiship system comprised of three missiles. The 3M-54E uses a subsonic first stage that incorporates a rocket-propelled second stage, which is released twenty–sixty kilometers from the target. This second stage, then accelerates to Mach 3 to defeat ship defenses. A land-attack capability is provided by the three-hundred-kilometer-range 3M-14E, which uses radar for terminal guidance. A long-range antisubmarine strike capability is provided the by small 91RE1 torpedo, which has a maximum fifty-kilometer range.[95]

During the December 2003 visit of Defense Minister Cao Guangchuan, there were Russian reports that Moscow was considering selling the PLA the ability to co-produce up to twenty more conventional submarines.[96] While there have been no subsequent reports, as the current Kilo contract nears completion it is likely that Russia will seek follow-on orders. If there are such orders or co-production, it can be expected that Russia will offer further improvements such as new AIP systems, more advanced weapons, or provision for larger vertical-launched missiles.

Type 041 Yuan SSK

In May 2004 Wuhan Shipyard launched the first of a new class of SSK, the Yuan class.[97] A second was reportedly launched in December 2004. This SSK has also been called the "Chinese Amur"[98] due to its resemblance to the Russian Project 677 Lada/Amur-1650 class. This similarity is apparent in the Yuan's overall dimensional ratios, the shape of the sail, and the use by both of a step on top of the hull, which may indicate a single-hull configuration. The "step" on the hull is used to facilitate aft-sail placement for vertical-launched antiship missiles in other versions of the Amur. The Yuan also appears to exhibit the Russian preference for excess buoyancy for better combat survivability.

Much less is known about the Yuan's engine, quieting, combat system, and weapons system outfit. A Rubin promotional video viewed in early 2006 indicates the Lada has broadband acoustics significantly improved over the Kilo 636.[99] If there were substantial Russian input into the hull design, it would then follow that Russian systems may also dominate the rest of the submarine, with the possible exception of using co-produced German marine diesel engines. The precedent of using Russian components for new weapons is not unknown, as demonstrated by the PL-12 active-guided air-to-air missile and the Type 052B Luyang I DDG. There is also the possibility that such a transfer was enabled by Chinese financial support for the Lada, which began as a private venture by the Rubin Bureau to produce a less expensive SSK for littoral missions. The fact that both were launched in 2004 may indicate that China was buying components as they were being developed for the Lada.

Should the Yuan approximate the capability and mission of the Lada, this SSK may be the ultimate replacement for the Type 035 Ming, assuming the littoral missions to allow the Kilos to venture further out to sea. However, this may not be the case should it prove that future Yuans incorporate new AIP systems, as is often rumored. In that case, they may join the Kilos on more distant missions.

Type 039/039A Song SSK

The 2003 DoD PLA report notes, "The SONG is a blend of Chinese and Western technology and has several key features that point to a major shift in diesel submarine design philosophy."[100] In 1997, ONI estimated that the PLAN would have about six Song submarines by 2005 and close to ten by

2010.[101] Other projections indicate that twelve may be launched by 2005. A higher rate of production is possible now that the Song is being built in two shipyards, Wuhan and Shanghai (Jiangnan).

However, for a period in the mid- to late 1990s, this submarine's future was in doubt as the first Type 039/Song was reported to have dissatisfied the PLAN, because it was too noisy and failed to successfully integrate German MTU diesel engines, Israeli electronics, French sonar, and (possibly) Russian weapons.

Improved Type 039A submarines, perhaps with Russian help, are reported to have been more successful, especially in reducing radiated noise.[102] Pictures of a new Project 039 released by the PLA in 2001 showed that it lacks the distinctive step sail of the first 039, thereby improving hull-noise dynamics. The Type 039 resembles the French Agosta-90B-class conventional submarine but there is no open reporting that indicates that France provided any assistance. The 039 is armed with a Chinese-designed antiship missile based on the YJ-81 and potentially, the longer-range YJ-82. It may carry the new C43 PRC-made wire-guided torpedo and the Russian Test-71ME wire-guided torpedo.[103] Chinese television coverage of the 2004 visit of a Song to Hong Kong illustrated its extensive use of digital systems in the control room, which suggests the utilization of more modern automatic combat control systems.

Russian Torpedoes

As the PLA Navy has come to rely on Russian submarines and related technology to propel its modernization, it follows that it has purchased several new types of Russian torpedoes for its new submarines. Two Russian torpedoes that reportedly arm Kilo submarines are the Test-71ME and the Set-65KE.[104] Both are wire guided, allowing the crew to direct the torpedo based on targeting data gathered either by ship sonar or from sonar on the torpedo. These two Russian torpedoes have the capability to home in on a ship's wake. Inasmuch as the Kilo 636 is equipped to fire the heavy TE-2 wire-guided torpedoes from two of its launch tubes, it is very possible that PLAN has that weapon. The TE-2 has a deadly four-hundred-kilogram warhead, which would be effective against large ships like aircraft carriers or provide a greater single shot kill probability against a submarine. While the U.S. Navy has an active antitorpedo torpedo program, it has not yet fielded a system capable of defending ships from wake-homing torpedoes.

Possible Sale of Russian Mobile Sea Mines

When discussing trends in PLA submarine modernization, the 2003 Pentagon PLA report notes, "A second major improvement entails the use of advanced mobile mines to augment the Navy's large inventory of submarine-laid mines."[105] While the Pentagon was not specific, this could be a reference to the possible purchase by the PLA of Russian mobile and deep water anti-submarine mines. Mobile mines can refer to mines which travel horizontally, like torpedoes, to a pre-set distance, or moored mines which detach a torpedo when a target is within range. The PLA Navy possesses a large inventory of mines, including the indigenous EM-52 and EM-55, which are both moored rocket-propelled mines.[106] It also has a self-propelled mine with a range of more than thirteen kilometers. The PLAN would likely seek Russian mines with similar capabilities to complement its growing inventory of Kilo submarines. The PMK-2 is a deep-water moored mine designed primarily for antisubmarine missions. This could be laid by Kilo submarines in the likely approaches that U.S. submarines might take to reach Taiwan. In addition, Russian SMDM self-propelled mines would be useful for attacking well-defended ports from a stand-off distance.

China's Sale of Modern Submarine Technology

When considering the impact of foreign technology on China's submarines it is also important to consider how this will better enable future Chinese submarine sales to others. Since at least the September 2004 Pakistan IDEAS arms show, China Shipbuilding has been marketing the Type 039 Song-class SSK. At that show Pakistani navy officials noted that they would be considering Chinese designs in addition to European designs for their next class of conventional submarine.[107] As Pakistani is suspected of having shared crashed U.S. Tomahawk cruise missiles to better help China assist the development of its new Babur land attack cruise missile,[108] it is possible that Pakistan would share advanced French submarine technologies with China. France has sold Pakistan its new Mesma AIP system to be placed in the latest Agosta submarines now being built in Pakistan. Onward transfer of this technology could improve future versions of the Song and Yuan, or help China to develop countermeasures to French and other Western submarines.

In addition, one cannot discount that China might also sell nuclear submarine technologies. This is at least suggested by China's record of selling Pakistan nuclear-bomb, solid-fuel ballistic-missile, and cruise-missile technologies. Should Pakistan desire to match a future Indian SSN capability, it is possible that China would oblige. Other countries seeking to build nuclear-powered submarines, like Brazil[109] (which already has extensive space and satellite cooperation with China), could be tempted to turn to China for nuclear submarine technologies as well.

Conclusion

Foreign submarines and related technology, especially from Russia, have been critical to the PLAN's ongoing rapid transformation of its submarine combat capabilities. While relatively little is known about the degree of Russian assistance to China's new SSNs and SSBNs, the prospect that they may contain—now or in the future—significant fourth-generation Russian technology should cause concern in the West. When considering the future Chinese submarine challenge to the United States and its allies, beyond any specific foreign technology, one emerging trend that should spark particular concern is the possibility that China may move toward a more Russian-style submarine design system featuring greater internal competition. This served to accelerate late Cold War Soviet submarine performance, and could similarly accelerate China's indigenous conventional and nuclear submarine development.

However, despite China's current dependence on foreign submarine technologies and influence, China's objective is to become an innovator or leader in submarine technology. Though a decade ago as the PLAN struggled with its SSK and SSN programs this prospect may have seemed distant, it would be unwise to underestimate China's determination to succeed or the willingness of China's current leadership to marshal the necessary resources. By mastering Russian technologies that may be associated with its third- or even fourth-generation submarines, it is possible that China could produce world-class submarines based largely on indigenous technologies within a decade. Mastery of advanced SSN and SSBN doctrine and operations is another matter, but given time and resources the PLAN will make rapid progress there as well.

Notes

1. While a full assessment of the impact of foreign technology on China's submarine modernization is limited by the paucity of open sources, the existing open data do allow for the assemblage of a rough estimate of conditions and trends. Of specific use have been public statements by the U.S. intelligence community, both in the

annual U.S. Department of Defense reports on the PLA and less frequent statements by the U.S. Office of Naval Intelligence, reports in the defense media, and interview data gathered by the author. This paper also builds on the author's previous study, *The Impact of Foreign Weapons and Technology On The Modernization of the People's Liberation Army, A Report for the U.S.-China Economic and Security Review Commission,* January 2004, http://www.uscc.gov/researchpapers/2004/04fisher_report/04_01_01fisherreport.htm.

2. For further background on China's recent submarine growth, see Lyle Goldstein and Bill Murray, "China's Subs Lead The Way," *U.S. Naval Institute Proceedings,* March 2003, 58–61; and "Undersea Dragons, China's Maturing Undersea Force," *International Security,* Spring 2004.

3. Charles Snyder, "Navy officer warns of Chinese subs," *Taipei Times,* July 27, 2004, 3.

4. As of 2006 the USN operates fifty-four SSNs. Future SSN force levels are uncertain, but are estimated to range from forty-five to thirty-seven. See Christopher P. Cavas, "U.S. Navy Lays Out 30-Year Fleet Plan," *Defense News* (March 28, 2005): 1; Bryan Bender, "Navy Eyes Cutting Submarine Force," *Boston Globe,* May 12, 2004.

5. You Ji, *The Armed Forces Of China* (London: IB Tauris, 1999), 164–65; Cole also considers the possibility of the PLAN's adopting a Bastion-like strategy if its Type 094 SSBN is successful, see Bernard D. Cole, *The Great Wall at Sea: China's Navy Enters the Twenty-First Century* (Annapolis, Md.: Naval Institute Press, 2001), 168–69.

6. Prasun Sengupta, "Full Steam Ahead," April 12, 2005, *Foreign Broadcast Information Service (FBIS),* Journal Code: 9302

7. A possible realistic estimate of a 5,400 NMI range for the JL-2 is graphically illustrated by the Office of Naval Intelligence, *Worldwide Maritime Challenges 2004,* 37.

8. Massimo Annati, "UUVs and AUVs Come of Age," *Military Technology* (June 2005): 72–78.

9. "Japan Eyeing Radar System to Defend U.S. From Missiles," *Asahi Shimbun,* October 18, 2005.

10. The Yulin nuclear submarine facility was first disclosed to the author as an underground nuclear submarine base by Asian officials in late 2002. The existence of this facility was subsequently confirmed by officials from two other Asian countries. In late 2004 the facility's existence was further confirmed to the author by a PLA General, who described it as an above-ground nuclear submarine facility. In early 2005 Internet-source photos showed a Han-class SSN visiting a South Sea Fleet base, presumed to be Yulin. This has also been reported to be an "underwater" base as well, see Sengupta, op. cit. In early 2006 the author was also able to view this new base on Google Earth, and confirmed that this facility did include a structure consistent with the opening for an underground submarine pen.

11. Interview with the author, November 2005.

12. Hualien has an international port, and is also nearby large underground air force basing facilities that could also support SSBN and SSN missions. In addition, the

often sheer rock coastal formations in this region may facilitate underground SSN/ SSBN basing. The PLA has significant experience in tunneling to create revetments.

13. Disclosed to the author by a PLA officer in November 2004.

14. Chin Chien-li, "PRC is preparing to form a space force," *Chien Shao*, July 1, 2005, 52–55; "China's 'Space Army' Is Taking Shape," *Hsiang Kang Shang Pao* (October 13, 2005): 4.

15. Under the names KT-1 (DF-21), KT-2 (DF-31), and KT-2A (DF-31A), these mobile land-based SLVs were marketed at the 2002 and 2004 Zhuhai Airshows.

16. Liu Huanyu, Dalian Naval Academy, "Sea-Based Anti-Satellite Platform," *Jianchuan Kexue Jishu* [Ship Science & Technology], February 1, 2004.

17. Interview, August 2005.

18. Russia's NPO Mashinostroyenia has sold China its >1m resolution KONDOR series of e/o and radar satellites, eight of which could be lofted by 2010, and at the 2002 Zhuhai Airshow the China Aerospace Corporation revealed two data-relay satellite designs.

19. Yihong Chang, "Is China Building a Carrier?" *Jane's Defence Weekly*, August 17, 2005; Vladimir Dzaguto, "From the Varyag into a Target," *Vremya Novostey*, October 18, 2005; interviews, Moscow Airshow, August 2005.

20. Interviews with the author, October and November 2004.

21. In a similar manner, the PLA's aircraft design sector benefited greatly from the adoption of the French Dassault CATIA computer-aided design and computer-aided modeling programs.

22. "094 Project Makes New Progress," *Kanwa Defense Review* (March 1, 2005): 3.

23. The importance to the Chinese of both open-source and espionage-gathered information on nuclear submarines, from the late 1950s onward, is amply illustrated in chapter three of John Wilson Lewis and Xue Litai, *China's Strategic Seapower* (Stanford Calif.: Stanford University Press, 1994), 47–73.

24. "Former Defense Agency Official Leaks Intelligence—Shadow of Subtle Chinese Espionage Activities," *Tokyo Shimbun*, April 26, 2005.

25. "Russian Customs Seize Submarine Being Exported to China for Scrap," *Agentstvo Voyennykh Novostey*, May 5, 2005.

26. Bill Gertz, "Four Arrests Linked to Chinese Spy Ring," *The Washington Times*, November 5, 2005; Greg Hardesty, "Spy Suspects Blended in, the FBI Believes Four In-Laws Were Involved in Stealing Information from an Anaheim Defense Contractor to Deliver to China," *The Orange County Register*, November 11, 2005.

27. "Money from Sea Depths, Submarines for Export," October 2005, http://www.kommersant.com/page.asp?idr=529&id=614878.

28. "Russia Helps China Take New SSNs into Silent Era," *Jane's Defence Weekly*, August 13, 1997, 14.

29. U.S. Office of Naval Intelligence, *Worldwide Submarine Challenges,* Washington, DC: U.S. Government Printing Office, February 1997, 23.

30. Report to Congress Pursuant to the FY2000 National Defense Authorization Act, *Annual Report on the Military Power of the People's Republic of China,* July 28, 2003, 27, hereafter called "DoD PLA Report, 2003," http://www.defenselink.mil/pubs/20030730chinaex.pdf.

31. *Worldwide Maritime Challenges 2004,* op. cit.

32. "CIA Report Reviews Weapons Proliferation Trends," http://www.cia.gov/cia/reports/721_reports/jan_jun2003.htm.

33. Norman Polmar and Kenneth J. Moore, *Cold War Submarines: The Design and Construction of U.S. and Soviet Submarines, 1945–2001* (Dulles, Va.: Potomac Books, Inc., 2003), 319.

34. Ibid.

35. *Worldwide Maritime Challenges 2004,* op. cit.; "Type 094 Class (SSBN)," *Jane's Fighting Ships Internet Edition,* posted 03 August 2005; Polmar and Moore, 319–21.

36. For example, in the early 1990s Russia refused to sell the Tupolev Tu-22M3 Backfire to China, but in August 2005 was reportedly in the middle of negotiations to sell this bomber to China.

37. This is an oft-heard refrain from Russians at numerous arms shows.

38. "Russia in a Hurry to Sell Arms to China," December 18, 2003.

39. The first Project 677 St Petersburg was reportedly inspected by the Chinese in mid-2005; see "Conference Announces Kilo-Class Subs Remain Russia's Top Naval Export," *ITAR-TASS,* July 1, 2005.

40. "China to Remain Largest Russian Arms Importer in Coming Years," *Interfax,* July 17, 2000; Pavel Felgenhauer, "No One Is Fooled by MND," *Moscow Times,* May 31, 2001; "Official says improved Russia-West ties have no effect on arms trade with China," *Moscow Agentstvo Voyennykh Novostey,* May 31, 2002 in FBIS, CEP20020531000249.

41. See Richard Fisher, Jr., "Military Sales to China: Going to Pieces," *Jamestown Foundation China Brief,* November 21, 2002.

42. The Malachite bureau was promoting both fuel-cell- and chemical-based AIP systems at the 2004 IDEX show while the Rubin bureau is promoting a fuel-cell-based AIP system for the new Lada/Amur SSK. Rubin has in the past offered hull-plug AIP insert modifications.

43. "094 Project Makes New Progress," *Kanwa Defense Review* (March 1, 2005): 3.

44. Robert Karniol, "China Buys Shkval Torpedo from Kazakhstan," *Jane's Defence Review* (August 26, 1998): 26.

45. Interview, Taiwan, December 2001.

46. Novator officials confirmed that China was a customer for the CLUB-S system at the 2005 Moscow Airshow.

47. "Solana says lifting of China arms embargo on long-term agenda," *Agence France Presse,* September 6, 2005.

48. Interview, November 2002.

49. Announcement, Second Sino-German Workshop on Fuel Cells, April 13–15, 2003, Guenzburg, Germany, http://www.zsw-bw.de/FuelCellWorkshop/general.php.

50. Joris Jansen Lok, "Germany's Submarines Combine Export Success with Propulsion Progress," *Jane's International Defense Review* (January 2002): 49.

51. Annati, "UUVs and AUVs Come of Age," 78–80.

52. In 2004 a German woman resident in Canada who was hired to translate weapons control documents related to the Type 212 was arrested in a Canadian counterintelligence "sting" after she offered to sell the documents to the Chinese embassy in Canada. The incident at least suggests knowledge of China's interest in the Type 212 by her German employers, see "German translator in Chinese espionage scandal involving the world's first fuel cell submarine," *Deutsch Presse Agentur,* December 15, 2004.

53. Hendrik Goesman, "Neue U-Boot Technologie," *Strategie und Technik,* October 2005.

54. Gertz, "Four Arrests Linked to Chinese Spy Ring."

55. Polmar and Moore, *Cold War Submarines,* 173, 285.

56. Lewis and Xue, *China's Strategic Seapower,* 56–57.

57. For example, see "Shape-memory alloys," *Binqi Zhishi* [*Ordnance Knowledge*], (September 2004): 75, which describes how the U.S. Navy may use this novel technology to move rudder/elevator functions to the propulsor shroud on SSN-774 class submarines, and that a full scale system may be available in 2007.

58. For U.S. submarine aspirations, see Mark Hewish, "Submarines to cast off their shackles, take on new roles," *Jane's International Defence Review* (March 2002): 35–43; Andrew Koch, "US Considers Alternative Submarine Propulsions," *Jane's Defence Weekly* (October 8, 2003): 6.

59. DoD PLA Report 2003, 27.

60. Interview, April 2004.

61. Interview, November 2005.

62. DoD PLA Report, 2003, 27.

63. Hui Tong, "093," *Chinese Military Aviation,* http://mil.jschina.com.cn/huitong/han_xia_kilo_song.htm.

64. A. D. Baker, *The Naval Institute Guide to Combat Fleets of the World: Their Ships, Aircraft, and Systems* (Annapolis, Md.: Naval Institute Press, 2002).

65. "Russia Helps China Take New SSNs into Silent Era," *Jane's Defence Weekly* (August 13, 1997) 14.

66. Artist projections of the Project 093 and 094 appeared in the PRC naval magazine *Guoji Zhanwang* and were viewed on the Internet in late 2000.

67. This possibility is reported by Anatoly Efimovich Taras, *Atomic Submarines, 1955–2005* (unknown Russian publisher), 2005, 194, viewed on the *Key Forum*, http://forum.keypublishing.co.uk/showthread.php?p=818044#post818044.

68. Rupert Pengelley, "Grappling for Submarine Supremacy," *Jane's International Defense Review* (July 1996) 51.

69. This estimate is provided by Polmar and Moore, *Cold War Submarines*, 319.

70. "Pumpjet Possibility for Russia's Private-Venture Amur," *Jane's International Defence Review* (February 1997): 19.

71. "Victor III (Project 671RTM(K))," IMDS 2003, International Maritime Defense Show, St. Petersburg, 25–29 June; see also Vladimir Shcherbakov, "Soviet Underwater Predators: A Story of the Victor Family Attack Submarines," *Arms Defense Technology Review (Moscow)*, 2 (15) 2003, 38.

72. Jian Je, "Shenhou Zhong de Xuangzi Zuo" (Myth of the Twins), *Guoji Zhanwang* (August 2002): 23, cited in Lyle Goldstein and Bill Murray, "China's Subs Lead the Way," *United States Naval Institute Proceedings* (March 2003): 59.

73. Andrew Koch, "Funding Curb Forces Virginia Reality Check," *Jane's Defence Weekly* (January 26, 2005): 4.

74. "Russia to build next generation submarine," *Xinhuanet*, February 8, 2006.

75. U.S. Office of Naval Intelligence, *Worldwide Submarine Challenges*.

76. DoD PLA Report, 2003, 31.

77. Bill Gertz, "China Tests Ballistic Missile Submarine," *The Washington Times*, December 3, 2004.

78. Hui Tong, "094," *Chinese Military Aviation*, http://mil.jschina.com.cn/huitong/han_xia_kilo_song.htm.

79. "Type 094 Class (SSBN)," *Jane's Fighting Ships Internet Edition*, posted 3 August 2005.

80. Ibid.

81. "Zhongwai He Qianting Bijiao" (A Comparison of Chinese and Foreign Nuclear Submarines), *Jianchuan Zhishi* (September 1998): 30, cited in Goldstein and Murray, "China's Subs Lead the Way."

82. Taras, *Atomic Submarines, 1955–2005*.

83. Steven Ashley, "Warpdrive Underwater," *Scientific American*, May 2001, 79.

84. Polmar and Moore, *Cold War Submarines*, 319.

85. "Akula (Project 971)," IMDS 2003, International Maritime Defense Show, St. Petersburg 25–29 June, 17.

86. David Miller, *Submarines of the World* (St. Paul, Minn.: MBI Publishing, 2002), 382.

87. A. D. Baker III, *Combat Fleets of the World, 2002–2003* (Annapolis, Md.: U.S. Naval Institute Press, 2002).

88. Rubin brochure.

89. Rupert Pengelly, "Grappling for Submarine Supremacy," *Jane's International Defense Review* (July 1996): 51.

90. "Russia, China 'Satisfied' With Joint Military Commission Meeting," *Interfax,* June 1, 2002, in FBIS, CEP20020601000050; "China Major Buyer of Russian Arms," *ITAR-TASS,* May 29, 2002, in FBIS, CEP20020529000144.

91. Mikhail Khodarenok, "Underwater Scandal," *Nezavisimaya Gazeta,* June 7, 2002, 6.

92. Vladimir Anufriyev, "Russia Inaugurates Construction of Submarines for China," *ITAR-TASS,* June 3, 2003, in FBIS, CEP20030603000328.

93. John Dikkenberg, "Regional Submarines: Just How Good Are the Kilos," *Asia-Pacific Defence Reporter* (November 2002): 17.

94. Ibid.

95. Military Parade, *Russia's Naval Ships, Armament and Equipment* (Moscow, 2006): 101–3; Novator brochures.

96. "Russia in a Hurry To Sell Arms to China," December 18, 2003.

97. Bill Gertz, "Chinese Produce New Type of Sub," *The Washington Times,* July 16, 2004; "YUAN (Type 041) (SSK)," *Jane's Fighting Ships Internet Edition,* posted 03 August 2005.

98. Term coined by Yihong Chang, see "Kanwa's Appraisal of New Chinese Submarine," *Kanwa Defense Review* (March 1, 2005): 13–14.

99. Rubin video viewed by author at the DEFEXP, New Delhi, February 2006.

100. DoD PLA Report, 2003, 21.

101. U.S. Office of Naval Intelligence, *Worldwide Submarine Challenges.*

102. Glen Levick, "China," in *Asian Navies Overview,* www.warships1.com, updated March 2000.

103. Mark Farrer, "Submarine force in change—the People's Republic of China"; *Kanwa News,* March 11, 1999.

104. Goldstein and Murray, "China's Subs Lead the Way," 58.

105. DoD PLA Report, 2003, 26.

106. The EM-52 is mentioned in the "Future Military Capabilities and Strategy of the People's Republic of China," Report to Congress pursuant to Section 1226 of the FY98 National Defense Authorization Act (Washington, D.C.: Department of Defense, November 1998), available at http://www.fas.org/news/china/1998/981100-prc-dod.htm.

107. Press Conference, IDEAS, Karachi, Pakistan, September 2004.

108. Robert Hewson and Andrew Koch, "Pakistan Tests Cruise Missile," *Jane's Defence Weekly* (August 17, 2005).

109. Pedro Paulo Rezende, "Brazil Closer to Fielding SSN," *Jane's Defence Weekly* (September 14, 2005).

Peter A. Dutton

International Law and the November 2004 "Han Incident"

A SUBMERGED HAN-CLASS NUCLEAR-POWERED SUBMARINE of the Chinese People's Liberation Army Navy (PLAN) entered Japanese territorial waters during the early morning hours of November 10, 2004, and passed submerged at about one hundred meters as it "wandered" in Japanese territorial waters for about two hours before exiting into international waters.[1] Moving from south to north, the submarine passed through the Ishigaki Strait, which separates the islands of Ishigaki and Miyako at the southwestern edge of Japan's Sakishima island chain.[2] The submarine was on its return to Meigezhuang Naval Base near Qingdao from its operating area in the Philippine Sea.

While the submarine was still operating well south of Japanese waters, the Japanese Maritime Self-Defense Force (JMSDF) was perhaps tipped to the presence of the submarine from U.S. Navy intelligence sources, and the JMSDF began passive tracking of the submarine and monitoring of its activities.[3] The Japanese continued to monitor the Han passively as it operated in international waters south of Ishigaki Island, but when the submarine turned north toward Japanese territorial waters, Japanese aircraft began using active sonar—which uses echoes from an emitted signal to provide trackers with a more precise location of their target submarine, and which is accepted among submariners as a warning signal.[4] The submarine chose to ignore the warning and kept on its northward path through the strait.

As a result of the submarine's incursion, the JMSDF was put on an unusually high-level alert by order of the defense agency director, General Yoshinori Ono, for only the second time since the end of World War II.[5] The JMSDF maintained track of the Han as it passed through the Strait and, once the alert order was issued, began more aggressive tracking of the Han in international waters until the submarine passed well beyond the Japanese coastline.[6] During this period the JMSDF tracked the submarine for more than two days with P-3C patrol planes, AWACS aircraft, and ASW-capable destroyers and SH-60J helicopters.[7]

The intriguing aspect of this incident is not that the Chinese chose to send a submarine through the Ishigaki Strait—for many reasons, maritime states with submarine fleets occasionally send their submarines on under-water excursions into another country's territorial waters.[8] Nor perhaps, in a region increasingly tense over economic rights, maritime boundaries, and political maneuvering, should Japan's assertive response have come as much of a surprise to anyone. What makes the Han's incursion especially inter-esting are the international law implications of the submarine's submerged passage through Japanese territorial waters and the strategic insights that attend them.

What Are the International Law Implications?

The Southwest Ryukyu Islands are Japan's westernmost outpost, strategi-cally located to protect Japan's maritime economic interests in the East China Sea from Chinese encroachment. The islands of Ishigaki and Miyako lie at approximately 24°30′ north latitude between approximately 124° and 125° east longitude (see Chart 1). They are relatively small islands, situated approx-imately one hundred nautical miles off the northeast coast of Taiwan and twelve hundred nautical miles southwest of Tokyo, with a combined land mass of less than three hundred square miles.

The water between the islands is bisected by tiny Tarama Island, which lies 18.2 nautical miles from Ishigaki Island and almost exactly 24 nautical miles from Miyako Island, in waters in which small coral islands and reefs abound.[9] It was through a relatively deep-water trench of Japanese waters that lies between Ishigaki and Tarama that the Han passed.

Under the United Nations Convention on the Law of the Sea (UNCLOS),

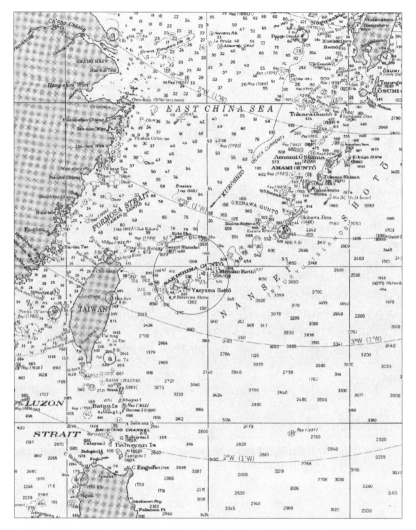

Chart 1. The southwestern Ryukyu Islands, depicted inside the circle, are a gateway to and from the resource-rich contested waters of the East China Sea. Source: U.S. Defense Mapping Agency WOPGN522.

coastal states have the right to establish sovereignty over adjacent waters out to a maximum of twelve nautical miles from the nation's coastline, including the coastline of offshore islands. These enclosed waters are known as the coastal state's territorial sea.[10] In 1996, the Japanese Government enacted a Territorial Sea Law that established its claim of sovereignty to the twelve-nautical-mile band of coastal waters around most of its shore line—including the Ishigaki, Tarama, and Miyako Islands—but claimed a lesser breadth for strategic reasons in five other key straits.[11]

In return for the expansion of sovereign control over waters that were formerly open to use by all states, UNCLOS provides seagoing states with certain rights of access. For instance, ships have the right of "innocent passage" through territorial seas. Innocent passage is generally the continuous and expeditious traversing through another state's territorial waters, for the purpose of passage, in a manner that is not prejudicial to the peace, good order, or security of the coastal state.[12] These broad terms are, of course, subject to significant variations of interpretation from one coastal state to the next, but UNCLOS does provide some specificity: without the permission of the coastal state, collection of intelligence and conducting research or survey activities are express violations of innocent passage.[13] Additionally, submarines exercising innocent passage are required to navigate on the surface and to show their flag.[14]

Another navigation regime, known as "transit passage," applies where opposing coastlines are situated twenty-four nautical miles apart or less. In these waters, known as international straits, the territorial sea claims of the coastal state or states overlap or abut to "close off" the strait of water between them, such that no corridor of international waters with high-seas freedoms remains between the opposing coasts. In these international straits, unlike in other territorial waters, all ships have the right to continuous and expeditious transit in the normal mode of operation. The normal mode of operation provides ships with much broader operating rights than in innocent passage and includes the right of submarines to pass through the strait submerged.[15] Transit passage applies in these straits as long as the strait connects two areas of high-seas freedoms, as is the case with the waters of the Ishigaki Strait between Ishigaki and Tarama Islands.[16]

In addition to the requirement that the strait connect two areas of high-seas freedoms, some states—Japan is one of them—apply an additional requirement before acknowledging a right of transit passage, including the right of submarines to pass through the strait submerged.[17] The Japanese look to UNCLOS language that specifies that transit passage "applies to straits which are used for international navigation,"[18] and recognize a right of transit passage only in those straits actually used for international navigation,[19] rather than in all straits capable of use for international navigation. This distinction is critical to understanding the assertive nature of the Japanese response to the presence of a submerged Chinese submarine in the Ishigaki Strait. The Japanese view is that a route of similar convenience in international waters applies to the west, between Ishigaki and Taiwan, making international transit through Japanese waters unnecessary and thereby nullifying the route between Ishigaki and Miyako as an international strait with rights of submerged passage for submarines.

The only definitive international law guidance concerning the rights of passage in an international strait is the 1949 Corfu Channel Case[20] involving a dispute between the United Kingdom and Albania over the right of British war ships to pass unhindered through the narrow waters between the Island of Corfu and the Albanian coastline. The case was heard before the International Court of Justice (ICJ), which determined that Albania could not hinder the passage of the British war ships through the Corfu channel because the strait's "geographical situation as connecting two parts of the high seas and the fact of its being used for international navigation," provided ships the right of passage as a matter of customary international law.[21]

In developing its policy concerning transit passage, the Japanese government relied on the language "used for international navigation" found in both the Corfu Channel case and in UNCLOS, and reasoned that only if the strait is routinely used for international navigation should the transit passage regime apply. The ICJ considered and specifically rejected an argument similar to Japan's position. Albania argued that for the right of unimpeded passage to apply, the strait must be "a necessary route between two parts of the high seas"; however, it was sufficient for the Court that the Corfu channel was merely "a useful route for international maritime traffic."[22] As might be expected, even the meaning of "useful route" is open to debate and interpretation. Maritime powers generally favor a broad interpretation of the term useful route and apply a right of transit passage to any qualifying strait capable of navigation by any international shipping—merchant or military—since the widest possible freedom of action is in the interest of such maritime powers. Contrarily, coastal nations with a sense of vulnerability from the sea naturally favor a much more restrictive view of the term useful route and acknowledge transit passage rights only in the relatively few world straits through which international shipping is routine and no other route of similar convenience is available, such as the straits of Gibraltar and Hormuz.

Perhaps not surprisingly, Japan, as an island state that has fought at sea with three major powers over the last century, advocates for the more restrictive application of the right of transit passage. As evidence of Japan's attempt to avoid a robust international right to transit passage between its islands, when the Japanese Government extended sovereignty over its coastal waters it took great pains to avoid creating international straits in areas where transit passage would apply under either definition. In the five international straits clearly affected by even the restrictive approach—the Tsushima Strait (in the waters between the Southern Island of Kyushu and the Korean peninsula, depicted in Chart 2), the Osumi Strait (between Kyushu and smaller islands off the coast), the La Perouse or Soya Strait (the northernmost strait between Hokkaido and Russia's Sakhalin peninsula), and the Tsugaru Strait (between Hokkaido and Honshu)—Japan limited its territorial sea claims to less than twelve nautical miles in order to leave a band of international waters with high seas freedoms sufficient for ships to pass without having to rely on a right of transit passage.[23]

Accordingly, from Japan's perspective, the Chinese Han-class submarine in submerged passage in the waters between Ishigaki-Shima and Tarama-Jima was in violation of Japan's sovereignty because it had no right to claim transit passage through those waters, which, though clearly capable of supporting international navigation, are not normally used for such purpose.

The United States does not accept the Japanese perspective that there are only five potential international straits through Japanese territorial waters. As a state with extensive maritime interests, and for which access to the world's oceans is critical to maintaining its national security, the United States has long interpreted UNCLOS and the Corfu Channel Case to mean that transit passage applies in all straits susceptible of international navigation.[24] This is a crucial distinction, in that under the U.S. definition every strait that is enclosed in territorial waters, but which connects two areas of high-seas freedoms, is fair game for transit passage of U.S. merchants and warships in the normal mode of operation—including submerged submarines. This vastly increases access to and through the world's littorals when compared with the restrictive Japanese views.

Like Japan, the PRC has long held the position that transit passage rights apply in only a very few international straits worldwide. This view is expressed in its PLA publication on international law for military officers, which says that the category of "straits for international navigation" is very narrow and only includes "those that straddle important international sea lanes" and which, through historical use or as evidenced by international

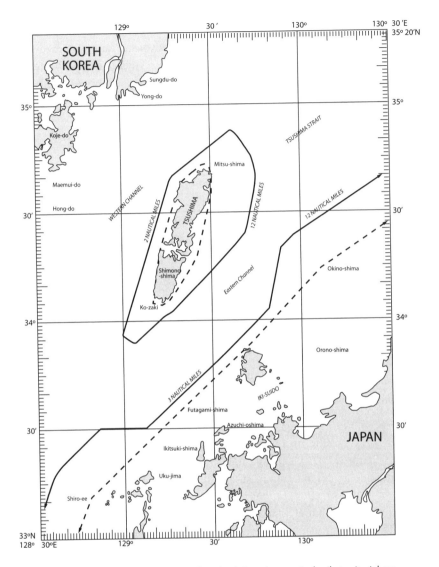

Chart 2.   The Japanese claimed less than the full twelve nautical mile territorial sea around Tsushima Island in order to channel international traffic in a high seas corridor. Source: *Limits in the Seas*, no. 120, *Straight Baseline and Territorial Sea Claims: Japan.* United States Department of State, Bureau of Oceans and International Environmental and Scientific Affairs (1998).

treaties, have "important implications for the national interests of certain countries."[25] Indeed, the language in which this section of PRC military guidance is written, while acknowledging that some straits are "open to international navigation," glosses over the UNCLOS right of transit passage and instead emphasizes the importance of coastal state sovereignty and jurisdiction over the waters in an international strait.[26]

Despite China's steady rise as a maritime power with substantial commercial and military interests at sea, during and after the diplomatic furor over the discovery of the submerged Han in Japanese waters the PRC remained officially wedded to its traditional restrictive right of transit passage. In response to the Japanese demands for a Chinese apology for the presence of the Han sub, the PRC officially "regretted" the intrusion, rather than moving its stance toward a broader right of transit passage.

If the PRC never intended to take this opportunity to shift its official position on the right of transit passage, why would the Chinese PLA Navy send an easily detected submarine through waters where, by its own doctrine and policy it acknowledges the submarine had no right to be? Han-class submarines are known to be fairly noisy and therefore easily detected, and this one passed through Japanese waters at the relatively shallow depth of less than one hundred meters.[27] Additionally, with PRC president Hu Jintao and Japanese prime minister Junichiro Koizumi scheduled to meet for a one-on-one side-summit at the Asia-Pacific Economic Cooperation Forum in Chile just days after the incident, why provoke the Japanese during the important weeks before the meetings?[28] Several possibilities suggest themselves—all of them instructive of the strategic implications of China's rise as a naval power.

The Strategic Implications of the "Han Incident"

The Incursion May Indeed Have Been Unauthorized or Due to a "Technical Reason"

The official explanation for the incident was that the submarine was returning from a routine patrol and blundered through the strait because of poor navigation stemming from a "technical reason." The explanation of navigational error, although officially accepted by Japan in order to diffuse political tensions, is implausible on its face. A glance at any chart of these waters makes clear that for the Han to pass through the Ishigaki Strait, it would have to have been fully seventy-five to one hundred nautical miles off a course that would have made its intended northern passage either between the islands of Taiwan and Ishigaki, or in the corridor of international waters southwest of Okinawa. On the contrary, the JMSDF track of the Han indicated that it passed through the strait cleanly, without noticeable navigational difficulty, and the submarine appeared as though it was piloted by someone familiar with the waters in that area.[29]

Additionally, all submarines operating in littoral waters use fathometers to measure depth. In this area there are ample underwater indications that, if the submarine were seriously off course, would alert the submarine commander to the danger. The applicable navigation chart, for instance, shows that the distance between the two-thousand-and-one-thousand-fathom-depth curves in the region of the strait is substantially shorter than in other waters through which the submarine might have intended to pass—the distance between curves is approximately ten nautical miles in the vicinity of the strait, as opposed to nearly fifty nautical miles elsewhere (see Chart 3). This unexpectedly rapid loss of water depth would have alerted the commander to course concerns and of possible grounding among the islands and their many coral reefs.[30] Had the submarine had actual concerns about its location or ability to navigate safely, it would have made a wide course correction well out to sea—certainly before it crossed the one thousand fathom curve just off Ishigaki Island. Clearly, the PRC story about navigational error and technical difficulties was a face-saving cover. Other more likely reasons for the submarine's decision to make passage through the Ishigaki Strait—and the Japanese response—have both legal and strategic significance.

The Action Could Have Been a Covert Mapping Exercise

For years the U.S. has been aware that the PLAN has been exploring various undersea routes through which to move its submarines into the central Pacific in the event of conflict over Taiwan.[31] By some reports, recent relaxations in trade and technology restrictions have allowed China to purchase advanced oceanographic mapping systems that allow it to make sophisticated maps of the ocean floor. These maps could be very useful to the PRC submarine force in the event of war over the status of Taiwan. Additionally, the maps could be useful in exploring the seabed for suitable locations to drill and explore for gas and oil. On these bases, some have suggested that the Han's passage was the latest excursion in a sustained effort to map the sea floor in the East China Sea and the approaches to it. Bolstering this perspective is the fact that after the submarine left Japanese territorial waters, the submarine was tracked passing through a disputed area of the East China

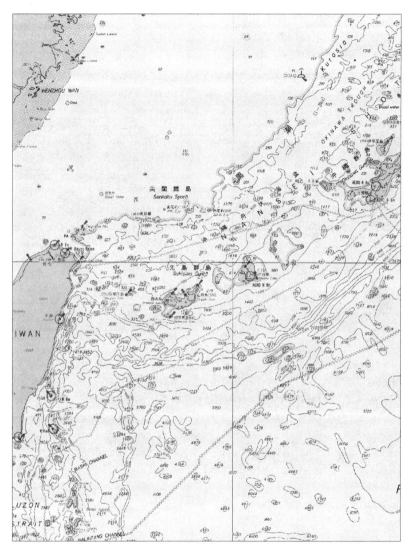

Chart 3.   The waters to the east and west of the Ishigaki Strait have dramatically different depth curves than the Strait itself, which would have alerted a submarine commander that he was off course. Source: U.S. Defense Mapping Agency INT509.

Sea in which China has an ongoing gas-exploration project that Japan considers an affront to its own claims.

If it is the case that the submarine was mapping Japanese territorial waters without Japan's permission or performing economic research in a disputed area, the PRC has some explaining to do. UNCLOS provides that "coastal states, in the exercise of their sovereignty, have the exclusive right to regulate, authorize and conduct marine scientific research in their territorial sea."[32] Furthermore, UNCLOS provides that "during transit passage, foreign ships . . . may not carry out any research or survey activities" without the prior consent of the coastal State, including hydrographic surveys.[33]

UNCLOS takes an equally stern stance regarding such activities during either innocent passage or transit passage. Concerning innocent passage, UNCLOS provides that "passage of a foreign ship shall be considered prejudicial to the peace, good order or security of the coastal State if in the territorial sea it engages in any act aimed at collecting information to the prejudice of the defense of the coastal State or the carrying out of research or survey activities."[34] UNCLOS also applies this prohibition to territorial waters covered by international straits by stating that "any activity which is not an exercise of the right of transit passage through a strait remains subject to the other applicable provisions of the Convention."[35]

Indeed, China itself gets rather prickly over just this issue—even in waters well away from its territorial sea. In March 2000 and again in September 2002, PLAN warships directed the USNS *Bowditch*—an unarmed oceanographic research vessel manned by twenty-five civilians—to exit an area of international waters well outside Chinese territorial waters in the Yellow Sea in which the *Bowditch* was performing hydrographic-performance acoustic data tests.[36] Such tests are performed using sonarlike equipment to determine the salinity, temperature, existence of currents, and other water characteristics that affect the movement of sound under the surface. The collected data is useful in tracking submarines, but is just as useful to submarines intent on avoiding detection. The waters in which the tests were being performed were within the PRC exclusive economic zone, but international law provides all states the right to exercise high-seas freedoms including conducting scientific research such as hydrographic surveys.[37] China's Foreign Ministry spokeswoman at the time refused to specify her country's specific basis for requiring *Bowditch* to depart, and cited only her state's "relevant rights" in the exclusive economic zone as a basis for the PLAN's actions.[38] Thus, comparing the two incidents, if indeed the Han's passage through the Ishigaki Strait was for the purpose of collecting hydrographic or intelligence data, then China's decision to send a submarine submerged through Japan's territorial waters was especially surprising, inasmuch as it performed in the territorial waters of Japan activities that by its own interpretation of international maritime law it would not countenance much further from its own shores in its exclusive economic zone.

International law does not leave states without legitimate remedies for true violations. UNCLOS provides that a coastal state has the right to "take the necessary steps in its territorial sea to prevent passage which is not innocent."[39] It also states that coastal states that discover warships in noncompliance with coastal state laws and regulations concerning passage through the territorial sea can request that the ship come into compliance and, if the ship does not, the coastal state may require it to leave the territorial sea immediately.[40] Additionally, the right of diplomatic protest preserves the coastal state's position on the state of the law. These remedies must of course be interpreted in light of the coastal state's right to use force in self-defense in response to an armed attack, but the clear intent of UNCLOS and international law is to avoid escalatory actions by coastal states toward nonhostile warships in their waters.

Put in this light, the submerged passage of the Han through the Ishigaki Strait, where it stood a reasonable chance of being detected by the Japanese, was counterproductive to the PRC's efforts to establish that a coastal state has relevant rights it may enforce by excluding others from information-gathering off its coasts. Additionally, since state practice is a primary source of international law, if China's purpose for the Han was to gather intelligence about the waters and sea bed in the Ishigaki Strait, then its own naval practices have defeated China's larger strategic purpose of advancing and shaping the law in favor of coastal state control over coastal waters.

The PLAN Was Demonstrating Its Sea Power

It is conceivable that the Chinese directed the submarine's submerged passage through Japanese waters as an intentional provocation to demonstrate to Japan and the United States the extent of the PRC's sea power and blue-water operations capability, and possibly to test the military response capabilities of the Japanese.[41] To the United States, China's message has consistently been to refrain from military support for Taiwan.[42] To Japan, China's message may be related to maritime boundary and resource disputes, making the Han incident one among a string of such messages over the past few years designed to demonstrate China's growing naval power. For instance, China increased its fleet activity significantly in the international waters within the Japanese EEZ in the East China Sea in the year before the Han incident—the submarine's passage through that area was reportedly the thirty-fourth such instance in 2004, up from only seven in 2003.[43] This increase could be attributed to a number of factors, including the need for new and deeper operations areas as the PRC submarine fleet's deep-water capabilities improve,[44] but the most plausible explanation is that China is using its navy to demonstrate its power to resolve disputes in its favor if neighbors or competitors should consider resorting to the use of force.

One of the reasons China may have taken this particular opportunity to demonstrate its naval capabilities is to strengthen its negotiating position in the disputed economic zones in the East China Sea. The Han incursion occurred amid tense disagreement between China and Japan over the PRC's gas exploration projects in the East China Sea inside an area that Japan claims is its exclusive economic zone.[45] As noted above, the submarine was tracked moving through the waters near those same PRC off-shore gas projects that are the subject of the controversy.[46] Japan protests the gas exploration because it claims that wells so near the boundary will inevitably take natural gas from the Japanese side of the border as well. In the days just after the Han's passage through this disputed region, Japan's trade minister openly questioned whether the presence of the submarine in those waters was meant by the PRC to send a not-so-veiled signal.[47] This is entirely plausible, since these waters continue to be the source of open threats by the Chinese against any Japanese interference. As recently as September 2005, for instance, a group of five PLAN ships were spotted operating for the first time in the area of the Chun Xiao gas field in the disputed area of the exclusive economic zones between China and Japan.[48] In order to make sure the message was clearly understood, one of the Chinese ships swiveled and aimed its 100mm bow gun at a JMSDF P-3 patrol plane patrolling the region in international airspace.[49] Such acts of intimidation are meant to reinforce China's claim to the resources under the entire continental shelf, and to encourage Japan not to interfere with operation of the Chinese gas field, which is located only about two kilometers from the Japanese-claimed EEZ boundary.

In preparation for the possibility that it may have to militarily defend its claims against Japan, it is possible that the PLAN sent the Han through sensitive Japanese waters in order to test the JMSDF antisubmarine warfare (ASW) response capabilities, an activity that states which view themselves as peer competitors or even as potential adversaries routinely conduct.[50] The slow speed and erratic course of the submarine as it passed through Japanese waters north of the Strait certainly suggest that it was testing the patrol and tracking capabilities of the JMSDF.[51] These mildly provocative naval operations were routine during the Cold War,[52] and China and Japan have recently accused each other of operating with a "Cold War mentality" based on the postures taken in recent national security strategy documents.[53]

That said, as with its stance against research and intelligence-gathering activities without consent, the PRC has expressed a clear and consistent policy that innocent passage within the territorial waters of a coastal state is not a matter of right for warships. Under Article 6 of the Territorial Waters and Adjoining Areas Act of the People's Republic of China, the Chinese government authorized merchant vessels the right of innocent passage through Chinese waters without prior permission, but specifically required that foreign military vessels seek permission of the Chinese government before entering its territorial waters.[54] Thus, in addition to weakening Chinese ability to limit research and intelligence gathering off its coasts, the passage of the Han through the Ishigaki Strait without Japan's consent also undermined China's efforts to shape international law in favor of coastal state control over the movement of war ships off its coasts.

In light of the political tensions in the East China Sea, and China's strict stance regarding passage by warships into its own territorial waters, the Japanese obviously followed the Han's path with particular interest. In fact, some sources reported the PRC submarine was initially detected leaving its home port, either by a U.S. satellite or through Taiwanese intelligence channels, then tracked by a U.S. submarine and U.S. Navy P-3C patrol planes as it operated off Guam.[55] The submarine continued to be tracked for more than four days as it operated south of the Ryukyus near the politically sensitive Japanese Okinotori Island and the Japanese stepped up monitoring activities as the submarine passed through its territorial waters in the ocean trench between Ishigaki and Miyako on its return trip.[56]

This is of particular interest to the U.S. and Japan because the Han's noisy movement through waters east of Taiwan and the Japanese island chain is an open demonstration that the PLAN is able to operate outside what it calls the "first defensive island chain" into the waters of the outer defensive perimeter, or approaching the "second island chain." These island chains are perceived as defensive spheres that the PRC intends to use to achieve sea supremacy and to deny the United States and allies freedom of action should armed conflict over Taiwan result.[57]

Indeed, over the past few years the PRC has systematically consolidated its position relative to Taiwan—both militarily and politically. Politically, the PRC has worked persistently to prevent international diplomatic recognition of Taiwan by offering economic incentives to underdeveloped states. Additionally, in March 2005 at the annual People's Congress, the PRC leadership pushed through "legislation" aimed at Taiwan that specifies that political separation is unlawful and may be responded to with the use of armed force.[58] Militarily, there is a noticeable trend of gradually increasing numbers of PLAN missions into waters disputed by China and Japan in the East China Sea, and now into Japanese waters themselves. These mounting military activities may be an effort by the PLAN to dissuade intervention in a cross-strait scenario, and the most recent incursion may well have been an intentional signal that China's navy has both the technology and operational ability to disrupt any efforts the United States and Japan might be inclined to undertake on Taiwan's behalf.

Given the international law and policy implications, it is intriguing that the PLAN's activities in Japanese waters do not appear to be well coordinated with the Foreign Ministry, and by implication the Chinese Communist Party. The PRC's delay in responding to Japan's official queries about the identity of the submarine and the purpose of its passage is telling. After initially denying to Japan that it had any knowledge of the developing situation,[59] the PRC government then remained silent about the incident for five days after reports of the submarine's presence in Japanese territorial waters were made public.[60] The PRC vice foreign minister eventually met with the Japanese ambassador and said the submarine was on "routine maneuvers" at the time of the incursion and that it had "accidentally strayed" into Japanese territorial waters and "expressed regret" over the incident, citing the cause as a "technical reason."[61] The five-day delay by the Chinese Foreign Ministry in providing an explanation of this event suggests that the Foreign Ministry was genuinely unaware of what the PLAN was doing and intimates that the PLAN leadership took the initiative to make an independent point to Japan (and possibly to other organs of the PRC government, as well).

Conclusions Concerning the Han Incursion and the Japanese Response

The status and interpretation of the international right of transit passage under international maritime law remain unchanged as a result of the Han's passage through the Ishigaki Strait. China and Japan still challenge the prevailing understanding that international straits include all "useful routes" for international navigation and each seeks to establish the position that only straits that are "necessary routes" for international navigation qualify as international straits. Additionally, neither country altered its view that transit passage applies only in all straits "routinely used for international navigation," rather than all straits that are "susceptible of international navigation." Only if China had followed the Han's underwater passage through the Ishigaki Strait with a political assertion that the submarine had an international law right to do so would the passage have qualified as the sort of state conduct on which customary international law is based. But the landscape of international law has changed nonetheless.

The Chinese spent at least a decade prior to the 2004 incident attempting to build its case for increased coastal state jurisdiction and control over the maritime zones off its shores. By preventing *Bowditch's* survey activities in their exclusive economic zone, for instance, the Chinese staked a position consistent with coastal state control. However, with one submarine's submerged passage through a neighbor's territorial waters in a manner that could not plausibly have been accidental, the Chinese undercut the legitimacy of their protectionist position on international law of the sea. This could have a profound effect on the development of maritime law as a whole, and at a minimum strengthens the hand of those states that accept minimum restrictions on the freedom of maritime navigation. Certainly, this incident will serve as a benchmark for the future when states seek to interpret acceptable practices in the coastal zones of other states in light of international maritime law. Thus, whether the Chinese sought to covertly map the seabed through the strait, or to demonstrate the PLAN's modern sea power, or to test the Japanese antisubmarine detection and response capabilities, the Chinese may well have made a short term tactical gain, but dealt themselves a long-term strategic loss.

In sharp contrast, Japan quickly saw an opportunity and took advantage of it. The Japanese forced the Chinese to express public regret over the incident, and thereby strengthened their own strategic position that Chinese submarines have no right to pass submerged through those waters. By choosing to actively pursue the submarine, rather than relying only on the de-escalatory measures contemplated by UNCLOS, Japan also clearly signaled to China that it is willing to flex military muscles of its own.[62] Thus, in the end, although international law remains mostly unchanged, Japan's strategic position is strengthened because its government demonstrated the ability to quickly respond to an emergent crisis, to grasp the strategic opportunity, and to take bold action.

Notes

1. "Japan continues tracking mystery sub," *Japan Times*, November 12, 2004; Kyodo World Service, "MSDF Ships Tracked Chinese Sub Cautiously Due to 'Possibility' of Attack," November 20, 2004.

2. Melody Chen, "Japan and US 'dissuade' China," *Taipei Times*, March 23, 2005, 2; Asian Political News, "China admits sub entered Japan waters, expresses regret," November 24, 2004; "China sub tracked by U.S. off Guam before Japan intrusion," *Japan Times*, November 17, 2004; "MSDF alert over mystery sub in waters off Okinawa," *Asahi Shimbun*, November 11, 2004; "'Intentional' or 'Navigational Error'?" *Japanese Defense Monthly*, February 1, 2005.

3. "Chinese sub tracked by U.S. off Guam before entering Japan waters," *Kyodo News*, November 16, 2004; "'Intentional' or 'Navigational Error'?" *Japanese Defense Monthly*, February 1, 2005.

4. "'Intentional' or 'Navigational Error'?" *Japanese Defense Monthly*.

5. "China admits sub entered Japan waters, expresses regret," *Asian Political News*, November 16, 2004; "Hosoda says Japan can't identify sub because it 'stays under water'," *Japan Today*, November 11, 2004. The first time the Japanese raised the military alert level to its highest state occurred in 1999 when two North Korean vessels approached the Noto Peninsula in the Sea of Japan.

6. "'Intentional' or 'Navigational Error'?" *Japanese Defense Monthly*.

7. "Hosoda says Japan can't identify sub because it 'stays under water'," *Japan Today*; "Japan Demands Apology over Chinese Submarine Intrusion," *The Sydney Morning Herald*, November 14, 2004; Yoso Furumoto, "Suspicious Submarine: Intrusion of Territorial Waters; JDA Sends AWACS to Surrounding Ocean; Watch Out for Chinese Fighter Jets," *Mainichi Shimbun*, November 13, 2004.

8. See, for instance, the discussion surrounding the 1981 incursions of Soviet submarines into Swedish waters in W. Michael Reisman and Andrew R. Willard, eds., *International Incidents: The Law that Counts in World Politics* (Princeton, N.J.: Princeton University Press, 1988), 40–67.

9. This information is derived from the Defense Mapping Agency's Tactical Pilotage Chart (TPC) H-12C, January 1996 edition. The distances referred to were measured by the author from the TPC H-12C.

10. United Nations Convention on the Law of the Sea, Article 3.

11. Law to Partially Amend the Law on the Territorial Sea (Law No. 73 of 1996), which entered into force on July 20, 1996.

12. United Nations Convention on the Law of the Sea, Articles 18, 19. Italics added.

13. UNCLOS, Article 19.

14. UNCLOS, Article 20.

15. UNCLOS, Articles 38, 39.

16. UNCLOS, Article 37.

17. Although UNCLOS does not further specify what the term "normal mode" means in reference to a submarine's passage through an international strait, this issue was clarified in the 1995 San Remo Manual on International Law Applicable to Armed Conflicts at Sea, in which the Round Table of scholars and officials expressed general agreement that the right of transit passage for submarines included subsurface passage: 105.

18. UNCLOS, Article 37.

19. Nakamura Susumu, e-mail of 10 May 2004, on file with the author.

20. 1949 I.C.J. 4, reprinted in U.S. Naval War College, *International Law Documents 1948–1949*, Blue Book series, 1950, vol. 46, 108. This case involved two British ships that struck naval mines in the Corfu Channel 1946, leading to the deaths of forty-five British sailors. Albania was adjudged responsible for ensuring that its territorial waters in the strait were safe for international navigation.

21. 1949 I.C.J., 28.

22. Ibid.

23. United States Department of State, Bureau of Oceans and International Environmental and Scientific Affairs, "Limits in the Seas No. 120, Straight Baseline and Territorial Sea Claims: Japan," April 30, 1998.

24. A. R. Thomas and James C. Duncan, eds., *Annotated Supplement to the Commander's Handbook on the Law of Naval Operations*, U.S. Naval War College International Law Studies, Blue Book series, vol. 73, 122 n. 36, citing Grunawalt, "United States Policy on International Straits," 18 Ocean Dev. & Int'l L. J. 445, 456 (1987).

25. Zhao Peiying, ed., *Basis of International Law for Modern Soldiers* (Beijing: PLA Press, 1996), 90.

26. Ibid., 90–91.

27. Lyle Goldstein and William Murray, "Undersea Dragons: China's Maturing Submarine Force," *International Security* 28, no. 4 (Spring 2004): 161–96.

28. Reiji Yoshida and Kanako Takahara, "China's Sub Intrusion Sparks Tokyo Protest," *The Japan Times*, November 13, 2004.

29. FBIS Report: "HK Phoenix TV Discusses PRC Submarine Intrusion, Japan's Reaction," Hong Kong Feng Huang Wei Shih Chung Wen Tai in Mandarin 0302 GMT 19 November 2004, FBIS# CPP20041122000100; Kyodo World Service, "MSDF Ships Tracked Chinese Sub Cautiously Due to 'Possibility' of Attack," November 20, 2004; "What the PRC Submarine Force is Aiming For," *Japanese Defense Monthly*, July 1, 2005.

30. "'Intentional' or 'Navigational Error'?" *Japanese Defense Monthly*.

31. "China sub tracked by U.S. off Guam before Japan intrusion." *The Japan Times*, November 17, 2004.

32. UNCLOS Article 245.

33. UNCLOS Article 40. See also Article 21(1)(g).

34. UNCLOS Article 19.

35. UNCLOS Article 38.

36. Mark Oliva, "Before EP-3, China Turned Away U.S. Research Ship in International Waters," *Stars and Stripes*, May 20, 2001; Erik Eckholm, "China Complains about U.S. Surveillance Ship," *New York Times*, September 27, 2002.

37. UNCLOS Articles 55, 58, and 87.

38. "Foreign Ministry Spokeswoman's Press Conference on September 26, 2002," at http://www.china-un.ch/eng/xwdt/t88395.htm.

39. UNCLOS Article 25(1).

40. UNCLOS Article 30.

41. "Chinese submarine intrusion considered an act of provocation," *Japan Times*, Nao Shimoyachi, November 13, 2004.

42. Max Boot, "China's Stealth War on the U.S.," *Los Angeles Times*, July 20, 2005.

43. "A strategically important area for China," *The Asahi Shimbun*, November 12, 2004.

44. Melody Chen, "Japan and US 'dissuade' China," *Taipei Times*, March 23, 2005, 2.

45. Reiji Yoshida and Kanako Takahara, "China's sub intrusion sparks Tokyo protest," *Japan Times*, November 13, 2004.

46. Steve Herman, "Japan Says Mystery Sub in Its Waters Was Chinese," *Voice of America*, November 12, 2004; Steve Herman, "Japanese Minister Links China's Sub Intrusion to Gas Exploration," *Voice of America*, November 14, 2004.

47. Steve Herman, "Japanese Minister Links China's Sub Intrusion to Gas Exploration."

48. Norimitsu Onishi and Howard W. French, "Japan's Rivalry with China Is Stirring a Crowded Sea," *New York Times*, September 11, 2005.

49. "Kyodo: Chinese Warship Pointed Gun at Japanese Patrol Plane in Sept," Tokyo Kyodo World Service, October 1, 2005.

50. "HK Phoenix TV Discusses PRC Submarine Intrusion, Japan's Reaction," FBIS Report.

51. "Japan continues tracking mystery sub," *Japan Times*, November 12, 2004; Nao Shimoyachi, "Chinese submarine intrusion considered an act of provocation," *Japan Times*, November 13, 2004.

52. See, e.g., W. Michael Reisman and Andrew R. Willard, *International Incidents: The Law That Counts in World Politics*, (Princeton, N.J.: Princeton University Press, 1988), chapter 3, which discusses Soviet submarine incursions into Swedish waters in 1981 and 1982, and the response by the Swedish government.

53. "China Denies Knowledge of Suspect Submarine in Japan," *The Manila Times*, November 12, 2004.

54. Zhao Peiying, ed., *Basis of International Law for Modern Soldiers* (Beijing: PLA Press, 1996), 87–88.

55. "China sub tracked by U.S. off Guam before Japan intrusion," *Japan Times*, November 17, 2004; "Chinese sub tracked by U.S. off Guam before entering Japanese

waters," *Kyodo News,* November 16, 2004; Melody Chen, "Taiwan 'regrets' Japan's stance on sub," *Taipei Times,* November 27, 2004, 3.

56. Melody Chen, "Japan and US 'Dissuade' China," *Taipei Times,* March 23, 2005, 2.

57. Ibid.

58. Alan A. Romberg, "Anti-Secession Bill Ups Cross-Strait Tensions," *Asia Times,* March 4, 2005, http://www.atimes.com/atimes/China/GC04Ad03.html.

59. "China denies knowledge of suspect submarine in Japan," *The Manila Times,* November 12, 2004.

60. "Japan Demands Apology over Chinese Submarine Intrusion," *The Sydney Morning Herald,* November 14, 2004.

61. J. Sean Curtin, "Submarine Puts Japan-China Ties into a Dive," *Asia Times Online,* November 17, 2004; unattributed article, "China Sub Tracked by U.S. off Guam before Japan Intrusion," *The Japan Times,* November 17, 2004; unattributed article, "Defense Official Doubts China's Explanation for Sub's Intrusion," *Tokyo Nihon Keizai Shimbun,* November 17, 2004.

62. "Japan's New Defense Outline Raises Concerns about China," *Muzi News,* November 16, 2004.

Andrew S. Erickson and Lyle J. Goldstein

China's Future Nuclear Submarine Force

Insights from Chinese Writings

Introduction

THE ADVENT OF THE YUAN-CLASS SSK in mid-2004 has had a major impact in transforming the assessments of Western naval analysts, and also of the broader community of scholars studying China's military moderniza-tion. In order to grasp the energy that China is now committing to under-sea warfare, consider that during 2002–04 China's navy launched thirteen submarines,[1] while simultaneously undertaking the purchase of subma-rines from Russia on an unprecedented scale. Indeed, China commissioned thirty-one new submarines between 1995 and 2005.[2] Given this rapid evo-lution, appraisals of China's capability to field competent and lethal diesel submarines in the littorals have slowly changed from ridicule to grudging respect of late.[3] China's potential for complex technological development is finally being taken seriously abroad.

Whereas the Yuan's debut allegedly surprised Western analysts, the emergence of China's 093 SSN and 094 SSBN have been anticipated for some time. Nevertheless, these programs remain shrouded in mystery and there is little consensus regarding their operational and strategic significance. In the broadest terms, it can be said that a successful 093 program will significantly enlarge the scope of Chinese submarine operations, perhaps ultimately serving as the cornerstone of a genuine blue-water navy. The 094 could take the survivability of China's nuclear deterrent to a new level, potentially enabling more aggressive posturing by Beijing in a crisis. Moreover, these platforms are entering the PLA Navy (PLAN) at a time when reductions are projected to occur in the U.S. Navy submarine force[4]—a fact duly noted by a senior PLAN strategist recently in one of China's premier naval journals.[5]

The PLA is notoriously opaque, posing major challenges for Western analysts. Official statements regarding the intentions of China's future nuclear submarine force are all but nonexistent.[6] Nevertheless, one of the most significant statements is contained in the 2004 PLA Defense White Paper's discussion of naval operations. Enhancing "nuclear counterattacks" capability was described as one of the PLAN's most important missions. Moreover, Chinese unofficial writings on defense issues are voluminous and growing more so. Among dozens of journals, magazines, and newspapers devoted to military affairs (not to mention hundreds of more technically oriented publications) are at least five focusing specifically on naval warfare.[7] This chapter will survey the available Chinese writings concerning the PLAN's future nuclear submarine force. Two caveats are in order. First, this chapter seeks to present the views of Chinese analysts, but does not render final judgment on the validity of those views. Such an approach will better acquaint a broader community of naval analysts with the essential primary source materials. Second, this is not a comprehensive study, but rather a preliminary research probe. These data need to be treated with a certain amount of caution and follow-on studies are necessary before major conclusions can be drawn.

The chapter begins with a brief survey of relevant elements from PRC writings concerning the PLAN's nuclear submarine history. A second section examines how PLAN analysts appraise developments among foreign nuclear submarine forces: what lessons do they glean from these other experiences? The third section concerns mission imperatives: what strategic and operational objectives are China's 093 and 094 submarines designed to achieve? The potential capabilities of these submarines are addressed in this chapter's fourth and final section.

Historical Perspectives

Chinese naval writings reveal an intense pride regarding Beijing's naval nuclear-propulsion program. These writings, in the "glorious genre" as it were, are well documented in John Wilson Lewis and Xue Litai's ground-breaking and authoritative classic *China's Strategic Seapower*.[8] This article will not attempt to examine Chinese writings to check for consistency with the conclusions in the detailed study by Lewis and Xue (though this is a worthwhile project and should be undertaken given the wide variety of new Chinese secondary-source data). Rather, this analysis highlights several important trends in contemporary PRC discussions of the first-generation nuclear submarines in order to assess the prospects for the next generation.

In his recent autobiography, published in Chinese by the official PLA press in 2004, Admiral Liu Huaqing provides a unique level of detail concerning the foundation for China's contemporary development of nuclear submarines.[9] Credited with an instrumental role in modernizing China's navy, Admiral Liu presided over a steady improvement and expansion of China's submarine force as both commander of the PLAN (1982–88) and vice chairman of the Central Military Commission (1989–97). In 1984, Admiral Liu emphasized: "We must place importance on submarines at all times. . . . Nuclear-powered submarines should be further improved and used as a strategic task force."[10] Liu viewed nuclear submarines not only as "a deterrent force of the nation" but also as "an expression of our country's overall strength." As commander of the PLA Navy, Liu emphasizes, "I paid exceptional attention to the practical work of developing nuclear-powered submarines. From 1982 through 1988, I organized various experiments and training sessions in this regard. I also considered developing a second generation of nuclear-powered submarines."[11] PLAN emphasis on submarine development continues today. As the 2005 edition of the PLA's first authoritative volume on strategy emphasizes, "Stealth warships and new-style submarines represent the modern sea battle platforms."[12]

Chinese periodicals shed light on more recent factors shaping Chinese nuclear submarine force development. One important 2004 PRC survey of China's emerging nuclear submarine program from the journal 世界航空航天博览 (*World Aerospace Digest*), reviews a series of inadequacies in China's submarine force which became starkly evident during the 1990s. According to this report, the 1993 *Yin He* incident was an important event for crystallizing the PRC commitment to a new generation of nuclear attack submarines. Thus, when the Chinese freighter was inspected in Saudi Arabia before proceeding to Iran, the PRC high command was apparently "extremely furious, but had no recourse" [怒火万分却毫无办法]. At that point, the leadership redoubled its efforts to build a "capable and superior nuclear attack submarine that could protect China's shipping in distant seas." The author notes that "at present, our country only has five Han-class nuclear attack submarines. . . . This number is insufficient and the capabilities are backward. . . . Thus, they are inadequate to cope with the requirements of the new strategic situation."[13]

The 2004 memoirs of former PLAN commander Admiral Liu appear to lend some credence to this sequence of events as they state that the Central Military Commission began development work on a "new generation nuclear submarine," probably the 093, in 1994.[14] "In 1990 the last [of the original five Han-class SSNs] was launched," Liu recalls:

> After I briefed President Jiang Zemin on this, he decided to personally inspect the launch of this submarine. At the time of inspection, he said resolutely: "Development of nuclear-powered submarines cannot be discontinued." On 29 May 1992, when forwarding the Navy's report on building nuclear-powered submarine units to President Jiang, I particularly stressed the need to continually develop science research and do successful safety work. President Jiang wrote a note on the report, giving his important instructions on this matter. Based on his instructions, in the course of developing nuclear-powered submarines, we formed a seamless and effective nuclear safety mechanism by drawing on the experience of foreign countries while taking our practical situation into account. The mechanism included regulations and rules, technological controls, and supervisory and examination measures. In 1994, in compliance with President Jiang's instructions, the Central Military Commission and its Special Committee adopted a decision to start developing a new generation of nuclear-powered submarines. Seeing that there were qualified personnel to carry on the cause and that new types of submarines would continue to be developed, I felt relieved.[15]

The above analysis in *World Aerospace Digest*, however, does cut against what appears to be conventional wisdom in China's naval literature, which tends to credit China's Han submarines with a significant role in the 1996 Taiwan Strait crisis. Thus, one report states that in mid-March 1996, "U.S. military satellites were unable to detect the position of [certain] Chinese nuclear submarines; it was as if they . . . had vanished." This narrative continues, "The U.S. carrier battle groups were unable to cope with the hidden, mobile, high-speed, undersea" threat posed by the Chinese nuclear submarines, and thus "were unable to approach the sea area within 200 nautical miles of Taiwan." Implying some uncertainty on this issue, the author asks, "Why did the U.S. carrier group suddenly change its original plan? Was it that they feared China's nuclear submarines?"[16] Another PRC report also alleges that U.S. military satellites lost track of China's SSNs and that the U.S. Navy was forced to retreat when confronted by the "massive threat of China's nuclear submarine force."[17] Given the Han-class SSN's reputation as a noisy vessel, these statements might well be viewed with suspicion—and, indeed, they are not reproduced here to suggest their truth.[18] Nonetheless, these Chinese conjectures are related here because they could be indicative of the intellectual context within which 093 and 094 development has occurred.

Most China scholars agree that the intellectual space for debate and disagreement in China is, and has for some time been, rather wide. In this respect, the analysis from *World Aerospace Digest* is once again noteworthy. While the vast majority of PLAN writings concerning the single Type 092 Xia SSBN heap praise on China's technical achievements, this analysis breaks new ground (in the PRC context) by drawing attention to the Xia's inadequacies. It notes candidly, "the Xia-class actually is not a genuine deterrent capability." Noting the symbolic value of the vessel, the author explains that the Xia was important to answer the question of "having or not having" a nuclear submarine, but then enumerates the platform's numerous problems: high noise levels and radiation leakage, not to mention the short range of the single warhead carried by China's first-generation submarine-launched ballistic missile (SLBM), the Julang-1. Forced to approach the enemy's shores, and vulnerable to enemy ASW, the Xia "cannot possibly serve as a viable nuclear, second-strike force." It is no wonder, the author explains, that China did not opt to build a "whole batch" of these problematic submarines.[19] No doubt, such candid observations suggest that Chinese strategists do not necessarily overestimate the capabilities of their first generation nuclear submarines, perhaps adding additional impetus to the building of a second generation.

Even more important than the observations concerning history cited above, however, are the views of China's "founding fathers" of naval nuclear propulsion. Two of these founding fathers recently offered interviews to the press, in which they expounded on the outlook for nuclear submarines in naval warfare. First, Peng Shilu, designer of China's first naval nuclear reactor, was interviewed in 国际展望 (*World Outlook*) in 2002. Although Peng drafted his first reactor designs more than three decades ago, this engineer is unwavering in his commitment: "In the First World War, the battleship was the most important vessel; and in the Second World War, it was the aircraft carrier. [But in] the future, I believe the most critical naval asset will be the nuclear submarine." For Peng, the SSN's primary strengths are: high power, fast speed, large carrying capacity for equipment and personnel, extended deployment capability, as well as excellent concealment possibilities. According to Peng, "Nuclear submarines can go anywhere . . . their scope of operations is vast [and they are therefore] most appropriate to meet the security requirements of a great power."[20] Drawing on another interview with Peng Shilu, an analysis published in 2005 by China's Central Party School Press concludes: "[Such is] the huge superiority of nuclear propulsion [that it] simply cannot be compared with conventional propulsion."[21]

An interview with the Han submarine's chief designer, Huang Xuhua, which appeared in the military periodical 兵器知识 (*Ordnance Knowledge*) in 2000, is more explicit regarding some of the dilemmas confronting China's naval nuclear propulsion program. Huang discusses the conundrum for naval strategists posed by the option to choose between development of AIP (air-independent propulsion) technology and nuclear propulsion. The interviewer asks Huang directly whether it makes sense to continue with nuclear propulsion development, given recent world-wide advances in AIP technology. Huang points out that nuclear propulsion offers far more power, is likely much safer and more reliable, and enables submarines to stay submerged for longer periods of time. Taking Sweden's *Gotland*-class AIP-equipped submarine as an example, he suggests that this submarine's two weeks of submerged operations at an average speed of four knots might not "be adequate for combat requirements." Huang accepts that certain bathymetric conditions are ideal for AIP-equipped diesel submarines, such as those prevailing in the Baltic Sea (a small, shallow area). For Sweden, therefore, Huang says, "It is scientifically logical to select this type of submarine." The implicit argument, however, is that China confronts rather different, if not wholly unrelated, maritime challenges and requirements.

In making an argument for Chinese nuclear submarine development, Huang draws a parallel to Britain's deployment of SSNs during the Falklands War. He notes that their high speed was critical to their success in deploying to a distant theater in a timely fashion. Indeed, other PRC naval analysts have been impressed by the sea-control capabilities that British SSNs afforded during this scenario—the most intense naval combat since the Second World War.[22] Huang then makes the observation that such high-speed submarines are critical for a nation, such as the United Kingdom, that—in contrast to the United States—no longer possesses a global network of bases.[23] For the PRC, which takes great pride in its lack of overseas bases, this would appear to be an argument for SSNs serving as the basis of a blue-water navy with considerable reach. Indeed, writing in China's most prestigious military publication, 中国军事科学 (*China Military Science*), PLAN Senior Captain Xu Qi goes so far as to state that China's "navy must . . . unceasingly move toward [the posture of] a 'blue-water navy' [and] expand the scope of maritime strategic defense. . . ."[24]

Comparative Perspectives

The Falklands War is hardly the only naval campaign of interest to Chinese strategists, as PRC analysts produce an extraordinary volume of analyses concerned with modern naval warfare—often generated by carefully dissecting foreign secondary sources. There is a large appetite for information regarding the United Kingdom's history of nuclear submarine operations[25] and even such nascent nuclear submarine powers as India.[26] However, Chinese naval strategists evidently prioritize analyses of the American, the French, and especially the Russian nuclear submarine fleets.

From a very early stage, PRC engineers demonstrated concretely that they were not averse to adopting American designs, as they conspicuously embraced the teardrop configuration for their first generation of nuclear submarines in contrast to then-current Soviet designs.[27] Today the threat component is also evident in PLAN analyses of the U.S. submarine force. Chinese researchers display intimate familiarity with all U.S. Navy submarine force programs, including the most cutting edge platforms, such as Sea Wolf[28] and *Virginia*.[29] Additionally, there is great interest in the ongoing transformation of some SSBNs into SSGNs.[30] Ample focus is also devoted to the capabilities of the *Los Angeles*-class as the backbone of the U.S. Navy submarine force.[31] Beyond platforms and programs, there is also a keen interest in America's industrial organization for nuclear submarine production and maintenance.[32]

Chinese analysts also closely monitor French nuclear submarine development.[33] They have paid particular attention to the manner in which France strives to maximize the effectiveness of its second-tier nuclear submarine force.[34] The September 2005 issue of 舰船知识 (*Naval & Merchant Ships*) features a lengthy report, apparently by a Chinese naval officer studying in France, who has made multiple visits to French nuclear submarines based in Brest. This report makes note of numerous details, from the vast support network at the base to France's tendency to support a high quality of life aboard its nuclear vessels. Concerning the value of France's SSBN force, which is noted to comprise "80% of France's nuclear weaponry," the author quotes a French military expert as saying, "France's SSBNs ensure national security, carry out strategic nuclear deterrence and [have] basic power for independent national defense." Other issues highlighted in this report include personnel practices (e.g., age limitations, two crews per submarine), operations cycles (a 2/2/2 pattern for SSBNs that matches other Chinese discussions—

see below), command and control arrangements, quieting technologies, and the small size of certain classes of French SSNs.[35]

It is with the Russian nuclear submarine force, however, that the Chinese navy feels the greatest affinity. This is not surprising and springs from historical, strategic, and perhaps even organizational-cultural affinities that appear to have been cemented since the passing of Sino-Soviet enmity in the late 1980s. Chinese analysts are well aware of the crisis that the Russian nuclear submarine force has suffered in recent years. They have written extensively on the *Kursk* tragedy and other accidents.[36] For instance, one source has documented the great embarrassment suffered during an SLBM test failure that was witnessed directly by Russian president Vladimir Putin in early 2004.[37] Chinese analysts note the vastly decreased building rate for Soviet nuclear submarines, and voice concern lest the legacy force be insufficient to contend with [抗衡] the United States.[38]

Nevertheless, respect for Russian nuclear submarine achievements has not diminished significantly.[39] A review of Soviet naval development that appeared in *China Military Science* in 1999 extols the virtues of nuclear submarines: "Relying on nuclear submarines, the Soviet Union rapidly overcame the unfavorable geostrategic situation, giving the USSR an ocean going navy with offensive capability."[40] Perhaps reflecting on internal debates in China regarding naval modernization, the author also describes how the Russian naval development encountered a major obstacle from a faction adhering to the notion that "navies have no use in the nuclear age" [核时代海军无用论].

Reflecting on today's Russian navy, 当代海军 (*Modern Navy*) lavished praise on the capabilities of a refurbished Typhoon-class SSBN, *Dmitry Donskoy*, that was relaunched in 2002;[41] it also hailed the 2001 launch of an Akula-class SSN, *Gepard*, which is described as the world's quietest nuclear submarine. The latter report also noted that *Gepard* has twenty-four nuclear-armed cruise missiles.[42] In a war game (of unknown origin) modeling a Russian-Japanese naval conflict, which was reported on in considerable detail in the October and November 2002 issues of *Naval & Merchant Ships*, the Russian nuclear submarine force overcame Japan's ASW forces and inflicted grave losses (thirteen ships sunk) on the Japanese navy.[43] This would appear to be a subtle argument that China also requires a substantial fleet of SSNs.

In Chinese naval periodicals, the affinity with the Russian nuclear submarine force is manifested by vast coverage of the most minute details of historical and contemporary platforms. In 2004–05, for example, the journal *Naval*

& Merchant Ships carried ten–fifteen-page special features, each devoted to outlining the development of a single class—such as the Victor, Delta, Oscar, and Alpha classes—complete with photo essays and detailed line drawings.[44] These features are suggestive of the volumes of data that have been made available over the last decade from the Russian side, and simultaneously the voracious appetite for such information within China's naval-studies community. Among such descriptions, perhaps no Russian submarine commands as much respect and interest as the massive Typhoon-class SSBN. Chinese analysts are captivated not only by this vessel's gargantuan proportions,[45] but also the efficiency of its reactors, its impressive quieting characteristics, the attention to crew living standards, as well as command and control equipment and procedures.[46] Evidently Chinese naval analysts appear to comprehend the strategic significance of a platform that could strike adversary targets from the "Russian-dominated Barents and Okhotsk seas."[47]

Western analysts have followed Russian arms transfers to China with an all-consuming interest. But the above discussions imply that one should not underestimate the transfer of software and expertise that has occurred in parallel with that of the hardware. The true dimensions of these intellectual transfers remain unknown.

Mission Imperatives

PRC writings concerning nuclear submarines do not hide the symbolic role of these vessels. One, for example, remarks on the precise correlation between membership in the UN Security Council and the development of nuclear submarines.[48] Indeed, it appears to be conventional wisdom in the PRC that nuclear submarines represent one of China's clearest claims to status as a great power [大国].[49] In 1989, after China's successful test of the JL-1 SLBM, then-Central Military Commission Vice Chairman Admiral Liu Huaqing stated,

> Chairman Mao said that "we will build a nuclear submarine even if it takes 10,000 years." . . . Our nuclear submarine [and its] stealthy nuclear missile both succeeded. This has [had] strong international repercussions. As Comrade Deng Xiaoping has said, if we did not have atomic bombs, missiles, [and] satellites, then we would not [enjoy] our present international status, and could not shape international great triangle relations [as a balancer to the Soviet Union]. Developing strategic nuclear weapons has therefore [had] great strategic significance for the nation.[50]

Beyond symbolism, however, what are the missions that Chinese strategists envision for the second generation of PLAN nuclear submarines?

In general, nuclear submarines are credited with having significant advantages over conventional submarines: "a large cruising radius, strong self-power [i.e., electrical power supply], high underwater speed, great diving depth, [relative] quietness and large weapons carrying capacity."[51] Perceived advantages of conventional submarines include "small volume, low noise, low cost, and mobility."[52] Underscoring the cost differential, an anonymous PLAN officer is cited as stating: "the price of one nuclear submarine can buy several, even more than ten, conventional submarines.... As a developing country, our nation's military budget is still quite low, and thus the size of the navy's nuclear submarine fleet can only be maintained at a basic scale [基本规模]."[53]

In 1989, as vice chairman of the Central Military Commission, Admiral Liu stated: "I believe that there are two issues in developing nuclear submarines: one is the development of SSBNs, and one is the development of SSNs. Both types of nuclear submarines should be developed, especially SSNs. Along with technological development, enemy ASW power has strengthened. Originally, using conventional submarines was sufficient to accomplish [our] missions, but now that has become problematic, [so] we must develop SSNs."[54]

To understand what strategic roles the 093 submarine might undertake, it is essential to return to the discussion initiated by both Peng Shilu and Huang Xuhua in part one of this chapter concerning the particular tactical and operational advantages of nuclear submarines. Indeed, the sophistication of PLA thinking on these issues is underlined by Huang's analysis of the different roles played by SSNs for each side during the Cold War. For the Americans, he says, they were a vital element of "global attack strategy" [全球进攻战略]. For the Soviets, by contrast, their roles were to stalk enemy carrier battle groups, as well as to defend Soviet ballistic-missile submarines.[55] Concurring with Peng and Huang, a third analysis from 国防 (National Defense) enumerates further advantages of nuclear submarines by emphasizing the all-important factor of the SSN's impressive power supply. Not to be underestimated, this supply of power can vastly improve the crew's quality of life (e.g., by providing for strong air conditioning) and support electronic combat systems. In terms of combat performance, it is said that SSNs can employ their speed to foil ASW attack, and are built solidly to absorb battle damage.[56]

A consistent theme in PRC writings concerning SSNs involves their ability to undertake long-range missions of extended duration. Consistent with the analysis above that cited the 1993 Yin He incident as lending significant

impetus for the 093 program, a recent discussion of China's nuclear submarine force in *Naval & Merchant Ships* refers to the enormous growth in
China's maritime trade as a factor in shaping China's emerging nuclear submarine strategy.[57] Likewise, another article from 现代舰船 (*Modern Ships*)
on PRC submarine strategy suggests, "Submarines are the PLAN's main
long-distance sea force. . . . Protecting China's sea lines of communication
has become an important aspect of maritime security. This is an important
new mission for the PLAN."[58] If nuclear submarines can "break through the
island chain blockade" [突破岛链封锁], they can conduct long-distance
operations without hindrance from the enemy's airborne ASW. In contrast
to diesel submarines, nuclear submarines are said to be far superior in combat situations in which air cover is lacking—a recognized vulnerability of the
PLAN in distant operations. But overall, there is a strong emphasis on the
imperative for Chinese nuclear submarines to function in a joint environment, thereby complementing other PLA strengths.[59]

Nevertheless, these same analyses also exhibit some conservatism, for
example suggesting explicitly that China's new nuclear submarines will not
operate beyond China's second island chain (running from the Japanese
archipelago south to the Bonin and Marianas Islands and finally to the Palau
group).[60] Indeed, nuclear submarines are also said to be critical in the struggle
to establish sea control [制海权] in the littoral regions and in China's neighboring seas. The linkage between the 093 program and the Taiwan issue (first
suggested in part one of this chapter) is relatively clear: "In order to guarantee the required national defense strength and to safeguard the completion
of national unification and to prevent 'Taiwan independence,' over the past
few years, China has increased indigenous production of new conventional
and nuclear submarines . . . " [emphasis added].[61] There is an acceleration of
not only the building rate, but also the pattern of submarine development:
"China's construction of a new generation of nuclear-powered attack submarines breaks with past practice, in which China would first build one vessel, debug it repeatedly, and then begin small batch production. In this case,
work on the later submarines began almost simultaneously with work on the
first. . . . China is doing it differently this time . . . because of the urgency of
the surrounding situation."[62] Consistent with the Taiwan scenario hinted at
above, it is said that China's nuclear submarines will be ideal for attacking a
likely enemy's lengthy seaborne supply lines.[63]

Disturbingly, one article actually does raise the possibility of a long-
range land attack and even a nuclear-strategic role for China's future SSN.[64]

But it is the 094 SSBN, of course, that is envisioned to have the primary role in the nuclear-strike/deterrence mission. Indeed, the same analysis suggests that, in contrast to Russia, China is planning to base a higher proportion—as many as half—of its nuclear warheads on submarines.[65]

One Chinese expert identifies bathymetry as influencing SSBN development and deployment. He suggests that countries with shallow coastal waters on a continental shelf (e.g., China) face strong incentives to develop smaller SSBNs in order to better operate in local conditions.[66] Among the reasons cited by Chinese strategists for continuing development of their nation's SSBN program are the inherent stealth and mobility of the submarine, which combine to make it the "most survivable type of (nuclear) weapon" [生存率最高的武器]. The PLAN is pursuing the 094, therefore, in order to 1) guarantee via deterrence that mainland China is not struck by nuclear weapons and 2) "to make sure, in the context of regional war, to prevent direct intervention by a third party" [阻止'第三者'直接介入的效果]. In this analysis, China's nuclear forces are viewed as being critical to deterring Washington in a Taiwan scenario, and the author is unusually candid: "At present, our country's nuclear deterrent forces are insufficient; [therefore] the potential for U.S. military intervention in a cross-Strait conflict is extremely high."[67] Another source, citing China's development of the 094 submarine, emphasizes that "If a war erupts across the Taiwan Strait one day, facing the danger of China waging nuclear war, it will be very difficult for America to intervene in the cross-strait military crisis."[68]

Another PRC analysis draws a direct link between the 094 and U.S. missile defense capabilities. It proposes: "In the face of the continual upgrade of the U.S. theater missile system and the excited U.S. research and development of all sorts of new antimissile systems, of course we cannot stand by idly and watch. . . . We must . . . [adopt] countermeasures. The most important of these countermeasures is to exert great effort on developing new types of nuclear-powered strategic missile submarines which are more capable of penetrating defenses . . ." Failure to do so, according to these authors, will increase the likelihood that "the opponent's nuclear cudgel may some day come crashing down on the heads of the children of the Yellow Emperor."[69]

A somewhat more subtle justification for the 094 makes the argument in quasi-legalistic terms. Since China currently has a no-first-use (NFU) policy for its nuclear forces, it is said to require the most survivable type of nuclear weapons (e.g. SSBN-based). The same analysis cautions that there is no need to build SSBNs in the excessive numbers that characterized the Cold War at sea. Rather, China will seek a "balanced" [均衡] nuclear force (both land- and sea-based), just as it will seek a balanced navy.[70]

Capabilities

For Western analysts, the most important details concerning the 093 and 094 submarines involve their projected deployment numbers and capabilities. Here we will examine both Chinese naval writings and related technical research to suggest a range of possibilities. It is imperative to reiterate that we do not endorse the estimates offered below, but are merely presenting the data for other scholars and analysts to consider.

A major theme of Chinese writings is that while China cannot yet build submarines that meet advanced Western standards in all respects, it is intent on building successful 093 and 094 submarines. According to one source, "The technology involved is relatively mature."[71] The situation is strikingly different from that surrounding China's first generation of nuclear submarines, which were built in the 1960s and 1970s when China was unstable, impoverished, isolated, and technologically backward. One author cites China's "successful economic reforms" over the "past twenty years" and the accompanying "technological progress" as providing the necessary expertise and adequate "resources" for successful nuclear submarine development.[72] China is finally poised to capitalize on its decades of experience with related development and manufacturing processes.[73] Because of these advances, China's new nuclear submarines will not necessarily be copies of either American or Russian submarines, but rather an indigenous Chinese effort that is informed by foreign best-of-breed technologies and practices. Nor will Chinese nuclear submarines necessarily be used in the same roles for which U.S. and Soviet submarines were optimized (e.g., antisubmarine warfare).[74]

The actual number of 093 and 094 submarines that China constructs and deploys will offer insight into its naval and nuclear strategies. One Chinese source suggests that by 2010, China will field a total of six 094 SSBNs, divided into patrolling, deploying, and refitting groups.[75] Consistent with this projection, another source suggests that these groups will comprise two SSBNs each.[76]

Another critical question concerns the 093 and 094 submarines' acoustic properties. Chinese sources universally recognize that noise reduction is one of the greatest challenges in building an effective nuclear submarine.[77] PRC scientists have long been conducting research concerning the fundamental sources of propeller noise. For instance, experts at China Ship Scientific Research Center developed a relatively advanced guide vane propeller by the late 1990s.[78] This, and the fact that China already has advanced seven-blade propellers with cruciform vortex dissipaters on its indigenous Song-class and imported Kilo-class diesel submarines, suggests that the 093 and 094 will have significantly improved propellers. A researcher in Qingdao's 4808 Factory also demonstrates Chinese attention to the need to use sound-isolation couplings to prevent transmission of vibrations to the ocean from major fresh-water circulating pumps in the steam cycle.[79] Advanced composite materials are credited with capability to absorb vibrations and sound.[80]

One Chinese researcher states that the 093 is not as quiet as the U.S. *Sea Wolf*-class or *Virginia*-class, but is on par with the improved *Los Angeles*-class.[81] Another analyst estimates that the 093's noise level has been reduced to that of the Russian Akula-class submarine at 110 decibels [分贝].[82] He states that the 094's acoustic signature has been reduced to 120 decibels. According to this report, this is definitely not equal to that of the *Ohio*-class, but is on par with that of the *Los Angeles*-class.[83] There is no additional information given to evaluate concerning the origins or comparability of these data.

It is conceivable, if unlikely, that the PRC has achieved a major scientific feat concerning the propulsion system for nuclear submarines. As Shawn Capellano-Sarver's contribution to this volume suggests, a wide variety of Chinese sources claim that China has succeeded in developing a high-temperature gas-cooled reactor (HTGR) [高温气冷堆] suitable for use in its new-generation nuclear submarines. This development is described as being a "revolutionary breakthrough" [革命性突破].[84] Another source elaborates: "HTGR is the most advanced in the world, [its] volume is small, [its] power is great, [its] noise is low—it is the most ideal propulsion system for a new generation of nuclear submarines. The United States and Russia have both not achieved a breakthrough in this regard. According to Western reports, in the first half of 2000, China successfully installed an HTGR on a nuclear submarine. If this information is true, the 093 uses this advanced propulsion technology."[85]

This same analyst suggests that the need to incorporate the new HTGR explains why 093 development has stretched out over a number of years.[86] HTGR development is indeed cited as a major component of China's 863 High Technology Plan [863高科技计划] to develop selected key technologies.[87] The Institute of Nuclear Energy Technology (INET) at Qinghua University has constructed a ten megawatt HTGR, HTR 10.[88] Qinghua and MIT signed a collaborative HTGR research agreement in 2003.[89] The Chief Scientist and Office Director in charge of energy technology development for the 863 Plan write that HTR 10's "high level results" make it "one of the most promising fourth generation systems."[90] In the area of nuclear reactor design, construction, and components, robust indigenous research has been supplemented by extensive technological assistance from such Western corporations as Westinghouse.[91]

As implied above, some Chinese analysts believe that the HTGR promises to give PLAN submarines unprecedented maximum speed.[92] China's Han submarines, by contrast, are said to have a maximum speed of twenty-five knots, while the Xia has a maximum surface speed of sixteen knots and underwater speed of twenty-two knots.[93] As mentioned before, however, Huang Xuhua believes that submarine speed is less important than concealment, which in turn depends on minimizing a submarine's acoustic signature.[94] Another possible benefit of advanced nuclear propulsion is increased reactor safety.

Despite the above speculation, there are substantial reasons to doubt that China would be willing or able to put such an immature technology in its second generation of nuclear submarines—as this would constitute a substantial risk on the investment. Moreover, as Shawn Capellano-Sarver points out, "The technical difficulties that would have to be overcome with the blowers (the need for magnetic bearings) and the fuel-loading system to make an HTGR compatible with a submarine are formidable. This makes the probability of the 093 being equipped with an HTGR small."[95]

As for armaments, the same analyst states that the 093 submarine may be equipped with "Eagle Strike" YJ-12 [鹰击-12] supersonic antiship cruise missiles.[96] The YJ-12 has been developed as part of a larger Chinese quest for improved cruise missiles, particularly submarine-launched variants.[97] The PLAN is presently working to equip "attack submarines with long distance, supersonic, low altitude missile travel, high accuracy, and strong anti-interference antiship missiles, with the combat capability to attack enemy surface ships from mid- to long-range."[98]

The 093 is said to have 65cm torpedo tubes.[99] In his interview, Huang discusses the engineering issues associated with torpedo tube diameter, explaining that "wider tubes support superior torpedoes and are *not* for . . . missiles or sound-dampening."[100] As for the number of missile tubes in the 094, two sources predict sixteen tubes compared with the Xia's twelve.[101] A third source forecasts between twelve and sixteen tubes.[102]

Admiral Liu Huaqing has recounted China's initial failure and ultimately successful effort to test launch the JL-1, or CSS-N-3, SLBM on 12 October 1982 from a submerged Golf-class submarine. This made China the fifth nation to have an undersea nuclear capability. "Launching carrier rockets from underwater has remarkable advantages, compared with using land-based or airborne strategic nuclear weapons," Liu emphasizes. "This is because the launching platform . . . has a wide maneuver space and is well-concealed. This gives it better survivability and, hence, greater deterrent power."[103] The JL-1 was test-fired successfully from the Xia on 15 September 1988.[104] According to one PRC analyst, "China believes that although the U.S. thinks the Xia-class submarine is too noisy and easy to detect, the Chinese navy is capable of going into the Pacific without detection because of its special tactics."[105]

The 094's JL-2 SLBM is projected to have a range of eight thousand kilo-meters,[106] compared to twenty-seven hundred kilometers for the JL-1.[107] There is also speculation that, in contrast to JL-1, JL-2 will have multiple independently targeted reentry vehicles (MIRVs). This would enhance nuclear deterrence by increasing China's number of undersea warheads and significantly bolstering their chances of penetrating an American national missile defense (NMD). One Chinese source predicts that each JL-2 SLBM will carry three to six warheads.[108] Another article makes the extremely ambitious claim that JL-2s already carry six to nine warheads each, and in the future will carry fourteen–seventeen.[109]

The question of how Beijing will communicate with its newly modernized submarine fleet constitutes a major operational challenge.[110] If China emulates other submarine powers, it is likely to pursue total redundancy for submarine command and control, relying on multiple means employing different physical principles. Extremely low frequency (ELF) communications have the advantage that messages can be received at depths of two to three hundred meters, thereby maximizing submarine stealth and survivability. There are major problems with ELF in practice, however, and it is not clear that China has mastered this technology. Most submarine communications are conducted across a wide range of frequencies, ranging from very low frequency to extremely high frequencies; submarines receive messages through exposed antennas while at periscope depth, or via floating or shallowly submerged antennas while near the surface. China might therefore create a dedicated maritime aircraft squadron for communications with its submarine fleet, if it has not already done so. A lengthy profile in *Naval & Merchant Ships* of the "U.S. Take Charge and Move Out" (TACAMO) air fleet, which supports American SSBN operations, may buttress the general conclusion that Beijing is determined to perfect its communications with its submarine fleet as it launches a new generation of nuclear vessels.[111]

The SSBN communications issue is especially acute, but China has been grappling with this particular problem for more than two decades. According to Admiral Liu Huaqing, China on 16 April 1984 used "the satellite communications system for our nuclear-powered submarines to test the channels" of the Dong Fang Hong-2 communications satellite, which had been launched eight days before. "The navy's satellite communication system for its nuclear-powered submarines was the first one to open a test communication line with the satellite," Admiral Liu reports. "The success of the nuclear-powered submarine's experiment on instantaneous transmission of messages via the satellite . . . pushed China's submarine communication to a new level."[112]

Centralization is arguably essential for SSBN command, control, and communication (C3), particularly in the highly centralized PLA. However, it is unclear to what extent this would be technologically possible for China. "At present China's communications infrastructure is vulnerable to a first strike," Garth Hekler, Ed Francis, and James Mulvenon contend. "As a result, the SSBN commander would require explicit and restrictive rules of engagement and . . . targeting data, lest crisis communications with Beijing reveal [the SSBN's] position to hostile attack submarines or if the submarine is cut off from Beijing after a decapitating first strike." On the broader question of submarine force command and control doctrine, it is suggested, "While the PLAN may recognize the effectiveness of decentralized C3 for certain types of submarine missions, it appears to be seeking to create a more tightly centralized submarine C3 system by developing command automation, network centric warfare strategies, and advanced communications technologies."[113]

Chinese naval planners realize that rapidly improving equipment is useless without corresponding improvement in human performance. The PLAN has for some time been pursuing nuclear submarine missions of extended duration. In his recently published memoirs, Admiral Liu relates that he raised the priority of long duration exercises for PLAN nuclear submarines in order to test all parameters of these new capabilities.[114]

Apparently as part of these expanded activities, current PLAN Chief of Staff Sun Jianguo reportedly commanded Han 403 during a mid-1980s mission of ninety days[115] that broke the eighty-four-day undersea endurance record previously set by USS *Nautilus*.[116] Chinese military medical journals evince a very clear interest in undersea medicine, and especially issues surrounding physical and psychological challenges related to lengthy submerged missions.[117]

An even more important challenge for nuclear submarine effectiveness is maintaining a cadre of quality technical personnel. According to one Chinese source, "The greatest problem facing submarine forces today is: it is difficult to have skilled technical operators; especially officers, because they must have good nuclear reactor equipment maintenance and repair skills."[118]

Conclusion

Chinese analysts acknowledge that America has long been dominant in undersea warfare, especially after the Cold War.[119] Many Westerners are therefore surprised that China would have the temerity to challenge the United States directly in this specialized domain of warfare. And yet PLAN analysts keep close tabs on U.S. Navy submarine build rates, and carefully probe for potential USN submarine force vulnerabilities.[120] They have monitored the 8 January 2005 accident involving USS *San Francisco* with great interest.[121] A 2006 article by a senior PLAN strategist suggests that "China already exceeds [U.S. submarine production] five times over" and that eighteen U.S. Navy submarines based in the Pacific might be at a severe disadvantage versus seventy-five or more Chinese submarines.[122] While these assessments are ultimately attributed to an American source, the PLA Navy analyst makes no effort to deny or reject these assessments.

It is widely held that the trajectory of Chinese nuclear propulsion may be one of the best single indicators of whether or not China has ambitions to become a genuine global military power.[123] With no need to surface in order to recharge batteries or any requirement for refueling, not to mention unparalleled survivability if acoustically advanced and properly operated, nuclear submarines remain ideal platforms for persistent operations in far-flung sea areas. They will form an efficient means for China to project power should it choose to do so. Available information on Chinese SSN and SSBN build rates currently suggests the continuation of a moderate development plan.[124] However, Washington should, at a minimum, develop contingency long-range planning for a determined PRC naval challenge, spearheaded by a new and formidable force of Chinese nuclear submarines.

Notes

1. Changing assessments are discussed, for example, in Jim Yardley and Thom Shanker, "Chinese Navy Buildup Gives Pentagon New Worries," *New York Times*, 8 April 2005, http://www.nytimes.com/2005/04/08/international/asia/08china.html? ex=1270612800&en=c76dc1da37f15f20&ei=5090&partner=rssuserland.

2. Ronald O'Rourke, "China's Naval Modernization: Implications for U.S. Navy Capabilities—Background and Issues for Congress," Congressional Research Service Report for Congress, updated 29 August 2006, Order Code RL 33153: 8.

3. See Yardley and Shanker, "Chinese Navy Buildup Gives Pentagon New Worries."

4. In a recent comprehensive, independent review, four of five proposed alternative force structures for the U.S. Navy envisioned substantial reductions in the submarine force. See *Options for the Navy's Future Fleet* (Washington, D.C.: Congressional Budget Office, May 2006), 39.

5. 杨毅 [Yang Yi], "谁的潜艇今后说了算?" ["Who Can Estimate the Future Number of Submarines?"], 舰船知识 [*Naval and Merchant Ships*] (July 2006): 28.

6. See PRC Ministry of Defense, "China's National Defense in 2004," http://www .chinadaily.com.cn/english/doc/2004-12/28/content_403913_4.htm. Other indications of increased prioritization of China's nuclear submarine force include personnel appointments. The previous PLAN Commander, Admiral Zhang Dingfa [张定发], a former nuclear submariner, may have been involved in China's development of naval strategic nuclear weapons. See Chi Hsiao-hua, "High-level Shuffle in the Navy is Not Aimed at the Taiwan Strait," *Sing Tao Jih Pao*, 8 January 2005, A30, FBIS document no. CPP20050108000049. Another nuclear submariner, Rear Admiral Sun Jianguo [孙建国], was selected to be chief of Naval Staff in January 2005.

7. These would include, at a minimum, 当代海军 [*Modern Navy*], 舰船知识 [*Naval and Merchant Ships*] 人民海军 [*People's Navy*], 舰载武器 [*Shipborne Weapons*], and 现代舰船 [*Modern Ships*].

8. See John Wilson Lewis and Xue Litai, *China's Strategic Seapower* (Stanford, Calif.: Stanford University Press, 1994).

9. 刘华清 [Liu Huaqing], 刘华清回忆录 [*The Memoirs of Liu Huaqing*] (Beijing: People's Liberation Army, 2004). All original quotations from Liu's autobiography were checked against the wording in the FBIS translation of Chapters 16–20, #CPP20060707320001001. Wording different from the FBIS translation is used whenever the authors felt that it better reflected Liu's meaning or would be more comprehensible to the reader.

10. Ibid., 468.

11. Ibid., 474.

12. Peng Guangqian and Yao Youzhi, eds., *The Science of Military Strategy* (Beijing: Military Science Publishing House, 2005), 411.

13. Data in this paragraph are derived from 林长盛 [Lin Changsheng], "我国核潜艇的战力" ["The Combat Power of China's Nuclear Submarines"], 世界航空航天博览 [*World Aerospace Digest*], no. 103 (September 2004): 31. *World Aerospace Digest*

is a semimonthly journal published by China Aerospace Technology Group, Inc. This article is perhaps the most comprehensive analysis to date of PRC nuclear submarine capabilities. Although this is a PRC source, Lin is actually a former Taiwanese military officer who recently spent time in the U.S. on a research fellowship. For Lin's background, see William Chien, "U.S. Military-Iraq," VOA News Report, 22 April 2003, www.globalsecurity.org/wmd/library/news/iraq/2003/iraq-030424-20194149.htm; http://www.1no.net/2004/12-22/0442319087-7.html. Lin's publications include "Counting China's ICBMs," *Studies on Chinese Communism* 37, no. 7 (July 2003): 80–90.

14. Liu Huaqing, *The Memoirs of Liu Huaqing*, 477.

15. Ibid., 476–77.

16. The above quotations in the paragraph are from 刘耿 [Liu Geng], "如果大陆不得不用武力解放台湾美国会武装干扰马?" ["Will the U.S. Interfere Militarily if Mainland China Has No Choice But to Use Force to Liberate Taiwan?"], 军事展望 [*Military Prospect*] (September 2002): 41–42.

17. 简杰 [Jian Jie], "神话中德双子座: 传说中的中国21世纪军事安全的海上长城—西方媒体报道中国下一代核潜艇" ["The Legend of the Virtuous Twins: Discussion of China's 21st Century Military Security Maritime Great Wall—The Western Media Cover China's Next Generation Nuclear Submarine"], 国际展望 [*World Outlook*], no. 448 (August 2002), editor's text box, 22.

18. 王逸峰, 叶景 [Wang Yifeng, Ye Jing], 从中日核潜艇事件看我核潜艇的突防 ["What the Nuclear Submarine Incident Between China and Japan Tells Us About the Ability of China's Nuclear Submarines to Penetrate Defenses, Part 1"], 舰载武器 [*Shipborne Weapons*] (January 2005): 27–31. For more on this episode, see Andrew Erickson, Lyle Goldstein, and William Murray, "'Gate Crashing': China's Submarine Force Tests New Waters," *Chinese Military Update* 2, no. 7 (April 2005): 1–4.

19. Data in this paragraph derived from 林长盛 [Lin Changsheng], "我国核潜艇的战力" ["The Combat Power of China's Nuclear Submarines"], 世界航空航天博览 [*World Aerospace Digest*], no. 103 (September 2004): 33.

20. 赵楚 [Zhao Chu], "与中国核潜艇之父面对面: 揭开共和国军备发展史上最神秘一页; 本刊副主编独家专访我国第一代核潜艇总设计师彭士禄院士" ["Face to Face with the Father of China's Nuclear Submarine: Revealing the Most Mysterious Page in the History of the Republic's Weapons Development; This Journal's Deputy Chief Editor's Exclusive Interview With Peng Shilu, Chief Designer of China's First Generation Nuclear Submarine"], 国际展望 [*World Outlook*] (2002): 18. *World Outlook* is a semimonthly journal published by the respected Shanghai Institute of International Studies (SIIS). This multidisciplinary research institute's seven departments covering national and regional studies and five issue-related research centers are dedicated to advancing China's knowledge of international affairs and improving its foreign policy-making.

For further information concerning Peng Shilu's role in China's nuclear submarine development, see 彭子强 [Peng Ziqiang], 中国核潜艇研制纪实 [*The Research and Development of Chinese Nuclear Submarines*], 中共中央党校出版社 [Chinese Communist Party Central Party School Press] (Beijing, 2005), 108–27;

李觉 [Li Jue], 当代中国的核工业 [*Modern China's Nuclear Industry*] (Beijing: 中国社会科学出版社 [China Social Sciences Press], 1987), 303.

21. 彭子强 [Peng Ziqiang], 中国核潜艇研制纪实施 [*The Research and Development of Chinese Nuclear Submarines*], 中共中央党校出版社 [Chinese Communist Party Central Party School Press] (Beijing, 2005), 111.

22. 严烈 [Yan Lie], "大海深处的感觉—访海军某核潜艇艇长闫保健" ["A Feeling for the Ocean Depths—A Visit with Naval Nuclear Submarine Commander Yan Baojian"], 航海 [*Navigation*] no. 1 (1998): 1.

23. Unless otherwise specified, all data from this and the preceding paragraph are derived from 吴锴 [Wu Kai], "攻击型核潜艇的计划思想—再访黄旭华院士" ["An Interview with Huang Xuhua: SSN Design Philosophy"], 兵器知识 [*Ordnance Knowledge*] 152, no. 6, (June 2000): 23–25. *Ordnance Knowledge* is a bimonthly journal of the China Ordnance Society.

24. *China Military Science* is published by the PLA's Academy of Military Sciences. See 徐起 [Xu Qi], "21世纪初海上地缘战略与中国海军的发展" ["Maritime Geostrategy and the Development of the Chinese Navy in the Early 21st Century"], 中国军事科学 [*China Military Science*] 17, no. 4 (2004): 75–81. Translation by Andrew Erickson and Lyle Goldstein published in *Naval War College Review* 59, no. 4 (Autumn 2006).

25. "英国机敏级攻击核潜艇立体剖视图" ["A Three-Dimensional Cutaway View of Britain's 'Swiftsure' Class Nuclear Attack Submarine"], 舰船知识 [*Naval & Merchant Ships*] 304, no. 1 (January 2005); 关朝江 [Guan Zhaojiang], "英国皇家海军的2010舰队" ["The United Kingdom's Naval Fleet in 2010"], 舰载武器 [*Shipborne Weapons*], no. 11 (2004); 世界核潜艇简介 (四) ["A Synopsis of World Nuclear Submarines (Part 4)"], 国外核新闻 [*Foreign Nuclear News*], no. 7 (2001): 10–12; 迎南 [Ying Nan], "透视英国 '水下核幽灵'" ["A Penetrating Look at England's 'Underwater Nuclear Spirit'"], 当代海军 [*Modern Navy*] no. 2 (1998): 37–38; 那刹 [Na Sha], 英国三叉戟导弹核潜艇将只携带96枚核弹头 ["England's Trident Guided Missile Submarine Only Carries 96 Nuclear Warheads"], 国外核新闻 [*Foreign Nuclear News*], no. 3 (1994): 11.

26. 杨力 [Yang Li], "印度核潜艇研制发展现状" ["The Present Situation of Indian Nuclear Submarine Development"], 国外核新闻 [*Foreign Nuclear News*], no. 11 (2002): 12–13; 袁海 [Yuan Hai], "'强大的蓝水海军' 计划最重要部分—印度自制核潜艇最新情" ["The Most Important Component of the 'Powerful Blue Undersea Navy' Plan—The Latest News on India's Self-Built Nuclear Submarine"], 国际展望 [*World Outlook*], no. 5 (2002): 25–27.

27. Peng Shilu discusses some details of this decision in 赵楚 [Zhao Chu], "与中国核潜艇之父面对面" ["Face to Face with the Father of China's Nuclear Submarine"], 国际展望 [*World Outlook*] (2002): 19.

28. 曹志荣 [Cao Zhirong], "枭雄梦断冷战 群狼险变抓狼 回眸SSN-21 '海狼'" ["The SSN-21 Sea Wolf"], 舰船知识 [*Naval & Merchant Ships*], no. 10 (2004): 16–19.

29. 河山 [He Shan], "'弗吉尼亚'号能否成为新世纪海上霸主" ["Can the Virginia Class Become the New Century's Maritime Hegemon?"], 当代海军 [*Modern Navy*], no. 10 (2004): 18–21.

30. 董露, 郭纲, 李文胜 [Dong Lu, Guo Gang, and Li Wensheng], "析美国战略导弹常规改装的动因及影响" [Analysis on the Motives and Effects of U.S. Strategic Missiles Armed with Conventional Warheads], 中国宇航学会 [China Space Institute], paper distributed but not presented at "10th PIIC Beijing Seminar on International Security," Program for Science and National Security Studies & Institute of Applied Physics and Computational Mathematics, Xiamen, China, 25-28 September, 2006; 林一平 [Lin Yiping], "美国海军改装部分弹道导弹核潜艇为巡航导弹核潜艇" ["The USN Refits a Portion of SSBNs into Cruise Missile SSNs"], 飞航导弹 [*Winged Missiles Journal*] no. 7 (2002): 13; 曹志荣 [Cao Zhirong], "'俄亥俄'变脸" ["The 'Ohio' Suddenly Turns Hostile"], 舰船知识 [*Naval & Merchant Ships*] 1 (2004): 46-48.

31. 止戈 [Zhi Ge], "别无选择 洛杉矶级:梦开始的地方" ["Don't Be Left Without Options: The Place Where the Dream Began"], 舰船知识 [*Naval & Merchant Ships*], no. 8 (2002): 31-37.

32. See, for example, 曹杰荣 [Cao Jierong], "美国核潜艇建造大哥大 百年老厂通用动力公司电船分公司" ["The Construction of USN SSNs: A Hundred Year Old Factory Jointly Used by General Dynamics and Electric Boat"], 舰船知识 [*Naval & Merchant Ships*] 1 (2005): 58-61.

33. See, for example, 伊凡 [Yi Fan], "法国梭鱼级攻击型核潜艇" ["France's 'Barracuda' Class Attack Submarine"], 全球军事 [*Militang*], no. 3 (2005): 17; no author, "法国梭鱼攻击核潜艇方案论证接近尾声" ["The Demonstration of France's Barracuda-Class Attack Submarine Nears a Conclusion"], *Intelligence Command Control & Simulation Techniques* 2, no. 27 (2005): 100.

34. 樊海刚, 尹文立 [Fan Haigang and Yin Wenli], "法国海基战略核力量探秘" ["Finding the Secret of the Strategic Nuclear Forces at France's Naval Bases"], 环球军事 [*Militang*], no. 10 (2005): 20-21.

35. 明周 [Ming Zhou], "零距离接触法国核潜艇" ["In Direct Proximity to French Nuclear Submarines"], 舰船知识 [*Naval & Merchant Ships*] 9 (2005): 18-21. *Naval & Merchant Ships* is a semitechnical monthly publication of the Chinese Society of Naval Architecture and Marine Engineering.

36. 春江 [Chun Jiang], "苏联/俄罗斯核潜艇的十二次重大事故" ["Twelve Major Accidents of Soviet/Russian Nuclear Submarines"], [*Quality and Reliability*], no. 5 (2000): 30; 宋宜昌 [Song Yichang], "从'库尔斯克'号事件看俄军事战略的变化" ["Looking at Russia's Military Strategic Change from the 'Kursk' Incident"], 舰船知识 [*Naval & Merchant Ships*] 253, no. 10 (2004): 13-14; 王子聿 [Wang Ziyu], "永远的'库尔斯克'号" ["The Eternal 'Kursk'"], 舰船知识 [*Naval & Merchant Ships*] 253, no. 10 (2004): 18-19.

37. 王晓龙 [Wang Xiaolong], "俄'台风'级战略核潜艇真的徒具虚名? 前北方舰队司令语出惊人" ["Does Russia's Typhoon Class Strategic Submarine Really Have an Undeserved Reputation? A Former North Sea Fleet Commander's Alarming Report"], 当代海军 [*Modern Navy*], no. 7 (July 2004): 54.

38. 吴健 [Wu Jian], "'北报巨鲸'在复苏—发展中的俄海军核潜艇部队" ["Reporting on a 'Huge Northern Whale' Coming Back to Life—The Russian Navy Nuclear Submarine Force Under Development"], 当代海军 [*Modern Navy*], no. 2 (1999): 29.

39. 辛文 [Xin Wen], "俄罗斯核潜艇惊心动魄四十年" ["The Soul Stirring Forty Years of Russian Nuclear Submarines"], 国外核新闻 [*Foreign Nuclear News*], no. 8 (2000): 11; 王存琳 [Wang Cunlin], "俄罗斯海上战略核力量的崛起—俄罗斯核潜艇舰队今昔" ["The Rise of Russia's Strategic Nuclear Power at Sea—The Past and Present of Russia's Nuclear Submarine Force"], 上海造船 [*Shanghai Shipbuilding*], no. 2 (2000): 53–64; "俄罗斯的核潜艇反应堆" ["Russian Nuclear Submarine Reactors"], 国外核新闻 [*Foreign Nuclear News*], no. 10 (1998): 12; 高艺, 黄展烽, 赵克文 [Gao Yi, Huang Zhanfeng, and Zhao Kewen], "游弋大洋深处的幽灵—扫描俄罗斯核潜艇" ["A Specter Cruising the Ocean Depths—Scanning Russia's Nuclear Submarines"], 中国民兵 [*Chinese People's Militia*], no. 6 (2005): 60–61.

40. 刘一建 [Liu Yijian], "核时代与戈尔什科夫 '核海军制胜论'" ["The Nuclear Age and Gorshkov's 'Winning Victory By Way of the Nuclear Navy'"], 中国军事科学 [*China Military Science*], no. 2 (1999): 154.

41. 吴大海 [Wu Dahai], "巴伦支海上刮起新'台风'" ["Raising a New 'Typhoon' on the Sea"], 当代海军 [*Modern Navy*] 109, no. 10 (2002): 25–26. *Modern Navy* is published by the official PLA Navy newspaper, *People's Navy*.

42. 海生 [Hai Sheng], "俄罗斯'猎豹'重拳出击" ["Russia's 'Gepard' Heavy Fist Launches an Attack"], 当代海军 [*Modern Navy*] 98, no. 11 (2001): 6.

43. 王新森 [Wang Xinsen], "俄罗斯核潜艇决战日本'八八舰队'(上)" ["Russian Nuclear Submarines Decisively Engage Japan's '88 Fleet' (Part 1 of 2)"], 舰船知识 [*Naval & Merchant Ships*] 278, no. 10 (October 2002): 25–29; 王新森 [Wang Xinsen], "俄罗斯核潜艇决战日本'八八舰队'(下)" ["Russian Nuclear Submarines Decisively Engage Japan's '88 Fleet' (Part 2 of 2)"], 舰船知识 [*Naval & Merchant Ships*] 278, no. 11 (November 2002): 27–32.

44. 王凌, 沈巍岗 [Wang Ling and Shen Weigang], "用钛合金建造潜艇" ["Using Titanium Alloy to Build Submarines"], 舰船知识 [*Naval & Merchant Ships*] 311, no. 8, (August 2005): 44–45; 王凌, 袁仲 [Wang Ling and Yuan Zhong], "A级核潜艇出笼的前前后后" ["The Whole Story Behind the Appearance of the A Class Nuclear Submarine"], 舰船知识 [*Naval & Merchant Ships*] 311, no. 8 (August 2005): 46–49; 王子聿, 王凌 [Wang Ziyu and Wang Ling], "A级攻击型核潜艇" ["A Class Nuclear Attack Submarine"], 舰船知识 [*Naval & Merchant Ships*] 311, no. 8 (August 2005): 50–53; 王子聿 [Wang Ziyu], "绝密: D级弹道导弹核潜艇: D-1型" ["Top-Secret: The D Class SSBN: Type D-1"], 舰船知识 [*Naval & Merchant Ships*] 298, no. 7 (July 2004): 25–28; "改发16枚弹道导弹的D-2型" ["Type D-2: Transformed to Fire 16 ICBMs"], 舰船知识 [*Naval & Merchant Ships*] 298, no. 7 (July 2004): 29; 王子聿 [Wang Ziyu], "首装分导弹头的D-3型" ["Type D-3: The First With MIRVed Warheads"], 舰船知识 [*Naval & Merchant Ships*] 298, no. 7 (July 2004): 30–32; 止戈 [Zhi Ge], "D级终结者: D-4型" ["The Last of the D-Class: The D-4"], 舰船知识 [*Naval & Merchant Ships*] 298, no. 7 (July 2004): 33–34; 王子聿 [Wang Ziyu], "V-1型: 苏联第一级水滴型核潜艇" ["Type V-1: The Soviet Union's First Teardrop-Shaped Submarine"], 舰船知识 [*Naval & Merchant Ships*] 294, no. 3 (March 2003): 17–20; 袁仲 [Yuan Zhong], "加大火力的V-2X型" ["Type V-2—With Added Firepower"], 舰船知识 [*Naval & Merchant Ships*] 294, no. 3 (March 2003): 21–22; 王子聿 [Wang Ziyu], "V-3型攻击核潜艇" ["The Type V-3 Nuclear Attack

Submarine"], 舰船知识 [*Naval & Merchant Ships*] 294, no. 3 (March 2003): 22–24; 王子聿, 王凌, [Wang Ziyu and Wang Ling], "奥斯卡级: 巡航导弹潜艇之魁" ["The Oscar Class: Chief Among Cruise Missile Submarines"], 舰船知识 [*Naval & Merchant Ships*] 279, no. 12 (2002): 18–21; 王子聿, 王凌, [Wang Ziyu and Wang Ling], "'花岗岩'历时16年的杰作" ["The 'Granit' Missile: A Masterpiece With a History of 16 Years"], 舰船知识 [*Naval & Merchant Ships*] 279, no. 12 (2002): 22–23; 钱普 [Qian Pu], "奥斯卡级: 反舰作战组织实施" ["The Oscar Class: Carrying Out Anti-Ship Battle Operations System"], 舰船知识 [*Naval & Merchant Ships*] 279, no. 12 (2002): 24–25.

45. 易佳言 [Yi Jiayan], "台风级的排水量" ["The Typhoon Class's Displacement"], 舰船知识 [*Naval & Merchant Ships*], no. 9 (2004): 15.

46. 王子聿 [Wang Ziyu], "世纪梦魇: 台风级战略导弹核潜艇" ["Nightmare of the Century: The Typhoon Class SSBN Nuclear Submarine"], 舰船知识 [*Naval & Merchant Ships*], no. 12 (2004): 26–31.

47. 吴健 [Wu Jian], "'北报巨鲸'在复苏—发展中的俄海军核潜艇部队" ["Reporting on a 'Huge Northern Whale' Coming Back to Life—The Russian Navy Nuclear Submarine Force Under Development"], 当代海军 [*Modern Navy*], no. 2 (1999): 30; 王子聿 [Wang Ziyu], "世纪梦魇: 台风级战略导弹核潜艇" ["Nightmare of the Century: The Typhoon Class SSBN Nuclear Submarine:], 舰船知识 [*Naval & Merchant Ships*], no. 12 (2004): 26; and 刘一建 [Liu Yijian], "核时代与戈尔什科夫'核海军制胜论'" ["The Nuclear Age and Gorshkov's 'Winning Victory By Way of the Nuclear Navy'"], 中国军事科学 [*China Military Science*], no. 2 (1999): 151.

48. 林长盛 [Lin Changsheng], "我国核潜艇的战力" ["The Combat Power of China's Nuclear Submarines"], 27.

49. No author, "于勇: 核动力的守护者" ["Valiant Yu: Guardian of Nuclear Power"], 人民海军 [*People's Navy*] (September 15, 2005): 3; see also 长风 [Zhang Feng], "核潜艇与中国海军" ["Nuclear Submarines and China's Navy"], 舰船知识 [*Naval & Merchant Ships*] (March 2005): 12.

50. Liu Huaqing, *The Memoirs of Liu Huaqing*, 476.

51. 吴毅平, 刘江平 [Wu Yiping, Liu Jiangping], "多面杀手—现代核潜艇" ["Multi-Faceted Assassin—The Modern Nuclear Submarine"], 当代海军 [*Modern Navy*], no. 5 (2002): 27.

52. 张学诚, 殷世江 [Zhang Xuecheng, Yin Shijiang], "常规潜艇将更有魅力" ["Conventional Submarines are Even More Fascinating"], 当代海军 [*Modern Navy*], no. 6 (2002): 9.

53. "钢铁鲨鱼" ["Steel Shark"], 三联生活周刊 [*Sanlian Life Weekly*] 20 (May 19, 2003): 29–30, as cited in Toshi Yoshihara, "U.S. Ballistic-Missile Defense and China's Undersea Nuclear Deterrent: A Preliminary Assessment," in this volume.

54. Liu Huaqing, *The Memoirs of Liu Huaqing*, 476.

55. 吴锴 [Wu Kai], "攻击型核潜艇的计划思想—再访黄旭华院士" ["An Interview with Huang Xuhua: SSN Design Philosophy"], 兵器知识 [*Ordnance Knowledge*] 152, no. 6 (June 2000): 22.

56. 高运 [Gao Yun], "核潜艇的优点及缺点" ["The Strengths and Weaknesses of Nuclear Submarines"], 国防 [*National Defense*], no. 6 (1996): 45. Researchers at a PLAN submarine base and China's Naval Engineering Academy have discussed methods to improve the repair of nuclear submarines in war. See 董富生, 赵新文, 蔡琦 [Dong Fusheng, Zhao Xinwen, and Cai Qi], "核潜艇战损修理研究" ["Study of Repair of Damaged Nuclear Submarines in War"], 中国修船 [*China Ship Repair*], no. 4 (1999): 35–37.

57. 长风 [Zhang Feng], "核潜艇与中国海军" ["Nuclear Submarines and China's Navy"], 舰船知识 [*Naval & Merchant Ships*] (March 2005): 12.

58. 沈游 [Shen You], "新世纪潜艇创新发展前瞻" ["Looking Ahead at the New Century's Nuclear Submarine Development and Innovation"], 现代舰船 [*Modern Ships*] no. 5 (2005): 15–16. *Modern Ships* is published by the state-owned China Shipbuilding Industry Corporation (CSIC). Directly supervised by China's State Council, CSIC is China's largest designer, manufacturer, and trader of military and civilian vessels and related engineering and equipment. CSIC's 96 enterprises, 28 research institutes, and 6 laboratories reportedly employ 170,000.

59. The three sentences above are all drawn from 长风 [Zhang Feng], "核潜艇与中国海军" ["Nuclear Submarines and China's Navy"], 12.

60. For the first and second island chains, see 徐起 [Xu Qi], "21世纪初海上地缘战略与中国海军的发展" [Maritime Geostrategy and the Development of the Chinese Navy in the Early 21st Century], 中国军事科学 [*China Military Science*] (Vol. 17, No. 4) 2004, pp. 75–81. Translation by Andrew Erickson and Lyle Goldstein published in *Naval War College Review* 59, no. 4 (autumn 2006), esp. map and translators' note 11.

61. 王逸峰, 叶景 [Wang Yifeng and Ye Jing], "从中日核潜艇事件看我核潜艇的突防" ["What the Nuclear Submarine Incident Between China and Japan Tells Us About the Ability of China's Nuclear Submarines to Penetrate Defenses, Part 2"], 舰载武器 [*Shipborne Weapons*] (February 2005): 40.

62. Ye Jing, "What the Nuclear Submarine Incident Between China and Japan Tells Us About the Ability of China's Nuclear Submarines to Penetrate Defenses," *Jianzai Wuqi* (March 1, 2005), FBIS #CPP20050324000211. The precise Chinese citation of the above article is: 王逸峰, 叶景 [Wang Yifeng and Ye Jing], "从中日核潜艇事件看我核潜艇的突防" ["What the Nuclear Submarine Incident Between China and Japan Tells Us About the Ability of China's Nuclear Submarines to Penetrate Defenses, Part 3"], 舰载武器 [*Shipborne Weapons*] (March 2005): 49.

63. 长风 [Zhang Feng], "核潜艇与中国海军" ["Nuclear Submarines and China's Navy"], 12.

64. 林长盛 [Lin Changsheng], "我国核潜艇的战力" ["The Combat Power of China's Nuclear Submarines"], 27–28.

65. Ibid., 27.

66. See 吴谐 [Wu Xie], "战略核潜艇设计方案简析" ["A Basic Analysis of SSBN Design Plans"], 兵器知识 [*Ordnance Knowlege*] 4, no. 198 (April 2004): 53, as cited in Toshi Yoshihara, "U.S. Ballistic Missile Defense and China's Undersea Nuclear Deterrent: A Preliminary Assessment," in this volume.

67. This paragraph is entirely drawn from ibid., 33.

68. "中国海上威慑进入一个崭新时代—093型，094型核潜艇最新消息" ["China's At Sea Deterrent: Entering a Brand New Era—The Latest Information on China's Type 093 and 094 Submarines"], 军事纵横 [*Military Overview*], no. 101, 53.

69. This paragraph is drawn entirely from Ye Jing, "What the Nuclear Submarine Incident Between China and Japan Tells Us About the Ability of China's Nuclear Submarines to Penetrate Defenses," *Jianzai Wuqi* (March 1, 2005), FBIS #CPP20050324000211. The precise Chinese citation of the above article is: 王逸峰, 叶景 [Wang Yifeng and Ye Jing], "从中日核潜艇事件看我核潜艇的突防" [What the Nuclear Submarine Incident Between China and Japan Tells Us About the Ability of China's Nuclear Submarines to Penetrate Defenses, Part 3], 舰载武器 [*Shipborne Weapons*] (March 2005): 51.

70. This paragraph is entirely drawn from 长风 [Zhang Feng], "核潜艇与中国海军" ["Nuclear Submarines and China's Navy"], 12.

71. Ye Jing, "What the Nuclear Submarine Incident Between China and Japan Tells Us About the Ability of China's Nuclear Submarines to Penetrate Defenses," *Jianzai Wuqi* (March 1, 2005), FBIS #CPP20050324000211. The precise Chinese citation of the above article is: 王逸峰, 叶景 [Wang Yifeng and Ye Jing], "从中日核潜艇事件看我核潜艇的突防" ["What the Nuclear Submarine Incident Between China and Japan Tells Us About the Ability of China's Nuclear Submarines to Penetrate Defenses, Part 3"], 舰载武器 [*Shipborne Weapons*] (March 2005): 49.

72. 林长盛 [Lin Changsheng], "我国核潜艇的战力" ["The Combat Power of China's Nuclear Submarines"], 31.

73. 长风 [Zhang Feng], "核潜艇与中国海军" ["Nuclear Submarines and China's Navy"], 13.

74. Ibid., 13.

75. 简杰 [Jian Jie], "神话中德双子座" ["The Legend of the Virtuous Twins"], 23.

76. 林长盛 [Lin Changsheng], "我国核潜艇的战力" ["The Combat Power of China's Nuclear Submarines"], 33.

77. See, for example, 高运 [Gao Yun], "核潜艇的优点及缺点" ["The Strengths and Weaknesses of Nuclear Submarines"], 国防 [*National Defense*], no. 6 (1996): 45.

78. 沈泓萃, 姚惠之, 周毅, 王锡良 [Shen Hongcui, Yao Huizhi, Zhou Yi, and Wang Xiliang], "增效降噪的潜艇前置导叶螺旋桨研究" ["Submarine Guide Vane Propeller for Increasing Efficiency and Reducing Noise"], 舰船力学 [*Journal of Ship Mechanics*] 1, no. 1 (August 1997): 1–7.

79. 赵洪江 [Zhao Hongjiang], "主循环水管路更换挠性接管技术" ["Study of Replacing Techniques for Flexure Joint-Pipe of Main Circulating Water-Piping"], 中国修船 [*China Ship-Repair*], no. 6 (1997): 21–23.

80. 任勇生, 刘立厚 [Ren Yongsheng and Liu Lihou], "纤维增强复合材料结构阻尼研究进展" ["Advances in Damping Analysis and Design of Fiber Reinforced Composite Material Structures"], 力学与实践 [*Mechanics & Engineering*] 26, no. 1 (February 2004): 9–16.

81. 简杰 [Jian Jie], "神话中德双子座" ["The Legend of the Virtuous Twins"], 23.

82. 林长盛 [Lin Changsheng], "我国核潜艇的战力" ["The Combat Power of China's Nuclear Submarines"], 33.

83. Ibid., 33. Decibel levels can be measured in various ways and thus are difficult to interpret out of context.

84. Ibid., 32.

85. 简杰 [Jian Jie], "神话中德双子座" ["The Legend of the Virtuous Twins"], 22–23.

86. Ibid., 22. An Internet source asserts, "plans to deploy this class of nuclear powered SSBNs are said to have been delayed due to problems with the nuclear reactor power plants." See "中国防务周刊对于094的介绍" [China Defense Weekly on the 094's Introduction], June 22, 2005, http://military.china.com/zh_cn /critical3/27/20050622/12422997.html.

87. 863 Plan Research has also focused on potential future propulsion technologies, such as magnetic fluid propulsion. This would use powerful electromagnets to quietly move sea water through a propulsor nozzle near the tail of a submarine. See 阮可强, 冯运昌 [Ruan Keqiang and Feng Yunchang], "863计划能源技术领域: 光辉十五年" ["The Energy Technology Domain of the 863 Plan: Fifteen Years of Brilliance"], 高科技与产业化 [High Technology & Industrialization], no. 1 (2001): 33.

88. See 吴宗鑫 [Wu Congxin] 先进核能系统和高温气冷堆 [An Advanced Nuclear Reactor System: The High Temperature Gas Cooled Reactor] (Beijing: Qinghua University Press, 2004), 204–6; Xu Yuanhui, "Power Plant Design; HTGR Advances in China," Nuclear Engineering International (16 March 2005), 22, http:// web.lexis-nexis.com/universe/printdoc; as cited in Shawn Cappellano-Sarver, "Naval Implications of China's Nuclear Power Development," in this volume.

89. Elizabeth Thomson, "MIT, Tsinghua Collaborate on Development of Pebble-Bed Nuclear Reactor," MIT press release 22 October 2003, available at http://web .mit.edu/newsoffice/2003/pebble.html. As cited in Shawn Cappellano-Sarver, "Naval Implications of China's Nuclear Power Development," in this volume.

90. 阮可强, 冯运昌 [Ruan Keqiang and Feng Yunchang], "863计划能源技术领域: 光辉十五年" ["The Energy Technology Domain of the 863 Plan: Fifteen Years of Brilliance"], 高科技与产业化 [High Technology & Industrialization], no. 1 (200): 32–33.

91. "西屋公司在中国赢得两项合同" ["The Westinghouse Corporation Gains Two Contracts in China"], 中国核信息网 [China Atomic Information Network], August 19, 2004, http://www.atominfo.com.cn/newsreport/news_detail.aspx?id=3149.

92. 林长盛 [Lin Changsheng], "我国核潜艇的战力" ["The Combat Power of China's Nuclear Submarines"], 33.

93. 简杰 [Jian Jie], "神话中德双子座" ["The Legend of the Virtuous Twins"], 22.

94. 吴锴 [Wu Kai], "攻击型核潜艇的计划思想—再访黄旭华院士" ["An Interview with Wang Xuhua: SSN Design Philosophy"], 兵器知识 [Ordnance Knowledge] 152, no. 6 (June 2000): 23.

95. Shawn Cappellano-Sarver, "Naval Implications of China's Nuclear Power Development," in this volume.

96. 吴锴[Wu Kai], "攻击型核潜艇的计划思想—再访黄旭华院士" ["An Interview with Wang Xuhua: SSN Design Philosophy"], 兵器知识 [*Ordnance Knowledge*] 152, no. 6 (June 2000): 23.

97. See, for example, 田金文 [Tian Jinwen], "如何提高巡航导弹生存能力和打击效果" ["How to Improve Cruise Missile Survivability and Attack Effectiveness"], 航天电子对抗 [*Aerospace Electronic Warfare*], no. 1 (2005): 12–14; 曹晓盼 [Cao Xiaopan], "中国的巡航导弹现状" ["The Current Status of China's Cruise Missiles"], 舰载武器 [*Shipborne Weapons*] (November 2004): 26–27.

98. 赵正业 [Zhao Zhengye], 潜艇火控原理 [*Principles of Submarine Fire Control*] (Beijing 国防工业出版社 [National Defense Industry Press], September 2003), 329, 332.

99. 简杰 [Jian Jie], "神话中德双子座" ["The Legend of the Virtuous Twins"], 23.

100. 吴锴 [Wu Kai], "攻击型核潜艇的计划思想—再访黄旭华院士" ["An Interview with Huang Xuhua: SSN Design Philosophy"], 25.

101. 简杰 [Jian Jie], "神话中德双子座" ["The Legend of the Virtuous Twins"], 14.

102. 林长盛 [Lin Changsheng], "我国核潜艇的战力" ["The Combat Power of China's Nuclear Submarines"], 33.

103. Liu Huaqing, *The Memoirs of Liu Huaqing*, 497.

104. For a history of JL SLBM development, see 台风 [Tai Feng], "'巨浪' 冲天举世惊中国海军潜射弹道导弹" ["'Great Wave,' A Shock Soaring Throughout the World: The PLAN's SLBM"], [*Shipborne Weapons*], no. 9 (2004): 32–35.

105. "终报震慑:中国的战略导弹"["EntirelyFrightful:China's Ballistic Missiles"], 军事纵横 [*Military Overview*], no. 101: 13.

106. 简杰 [Jian Jie], "神话中德双子座" ["The Legend of the Virtuous Twins"], 23.

107. One Internet source speculates that the JL-2 is an underwater variant of China's DF-31. See "漏斗子关于094和巨浪言论" ["Opinions Regarding 094 and Julang"], 读卖新闻 [*Mainichi Daily News*], June 21, 2005, http://military.china.com/zh_cn/critical3/27/20050621/12418878.html.

108. 简杰 [Jian Jie], "神话中德双子座" ["The Legend of the Virtuous Twins"], 23. An unofficial posting on China Central Television's website claims seven–eight warheads per JL-2. See "现在中国的巨浪二型潜射弹道导弹" ["China's Current JL-2 SLBM"], 央视国际首页 > 论坛首页 > 网评天下 [China Central Television International Lead Page > Forum Lead Page > China Commentary Network, August 4, 2004, http://bbs.cctv.com.cn/forumthread.jsp?id=4513301.

109. 严烈 [Yan Lie], "大海深处的感觉—访海军某核潜艇艇长闫保健" ["Becoming Aware of the Ocean Depths—Visiting a Certain Naval Nuclear Submarine's Captain Yan Baojian"], 航海 [*Navigation*] no. 1 (1998): 1, 27. By way of comparison, when first deployed in 1971 the U.S. Navy's Poseidon SLBM could reportedly carry as many as fourteen MIRVs. France's M-4 SLBM reportedly carries up to six MIRVed warheads. In 2001, a noted Chinese nuclear expert claimed that "China

has the capability to develop . . . MIRVs . . . but has not done so. . . ." See Li Bin, "The Impact of U.S. NMD on Chinese Nuclear Modernization," Working Paper, Pugwash Workshop on East Asian Security, Seoul, April 2001.

110. This entire paragraph is drawn from Stephen Polk, "China's Nuclear Command and Control," chapter 1 in Lyle Goldstein and Andrew Erickson, eds., *China's Nuclear Force Modernization*, U.S. Naval War College Newport Paper no. 22, April 5, 2005, 19–20.

111. 王新森 [Wang Xinsen], "魔鬼的天籁: 对潜通信中继机" ["The Call of the Devil: Submarine Communications Aircraft"], 舰船知识 [*Naval & Merchant Ships*], no. 287 (August 2003): 42–45.

112. Liu Huaqing, *The Memoirs of Liu Huaqing*, 501–2.

113. Garth Hekler, Ed Francis, and James Mulvenon, "C3 in the Chinese Submarine Fleet," in this volume.

114. Liu Huaqing, *The Memoirs of Liu Huaqing*, 474–77, 494.

115. 彭子强 [Peng Ziqiang], 中国核潜艇研制纪实施 ["The Research and Development of Chinese Nuclear Submarines"], 中共中央党校出版社 [Chinese Communist Party Central Committee Party School Press] (Beijing, 2005), 286.

116. 黄彩虹, 寒羽 [Huang Caihong, Han Yu], 核潜艇 [*Nuclear Submarines*] (Beijing: People's Press, 1996), 91, Caltech Chinese Association online library at http://caltechc.caltech.edu/~caltechc/clibrary/CD%20056/ts056058.pdf, accessed on 1 March 2005.

117. 吕家本，王盛龙，刘文 [Lu Jiaben, Wang Shenglong, Liu Wen, et al.], "'银参冲剂'对核潜艇远航艇员保健效能的评价" ["Evaluation of Health Protective Effects of 'Silver Ginseng Medicine' on the Crew of a Nuclear Submarine During a Long Voyage"], 中华航海医学杂志 [*Chinese Journal of Nautical Medicine*] 5, no. 4 (December 1998): 241–44; 房芳, 吴力克, 毕可玲, 梁冰, 赵红 [Fang Fang, Wu Like, Bi Keling, Liang Bing, and Zhao Hong], "水面舰艇和核潜艇对艇员血液细胞成份和某些流变学指标的影响" ["The Effects of Long-Term Voyages on the Blood Cell Components and Rheology of Sailors on Naval Ships and Nuclear-Powered Submarines"], 解放军预防医学杂志 [*Chinese People's Liberation Army Journal of Preventive Medicine*], no. 4 (2004): 261–64; 马彩娥, 吕发勤, 宓传刚, 杜莉, 孙湖山 [Ma Cai'e, Lu Faqin, Mi Chuangang, Du Li, Sun Hushan], "核潜艇艇员远航后心脏超声心动图随访观察" ["Echocardiographical Follow-up Studies of the Hearts of Nuclear Submarine Sailors After Lengthy Voyages"], 心脏杂志 [*Chinese Heart Journal*], no. 1 (2004): 71–75; 赵红, 吴力克, 梁冰, 刘文, 房芳, 杨朋 [Zhao Hong, Wu Like, Liang Bing, Liu Wen, Fang Fang, and Yang Peng], "水面舰艇及核潜艇长航对艇员心里健康水平的影响" ["The Effects of Long-Term Voyages on the Psychological Health of Sailors on Naval Ships and Nuclear-Powered Submarines"], 解放军预防医学杂志 [*Chinese People's Liberation Army Journal of Preventive Medicine*] 20, no. 5 (October 2002): 332–35; 余浩, 项光强 [Yu Hao and Xiang Guangqiang], "核潜艇艇员个性心理特征分析" ["Analysis of Submariners' Personalities"], 海军医学杂志 [*Journal of Navy Medicine*] 21, no. 1 (March 2000): 7–8.

118. 高运 [Gao Yun], "核潜艇的优点及缺点" ["The Strengths and Weaknesses of Nuclear Submarines"], 国防 [*National Defense*], no. 6 (1996): 45.

119. 赵大勋, 李国兴 [Zhao Daxun and Li Guoxing], 美国海军潜艇设计特点及质量控制 [*USN Submarines' Design Characteristics and Quality Control*], 哈尔滨工程大学出版社 [Harbin: Harbin Engineering University Press], 2000, 2.

120. 河山 [He Shan], "'弗吉尼亚'号能否成为新世纪海上霸主" ["Can the Virginia Class Become the New Century's Maritime Hegemon?"], 当代海军 [*Modern Navy*], no. 10 (2004): 18–21.

121. 止戈 [Zhi Ge], "'旧金山'号核潜艇事故分析" ["An Analysis of the 'San Francisco' Nuclear Submarine Accident"], 舰船知识 [*Naval & Merchant Ships*], no. 3 (2005): 59.

122. 杨毅 [Yang Yi], "谁的潜艇今后说了算?" ["Who Can Estimate the Future Number of Submarines?"], 舰船知识 [*Naval and Merchant Ships*] (July 2006): 28.

123. This paragraph draws on the introduction to this volume.

124. After launching the first 093 in 2002, China now may be working on hull three of that class. The first 094 was reportedly launched in 2004. See Richard Fisher, "Submarine Incident Highlights Military Buildup," *Asian Wall Street Journal*, 17 November 2004, http://www.strategycenter.net/research/pubID.51/pub_detail.asp.

Garth Hekler, Ed Francis, and James Mulvenon

C3 in the Chinese Submarine Fleet

Introduction

CHINA'S SUBMARINE FLEET IS EXPANDING RAPIDLY, with the development of second-generation nuclear-powered attack and ballistic-missile submarines (the 093 and 094 respectively), as well as the US$ 1.6 billion purchase of eight Russian Kilo-class conventional submarines.[1] With an increasingly complex submarine fleet, the People's Liberation Army Navy (PLAN) will need to develop a system to control its forces. While command, control, and communications (C3) have challenged military leaders for centuries, submarines present a unique set of obstacles because of the nature of submarine warfare. A submarine's key tactical advantage is its ability to act undetected beneath the ocean surface. However, communications are limited by the fact that seawater rapidly attenuates the signal strength of all but the longest radio wavelengths. A submarine wishing to send and receive information beyond basic time and navigation data must rise to shallower depths for transmission, trading stealth for connectivity. Submarine communications therefore come with a trade-off: a submarine can either stay hidden but act alone, or it can act in concert with the rest of the navy but with limited stealth.

This chapter will analyze China's submarine C3 system, paying particular attention to the level of centralization and trends in the development of communication technologies. We will begin by discussing the relative merits of centralized and decentralized C3 systems. After that, we will examine the PLAN and its approach to submarine C3. While the PLAN may recognize the effectiveness of decentralized C3 for certain types of submarine missions, it appears to be seeking to create a more tightly centralized submarine C3 system by developing command automation, network-centric warfare strategies, and advanced communications technologies.

Definition of Terms: Centralized versus Decentralized C3

Before embarking on a discussion of Chinese submarine C3, it is first necessary to compare what is meant by centralized versus decentralized C3. In a decentralized C3 system, tactical decisions are made at the lowest level possible, relying heavily on well-trained officers at the tactical level who are able to act without guidance from the central commander. Such a system requires established rules of engagement and frequent training exercises in preparation for battle, including battle simulations and real-time exercises designed to prepare individual soldiers to act in unexpected circumstances. Decentralized C3 systems still take advantage of high communications connectivity, but individual tactical nodes are entrusted with greater autonomy in the event of a collapse in the communications infrastructure.

By contrast, in a centralized C3 system, decisions are made at the top of the command chain. Centralized C3 systems seek to empower a central commander to collect and process enormous amounts of information, and issue orders to guide the actions of subordinate command units. Centralized C3 requires a reliable communications system so that the central commander can remain in constant contact with his subordinates. The system requires training, consisting of rote drills and scripted exercises designed to get officers at the tactical level to follow orders, rather than to react independently and/or solve problems as they arise.

In *Command in War*, Martin van Creveld analyzed the historical development of C3 in land warfare,[2] and found that decentralized C3 systems have generally proven to be more adaptable and effective than centralized C3 systems. Michael Palmer came to similar conclusions with regard to naval C3 in his recent book *Command at Sea: Naval Command and Control Since the Sixteenth Century*.[3] Their conclusions were based on an assessment that, despite advances in surveillance and communications technologies, the wartime battlefield environment remains significantly uncertain. Real-world commanders act under pressures of limited time, imperfect knowledge, and haphazard communications. Decentralized C3 systems are generally better suited to overcoming these challenges. This is reflected in the U.S. Navy's endorsement of decentralized control in "Naval Doctrine Publication 6: Naval Command and Control."[4] The Second World War provides two historical examples of centralized and decentralized C3 for submarines.

The German submarine campaign in the Atlantic made use of a relatively centralized C3 approach. The German approach involved sending submarines to different points in the Atlantic. When allied ships were located, the submarines would send the coordinates to headquarters. Headquarters would then order several submarines to converge on a select point where they would attack as a "wolf pack." By most accounts this strategy was effective in that Germany was able to sink a respectable quantity of allied shipping.[5] However, as the war continued, Germany suffered progressively greater losses to its submarine force. By the end of the war, according to the analysis of Karl Lautenschlaeger, Germany had lost 67 percent of its submarine forces while sinking approximately 17.4 percent of Great Britain's merchant shipping.[6]

We see a very different approach to submarine C3 in the U.S. submarine campaign against Japan. The U.S. approach involved sending several submarines into Japanese shipping channels. Rather than communicating with headquarters, these submarines were expected to attack alone, and to take targets of opportunity as they presented themselves.[7] The U.S. campaign devastated Japanese shipping, sinking approximately 48.5 percent of Japan's merchant fleet as measured in tonnage, with losses to U.S submarine forces of approximately 15.4 percent.[8]

While decentralized C3 appears to be the superior approach, this endorsement is not without caveats. Decentralized C3 demands a well-trained officer corps. In the absence of such well-trained officers, delegation of authority can be far worse than micromanagement. While a well-functioning decentralized C3 system may be the ideal, it may not be practical if tactical commanders are not up to the challenge. It is therefore possible that centralized C3 could be preferable under certain circumstances.

It should also be noted that certain types of missions demand centralized C3 by their very nature, the most important example being the deployment of nuclear ballistic-missile submarines (SSBNs). In this case, the goal is not so much victory on a naval battlefield or the destruction of enemy shipping, but rather deterrence from engaging in nuclear warfare. Under these circumstances, centralized C3 is preferable, and during the Cold War, both the United States and the Soviet Union maintained constant centralized control over their submarine forces.[9]

PLAN Submarine Command and Control: Context and Challenges

The most important political-military challenge and the most likely flash-point for Sino-US conflict is Taiwan. Should the situation deteriorate into direct military conflict, the People's Liberation Army (PLA) since 1992 has been hard at work bolstering the hedging options of the leadership, developing advanced campaign doctrines, testing the concepts in increasingly complex training and exercises, and integrating new indigenous and imported weapons systems. At the strategic level, the writings of Chinese military authors suggest that there are two main centers of gravity in a Taiwan scenario, both of which directly involve China's increasingly formidable submarine force. The first of these is the will of the Taiwanese people, which they hope to undermine through exercises, submarine blockades, missile attacks, Special Operations Force (SOF) operations, and other operations that have a psychological warfare focus. Based on intelligence from the 1995–96 exercises, as well as public opinion polling in Taiwan, China appears to have concluded that the Taiwanese people do not have the stomach for conflict and will therefore sue for peace after suffering only a small amount of pain. The second center of gravity is the will and capability of the United States to intervene decisively in a cross-strait conflict. In a strategic sense, China may believe that its ICBM inventory, which is capable of striking the continental United States, will serve as a deterrent to U.S. intervention, or at least a brake on escalation. In the future, deployment of the next-generation SSBN will enhance the stability of China's second-strike deterrent. Closer to Taiwan, the PLA has been engaged in an active program of equipment modernization, purchasing and indigenously developing niche anti-access, area-denial capabilities such as long-range cruise missiles and quiet diesel-electric and nuclear-powered attack submarines to shape the operational calculus of the American carrier battle group commander on station.

At the same time, China's emerging submarine force, much like its road-mobile conventional and nuclear missile force, pose significant C3 challenges to the Chinese military and national command authority, as they will be the primary units operating at the dynamic edges of a system accustomed to maintaining strong, active control via internal lines of communication. Traditionally, the Chinese C3 system has delegated little authority to lower levels, requiring central-level approval for the movement of even company-size ground force units.[10] The traditional command culture has also emphasized caution and discouraged initiative without explicit instructions from above, suggesting that units cut off from their chain of command would remain passive rather than acting without clear guidance. These traditional concepts and operational codes are perceived by the PLA leadership as an impediment to full exploitation of the PLA's emerging advanced C3 system, characterized by multiple, redundant, secure channels of communication.[11] Moreover, the combination of this traditional command culture and advanced information technology could result in the perverse outcome of *greater centralization* of control rather than decentralization and flexibility at lower levels, as senior military leaders use their greater battlespace awareness to exercise closer control at tactical levels.

In the context of these contradictions between central desire for control and the liberating effect of information technology, submarine command and control poses a particularly thorny challenge. A few examples illustrate the dilemma. For the diesel-electric and nuclear-powered attack boats expected to operate east of Taiwan and hunt for carrier strike groups (CSGs), it is unreasonable to expect them to surface and transmit a request for guidance from Beijing after finding the CSG, especially in such a hostile ASW environment. Instead, it is more reasonable to deduce that the submarines (and mobile missile units) would be given rules of engagement to be used when they cannot communicate with Beijing, either because it would be too dangerous or their C3 support infrastructure had been destroyed. However, this scenario places tremendous responsibility in the hands of a submarine commander, particularly given the possible strategic consequences of sinking a U.S. ship.

Indeed, one must assume that a similar dynamic is at work with the imminent deployment of China's next-generation SSBN. Decades of lessons from the Cold War about operating a successful nuclear deterrent suggest that a stable, survivable C3 system is critical so that headquarters could reliably authorize a second strike in the event of any first strike. At present, China's communications infrastructure is vulnerable to a first strike. As a result the SSBN commander would require explicit and restrictive rules of engagement and even targeting data, lest crisis communications with Beijing reveal its position to hostile attack submarines, or if the submarine is cut off from Beijing after a decapitating first strike. Both of these illustrative cases highlight C3 challenges that will likely stress both the Chinese C3 and decision-making systems.

PLAN Submarine Command-and-Control Structure

The PLAN is part of the greater PLA, which is divided according to services—the PLAN, People's Liberation Army Air Force (PLAAF), and the 2nd Missile Brigade—and seven military regions (MR).[12] The PLAN itself is subdivided into three fleets: the North Fleet, headquartered in Qingdao (Shandong Province, Jinan MR); the East Fleet, headquartered in Ningbo (Jiangsu Province, Nanjing MR); and the Southern Fleet, headquartered in Zhanjiang (Guangdong Province, Guangzhou MR). The PLAN can also be divided into five categories of units: naval surface vessel units, naval submarine units, naval aviation units, naval coastal defense units, and marines.[13]

In peacetime, PLAN fleet commanders are subject to multiple lines of authority from the PLAN headquarters,[14] the leaders of their respective MRs, as well as the relevant offices of the four General Departments (Staff, Political, Logistics, and Armament), especially the naval bureaus under the operational and planning departments of the General Staff Department (GSD). PLAN headquarters is organized along the same lines as PLA headquarters with its own general staff, political, logistic, and armament departments. This pattern is repeated at the level of PLAN regional fleets as well. Under this system, each commander is directly subordinate to numerous superiors. Many articles written by PLA members have described this system as being inadequate to the needs of modern war, because subordinate commanders simply cannot respond to multiple, often-conflicting orders.[15]

Because of this weakness, the PLA supreme command (*tongshuai bu*) is supposed to establish a streamlined joint wartime command structure during times of war. The process begins with the designation of a war zone[16] (*zhanqu*) and the establishment of a Joint Campaign Command (*lianhe zhanyi zhihui jigou*). The joint campaign command then takes over control of campaign execution, including planning, logistics, battlefield control, and coordination among the PLA services.[17] The desired effect of this transition is removing redundant lines of authority from the service headquarters and GSD departments. It is important to note that these reforms are not an effort to delegate tactical decision making down to the tactical level. Rather, the Chinese reforms appear to be focused on achieving unity of command.

This push for greater central control is reinforced through a move toward greater reliance on technology in submarine command automation. *Naval Operational Command Theory,* an internal publication of the PLAN, deals with principles of naval operational command. It lists several things that are necessary for an effective command system, including strengthening "jointness (*lianhe*)" and "synthesis (*hecheng*)" in the command system, and adopting modern technological methods of command. One striking suggestion concerns improving the quality of commanders: "currently the most important thing is to strengthen the commander's knowledge of science and technology at all levels. . . . Science and technology has materialized within intelligence, communication, command and control systems, and if commanders do not master high-technology knowledge, they will not be able to use automated command tools, and will not be able to truly implement operational command automation." In other words, a quality commander is one who can properly use command automation equipment, not one who can take initiative.

Naval Operation Command Theory[18] does acknowledge the potential usefulness of decentralized C3, even going so far as to remark on its potential application for submarines: "delegation-style [*weituoshi*—explained as decentralized C3] command methods are especially useful for opening naval *sabotage/guerilla warfare (poxi youji zhan)*, as it is good for fully realizing the initiative, flexibility, rapidity, quick decision, and fluidity of naval sabotage/guerilla warfare. It is more advantageous for *submarines*, air power, and small scale surface ships, when executing activities in small aircraft units, flotillas, or even as *single* boats or aircraft" (emphasis added).[19] Based on this statement, it appears that submarines could operate with substantial autonomy down to the level of single vessels. In short, this passage would support the assertion that delegation-style command is very possible in the context of the PLA's very centralized C3 system. However, closer review of Chinese writings on submarine command automation (*zhihui zidonghua*), network centric warfare (*wangluo zhongxin zhan*), and efforts to develop joint capabilities within PLA/PLAN provide some evidence that the PLAN may be seeking to develop tighter central control over its submarine forces.

Several articles extolling the benefits of submarine command automation have appeared in Chinese academic journals. An article in *Ship Engineering* presents a model for submarine decision making based on fuzzy neural networking theory. The author argues that submarine commanders would be able to enter a series of incomplete inputs into a program, which would then provide advice on the most expeditious course of action.[20] Other examples include an article in *Fire Control and Command and Control*, discussing the applicability of analytic hierarchy processing and fuzzy mathematics,[21] and a third article, which appeared in *Ship Electronic Engineering*, pointing to quality function deployment (QFD) as a way of improving command automation in submarines.[22] These discussions emphasize data entry and execution of computer-generated decisions. While submarines would operate independent of central command, tactical decision making in this construct would still be outside the hands of the submarine commander. While this information is by no means doctrinal information, it does indicate that there are people doing work on technologies that would do at least some of the work of a submarine officer, and does not indicate a high level of trust in individual submarine commanders.

Besides command automation, the PLA/PLAN is seeking to develop network-centric warfare (NCW) capability. Given China's penchant for centralized command, the enhanced connectivity inherent to NCW would probably lead to even greater interference in submarine tactical decision making. Several journal articles hint that centralization is the intended outcome of Chinese NCW development. One article in *Sensor & Control Technology* explicitly states that the goal of network-centric warfare is to "implement centralized long distance control over military forces."[23] The same article also noted the importance of combining NCW with command automation technology. Another article that appeared in *Information Command Control System & Simulation Technology* also made the point that NCW should be used in conjunction with greater command automation to better integrate submarine, surface, air, and land forces.[24] Based on these articles it appears that China's efforts to bring submarines into NCW will probably lead to less decision-making responsibility among subordinate officers.

Submarine Communications

While the PLAN may want to exercise tighter control over its submarine fleet, its current communications technology presents a significant obstacle. Until the PLAN is able to develop more advanced means of communication, it will probably be forced to exercise a more decentralized form of C3 with its submarine force. China's research and development in communications technology will be an important factor in determining how China will execute C3 with its submarine force.

Organization

At the national level, the communications aspects of C3 in the PLA are very likely led by the General Staff Department Communications Department (*Zong canmoubu/tongxin bu*). This unit (hereafter referred to as GSD/ Comms) is the PLA's signal corps, responsible for building, operating, and protecting the military's communications infrastructure. The navy communications system is connected to the national military communications system in both vertical and horizontal ways, paralleling the multiple lines of command and control in peacetime. The PLAN Headquarters in Beijing, for example, has its own communications department, which supervises subordinate communications departments in the three regional fleets. The fleet communications departments, in turn, exercise guidance over communications units in all lower echelons, culminating in the communications personnel on individual naval ships.

Communications Infrastructure

An early article from *Xinhua* describes the PLA's communications system as comprising underground networks of fiber optic cables, communications satellites, microwave links, shortwave radio stations, and automated command and control networks.[25] A series of articles in *Liberation Army Daily* between 1995 and 1997 is more specific, describing the C3 system as being composed of at least four major networks: a military telephone network, a confidential telephone network (alternatively described as "encrypted"),[26] an all-army data communications network (also known as the "all-army data exchange network" or "all-army public exchange network"),[27] and a "comprehensive communication system for field operations."[28] A third account merges the two accounts, arguing that the PLA's underground networks of optical fiber cables, communications satellites in the sky, and microwave and short-wave communications facilities in between form the infrastructure for a military telephone network, a secure telephone network, an all-army data communications network, and the integrated field communications network.[29]

In terms of submarine communications, China currently has long-range high frequency (HF)—also known as shortwave—and very low frequency (VLF) communication capability.[30] China's first submarine communications technology was long-range HF radios from the Russians. In 1958, Russia agreed to construct a high-power VLF site. In addition, the South Fleet made use of a low frequency (LF) station located in Zhanjiang. The first high-power LF station was built in Hainan in 1965. By 1980, China had VLF transmitters in both Zhanjiang and Yulin.[31] Reportedly, China has twelve VLF stations with twenty-two operating frequencies, of which only two appear to be in active use.[32]

Each technology has advantages and disadvantages, and each is useful for different purposes. VLF allows shore commanders to contact submarines submerged to depths between ten and forty meters, or greater if the submarine deploys a buoyant cable antenna. VLF transmitters operate continuously to provide submarines with basic navigation and time data while maintaining an open channel for sending other alerts. These advantages are balanced by several limitations. First, VLF communications are one-way—the transmitters are too large to house on a submarine. Second, VLF signals are less useful for sending large amounts of data because they operate with limited bandwidth compared to HF transmissions—VLF communications are typically transmitted at fifty to two hundred baud, compared with up to twelve hundred baud for high frequency (HF) transmissions. Third, besides functional issues, VLF transmitters are vulnerable to enemy attack because of their immense size.

The advantages of HF transmissions are that they allow the submarine to engage in two-way communications, and they are capable of supporting higher data-rate transmissions. HF transmissions allow for communications over great distances without using relays. However, in order to communicate, the submarine must rise to periscope depth, exposing the submarine to detection and the adversary's ASW forces. HF transmissions can also expose the submarine's location by allowing ASW forces to track the submarine's signals—a problem that China has addressed using instantaneous HF transmission technology based on the Soviet Akyha 900 communication system.[33] Another problem with HF communication is its reliability. HF transmissions rely on the ionosphere to reflect HF waves over distances and are therefore susceptible to disruption by solar wind and other atmospheric disruptions, including high-altitude nuclear detonations.

Several articles in Chinese academic journals have addressed trends in the development of submarine communication technology. An article in *Ship Electronic Engineering* discusses the vulnerability of China's shore-based VLF transmitters, suggesting that China should develop a system of airborne VLF transmitters, similar to the U.S. Navy's Take Charge and Move Out (TACAMO) system.[34] Another article addresses ways of preventing enemy detection of submarine-to-shore transmissions, specifically suggesting developing satellite technology, frequency hopping, and spread spectrum transmissions.[35] Research on spread spectrum technology is clearly in progress as indicated by a recent article reporting experimental findings in this area.[36] Research is also being conducted on improving China's HF instantaneous communications technology.[37] Beyond this, several articles also address the development of extremely low frequency (ELF) and blue-green laser technology.[38] However, China does not appear to be ready to develop either an ELF system or a laser communications system.[39]

Communications Research

The Chinese military and defense-industrial base possesses numerous subordinate research institutes that focus on topics related to C3 systems. Among the General Staff Department institutes, the 54th Research Institute is a long-established center for research on communications and monitoring technologies, including microwave relay communications, wireless communications, scatter communications, satellite communications, satellite broadcast access, remote sensing, telemetry, surveys, communications countermeasures, intelligence, and reconnaissance. The institute produced China's first fully digital satellite, communications ground station, first large shipborne satellite, communications ground station, first area air defense communications network, and first man-made satellite monitoring equipment.[40] The 56th Research Institute develops computer systems. The 61st Research Institute reportedly develops command automation systems, as well as C3 systems, and hosted the 1997 Defense Information Modernization Symposium.[41] The 62nd Research Institute performs research and development on communications equipment, computers, and command automation. The former 63rd Research Institute (now merged into the PLA Science and Engineering University) in Nanjing reportedly conducted research into microwaves and possibly encryption. One of these institutes was likely the subject of a 1999 article describing "a certain communications technology research institute under the General Staff Department" that had developed a phased-array antenna for satellite communications, thereby achieving "the goal of mobile communications and improving the rapid-reaction capability of its troops."[42]

A narrower strata of the military and defense-industrial R&D base is principally concerned with naval communications. The China Shipbuilding Industry Corporation (CSIC), a state-owned conglomerate that designs, manufactures, and sells both military and civilian ships, is a major source of submarine C3-enabling research and development. One of CSIC's principle research facilities for naval communications systems and network technology is CSIC No. 722 Research Institute, also known as the Wuhan Maritime Communications Research Institute. The institute was responsible for developing China's high-power VLF[43] and instantaneous HF communication technology.[44] The institute has also done research to determine the minimum shift key (MSK) for ELF communication, as well as buoyant antenna technology,[45] and a wide range of hard communications hardware including antennae.[46]

The CSIC 716 Research Institute, also known as the Jiangsu Automation Research Institute, investigates command automation, target processing, and C3 networking. Notably, the 716 research institute is particularly vigilant in monitoring foreign trends in naval C3-I, publishing numerous studies on the state of technology in other advanced nations.[47]

Among academic institutions, the Dalian Naval Academy and the Naval Submarine Academy at Qingdao stand out as key loci of submarine C3 research. While many of China's foremost technical universities are engaged in research on topics with tangential implications for submarine C3, these two academies are particularly notable because their programs of study include both technical and naval officer training. The variety of research published by these schools reflects this dual mission. Researchers at the Dalian Naval Academy have published numerous studies on communications technology topics applicable to submarine communications. The Academy's C3I Department, Automation Department, and Information Engineering Department all engage in naval communications research. Most recently, the academy appears to be particularly active in the fields of high-frequency communication, and frequency hopping and management techniques.[48] Also, as Dalian Naval Academy's primary mission is to train the PLAN officer force (80 percent of PLAN officers graduate from the Dalian Naval Academy),[49] the academy also publishes on topics relating to officer training reform and some naval C3 theory.

Submarine C3 research at the Naval Submarine Academy in Qingdao has recently focused on command automation systems and computer control models for submarine-commander decision making.[50] Other C3-related topics covered in recent publications include submarine-specific VLF communication,[51] and theoretical laser communications. The Submarine Academy has also published broader C3 literature considering the role of submarines in network-centric warfare and indexing worldwide trends in submarine C3 development.

Conclusions and Implications

Due to the limitations of submarine communications technology, the PLAN currently can only exercise relatively limited tactical control over its submarines. This makes China's submarine force an anomaly in the PLA, which has a tradition of highly centralized decision making. Although some Chinese military publications support the idea that submarines might be effective as relatively autonomous guerilla sabotage units, this concept is at odds with the PLA's wartime joint command structure, which is designed to move the locus of tactical decision making closer to central command. It seems likely that submarine autonomy is a second-best solution driven more by questions of what is possible than by what is most desirous.

There have been many articles published in Chinese journals that indicate an interest in developing improved command automation technologies and greater network-centric warfare capability. Both developments hinge on the ability of the submarine force to share information and coordinate action with other PLAN vessels. The greatest obstacle to this interactive role is communications technology. Chinese research organizations and universities are currently working to develop better satellite and high-frequency communication systems, and a survivable VLF system. Advances in these technologies will facilitate greater connectivity between submarines and the rest of the PLAN fleet, providing military leaders with the option to exercise greater control over tactical decision making.

It remains to be seen how these technical developments will change the degree of centralization in China's submarine force C3. While it is *highly likely* that the PLA will seek to strengthen centralized control over its fleet of nuclear ballistic-missile submarines, it is less obvious what will happen to the command structure of its attack submarines. Lessons drawn from historical comparison of United States and German submarine fleet effectiveness clearly favor decentralized C3, but this would be a highly unusual mode of operation within the greater PLA so accustomed to centralized decision-making. As improved communications technology makes centralized C3 a real option, it is difficult to say whether or not submarine forces will be able to resist the prevailing tendency toward greater centralization.

Notes

1. See Lyle Goldstein and William Murray, "Undersea Dragons: China's Maturing Submarine Force," *International Security* 28, no. 4 (Spring 2004): 165–66.

2. Martin Van Creveld, *Command in War* (Cambridge: Harvard University Press, 1985), 261–75.

3. Michael Palmer, *Command at Sea: Naval Command and Control Since the Sixteenth Century* (Cambridge: Harvard University Press, 2005), 319–22.

4. "Naval Doctrine Publication 6: Naval Command and Control," accessed at http://www.dtic.mil/doctrine/jel/service_pubs/ndp6.pdf.

5. Michael Palmer provided comparative descriptions of the German and U.S. approaches to to submarine C3 during World War II: Michael Palmer, *Command at Sea: Naval Command and Control Since the Sixteenth Century*, 275–79.

6. Karl Lautenschlager, "The Submarine in Naval Warfare, 1901–2001," *International Security* 11, no. 3 (Winter, 1986–87): 122.

7. Michael Palmer, *Command at Sea: Naval Command and Control Since the Sixteenth Century*, 275–79.

8. Karl Lautenschlager, "The Submarine in Naval Warfare, 1901–2001," 122.

9. Michael Palmer, *Command at Sea: Naval Command and Control Since the Sixteenth Century*, 300–303. For further discussion on nuclear command and control see Stephen Polk, "China's Nuclear Command and Control," in Lyle J. Goldstein and Andrew S. Erickson, eds., *China's Nuclear Force Modernization*, U.S. Naval War College, *Newport Paper No. 22*, 2005.

10. Michael Swaine, *The Military and Political Succession in China: Leadership, Institutions, Beliefs* (Santa Monica, Calif.: RAND, 1992), R-4254-AF.

11. James Mulvenon, "Chinese C4I Modernization: An Experiment in Open-Source Analysis," in James Mulvenon and Andrew N. D. Yang, *A Poverty of Riches: New Challenges and Opportunities in PLA Research* (Santa Monica, Calif.: RAND, 2003), CF-189-NSRD.

12. The seven military regions are Beijing, Nanjing, Guangzhou, Lanzhou, Shenyang, Chengdu, and Jinan.

13. Bernard C. Cole, "The Organization of the People's Liberation Army Navy (PLAN)," in James C. Mulvenon and Andrew N. D. Yang, eds., *The People's Liberation Army as Organization: Reference Volume v1.0* (Santa Monica, Calif.: RAND, 2002), CF-182-NSRD, 482–83.

14. The previous commander of the PLAN was Admiral Zhang Dingfa, himself a former submariner. See Lyle Goldstein and William Murray, "Undersea Dragons: China's Maturing Submarine Force," *International Security* 28, no. 4 (Spring 2004): 161–96.

15. See Zhang Peigao, ed., *Joint Campaign Command Teaching Materials* (Beijing: Beijing Military Science Press, 2001), 49. See also Li Wei, ed., *An Introduction to War Zone Joint Campaign Command* (Beijing: National Defense University Press, 2000), 69.

16. A war zone is described as a relatively independent battle field, encompassing a wide battle space possibly encompassing land, sea, and air elements. See Kevin Pollpeter, Michael Lostumbo, Eric Valko, and Michael Chase, *Joint Campaign Command, Control and Coordination in the Chinese Military* (Santa Monica, Calif.: RAND, April 2004), 27–28.

17. It is important to note that service coordination in the Chinese sense is very different from joint operations in the U.S. sense, in that there is little actual integration of forces across services. For example, navy air forces would not fall under a coordinated command with air force, or army air units. Rather, each service would maintain control over their land, sea, and air units, but under the guidance of the joint

campaign command. See Pollpeter et al., *Joint Campaign Command, Control and Coordination in the Chinese Military,* 49–53.

18. Yang Genyuan, ed., *Naval Operational Command Theory (Haijun Zuozhan Zhihui Gailun)* (Beijing: National Defense University Publishing House, 2002).

19. Ibid., 158–59.

20. Lu Minghua and Zhao Lin, "Submarine Command Decision Control Model and Simulation Research," *Ship Engineering (Chuanbo Gongcheng)* 27, no. 3 (2005).

21. Cai Guangyou and Song Yunong, "AHP and Its Application in the Field of Submarine Command," *Fire Control & Command and Control* 28 (5 October 2003).

22. Yang Jian and Song Yunong, "Operations Analysis about Submarine Command Automation System Based on QFD," *Ship Electronic Engineering (Chuanbo Dianzi Gongcheng)* 25, no. 4 (April 2005).

23. Qiu Xiaohui and Qiu Xiaohong, "Study on Network Centric Warfare and Its Command and Control System," *Sensor and Control Technology* 23, no. 4 (2004): 67.

24. Meng Zhaoxiang, "Submarines Engaged in NCW Require More Advanced C4ISR," *Information Command Control System & Simulation Technology (Qingbao Zhihui Kongzhi Xitong Yu Fangzhen Jishu)* 27, no. 1 (February 2005).

25. Li Xuanqing (*Jiefangjun bao*) and Ma Xiaochun (*Xinhua*), "Armed Forces Communications Become Multidimensional," *Xinhua* (16 July 1997).

26. Liu Dongsheng, "Telecommunications: Greater Sensitivity Achieved—Second of Series of Reports on Accomplishments of Economic Construction and Defense Modernization," *Jiefangjun bao* (8 September 1997): 5, in *FBIS,* 14 October 1997.

27. See Tang Shuhai, "All-Army Public Data Exchange Network Takes Initial Shape," *Jiefangjun bao* (18 September 1995) (FBIS).

28. Cheng Gang and Li Xuanqing, "Military Telecommunications Building Advances Toward Modernization with Giant Strides," *Jiefangjun bao* (17 July 1997) (FBIS).

29. Chen Jun, Hong Jie, and Tian Hong, "Regarding War Preparation, Emergency Communications, Research on Tax Exemption Questions," *Electronics Window (Dianzi zhi Chuang),* 08-2005, 51–54; Situ Mengtian "A Superficial View on the Construction of Our Army's Emergency Communication System," *Journal of Military Communications Technology (Junshi Tongxin Jishu)* (September 2001): 31–33.

30. Zheng Ruixun, "Navy Ship Communication Technology and Development Trends," *Ship Electronics Engineering (Chuanbo Dianzi Gongcheng),* no. 5 (August 1997).

31. James C. Bussert, "Chinese Submarines Pose a Double-Edged Challenge," *SIGNAL Magazine,* December 2003, accessed at: http://www.afcea.org/signal/articles/anmviewer.asp?a=93&z=22.

32. http://www.vlf.it/trond2/25-30khz.html, viewed January 15, 2006.

33. Zheng Ruixun, "Navy Ship Communication Technology and Development Trends."

34. Qu Xiaohui, "A Brief Look at the Direction of Domestic Submarine Technology Development," *Ship Electronic Engineering (Chuanbo Dianzi Gongcheng)* (May 2000): 43.

35. Mi Chen and Lai Jungao, "Submarine Communications Reconnaissance and Deception," *Information Command and Control System & Simulation Technology (Qingbao Zhihui Kongzhi Xitong Yu Fangzhen Jishu)* 26, no. 4 (August 2004): 63.

36. Fan Youwen, "Analysis of Multiple-Access Interference for Spread Spectrum Communications in Modern Submarines," *Ship Science and Technology* 26 (Supplement, 2004): 62–65, 74.

37. Zheng Ruixun, "Navy Ship Communication Technology and Development Trends," 34.

38. See Dan Xianyu, "Exploration and Partial Experiments on the Principles of Underwater Laser Communications Technology," *Physical Experiment of College (Daxue Wuli Shiyan)* 15, no. 4 (December 2002). See also Qu Xiaohui, "A Brief Look at the Direction of Domestic Submarine Technology Development," *Ship Electronic Engineering* (May 2000): 43.

39. ELF communications systems have only been built by the United States and Russia, as the systems are very large and difficult to keep in operation. Because of the expense involved, it appears unlikely that China will develop an ELF communications system.

   For its part, blue-green laser communications technology, if successfully developed, would theoretically allow for high-speed transmission of information to submarines at exceptional ocean depths. However, there are several technological challenges that prevent the technology from working. Examples include atmospheric and aquatic scatter, as well as interference from sunlight. To date there is no known blue-green laser communication system.

40. *China Electronic News (Zhonguo Dianzi Xinwen)* (22 September 2000).

41. Liang Zhenxing, "New Military Revolution: Information Warfare," *Zhongguo dianzi bao* (24 October 1997): 8, in *FBIS*, 12 January 1998.

42. "PLA Develops Mobile Satellite Communications Antenna," *Xinhua* (14 December 1999) (FBIS).

43. Stephen Pollack, "China's Nuclear Command and Control," from Lyle Goldstein and Andrew Erickson, eds., *China's Nuclear Force Modernization* (Newport, R.I.: Naval War College Press, 2005).

44. Zheng Ruixun, "Navy Ship Communication Technology and Development Trends," 34.

45. Ibid., 37.

46. Ibid., 35.

47. See examples: Dong Zhirong, "Teams and Academic Contribution on Submarine Concealed Attack Research," *Information Command Control System & Simulation*

Technology (Qingbao Zhihui Kongzhi Xitong Yu Fangzhen Jishu) 26, no. 1 (February 2004); Zhang Yisheng, "Development of New Russian Shipboard C-3I," *Intelligence Command Control and Simulation Techniques (Qingbao Zhihui Kongzhi Xitong Yu Fangzhen Jishu)* (June 2004); Wang Ya, "EMC Design of the Maneuverable C4-I System," *Fire Control and Command Control (Huoli yu Zhihui Kiongzhi)* (March 2005).

48. Examples include: Zhao Wenxiang, "Shortwave Communications Challenges for a Naval Island Blockade," *Ship Electronic Engineering (Chuanbo Dianzi Gongcheng* (February 2003); Wang Yu, "Reconnaissance Probability of Shipboard Frequency Hopping Radio," *Ship Science and Technology (Chuanbo Dianzi Gongcheng)* 27, no. 2 (April 2005); Li Guojian, "Software Radio and Its Applications in the Networking of Frequency Hopping Radio," *Ship Science and Technology (Chuanbo Kexue Jishu)* 26, no. 6 (December 2004).

49. Statistic provided by Dalian Naval Academy website: http://www.dljy.edu.cn/.

50. For example: Cai Guangyou, "Analytic Hierarchy Processing and Its Application in the Field of Submarine Command," *Fire Control & Command Control (Huoli yu Zhihui Kongzhi* 28, no. 5 (October 2003); Yang Jian, "Operations Requirement Analysis about Submarine Commands Automation System Based on QFD," *Ship Electronic Engineering (Chuanbo Dianzi Gongcheng),* no. 148 (April 2005).

51. Yan Haijiao, "INS Output Revising Based on Differential VLF Position," *Ship Electronic Engineering (Chuanbo Dianzi Gongcheng)* 25, no. 3 (March 2005).

Andrew S. Erickson and Andrew R. Wilson

China's Aircraft Carrier Dilemma

Introduction

CHINA'S NATIONAL LEADERSHIP is facing a dilemma that has bedeviled many other powers in modern history. The challenge—an especially difficult one in an era of rapid technological change—is discerning when and how to spend finite military budgets on new technology, organization, doctrine, and force structure. The history of navies trying to anticipate and prepare for the next war is replete with both positive and negative analogies to which Beijing can turn. These include Germany's attempts prior to World Wars I and II to strike the right balance between fleet-on-fleet and *guerre de course*, and missing on both counts; Japan's pattern prior to World War II of innovating with aircraft carriers and amphibious warfare but keeping the battleship firmly at the center of its naval doctrine; and even China's own naval embarrassments in the 1884–85 Sino-French War and the 1894–95 Sino-Japanese War, in which poor standardization, divided political and military leadership, and slow mobilization cost the Qing Dynasty two very expensive fleets.

The numerous sources available suggest that these issues weigh heavily on China's naval strategists today. Writing in China's most prestigious military journal, 中国军事科学 (*China Military Science*), People's Liberation Army Navy (PLAN) Senior Captain Xu Qi emphasizes that "Entering the twenty-first century, China's . . . maritime geostrategic relationships . . . are undergoing profound change. . . . China's navy must make [important] strategic choices."[1] Getting the answers right in the near term will appropriately shape China's force structure and inform training and doctrine in anticipation of the most likely scenarios. Obviously, analyses regarding the nature of the next war, the relative strengths and weaknesses of the possible belligerents, and the characteristics of the likely theater will determine those answers. In other words, strategic focus and concentration on the nature of the next war can spur modernization. Taiwan scenarios certainly dominate Beijing's attention, but while they narrow the decision sets, they do not resolve the central dilemma facing China's maritime strategists.

Of the issues that confront Chinese naval modernization, the most comprehensive and far-reaching is the extent to which Beijing has faced a choice between a navy focused on large-deck aviation versus one based fundamentally on submarines. The answer is the simplest possible—not at all. China has yet to confront the issue in any meaningful way, and that is so because its technology, assets, and facilities are far from a state that might force the issue.

Whether it makes sense now for Beijing actually to develop an aircraft carrier has apparently been the subject of considerable debate in China.[2] Hong Kong's Phoenix Television has quoted Song Xiaojun, editor in chief of 舰船知识 (Naval & Merchant Ships), as stating that a PLA faction advocates aircraft carrier development but must compete with elements urging submarine and aerospace industry development.[3] One Chinese analyst states that Beijing, reflecting the interests of the submarine faction, is currently focused on developing new types of submarines in part precisely because they can attack carrier strike groups (CSGs), presumably those of the United States. Carriers present large targets, have weaker defenses than (and cannot easily detect) submarines. Submarines can attack CSGs with "torpedoes, sea mines, and missiles," thereby rendering sea lines of communication (SLOC) and seaborne trade itself vulnerable to undersea attack.[4] The analyst contends that China's Type 093 and 094 submarines will increase the sea-denial capabilities, strategic depth, coastal defense, and long-range attack capability of the People's Liberation Army Navy (PLAN).[5] In a recent meeting with the authors, a senior Chinese official elaborated that although he had "been an advocate of aircraft carriers for many years because we need them," until recently carriers had "not been the best use of national resources" because China "lacks an escort fleet," thereby making any carrier a vulnerable target. China has therefore invested instead in "submarines, mid-sized ships, and fighters [aircraft]."[6]

At the same time, however, dismissing China's carrier aspirations could be myopic, given its rapid development of all other major aspects of its navy over the past few years. Submarines currently dominate China's naval development, but they might not do so indefinitely. Contending that submarine force development is not a panacea for the PLAN, one Chinese analyst calls for "rethinking the theory that aircraft carriers are useless and [that one should] rely solely on assassin's maces," or asymmetric silver bullet-type weapons: "Allied ASW is very strong.... The U[nited] S[tates] and Japan carefully monitor PLAN submarine activities.... PLAN submarines' 533 mm torpedoes are insufficient to constitute a strong threat to a U.S. aircraft carrier [and] PLAN submarine-carried guided missiles are insufficient to wound an aircraft carrier."[7]

The aforementioned Chinese official stated to the authors in 2006 that "China will have its own aircraft carrier" in "twelve to fifteen years." In 2004, however, he had declared to a group of western academics that there was an internal political and military consensus that China had no intention of developing an aircraft carrier (CV). When asked to explain this apparent contradiction, the official stated that over the past two years the subject of aircraft carrier development has become a "heated internal debate" in Beijing as Chinese national interests have grown, SLOC security has become ever more important, the need to rescue Chinese citizens overseas has become increasingly apparent, and "air coverage" is viewed as an essential component of "balanced naval forces."[8]

China has made great progress in many dimensions necessary to support the development of aircraft carriers, though in some areas it is unclear whether substantial efforts have been made at all. The PLAN's submarine program is far ahead of its carrier program. In India, by contrast, the CV program is far ahead of the ballistic-missile submarine (SSBN) program; Spain, Japan, and Thailand have carriers though they lack SSBNs entirely, whereas the United Kingdom and France deploy both carriers and SSBNs. The Chinese literature notes all of these potential force structure models and the disparities in capabilities and experience between not merely the PLAN and the world's leading navies, but most notably between the PLAN and its regional peers, the Japan Maritime Self-Defense Force (JMSDF) and the Indian navy. In that literature the discussion of submarines, both as machines and as operational and strategic platforms, is much more advanced and grounded in reality than that of carriers—which is still notional, if not romantic, and largely comprises rather generic analyses of possible ship configuration options.[9] Certainly, there is logic, reinforced by the German and Japanese examples from the early twentieth century, in not playing to the adversary's strength. If the greater payoff is to be found in an asymmetric silver bullet or assassin's mace that SS/SSNs or mine warfare seem to offer, why should Beijing invest in a war-fighting specialty—that is, power-projection carrier operations—in which the PLAN is so clearly outmatched by the U.S. Navy and which appears ill suited to China's overall defensive posture?[10]

This, however, does not mean that the way ahead for the Chinese navy— which currently has a submarine-centered force structure and doctrine—is cast in stone or that the choice need be mutually exclusive. In fact, while submarines seem to be ascendant, the Chinese are still actively engaged with the carrier question and are reframing the terms of the debate. That debate, moreover, has been reinvigorated by recent events, notably the 2004 Southeast Asian tsunami, which the above cited Chinese official averred had "definitely" changed Chinese thinking about the utility of aircraft carriers, and by the advent of China's eleventh "five-year plan," for the period 2006–10. This chapter examines China's progress thus far, the road ahead, and a range of ways in which an aircraft carrier might ultimately fit into the PLAN's emerging order of battle.

China's Carrier Development History and Future Options

The aircraft carrier has long had determined, if not numerous, advocates at the highest levels of the Chinese military. Admiral Liu Huaqing, a student of Soviet admiral Sergei Gorshkov at the Voroshilov Naval Academy in Leningrad (1954–58), championed the aircraft carrier when he became commander of the PLAN (1982–88) and vice chairman of the Central Military Commission (1989–97). "Building aircraft carriers has all along been a matter of concern for the Chinese people," Admiral Liu insisted. "To modernize our national defense and build a perfect weaponry and equipment system, we cannot but consider the development of aircraft carriers."[11]

Liu has been credited with an instrumental role in modernizing China's navy and with conceiving ambitious goals for its future power projection, in the framework of "island chains."[12] Chinese analysts view the "island chains" alternatively as benchmarks of China's progress in maritime force projection and as fortified barriers that China must continue to penetrate to achieve freedom of maneuver in the maritime realm. As PLAN Senior Captain Xu Qi emphasizes, China's "passage in and out of the [open] ocean is obstructed by two island chains. [China's] maritime geostrategic posture is

[thus] in a semi-enclosed condition."[13] Liu and others have defined the first island chain, or current limit of most PLAN operations, as comprising Japan and its northern and southern archipelagos (the latter disputed by China), South Korea, Taiwan, the Philippines, and the Greater Sunda Islands. The second island chain, which Liu envisioned as being fully within the scope of future PLAN activities, ranges from the Japanese archipelago south to the Bonin and Marianas Islands (including Guam) and finally to the Palau group. Some unofficial Chinese publications refer to a third island chain centered on America's Hawaiian bases, viewed as a "strategic rear area" for the U.S. military.[14] The ultimate goal is a Chinese navy that can perform a mix of sea-denial, area-denial, and varying degrees of power-projection within and out to these island chains.

In his 2004 autobiography, coverage of which by China's Xinhua press agency implies quasi-official endorsement, Admiral Liu described in some detail his association with, and aspirations for, efforts to develop an aircraft carrier.[15] As early as 1970 Liu "organized a special feasibility study for building aircraft carriers as instructed by the higher authorities and submitted a project proposal to them."[16] In May 1980 Liu became the first PLA leader to tour an American aircraft carrier, USS *Kitty Hawk* (CV 63). This experience left him "deeply impressed by its imposing magnificence and modern fighting capacity."[17] Liu stated that he emphasized to the PLA General Staff the need to devote great effort to "two large . . . key issues" essential not only to "long range combat operations" in "wartime but also to deterrence power in peacetime": development of aircraft carriers and of SSBNs.[18]

Liu recalled that the question of Chinese aircraft carrier development had weighed particularly heavily on him when he became PLAN commander in 1982. "With the development of maritime undertakings and the change in the mode of sea struggles, the threats from sea we were facing differed vastly from the past," Liu assessed. "We had to deal with SSBNs and ship-based air forces, both capable of long-range attacks. To meet that requirement, the strength of the Chinese navy seemed somewhat inadequate. Despite our long coastal defense line, we had only small and medium-sized warships and land-based air units, which were merely capable of short-distance operations. In case of a sea war, all we could do was to deplore our weakness." But "by developing aircraft carriers," Liu believed, "we could solve this problem successfully."

In early 1984, at the First Naval Armament and Technology Work Conference, Liu recalled stating, "'Quite some time has elapsed since the navy had the idea of building aircraft carriers. Now, our national strength is insufficient for us to do this. It seems that we have to wait for some time.'" In 1986, however, "when briefed by leaders of the Navy Armament and Technology Department," Liu revisited the issue. "I said that we had to build aircraft carriers," Liu recalled, and that "we must consider this question by 2000. At this stage . . . we need not discuss the model of carriers to be built, but should make some preliminary studies." The Gorshkov-educated Liu saw an historical analogue: "The Soviet Union spent thirty years developing carriers. At the beginning, there were different opinions about building carriers. The Central Committee of the Soviet Communist Party did not have a firm determination to do this, but the Soviet people wanted carriers. Shortly afterward, they started building carriers. Judging from our present situation, even for defense purposes only, we are in need of carriers." Following Liu's entreaty, "the leaders of the Navy Armament and Technology Department promptly passed [his] idea to the Naval Armament Feasibility Study Center. Then, the two departments teamed up to organize a feasibility study in this respect."[19]

Liu suggested that in 1987 China was finally on track to address the "key question" of the carrier platform and its aircraft.[20] On 31 March of that year, he reported to the PLA General Staff that Chinese aviation and shipbuilding industry leaders and experts assessed that their country was "technologically capable of building carriers and ship-borne aircraft." "With regard to some special installations, of course, there are questions that we must deal with seriously," Liu allowed. "But they can be solved." Liu suggested that China begin aircraft carrier development "feasibility studies in the Seventh Five-Year Plan period, do research and conduct preliminary studies of the platform deck and key questions on the aircraft during the Eighth Five-Year Plan period, and decide on the types and models in 2000."

Liu contended that "the annual spending for the present and the following years will not be too much" and that "technologically [the plan had] many advantages." These included catalyzing "the development of technologies required by the state and by national defense." Moreover, "through the preliminary studies, we can get a deeper understanding of the value of aircraft carriers and the need for their existence in war preparations. This understanding will be conducive to making a final scientific policy decision." Liu maintained that his "report had a certain effect on the PLA General Staff Department and the Commission of Science, Technology, and Industry for National Defense [COSTIND]. After that, the science research units concerned and the Navy's armament department started to make relatively in-depth feasibility studies for developing aircraft carriers under the auspices of [COSTIND]."

Throughout his vigorous promotion of aircraft carriers, Liu insisted, he weighed overall naval and national interests carefully. "During the feasibility studies . . . I stressed the need to make a combat cost comparison between using aircraft carriers and ship-borne aircraft and using land-based air divisions, aerial refuellers, and land-based aircraft," he continued. "Later, when I was working with the Central Military Commission, I continued to pay attention to this matter. I asked [COSTIND] and the Armament Department of the PLA General Staff Department to make an overall funding plan for developing carriers, including the funds needed for preliminary studies, research, and armament." Liu stated that the aforementioned plan "should be listed along with the plans for developing warships, aircraft, weapons, and electronic equipment rather than included in the aircraft carrier development program so as to avoid creating an excessively large project that the higher authorities could not readily study. I told them clearly that any plan they made should be discussed by the Central Military Commission."[21]

As for foreign technology, Liu reports,

> I gave approval for experts of the Navy and related industries to visit such countries as France, the United States, Russia, and Ukraine to inspect aircraft carriers. During that period, departments related to the national defense industry invited Russian carrier design experts to China to give lectures. Technical materials on carrier designs were introduced into our country, and progress was made in preliminary studies concerning key accessories aboard carriers. Under arrangements made by the PLA General Staff Department and [COSTIND], findings obtained from the inspection trips, materials introduced from abroad, and the results of our own preliminary studies were analyzed, studied, and appraised. This enabled many leaders and experts within and outside the military to enhance their understanding of the large systems engineering [required] for [developing] carriers and ship-borne aircraft.[22]

In his retirement Liu was to recall that he had "fulfilled [his] responsibility for making some plans for developing an aircraft carrier for China."[23] In 2005, retired Vice Admiral Zhang Xusan stated, "I certainly advocate having an aircraft carrier soon. . . . When I was [Deputy Commander of the PLA] Navy I advocated that, and at that time Commander . . . Liu Huaqing advocated it too, but for many reasons it was postponed. I believe that it will not be too long before we will have an aircraft carrier. When, what year, I can't say, because I'm not in charge of that matter now. But I feel we will have one in the not too distant future."[24]

It remains unclear to what extent Liu's advocacy of carriers, which he termed the "core of the Navy's combined battle operations" and considered a symbol of overall national strength that many other countries had already developed, has actually influenced PLAN development.[25] As Liu himself was careful to emphasize, "the development of an aircraft carrier is not only a naval question, it is also a major question of national strategy and defense policy. It must emerge from the exact position [of] and prudent strategy [concerning] comprehensive national strength and overall national maritime strategy."[26] In light, however, of both Beijing's determination to be respected universally as a great power and its growing maritime interests, China's navy has clearly been contemplating various alternatives for developing aircraft carriers—research that provides critical indicators of Beijing's emerging maritime strategy.

Overseas New Construction

When it comes to obtaining a working aircraft carrier, China has several options, but each largely limits what the carrier could be used for. Buying a big-deck, Western strike platform akin to the *Enterprise* or *Nimitz* has apparently never been seriously considered. It would simply not be within the realm of the possible to acquire such a ship from the West—including, apparently, even Russia, which China reportedly approached in the early 1990s.[27] Moreover, operating a *Nimitz*-class aircraft carrier or equivalent is among the most complex tasks of modern warfare. Matching American or French expertise at large-deck power projection would involve incredible cost and many years of trial and error. China may be weighing the costs and benefits of vertical-and-short-takeoff-and-landing (VSTOL) and catapult carriers, the latter of which could support larger aircraft with greater payloads. Specialists at China's Naval Engineering University and Naval Aeronautical Institute have conducted research on steam-powered catapults, but it appears to be theoretical in nature.[28] Only a few navies, notably those of the United States and France, have solved the perplexing mechanics and daunting upkeep of steam catapults or the subtleties of arresting gear, and they are unlikely to sell them to foreign powers. When it comes to aircraft for a conventional deck, only the United States and France have third-generation catapult-capable planes (we will return to aircraft below).

Another option for overseas purchase would be a small-to-midsized VSTOL-capable carrier from a European producer, such as Spain's Navantia, the builders of Thailand's ten-thousand-ton *Chakri Naruebet*.[29] In fact, there were some tentative moves in this direction in the mid-1990s, but nothing developed from them. Empresa Nacional Bazán, which merged with Astilleros Españoles S.A. (AESA) to form Navantia in 2000, reportedly attempted to market its SAC-200 and -220 light conventional-takeoff-and-landing (CTOL) designs to China in 1995–96, but apparently Beijing was interested in obtaining design plans, as opposed to a prebuilt carrier.[30] Given the continuation of the post-Tiananmen U.S.-EU arms embargo on the People's Republic of China (PRC), the acquisition of operational carriers from overseas seems highly unlikely for the foreseeable future.

Notwithstanding all of this, however, buying a carrier undeniably saves time, trouble, and expense, by capitalizing on the expertise of others and securing a proven commodity, and it is notable how the Chinese debate has accommodated to this reality.

Indigenous New Construction

This approach would appear to offer a wider range of options and would allow the Chinese to take engineering and architectural clues from other navies and tailor the ship more closely to China's anticipated naval doctrine and aspirations. Nonetheless, start-up costs are very high, and the delta between plans and construction is large. China would confront such challenges as a long timetable and a lack of relevant experience. Prestige issues would seem to push China toward the biggest ship possible, but lately there have been signs of favoring a more modest ten- to twenty-five-thousand-ton ship that would carry helicopters or VSTOL aircraft, like the British Harrier or newer versions of Russia's Yak-141. These discussions include some speculation that such a ship might even be nuclear powered, although conventional power seems more realistic. This proposal has drawn intense interest within China's navy and in the opinion of the authors is the most realistic course of action if the PLAN is to bring aircraft-carrying naval vessels into service in the near future.

However, according to sources of varying credibility, a more ambitious construction plan, sometimes referred to as "Project 9935," is underway that would produce a large-deck, conventionally powered CTOL carrier in the fifty-thousand-ton range capable of launching and retrieving carrier-capable versions of Russian Su-30 aircraft, possibly within the next few years. While these aspirations are not to be lightly dismissed, Chinese-language sources reflect little attention to such a program, far less than to smaller helicopter and VSTOL-carrying ships. If a vessel along the lines of the 9935 concept were to come down the ways in a Chinese shipyard, it would be likely to do so under the twelfth five-year plan, which will begin in 2011. In the near term, it is critical to monitor the purchase or production of support ships, aircraft, and shipboard systems that would be required to support an operational CSG regardless of whether the notional 9935 carrier or some other vessel is to constitute its core.

Rebuilding

China has already purchased four decommissioned aircraft carriers, to considerable Western media speculation. In 1985 China purchased for scrap the Australian carrier HMAS *Melbourne*, from which it may have learned engineering principles—albeit limited and perhaps antiquated ones—when dismantling it. The ex-Russian *Minsk,* acquired by front companies in 1998, is now the centerpiece of a Chinese "military education" amusement park in Shenzhen.[31] A ship of the same class, *Kiev,* arrived in Tianjin in 2000;[32] it was subsequently renovated to attract tourists as the center of "China's largest national defense education base" and "the world's largest military theme park."[33] A visit to *Kiev* in June 2006 revealed a replica of a PRC J-10 aircraft, of which China may be developing a carrier-compatible version, below deck. The vessel itself, however, appeared to receive only cosmetic maintenance and is therefore likely in no condition to go to sea.[34] Finally, the Russian "heavy aircraft-carrying cruiser" *Admiral Kuznetsov*-class *Varyag* (purchased from Ukraine in 1998 for $20 million and delivered in 2002) has attracted renewed international attention after having recently received a fresh coat of PLAN silver-gray paint, and possibly other renovations, at Dalian Shipyard.[35] The subject of much press speculation, *Varyag* is the most likely candidate if a decommissioned carrier is to be made operational. At the very least, its expensive acquisition and lengthy refurbishing seems to contradict the stated intention of its original buyer, Macao's Agencia Turisticae Diversoes Chong Lot Limitada, to use it as a floating casino. There have even been claims that by 2008 *Varyag* will be operational and based in Yalong Bay, Sanya City, on Hainan Island, to protect the Spratlys and the Taiwan Strait.[36] A senior Chinese official has told the authors that "some naval officers want" to refit *Varyag* and that "there is still a heated debate."[37] The significance of this insight is that operationalizing *Varyag* is not a dead letter in senior naval circles and that debate over its general utility and possible future roles continues.

Many of *Varyag's* apparent disadvantages as a first carrier for China can be viewed in fact as advantages. *Varyag* was delivered without weapons, electronics suites, or propulsion, so although start-up costs would be high, the potential for customization is considerable. Further in its favor, *Varyag* is a very large ship, designed to displace 67,500 tons fully loaded; it can therefore be equipped with a variety of aircraft and shipboard systems. It is also a known quantity, in that the Soviets experimented with similar carriers and thought through related doctrinal issues. Finally, off-the-shelf aircraft, including helicopters, CTOL and VSTOL, already exist that are known to work with the design and have been deployed aboard *Varyag's* sister ship, *Admiral Kuznetzov*.

On the downside, and though the Chinese can build a conventional power plant as well as shafts and screws sufficient to propel *Varyag*, it seems unlikely that the reverse engineering this effort would entail could be easy or fast. In addition, a large conventionally powered carrier could not operate far from Chinese home waters without a combination of friendly foreign ports (to which access is presently uncertain) or a robust underway-replenishment capability. On this latter point, the PLAN regularly performs resupply and even repairs at sea and could obviously learn from the practice of navies that now deploy conventional carriers. The Chinese, no doubt, are closely watching Indian efforts at purchasing and eventually operationalizing the former Soviet *Kiev*-class VSTOL carrier *Admiral Gorshkov*. Since India has operated ex-British carriers for years, it already has a great deal of carrier experience; by contrast, China will inevitably start far behind India's level of expertise in actual carrier aviation and operation.

China's old carriers, especially *Minsk* and *Kiev*, were probably purchased as "cadavers" to be dissected to inform indigenous design. *Varyag*—while it will certainly serve that purpose, especially as it reflects the largest and most advanced Soviet carrier design—may ultimately also be used for pilot and deck crew training, as well as a "test platform" for general research and the development of catapults, arresting gear and other ship-board systems.[38] To this end, *Varyag* may be retrofitted with a power plant, shafts, and screws so that it can go to sea under its own power, but training and equipment experimentation will likely be the extent of its capabilities in the near term. Further out, a modestly capable *Varyag* may become a centerpiece of Beijing's naval diplomacy and, in addition to training (following the model of the *Shichang*, discussed below), could potentially be used for humanitarian operations and disaster relief. But as with everything concerning *Varyag*, these projections are highly speculative.

Commercial Conversion

A final option would be to reconfigure a large commercial vessel as an aircraft carrier. A possible indication of austerity, flexibility, and commercial orientation is apparent Chinese interest in Australian shipbuilding corporation INCAT's Evolution One12. This wave-piercing catamaran is claimed to be "the world's largest diesel-powered fast craft," a distinction corroborated by INCAT. INCAT has reportedly proposed a multifunction VSTOL and helicopter ship for the Royal Australian Navy.[39] Were it to pursue a parallel course of development, China could exploit its large and rapidly advancing shipbuilding sector, projected to become soon the world's largest.[40] China's shipbuilding industry appears to combine economic dynamism and broad-based Western technology assimilation with close military coordination.[41] Indeed, Shanghai's Jiangnan shipyard—China's largest and perhaps soon the world's largest—already contains both commercial facilities and others for advanced submarines and surface warships.

Indeed, while commercial technology is not directly applicable to military vessels—substantial modifications are necessary—China might prove more adept at this process than many other nations. It is conceivable that carrier-relevant research, development, and even production could proceed at one or more of China's major shipyards on a scale and with a rapidity that might surprise foreign analysts. Certainly, however, there would be extraordinary challenges in converting a merchant ship into a combat-ready carrier. Producing a ship capable of ferrying helicopters would be comparatively straightforward, but even then the final result would likely be of minimal tactical utility and a tempting target for an adversary. Ultimately the aircraft carrier itself is simply a platform for air operations—the system of systems that allows for the projection of air power from the sea. The acquisition of a Chinese carrier vessel would be simply one step, and a relatively simple one at that, along a complex continuum that might someday lead to a truly operational Chinese aircraft carrier. The subsequent steps would involve hardware, software and training.

The Carrier Hardware Package

All of these options would rely on conventional propulsion. While a theoretical possibility, nuclear propulsion makes little sense for the Chinese, who do not currently need surface combatants with the range of U.S. nuclear-powered carriers. Conventional propulsion is technologically much simpler and significantly more economical. Still, a carrier that can go to sea under its own power is one thing; a fully operational carrier is another matter entirely. As we have seen, there are many other technological and doctrinal questions to be answered.

Carrier operation demands a full complement of such elements as aircraft, deck elevators, radars, and defenses. Already, Chinese specialists have conducted extensive research in many major relevant areas. Experts at Beijing University of Aeronautics and Astronautics have studied carrier-aircraft landing gear.[42] Harbin Engineering University's Naval Architecture Department has examined the structural demands of flight decks.[43] Other experts have analyzed ski-jump configurations (similar to those of *Kuznetzov* and some European VSTOL carriers)[44] and other takeoff issues, deck-motion compensation, wake turbulence, wave-off procedures, landing decision aids, as well as aircraft-critical technologies and command and control.[45] In addition to detailed analyses of the requirements of current carrier operations, there is discussion of potentially revolutionary technologies that could be employed on next-generation carriers, including electromagnetic catapults and "integrated full-electric propulsion" (IFEP).[46] Nearly all of this research appears to be theoretical in nature, however, and none of it proves that China has made actual progress in developing its own aircraft carrier—or even has made an official decision to do so. Rather, it seems to indicate that Chinese experts have followed closely major foreign aircraft carriers and are gaining increasing understanding of the systems and technologies that other navies employ. Moreover, much of the research is at least indirectly applicable to targeting enemy carriers more effectively.[47] In June 2006, a second Chinese official informed the authors that in PLA internal meetings, Taiwan scenarios and how to target U.S. CSGs are often discussed.

With respect to carrier aircraft, pilot training would be particularly problematic for VSTOL and VTOL aircraft, given China's lack of relevant experience, if less so for helicopters, though rotary-wing operations are now very modest in the PLAN. In general, however, there has been incremental progress in Chinese naval aviation, albeit from a rather low baseline. The PLA Naval Air Force (PLANAF) is increasingly aggressive and confident in its basic homeland defense and interdiction missions, and its experience in nighttime over-water training and patrol is growing. Leading indicators of serious aircraft-carrier preparations include the development of special air control radars and reinforced landing gear. According to a 2004 article, Chengdu Aircraft Industry Corporation has been working on a carrier variant of the J-10 but still faces many technological shortfalls.[48] Another recent source claims that China may be seeking Russian thrust-vectoring-controlled AL-31FN engines to render the J-10 better capable of takeoff from a ski-jump deck and to reduce its landing speed.[49] However, additional large purchases or licensing agreements for naval variants of Russian aircraft suitable for carrier operations—such as the Yak-141, the Su-30MKK, or the Su-33 (the last an Su-27 variant designed for *Kuznetsov*-class carriers, and hence appropriate for *Varyag*)—would be one of the better indicators of where China's aircraft carrier program is moving.[50]

Obtaining aircraft would not in itself, however, mitigate the lack of practical experience with them in a carrier environment. Great leaps forward in operational capabilities solely through acquisition are unlikely. More incremental improvements—akin to Japan's gradual approach to its helicopter-carrying *Osumi*-class, and next-generation landing ship tanks (LSTs) (which some speculate may deploy fixed-wing aircraft, possibly the Joint Strike Fighter)—are more realistic. In this regard, Thailand's acquisition of the Spanish-built *Chakri Naruebet* may serve as a tangible lesson. Bangkok acquired this fully outfitted, very expensive ship in 1997 but due to financial constraints and lack of experience has rarely deployed it.

Therefore, there are many reasons for the Chinese to pace themselves rather than rush to deploy an operational carrier. The most that a major purchase of new aircraft, such as the Russian two-seat Su-30MKK, or the Chinese version, the MKK2, can offer the PLANAF is greater ability to perform its basic missions. Better weapons and more experience with air-to-surface attack can extend area-denial and interdiction incrementally, but significant growth of that envelope is unlikely without sea-based aviation and land-based, over-water, midair refueling capability, in addition to some means of coordination and defense (e.g., an AWACS equivalent).[51] Both of these capabilities appear to be high priorities for the PLAN. China purchased Russian A-50 AWACS-type aircraft in 2000, following cancellation of Israel's Phalcon sale amid mounting American pressure. China is also reportedly developing the KJ-2000, and indigenous AWACS-type aircraft.[52] "While the larger, more advanced" KJ-2000 is envisioned to conduct "long-range, comprehensive aerial patrolling and control roles," the smaller KJ-200/Y-8 airborne early warning (AEW) aircraft (nicknamed Balance Beam in the West), with an electronically steered phased array, offers "a less expensive platform for tactical airborne early warning and electronic intelligence missions."[53] Various sources report that a KJ-200 aircraft crashed on 4 June 2006, killing forty people and possibly setting back the program.[54] China is also reportedly considering Russia's Kamov Ka-31 helicopter for carrier-based AEW.[55]

China still relies on Russian aerial refueling tankers (for instance, the Il-78), but is struggling to achieve domestic production capabilities even there.

If the experience of other navies is any measure, the Chinese also need to realize that getting carrier operations right will involve the loss of expensive aircraft and hard-to-replace pilots. In 1954 alone, in working to master jet aviation off carriers, the U.S. Navy lost nearly eight hundred aircraft. In 1999 the Navy lost only twenty-two, but these were the most advanced aircraft flown by the world's most experienced aviators.[56] While the Chinese will certainly benefit from improvements in technology and will not be attempting a scale of operations even close to that of the United States during the early Cold War, they must realize that their CV learning curve will be costly in terms of blood and treasure. Moreover, the PLANAF has traditionally been poorly funded and its pilots have only a fraction of the flying hours that their peers in the United States, Japan, and even India have. These factors will make China's mastery of carrier aviation even more costly in human terms.

Quantum leaps forward are required not only in sea-based aviation and midair refueling but also in PLAN doctrine and antisubmarine warfare (ASW) as well as in PLANAF service culture if China's aerial power-projection capabilities are to be improved dramatically. As the 2005 edition of the PLA's first authoritative volume on strategy acknowledges, "because the borders and coasts are far away from our central inland, some at a distance of hundreds or even thousands of kilometers, it is very difficult for the projection of forces, operations, logistics and supports."[57] Without major improvements in ASW, for instance, any Chinese CV would be an easy target for a diesel-electric or nuclear-powered attack submarine (SS/SSN). Chinese ASW capabilities, while slowly improving, cannot yet be counted on to provide a reasonable degree of security in open waters. In a crisis scenario, many air support tasks would be performed by the People's Liberation Army Air Force (PLAAF). This means that unlike a U.S. carrier strike group, a Chinese CSG would not need to be wholly self-supporting. But it remains unclear how capable of joint coordination China's different services are in operations over water. Integrating operations between a highly regimented and rigidly structured PLAAF and an immature and sea-based PLAN contingent would require technological and service-culture innovations, as well as exercises less carefully scripted than has been usual, to develop the requisite interoperability and inter-service coordination. Significant additional research is required to gauge how much coordination exists within the PLAN between its ground-based naval air and surface/subsurface assets. This is all the more critical as the type and degree of coordination will necessarily vary depending on maritime mission (i.e., humanitarian, interdiction, area denial, sea control, or strike power projection).

China's navy must also determine what mix of surface vessels and submarines would be necessary to support a carrier. Here the evolution of the overall naval order of battle may offer insights. China might be unlikely to commit itself to a militarily useful carrier until it could fill out the strike group without compromising its ability to execute other missions. Analysis here requires nuanced understanding of exactly what it takes to operate a carrier and what mixes of indigenous products and off-the-shelf technologies could be combined in a Chinese strike group. CVs are highly vulnerable even with supporting strike groups, especially to the submarines of the United States and other regional competitors; the time and expense of deploying a carrier will be for naught if it cannot be protected.

As they currently stand, China's capabilities are sufficient to give the United States pause if a Taiwan conflict scenario were to erupt, but truly controlling the battle space against a determined and capable adversary remains a Chinese aspiration, not a demonstrated capability.

The Role of a Carrier in Chinese Naval Doctrine

If China were to achieve any of the acquisition options outlined above and outfit a carrier, such a ship, while expensive and complicated, would indeed be a useful asset. It would have little role in a near-term Taiwan scenario, however, as land-based PLAAF and PLANAF aircraft would be called on to handle all of the required air operations across the narrow Taiwan Strait. Unless China is able to produce and incorporate a range of carriers in a cohesive and effective concept of operations, it is difficult to envision them as the centerpiece of Chinese naval doctrine in future decades. In his memoirs, Admiral Liu Huaqing described aircraft carriers as providing air coverage essential to offshore defense.[58] An aircraft carrier would thus facilitate Chinese air operations in the Taiwan Strait by obviating the need for short-range fighters to sortie from land bases. This, Liu believed, would maximize the utility of China's existing aircraft.[59] However, Liu made these statements in 1987, before modern precision weaponry had demonstrated its startling effectiveness in the first Gulf War. Indeed, a concomitant shift in operational scenarios may at least partially explain apparent indecision in China concerning aircraft carrier development. Though periodically considered, it may have been repeatedly postponed in favor of submarines. Even Liu acknowledged that nuclear submarines are "one of the very most important pieces of naval equipment."[60] A senior Chinese official has further emphasized to the authors that "China will not try to compete with the U[nited] S[tates] in the open sea. Even twenty PRC carriers cannot compete with U.S. nuclear carriers."[61]

That said, there are two general categories of potential carrier roles in the PLAN. The first is as a discrete capability to support secondary missions. The second is as a complement to China's submarine-centered fleet. As to using carriers as a discrete platform, the most basic motivation is prestige. Senior Captain Xu Qi views China's navy as a vehicle for the assertion of Chinese sovereignty abroad: "Naval vessels are symbols of state power and authority [which] can act as 'mobile territory' and freely navigate the high seas of the world . . . their mission is not limited to offshore defense."[62] The prestige value of aircraft carriers would be particularly attractive to a great power still seeking to right the wrongs of its devastating national weakness since 1840. As one Chinese analysis emphasizes,

> The enterprise of China's ocean development has a splendid history dating back to [Ming Dynasty Admiral] Zheng He's seven voyages to the West. But its previous feudal rulers locked their doors against the world. They fettered the Chinese Nation's vigorous ocean-based development. This included especially the Ming and Qing Dynasty's severe prohibition of maritime [focus] for over 400 years. This repeatedly caused the Chinese Nation to miss favorable opportunities [that would have stemmed from] developing civilization from the sea. Then the Western gunships bombarded their way through the gate that China's feudal rulers had locked. Thenceforth, a succession of wars of invasion from the sea visited profound suffering as well as galling shame and humiliation on the Chinese Nation. The beautiful, abundant ocean gave forth only sorrow and tears.[63]

Chinese interlocutors often tell Westerners that "a nation cannot become a great power without having an aircraft carrier." Lieutenant General Wang Zhiyuan, deputy director of the PLA General Armament Department's Science and Technology Commission, stated in a 2006 interview that the PLA "will conduct research and build aircraft carriers on its own, and develop its own carrier fleet. Aircraft carriers are a very important tool available to major powers when they want to protect their maritime rights and interests. As China is such a large country with such a long coastline and we want to protect our maritime interests, aircraft carriers are an absolute necessity."[64]

Zhang's conception of China as facing both challenges and opportunities from the sea is prevalent among Chinese analysts.[65] As PLAN Senior Captain Xu Qi states, "the ocean is an important realm for [China] to participate in international competition. It is the nation's main artery of foreign trade." Xu also stresses: "The maritime security threat comes from the open ocean. [This] requires the navy to cast the field of vision of its strategic defense to the open ocean [and to] develop attack capabilities for battle operations [on] exterior lines, in order to hold up the necessary shield for the long-term development of national interests."[66]

Carrier acquisition can also be seen as part of regional power competition. When the Japanese deploy their larger version of the *Osumi*-class LST, or when the Indian navy puts a refurbished *Gorshkov* to sea, the Chinese may be compelled to accelerate their carrier program to maintain the appearance of a great power. But this is more than simply an issue of face. Showing the flag is important, but as Japan itself maintains, some form of carrier is needed for peacekeeping operations, as well as for humanitarian intervention and for defense of vital and lengthy sea lines of communication.

This unique role for aircraft carriers was demonstrated by the 2004 tsunami, after which the PLAN found itself on the outside looking in, especially compared to the U.S. Navy, but more painfully to the Indian navy and, even more unbearably, the JMSDF.[67] An article in the PLAN publication 当代海军 (*Modern Navy*) assessed that Japan's "first dispatch of a warship overseas [for] search and rescue . . . demonstrated its status as a 'great power of disaster relief.'" The article noted that the United States "dispatched [the *Lincoln*] carrier battle group to the rescue" and that India's "navy served as the daring vanguard." It concludes, "The rescue activities following the Indian Ocean tsunami abundantly illustrated that the use of armed forces is not only to prevent conflict or to wage wars, but also brings into play the key actions of national construction, disaster relief, and rebuilding." Aircraft carriers and helicopters, it suggests, are vital for such "non-combat military operations."[68]

The final category of potential Chinese carrier missions includes collective maritime security (e.g., sea-lane protection and counterpiracy). This collective-security force structure is obviously a secondary mission of the PLAN, and it would be oriented toward friends and rivals in the South China Sea and the Indian Ocean. Deployment of an aircraft carrier would enable modest force projection to assert Chinese claims in the South China Sea. In this vision, *Varyag* or an indigenous carrier in the mold of India's older *Viraat*, its refurbished *Gorshkov*, Thailand's *Chakri Naruebet*, or Japan's *Osumi*-class would be all the Chinese would need. A more robust and capable CSG might be needed to defend properly Chinese sea lanes and energy access through the Strait of Malacca to the Indian Ocean, but even an ability to show the flag in this fashion could have valuable psychological effects. In an important article in 1998, noted China Institute of Contemporary International Relations scholar Zhang Wenmu contended that America has historically pursued a strategy of monopolizing access to oil. Land-accessible energy resources in Central Asia offer an important hedge against Chinese reliance on sea-based energy supply, which is far easier for U.S. forces to control and disrupt, he argued.[69] But Zhang strongly believed that China must control its sea-based oil supplies as well:

> China is facing fierce competition overseas in obtaining its share of crude oil.... [U]nder globalization a nation's energy security is no longer an economic issue alone. Instead, it is also a political issue, as well as a military issue.... [It is therefore necessary to] build up our navy as quickly as possible.... We must be prepared as early as possible. Otherwise, China may lose everything it has gathered in normal international economic activities, including its energy interest, in a military defeat.[70] China should strive to develop its naval power. China should not only strengthen its naval power and defense to protect imported oil, but also expand its navy to achieve its influence over the offshore resources in the Asia Pacific region with [its] complex rights dispute[s]. [Sea] power has a permanent [significance for] the trade of coastal countries, and the backup of a country's [sea] power is its navy. Therefore, the long term approach toward ensuring open sea lane and potential ocean resources is to [develop] a modern oceangoing navy.[71]

Zhang strongly contended that China needs aircraft carriers—although nuclear submarines are even more important (at least at present).[72]

In any case, SLOC security does appear to be a growing Chinese concern. "In 2001, major maritime industry increased in value to 3.44 percent of [China's] GDP, [and is] estimated to reach approximately 5 percent by 2010.... [China's] open ocean transport routes pass through every continent and every ocean [and] through each important international strait [to] over six hundred ports in over 150 nations and [administrative] regions," PLAN Senior Captain Xu Qi writes. "By 2020, China's maritime commerce will exceed U.S. $1 trillion. It may be[come] necessary to import three-quarters of [China's] oil from overseas."[73] According to another PLA analysis, to "ensure the security of our strategic energy supply is . . . of great significance to our development in the long run."[74]

As to the issues of complementary capabilities in Chinese submarine doctrine, the Soviet model might be illustrative. Soviet deck aviation had an important ASW component. In the 1970s and 1980s the Soviet navy considered bastion strategies of protecting SSBNs, as well as performing area-denial and ASW, centered on helicopter carriers such as *Minsk* and *Moskva*. The original approach was later supplemented by the *Kuznetzov/Varyag*, designed for force-on-force operations.[75] There is some evidence that China might follow this pattern of integrated air and undersea warfare doctrine, but like all carrier discussions, this is still very hypothetical.

In the near term, if China cannot solve the extended-deployment issue and its SSBNs have to stay close to home, there might be logic in the carriers protecting an SSBN bastion in the Yellow Sea, Bohai Gulf, or South China Sea. But pursuit of such a strategy was arguably problematic for the Soviet Union. A bastion strategy might be even more counterproductive for China; forces devoted to supporting and defending a carrier are better spent elsewhere if fixed-wing ASW assets cannot be developed and deployed either from land bases or onboard ship. Even then, force protection, as it is in the U.S. Navy, would be a major drain. In an era in which long-distance precision strike has been emphasized—particularly by the U.S. military—it is far from clear how survivable Chinese aircraft carriers might be, particularly in a concentrated bastion, where they would offer dense targeting options for a wide variety of adversary platforms, although targeting the right vessel would still be a complex problem for the adversary.

A Smaller Helicopter Carrier: China's Interim Compromise?

China already has some experience with a ship that can support multiple helicopters, albeit an extremely modest one. The multirole aviation training ship 0891A *Shichang* (世昌, PLAN Hull 082) has a large aft helicopter deck, accounting for two-thirds of its 125-meter (410-foot) length. The deck has dual landing spots for Harbin Zhi-9A helicopters. Removing equipment containers (designed for rapid reconfiguration) aft could make space for a total of three helicopters. *Shichang* was conceived as both "China's first aerial service capacity ship" and "first national defense mobilization warship" as part of a larger plan to refit merchant vessels rapidly for defense mobilization.[76] This initiative apparently began in 1989, and was motivated in part by British and American use of commercial vessels in the Falklands War and later by Operation Desert Storm, respectively.[77] *Shichang* is entirely indigenous in its development and production, and reportedly meets all relevant domestic and international standards.[78]

Shichang, which resembles the Royal Navy's Royal Fleet Auxiliary aviation training and primary casualty reception ship *Argus*, was launched on

28 December 1996 in Shanghai; it was dispatched to the Dalian Naval Academy in 1997 following rigorous sea trials, prioritized by the PLAN leadership, ranging as far away as the South China Sea.[79] According to an article that originally appeared in China's *PLA Daily*, *Shichang*, together with the naval cadet training ship *Zheng He* (Hull 081), serves as an "at sea university," one that has trained two of every three current PLAN officers.[80] *Shichang's* ninety-five-hundred-ton displacement, 17.5-knot speed, crew of two hundred, and range of eight thousand nautical miles suggest a serious effort to develop some limited form of deck aviation.[81] It is at sea two hundred days per year, and its crew is accustomed to handling typhoons and thirty-degree rolls.[82] It supports "simultaneous operations of multiple helicopters," which "facilitates training for shipboard helicopter operations, as well as amphibious assault training."[83] *Shichang* "is widely regarded as the prelude to construction of a [true] helicopter carrier or amphibious assault vessel [presumably LPD- or LPH-type ships], and provides a basis for perfecting fixed-wing aircraft carrier operational concepts." With its helicopter module, it can serve as a "transfer station" for "a group of helicopters in wartime."[84] *Shichang* is also envisioned as having an ASW mission.[85]

A detailed 2005 analysis of China's prospects for developing a helicopter carrier states that "arrogant intervention of hostile great power(s) in the cross-Strait divide requires us to prepare for successful military struggle. Moreover, China still has some significant maritime territorial disputes with some peripheral countries." Its author believes that a coastal defense strategy is increasingly inadequate for China's future needs, which include "energy security, economic development, and political stability," all of which "are increasingly intimately connected with the international situation." Developing a helicopter carrier is therefore China's best "springboard" for such a "development strategy."[86]

> Considering funding, technology, and tactical issues, a helicopter carrier's displacement should be approximately 15,000 tons when fully loaded. It should be able to accommodate approximately 15 helicopters (12 ASW helicopters [and] 4 advance warning helicopters. . . .) The [hurdle] of 10,000 ton ship technology is small. China has previously constructed the *"Shichang"* training ship of around 10,000 tons. . . . As a result of limited tonnage, the equipment demands of a helicopter carrier are lower than those of a large or medium aircraft carrier, [helicopter carriers] can use [the] Commercial Off the Shelf Technologies (COTS) method in their construction, and [their] costs can be greatly reduced.[87]

Further, "China's opportunity, funding, and technology for developing a helicopter carrier are all mature. Because the superpowers have encircled China's periphery, and the opportunity for developing a fixed-wing aircraft carrier is not mature, the author believes that firmly grasping the opportunity to develop a helicopter carrier is the correct choice. China's Navy should reasonably call [the carrier] its own *Moskva* class. I hope this day arrives soon!"[88] Among the models reportedly under consideration is a fifteen- to twenty-thousand-ton LHD-like amphibious assault ship, featuring a large deck that can handle heavy transport helicopters and a mix of amphibious landing craft.[89]

The wide range of challenges inherent in developing a successful large-scale carrier and questions concerning its mission utility suggest that China may take a creative approach to carrier development, as it has done in other areas. Here it may be useful to examine other platform developments to seek patterns that would reveal PLA decision-making methods and practices.

One notable trend in PLAN development has been the production of single, or short-series, platforms. Examples include emulation of Soviet efforts to build a dedicated mine-laying vessel.[90] China's initial Xia SSBN is another potential example. Some Western analysts might ascribe such activity to mere copying of Soviet failures or to a PLAN experiencing growing pains that reduced its ability to plan for and produce an effective fleet. But another interpretation, one that is supported by some Chinese sources, is that such small-scale experimentation deliberately facilitates learning independent of immediate combat relevance. Viewed in this light, the Chinese navy might attempt to retrofit *Varyag* to begin experimentation with naval aviation—perhaps with little or no intention of ever using the resulting platform in battle.[91]

Such a vessel might also be used to practice operations against foreign carriers. Chinese specialists are acutely aware of aircraft carrier vulnerabilities, having conducted a wide variety of research apparently directed toward threatening aircraft carriers with ballistic and cruise missiles, submarine-launched torpedoes, and sea mines.[92] One Chinese article emphasizes these trump cards as well as "neutron bombs [and] stealth missile ships."[93] China's rapidly developing navy might view a carrier-based force posture as entirely premature yet also see the need to begin preparing for a future in which China's maritime interests are more wide-ranging and its capability to defend those interests greatly advanced. By that time, improvements in intelligence, surveillance, and reconnaissance (ISR), as well as in precision weaponry, might conceivably have rendered aircraft carriers and other surface vessels ineffective for some missions—as the "floating coffins" that Nikita Khrushchev foresaw.[94] But by cultivating a nascent capability, however modest, the PLAN would have hedged its bets.

A second trend has been to improvise and compromise. A case can be made that the PLAN has long recognized its limitations in capability and lived within them. Some Western analysts appear to engage in mirror imaging in assuming that China will automatically emulate American and Soviet large-deck aviation trajectories. But even a serious Chinese carrier development program might look substantially different from that of the superpowers. In August 1986, Admiral Liu Huaqing recalled, "when I was briefed by the leaders of the Naval Armament and Technology Department and the Feasibility Study Center, I assigned them a task regarding the development of carriers. I said, 'The method of building an aircraft carrier is a matter of overall naval construction. Whether [we are to build] helicopter carrier(s) and escort carriers in different stages, or [to] directly build escort carriers [is a matter that we] must assess carefully.'"[95] Recently, the Chinese have been surprisingly open minded as to the definition of a "carrier," running as it does the gamut from amphibious warfare ships through helicopter and hybrid carriers, up to the U.S. supercarriers.[96] A senior Chinese official stated to the authors that "China will not develop *Nimitz*-class carriers but rather mid-sized carriers."[97] In this regard, France may be a model for China. According to one article, "Since the 1970s, China has dispatched a large number of military personnel to each of the French Navy's research institutes for exchange. [They] have conducted thorough analysis on aircraft-carrier-related technology. Many people follow France's aircraft carriers carefully, even learning from personal experience how to pilot carrier-based aircraft for deck landings."[98]

Numerous literature and analyses concerning foreign helicopter carriers suggest that this might be a more logical arc for the PLAN.[99] These smaller, simpler carriers would be substantially easier to build and operate. Helicopter carriers might also better serve Chinese operational requirements, ranging from augmenting China's currently anemic airborne ASW capability to logistical support and even humanitarian missions.[100]

The major obstacle to successful Chinese development of helicopter carriers is the continuing backwardness of its rotary-wing aircraft development and inventory. The entire People's Liberation Army today reportedly possesses fewer than 350 helicopters (roughly three hundred in the PLA and forty in the PLAN). Most platforms in the PLA's disproportionately small fleet are either imports (for instance, Super Frelons) or copies of foreign models (like the Z-8 Super Frelon derivative). The only remotely capable versions are based on French platforms, such as the Dauphin (Z-9). China also operates some Russian imports, e.g., the Ka-28 Helix.[101] It is finally beginning to address this lack by entering into joint ventures with Eurocopter to produce more capable machines and to obtain related technology and expertise. Reportedly, China is developing its first indigenous assault helicopter, the WZ-10 attack variant.[102] For the foreseeable future, however, China may prefer to purchase European helicopters. One Chinese analyst expresses particular interest in acquiring the Anglo-Italian EH101 and the multirole NATO NH-90 helicopter, developed by a joint venture of Italian, French, German, Dutch, and Portuguese corporations.[103] This prospect would be greatly strengthened if the EU's post-Tiananmen arms embargo were to be further weakened or lifted in the near future. In any case, the state of China's rotary-wing capability and inventory will likely serve as a leading indicator of any substantial helicopter carrier initiatives.

The long PRC record of avowedly defensive military development, recently strained by China's rising comprehensive national power and Japanese nationalism, suggests that Beijing would carefully weigh the costs and benefits of deploying so explicit a concept of force projection as a large-deck aircraft carrier.[104] Other methods and platforms might accomplish many of the same ends without alienating neighboring countries. Submarines are less conspicuous than many other major naval platforms. Diesel submarines may be interpreted as defensive in nature. Sea mines, better still, are often invisible even to foreign militaries.[105] Perhaps that is one reason—aside from survivability and cost-effectiveness—why China has recently placed so much emphasis on these platforms. Aircraft carriers, by contrast, are impossible to hide; even to some Chinese leaders they connote gunboat diplomacy and imperialism, particularly in an East Asia still consumed by memories of Japan's bloody attempts to rule it.[106] In fact, it is for precisely these reasons that the Japanese refer to the *Osumi*-class as LSTs. The Japanese public could also become alarmed by Chinese carrier development and be stimulated to support constitutional revision, increased military spending, and even nuclear weapons development. Any form of an arms race with so capable and strategically situated a nation as Japan is clearly something that China would prefer to avoid. These are not reasons why China would *never* develop aircraft carriers, but they do suggest that China will do so only cautiously and with full cognizance of opportunity and contingency costs.

No doubt these issues have engendered substantial debate within China's civilian and military leadership, debate reflected at least in part by the diverse opinions of Chinese analysts in open sources. Perhaps some of the rumors and activities that make the question of Chinese aircraft carrier development so fascinating can be ascribed to just such a process. If and when China does embark on an unmistakable course of acquisition, we can expect to see sophisticated attempts to explain why China's carriers are different from, and serve different purposes than, their Japanese, Soviet, and American predecessors or their Indian, Japanese, Thai, American, and European contemporaries. Whatever carrier China does manage to deploy will likely be framed within peaceful rhetoric. "Our purpose in manufacturing aircraft carrier(s) is not to compete with the United States or the [former] Soviet Union, but rather to meet the demands of the struggle [to recover] Taiwan, to solve the Spratly Islands disputes and to safeguard [China's] maritime rights and interests," Admiral Liu Huaqing emphasized in his memoirs. "In peace time, [aircraft carriers] could be used to maintain world peace, thereby expanding our international political influence."[107] Here it is important to note that, according to a major PLA assessment, "Totally, our disputed water area with other countries amounts to 1,000,000 square kilometers, one ninth of China's national land territory. As far as the number of countries in dispute with or the expanse of the disputed are concerned, China is one of the most prominent states in the world."[108] In particular, PLA strategists see the issues of Taiwan's recovery as "the largest and the last obstacle which we must conquer in the Chinese people's path to rejuvenation in the twenty-first century" and "the most important [consideration] in our national security strategy." The return of Taiwan is regarded as imperative not only for reasons of national unity and political legitimacy but also also of national security and development:

> It is where we can breach the chain of islands surrounding us in the West Pacific to the vast area of the Pacific, as well as a strategic key area and sea barrier for defense and offense. If Taiwan should be alienated from the mainland, not only our natural maritime defense system would lose its depth, opening a sea gateway to the outside forces, but also a large area of water territory and rich reserves of ocean resources will fall into the hands of others. What's more, our line of foreign trade and transportation which is vital to China's opening up and economic development will be exposed to the surveillances and threats of separatist and enemy forces, and China will forever be locked to the west side of the first chain of islands in the West Pacific.[109]

PLAN Senior Captain Xu Qi echoes this emphasis on securing access to ocean resources to fuel national development: China's "coastal seas and continental-shelf areas [combine to] approach 273 million hectares. This area is more than two times that of China's total arable land . . . for China, with the world's largest population and relatively deficient resources . . . the sea can serve as a strategic resource replacement area."[110]

Like other aspects of Chinese maritime development, however, that of Chinese aircraft carriers would likely be imbued with shades of the Zheng He metaphor, "peaceful" voyages of discovery and goodwill commanded by the fifteenth-century eunuch admiral.[111] A recent series in China's official navy newspaper, 人民海军 (*People's Navy*), to commemorate the six hundredth anniversary of Zheng He's voyages emphasized precisely these factors.[112] In fact, Chinese commentators make the case that while China has historically been able to build great ships, it has never used them to dictate terms to others.[113] For instance, the senior Chinese official we interviewed in mid-2006 emphasized that "a Chinese aircraft carrier would not be used to seek hegemony."[114] While the merits of such claims are open to debate, they do hint at one way in which naval power is conceptualized in the contemporary PRC. In a more immediate sense, U.S., Japanese, Indian, and Thai operations in the aftermath of the 2004 tsunami have convinced many Chinese that good carriers make good neighbors and that they are a necessity if China's force structure available for deployment to Southeast Asia is to match and complement its diplomatic initiatives.[115]

In May 1998, for instance, *Shichang* visited Sydney, Australia, with the destroyer *Qingdao* and the hospital ship *Nancang*.[116] This is part of a larger mission of *Shichang* and fellow training ship *Zheng He*—to "reveal the graceful bearing of a new generation of PLAN officers, spread the arena of friendship, understand the world, open the window of a [new] a field of vision, increase experience, [and become] a study platform" by visiting over sixty sea areas and ports, including Hawaii and Vladivostok.[117] *Shichang* has also visited New Zealand and the Philippines.[118] It is designed specifically to deploy to disaster areas. Under Captain Wang Gexin, its hospital unit has also participated in domestic flood relief efforts.[119] *Shichang* conducted a national defense mobilization drill near Xiamen on 28 July 1999.[120] *Shichang* has proven capable of long-distance open-ocean navigation. In July–August 1999 "it carr[ied] out at-sea defense drills, [the] largest, furthest, and longest in PLAN history."[121] Perhaps *Shichang* was not deployed to help with tsunami relief in 2004 because it is indispensable to PLAN training. If that is the case, maybe China would consider such a role in the future if its helicopter carriers become more sophisticated and numerous.

The logic Chinese sources outline for the utility of a small carrier for regional purposes raises the interesting ideas of both a naval ecosystem and a modern, regional basis for capital-ship calculations. Chinese calculations of a small carrier's utility in regional diplomacy vis-à-vis the Indian navy and the JMSDF are very similar to the logic that Alfred Thayer Mahan used when calculating how many battleships should be posted on America's West Coast vis-à-vis the Royal Navy and French and German navies, to prevent adventurism on the west coast of South America. In a Chinese context, the idea might be to complicate the calculations of others with claims to the Spratly Islands or other contested areas. The tactical utility of these platforms as disaster relief sea bases offers a positive spin-off for diplomacy. The idea of a regional naval ecosystem is of great potential importance to the development of a global maritime security network, as the U.S. Navy goes about rendering naval security assistance. All U.S. actions will have second and third order effects on these systems. Awareness of such ramifications will be essential for the conduct of effective Phase Zero (precursor) operations.[122]

A New Gold Standard

In their excellent article in the Winter 2004 issue of *Naval War College Review*, You Ji and Ian Storey concluded that, "With the retirement of Liu in 1997 . . . the aircraft carrier lost its champion in the Chinese navy. At the same time, the need to control the South China Sea as a strategic priority was downgraded as reunification with Taiwan hurtled to the top of Beijing's agenda. In that context, given the relative closeness of Taiwan and improvements in the capabilities of the Chinese air force and missile arsenal, aircraft carriers are not now considered vital."[123]

This and similar U.S. Defense Department assessments of recent years that China's carrier program was sidelined were apparently correct and would likely have been confirmed by senior Chinese officials at the time. Following the 2004 tsunami and especially with the advent of the eleventh five-year plan, however, those priorities seem to be changing. What even a modest carrier can do in the near term caught the Chinese by surprise in early 2005, when they watched Indian and Japanese carriers conduct post-tsunami relief operations. Thus, in reconceptualizing the PLAN carrier, China's two potential role models—and competitors—are not the United States and the former Soviet Union but rather India and Japan. Fixating on the global gold standard for aircraft carriers is no longer the only, or even the most appealing, option for China. Beijing's strategic focus on Taiwan militates against developing aircraft carriers, except for small helicopter carriers serving as antisubmarine-warfare platforms, for that specific scenario. To China's south and southwest, however, especially along the lengthy SLOCs, aircraft carriers of all variations could play more useful operational and diplomatic roles. A carrier as a discrete capability fulfilling secondary roles, such as sea-lane security and for humanitarian and disaster relief missions, is therefore the most likely trajectory.

Nevertheless, once China has multiple carriers in operation, there is no reason to think that new technologies and doctrines will preclude Beijing from linking the carrier to its more capable and far more numerous submarines. As many as twelve to fifteen helicopter carriers or a mix of modest carriers and somewhat larger variants would represent a significant shift in ASW capability and may better complement the submarine-centered navy, which China is clearly developing at present, than would large-deck fixed-wing alternatives. With the wealth of new models of foreign carriers and operational concepts available to watch, the carrier discussion in China—while still theoretical—has matured. On paper at least, the Chinese have avoided the pitfall of spending too much on the wrong platforms at the wrong time. It remains to be seen, however, exactly what place aircraft carrier development will have in what has been a prolonged, publicized, and increasingly successful attempt by China to become a maritime power.

One thing is clear: Beijing will continually search for the most effective platforms with which to assert control over its maritime periphery. As a recent article in the *PLA Daily* emphasizes,

> We must absolutely no longer be the least bit neglectful regarding the "world without markers" of our vast sea area, our blue frontier. We must no longer customarily assert that the total area of our national territory is 9.6 million square kilometers. To that we must add our sea area of 3 million square kilometers, our blue frontier. Who will protect this vast blue frontier? How should it be protected? Those are questions which every Chinese person, and especially every member of the Chinese armed forces, must ponder carefully. During China's era of weakness and degeneration in the past, in the face of power backed up by gunboats, we lost many things which we should not have lost. It is a different era now. We must not lose anything. We must fight for every inch of territory, and never give up an inch of sea area! We must build a powerful Navy, and protect our coastal defenses, our islands, our vast blue frontier, and everything within the scope of our maritime rights and interests. Cherishing and protecting the seas and oceans is the sacred duty and responsibility of our republic's military personnel. Every intangible "boundary marker" and "sentry post" at sea must always be clearly visible in the minds of every one of us.[124]

Notes

The authors thank Dr. Lyle Goldstein, Cdr. Thomas Lang, USN, Cdr. Dan Monette, USN, Professor William Murray, Professor Robert Rubel, and Capt. Michael Sherlock, USN, for their incisive comments.

1. *China Military Science* is published by the PLA's Academy of Military Sciences. 徐起 [Xu Qi], "21世纪初海上地缘战略与中国海军的发展" ["Maritime Geostrategy and the Development of the Chinese Navy in the Early 21st Century"], 中国军事科学 [*China Military Science*] 17, no. 4 (2004): 75–81. Translation by Andrew Erickson and Lyle Goldstein published in *Naval War College Review* 59, no. 4 (Autumn 2006).

2. See, for example, 王振文 [Wang Zhenwen, editor], "'明思克'号传奇" [*The Legend of the* Minsk], (南海出版公司 [South China Sea Publishing Company], 2002), 238. The works of such premier scholars as Tang Shiping of the Chinese Academy of Social Sciences (CASS) emphasize the need for China's leaders to focus on resolving domestic problems and to "make positive advances while not rushing forward blindly . . . to seek a balance between progress and prudence." This would seem to problematize a rapid large-deck carrier program. 唐世平 [Tang Shiping], "2010–2015 年的中国周边安全环境—决定性因素和趋势展" [China's Peripheral Security Environment in 2010–2015: Decisive Factors, Trends, and Prospects], 战略与管理 [*Strategy & Management*], no. 4 (2001): 37, Foreign Broadcast Information Service (FBIS) CPP20021017000169. See also 唐世平 [Tang Shiping], "再论中国的大战略" [Reconsidering China's Grand Strategy], 战略与管理 [*Strategy & Management*], no. 4 (2001).

3. "Observation Post of the Military Situation" program, Feng Huang Wei Shih Chung Wen Tai [Phoenix Television], 15 March 2006, FBIS CPP20060317515025. *Naval & Merchant Ships* is a semitechnical monthly publication of the Chinese Society of Naval Architecture and Marine Engineering.

4. 赵卫 [Zhao Wei], 超空泡高速鱼雷技术综合分析 ["A Comprehensive Analysis of High-Speed Supercavitating Torpedo Technology"] (master's diss., Harbin Engineering University, 1 January 2001): 64.

5. Ibid.

6. Authors' interview, Beijing, June 2006.

7. 吴红民 [Wu Hongmin], "龙游五洋: 中国海军发展新论" ["The Dragon Swims the Five Seas: New Ideas on China's Naval Development"], 舰载武器 [*Shipborne Weapons*] (September 2005): 18.

8. Ibid.

9. For scholarship concerning China's carrier development, see Ian Storey and You Ji, "China's Aircraft Carrier Ambitions: Seeking Truth from Rumors," *Naval War College Review* 57, no. 1 (Winter 2004): 77–93. This article has been translated into Chinese as 张宏飞 [Zhang Hongfei], "中国人为什么需要或不需要航母?—看清中国的航母雄心 外国专家从传言中探寻真相" "[Why Do the Chinese People Need, or Not Need, an Aircraft Carrier?—Foreign Experts Seek from Rumors to

Clearly See the Truth about China's Aircraft Carrier Ambitions"], 国际展望 [*World Outlook*], no. 16 (August 2004): 16–21.

10. This is not to imply that the Chinese have across-the-board advantages in either submarine or mine warfare, especially compared to the U.S. Navy, but rather that focused investments in these warfighting specializations seem to promise the highest rate of strategic return in the near term.

11. 刘华清 [Liu Huaqing], 刘华清回忆录 [*The Memoirs of Liu Huaqing*] (Beijing: People's Liberation Army, 2004), 481. All original quotations from Liu's autobiography were checked against the wording in the FBIS translation of chapters 16–20, CPP20060707320001001. Wording different from the FBIS translation is used whenever the authors felt that it better reflected Liu's meaning or would be more comprehensible to the reader.

12. See Liu Huaqing, *Memoirs of Liu Huaqing*, 437; Alexander Huang, "The Chinese Navy's Offshore Active Defense Strategy: Conceptualization and Implications," *Naval War College Review 47*, no. 3 (Summer 1994): 18; Bernard D. Cole, *The Great Wall at Sea: China's Navy Enters the Twenty-first Century* (Annapolis, Md.: Naval Institute Press, 2001), 165–68. Because neither the PLA Navy nor any other organization of the PRC government has publicly made the island chains an integral part of official policy or defined their precise scope, however, Chinese references to island chains must be interpreted with caution.

13. 徐起 [Xu Qi], "21世纪初海上地缘战略与中国海军的发展" ["Maritime Geostrategy and the Development of the Chinese Navy in the Early 21st Century"], 中国军事科学 [*China Military Science*] 17, no. 4 (2004): 75–81. Translation by Andrew Erickson and Lyle Goldstein published in *Naval War College Review 59*, no. 4 (Autumn 2006).

14. For a detailed graphic from the PRC naval studies community that shows all three "island chains," see 阻明 [Zu Ming], "美国驻西太地区海军兵力部署与基地体系示意图" [A Schematic Diagram of the U.S. Naval Forces Deployed and System of Bases in the Western Pacific], 舰船知识 [*Naval & Merchant Ships*], no. 2 (January 2006): 24. A recent issue of China's official *People's Daily*, however, mentions only two island chains, the first and the second. See "美军忙著大调整" ["U.S. Navy Preoccupied with Major Adjustment"], 人民日报 [*People's Daily*], 9 July 2004. Also, "美国鹰派人物再放狂言—透视美国空中打击中国计划" ["Members of the U.S. 'Hawk Faction' Rave Again: A Perspective on a U.S. Plan to Attack China from the Air"], 国际展望 [*World Outlook*], no. 9 (May 2005): 27–28.

15. "Memoir of Senior Military Leader Published," *Xinhua*, 8 October 2004, FBIS CPP20041008000177; "'刘华清回忆录' 已由解放军出版社出版" ["Memoirs of Liu Huaqing" (former Central Military Commission vice chairman) Published], *Jiefangjun Bao*, www.chinamil.com.cn/site1/xwpdxw/2004-10/03/content_28915.htm.

16. Liu Huaqing, *Memoirs of Liu Huaqing*, 477.

17. Ibid., 477.

18. Ibid., 479.

19. This paragraph is drawn entirely from Ibid., 478.

20. Ibid., 480.

21. Information from this and the preceding paragraph is derived from ibid., 480–81.

22. Ibid., 481.

23. Ibid.

24. "Former Deputy Commander of the PLA Navy Vice Admiral Zhang Xusan Is Guest of Sina.com," *Jianchuan Zhishi* (Internet version), 11 July 2005, FBIS CPP20050713000187.

25. For the quote, Liu Huaqing, *Memoirs of Liu Huaqing*, 481. For symbolism, ibid., 477. For developments in other countries, ibid., 479.

26. Ibid., 481.

27. See "Aircraft Carrier Programme," *Chinese Defence Today*, available at www .sinodefence.com/navy/aircarrier/default.asp.

28. 余晓军, 高翔, 钟民军 [Yu Xiaojun, Gao Xiang, and Zhong Min], "蒸汽弹射器的动力学仿真研究" ["Simulation of Dynamics of the Steam-Powered Catapult"], 船海工程 [*Ship & Ocean Engineering*] 166, no. 3 (2005): 1–4; and 贾忠湖, 高永, 韩维 [Jia Zhonghu, Gao Yong, and Han Wei], 航母纵摇对舰载机弹射起飞的限制研究 ["Research on the Limitation of Vertical Toss to the Warship-Based Aircraft's Catapult-Assisted Take-off"], 飞行力学 [*Flight Dynamics*] 20, no. 2 (June 2002): 19–21.

29. The Thai carrier has a full load displacement of 11,486 tons, making it one of the smaller, if not the smallest, operational aircraft carriers. See "Chakri Naruebet Offshore Patrol Helicopter Carrier, Thailand," www.naval-technology.com/ projects/chakrinaruebet/.

30. See "Aircraft Carrier Programme."

31. For "military education," 天鹰 [Tian Ying], "1979年中国海军迫近'明斯克'号" ["In 1979 the PLAN Approached the Minsk Aircraft Carrier"], 舰载武器 [*Shipborne Weapons*] (January 2005): 87–89; and 区国义 [Ou Guoyi], "前苏联'明斯克'号航母的改装" ["The Re-Equipping of the Soviet Aircraft Carrier 'Minsk'"], 中国修船 [*China Ship Repair*], no. 4 (2000): 15. Also, 吴伦楷 [Wu Lunkai], "'明思克'航空母舰成功系泊之所在" ["The Reason of the Successful Mooring of the Aircraft Carrier 'Minsk'"], 船舶 [*Ship & Boat*], no. 6 (December 2001): 54–57.

32. 李伟群 [Li Weiqun], "'基辅'号闯关记" ["Record of the Retired Russian Aircraft Carrier 'Kiev' Braving the Journey"], 中国远洋航务公造 [*China Ocean Shipping Monthly*], no. 10 (2000): 62–64.

33. For tourists, 张俊杰 [Zhang Junjie], "不露文章世已惊—扫描 '基辅'航母世界" ["Astonish the World before Publicity: A Glance over the Aircraft Carrier 'Kiev'"], 中国船检 [*China Ship Survey*] no. 8 (2001): 26–27. Also, 安飞 [An Fei], "'基辅'号航母探秘" ["A Probe into the Aircraft Carrier 'Kiev'"], 中国船检 [*China Ship Survey*], no. 10 (2003): 39.

34. Author's visit, 滨海航母主题公园 [Binhai Aircraft Carrier Theme Park], June 2006.

35. Maubo Chang, Taiwan Central News Agency, 2 April 1998, FBIS FTS19980402001018. According to one source: "The contract with Ukraine stipulated that the buyer can't use the carrier for military purposes, and that any equipment that could be used to build other warships were removed from the craft." The extent to which this was a binding stipulation is unclear, especially as the company that originally purchased Varyag from Ukraine no longer exists. Moreover, whether "military purposes" includes training and experimentation is equally unclear. A close examination of the specifics of the contract as well as the larger legal issues of operationalizing the Varyag is definitely warranted but is beyond the scope of the current work. "Aircraft Carrier Project," GlobalSecurity.org, available at www.globalsecurity.org/military/world/china/cv.htm.

36. See Xie Qiong, "Chinese Navy's First Aircraft Carrier Strike Group in Commission Within Two Years," Duowei Xinwen, 1 May 2006, FBIS CPP20060512501008.

37. Authors' interview, Beijing, June 2006.

38. For a Chinese claim that Varyag may be used for "training," see Wu Hongmin, "Dragon Swims the Five Seas," 20. According to recent Chinese Internet rumors, Varyag will be renamed 施琅 [Shi Lang], given hull number 83, and be used as an education and training facility attached to the Dalian Naval Academy. Admiral Shi Lang (1621–96) served as commander-in-chief of the Qing fleet of 300 warships and 20,000 troops which conquered Taiwan through amphibious invasion in 1683. Shi advocated the formal integration of Taiwan into Qing administration. Following Shi's victory, Taiwan formally became a prefecture of China's Fujian province. For historical background, see 吴温暖 [Wu Wennuan], "施琅 '恭陈台湾弃留疏' 的战略指导价值" ["The Strategic Value of Shi Lang's Memorial to the Emperor on the Taiwan Issue"] 厦门大学学报 (哲学社会科学版) [Journal of Xiamen University (Arts & Social Sciences Edition)], no. 1 (2004): 79–84.

39. See 苏红宇 [Su Hongyu], "是航母? 还是" ["Is It an Aircraft Carrier, Or . . . ?"], 船舶工业技术经济信息 [Ship Building Industry Technological & Economic Information], no. 3 (2005): 50–55; and "A Vessel of Choice," INCAT News, 22 May 2003, www.incat.com; Michael Lowe, "INCAT's Aircraft Carrier Plans," Examiner, 30 July 2003, available at www.examiner.com.au/story.asp?id=188186.

40. For evidence that the shipbuilding sector is among China's most advanced military sectors, thanks in part to its robust civilian counterpart, see "China's Shipbuilding Industry," chapter 3 of Evan S. Medeiros, Roger Cliff, Keith Crane, and James C. Mulvenon, A New Direction for China's Defense Industry (Arlington, Va.: RAND, 2005), 109–54.

41. See, for example, such periodicals as 中船重工 [China Shipbuilding Industry], 船舶工业技术经济信息 [Technological and Economic Information of the Shipbuilding Industry], and 中国港口和码头 [Chinese Harbors and Wharves].

42. 励缨, 温玮, 金长江 [Li Ying, Wen Wei, and Jin Changjiang], "舰载飞机逃逸复飞动力学特性研究" ["The Study of the Dynamic Character of Bolting and Going-Around for Carrier Aircraft"], 飞行力学 [Flight Dynamics] 12, no. 2 (June 1994): 1–9.

43. 姚熊亮, 瞿祖清, 陈起富 [Yao Xiongliang, Qu Zuqing, and Chen Qifu], "飞机在航母飞行甲板上着舰时的冲击轮载" ["Landing Loads of Airplane Gear on the Deck of Aircraft Carriers"], 哈尔滨工程大学学报 [*Journal of Harbin Engineering University*] 18, no. 2 (April 1997): 8–15; and 姚熊亮, 瞿祖清, 陈起富 [Yao Xiongliang, Qu Zuqing, and Chen Qifu], "爆炸载荷下航母飞行甲板" ["The Elastoplastic Responses of Flight Decks of Aircraft Carriers Subjected to Air Blasts"], 哈尔滨工程大学学报 [*Journal of Harbin Engineering University*], no. 3 (1996): 21–30.

44. A "ski-jump" is a ramp, typically twelve degrees, at the bow, that helps impart lift and permits heavier aircraft to become airborne after a short takeoff run. This allows for greater range and weapon payload than nonramped vertical/short take-offs, but still not on par with the range and payloads of aircraft launched by steam catapult.

45. For VSTOLs, 金长江, 车军 [Jin Changjiang and Che Jun], "斜板滑跳起飞动力学特性研究" ["Study of the Dynamic Characteristics of Ramp Ski Jump Takeoffs"], 北京航空航天大学学报 [*Journal of Beijing University of Aeronautics and Astronautics*] 23, no. 3 (June 1997): 356–61. For takeoff issues, 曲东才, 周胜明 [Qu Dongcai and Zhou Shengming], 载机起飞技术研究 ["Study of Technologies of Shipboard Plane Taking Off"], 航空科学技术 [*Aeronautical Science & Technology*], no. 4 (2004): 25–29. For deck motion, 余永, 杨一栋 [Yu Yong and Yang Yidong], "基于卡尔曼滤波理论的甲板运动预估技术研究" ["Deck Motion Prediction Technique Based on Kalman Filtering Theory"], 数据采集与处理 [*Journal of Data Acquisition & Processing*] 17, no. 4 (2002): 381–84; and 要瑞璞, 赵希人 [Yao Ruipu and Zhao Xiren], "航母运动姿态实时预报" ["Real-Time Prediction of Aircraft Carrier Motion"], 海洋工程 [*Ocean Engineering*], no. 3 (1997): 26–31. For air wake, 彭兢, 金长江 [Peng Jing and Jin Changjiang], "航空母舰尾流数值仿真研究" ["Research on the Numerical Simulation of Aircraft Carrier Air Wake"], 北京航空航天大学学报 [*Journal of Beijing University of Aeronautics and Astronautics*] 26, no. 3 (June 2000): 340–43. For landing decisions, 余勇, 杨一栋, 代世俊 [Yu Yong, Yang Yidong, and Dai Shijun], "舰载飞机复飞决策技术研究与实时可视化仿真" ["Study on Wave-Off Decision Techniques and Real-Time Visible Simulation of Carrier-Based Aircraft"], 飞行力学 [*Flight Dynamics*] 20, no. 2 (June 2002): 31–38. For key technologies, 王钱生 [Wang Qiansheng], "舰载机总体设计主要关键技术概述" ["Critical Technologies in Carrier-Based Aircraft Design and Development"], 飞机设计 [*Aircraft Design*], no. 2 (June 2005): 6–10. For command and control, 郭蕾, 王矩 [Guo Lei and Wang Ju], "航母舰载机战斗群航空作战指挥控制系统初步研究" ["Primary Study on Command & Control System for Aerial Combat of Carrier-Based Aircraft"], 电光与控制 [*Electronics Optics & Control*] 12, no. 3 (June 2005): 6–8.

46. For levitation ejectors, "为什么新一代航母要用磁悬浮弹射装备" ["Why the Next-Generation of Aircraft Carriers Will Use Magnetic Levitation Ejectors"], 国防科技 [*National Defense Science & Technology*], no. 4 (2004): 83. For IFEP, 石艳, 徐惠明 [Shi Yan and Xu Huiming], "21世纪结合全电力推进的航母" ["Aircraft Carrier with IFEP for the Twenty-first Century"], 船电技术 [*Marine Electric Technology*], no. 2 (2005): 4–5, 9. Emerging technologies may be able to provide

significant combat capability suitable for the Chinese strategy even with a smaller deck. For insight into propulsion and catapult alternatives, see navy-matters.beedal .com/cvf3-2.htm.

47. For an explicit example, see 冯宁 [Feng Ning], "成像型制导系统舰船目标自动 识别技术的研究" ["Research Concerning Automatic Vessel Target Recognition Technology in Imaging-type Guidance Systems"] (master's diss., 哈尔滨工程大学 [Harbin Engineering University], 2 February 2005).

48. 流星 [Liu Xing], "中国迫切需要航空母舰吗" ["Does China Urgently Need an Aircraft Carrier?"], 舰载武器 [Shipborne Weapons] (January 2004): 27. For a Shenyang Aircraft Design & Research Institute expert's analysis of relevant technological demands, see Wang Qiansheng, "Critical Technologies in Carrier-Based Aircraft Design and Development," 6–10. For other challenges inherent in developing aircraft suitable for a Chinese aircraft carrier, see 宇垣　大成 [Ugaki Taisei], "中国空母はいつ出現するか" ["When Will a Chinese Aircraft Carrier Appear?"], 世界の艦船 [Ships of the World] (April 2005): 112.

49. See "Aircraft Carrier Programme."

50. Ibid. As of June 2006, China had received 24 Su-30 MKK/MK2s. While this is a significant purchase, it might not be sufficient to outfit a CSG.

51. "AWACS" refers to the U.S. Airborne Warning and Control System, carried by the E-3A aircraft.

52. "KJ-2000 Airborne Warning & Control System," Chinese Defence Today, available at www.sinodefence.com/airforce/specialaircraft/kj2000.asp.

53. "Y-8 'Balance Beam' Airborne Early Warning Aircraft," Chinese Defence Today, available at www.sinodefence.com/airforce/specialaircraft/y8balancebeam.asp.

54. See, for example, "Observation Post of the Military Situation," HK Phoenix TV, Military News, FBIS CPP20060626715001, 21 June 06.

55. See "Aircraft Carrier Programme."

56. Sandra I. Erwin, "Navy Aims to Curtail Aviation Mishaps Caused by Crew Error," National Defense, October 2000, www.nationaldefensemagazine.org/ issues/2000/Oct/Navy_Aims.htm.

57. Peng Guangqian and Yao Youzhi, eds., The Science of Military Strategy (Beijing: Military Science Publishing House, 2005), 449.

58. Initially, the PLA Navy was a coastal defense force. During the late 1970s, the PLAN sent submarines into the South China Sea and beyond the First Island Chain into the Pacific Ocean for the first time. By the mid-1980s it had developed broader ability to conduct "近海作战" [offshore operations] as part of a larger "海军战略" [naval strategy] of "近海防御" [offshore defense] approved by Deng Xiaoping and articulated and implemented by PLA Navy commander Admiral Liu Huaqing. The Chinese term 近海 (jinhai) is often translated as "offshore." In contrast, the term 远海 (yuanhai), like its rough synonym 远洋 (yuanyang), may be translated as "open ocean." Related terms 沿海 (yanhai) and 海岸 (haian) may be translated as "coastal"; 滨海 (binhai) and 近岸 (jinan) as "inshore" (between "coastal" and "offshore"); and 中海 (zhonghai) perhaps as "mid-distance seas" (between "offshore"

and "open ocean"). For a detailed diagram and explanation of these terms, see Alexander Huang, "The Chinese Navy's Offshore Active Defense Strategy: Conceptualization and Implications," *Naval War College Review* 47, no. 3 (Summer 1994): 16–19. These terms do not relate to specific geographic distances *per se*, but rather to conceptual areas for naval defense and power projection progressively further from shore. The distance ranges to which these terms pertain, while relative as opposed to absolute, do appear to have expanded in scope in parallel to growth in the PLA Navy's capabilities. To date, however, perhaps to preserve strategic flexibility, neither the PLA Navy nor any other organization of the PRC government has publicly defined the precise meaning of these terms.

59. Liu Huaqing, *Memoirs of Liu Huaqing*, 480.

60. Ibid., 474.

61. Authors' interview, Beijing, June 2006.

62. 徐起 [Xu Qi], "21世纪初海上地缘战略与中国海军的发展" ["Maritime Geostrategy and the Development of the Chinese Navy in the Early 21st Century"], 中国军事科学 [*China Military Science*] 17, no. 4 (2004): 75–81. Translation by Andrew Erickson and Lyle Goldstein published in *Naval War College Review* 59, no. 4 (Autumn 2006).

63. 李兵 [Li Bing] 海军英豪: 人民海军英模荟萃 [*Naval Heroes: An Assembly of Heroic Models from the People's Navy*] (Beijing: Sea Tide, 2003), 1.

64. "Senior Military Officer: China to Develop Its Own Aircraft Carrier Fleet," *Wen Wei Po*, 10 March 2006, FBIS CPP20060310508004.

65. See, for example, Li Bing, *Naval Heroes*, 1–3.

66. 徐起 [Xu Qi], "21世纪初海上地缘战略与中国海军的发展" ["Maritime Geostrategy and the Development of the Chinese Navy in the Early 21st Century"], 中国军事科学 [*China Military Science*] 17, no. 4 (2004): 75–81. Translation by Andrew Erickson and Lyle Goldstein published in *Naval War College Review* 59, no. 4 (Autumn 2006).

67. Author's interviews, Beijing, December 2005.

68. *Modern Navy* is published by the official PLA Navy newspaper, *People's Navy*. 陈张明, 王积建, 冯先辉 [Chen Zhangming, Wang Jijian, and Feng Xianhui], "印度洋海啸中的海军行动" ["Naval Operations in the Indian Ocean Tsunami"], 当代海军 [*Modern Navy*], no. 3 (2005): 44–45. For "non-combat," "让'非战争军事行动'阳光起来" ["Letting 'Non Combat Military Operations' Shine Forth"], 当代海军 [*Modern Navy*], (March 2005): 1.

69. 张文木 [Zhang Wenmu], "美国的石油地缘战略与中国西藏新疆地区安全—从美国南亚和中亚外交新动向谈起" ["America's Geopolitical Oil Strategy and the Security of China's Tibet and Xinjiang Regions: A Discussion Based on New Trends in America's South and Central Asian Diplomacy"], 战略与管理 [*Strategy & Management*] 27, no. 2 (1998): 100–104.

70. Zhang Wenmu, "China's Energy Security and Policy Choices," *Shijie Jingji Yu Zhengzhi* [*World Economics & International Politics*], no. 5 (May 2003): 11–16, FBIS CPP20030528000169.

71. Liu Xinhua and Zhang Wenmu, "China's Oil Security and Its Strategic Options," *Xiandai Guoji Guanxi* [*Contemporary International Relations*], no. 12 (December 2002): 35–37, 46, FBIS CPP20030425000288.

72. 张文木 [Zhang Wenmu], "试论当代中国 '海权' 问题" ["Discussing Modern China's Problem of Maritime Rights"], 中国远海航务公告 [*Maritime China*], no. 5 (2005): 50. For a more moderate view concerning the most effective means of promoting Chinese energy security, see People's University scholar 查道炯 [Zha Daojiong], "中美能源合作及对东亚合作的影响" ["Sino-American Energy Cooperation and Its Impact on Cooperation in East Asia"], 外交评论 [*Journal of the Foreign Affairs College*], no. 6 (2005): 34–35.

73. 徐起 [Xu Qi], "21世纪初海上地缘战略与中国海军的发展" ["Maritime Geostrategy and the Development of the Chinese Navy in the Early 21st Century"], 中国军事科学 [*China Military Science*] 17, no. 4 (2004): 75–81. Translation by Andrew Erickson and Lyle Goldstein published in *Naval War College Review* 59, no. 4 (Autumn 2006).

74. Peng Guangqian and Yao Youzhi, eds., *The Science of Military Strategy*, 446.

75. For a Chinese analysis of Soviet successes and failures in carrier design and construction, see 王存琳 [Wang Cunlin], "俄罗斯航空母舰的兴衰" ["The Prosperity and Decline of Aircraft Carriers in Russia"], 上海造船 [*Shanghai Shipbuilding*], no. 2 (1999): 55–60.

76. "'世昌'号—中国海军的新式空中勤务舰" ["'Shichang': China's Navy's New Type of Aerial Service Ship"], 船舶电子工程 [*Ship Electronic Engineering*] 107, no. 5 (1998): 41.

77. 曹金平 [Cao Jinping], "'世昌'号,中国第一艘国防动员舰" ["'Shichang': China's First National Defense Mobilization Ship"], 航海 [*Navigation*], no. 1 (1998): 21.

78. Cao Jinping, "Shichang," 22.

79. For the *Argus* similarity, "The Rusted 'Viking' Lives Again: The Strange Tale of a Former Soviet Aircraft Carrier," *Sitrep* (Royal Canadian Military Institute) 65, no. 6 (November/December 2005): 15. For the Dalian visit, 曹金平 [Cao Jinping], "探营国防动员舰" ["Visit and Operate National Defense Mobilization Ship"], 解放军报 [*PLA Daily*], 29 July 2003, www.pladaily.com.cn/gb/defence/2003/07/29/2 0030729017107_gfgj.html. For trials, 海司院校部 [Naval Department Academic Section], "世昌'舰完成首次远航实习任务" ["'Shichang' Vessel Accomplishes Its First Extended Sea Trial Mission"], 海军院校教育 [*Education of Naval Academies*] 217, no. 3 (1999): 12.

80. "我海军院校学员实践性课目训练都在训练舰上完成" ["Our Naval Academy Students Accomplish Practice of All Their Training Subjects on Training Vessels"], 解放军报 [*PLA Daily*], as reprinted in 人民日报 [*People's Daily*], 27 September 2004, available at www.people.com.cn/GB/junshi/1076/2810389.html.

81. *Shichang* is named for Qing dynasty hero and Beiyang navy general Deng Shichang (Cao Jinping, "Shichang," 21). Deng died a hero's death in the Sino-Japanese War's Yellow Sea Battle after ramming an enemy ironclad when his ammunition had run out. Ammunition supplies were inadequate because of official corruption. Also 陈国芳, 李朝贵, 陈万军. [Chen Guofang, Li Zhaogui, and Chen Wanjun],

"'世昌号', 我们热烈欢迎您—我国第一艘国防动员船诞生记" ["'Shichang,' We Warmly Welcome You: A Record of the Emergence of China's First National Defense Mobilization Ship"], 中国民兵 [*China Commando*], no. 4 (1997): 26.

82. Cao Jinping, "Visit and Operate National Defense Mobilization Ship."

83. Unless otherwise specified, this quotation and other information in this paragraph derives from "Shichang (Multirole Aviation Ship)," GlobalSecurity.org, www .globalsecurity.org/military/world/china/shichang.htm.

84. Ibid. Addition of medical treatment and hospital ward modules allows *Shichang* to serve as a "true 'at-sea mobile hospital,'" with dimensions similar to a land-based equivalent. With its transport container, it can become a larger transport ship. *Shichang* boasts 108 rooms and compartments. Cao Jinping, "Visit and Operate National Defense Mobilization Ship."

85. 鞭激 [Bian Ji], "中国的航母雏形—'世昌舰'" ["China's Embryonic Aircraft Carrier: 'Shichang'"], 船舶电子工程 [*Ship Electronic Engineering*] 113, no. 5 (1999): 59.

86. 尹岭 [Yin Ling], 中国直升机航母前瞻 ["The Outlook for Chinese Helicopter Carrier(s)"], 舰载武器 [*Shipborne Weapons*], no. 8 (2005): 43.

87. Ibid., 45.

88. Ibid., 49.

89. See "Amphibious Assault Ship (LHD) Programme," *Chinese Defence Today,* www.sinodefence.com/navy/amphibious/lhd.asp.

90. See Ling Xiang, "扬威海上的中国水雷战舰艇" ["Chapter 6: Raise Mighty Chinese Sea Mine Warfare Ships on the Sea"], in 当代水雷战舰艇大观 [*Modern Sea Mine Warships Spectacle*], 当代军舰大观系列丛书之五 [Modern Warship Spectacle Book Series, vol. 5] (Beijing: World Knowledge Press, 1995), 160; and 林长盛 [Lin Changsheng], "潜龙在渊: 解放军水雷兵器的现状与发展" ["The Hidden Dragon in the Deep: The Present Situation and Development of PLA Mine Weaponry"], 国际展望 [*World Outlook*], no. 9 (May 2005): 32.

91. Taiwan military spokesman Liu Chih-chien is quoted as stating that the *Varyag* will be "used as a training ship in preparation for building an aircraft carrier battle group"; David Lague, "An Aircraft Carrier for China?" *International Herald Tribune,* 31 January 2006, www.iht.com/articles/2006/01/30/business/carrier.php.

92. For ballistic missiles, "攻击航母的武器装备" ["Weapons for Attacking Aircraft Carriers"], 当代海军 [*Modern Navy*] (October 2004); 顾险峰, 钱建平, 马远良 [Gu Xianfeng, Qian Jianping, and Ma Yuanliang], "鱼雷武器远程精确打击导引模式和技术架构初步探索" ["Preliminary Research on the Guidance Pattern and Technique Framework of Long-Range Accurate Attack Torpedo Weapons"], 舰船科学技术 [*Ship Science & Technology*], March 2003: 7–11; 催绪生, 关国枢, 周德善 [Cui Xusheng, Guan Guoshu, and Zhou Deshan], "接受海战的历史教训—加强新世纪的鱼雷研制工作" ["Draw Useful Lessons from History and Strengthen R&D of Torpedoes in the New Century"], 舰船科学技术 [*Ship Science & Technology*] (March 2003): 4–6; 李光普 [Li Guangpu], "美国航母的今昔及与其对抗问题的分析" ["An Analysis of American Aircraft Carriers Past and Present

and the Problems They Have Faced"], 飞航导弹 [*Winged Missiles Journal*] (March 2002): 1–5; 张国华, 袁乃昌, 庄钊文 [Zhang Guohua, Yuan Naichang, and Zhuang Zhaowen], "基于前元法的航母雷达散射截面计算" ["Calculation of the Radar Cross Section of an Aircraft Carrier Based on the Plate-Element Method"], 国防科技大学学报 [*Journal of the National University of Defense Technology*] 23, no. 5 (2001): 79–83; and "海上霸王—航空母舰" ["Maritime Hegemon: The Aircraft Carrier"], *Science Initiation* (March 1996). For cruise missiles, 王剑飞, 武文军, 彭小龙, 熊平 [Wang Jianfei, Wu Wenjun, Peng Xiaolong, and Xiong Ping], "美军航母战斗群空袭火力及其效能分析" ["Analysis on Effectiveness of the Air-Attack Firepower of a U.S. Carrier Fighting Group"], 情报指挥控制系统与仿真技术 [*Intelligence, Command, Control, and Simulation Technology*] 27, no. 1 (February 2005): 24–30; 吴强 姜玉宪 [Wu Qiang and Jiang Yuxian], "反舰导弹综合突防技术" ["Research on the Integrated Penetration of Antiship Missiles"], 北京航空航天大学学报 [*Journal of Beijing University of Aeronautics and Astronautics*] 30, no. 112 (December 2004): 1212–15; and 何文涛, 吴加武 [He Wentao and Wu Jiawu], "航母编队特点及对策研究" ["A Study on Countering Aircraft Carrier Battle Groups"], 现代防御技术 [*Modern Defense Technology*] 32, no. 5 (October 2004): 18–20, 29. For submarines, [Qin Hang, Lin Hua, and Zhou Feng], "响潜艇战斗群作战性能技术因素分析" ["Analysis of Some Technical Factors That Affect the Combat Characteristics of a Group of Submarines"], 海军工程学院学报 [*Journal of the Naval Engineering Academy*] 89, no. 4 (1999): 60–63. For torpedoes, 石敏, 刘晓亮, 逄妍立, 石勇 [Shi Min, Liu Xiaoliang, Pang Yanli, and Shi Yong], "反航母鱼雷远程制导技术的现状和发展" ["The Present Situation and Development of Long-Range Homing Technology on Anti–Aircraft Carrier Torpedoes"], 舰船科学技术 [*Ship Science & Technology*] 27, no. 1 (2005): 17–20; and 顾险峰, 钱建平, 马远良 [Gu Xianfeng, Qian Jianping, and Ma Yuanliang], "鱼雷武器远程精确打击导引模式和技术架构初步探索" ["Preliminary Research on Guidance Patterns and Technique Framework of Long-Range Accurate Attack Torpedo Weapons"], 舰船科学技术 [*Ship Science & Technology*] 25, no. 3 (2003): 7–11.

For sea mines, 刘衍中, 李祥 [Liu Yanzhong and Li Xiang], "实施智能攻击的现代水雷" ["Carrying Out Intelligent Attacks with Modern Sea Mines"], 当代海军 [*Modern Navy*] (July 2006): 29; Jiao Fangjin, "双头鹰的水中伏兵" ["The Double-Headed Eagle's Ambush at Sea"], 国防科技 [*Defense Science*] (July 2003): 91; Wang Wei, "历久弥新话水雷" ["Enduring and Yet Fully Relevant: A Discussion of Sea Mines"], 国防 [*National Defense*] (November 2002): 58; Fu Jinzhu, 水雷战 不容忽视 ["Mine Warfare Must Not Be Ignored"], 现代舰船 [*Modern Ships*], no. 156 (November 1998): 1.

93. 宜恒, 新华 [Yi Heng and Xin Hua], "航母煞星: 对付航母的六大撒手锏" ["Six Trump Cards to Cope with Aircraft Carriers"], 国际展望 [*World Outlook*], no. 3 (February 2001): 60–61.

94. For a Chinese account of the influence of Khrushchev's "航空母舰棺材论" [aircraft carrier coffin theory], see Wu Hongmin, "Dragon Swims the Five Seas," 17.

95. Liu Huaqing, *Memoirs of Liu Huaqing*, 478. In a March 1987 report to the PLA General Staff, Admiral Liu offered possible clarification of what he meant by "escort carriers": "our analysis shows that, without developing aircraft carriers, the

Navy still has to develop destroyers and escort ships in order to make up a mobile force at sea. If aircraft carriers are developed, these ships can serve as escorts for the aircraft carriers and also as mobile combat vessels." Ibid., 480.

96. The Chinese colloquial abbreviation for aircraft carrier, 航母, is also used extensively to describe flagship enterprises and other great achievements. See, for example, 张权 [Zhang Quan], "打造锰业航母—做大做强锰业" ["Build Up the Aircraft Carrier of the Manganese Industry and Make the Manganese Industry Stronger"], 中国锰业 [*China's Manganese Industry*] 23, no. 3 (August 2005): 54–55. For use of the term "aircraft carrier" metaphorically to describe a space station, see 卢天贶 [Lu Tiankuang], "居高临下的太空武器" ["Space Weapons: Occupying Commanding Heights"] (天津科学技术出版社 [*Tianjin Science & Technology*] (2003): 56. For use of the term "aircraft carrier" to symbolize an educational institution, see 顾明远 [Gu Mingyuan], "挑战与应答: 世纪之交的中国教育变革" ["Challenges and Answers: A Century of Chinese Educational Transformation"], (福建教育出版社 [*Fujian Education*] (2001): 96. These examples suggest a larger Chinese penchant for metaphorical writing that makes literal interpretation of interesting rumors problematic.

97. Authors' interview, Beijing, June 2006.

98. 克里斯蒂.曼巴尔. 丹杰. [Christie Manbar (as transliterated), France, trans. and ed. Dan Jie], "中国早期航空母舰设想" ["China's Early Stage Conception of Aircraft Carrier(s)"], 舰载武器 [*Shipborne Weapons*] (July 2005): 18–21. For an article documenting a PLAN officer's attendance at a five-day exercise on the *Charles de Gaulle*, see 纪明周 [Ji Mingzhou], "我随'戴高乐'号出航" ["I Set Sail with the 'Charles de Gaulle'"], 舰船知识 [*Naval & Merchant Ships*] (November 2005): 18–22.

99. For a Chinese analysis of the British ASW helicopter carrier HMS *Invincible* (R05), see 陈坚主 [Cheng Jianzhu], 武器装备完全图美册: 英国 [*Complete Guide to Weapons: England*], (Nanning: 广西人民出版社 [Guangxi People's Press], 2003), 74.

100. See 尹岭 [Yin Ling], "中国直升机航母前瞻" ["The Outlook for a Chinese Helicopter Carrier"], 舰载武器 [*Shipborne Weapons*] (August 2005): 43–49.

101. See *Chinese Defence Today*, at sinodefence.com/airforce/helicopter/z9c.asp and sinodefence.com/airforce/helicopter/ka28.asp.

102. "WZ-10 Attack Helicopter," *Chinese Defence Today*, www.sinodefence.com/airforce/helicopter/wz10.asp.

103. 银河 [Yin He], "飞向大洋: 中国海军舰载直升机的发展与问题" ["Flying toward the Ocean: The Development and Problems of the PLAN's Ship-Based Helicopters"], 舰载武器 [*Shipborne Weapons*], no. 7 (July 2005): 30.

104. A third PLAN development trend has been careful consideration of the political impact of its development and deployment activities. China's leaders took great pains to characterize their successful detonation of an atomic bomb in 1964 as "prevention of nuclear blackmail" and the liberation of other developing nations by breaking a "superpower monopoly." In sharp contrast to Soviet expansion-

ism, Chinese leaders insisted, China's military development was inherently defensive. Beijing went so far as to describe the 1978 invasion of Vietnam as a "defensive counterattack." As China has grown more powerful in recent years, Beijing has characterized its rapid military development as a "peaceful rise" designed merely to restore China to its former position of benevolent greatness. Even that slogan was recently deemed too provocative; it has been replaced with the concept of "peaceful development."

105. See, for example, 林长盛 [Lin Changsheng], "潜龙在渊: 解放军水雷兵器的现状与发展" ["The Hidden Dragon in the Deep: The Present Situation and Development of PLA Mine Weaponry"], 国际展望 [*World Outlook*], no. 9 (May 2005): 22.

106. For acknowledgment of this issue, and a claim that it will not stop China from refitting the *Varyag* as an operational aircraft carrier, see "First Aircraft Carrier in Service Three Years from Now," *Tung Chou Kan,* no. 135 (28 March 2006): 54–56, FBIS CPP20060403510006.

107. Liu Huaqing, *Memoirs of Liu Huaqing,* 479.

108. Peng Guangqian and Yao Youzhi, eds., *The Science of Military Strategy,* 441.

109. Ibid., 443.

110. 徐起 [Xu Qi], "21世纪初海上地缘战略与中国海军的发展" ["Maritime Geostrategy and the Development of the Chinese Navy in the Early 21st Century"], 中国军事科学 [*China Military Science*] 17, no. 4 (2004): 75–81. Translation by Andrew Erickson and Lyle Goldstein published in *Naval War College Review* 59, no. 4 (Autumn 2006).

111. For an example of this differentiation, see Wu Hongmin, "Dragon Swims the Five Seas," 12–21.

112. See (all in 人民海军 [*People's Navy*]), 虞章才, 李慧勇 [Yu Zhangcai and Li Huiyong], "闪光的航迹—郑和七下西洋的真实历程" ["A Gleaming Wake: The True Course of Zheng He's Seven Voyages to the West"] (5 July 2005): 3; 林一宏 [Lin Yihong], "经略海洋—郑和下西洋对建立现代海洋观的启示" ["The Inspiration of Zheng He's Voyages to the West in Establishing a Modern Maritime Outlook"] (7 July 2005): 3; 陆儒德 [Lu Rude], "捍卫海上利益—郑和下西洋对海军建设的启示" ["Defending Maritime Interests: The Inspiration of Zheng He's Voyages to the West in Naval Construction"] (9 July 2005): 3; 吴瑞虎, 马晓静 [Wu Ruihu and Ma Xiaojing], "中国的'航海日'诞生了!" ["China's 'Navigation Day' Is Born!"] (9 July 2005): 1; and 徐起 [Xu Qi], "敦睦友邻—郑和下西洋对中国和平崛起得启示" ["A Friendly Neighbor Promoting Friendly Relations: The Inspiration of Zheng He's Voyages to the West in China's Peaceful Rise"] (12 July 2005): 3. *People's Navy* is a daily newspaper published by the political department of the PLA Navy.

113. Author's interviews, Beijing, December 2005.

114. Authors' interview, Beijing, June 2006.

115. Ibid.

116. Lonnie Henley, "PLA Logistics and Doctrine Reform, 1999–2009," in *People's Liberation Army after Next,* ed. Susan M. Puska (Carlisle, Pa.: U.S. Army War College, 2000), 67.

117. "Our Naval Academy Students Accomplish Practice of All Their Training Subjects on Training Vessels."

118. "'Shichang': China's Navy's New Type of Aerial Service Ship," 41.

119. Cao Jinping, "Visit and Operate National Defense Mobilization Ship."

120. Bian Ji, "China's Embryonic Aircraft Carrier," 59.

121. 韩学利, 李耸岩, 尹承宇 [Han Xueli, Li Songyan, and Yin Chengyu], "'世昌'舰海上卫勤演练中医疗救护的几点体会" ["Several Realizations from Experience Concerning 'Shichang' Medical Treatment During At-Sea Defense Drills"], 海军医学杂志 [*Journal of Navy Medicine*] 22, no. 2 (2001): 139.

122. The authors are indebted to Professor Robert Rubel for the ideas expressed in this paragraph.

123. See Storey and You Ji, "China's Aircraft Carrier Ambitions," available at www.nwc.navy.mil/press/review/2004/Winter/art6-w04.htm.

124. Yu Xiao, "Pay Attention to a 'World without Markers,'" *Jiefangjun Bao* (18 June 2006): 2, FBIS CPP20060619710001.

James Patton

Cold War SSN Operations

Lessons for Understanding Chinese Naval Development

Introduction

EVEN THE FINAL EVENTS of what noted author Norman Friedman documented in his award-winning book *The Fifty-Year War*[1] are now approaching an age of two decades. Another book which purported to describe Cold War events from a point of view more specifically submarine-oriented was published in 1998,[2] at which time it caused quite a stir because of certain covert operations implied. A year or so later, in a landmark exhibit called "SSNs and Boomers" at the Smithsonian Institution's American History Museum and vetted by the Office of Naval Intelligence, some of these alleged events seemed to be validated.[3] It is perhaps appropriate at this point, the Cold War being far enough distant to be in focus, yet not so far removed to be addled by imperfect memory, to review them in some detail for possible application as lessons learned in support of today's existing and evolving strategic environment.

Of particular interest would be any possible correlation to events unfolding in the Far East, as China rapidly evolves through the point of being a formidable regional power, toward superpower status. Whereas economic and military competitions are inevitable (and existing), it is greatly desirable, as with the Soviet Union, to deter and dissuade conflict. Undoubtedly, China's political and military leaders are or have already closely reviewed Cold War events looking for ways and means to achieve their goals without suffering economic collapse or military defeat.

The perspective of this author is as one who reported aboard USS *Scorpion* (SSN589), then the twelfth U.S. nuclear submarine, at the end of her post-shakedown availability in the fall of 1961. The following reflections of Cold War SSN operations, and how they might relate to evolving relations with China, are based on the ensuing twenty-four years of active duty on seven U.S. Navy submarines and submarine-related shore tours, and stem largely from performing intelligence, surveillance, and reconnaissance (ISR) missions and preparing or training others to conduct antisubmarine warfare (ASW) combat—the first mission being strongly supportive of the second.

Background

When the Berlin Wall fell and the Soviet Union imploded in 1989–92, the U.S. submarine force found itself in a similar position to that it had experienced at the end of World War II. In both cases the force was recognized as having made a major contribution to victory, but was also recognized as being too large and expensive for post-conflict national needs. Each time, Moscow (or third world countries) lacked sufficient numbers of merchant ships (or modern submarines) to warrant retaining such expensive assets. In both instances, however, the submarine force quickly and effectively reinvented itself to demonstrate a superior capability in a new "most important" mission area.

Shortly after World War II, the newly established Submarine Development Group Two (later renamed Submarine Development Squadron Twelve—more commonly referred to as DEVRON 12) was tasked with developing the tactics, techniques, and procedures that would allow the submarine force to become the nation's premier ASW element. After the fall of the Soviet Union, the same organization developed, disseminated, and continually improved and updated the tactics, techniques, and procedures that enabled submarines to perform as meaningful elements of carrier battle groups and amphibious ready groups. This included becoming a leading choice for executing land attack strike missions with Tomahawk cruise missiles.

Throughout its post-WWII history, however, the U.S. submarine force has executed a far less heralded, but true core competency of conducting ISR missions. During the Cold War, submarines remained poised to conduct offensive operations against the Warsaw Pact—much as they had, albeit in different circumstances, against Japan during the early 1940s. It should be noted, however, that this combat readiness was itself a result of submariners' continuous ISR operations.

The Evolution of U.S. Navy SSN Missions

There are two sets of missions for any warship—the peacetime mission and the wartime mission. More so than for other platforms, the philosophy of the U.S. submarine force has been (with the notable exception of weapon release) to operate in peacetime where and how they expect to have to operate in war.

There are some allegations in open literature that U.S. submarines conducted peacetime ISR missions in international waters contiguous to Soviet naval bases since the late 1940s.[4] The United States has certainly been forthcoming in recent years in admitting (and asserting a right) to conducting submarine ISR missions in international waters close to a variety of foreign shores. It is not a leap of logic to assume that the execution of such missions shifted entirely to nuclear submarines as these ships became more numerous in the mid-1960s.

In the early 1960s, U.S. SSNs and diesel-electric submarines would have been assigned to barrier roles in places such as the Greenland-Iceland-United Kingdom (GIUK) Gap as a wartime mission. A typical barrier station might have been a few tens of miles wide and fifty to one hundred miles deep—not a very big slice of ocean for a nuclear submarine. An SSN would likely also have had a U.S. diesel-electric submarine stationed on either side of its patrol zone. This positioning was meant to be in support of a kind of containment attempt to keep the USSR's more than three hundred diesel-electric submarines out of the open oceans where they could threaten the sea lines of communication (SLOC) to NATO and other allies in a WWI/WWII analogue. This concept did not optimally employ the SSN's stealth, mobility or endurance. It further assumed that the Soviet submarines would not have predeployed in advance of any political-military crisis. It took several decades and the GLOBAL-series of war games at the U.S. Naval War College to determine that the special qualities of a U.S. SSN, coupled with nominal intelligence expectations, would permit the bulk of the force to be assigned to operate in waters adjacent to the Soviet Union before hostilities commenced.[5]

During this period—the early 1960s—the offensive capability of even nuclear submarines remained largely oriented toward antisurface ship warfare (ASUW) as DEVRON 12 was just beginning to determine how best to conduct ASW. In fact, the ASW weapon that *Scorpion* deployed with in 1961 was the Mk 27 torpedo. This weapon used a lead-acid battery, and was derived from a WWII German weapon. The torpedo was slow (twelve knots) and very short-ranged. With only a passive acoustic homing capability, the *only* submarine the Mk 27 was capable of finding and attacking was a snorkeling diesel submarine, and even then its poor detection ranges obliged the crew to employ the weapon in salvos of three, orbiting in intersecting circles just ahead of the target in what was called the "Ballantine spread" after the logo of a then-popular beer. There was then simply no submarine weapon available to attack an SSN unless it was on the surface.

What appeared to be a major improvement in submarine-launched ASW weapons appeared shortly thereafter. The Mk 37 torpedo was still electrically powered, but used a high-energy-density one-shot potassium hydroxide/silver-zinc battery that essentially doubled both the speed and range of the Mk 27. Another improvement was its organic active sonar, which allowed the torpedo to detect and home on quiet targets. If an SSN target detected the incoming weapon, however, it was generally easy for the targeted submarine to accelerate quickly enough to invalidate the torpedo's firing solution, and escape the weapon's detection cone before the weapon acquired and homed. The somewhat lengthened Mk 37 Mod 1, in turn, incorporated wire guidance in an attempt to allow the firing submarine to correct the torpedo heading to compensate for postlaunch maneuvering by the target. At about the same time, however, engineers discovered that the magnetostrictive transducer on the weapon did not function below four hundred feet due to static backpressure, and a new ceramic transducer was backfitted. Other problems such as low power, turn-rate limitations, and maneuverability restrictions on the firing ship continued to plague the Mk 37 family of ASW weapons throughout their life. Perhaps revealing frustration, the U.S. deployed nonhoming, nuclear-warheaded torpedoes[6] and even a rocket capable of lobbing a rather large thermonuclear warhead.[7] The desired range of this weapon, however, exceeded the localization capability of the solitary submarine from which it was fired.[8] These and other limitations resulted in the weapon being removed from inventory after a relatively short time.

If it is a reasonable assumption that Soviet submarine-launched ASW weaponry was no better than that of the United States during the 1960s and 1970s, then a non-nuclear ASW war between them at that time would have been—in Shakespeare's words—"much ado about nothing," since neither side's SSNs would have been much threat to the other for lack of an effective weapon. Since U.S. SSNs were clearly a deterrent to the USSR, it was their perceived, not actual, offensive capability that produced this desirable effect. This perceived deterrent value was greatly enhanced by U.S. SSNs' demonstrated ability to stealthily operate unmolested in Soviet home waters. Rather than their ASW potential, it was actually U.S. SSNs' ISR product from these missions that represented concrete return on investment for the United States.

The offensive capability of U.S. SSNs skyrocketed in the early 1970s with the introduction of the Mk 48 dual-purpose torpedo. With a warhead large enough to also serve as an ASUW weapon, it additionally had very high speed, long range, excellent maneuverability, and a superb active and passive sonar capability. Unlike previous submarine-launched ASW weapons, the Mk 48 could be launched throughout the ship's speed range.[9] Unlike the Mk 37 Mod1, which only allowed post-launch course and enabling run changes, all weapon parameters except those related to the launching ship's own safety could be changed over the Mk 48's umbilical wire. The Mk 48 torpedo features a powerful thermal system that is fueled by what is essentially a stabilized form of nitroglycerin. The combined features and continued upgrades to this system continue to provide a potent ASW and ASUW weapon for U.S. and some allied forces.

A similar technological development occurred in the field of submarine passive sonars. Both the U.S. and the Soviet Union started the Cold War with copies and derivations of the passive sonars found in the Germany's late-WWII Type XXI U-Boat. This system consisted of a right circular cylinder approximately four feet in both diameter and height. As much better knowledge of acoustics and the ocean environment was gained—predominantly by the Navy Underwater Sound Lab in New London, Connecticut, working closely with Submarine Development Group Two—it became apparent that sound energy frequently arrived at other than in a horizontal plane. Engineers also determined that much larger arrays were needed if greater sensitivity at lower frequencies and against quieter targets were to be obtained. As a result, the diminutive USS *Tullibee* (SSN597) boasted a fifteen-foot diameter spherical sonar whose listening beam could be mechanically trained in the vertical as well as the azimuthal direction when that vessel was commissioned in late 1960. This array occupied the space in the bow of the boat in which torpedo tubes were normally located. As a result, the *Tullibee's* torpedo tubes were located aft and canted out, where they remain on all subsequent U.S. submarines.

The *Tullibee's* sonar system, though a great improvement over previous systems, was soon eclipsed. Further advances in U.S. sonar systems in the 1970s used computers to perform simultaneously the operations that previously had to be performed manually.

Another disruptive technology that appeared in this timeframe was the innovative towed array—introduced to provide submarines with an acoustic antenna hundreds of feet long which enabled a far greater ability to detect and resolve bearings to low frequency components of an adversary submarine's acoustic signature. These two developments contributed greatly to further extending the acoustic advantage U.S. submariners enjoyed over their Soviet counterparts.

The fact that the development of a U.S. military weapon or sensor system typically takes seven to ten years does not mesh well with Moore's Law—that computer capabilities double every eighteen months. This meant that new systems entered the fleet some five to seven generations behind state of the art. An absolutely brilliant program has been instituted for submarine sonar systems in recent years called acoustic rapid commercial off-the-shelf (COTS) insertion, or ARCI. In essence, every couple of years, a group of people inexpensively, rapidly, and dramatically improve each submarine's sonar system through hardware and software modifications. Requirements such as military specification concerning temperature, humidity, or shock resistance, are met to the maximum extent possible by the cabinets and racks into which commercial equipment is installed. ARCI has been held up to the rest of the U.S. Navy as an exemplar of transformational improvement, and other organizations are scrambling to emulate it.

Soviet Nuclear Submarines: Successes and Failures

The primary success achieved by the Soviet submarine force was that so many nuclear submarines could be built and manned so quickly. Their primary failure was that they were generally not well constructed.[10] Another failure was the lack of value Soviet designers placed on quieting. This last weakness was remedied shortly after the Walker-Whitworth espionage affair revealed to the Russians just how inferior Soviet submarines were in the domain of acoustic stealth.

For a time, the fact that nearly all Soviet nuclear submarines had been built with two reactors (as opposed to one) generated undue U.S. concern.[11] What has come to light, however, is that the Soviets failed to either understand or demand the same level of attention to water chemistry and corrosion control that the U.S. nuclear Navy mandated. In Soviet ships, therefore, the eight primary coolant loops and associated steam generators (each reactor having four) were routinely sequentially isolated as associated leaks released unacceptable levels of radioactivity into the ship's atmosphere. When only one or two cooling loops were left operable, the submarine would enter an extended shipyard availability in which loops and steam generators would be cut out, disposed of, and replaced.

The culture of intensive cross-rate crew training that has long been a U.S. hallmark did not exist in the Soviet navy. Instead, the operation and maintenance of complex propulsion and combat systems was almost entirely accomplished by the highly, but narrowly trained Michman—or what the U.S. Navy would classify as a warrant officer. A significant degree of automation was engineered into systems, and the crew size of a Soviet nuclear submarine was significantly less than that of a comparable U.S. nuclear submarine. Many of the disasters suffered by the Soviet submarine force can be directly attributed to inadequate training, undermanning, or a combination of both. This includes the recent loss of *Kursk* in the Barents Sea,[12] in which reportedly there was no person stationed in the torpedo room where the problem occurred. The *Komsomolets* (Mike-class SSN) was lost off of North Cape, Norway, in 1989 after a fire broke out in the aftermost engineering spaces where there was but one watchstander. He was unable to contain the fire, which eventually sank the ship. Finally, a Yankee-class SSBN had a missile explode in its tube while on patrol off Bermuda in 1986 during abortive damage control efforts by unknowledgeable crewmembers following the death of the weapons officer during the early stages of a missile liquid-fuel leak.[13] The Yankee sank three days later as it was being towed back toward its base in the Barents.

Although Admiral Sergei Gorshkov's reputed mantra of "better is the enemy of good enough" was intrinsically tolerant of some degree of U.S. nuclear submarine superiority, the Soviets did not really appreciate the degree of their inferiority until the Walker-Whitworth espionage operations revealed to them the extent and repercussions of their weakness. In command of a *Sturgeon*-class SSN in the late 1970s, for example, I enjoyed a 40 dB acoustic advantage over likely adversaries—a 10,000:1 ratio.[14] These are exactly the odds desirable when seeking to avoid a fair fight. Faced with this evidence, the Soviets embarked on a costly and extensive effort—comparable in cost and priority to the U.S. Manhattan Project in World War II—to reduce the acoustic signatures of their submarines.[15] These Herculean efforts resulted in a 15–20 dB improvement, which represents a noteworthy achievement. Soviet joy in this accomplishment, however, was short-lived when the technologies associated with the *Seawolf*-class (and therefore *Virginia*s) raised the acoustic advantage competition to a more demanding and even more expensive realm.

In his book *Strategic Antisubmarine Warfare and Naval Strategy*, Tom Stefanick concludes that (primarily due to the differences in stealth) U.S. SSBNs were virtually invulnerable to Soviet ASW attempts while Soviet SSBNs were totally at risk to U.S. SSNs.[16] This imbalance manifested itself dramatically both at the tactical and strategic level. As the extent of the acoustic vulnerability of their SSBNs became apparent, and as the ranges of their submarine-launched ballistic missiles become greater, Soviet SSBNs withdrew deeper and deeper into home waters, drawing tactical platforms such as SSNs and SSKs with them into so-called bastions. This retraction of forces dramatically reduced the wartime submarine threat to Western SLOCs as an unintended consequence.

From the perspective of a U.S. submariner, these bastions created a target-rich environment that greatly simplified hunting for Soviet SSBNs, albeit at the increased risk of encountering defensive forces such as SSKs, SSNs, ASW surface ships, and sea mines. U.S. SSBNs, on the other hand, relied on their acoustic stealthiness and longer missile ranges to more freely roam a greater extent of the open oceans.

In fairness to the Soviet submarine force and the Soviet navy, both organizations were always subject to overriding considerations imposed upon them by the Red Army and the land-based Rocket Forces. One of these considerations bordered on near-paranoia concerning Russia's northern flank—the Barents Sea—and how the U.S. Strategic Air Command (SAC) aircraft could pass over it via the Arctic. Because of this concern, most of the Soviet navy's magnificent surface-to-air missile (SAM)-capable warships seemed to have been relegated to extending the Soviet Union's early warning and air defenses to the north—adding again to the target set for U.S. SSNs.

In light of the post-9/11 furor and homeland defense concerns, the United States stands to learn from the Soviet navy of the 1980s. Navies are intrinsically offensively oriented organizations and should be kept, and engaged, forward. A first sign of their imminent worthlessness is when they are pulled back into a defensive role.

Prospective Chinese SSN Operations

The most apparent difference between the geography of Russia and China is that Russia has access to both the Atlantic and Pacific oceans, whereas China's coast borders only the Pacific. The Soviet Union's access, however, was constrained by the Norwegian Sea, the Sea of Okhotsk, and the Sea of Japan—all of which would have seen significant naval actions had the Warsaw Pact and NATO gone to war. China does have to deal with the shallow Yellow Sea, but there appears to be abundant access to deep Pacific waters for most of China's almost twenty-seven hundred miles of coastline.[17] Specifically, China's submarine bases on the island of Hainan seem exquisitely positioned for many of Beijing's emergent needs. These include access to the purportedly oil-rich Spratly and Paracel island groups in the South China Sea,[18] and protection of their SLOCs through the Strait of Malacca.[19] Any Chinese tendencies to limit SSBN patrols to the northern extreme of the crowded, noisy, and very shallow Yellow Sea would be reminiscent of Soviet SSBN bastions, but might perfectly suit a need to preserve a nuclear-capable and difficult to target submarine "fleet-in-being" used to deter more than one potential adversary. In fact, through swarm tactics, the hundreds of vessels in Chinese (likely state-controlled) fishing fleets could so complicate any acoustic environment to as make detection of even a relatively noisy SSBN extremely problematical.

In examining all the waters shallower than twenty fathoms along the East Asian littoral, it becomes clear why the term "first island chain" is so prevalent in available Chinese strategic musings. China indeed has good access to three potential *maria nostra* (somewhat analogous to the smaller Soviet ones of the Barents Sea and the Sea of Okhotsk)—the Sea of Japan, the Yellow/East China Sea, and the South China Sea. Given appropriate defensive naval assets, the constrained access to these waters can be exploited as a barrier to an adversary's maritime power. However, from the inside looking out, and if any ambition for global maritime influence exists, these same narrow portals become severe liabilities. One other significant point becomes apparent by looking at the region's particular bathymetry. If a global maritime presence is a national goal, as it almost has to be given China's growing strategic dependence on trans-Pacific SLOCs, then the east coast of Taiwan stands out as the only part of "China" with unfettered access to the deep Pacific.

Can Beijing rely on submarines to police its vulnerable SLOCs? Nuclear submarines could perhaps do so, but diesel submarines (even if equipped with air-independent propulsion) will not be effective in this role. SSNs excel at sea denial and therefore can be extremely effective against surface forces, and in the absence of credible cuing (none exists in the South Pacific at present) they are virtually immune from air attack, unlike any escorting surface forces. With encapsulated weaponry from other services rapidly being developed, even a rudimentary air defense capability (from a covert stance) would go a long ways toward deterring air attack against those SLOCs being guarded.

The question of how China's SSNs contribute to overall naval strategy would be easier to answer if there were a definitive understanding of China's naval and maritime goals. The only apparent valid assumption is that these naval and maritime goals must support a larger set of national goals. Given in particular the success of China's economic development and its reliance on international trade, there is little incentive for forcing a confrontation with the United States over Taiwan or any other issue. Indeed, one can easily imagine a scenario in which eventual economic incentives encourage Taiwan to voluntarily seek closer ties to the mainland. In such a case, neighboring countries could view a powerful but benevolent China as a guarantor of regional stability and economic well being. That scenario could set the stage for a Chinese version of the Monroe Doctrine in which China would demand, and be able to enforce, the withdrawal of foreign military forces from the region. Such a turn of events would doubtless dramatically affect all aspects of U.S. foreign policy, including especially the force structure and roles of the U.S. Navy.

There is an interesting historical analogy relating to the above discussion—that of England tolerating market competition from a brash and expanding U.S. economy. Was that tolerance inspired by a common heritage and language? Obviously, that would not be a mitigating factor in this emergent Pacific Rim rivalry. Other considerations require no speculation at all. China is energy-hungry, and will increasingly become more so. Without much fanfare, China has entered into extensive energy agreements with many Middle Eastern and African nations. Although the United States tends to instinctively think of Japan as being dangerously vulnerable to perturbations in the oil SLOCs through the Strait of Malacca, China has become no less so. In addition, China has entered into extensive trade and energy agreements with South American countries on both the Atlantic and Pacific coasts and will soon have vital Trans-Pacific SLOCs to be concerned with in addition to those of the Indian Ocean/Strait of Malacca. China's aspiring to acquisition of a strong open-ocean navy could be indicative of nothing more than Beijing's appreciating the logic of Mahan—that if a nation depends on maritime trade it must have a navy with which to protect those ships and routes, or else be closely allied with another country that already has that capability.

The national desire to deploy SSNs is *not* by itself a clear indication of creating regional antiaccess capabilities, since a powerful argument can be made that a more cost-effective way to provide for the defense of home waters is by means of modern non-nuclear submarines (preferably AIP versions). A more certain conclusion to be drawn from a nation acquiring an SSN fleet is a desire to obtain a significant degree of global maritime influence. Just as AIP diesel-electric submarines are a relatively affordable way to provide *regional* antiaccess/area denial (AA/AD; also known as sea control/sea denial) capabilities, the SSN is actually the most cost-effective way to impose maritime AA/AD on short notice with minimum platforms at some place far removed from one's home waters.[20] If such SSNs are equipped with a land-attack as well as an ASUW/ASW capability, then they represent a survivable power-projection capability that can deter, delay, or dissuade until heavier forces arrive. The U.S. Army may have embraced the enlistment mantra of "An Army of One," but in a very real sense, a modern SSN comes close to being "A Battle Group of One."

A preliminary sketch of China's submarine strategy might include the following points. China will continue to build a mix of top-end non-nuclear (probably AIP) submarines and near top-end nuclear (Victor III) equivalents. Unlike the United States, China does need a mix since it has a requirement to defend local waters with AIP boats, while also having a need to create an eastern Pacific (if not global) naval presence, achieved most efficiently with nuclear submarines. China will have learned well the dangers of low-balling such elements as levels of stealth and depth of training, and will leapfrog several generations of platform/personnel capabilities and characteristics.[21] Beijing is likely to seek an established out-of-area SSN deployments and so we should watch for a port visit in Columbia, Ecuador, Peru, or Chile by a Type 93 SSN in this decade. Having established an eastern Pacific (global) presence, a further step might well include economic support for a Kiribati-like South Pacific entity to host a deployed SSN/SSBN—perhaps a submarine tender oriented similar to U.S. Navy deployments to Holy Loch, Scotland, and La Madellena, Sardinia.

U.S. planners may be deluded into believing that China will surge large numbers of submarines against carrier and amphibious battle groups for torpedo attacks. In fact, Beijing would be wiser to plan to dilute the American ASW efforts with large numbers of boats deployed, but not attempting to penetrate ASW defenses. Submarine attacks against surface targets would instead be directed by third-party targeting fire with long-range antiship cruise missiles (ASCMs) from submarines in relatively safe locales awaiting targeting data. Chinese submarines should avoid any direct confrontation with U.S. SSNs, but instead would hope that the U.S. SSNs are wasted by being tasked to conduct time-consuming searches for dispersed and quiet units, rather than being employed in their other multitudinous roles to include ISR, ASUW, land attack, and SOF support. PLAN admirals will likely deploy top-end SSNs to break out into deep Pacific waters to conduct cavalry-like raids on trans-Pacific U.S. Navy logistic tails. If U.S. planners refused to fall into the temptation of placing their SSN assets into ASW search mode, but rather positioned even but a half-dozen in the Taiwan Strait, they could effectively defeat any attempt at an amphibious assault.

Concerning the broader rivalry, it is worth noting that playing the no-limit fiscal poker game in defense spending that crippled the Soviet economy probably will not work with the burgeoning economic machine China has become. But unlike with the Soviet Union, there is an almost inextricable entwining of the U.S. and Chinese economies—a fact that will go far to mitigate the possibilities of military conflict. On the other hand, there is a very real capabilities-based force level requirement that has to be acknowledged, and this is probably not the time to let levels of key access-insensitive platforms—especially submarines—fall below levels where their unique abilities to thwart any maritime adventurism, such as an invasion of Taiwan, can be perceived as less than credible.

Conclusions

In a landmark article several years ago, Barry Posen described the current and future security environment as one in which it is not only desirable, but essential for the U.S. to "control the maritime commons."[22] What the U.S. WWII submarines did in the 1940s, *Sturgeon*-class SSNs did in the 1970s, and *Los Angeles*-class submarines do today is precisely that. The phenomenon has also been called sea control and sea supremacy, or even during the eighteenth century, ruling the waves. It is at heart a realization that in the current globalized world that all nations are maritime nations, and that only one among them will be the dominant maritime power. Possessing that title and its associated responsibilities, as the United States does, is, and always has been a frightfully expensive proposition, but less expensive than neglecting that responsibility, as both Mahan[23] and John Keegan[24] have stated. There is certainly no law of nature that requires the dominant maritime power to be the United States, but one must ask "if not America, then whom?"

Notes

1. See Norman Friedman, *The Fifty-Year War* (Annapolis, Md.: Naval Institute Press, 2000).

2. *Chicago Tribune* reporters Christopher Drew and Sherry Sontag originally undertook an investigation concerning what, if any, correlation existed between cancer of various types and extensive duty aboard nuclear submarines. They interviewed a significant number of submariners for this project, including this author, but eventually became intrigued by vague references concerning the nature of Cold War submarine operations. In their book Drew and Sontag alleged that U.S. submarines "trailed" many Soviet SSNs, SSGNs, and SSBNs for extended periods, maintained a virtually continuous presence in international waters just off all major Soviet naval ports, and performed other clandestine services. Christopher Drew and Sherry Sontag, *Blind Man's Bluff* (New York: Perseus Book Group, 1998).

3. This exhibit, which closed in 2003, graphically displayed and discussed an eighty-day trail by USS *Batfish* (SSN681) of a Soviet Yankee-class SSBN from the Greenland/Iceland/United Kingdom (GIUK) "gap" to and throughout its patrol near Bermuda and back. The exhibit also displayed video recordings made through U.S. SSN periscopes. The first captures the preparations, launch, and target drone impact of a surface-to-air missile fired from a Soviet cruiser in littoral Soviet operating areas. The second recorded the undetected underhull survey of an underway warship by a U.S. SSN—up one side and down the other, with the optics of the periscope probably no more than six to ten feet away from the ship's hull.

4. See Drew and Sontag, *Blind Man's Bluff*, 1–24, concerning USS *Cochino* (SS345) and USS *Tusk* (SS426).

5. See James D. Watkins, "The Maritime Strategy," *U.S. Naval Institute Proceedings*, January 1986. At the beginning of the GLOBAL War Games series, conventional wisdom held that in a NATO/Warsaw Pact war, the U.S. fleet in the Mediterranean Sixth Fleet would be destroyed in hours or days, and that the remainder of U.S. naval forces would be ill advised to transit more than halfway across the Atlantic. Submarines, both nuclear and conventional, would be passively employed in barriers in the GIUK gaps. By the time the Berlin Wall fell, the Sixth Fleet was projected to have nothing to do after the first few days as a result of offensive actions associated with the Maritime Strategy that would have quickly destroyed threatening forces. Nuclear submarines were tasked to immediately engage Soviet submarines and surface forces in the Barents Sea, carrier battle groups were operating off the coast of northern Norway, and amphibious units were landing on the western coast of Jutland.

6. It is interesting to note that the accepted story behind the Mk 45 Astor torpedo was that it was developed on the basis of a Penn State Applied Research Lab-

oratory study concerning the optimum torpedo to be employed against a carrier battle group—of which the USSR had none.

7. There has even been a rather cynical view expressed that during this time period if your weapons platform did not have a nuclear capability, you were somewhat second-rate citizens, and not invited to a lot of Pentagon meetings. The weapons themselves were considered a bother by most submariners because of the extra inspections and greatly increased security measures involved. In the case of the SUBROC rocket-propelled weapon, there were nagging safety issues regarding the torpedo room presence of large solid-fuel rocket motors—an issue hauntingly remembered following the *Kursk* disaster.

8. The proposed answer to this rather disturbing non sequitur resulted in an essential design feature of the *Thresher*-class SSN. Designers assumed that two such ships would operate in consort, and would share bearing data through secure underwater communications. This would, it was believed, allow triangulation to achieve an adequately accurate target position. The secure underwater communications system (SESCO), upon which this concept depended, worked well in the benign, freshwater lake testing environment, but failed to perform adequately in the much harsher acoustic environment of the open ocean.

9. Earlier submarine ASW weapons were nineteen-inch-diameter versions that swam out of twenty-one-inch diameter torpedo tubes. These weapons literally left the firing ship under their own power and could only be launched successfully at slow speed. The Mk 48 torpedo, conversely, is a twenty-one-inch weapon that was ejected, just as legacy ASUW weapons were, and started only after this water ejection impulse. Most Soviet submarines, on the other hand, were hampered in releasing weapons by relying on compressed air to eject. Russian submarines, therefore, could only launch their weapons from relatively shallow operating depths.

10. Even though the movie *K-19, The Widowmaker*, was, by Hollywood necessity, highly dramatized, there are elements of truth in the insinuations that Soviet submarine fabrication and crew training were often victims of expediencies.

11. The U.S. submarine force only built one two-reactor submarine—the *Triton*, famous for its submerged circumnavigation of the world in 1960. Built as a radar picket submarine (SSRN), its design raison d'être vanished when carriers began flying their own airborne radar early-warning aircraft. It was subsequently redesignated as an SSN. One feature of this vessel was its large combat information center, and for three years in the mid-1960s the submarine served as what would have been the U.S. president's secure command post in the event of a nuclear attack. The *Triton* is often used as an example of the hazards associated with building purpose-specific instead of multipurpose submarines.

12. See Robert Moore, *A Time to Die* (New York: Crown Publishers, 2002), 271.

13. Early in the U.S. Polaris program it was decided that liquid-fueled rockets would be too hazardous aboard submarines. The art and science of solid-fueled ballistic missiles was invented on schedule to support the program. The Soviets did not do this, and the missiles on the Yankees were fueled essentially the same as the German

V-2—with red fuming nitric acid as the fuel and concentrated hydrazine as the oxidizer—both highly dangerous in their own right, and spontaneously explosive when mixed. See Igor Kurdin and Wayne Grasdock, "Loss of a Yankee SSBN," *Undersea Warfare* (Fall 2005), www.chinfo.navy.mil/navpalib/cno/n87/usw/issue_ 28/yankee2.html.

14. For an excellent open source discussion about comparative characteristics of U.S. versus Soviet nuclear submarines, see Tom Stefanick, *Strategic Antisubmarine Warfare and Naval Strategy* (Lexington, Mass.: Lexington Books, 1987), 384.

15. This analogy was used by several Soviet-era submarine officers and designers who spoke at the U.S. Naval War College's May 2004 Cold War at Sea Conference. Russian attendees included Vice Admiral Yuriy Sysuev, Chief of Kuznetsov Naval Academy in St. Petersburg; Rear Admiral (Ret.) Lev Chernavin, submariner and past commander of the Mediterranean Squadron; Rear Admiral (Ret.) Bogdan Malyarchuk; and several active duty and retired senior captains, including the colorful Captain Ryurik A. Ketov, who commanded both the only Foxtrot diesel submarine involved in the 1962 Cuban Missile Crisis that was not surfaced by U.S. ASW forces, and a Victor-class SSN that had been involved in a collision with a U.S. SSN.

16. Tom Stefanick, *Strategic Antisubmarine Warfare and Naval Strategy*, 32–79.

17. To put this into context, the Pacific coastline (excluding Alaska) of the U.S. is about twelve hundred miles, the Atlantic coast about eighteen hundred, and the Gulf coast about fifteen hundred.

18. These islands—often no more than rocky outcroppings, are the subject of intersecting territorial claims by China, Vietnam, Indonesia, Malaysia, Brunei, and the Philippines. In addition, they straddle the SLOCs by which oil is delivered through the straits of Malacca to Japan and others.

19. The Strait of Malacca is an interesting oceanic (as the Himalayas are a terrestrial) seam between China and another entity that aspires to global maritime influence through possession of SSNs—India.

20. As unintuitive as it might seem, it can be shown mathematically that if a constellation of some twelve to fourteen SSNs is somewhat homogeneously deployed in the world's oceans, the probability of one being within Tomahawk range (and but two days steaming) of any point of the littorals approaches unity. If typically 25 percent or so of such a fleet is actually deployed, then the force level to enable such a "Great Black Fleet" would be in the order of forty-eight to fifty-six units.

21. What should serve to emphasize to China the critical aspect of training and maintenance as essential elements of submarine operations is the recent apparent asphyxiation of the entire crew of a Romeo-class SSK when, it would appear, the head valve (through which air is drawn into the boat to replace that being pumped overboard by the running diesels) shut during snorkeling operations, did not reopen, and the diesels did not shut down on low vacuum as they should. This series of events would result in the effective altitude inside the submarine to increase in the order of one thousand feet per second, reaching the equivalent of a jet airliner losing cabin pressurization in less than a minute, by which time all would have lost consciousness.

22. See Barry Posen, "Command of the Commons," *International Security* 28, no. 1 (Summer 2003): 5–46. Posen argues that the United States presently commands the space, airspace, and maritime "commons."

23. See Alfred Thayer Mahan, *Influence of Sea Power upon History, 1660–1805* (abridged ed.) (Englewood Cliffs, N.J.: Prentice-Hall, 1980), 256.

24. See John Keegan, *The Price of Admiralty* (New York: The Penguin Group, 1988), 292.

Robert G. Loewenthal

Cold War Insights into China's New Ballistic-Missile Submarine Fleet

Introduction

AT THE END OF WORLD WAR II, only diesel submarines existed in the world. There were no nuclear submarines or submarines armed with ballistic missiles. In the 1950s, both the United States and the Soviet Union conducted very intensive development of ballistic-missile submarines. This was a completely new weapons system. There was no experience in its use. Progression from diesel to nuclear power, from surface launch to submerged launch of missiles, navigation and missile-guidance improvements, and increasing missile ranges facilitated improvements in operational use. Examining how the fleet ballistic-missile submarines and their weapons were developed during the Cold War leads to reflections on the changes in their operations. In considering the historical development of this weapon system and comparing the various employment doctrines of the superpowers, this chapter will seek to provide possible insight into how China is developing and may use its new force of SSBNs.

In 1955, the USS *Nautilus* proved that nuclear power would greatly expand the capabilities of submarines and make them free from the earth's atmosphere for long periods of time. In 1960, the 5,900-ton nuclear-propelled USS *George Washington*, carrying sixteen Polaris A-1 missiles, put to sea. This accomplishment required phenomenal technical developments in a short period of time. By 1967 the United States had forty-one ballistic-missile nuclear submarines (SSBNs), called "Forty-One for Freedom," available for operations. Later, more advanced ships and missiles were developed, and Trident-class submarines with their twenty-four missiles still conduct patrols today.

The U.S. goal was to keep each SSBN at sea for as many patrols as possible, considering refit requirements and overhaul intervals. At sea, "continuously ready," was the watchword for SSBNs patrolling the Atlantic and Pacific Oceans, as well as the Mediterranean Sea. From 1960 to 1991, 2,427 Polaris and Poseidon patrols were conducted.

Operating an SSBN is not an easy task. To suppose that one simply hides and waits for orders to launch their weapons is too simplistic. These are nuclear-powered submarines submerged in a hostile environment twenty-four hours a day, seven days a week, for patrols of seventy days or longer. The author made three patrols in the Pacific and one in the Atlantic in USS *Daniel Boone* (SSBN 629), a Polaris submarine, and five patrols in the Mediterranean as commanding officer of USS *George Bancroft* (SSBN 629), a Poseidon-armed submarine.

SSBNs are required

- to remain undetected by anyone, friend or potential foe, essentially in a wartime posture;
- to remain able to receive radio messages continuously;
- to maintain navigation accuracy beyond anything one could have conceived just a few short years before the Cold War; and
- to take the crew through missile launch sequences, with no previous notice on orders received any time day or night, either for an exercise or for a tactical launch. The requirement was to have all preparations completed and ready to launch in less than fifteen minutes.

The Soviet Union also started developing submarine-launched ballistic-missile systems in the 1950s. They developed diesel-powered ballistic-missile submarines (SSBs), and later, nuclear-powered SSBNs. They deployed their first sixteen-missile SSBN, the Yankee-class, in 1967.

In the early years, with so many different classes of submarines, and different missile ranges, the Kremlin operated its SSBN fleet more on an individual deployment basis. Soviet SSBNs sailed out of the Northern Fleet and the Pacific, and conducted patrols off of the coast of the United States for periods of some weeks. Later, when longer-range missiles were available, they stayed closer to home, in so-called "bastions," and conducted more continuous patrols.

The price of the intense submarine operations during the Cold War was not cheap, in human lives or in submarines. The United States lost two nuclear attack submarines, USS *Thresher* (SSN 593) and USS *Scorpion* (SSN 589). The Soviet Union lost several submarines in the earlier years, including a November-class SSN in 1970. In the 1970s and 1980s, they lost several more submarines including a Yankee-class SSBN.

In 1981, China launched its very first ballistic-missile submarine, Type 092, NATO Code Xia-class. China tested a submarine-launched ballistic missile (SLBM) in 1988 and the submarine is still deployed with the Peoples Liberation Army Navy (PLAN) North Sea Fleet. A new class of SSBN, the Type 094, was launched in July 2004. It is reported that it will carry twelve ballistic missiles.

China's People's Liberation Army Navy (PLAN) is now, or will shortly have, the capability to deploy an SSBN for individual patrols in open ocean areas within range of targets in the United States or other countries. If Beijing desires to have a continuous SSBN on station in a strategic deterrent posture, that will require more assets. To have one SSBN on patrol requires at least three and probably four SSBNs in the fleet. If the current estimates are correct, China could have that capability by 2010 to 2015, with five or six Type 094 submarines. If the new Jl-2 missile with an estimated range of 8,000 kilometers (4,900 NM) is available, China's SSBNs can remain reasonably close, in the open ocean off China's coast, for patrols. The PLAN will have to develop longer range missiles to conduct patrols in bastions in the South China or East China Sea, however, and still be able to cover targets in the continental United States.

The PLAN may indeed opt to deploy SSBNs in bastions similar to the doctrine of the Soviet navy in the later stages of the Cold War. It is an advantage to be protected by friendly air and surface forces. But being in a bastion is not particularly useful if both the SSBN and its protector, possibly an SSN, are both under an acoustic disadvantage to an enemy who will come in to the bastion and be ready to attack.

China has now genuinely become the fifth member of the ballistic-missile submarine club after the United States, Great Britain, France, and Russia. It is an elite group possessing a very sophisticated weapons system. SSBNs and their weapons systems are expensive to build and expensive to maintain. They require a high level of technology, and above all, exquisite and regular crew training to exceedingly high standards. Continuous demonstration of the ability for the entire weapon system to work is required for them to form a credible strategic deterrent.

China has the resources, the access to technology and, seemingly, the will to create a viable SSBN force. But it will take time, serious training, extensive support facilities and a lot of experience at sea to be truly successful in this endeavor.

U.S. Ballistic-Missile Submarines During the Cold War

Development

In the 1950s, the idea of launching ballistic missiles from nuclear submarines was conceived. Many, particularly submariners, viewed this initiative with great skepticism. The United States had cruise-missile submarines which were tested and deployed, although they had to surface to fire their missiles and these weapons were of short range. In 1955, the Navy's ballistic-missile program commenced as part of the Army-Navy Jupiter Program. In 1956, the Navy under Adm. Arleigh Burke, then Chief of Naval Operations (CNO), received approval to initiate its own Polaris fleet ballistic-missile (FBM) program and terminate its involvement in the joint liquid-fuel Jupiter missile program.[1] Due to the surprise and anxiety in Washington concerning Moscow's success with space launches, the so-called missile gap was perceived by U.S. leaders to exist and we found ourselves in a missile race with the Soviet Union. The goal for the U.S. Navy to develop a ballistic-missile system was set for four years.

Only four years later, in 1960, the fifty-nine-hundred-ton nuclear-powered USS *George Washington,* carrying sixteen Polaris A-1 missiles, put to sea. The technical challenges to accomplish this were monumental. The primary challenges were in six areas: the ship, the missile, ship navigation, missile guidance, the fire control system, and missile launchers.

The challenge was to design, build, and test a submarine of revolutionary design in an extremely short amount of time. It was decided to use a modified *Skipjack* (SSN) hull. A submarine in construction, the *Scorpion,* was actually cut in half, a one-hundred-thirty-foot-long missile compartment containing sixteen vertical launch tubes was added, and this became the fleet ballistic-missile submarine, USS *George Washington.*

With respect to the nuclear-armed missile, Jupiter had been a liquid-fueled missile. The Navy felt that a liquid-fueled missile was too large and inherently more cumbersome and dangerous than a missile with solid propellant. At the time, however, solid propellant was not a mature technology.[2] In spite of inevitable missile failures from the test pads—and some were spectacular—the solid fuel motors were developed successfully.

The existing missile guidance systems were too large for the Polaris missile so a new system had to be developed. MIT and General Electric worked together to miniaturize inertial components to be integrated into the guidance system. To guide a ballistic missile more than one thousand miles, greater navigational accuracy than available by traditional means was needed. One must know the ship's position at all times between navigational fixes and the azimuth to target with the required accuracy. Fixing techniques using radio navigation, bottom contour navigation and, later, satellite navigation were developed. Also, a dead reckoning system, called the ship's inertial navigation system (SINS), which provided the between-the-fix accuracy, was developed. Finally, to provide the very accurate heading information needed, a periscope sextant, the Type XI, was developed. In the mid-1960s improved SINS systems made it so that dependence on the periscope sextant was no longer required. Finally, a digital fire control system was developed (MK 80) that solved the ballistic missile fire control problem.[3]

With respect to the process of launch, propelling the missile through the water while keeping it dry was no small feat. A method of ejecting the missile through a frangible diaphragm using compressed air was developed. The diaphragm kept the missile dry when the hatch was opened for a launch. Once launched, the missile actually surfaces in an envelope of air and does not ignite until it is above the surface. Later, a gas generator using the exhaust and steam from the combustion was used. While already going at slow speed and quickly launching a missile weighing thousands of pounds, the SSBN becomes instantly very light. Depth control becomes a serious problem. A method of hovering the submarine in place and quickly compensating for the loss of weight on missile launch was developed.

These were impressive technical developments in a short period of time. By 1967 the United States had forty-one SSBNs available for operations. But all was not rosy. There were many stumbling blocks, such as early missile test failures. Also, in the early years there was a very steep learning curve in building proficiency in operating these submarines. A very careful way to test the entire system was developed: communications, transmitting and receiving a launch order, verification of the order, placing the submarine at depth and speed to launch, energizing the missile fire control systems, verifying the fire control inputs to be correct, and finally simulated launch. This system is tested, practiced, and proven continuously. It has to be so for the credibility of the weapons system to be believed, especially by potential adversaries.

In the 1970s a new submarine, the *Ohio*-class, was designed and built. Carrying twenty-four Trident D-5 missiles with a range of 5,000 miles, 560 feet long, and displacing 16,747 tons, the first *Ohio*-class deployed on patrol in October 1982.

Operations

Operating an SSBN for a patrol is not a simple task. These are nuclear-powered submarines. They are submerged in a hostile environment twenty-four hours a day, seven days a week, for patrols of seventy days or longer. They experience damage to equipment that must be repaired by the crew.

They are required

- *To remain undetected by anyone, friend or potential foe.* All sonar contacts were continuously tracked, and avoided. If it was necessary to come to periscope depth for some reason, although seldom, it could be a challenge to find a vacant piece of ocean. This was especially true in the crowded Mediterranean where the author made five SSBN patrols.

- *To remain able to receive radio messages continuously.* One of several types of antennas had to be close to the surface in the Cold War days. Casualties to the somewhat fragile antennae were common and had to be dealt with by deploying spares or alternate types.

- *To maintain navigation accuracy beyond anything one could have conceived just a few short years before the SSBNS were built.* Until the mid-1960s, the Type XI periscope sextant had to be used to provide the very accurate heading information needed. This meant going to periscope depth to shoot stars. Again, it could be a challenge to accomplish that and return to patrol depth undetected. Present-day systems are extremely accurate due to the introduction of GPS and improvements in the SINS systems, so excursions to periscope depth are required much less often.

- *With no previous notice, on orders received any time day or night, take the crew through a missile launch sequence either for an exercise or for a tactical launch.* Once the launch message was received, the ship would be brought to launch depth and prepared to slow and almost hover in place. The missile systems would be spun up and the launcher systems prepared. The requirement was to have all preparations completed and ready to launch in fifteen minutes. Exercise messages would be sent often by higher authority. Invariably, it seemed, this occurred in the middle of the night. The ship and crew went through the whole simulated missile launch sequence exercise every time.

In order to keep the submarines at sea for the maximum time, the two-crew concept was initiated. This allowed the submarine to be refitted and to return to sea immediately with the counterpart crew on board. It was a unique concept, a complete break with Navy tradition. The turn-over period between crews was only four days and the crew having just completed a patrol flew back to their home port in the United States for rest and recreation, followed by intensive training, only to return to the refit site three and a half months later.

Soviet Ballistic-Missile Submarines During the Cold War

Development

The Soviet Union's program developed differently from ours. They used diesel ballistic-missile submarines (SSBs) for a time even after they had developed nuclear power for submarines. They commissioned many different classes, making incremental improvements rather than great technological breakthroughs.

The Soviet Union created the world's first ballistic-missile submarine with its project 611 (NATO code name Zulu). One was equipped with a single Scud missile. Five more were converted to carry two of the Scud missiles in tubes in the enlarged sail. The submarine B-67 launched a missile on September 16, 1955. The missile was the R-11FM missile designed by Sergei Korolev, using kerosene and nitric acid for fuel. The Scud missile was derived directly from German V-2 technology, and continued to haunt the world as it migrated down the power chain to rogue nations of the Middle East.[4]

The Zulu was a diesel-powered submarine and had to surface to launch missiles. They had their problems. The author was a young lieutenant stationed at the U.S. Navy's Scientific and Technical Intelligence Center in Washington in 1963 and 1964, assigned as the submarine and submarine-launched missile analyst. A picture, taken by a third country source, came across my desk which showed a Zulu-class submarine returning to port, a missile at the top of the sail and blackened charred areas all around the openings at the bottom of the sail. Evidently, it was a failed launch in which the missile motor ignited but did not leave the top of the sail. We analysts all felt the ship was fortunate to make it home.

The first Soviet submarine, designed from the outset as a ballistic-missile submarine, was the Golf-class (1958). The Golf-class was diesel-powered and carried three SS-N-4 ballistic missiles in an extended sail structure. The SS-N-4 could only be fired from the surface, and required a time-consuming prelaunch setup period.

The Soviets had a very ambitious nuclear submarine program which led to the production of three classes of nuclear submarines between 1958 and 1960, with no fewer than twenty-six of all types being built by 1963. These were the November-class, an SSN; the Echo-class, an SSGN; and the Hotel-class, an SSBN. The Hotel-class was the world's first nuclear-powered ballistic-missile submarine; with the first hull completed in 1959, slightly ahead of the United States' first, USS *George Washington*. The Hotel versions I and II carried three missiles. The Hotel III carried six. The later Hotel classes (1962) could launch their missiles from the submarine while submerged.[5]

Through the early 1960s, the U.S. intelligence community was continuously asked: Are the Soviets developing a more advanced capability than the Hotel-class? The answer was: "Not that we can determine." On a Saturday morning in 1963, the author, still stationed at the Scientific and Technical Intelligence Center, received a call from a fellow analyst at the Naval Photographic Intelligence Center. He said, "You need to get over here—now." After arriving, we gazed at a picture of a submarine in a building yard that looked very similar to our *George Washington*-class SSBN. But it was a Soviet building yard. It was Project 667 (a NATO-designated Yankee-class submarine). This was the first Soviet submarine to approach any thing like our Polaris submarines. It had a streamlined hull, and so was faster than previous Soviet SSBNs. It had sixteen launch tubes, and could launch while the submarine was submerged. The first Yankee class was commissioned in 1967. Thirty-four hulls of this class were built.

The Soviets continued to build larger and improved SSBNs. Between 1972 and 1992, they built forty-three of the Delta-I though Delta-IV submarines. This class is one of the most successful of all SSBNs. It had increasingly improved missiles and went from twelve missiles in the Delta-I to sixteen in the Delta-II, -III and -IV. With the forty-eight-hundred-nautical-mile-range

SS-N-8 missile, the Soviets were truly able to threaten the United States from bastions in the Sea of Okhotsk and the Barents Sea, close to their own shores.[6]

In 1983 the Soviets came out with the Typhoon-class, the largest SSBN in the world, 566 feet long and displacing 33,800 tons submerged. The Typhoon carries twenty 4,470-nautical-mile solid-fuel missiles. A total of six Typhoons were built.

Soviet SSBN Operations

In the early Golf- and Hotel-class submarines, Soviet missiles were in the one thousand- to thirteen hundred-mile range, which required them to patrol off the east and west coasts of the United States in order to cover targets. These presented a significant threat to major U.S. military targets, as they were within just minutes of flight time for the missiles. However, the submarines were noisy and easily tracked by American SSNs and the SOSUS (sound surveillance system).[7]

The eight years between the first Hotel-class and the first Yankee-class allowed for some major changes in Soviet strategy. The Hotel-class was stopped after only eight units were built, a reflection of the ascendance of the Strategic Rocket Forces that Nikita Khrushchev had established in December 1959. This new service, as dramatic in its debut as the United States Air Force had been in September 1947, took over the first land-based ICBMs as well as the medium-range missile units that formerly had been under the control of Long Range Aviation or reported directly to the Supreme High Command.[8] The *George Washington*-class had to be matched, however, and the Central Design Bureau No. 18 responded with Project 667A, which became the Yankee class.[9]

With a streamlined hull, added speed, and sixteen vertical launchers, the strategic effect of the Yankee-class was dramatic. The Soviets now had a fast nuclear submarine, armed with sixteen ballistic missiles with a range of fifteen hundred nautical miles, which could launch submerged. It was a serious threat to the United States. However, once again, they were relatively noisy and could be tracked by U.S. SSNs and the SOSUS system.[10]

Over the next years the very serious business between the United States and the Soviet Union of trying to track each other and trying to establish a method of neutralizing each other's SSBNs was conducted. In the colorful prose of Gary Weir and Walter Boyne: "Cold War oceans were filled with the tumult of submarine versus submarine encounters, any of which could have resulted in disaster and some of which did result in collisions. To the United States and the Soviet Union, the threat of a ballistic-missile submarine was so great that each one had to be identified, shadowed, and marked for instant destruction in the event of war. It was a demanding task, and required extraordinary equipment and crews in both navies."[11]

As their missile ranges improved, the Soviets elected to patrol closer to home in their bastions, where they felt their SSBNs could be protected by their forces. This could only be successful if their submarines, both SSBNs and SSNs, were quiet enough to have an advantage over an adversary in contact with their SSBN.

The High Price of Submarine Operations During the Cold War

The price of intense submarine operations during the Cold War was not cheap, either in human lives or in submarines. Submarines were lost during the Cold War, not to hostile action, but to failures of equipment, fires, collisions, and other casualties.

The United States lost two nuclear attack submarines, USS *Thresher* (SSN 593) and USS *Scorpion* (SSN 589). USS *Thresher* was lost during post-overhaul sea trials in 1963. The investigation indicated that the vessel probably suffered a flooding casualty, which resulted in short-circuiting some electrical equipment, causing the reactor to shut down. Although the crew blew the main ballast tanks, the blow stopped, possibly due to ice forming in strainers in the blow valves.[12] Many changes in submarine piping systems design and fabrication, as well as to operational procedures, directly resulted from the loss of *Thresher*.

USS *Scorpion* was lost returning from a deployment to the Mediterranean in the mid-Atlantic in 1968. In the investigation report, the Commander Submarine Force, U.S. Atlantic Fleet postulated that *Scorpion* was lost "as a result of a flooding type casualty, which originated at a depth of XXX feet or less; that for undetermined reasons the flooding caused the ship to sink near or beyond the hull designed collapse depth."[13]

The book *Blind Man's Bluff* documents the findings and investigation by Dr. John Craven, who directed the search for *Scorpion*. Craven felt that a likely cause of its loss was a faulty torpedo battery overheating. The Mk46 battery used in the Mark 37 torpedo had had a thin foil barrier separating two types of volatile chemicals. When mixed slowly and in a controlled fashion, the chemicals generated heat and/or electricity, powering the torpedo motor. But vibrations normally experienced on a nuclear submarine had been found to cause the thin foil barrier to break down, allowing the chemicals to interact intensely. In one case, vibration tests in a torpedo test lab had caused a fire in the lab that was strong enough to have caused a low order detonation of a warhead (a dummy warhead was installed for lab tests) had the fire not been extinguished quickly. Such a detonation may have occurred in *Scorpion*, opening the torpedo loading hatch and causing *Scorpion* to flood and sink. Indeed, the Court of Inquiry looking into the disaster, *when their detailed findings were finally released in 1993*, showed that the court had concluded that the top three probable causes of *Scorpion*'s loss all involved torpedo accidents.[14]

The Soviet Union lost several submarines in the earlier years, including a November-class SSN in 1970.[15] In the 1970s and 1980s, the Soviets lost several more submarines including a Yankee-I class SSBN northeast of Bermuda. In that submarine, K-219, a missile hatch leaked, allowing in seawater that reacted with liquid missile fuel that had leaked in to the missile tube. The resulting explosion and fires killed four crew members. All others aboard were rescued. After extensive efforts to save the ship and to tow her, the ship sank due to the extensive damage and resulting flooding.[16]

Perhaps the most well-known Soviet submarine accident, until the tragic loss of the *Kursk*[17] and its crew in 2000, was that of the Hotel-1-class K-19 in July of 1961. Coolant piping for one of the reactor plants failed. The submarine surfaced and tried to radio for help at that time, but the long-range radio antenna was flooded and useless. Volunteers were requested and a team of eight courageous crewmen entered the reactor compartment to make repairs, which they knew would mean their death from radiation exposure. The ship's freshwater system was rigged to provide cooling, which prevented a catastrophic accident. The crew was eventually evacuated to a Russian submarine. Nevertheless, the whole ship was highly contaminated and many of the crew later died. K-19 was towed to port, decontaminated, new reactors installed, and put back in to service. Crew members who served in the submarine in later years called it "Hiroshima."[18]

China's Fleet Ballistic-Missile Submarines[19]

The Type 092 Xia-class was China's first SSBN. The first ship, *Changzheng 6* (406), was launched in 1981, and became operational in 1983, though the JL-1 SLBM did not conduct a successful test launch until 1988 due to problems with its fire-control system. The Xia-class submarine is outfitted with twelve submarine-launched ballistic missiles with two-stage solid-fuel rocket motors and a maximum range of approximately two thousand kilometers (eleven hundred nautical miles).

The first test launch of the JL-1 SLBM took place on 30 April 1981 from a submerged pontoon near Huludao. A second missile was launched on 12 October 1982 from a Golf-class diesel trial submarine. The first launch from Type 092 in 1985 was unsuccessful, delaying the final acceptance into service of this submarine. It was not until 27 September 1988 that a satisfactory launch took place. Currently the 406 is deployed in the PLAN North Sea Fleet based at Qingdao. It started a major set of upgrades in late 1995 at Huludao Shipyard. This modernization was completed in 2001. The upgrades reportedly include replacing the original JL-1 SLBM with the improved JL-1A, which has an extended range of 3,000–4,000 kilometers (1,640–2,187 NM).[20]

With only one single Type 092 SSBN, it is not possible for the PLAN to establish an effective underwater nuclear strike capability, which can guarantee that at least one SSBN is ready to launch at any time. However, the boat has served as a stepping stone in the development of a more comprehensive Chinese SSBN force in the future.

Operations of the Type 092 SSBN have been limited and the boat has never sailed beyond Chinese regional waters. Despite a potential for operations in the Pacific Ocean, capabilities would be very limited against modern ASW capabilities.

The first of a new class SSBN, the Type 094, was launched in July 2004.[21] It is estimated that four or five of the Type 094 will be built by 2010. Type 094 will have twelve of the new Jl-2 missiles with an estimated range of seventy-five hundred kilometers (forty-seven hundred nautical miles).[22] Estimates from various sources show the JL-2 missile with ranges quoted from seventy-five hundred kilometers to eighty-six hundred kilometers. Eight thousand kilometers is used for subsequent analysis of Chinese SSBN capabilities in this chapter.

China's Strategy for Fleet Ballistic-Missile Submarines

Recently, the Chinese and Russians conducted eight days of joint "maneuvers" centered on the Shandong Peninsula, across the Yellow Sea from the Korean Peninsula. The drills were conducted with ten thousand military personnel on land, at sea, and in the air; about eighty-five hundred of them Chinese.[23]

In an interview in August 2005 concerning the exercises, Adm. Gary Roughhead, the new commander of the U.S. Pacific Fleet, suggested that he was more interested in the Chinese than the Russian navy, much of which has been sidelined by a lack of funds. "Clearly, the Chinese are developing a very capable modern military, especially the navy. The question is: What do they see as the intended use of that navy? If it is to ensure the free flow of commerce, that would not be surprising," he said, nodding toward the sea lanes in the South China and East China Seas through which pass the oil and raw materials that feed China's burgeoning economy, not to mention its soaring imports. The Admiral added, however: "What if the intent is not purely to defend the sea lanes?"[24]

At the Naval War College, it is taught that a nation's national objectives lead to policy, which leads to strategy. Strategy leads to the procurement and allocation of resources and their operational use. How does that relate to Chinese naval strategy, and specifically, development and deployment of ballistic-missile submarines?

An insight into this initiative might be gleaned from an interview of Vice Chairman of the Standing Committee of the National Peoples Congress, Cheng Siwei, in June of 2005.[25] Although the subject was the Chinese economy and this discussion specifically concerned U.S. pressure on China to revaluate their currency, which they partially did later, the statements by Cheng reveal the Chinese sensitivity to treatment as an equal world power: "If you take us as a friend, you will have a friend. If you take us as an enemy, you will have an enemy. So we don't want to fight with you. So please don't put pressure to us. . . . We would like to solve these problems through dialogue and consultation rather than confrontation. But, you know, we have our own dignity."

China is the fourth largest country in the world and has a population of over 1.2 billion people, about one-fifth of the world's population. It has a rapidly expanding industrial base and economy. China certainly must be taken seriously and is, because of a painful historical legacy, quite obsessed with defense against external threats. That China is developing an expanding navy with increasing and varied weapons systems and capabilities is not surprising. Ballistic-missile submarines are part of the mix.

Capt. Brad Kaplan, the naval attaché to China at the time, seemed to capture the essence of the Chinese strategy for the PLA Navy when he wrote in December 1999:

In recent years, the PLAN's maritime mission has evolved from a role of static coastal defense to one of "active offshore defense." In this capacity, the PLAN can be used both as a tactical force and to support strategic national defense. The objectives of this new strategy are to assert China's role as a regional maritime power, to protect coastal economic regions and maritime interests, and to optimize the Navy's operations for national defense. The PLAN's responsibilities now include capture and defense of islands, and protection and blockade of sea-lanes of communication. Moreover, the PLAN is increasingly viewed by senior PLA leadership as integral to resolution of the Taiwan issue—should force be required—and for safeguarding China's "Xisha" [Paracels] as well as claims to the "Nansha" [Spratly] islands in the South China Sea. Finally, the PLAN is likely to be increasingly used as an instrument of overseas diplomacy through participation in goodwill cruises and port visits.

It seems that as far as national policy and overall strategy are concerned, the Chinese are intent on increasing their ability to be a serious player on a larger and larger part of the Pacific Ocean stage.

Some Operational Considerations for SSBNs

The Chinese Navy has now or will shortly have the capability to deploy an SSBN for individual patrols to open ocean areas. If it desires to continuously have an SSBN on station in a strategic deterrent posture, it will require more SSBNs. To have one SSBN on patrol would require at least three, probably four, SSBNs in the fleet. If current estimates are correct, China could have that capability by 2010 to 2015. If the new Jl-2 missile with an estimated range of eight thousand kilometers (forty-nine hundred nautical miles) were available, Chinese SSBNs could range in the open ocean distant from their targets, using the vast reaches of the Pacific for their operations.

Training and Demonstration of Weapons System Capability

If one assumes that the Chinese desire to have a credible SSBN weapons system with capability for a continuous strategic deterrent posture, they must not only have a sufficient number of SSBNs but also pursue rigorous training and practical demonstrations of the system on a regular basis. Once the decision is made to launch, that must be transmitted to the submarines by a robust and survivable communications system. A system of authenticating that order on the ship must be totally dependable. The ship itself has to rigorously practice the preparations for launch, gaining proper depth and speed rapidly and, finally, the missile and guidance systems must be able to be exercised and verified right up to a simulated launch. All of this training must be done routinely and often. Some sort of test program with a periodic launch from an operational submarine of a missile with dummy warheads is also essential. This is necessary to prove the reliability and accuracy of the system.

If a two-crew concept is used, the crew that is ashore cannot allow their skills to be neglected, so training must resume during their off-crew period, after suitable leave. This requires sophisticated facilities ashore.

Patrol Areas and Bastions

If the Chinese were to desire to patrol in bastions, similar to Moscow's strategy in the later stages of the Cold War, the mode of operations would secure the protection of Chinese air and surface assets. With the JL-2 missile range of only eight thousand kilometers, the new 094 probably cannot stay close in the South China or East China Sea. If they want to cover targets in the United States, for instance, they must patrol in more distant areas, for example about twenty-four hundred kilometers (fifteen hundred nautical miles) in the open ocean due east of Taiwan. The ranges to some U.S. West coast cities and Washington, D.C., are shown in Table 1.

If China develops longer-range missiles, so that its SSBNs can stay in bastions closer to their homeland, Chinese SSBNs would enjoy additional protection. Also, those areas are saturated with merchant and fishing boat noise. Such noise can facilitate the hiding of an SSBN, but it can also make the sonar picture for the SSBN very complex. Having literally tens or hundreds of sonar contacts in such an area is not uncommon. Sorting through

Table 1. Missile Ranges From a Point at 20°N 150°E in the Open Ocean, about 2,400 Kilometers (1,500 nautical miles) East of Taiwan

City	Latitude	Longitude	Distance (km)	Distance (NM)
Los Angeles	34° 00'N	118° 30' W	7,738	4,808
San Francisco	37° 30'N	122° 00' W	7,382	4,587
Seattle	48° 00'N	123° 00' W	7,081	4,400
San Diego	32° 30'N	117° 00' W	7,900	4,909
Washington, D.C.	38° 30'N	77° 00' W	10,309	6,406

them and monitoring the contacts of interest can be a challenge. Also, with respect to being protected from an adversary SSN by one's own friendly SSN, this is a matter of acoustic advantage. Being in a bastion is not particularly useful if both the SSBN and its protector SSN suffer an acoustic disadvantage to the enemy who will come in to the bastion and be ready to attack. As a submariner friend of the author recently said, "If he operates his submarine correctly, he who is quieter will win."

Conclusions

There are lessons learned during the Cold War development of SSBN forces that can provide insight into what the Chinese face in creating an SSBN weapons system of strategic deterrent capability. China is modernizing its navy at an accelerated pace as it certainly desires to become a major power to be reckoned with in the world strategic picture. SSBNs are part of that modernization. The Chinese navy has demonstrated that it can build an SSBN and operate it at sea. It has built a second-generation SSBN with significant improvements and increased missile range. All indications are that this program will continue, but exactly how it fits into the Chinese policy and strategy remains to be seen. Beijing has the resources, the access to technology, and seemingly, the will to continue to create a viable SSBN force of some number of ships. But it will take time, serious training of personnel at very high standards, creation of significant support and training facilities ashore, and considerable experience at sea to make that force a legitimate SSBN weapons system to support a deterrent strategy.

Notes

1. Richard T. Wright, "Submarines in Strategic Deterrence," in *United States Submarines* (Waterford, Conn.: Sonalysts Inc.; and Annandale, Va.: Naval Submarine League, Hugh Lauter Levin Associates, 2002), 208. This article provides an excellent overview of the development and history of the United States strategic deterrent submarine force by one who was directly involved for the whole time.

2. Ibid., 214.

3. Ibid., 217

4. Gary Weir and Walter J. Boyne, *Rising Tide: The Untold Story of the Russian Submarines That Fought the Cold War* (New York: Basic Books, 2003), 288.

5. Ibid., Appendix 2, 280.

6. David Miller, *Submarines of the World* (St. Paul, Minn.: MBI Books, 2002), 427.

7. NOAA VENTS program, articles approved by the Navy for publication in open literature. Claude E. Nishimura and Dennis M. Colon, "IUSS Dual Use: Monitoring Whales and Earthquakes Using SOSUS," *Marine Technology Society Journal* 27, no. 4 (1994): 13–21. "The U.S. Navy developed and operates the SOund SUrveillance System, or SOSUS. It is a fixed component of the U.S. Navy's Integrated Undersea Surveillance Systems (IUSS) network used for deep ocean surveillance during the Cold War. Installation of SOSUS was begun in the mid-1950s by the U.S. Navy for use in antisubmarine warfare. SOSUS consists of bottom-mounted hydrophone arrays connected by undersea communication cables to facilities on shore. The individual arrays are installed primarily on continental slopes and seamounts at locations optimized for undistorted long range acoustic propagation. The combination of location within the oceanic sound channel and the sensitivity of large-aperture arrays allows the system to detect radiated acoustic power of less than a watt at ranges of several hundred kilometers."

8. Gary Weir and Walter J. Boyne, *Rising Tide,* 293.

9. Ibid.

10. Ibid., 294.

11. Ibid., 188.

12. Francis Duncan, *Rickover, the Struggle for Excellence* (Annapolis, Md.: Naval Institute Press, 2001), 194–96.

13. Navy press release of Court of Inquiry findings, 26 October 1993, obtained by the USS *Scorpion* Veterans, http://www.txoilgas.com/589-court.html.

14. Sherry Sontag and Christopher Drew, *Blind Man's Bluff, The Untold Story of American Submarine Espionage* (New York: Perseus Books Group, 1998), 88–107. A full chapter of this book is dedicated to the discussion of the loss of *Scorpion.* It has excellent detail of Dr. Craven's efforts to locate *Scorpion* and his theory of the cause of her loss.

15. James Oberg, *Uncovering Soviet Disasters* (New York: Random House, 1986), 3.

16. See an interesting article written by Wayne Grasdock in collaboration with Igor Kurdin of the Russian navy, who was the executive officer of K-219 at the time. See Igor Kurdin and Wayne Grasdock, "Loss of a Yankee SSBN," *Undersea Warfare* (Fall 2005), www.chinfo.navy.mil/navpalib/ cno/n87/usw/issue_28/yankee2.html.

17. The Russian submarine *Kursk* sailed out to sea to perform an exercise of firing dummy torpedoes at a Kirov-class battlecruiser. On August 12, 2000, the missiles were fired, but an explosion occurred shortly after on the *Kursk*. Monitoring equipment showed an explosion equivalent to one hundred kilograms of TNT and registered 1.5 on the Richter scale. Despite a rescue attempt by Russian and Norwegian teams, all sailors and officers aboard the *Kursk* were lost. The *Kursk* was eventually recovered from her grave by a Dutch team, and 115 of the 118 dead were recovered and laid to rest in Russia. See Wikipedia, http://en.wikipedia.org/wiki/Russian _submarine_Kursk_explosion_%282000%29.

18. Gary Weir and Walter J. Boyne, *Rising Tide,* 73.

19. Information on the Type 092 (Xia-class) was obtained mainly from www .sinodefence.com, September 30, 2005.

20. *Chinese Defence Today*, www.sinodefence.com, September 30, 2005.

21. "Navy," *Jane's Sentinal Security Assessment—China and Northeast Asia,* 20 October 2006, www.janes.com.

22. *Chinese Defence Today*, www.SinoDefence.com, 28 February 2006.

23. Richard Halloran, "China's navy prompts US concern," *Taipei Times,* August 27, 2005, 8.

24. Ibid., 9.

25. *Online News Hour with Jim Lehrer,* October 12, 2005, http://www.pbs.org /newshour/bb/asia/july-dec05/china_10-12.html#.

Peter M. Swartz

Meeting the Chinese Naval Challenge

Lessons from the 1980s

Introduction

THE U.S. NAVY AT THE DAWN of the twenty-first century is grappling with the development of an appropriate strategy to help guide its operations, exercises, doctrine, and programs. That strategy—the naval component of the national strategy—must take numerous elements and trends into account, particularly the overall national security, defense, and military strategies.[1] Among the most salient strategic issues, the U.S. Navy must address is its roles vis-à-vis the People's Republic of China (PRC), the Peoples Liberation Army Navy (PLAN), and the PLAN's nuclear submarine force, now and in the future.[2]

The U.S. Navy has had long experience in positing appropriate U.S. maritime and naval strategies with regard to other world and regional powers.[3] Civilian and uniformed U.S. Navy leaders throughout the nineteenth century would periodically ponder the proper approaches for America's Navy to take in the event of war with Great Britain or France. The lectures and writings of Capt. Alfred Thayer Mahan at the end of that century gave this planning particular elegance, coherence, and power. Specifically, strategic naval planning in the 1890s against Spain proved both prescient and useful as the century ended.

Strategic naval thinking in the first few decades of the twentieth century was carried out within the bounds of the various joint "color plans," the most important of which were Plan Black (against Imperial Germany), Plan Red (against the British Empire), and Plan Orange (against Imperial Japan). Before and during World War II, Navy strategic planning against the Axis powers was conducted within a joint strategic planning framework and in accordance with the Europe First precepts laid out in 1940 by the Chief of Naval Operations (CNO) in Plan Dog.

Following World War II, U.S. Navy strategic thinking focused on the Navy's role in joint and combined operations against the Soviet Union and its allies, within the contexts of the Cold War and evolving joint and allied strategic planning systems.[4] The Navy envisioned global wartime forward offensive naval sea control and power projection operations in the Mediterranean, the North Atlantic, and the Western Pacific. By the late 1970s, the salience of naval operations in the Indian Ocean and the Persian Gulf had become an important strategic issue as well.

During the 1980s, U.S. Navy Cold War strategic thought was crystallized into a construct that became known as The Maritime Strategy, written down and disseminated in both classified and unclassified forms.[5] The Maritime Strategy, however, was more than just a set of documents. It represented a global, forward, offensive, joint, and combined approach to the use of naval power against the Soviets and their allies that the Navy's leaders and staff officers used to inform the national and regional strategic planning documents and war plans of the day. It also provided the objectives of many joint, combined, and naval operations and exercises of the period, and of much of the Navy's operational and tactical training.[6]

The Maritime Strategy thus represents a major recent Navy strategic planning effort, and one of the most significant such efforts in its history.[7] It was the product of a decade in which the U.S. Navy made a conscious effort to think through the utility of naval power to deter and defend against a major perceived threat to the country. Therefore, it may prove useful to examine the U.S. Navy's experience with The Maritime Strategy, to illuminate aspects of the Navy's current and potential interest in the PRC, the PLAN, and the PLAN's nuclear submarine force.

Such an examination, if done comprehensively, could address dozens of issue areas and fill enough pages for a book. This preliminary effort will not be that extensive, and will cover only a sampling of possible topics:

- Nature of the threat
- Intelligence on the threat
- Time frame
- Geography
- Jointness
- Allies
- Domestic political and bureaucratic factors
- Competing strategic approaches
- Force structure and technology
- Nuclear strategy
- Perception management
- Uncertainties

Conducting this exercise should in no way suggest that the Soviet Union of the 1980s and the PRC of the present and future represent identical threats to the United States. They do not. A major reason to undertake such comparisons, however, is to identify key differences, as well as occasional similarities.

Nature of the Threat

The Soviet Union posed, by the 1980s, a generally accepted military threat to the United States and its allies. Almost everyone—the public, the President, the Congress, the State Department, the other services—saw the Soviets as opponents, to a greater or lesser degree. President Reagan publicly damned them as the "Evil Empire"—a characterization that stirred up some controversy at home and abroad, but which resonated with a large segment of the American electorate. The Maritime Strategy was therefore unexceptional in its view of the Soviet military, especially the Soviet navy, as its principal projected wartime target, in both its classified and unclassified formats. The Navy's—and the nation's—public and secret stances were thus quite similar, and major aspects of The Maritime Strategy could be—and were—freely debated in the press, in open academic and trade publications, and at numerous conferences and meetings, by civilians and naval officers alike.[8] This included some quite sophisticated public discussions of Soviet, American, and allied nuclear-powered attack submarine (SSN) and nuclear-powered strategic ballistic-missile submarine (SSBN) operations. The Maritime Strategy was embedded in a wide and rich public discussion and consensus.

China at the beginning of the twenty-first century represents a quite different case. There is no such sense of agreement in the nation or among its allies that China currently represents a military threat to the United States, although there appears to be a consensus supporting the nation's announced policy to oppose a use of force by the PRC to incorporate Taiwan into its domain. The evolving public face of U.S. official government positions regarding China does not conform to the stance that would have to be taken behind closed doors to undertake serious operational military planning against that country, beyond the Taiwan contingency. Therefore, public discussions of war planning in relation to China are—and must be—muted, seldom informed by actual planning being conducted by the military, and almost never with serving U.S. officers as discussants. By the same token, whatever prudent military planning may or may not be currently underway involving the PRC, it is not being informed by a public and professional debate on naval policy and strategy as open as that which characterized The Maritime Strategy.

The situation today may be in some ways more analogous to that of the 1920s and 1930s, when the U.S. military developed and exercised its color plans, especially Plan Orange, in the absence of any clear direction to do so from the President and his cabinet, and without a similar approach being taken toward the threat (in that case, Imperial Japan) by the State Department.[9] On the other hand, the richness of the current public debate on U.S. China policy by academics, policy experts, journalists, and others—but not many active duty military officers—seems to derive in part from America's Cold War experience and the development of important policy-oriented communities. During the 1920s and 1930s, the number of policy specialists had been far less, their writings were far fewer, and most of the public paid them scant attention.

Intelligence on the Threat

One significant aspect of The Maritime Strategy was the extent to which it relied on sophisticated high-level intelligence products agreed across the intelligence community, obtained in part through deep penetration of the adversary.[10] The nature of the Soviet naval threat—including that posed by its SSN and SSBN force—had been a hotly debated topic as late as the 1970s, with sharp internal disagreements among the various intelligence agencies that could be discerned even in the public statements of senior agency and service leaders. By the 1980s, almost all of these disagreements had been resolved, due in large part to the credibility of certain sources. A heretofore fractious intelligence community now put forward a single, coherent view of the nature of the Soviet threat at sea that simplified greatly the problem of crafting a coherent family of joint, allied, and service strategies to counter that threat. That unified view by the intelligence community, rendered even more powerful by the memory of previous disagreements, provided a firm foundation that contributed greatly to the success of The Maritime Strategy as an organizing concept for the application of U.S. naval power.[11]

The public face of internal U.S. government estimates on the nature of a Chinese military threat to the United States—if indeed China is considered to pose a threat at all—is far more opaque today than was true of U.S. intelligence community views of the Soviets two decades ago.[12] The 2006 *Quadrennial Defense Review* flatly declares that "Secrecy, moreover, envelopes most aspects of Chinese security affairs. The outside world has little knowledge of Chinese motivations and decision-making or of key capabilities supporting its military modernization."[13] There is little public understanding of whether or not the U.S. intelligence community is internally united or divided regarding China. Whatever the actual situation, however, it is important for this discussion to remind that much of the power of The Maritime Strategy derived from that of the unified intelligence estimate on which it was based, which in turn rested on confidence in a certain set of highly credible sources. If such a unified estimate cannot be said to exist today regarding the Chinese and their projected use of naval power, the power and influence of U.S. joint and naval strategies devised to confront China will be weaker.

Time Frame

The Maritime Strategy presumed that war with the Soviet Union could break out at any time—today, tomorrow, or far into the future. Whenever it broke out, however, its basic underlying strategic principles were presumed to remain the same, or at least to evolve in a slow and steady fashion. The enemy thus could be the Soviet Union of the 1980s, or the 1990s, or the twenty-first century, and that enemy would evolve at a pace that would be understood and countered by the United States and its allies. The Soviets would continue to grow in power, as would we. Current symmetries and asymmetries would probably be maintained in the foreseeable—and even unforeseeable—future. The allocation of American and allied military resources for war with the Soviets had to be spread over current and future contingencies, with the future not looking all that different from the present.

There is no such predicted steadiness in the evolution of the American-Chinese power relationship. The explosive growth of the Chinese economy—and its interdependence on that of the United States—has spawned a variety of predictions on its future character. China today is not considered a military enemy by the U.S. Government nor the American people, but few predict that that view will necessarily hold ten, twenty, thirty, or forty years hence. As China's future economic and military power grows and as Chinese foreign policy evolves, the relationship of China to the United States may well not remain stable and similar to that which now exists. The Maritime Strategy seemed (at the time) eternal, so future radical changes were not foreseen or developed. Few believe that current U.S. maritime strategy regarding the China of 2006 will be the same as one regarding the China of 2016 or 2026 or beyond.

Geography

The Soviet Union was a global superpower spanning a dozen time zones itself, from the North Atlantic to the North Pacific, and tightly allied through the Warsaw Pact with Baltic and Black Sea littoral satellite nations. Moreover, it had military outposts of varying kinds in Cuba, Vietnam, and elsewhere, plus the availability of facilities and perhaps indigenous allied forces in such locales as North Korea, Syria, Libya, Ethiopia, and Angola. The Soviet navy was deployed on a global scale, with fleets in the North Atlantic, Black Sea, Baltic Sea, and Pacific, and squadrons in the Mediterranean, the Caribbean, the South China Sea, the Indian Ocean, and African waters. The Maritime Strategy was therefore likewise global: contemplating forward offensive U.S. operations in the North Atlantic, North Pacific, Arctic, and Mediterranean; allied operations in the Baltic and Black Seas and the Sea of Japan; and perhaps operations in the Caribbean, the South China Sea, the Indian Ocean, and the South Atlantic as well.

The Chinese situation is nothing like that of the Soviet Union—or, for that matter, the Russian Federation today. While a vast East Asian nation, as has been the case for millennia, China is just that—an East Asian power. The PRC's extensive coastline fronts only one ocean area—the western Pacific. While it is certainly within the realm of possibility that a China of the future could acquire allies, forward bases far afield, and a global naval reach—

especially with SSNs—there is almost nothing in Chinese history that indicates such an impulse. Thus, a U.S. maritime strategy vis-à-vis China would be almost exclusively a western Pacific strategy, unlike The Maritime Strategy of the 1980s.

Moreover, despite the probable regional nature of a conflict with China, the United States remains and will remain a global superpower, deploying and using its navy in many regions of the world. For example, during the entire post–Cold War era to date, despite the unquestioned importance of the western Pacific, U.S.-Chinese defense and military relationships, and U.S. forward-deployed forces off the East Asian rim, the center of gravity for U.S. naval operations has actually been elsewhere—in and around the Persian Gulf and the Arabian Sea. And significant U.S. naval deployments occurred routinely in the Caribbean, around Latin America, off Africa, and in European waters. These non-East Asian deployments have been driven by political, diplomatic, and defense considerations far different from those driving deployments to the western Pacific, and often with differently configured force packages.

During a hypothetical future conflict with the Chinese, at least some non-Chinese-related U.S. Navy deployments could be expected to persist, given the continuing significant worldwide interests of the United States. What forces would they require? During the era of The Maritime Strategy, most U.S. Navy forces planned to engage similarly-configured Soviet forces wherever they deployed in the North Pacific, North Atlantic, or Mediterranean. Consequently, U.S. Navy force packages in those areas were similarly configured, centering on carrier battle groups, amphibious ready groups, and independently operating submarines. Would future conflict with the Chinese, however, require force packages significantly different from those needed to pursue U.S. military goals in other parts of the world? Should the U.S. Navy therefore, from here on out, plan, organize, equip, and exercise different forces for different regions?

Jointness

The Maritime Strategy was an avowedly joint concept. It fully discussed the contributions to be made by U.S. Navy, Marine Corps, and Coast Guard forces in its implementation. Moreover, it incorporated the vital roles in U.S. strategy played in peacetime, crises, and war by the U.S. Army and Air Force. And it explored the wartime relationships among U.S. naval, ground, and air forces, and the synergies and mutual support that were both necessary and expected.[14] Examples included the employment of Army missile batteries and Air Force fighters in Iceland, the availability of Air Force tanker aircraft and minelaying bombers, and the central necessity for the protection of reinforcement and resupply shipping from North America to Europe. Fleet commanders regularly exercised aspects of The Maritime Strategy with elements of the other services, especially the Air Force. Many of the Global War Games conducted at the Naval War College in Newport during the 1980s strove to include as much ground and air play as naval operations.[15]

To the Navy, however, jointness meant conducting operations that maintained autonomous Navy commands conducting maritime campaigns, but coordinating these with air-land and air campaigns being waged ashore. The Navy remained wary of more integrated joint forces, and of placing naval sea, air, and amphibious forces under the immediate operational command of Army or Air Force generals.

Interestingly, The Maritime Strategy often was castigated by its opponents as being a U.S. Navy go-it-alone strategy. This parochial reputation of one of the least parochial documents in the Navy's history had at least two possible explanations:

- While the Navy was hard at work ensuring that The Maritime Strategy stressed joint cooperative operations, the Navy was simultaneously waging a bitter campaign on Capitol Hill to defeat passage of the Goldwater-Nichols Act, with its numerous requirements for a more *integrated* total U.S. defense force.[16] The Navy's reputation as an organization focused on retaining the autonomy of its forces thus overshadowed whatever steps toward *cooperative* jointness were being made by the Navy's fleet commanders, war gamers, and strategists in articulating and exercising The Maritime Strategy.[17]

- For those caught up in the internal bureaucratic battles over budget share in the Pentagon, imbued with the ethos of zero-sum games, all perceived successes by one service on any front were considered defeats by the other services.[18] As The Maritime Strategy received publicity and even accolades in various quarters, some civilian analysts in the Office of the Secretary of Defense (OSD) and some U.S. Army and Air Force programmers decried its success and criticized it on general principles, stressing its Navy Department origins, and refusing to consider its merits.[19]

In developing The Maritime Strategy, one of the Navy's goals was to articulate well its roles as it saw them in any confrontation between the

United States and the Soviet Union. The Navy was concerned that the narrow focus that some analysts and planners took toward such a confrontation—concentrating almost all attention on the NATO-Warsaw Pact border in Central Europe—inevitably led toward a view that only the Army and Air Force could fundamentally contribute to such a conflict. The Navy sought to explain not only how its forces would coordinate with those of the other services in peace, crises, and war, but also the variety of critical roles it envisioned naval forces playing across that spectrum of activity, especially on the NATO flanks and in the Arctic and Pacific.

The role of the forces of each of the services will be an important consideration in planning with regard to China. The oft-repeated cliché that "the U.S. will engage in no more land wars in Asia" implies little role for the U.S. Army should hostilities occur—unless they occur in Korea. Thus the Army as an institution could plausibly have little concern for non-Korean East Asian contingencies, focus its attention elsewhere—like the Middle East—and urge civilian policy-makers to do likewise. Or the Army could take an opposite tack and seek to cut out for itself unrealistic roles in East Asia.

The Navy, by contrast, might counter that it is the Navy that is the nation's hedge force against a militarily assertive China, and that the major roles envisaged for naval forces in the western Pacific argue for Navy-dominated command structures and larger Navy budget shares. In some ways, current and future positions of the Army and Navy on East Asian contingencies could be the obverse of what they were during the Cold War regarding European contingencies. While during the Cold War the Navy often felt that its relevance to deterring and—if necessary, fighting—the Soviets was questioned by some, the Navy has no such concerns today, given the dearth of U.S. forward land-based forces south of Northeast Asia, and the critical necessity in many possible scenarios to control the sea-air battlespace in the western Pacific.

At the end of the day, however, any operation undertaken by the U.S. military, against China or any other power, will be a joint one, involving all the services in varying degrees. Sorting out individual service roles within joint campaigns will merit close attention.

One possible significant difference between the Cold War and a future confrontation with China emerges from this discussion: It is unclear whether there would be significant reinforcement and resupply shipping that the U.S. Navy would be required to protect, in the event of hostilities with China. True, a significant U.S. Army, Marine Corps, and Air Force presence is likely to remain forward on the ground in East Asia, in Korea, Japan, and Guam.

In the event of a limited conflict confined to, say, the Taiwan Straits or the South China Sea, however, the threat to the military sea lines of communication supporting those forces might prove to be only a tertiary consideration. The Navy would probably then only need to protect its own forces and logistics against a PRC SSN force, not the lifelines of its sister services as well.[20]

Allies

The Maritime Strategy was, despite ill-informed claims to the contrary by its detractors, conceived to be part of an immense allied cooperative endeavor.[21] Allied naval and air forces around the globe were viewed as vital partners in the effort to protect U.S. and allied reinforcement and resupply shipping and to sink the Soviet navy. U.S. naval forces were to implement the Maritime Strategy embedded in allied and coalition military structures derived from the North Atlantic Treaty, the Rio Pact, the ANZUS and Southeast Asia treaties, and bilateral defense agreements with Japan, South Korea, the Philippines, and Thailand.

NATO itself developed a Concept of Maritime Operations (CONMAROPS) in the 1980s that echoed the principles underlying The Maritime Strategy, especially the importance of forward operations.[22] For example, British and Dutch submarine forces were expected to operate forward in the Northeastern Atlantic; and German and Turkish naval forces anticipated forward operations in the Baltic and Black Seas respectively.[23] Meanwhile, the Japanese Maritime Self-Defense Force was expected to help keep the waters around Japan—and therefore off the Soviet Pacific Coast—free of Soviet naval forces; and friendly Latin American navies planned on supportive naval control and protection of shipping (NCAPS) operations in the South Atlantic and Eastern Pacific. Significant specialized areas of naval endeavor, such as NCAPS and mine countermeasures, lacking major U.S. Navy resources, had become largely the domain of allied forces.

Planning for and exercising these wide-ranging and disparate cooperative operations preoccupied U.S. and allied naval forces alike, supported—and directed—by national governments and international military institutions.[24] Significant debates on the efficacy and modalities of The Maritime Strategy, CONMAROPS, and complementary allied national naval strategic concepts roiled the domestic political scenes in Britain, Norway, Iceland, Australia, Canada, and elsewhere.

What of possible hostilities with China? Who would America's allies be? What forces could they bring to bear to complement or supplement U.S.

Navy ships and aircraft, including for operations against Chinese SSNs? What antisubmarine warfare planning and exercising would need to be done beforehand? In this case, unlike The Maritime Strategy, far fewer allied assets could be expected to be made available, and from far fewer allies (Taiwan? Japan? Australia? South Korea?). Australia and its navy are today among the very closest of America's allies; and U.S.-Japanese relationships appear to be strengthening, including naval cooperation at sea. U.S.-Singapore naval relations are quite close, and new bonds between the U.S. and Indian navies are currently being forged. On the other hand, not many allied assets might be needed in many hypothetical United States-PRC contingencies.

Nevertheless, increased attention to fostering allied and friendly nation capabilities at sea has become a hallmark of the initial year in office of the current chief of naval operations of the U.S. Navy, Adm. Michael Mullen. While the announced policy appears to be global and generic, with a focus on maritime security issues such as maritime domain awareness rather than war-fighting, it does support active efforts to build even closer ties among Pacific navies that might prove useful in a contingency involving the PRC.[25]

Domestic Political and Bureaucratic Factors

U.S. naval policy and strategy derives from national policy and strategy. The Maritime Strategy was strategically forward, tactically offensive, widely advertised as such, and required significant power to implement. It nested comfortably within publicly-supported Reagan administration policies that branded the Soviet Union as an evil empire, conceded it nothing, sought to deter it through declarations and demonstrations of strength, and poured money into the defense budget for several years to improve fleet force levels and readiness.[26] John Lehman, President Reagan's first secretary of the Navy and a well-connected Republican, was arguably the major public spokesman for The Maritime Strategy. Lehman was no figurehead or mere mouthpiece, however. He was a major ideological influence on and spokesman for overall administration defense policy and strategy, and embodied the close linkage between national strategy and its implementation by the Navy. The tone and substance of Reagan-era national security strategy and documents fit well with that of The Maritime Strategy, and the Navy became central to the country's overall defense strategy and posture. Consequently, the Navy's claim on the nation's defense resources also increased.

It is true that The Maritime Strategy represented the preferred strategic outlook of the uniformed leadership of the Navy regarding the sensible use of their service in time of war, but that outlook was able to be translated into policy because it found a resonance within the Reagan administration—which also saw it as sensible. The Navy's strategic preferences had not found such resonance in the previous Democrat-controlled White House of President Jimmy Carter and Secretary of Defense Harold Brown. During the Carter years, the Navy as a bureaucratic actor often found itself on the defensive in internal administration policy debates, especially regarding the relative importance of sea power, operations in the Pacific, carrier strike capabilities, and anti-SSBN operations in a possible future conflict with the Soviets. Consequently, Carter-era national security strategy documents often provided little in the way of solid underpinnings for Navy views.[27] While the aggressive concepts that emerged in The Maritime Strategy were certainly current in internal U.S. Navy thinking during the 1970s, their articulation was necessarily muted in the keystone Navy strategy and policy documents of the period, such as "The Strategic Concept of the U.S. Navy" (NWP-1). Also, the tight defense budgets of the 1970s reflected the Navy's problematic status within the Defense Department, with under-funding—as the Navy saw it—of significant Navy programs and a perceived "tilt" toward improving Army and Air Force postures at the expense of the Navy.

What is the situation today? The Bush administration famously exercises fairly tight control over the development and implementation of U.S. defense strategy and policy. The administration came into office much concerned with the unfolding prickly defense relationship with the PRC, and aiming to shore up the nation's defense posture in the Pacific, including its naval posture.[28] The 9/11 terrorist attacks and the subsequent conflicts in Afghanistan and Iraq drastically shifted the center of gravity of the Bush administration's defense thinking and activity to the Middle East, but while administration rhetoric in relation to China may have become muted, concerns over the growth of China's military muscle and over her policies toward Taiwan, the South China Sea, and Northeast Asia remain.

The official 2006 Defense Department *Quadrennial Defense Review* (QDR) characterized China as having "the greatest potential to compete militarily with the United States and field disruptive military technologies that could over time offset traditional U.S. military advantages absent U.S. counter strategies," and called attention to Chinese military modernization programs. It also announced an increased U.S. Navy focus on the Pacific, with six operational aircraft carriers to be deployed there, along with 60 percent of the total Navy submarine force; and a policy of attempting to "dissuade any military competitor from developing disruptive or other capabilities that could enable regional hegemony or hostile action against the United States or other friendly countries, and it will seek to deter aggression or coercion." On the other hand, the same document declared that "U.S. policy remains focused on encouraging China to play a constructive, peaceful role in the Asia-Pacific region and to serve as a partner in addressing common security challenges," and that "U.S. Policy seeks to encourage China to choose a path of peaceful economic growth and political liberalization, rather than military threat and intimidation."[29]

The Navy provides important but secondary forces to the global war on terrorism (GWOT), especially the wars in Afghanistan and Iraq. The Army, Marine Corps, and Special Operations Forces occupy center stage there and have first claim—in their view—on the nation's defense resources. What may emerge in policy and budget debates within the administration and on Capitol Hill is a sense that GWOT and Middle East wars require strong ground (and special) forces—even at the expense of funding other forces, like those of the Navy—while the appropriate defense posture in East Asia requires significant and powerful naval and air forces, even at the expense of funding ground forces. If the nation's focus continues to be on the ground in the Middle East, what are the implications for future naval strategy and policy—and resources—focused on the rising power of the PRC, including its emerging SSN force? If the United States were to disengage from the Middle East, would that free up resources to bolster the Navy, and increase Navy influence in the halls of the Pentagon? And would another terrorist attack on the U.S. homeland cause a shift in resource allocation to more close-in homeland defense measures, like continental air defense, or sea defense of the approaches to North America?

Competing Strategic Approaches

The concepts underpinning The Maritime Strategy were not the only ones that the nation and its defense establishment could have adopted in the 1980s. At least two other strategic concepts competed with The Maritime Strategy at the time:

- *Convoy escort primacy:* This view saw the Navy's wartime role as principally one of ensuring the safety of reinforcement and resupply shipping for U.S. ground and air forces in Germany, largely through the organization and protection of convoys, and the establishment of submarine barriers. Strike operations on the NATO flanks were ignored or condemned as unproductive sideshows. Strike operations against the Soviet Union itself, including its naval air bases in the Crimea and the Kola Peninsula were dismissed as dangerously escalatory, as were forward attack submarine operations. Operations in the Pacific to secure lines of communication to U.S. forces in Northeast Asia, to draw or keep Japan in the conflict, and to force the Soviets to fight a global war in all theaters were downplayed or ignored. Strike or amphibious operations against the Soviet Far East deliberately to tie down the large Soviet air forces deployed there were dismissed as fanciful. Not only was NCAPS in the North Atlantic the only preferred mission for U.S. Navy forces, but all other types of ASW operations beside convoy escort and submarine barriers there were considered wasteful. Proponents of this strategic view had held sway in the U.S. Department of Defense during the Carter administration, and permeated strategic thinking in the U.S. Army, much of the U.S. Air Force, and among most staff officers of the U.S. European Command and Supreme Headquarters Allied Powers Europe (SHAPE). Not many in the U.S. Navy espoused such a position, however.[30]

- *Third World contingency primacy:* This countervailing view saw most concerns with the U.S.-Soviet military balance and preparation for war with the Soviets as irrelevant. Proponents regarded the Cold War balance between NATO and the Warsaw Pact as stable and unchanging, guaranteed by the nuclear balance of terror and the phenomenon of strategic deterrence. The real threats facing the United States were not seen as being on the Inner-German Border (IGB), in the Mediterranean, or under the Norwegian Sea, but rather in the deserts and jungles of the Middle East, Africa, Southeast Asia, and Latin America. There indigenous forces, Soviet proxies, and perhaps even Soviets themselves some day posed the real current and future threats to U.S. interests, and there U.S. forces had to be prepared to fight in low intensity conflicts (LIC). This view informed the so-called "Iklé Study," *Discriminate Deterrence*, and became U.S. Marine Corps policy once Gen. Al Gray took the helm of that service in 1987.[31] It was also held by a small minority of serving U.S. Navy officers (including some flag officers). In this view, amphibious forces needed major increases, and aircraft carriers were quite useful, but largely to support ground forces ashore. Spending on submarines, the SOSUS net, and maritime patrol aircraft was seen as simply profligate. In terms of current operations, the fleet should be ready to perform presence and crisis response operations throughout the globe, but should throttle back its extensive planning and exercise program for war with the Soviets.

During the 1980s, these two alternative strategies were often discussed and debated in academia and at think tanks, but The Maritime Strategy maintained its conceptual power and priority in administration and U.S. Navy thinking until the collapse of the Warsaw Pact at the end of the decade.[32]

The premise of this chapter is that a focus on the PRC and its potential threat to U.S. interests is one of the important strands of strategic and naval thought in the United States—including the U.S. government—today.[33] What equivalent strategic concepts compete for policy approval and resource allocations today with this view? There seem to be at least four at this time:

- One view holds that the United States should embrace rather than oppose China, and touts one of the major differences between the current U.S.-PRC relationship and that between the United States and the Soviet Union during the Cold War: the huge—and increasing—economic interdependence between the United States and China, especially the enormous and increasing volume of trade and investment flows between the two countries. (By contrast, U.S.-Soviet trade was miniscule, and U.S. investment in the Soviet Union almost nonexistent.) In this view, the United States should focus its defense concerns elsewhere—and if that means acknowledging Chinese sway over Taiwan and other areas in East Asia, so be it. Thus a U.S. Navy priority on antisubmarine warfare—whose targets would mostly be Chinese— seems ill-advised.[34]

- Another view holds that, in any event, it is the Middle East, not East Asia, that should hold center stage in American military thinking. The United States should hedge against problems with China, but the real focus of U.S. policy should be on reconstructing the Middle East and opposing the various threats to America and its partners that emanate from there. For this the United States needs stronger ground, diplomatic, intelligence, special operations, "brown water," and maritime intercept forces, with submarine and antisubmarine forces among the bill payers.

- A third view would have the United States pull in its forces and establish a close-in defense perimeter around the North American continent. This view sees homeland security and homeland defense as the major focus for U.S. military forces—a focus often stated in contemporary administration defense rhetoric. (Administration statements, however, seem to be translated into forward homeland-defense operations that seem indistinguishable from the forward naval presence and crisis-response operations that have characterized the employment of U.S. naval forces for more than a decade.) The primary threats here are seen to be terrorists and ballistic missiles, so U.S. naval forces optimized for maritime domain awareness, coastal warfare, and ballistic-missile defense would receive priority; forces optimized for forward deployments would not.

- A fourth view holds that the world is much too uncertain a place right now to be able to optimize strategic thinking or forces along one particular line. China, the Middle East, Iran, North Korea, drug lords, terrorists, and pirates are all significant current or potential dangers. With limited defense resources available, the United States should therefore invest in a variety of military capabilities to defend against as many of these threats as possible. Putting more resources into ASW to guard against PRC SSNs is seen as a good idea, but one that must be balanced against the competing demands of carrier aviation, missile defense, maritime intercept, "brown water operations," and maritime domain awareness. A balanced fleet is what is needed, and no one part of the balance will, probably, be able to be optimized against a particular threat.[35]

It currently appears that no one focused strategic strand is predominant in U.S. defense or naval thinking right now, unlike the era of The Maritime Strategy.[36] The cacophony of contemporary competing strategic visions will affect the nation and the U.S. Navy's approach to the PRC, the PLAN, and the emerging PLAN nuclear submarine force.

Force Structure and Technology

The Maritime Strategy provided a threat-based template with which to develop U.S. Navy force structure. To implement The Maritime Strategy, the Navy developed some capabilities that were primarily of use in deterring or fighting the Soviets in a general war, and some that were useful across a much wider spectrum of conflict, especially for forward presence and crisis-response operations. SSBNs, SSNs, maritime patrol and Tomcat aircraft, the SOSUS net, and much of the naval intelligence establishment were necessarily focused almost exclusively on a Soviet enemy that had many characteristics unique to itself. Likewise, many of the Navy's advanced bases—like Iceland, Bermuda, London, the Azores, Adak, and La Maddalena—existed primarily to support an anti-Soviet posture. U.S. Navy carrier battle groups (CVBGs), amphibious ready groups (ARGs), and surface action groups (SAGs), on the other hand, had a broader range of potential uses.

During the 1990s, following the demise of the Soviet Union, the more specialized anti-Soviet forces were refocused on other threats, but were also cut substantially. Forward bases focused solely on the Soviets were consolidated or closed down. CVBGs, ARGs, and SAGs were pared less severely, and their capabilities were greatly enhanced.

China today exhibits its own unique set of geographic, political, and military characteristics. If China is the significant emerging threat, then U.S. forces—including naval forces—and America's forward basing posture should be optimized against the PRC and its particular antiaccess, force projection, and nuclear weapons delivery systems. This would mean focusing the U.S. Navy's strike, antiair, antimissile, antisurface, antisubmarine, and mine and information warfare capabilities on neutralizing or killing specific PRC systems or systems of systems. Today's Pentagon, however, has sought a more generic, country-neutral, capabilities-based approach to developing force structure and fielding new military and naval technology.

Nuclear Strategy

The deterrent role of nuclear weapons was central to strategic thinking throughout the Cold War, inside and outside governments. As part of the overall nuclear balance, Soviet, U.S., and NATO allied forces deployed strategic and theater nuclear weapons at sea, targeting opposing naval and other military and civilian forces, facilities, and centers. Thinking about both deterrent and war-fighting roles of nuclear weapons—and especially about anti-SSBN campaigns—was one of the central characteristics of The Maritime Strategy.[37]

The threat of nuclear weapons use loomed large over calculations regarding all levels of confrontation between the United States and the Soviets: from peacetime exercises at sea through Third World crises through potential flashpoints on the NATO flanks and at sea through possible conflict in central Europe. The designers of The Maritime Strategy had to develop and articulate clear and compelling views on the possibilities and dangers of nuclear escalation—an issue that became central to policy debates on the strategy among defense experts.[38]

No such overwhelming nuclear concerns characterize U.S.-PRC defense relations today. While both powers possess nuclear weapons and launchers, the arsenal of the United States far outstrips that of the Chinese. On the other hand, U.S. naval and other forces deploy a far smaller nuclear battery than had been the case during the Cold War. The role that nuclear weapons could play in a U.S.-China crisis seems much more questionable than during both real and hypothetical U.S.-Soviet Cold War crises. Moreover, while the United States and U.S. Navy of the Cold War era faced the possibility of waging war that could obliterate one or both sides, plausible future war scenarios between the United States and China (over Taiwan, sea lines of communications, threats to U.S. allies, etc.) lack this Armageddon-like quality. Thus, nuclear considerations probably play a considerably smaller role in developing U.S. Navy strategies vis-à-vis the PLAN than they did during the era of The Maritime Strategy.

That said, the Navy has a responsibility to develop as wide a range of operational and tactical surveillance, targeting, and kill capabilities as national military policy allows—probably including the ability to trail and attack PRC SSBNs. The enormous differences between the geography, force levels, and operational skills of contemporary China and those of the Soviet Union of the 1980s, must necessarily drive the U.S. Navy to develop very different operational and tactical approaches to any anti-SSBN measures it may contemplate.

Perception Management

Perception management was one of the naval roles articulated in The Maritime Strategy; and promulgation and exercising of The Maritime Strategy was itself part of the nation's perception management efforts with regard to the Soviet Union in the 1980s. Perception management—what would be called information operations today—was an integral part of the Reagan administration's foreign and defense policies.[39] The administration sought to convince the Soviet Union that America was resolved, powerful, and militarily superior.[40] Above all, it sought to deter Soviet aggression and weaken Soviet resolve. For deterrence to work, however, an adversary has to have a certain understanding of American capabilities and intentions. This understanding is based—at least in part—on deliberate conveying of information about those capabilities and intentions to the adversary.

Trumpeting America's naval prowess through publication of The Maritime Strategy and the actual conduct of related operations at sea were the results of calculated policy decisions, not random products of bureaucratic interservice rivalries or personally pugnacious naval leaders.[41] The public announcement of America's anti-SSBN capabilities and intentions was part of the perception management campaign, as were multi-carrier battle force exercises in far northern waters, periodic surge deployments of U.S. submarines from their home ports, submarine surfacings through the Arctic ice, and overt intelligence-gathering operations off Soviet and other Warsaw Pact members' coasts.

Successful perception management requires accurate intelligence as to the perceptions that matter most for an adversary, and how they might be managed. The high confidence in its intelligence on the Soviet navy was a powerful underpinning to the perception management campaign waged by the naval leaders who created The Maritime Strategy.

Perception management is presumably a function of U.S. naval strategy today, especially in relation to China. U.S. naval pronouncements, deployments, and other activities may well be parts of orchestrated national military information operations campaigns. The perception management campaign toward the Soviets, including The Maritime Strategy, was considered highly successful by administration and U.S. Navy leaders and analysts. It is an effort that should be carefully studied and perhaps emulated today.

Uncertainties

One of the hallmarks—and great strengths—of The Maritime Strategy was its crucial treatment of *uncertainty*. The Maritime Strategy was written in narrative form. It unfolded like a story:

- U.S. Navy and other joint and allied forces were used to perform forward peacetime presence missions to help try to deter the outbreak of crises or war.

- Should this deterrence fail, the Navy would provide vital afloat forces to the nation's joint unified commanders to respond to crises or begin the move toward general war with the Soviets.

- Should the forward surge deployment of American and allied naval and other forces fail to deter the Soviets from aggression, the U.S. Navy and others would engage the Soviets as far forward as possible, sinking their fleet—including SSNs and SSBNs—and defending against and attacking Soviet forces invading allied countries on the European flanks and in the Pacific.

- If called upon by the national command authorities, significant Soviet forces on the perimeter of the Soviet homeland itself would be attacked and defeated, in the Arctic, the Mediterranean, and/or the North Pacific.

- Meanwhile, reinforcement and resupply of ground and air forces in central Europe would flow, protected by a combination of largely American forward operations against deploying Soviet subsurface, surface, and air forces, and heavily allied area antisubmarine operations, close-in convoy escort, and forward port security.[42]

- The Soviet Union would presumably call off the war, having been stymied at sea by implementation of The Maritime Strategy and CONMAROPS, and on land by operations that had unfolded in accordance with NATO's Follow-On Forces Attack (FOFA) doctrine, U.S. Army's AirLand Battle Doctrine, and the U.S. Air Force's Aerospace Doctrine.

The authors of The Maritime Strategy insisted, however, that while this was the baseline story of the strategy, they hardly expected things to flow so smoothly. They recognized—and did so as an integral part of their documents—that they had made numerous assumptions in weaving their tale, but that many of these assumptions could fail to pan out, in which case the ability of The Maritime Strategy to play itself out as written would be uncertain. Many versions of The Maritime Strategy explicitly listed many of these uncertainties.[43] The Navy paid a great deal of attention during the 1980s to exercising, gaming, and analyzing the effects of various manifestations and combinations of these uncertainties on implementing the strategy, and how to counter or mitigate these effects.

The various uncertainties analyzed included:

- *Political decisions:* What would they be? When would they be taken? How would they change prewar plans? What constraints would be placed on the use of naval forces, if any? Would the territory of the Soviet Union and/or Soviet strategic nuclear forces be considered inviolate? Would early operations against Soviet SSBNs be authorized?

- *U.S. allies:* Which would join the United States? Which would not? Which would need protection? Which would provide what forces? How might their operations be restricted?

- *Soviet strategy:* Was the National Intelligence Estimate (NIE) correct? What if the Soviets did something different? What if they employed their SSNs differently? Their SSBNs? Their naval aviation?

- *Soviet forward allies:* Would North Korea attack the South? Would Cuba, Libya, Syria, Angola, or Vietnam support and assist the Soviet navy? What effect would that have on U.S. operations? Which of them might have to be neutralized? How and when?

- *China:* What role would the PRC play? Stay neutral? Join the United States? Join the Soviets?[44]

- *Other U.S. services:* Would the U.S. Army and U.S. Air Force devote the forces to the maritime and flank campaigns that they had planned before the war? Would they need naval assistance in Central Europe?

- *Nuclear escalation:* Would it occur? When? How? Would it operate differently at sea than on land?

- *Chemical and biological warfare:* Would it occur? What effect would it have at sea and on the littorals?

- *War termination:* What would U.S. war aims be? How would war termination occur? What roles would naval places play during and after war termination?

The situation today and in the future vis-à-vis China is arguably rife with even more uncertainties. Whatever the agreed baseline scenario of the maritime portions of a joint campaign of some type against the PRC, the implications of its underlying assumptions not panning out should be the subject of close examination. For example: What are the key uncertainties regarding hostilities with China? How do they differ from those of the past? How can they be mitigated? What would Russia's position be, or Japan's? Will the President see the Chinese mainland as immune from attack? What about Chinese strategic nuclear forces? As was true in the 1980s, to best serve their country, contemporary American strategists will have to work their way through an analysis of the most significant uncertainties regarding a conflict with the Chinese—including those pertaining to PLAN employment of its SSN and SSBN forces, and U.S. policy, strategy, and tactics to counter them.

Conclusion

This treatment of The Maritime Strategy has been brief and selected. Those aspects of The Maritime Strategy chosen for discussion were done so with a view of highlighting some salient issues addressed by its authors in the U.S. Navy with regard to the Soviet Union and Soviet navy of the 1980s, so as to illuminate related issues that may be faced by civilian, military, and naval planners and operators today, as they ponder the nation's correct naval response to the challenges presented by the rise of PRC military power today and tomorrow, and especially by its prospective deployment of a sophisticated PLAN submarine force.

Notes

1. These are both informal bodies of strategic policy as well as series of formal documents issued every year or so by the President, the Secretary of Defense, and the Chairman of the Joint Chiefs of Staff.

2. The author is indebted to the comments of Henry H. Gaffney, Michael A. McDevitt, and David Perin—colleagues at the Center for Naval Analyses (CNA)—for their pointed and helpful comments on an earlier draft of this paper.

3. For an excellent overview, see George W. Baer, "U.S. Naval Strategy 1890–1945," *Naval War College Review* 44 (Winter 1991): 6–33.

4. A thoughtful analysis of the evolution of post–World War II U.S. naval strategic thinking is in Mackubin Thomas Owens, "U.S. Maritime Strategy and the Cold War," in Stephen J. Cimbala, ed., *Mysteries of the Cold War* (Aldershot, U.K.: Ashgate, 1999), 147–241. A briefer overview is George W. Baer, "Purposes and Platforms in the U.S. Navy," in Phillips Payson O'Brien, ed., *Technology and Naval Combat: In the Twentieth Century and Beyond* (London: Frank Cass, 2001), 200–215. On the late 1940s and early 1950s, see Michael A. Palmer, *Origins of the Maritime Strategy: American Naval Strategy in the First Postwar Decade* (Washington, D.C.: Naval Historical Center, 1988), Contributions to Naval History No. 1. Navy strategic thought in the 1950s and 1960s is analyzed in Richard Erik Hegmann, "In Search of Strategy: the Navy and the Depths of the Maritime Strategy" (Ph.D. diss.: Brandeis University, 1991); and Hegmann, "Reconsidering the Evolution of the U.S. Maritime Strategy 1955–1965," *Journal of Strategic Studies* 14 (September 1991): 299–336.

5. Classified versions of The Maritime Strategy have yet to be declassified. The unclassified version was issued as a special supplement to the U.S. Naval Institute *Proceedings* 112 (January 1986).

6. The best single work on The Maritime Strategy is John B. Hattendorf, *The Evolution of the U.S. Navy's Maritime Strategy, 1977–1986* (Newport, R.I.: Naval War College Press, 2004), Newport Paper Number Nineteen. See also David A. Rosenberg, "Process: The Realities of Formulating Modern Naval Strategy," in James Goldrick and John B. Hattendorf, eds., *Mahan is Not Enough: The Proceedings of a Conference on the Works of Sir Julian Corbett and Admiral Sir Herbert Richmond* (Newport, R.I.: Naval War College Press, 1993), 141–75. On submarine warfare strategies during The Maritime Strategy era, before, and since, see Owen R. Coté, Jr., *The Third Battle: Innovation in the U.S. Navy's Silent Cold War Struggle with Soviet Submarines* (Newport, R.I.: Naval War College Press, 2003), Newport Paper Number Sixteen.

7. The Navy has continued to develop and codify its strategic concepts following the end of the Cold War. See, for example, Edward Rhodes, '. . . From the Sea' and Back Again: Naval Power in National Strategy in the Second American Century," in Pelham G. Boyer and Robert S. Wood, eds., *Strategic Transformation and Naval Power in the 21st Century* (Newport, R.I.: Naval War College Press, 1988), 307–53; Edward A. Smith, Jr., "What '. . . From the Sea' Didn't Say," *Naval War College Review* 48 (Winter 1995): 9–33; Bradd C. Hayes, "Keeping the Naval Service Relevant," U.S. Naval Institute *Proceedings* 119 (October 1993): 57–60; Stewart Fraser, *US Maritime Strategy: Issues and Implications* (Lancaster, U.K.: Lancaster University, Centre for Defence and International Security Studies, 1997); Thomas P. M. Barnett, *The Pentagon's New Map: War and Peace in the Twenty-first Century* (New York: Putnam's Sons, 2004), 63–79; and Jason Sherman, "Getting it Right," *Seapower* 48 (June 2005): 14–16.

8. For an attempt to capture the extent of the public discourse, see Peter M. Swartz, "The Maritime Strategy Debates: A Bibliographic Guide to the Renaissance of U.S. Naval Strategic Thinking in the 1980s," in Hattendorf, *The Evolution of the U.S. Navy's Maritime Strategy*, 185–277.

9. For naval planning in the interwar period, see especially Edward S. Miller, *War Plan Orange, 1897–1945: The Naval Campaign through the Central Pacific* (Annapolis, Md.: Naval Institute Press, 1988).

10. On the role played by naval intelligence in the development and implementation of The Maritime Strategy, see Christopher A. Ford and David A. Rosenberg, "The Naval Intelligence Underpinnings of Reagan's Maritime Strategy," *The Journal of Strategic Studies* 28 (April 2005): 379–409.

11. The declassified secret National Intelligence Estimate (NIE) *Soviet Naval Strategy and Programs through the 1990s* is reprinted as Appendix I in Hattendorf, *Evolution of the U.S. Navy's Maritime Strategy*, 101–84.

12. In response to Congressional direction, the U.S. Department of Defense publishes an annual unclassified assessment of Chinese military policy and strategy. The latest edition is *Annual Report to Congress: The Military Power of the People's Republic of China: 2005* (Washington, D.C.: Office of the Secretary of Defense, 2005).

13. Secretary of Defense Donald Rumsfeld, *Quadrennial Defense Review Report* (Washington, D.C.: Department of Defense, February 6, 2006), 29.

14. On the complementarity of Army, Navy, and other service concepts, see William Pendley, "The U.S. Navy, Forward Defense, and the Air-Land Battle," in Robert Pfaltzgraff, Jr., et al., eds., *Emerging Doctrines and Technologies* (Lexington, Mass.: Lexington Books, 1987).

15. On the Navy's efforts to game The Maritime Strategy, see Bud Hay and Bob Gile, *Global War Game: The First Five Years* (Newport, R.I.: Naval War College Press, June 1993), Newport Paper Number Four; and Robert H. Gile, *Global War Game: Second Series, 1984–1988* (Newport, R.I.: Naval War College Press, 2004), Newport Paper Number Twenty.

16. The Navy was not alone in its opposition to Goldwater-Nichols. Secretary of Defense Weinberger and others were also against its passage.

17. On the Navy's dogged opposition to the Goldwater-Nichols Act, see James R. Locher III, *Victory on the Potomac: The Goldwater-Nichols Act Unifies the Pentagon* (College Station, Tex.: Texas A&M University Press, 2002).

18. Ambassador Robert W. Komer, a major critic of The Maritime Strategy, argued that among its vices was its potential diversion of defense budget resources from the Army to the Navy. See his *Maritime Strategy or Coalition Defense?* (Cambridge, Mass.: Abt Books, 1984). John Mearsheimer made similar arguments in his more sophisticated critique "A Strategic Misstep: *The Maritime Strategy* and Deterrence in Europe," *International Security* 11 (Fall 1986): 3–57.

19. U.S. Army concerns that it was not doing as well as the Navy in strategic planning caused Army leaders to commission a study by Carl H. Builder, *The Army in the Strategic Planning Process: Who Shall Bell the Cat?* (Bethesda, Md.: U.S. Army Concepts Analysis Agency, October 1986). The study was revised and reissued as a RAND Corporation publication in 1987. It was further revised and republished as the influential *The Masks of War: American Military Styles in Strategy and Analysis* (Baltimore, Md.: Johns Hopkins University Press, 1989).

20. I am indebted to Owen Coté and Michael McDevitt for nuances on this point.

21. Note the specious title of Ambassador Komer's critique of The Maritime Strategy: *Maritime Strategy or Coalition Warfare?*

22. On CONMAROPS, see Peter M. Swartz, "Preventing the Bear's Last Swim: The NATO Concept of Maritime Operations (ConMarOps) of the Last Cold War Decade," in *NATO's Maritime Power 1949–1990* (Piraeas, Greece: European Institute of Maritime Studies and Research [INMER], 2003), 47–61.

23. On coordinated Royal Navy forward submarine plans and operations, see Jim Ring, *We Come Unseen: The Untold Story of Britain's Cold War Submariners* (London: John Murray, 2001). On complementary Federal German Navy far forward operational intentions in the Baltic, see Rear Admiral Vice Admiral Helmut Kampe, Federal German Navy, "Defending the Baltic Approaches," U.S. Naval Institute *Proceedings* 112 (March 1986): 93; and Rear Admiral Gerhard Bing, Federal German Navy, "Tornado in the Naval Role," *NATO's Sixteen Nations*, Special Edition (April 1990): 23–24.

24. On exercising The Maritime Strategy and CONMAROPS, see Henry C. Mustin, "The Role of the Navy and Marines in the Norwegian Sea," *Naval War College Review* 39 (March–April 1986): 2–6; and Eric Grove, with Graham Thompson, *Battle for the Fiords: NATO's Forward Maritime Strategy in Action* (Annapolis, Md.: Naval Institute Press, 1991).

25. On Admiral Mullen's initiative to strengthen alliance and coalition integration at sea, see John G. Morgan and Charles W. Martoglio, "The 1,000-Ship Navy: Building a Global Maritime Network," U.S. Naval Institute *Proceedings* 131 (November 2005): 14–17. For responses by commanders of other navies—including the commanders of the Australian, Indian, Indonesian, and New Zealand navies and the Japanese Maritime Self-Defense Force—see "The Commanders Respond," U.S. Naval Institute *Proceedings* 132 (March 2006): 34–51.

26. On Reagan administration defense policies, see Dale R. Herspring, *The Pentagon and the Presidency: Civil-Military Relations from FDR to George W. Bush* (Lawrence, Kans.: University Press of Kansas, 2005), 265–96; and John Lewis Gaddis, "National Security: Strategies of Containment, Past and Future," *Hoover Digest* no. 2 (2001).

27. For an analysis of the difference in outlook between the Carter administration and its U.S. Navy leadership, see Thomas H. Etzold, "The Navy and National Security Policy in the 1970s," in Harry R. Borowski, ed., *Military Planning in the Twentieth Century: Proceedings of the Eleventh Military History Symposium: U.S. Air Force Academy: 1984* (Washington, D.C.: U.S. Government Printing Office, 1986), 275–94.

28. For an assessment of initial Bush administration attitudes toward China, see Michael A. McDevitt, "The China Factor in Future U.S. Defense Planning," in Jonathan D. Pollack, ed., *Strategic Surprise: U.S. China Relations in the Early Twenty-first Century* (Newport, R.I.: Naval War College Press, 2003), 149–57.

29. *Quadrennial Defense Review Report*, 29–30.

30. But see R. A. Bowling, "Keeping Open the Sea-Lanes," *U.S. Naval Institute Proceedings* 111 (December 1985): 92–98; and E. Cameron Williams, "The Four 'Iron Laws' of Naval Protection of Merchant Shipping," *Naval War College Review* 39 (May–June 1986): 35–42.

31. The high-level and influential "Iklé Study" tried to refocus American strategic attention on the Third World. See Commission on Integrated Long-Term Strategy, Fred C. Iklé and Albert Wohlstetter, cochairmen, *Discriminate Deterrence: Report of the Commission on Integrated Long-Term Strategy* (Washington, D.C.: The Commission, January 1988). On the Marines' refocusing away from The Maritime Strategy under General Gray (and their endorsement of *Discriminate Deterrence*), see John C. Scharfen, "The Marine Corps in 1987," *U.S. Naval Institute Proceedings* 114 (May 1988): 160–64; "Interview with USMC Commandant Gen. A. M. Gray," *Seapower* 31 (November 1988): 19–21; and Allan R. Millett, *Semper Fidelis: The History of the United States Marine Corps: Revised and Expanded Edition* (New York: The Free Press, 1991), 630–34.

32. Stansfield Turner argued that both alternatives were needed, and in combination were preferable to The Maritime Strategy. See his "U.S. Naval Policy," *Naval Forces* no. 3 (1985): 15–25.

33. For an example of an unofficial view in this vein, see John J. Tkacik, Jr., "China's Submarine Challenge," Heritage Foundation Web Memo #1001, March 1, 2006, www.heritage.org/Research/AsiaandthePacific/wm1001.

34. Thomas P. M. Barnett has become a leading exponent of this view. See his *Blueprint for Action: A Future Worth Creating* (New York: Putnam, 2005).

35. This seems to be the current U.S. Navy public view. See Michael Mullen, "Edited Remarks As Delivered," Surface Navy Association National Symposium (10 January 2006).

36. For another analysis of rival contemporary U.S. defense and naval concepts and strategies, see Barnett, *Blueprint for Action*, especially 8–9, 39, 172–76.

37. Nuclear considerations behind The Maritime Strategy were publicly laid out in Linton F. Brooks, "Naval Power and National Security: The Case for the Maritime Strategy," *International Security* 11 (Fall 1986): 58–87; and "The Nuclear Maritime Strategy," U.S. Naval Institute *Proceedings* 113. See also "Comment and Discussion," *Proceedings* (May 1987): 14, 17; and *Proceedings* (August 1987): 27–28.

38. Two of the best known contemporary critiques of the allegedly escalatory nature of The Maritime Strategy were Barry A. Posen, "Inadvertent Nuclear War? Escalation and NATO's Northern Flank," *International Security* 7 (Fall 1982): 28–54; and Mearsheimer, "A Strategic Misstep."

39. For an overview of perception management as an American military tool, see Pascale Combelles Siegel, "Perception Management: IO's Stepchild?" *Low Intensity Conflict & Law Enforcement* 13 (Autumn 2005): 117–34.

40. On Reagan administration perception management efforts, see Caspar W. Weinberger, "U.S. Defense Strategy," *Foreign Affairs* 64 (Spring 1986): 677–78; Ben B. Fisher, *A Cold War Conundrum: the 1983 Soviet War Scare* (Washington, D.C.: Central Intelligence Agency, Center for the Study of Intelligence, 1997), 6–11; Peter Schweizer, *Victory: The Reagan Administration's Secret Strategy That Hastened the Collapse of the Soviet Union* (New York: Atlantic Monthly Press, 1994), xii–xix, 6–9, 190–91, 235–36; Peter Schweizer, *Reagan's War: The Epic Story of His Forty-Year Struggle and Final Triumph over Communism* (New York: Doubleday, 2002), 130–33, 141, 205–7, 216–17; William E. Burrows, *By Any Means Necessary: America's Secret Air War in the Cold War* (New York: Farrar, Straus and Giroux, 2001), 294–96.

41. On the Navy's perception management efforts during The Maritime Strategy era, see Ford and Rosenberg, "The Naval Intelligence Underpinnings of Reagan's Maritime Strategy"; Coté, *The Third Battle*, 70–76; and Tom Brooks and Bill Manthorpe, "Setting the Record Straight: A Critical Review of *Fall from Glory*," *Naval Intelligence Professionals Quarterly* 12 (April 1996): 1–2.

42. On the residual role of the U.S. Navy in convoy escort, within the larger context of The Maritime Strategy, see Stuart D. Landersman, "Naval Protection of Shipping: A Lost Art?" *Naval War College Review* 39 (March–April 1986): 23–34. See also his "I Am a . . . Convoy Commodore," U.S. Naval Institute *Proceedings* 112 (June 1986): 56–63.

43. On The Maritime Strategy and its uncertainties, see, for example, Linton F. Brooks, "Naval Power and National Security: The Case for the Maritime Strategy," *International Security* 11 (Fall 1986): 58–87; and Lee Baggett, Jr., "U.S. Maritime Strategy," in Ellmann Ellingsen, ed., *NATO and U.S. Maritime Strategy: Diverging Interests or Cooperative Effort* (Oslo: The Norwegian Atlantic Committee, 1987), 5–28.

44. On Chinese-U.S. Navy relationships during the 1980s, see Andrew C. A. Jampoler, "The Politics of Port Visits," U.S. Naval Institute *Proceedings* 130 (August 2004): 66–69.

Toshi Yoshihara

U.S. Ballistic-Missile Defense and China's Undersea Nuclear Deterrent

A Preliminary Assessment

Introduction

IN JULY 2005, THE DIRECTOR of the U.S. Missile Defense Agency (MDA), Air Force Lt. Gen. Henry Obering, made remarks to the Defense Writers Group about his agency's view of the Chinese missile threat. Subsequent media reports of his speech raised some eyebrows within the U.S. policy community. As reported by the *Washington Post*, Obering stated, "What . . . we have to do is, in our development program, be able to address the Chinese capabilities, because that's prudent."[1] Taken at face value, the statement represented a remarkable shift in U.S. policy, which had until then insisted that missile defense was not directed at the People's Republic of China (PRC).[2] Subsequent clarification from the MDA showed that Obering's full remarks, which the *Post* omitted, were consistent with existing national policy.[3]

Obering asserted that the MDA did not intend to develop the ballistic-missile defense (BMD) system to counter Chinese missiles. Washington's rationale for monitoring China's missile capabilities, he reasoned, is premised on the risk that technologies developed by the Chinese might fall into the hands of other countries hostile to the United States. In other words, proliferation (whether intended or unintended), rather than China's own strategic forces, was what most concerned the MDA. In any event, fears that Obering had committed a diplomatic faux pas proved unwarranted.

Nevertheless, this minor nonevent raises some important issues that deserve further examination. First, a great deal of ambiguity continues to surround Sino-U.S. relations in respect to Washington's controversial missile defense system. Obering's carefully phrased statement and the apparent readiness of some observers to jump to the most extreme conclusions about U.S. missile defense planners reflect great sensitivity of Chinese perceptions regarding American intentions. Second, what exactly did Obering mean by "prudent"? How will the United States prudently design its missile defense system in a manner that avoids alarming Beijing? Third, even if Obering's rationale for watching China's missile developments was sincere, the expected outcome—a more capable shield against Chinese capabilities—could still potentially harm Beijing's security interests. How, then, might the PRC respond?

These questions acquire increasing policy urgency as new generations of intercontinental land- and sea-based strategic weaponry are expected to bolster China's nuclear posture. In particular, the potential capacity of the new strategic missile submarine (Type 094) to virtually guarantee a second-strike capability has been a subject of scrutiny within the U.S. policy community. The level of interest will likely intensify given that Washington's determination to deploy ballistic-missile defense adds a complicating factor to China's nuclear calculus and will almost certainly shape Chinese thinking about deployment options for its nascent undersea force.

To address the potential interactions between the future of U.S. BMD system and the emerging Chinese undersea strategic missile submarine fleet, this chapter seeks to examine: 1) Chinese attitudes toward missile defense; 2) the BMD program's potential impact on Chinese perceptions and responses; 3) factors that are likely to influence the PRC's nuclear force structure, particularly the strategic submarine force; and 4) operational considerations for China's emerging undersea fleet.

Chinese Perceptions of U.S. BMD

China's position on ballistic-missile defense, both official and unofficial, has centered primarily on five objections.[4] First, Beijing worries that missile defense could undermine the credibility of its nuclear deterrent. Chinese analysts have often asserted that even a modest configuration of the proposed system could neutralize China's small nuclear force.[5] Currently, the mainstay of PRC's strategic rocket forces consists of twenty or so aging single-warhead intercontinental ballistic missiles (ICBMs).[6] Given that the warheads and the liquid propellants are stored separately and that a portion of the missile force is dispersed in caves, launch preparations are a time-consuming challenge.[7] It is generally assumed that such a posture suffers from low levels of readiness. Observers have long noted that this absence of responsiveness exposes the Chinese deterrent to a disarming first strike. Missile defense, it is argued, threatens to further exacerbate this vulnerability.[8]

However, the validity of this argument, to which Chinese opponents of U.S. BMD often turn, could gradually erode as a new generation of rail or road mobile ICBMs enters service.[9] The DF-31 ICBM boasts a range of eight thousand kilometers.[10] The mobility of these missiles promises greater survivability compared to their predecessors and thus a more credible second-strike capability. However, reports on the operational status of the DF-31 remain fragmentary at best and often contradictory.[11] Since late 2001, the International Institute for Strategic Studies has claimed that the 2nd Artillery Corps has deployed a brigade of eight DF-31s.[12] Jane's speculates that two brigades armed with eight launchers each may be operational in southern and central China.[13]

In contrast, official reports suggest that the DF-31s are either just entering service or are some years away from deployment. The Pentagon's latest annual report on Chinese military power places initial operational capability in the 2005–06 timeframe.[14] In a hearing at the Senate Select Committee on Intelligence, the Director of the Defense Intelligence Agency, Vice Adm. Lowell Jacoby, testified that the DF-31 was still under development and provided no indications that the ICBM was operational.[15] Until a clearer picture of this new missile force emerges, determining whether limited numbers of DF-31s are in service or not remains a speculative exercise. What is less disputable is that as the missiles are fielded over time, China's second-strike capability will gradually improve in the coming years (the implications of which are more fully explored below).

Second, some of the strongest objections to BMD have been directed at potential U.S. transfers of theater missile defenses to Taiwan. The Chinese contend that the psychological benefits of deploying missile defense regardless of actual effectiveness might embolden the independence movement on the island. The delivery of such a system would significantly enhance U.S.-Taiwan military interoperability and so would contradict Washington's "One

China" principle. As one Chinese scholar points out, "China is opposed to the provision of a missile defense system or its related technology to Taiwan in any form by the U.S., because the essence of such a move would put Taiwan under the U.S. umbrella of military protection, which would be tantamount to the restoration of a quasi-military alliance between the U.S. and Taiwan."[16] An effective BMD that enhances American invulnerability to a Chinese nuclear deterrent might also increase the likelihood of U.S. intervention in a China-Taiwan conflict.

Third, the Chinese have consistently expressed strong opposition to Japan's codevelopment of theater missile defense technologies with the United States. To some Chinese observers, Japanese advances in missile defense capabilities could provide an important political and technological foundation for remilitarization.[17] Others contend that American and Japanese collaboration would enhance the capacity of the alliance to contain China. Chinese protests have also been couched in terms of Taiwan. Given that allied missile defense involves very high levels of interoperability, an objective enshrined in the 1997 U.S.-Japan defense guidelines, Tokyo might be forced or dragged into a U.S. intervention over a Taiwan crisis. Still others believe that Japan's interest in missile defense reflects Tokyo's determination to intervene in a future contingency over Taiwan.[18]

Fourth, Chinese analysts have pointed to the adverse effects that missile defense could have on arms control regimes and the global disarmament agenda. They contend that missile defense would prompt states to accelerate proliferation, engage in arms races, and weaponize space. While this moral posturing is consistent with the PRC's long-standing rhetoric on nuclear matters, it implicitly admits to China's likely response to missile defense: a countervailing buildup of its nuclear forces. Finally, China has long opposed American unilateralism. Beijing fears that missile defense will add to Washington's freedom of maneuver on the world stage and thereby cement U.S. hegemony.

It is noteworthy that most of the objections tend to underscore the political nature of the PRC's concerns. For example, ambivalence toward Japanese participation in U.S. missile defense development largely reflects Chinese anxieties about Tokyo's long-term strategic direction. Even in the case of Taiwan, where an actual military contingency is conceivable, missile defense does not rank high in Chinese thinking as an operational concern. China boasts the capacity to saturate theater- and tactical-level missile defenses on the island with its large (and growing) arsenal of short-range ballistic-missiles,[19] which are in any event not vulnerable to ground-based, midcourse interceptors designed to protect the U.S. homeland from long-range missiles. In contrast, the longer-term viability of China's strategic deterrent vis-à-vis the United States is the one central issue that could necessitate concrete responses on the part of Beijing.

Post-ABM Treaty Perceptions of BMD

The PRC's vocal opposition to U.S. BMD throughout the 1990s abruptly ended following Washington's formal withdrawal from the Anti-Ballistic Missile (ABM) Treaty in 2002. Indeed, China's diplomatic posture toward missile defense developments has remained consistently restrained. Several factors explain this outward silence.

First, China had to acquiesce to what amounted to a fait accompli. The determination with which the Bush administration sought to leave behind the ABM treaty convinced the Chinese that some type of missile defense deployment was a foregone conclusion. The collapse of the Sino-Russian pact against U.S. missile defense plans further undercut the PRC's diplomatic leverage. Beijing probably concluded that continued opposition would strain its relations with Washington without producing any favorable outcomes. Chinese decision makers may have also feared that stubborn public displays of displeasure might backfire, thereby driving American proponents of missile defense to embrace arguments favoring BMD systems designed specifically for China. Finally, a steady stream of official American reassurances and China's own decision to pursue a more constructive relationship with the United States appear to have played an important role in changing Beijing's calculus.[20]

Second, the failure of diplomacy to deter or delay U.S. policy ushered in a new phase in China's reactive strategy focused on concrete responses to the prospective challenge. Political reassurances by U.S. officials notwithstanding, Beijing (or any responsible state for that matter) will almost certainly assume that the BMD might be technically configured to degrade Chinese capabilities.[21] According to one Chinese observer, "No matter how the Bush administration explains its motivations for deploying NMDs, there is no denying the fact that America's NMDs would have the ability to intercept and defend against China's ICBMs."[22] Based on many conversations with their counterparts in China, American analysts have also concluded that the Chinese uniformly reject the argument that missile defenses are designed only for rogue states.[23]

One obvious response is to sustain the credibility of China's nuclear deterrent in the coming years. Given that China has been engaged in the development of second-generation nuclear capabilities for the past two decades, the extent to which change in the PRC's nuclear posture can be attributed to missile defense is somewhat uncertain. Nevertheless, the Chinese have made it abundantly clear that Beijing will respond to BMD. For at least the past five years, Chinese strategists have openly speculated about how China could tailor its nuclear forces to defeat missile defense. Li Bin, a well-respected Chinese analyst on nuclear strategy, called for a moderate buildup of China's deterrent focused on survivability.[24] In another article, he assured his readers that the Chinese leadership has and will continue to study all options in order to counter the missile shield.[25]

Third, some have argued that the expected *near-term* capabilities that the United States can realistically field will not adversely affect China's deterrence calculus. According to one analysis, "Chinese security managers currently are convinced that the offense-dominant global nuclear regime is highly robust from a technological point of view."[26] Shen Dingli, for example, argued that the expected deployment of six to ten interceptors in 2004 would not impact the current size of China's ICBMs.[27] In other words, Beijing has probably concluded that it has the time and capacity to respond to the evolving BMD system. Thus, fears of Chinese over-reaction that could in turn trigger an "arms race" are likely exaggerated.

Key Drivers Behind China's Likely Responses to BMD

Gauging specific Chinese responses to defeating the emerging U.S. BMD architecture remains problematic. The opened-ended nature of missile defense development (detailed below) renders predictions about the final state of the system virtually moot. In other words, a benchmark with which to measure against the range of Chinese options to counter BMD remains absent.[28] Without sufficient data on the expected defensive capabilities of missile defense, Beijing has little basis to make accurate judgments about the types and numbers of offensive systems it would have to acquire to bolster its second strike capability. As such, the offense-defense interactions between the United States and China will remain in flux until the various components of missile defense system mature further.

An assessment of the philosophies and assumptions underlying the missile defense program provides one method for discerning whether China might feel compelled to act quickly or overreact in the face of a looming defensive shield. Given that BMD development has occupied a major place in defense planning under the Bush administration, an exercise of this kind is particularly instructive. Indeed, a closer look at Washington's current approach to missile defense reveals that the program contains features that are likely to both exacerbate and dampen Chinese fears.

On the one hand, the potential for the BMD program to achieve significant breakthroughs and successes will almost certainly produce incentives for Beijing to accelerate the qualitative and quantitative improvements of its nuclear arsenal. The Bush administration deliberately blurs the operational line dividing national and theater missile defenses. The goal is to create an integrated, multilayered (or "thick") defensive system designed to intercept a ballistic missile at every stage of its trajectory from boost to terminal phases. The program conspicuously avoids specificity regarding the final status of the missile defense architecture. Proponents of BMD have argued that an undefined "end state" provides the United States with the flexibility to respond and adapt to new and emerging threats in the security environment.[29]

In theory, such an unrestrained research and development strategy could produce far more effective missile defense systems that are capable of protecting the U.S. homeland from threats beyond those posed by rogue states and accidental launches. This possibility is a principal reason for the PRC's objections to missile defense. Indeed, throughout the late 1990s, Chinese and American analysts warned repeatedly that even a modest BMD configuration would have required China to depart from its leisurely nuclear posture.[30] Further, as noted above, the Chinese do not believe American claims that the BMD system is designed to serve limited objectives. Beijing's suspicions of U.S. intent and capability could spur it to keep pace with potential BMD as a strategic hedge, especially if the Chinese perceive a shift in the offense-defense balance. In this context, China's emerging second-strike capabilities and other countermeasures against missile defense (detailed below) will play complementary roles in maintaining the integrity of its deterrent posture.

On the other hand, the technical and financial obstacles that stand in the way of the BMD program's success will moderate worst-case scenario thinking and the potential for overreaction. Debates about the effectiveness of missile defense against China are still largely theoretical. Hobbling problems associated with technical feasibility and with the current acquisition strategy persist and will likely spill over to the operational viability of the proposed BMD. Technological impediments remain a major problem. The series of test failures that occurred in highly favorable (if not unrealistic) conditions in the past few years point to the technical difficulties inherent to missile defense.[31] The test record for the ground-based, midcourse interceptor, which is central to intercepting long-range ballistic missiles, has proved sobering: five of the ten "kinetic kill" tests have thus far failed. More recent successes have been based on even less rigorous testing conditions, such as simulating the flight of an imaginary enemy target.[32]

Critics of missile defense in the United States have also pointed to major flaws in the current acquisition strategy that the Bush administration has adopted. Known as "spiral development" within the policy community, it is at the heart of the open-ended character of the BMD program.[33] Under this evolutionary approach, various elements of the missile defense architecture would be developed, tested, and deployed along parallel tracks. As each component becomes technically feasible, it would be integrated to enhance the existing architecture.[34] Refinements and improvements on existing and future systems would continue in an iterative process. Premised on the Pentagon's capabilities-based planning process, the architecture would evolve continually until it could cope with the entire range of conceivable missile threats.[35]

This development philosophy stands in sharp contrast to the traditional acquisition standard that sets out clear operational requirements against which testing and deployment decisions are made. While an undefined architecture provides flexibility to build a robust BMD system tailored to the prevailing threat environment, it also accentuates the risks of unleashing cost overruns that have in turn increased anticipation of greater congressional scrutiny. In other words, the financial sustainability of this approach over the long term could become increasingly questionable.

The technical and financial challenges that the United States confronts have not gone unnoticed in China.[36] Some Chinese analysts confidently predict that missile defense would not likely be effective.[37] Others suspect that the program was intended as a deception to lure Beijing into a fruitless, costly arms race—resembling the Cold War superpower competition—designed to bankrupt China.[38] To some degree, then, there is recognition that time is on China's side and that Beijing has a choice in how it responds. Short of a radical strategic technical surprise, then, the PRC will be able to pace and match U.S. developments without fear of losing its deterrent credibility in the near term.

The various ambiguities surrounding missile defense suggests that Beijing's responses will be far more measured than what some Chinese analysts themselves have warned about or threatened. It appears unlikely that China would hastily forecast a highly capable BMD threat until sufficient empirical evidence emerges about the true nature of the proposed missile defense system. Equally important, Beijing would not likely seek to out-build any system that could produce unintended reactions from its alarmed neighbors or from the United States. In particular, the PRC has strong incentives to avoid moves that could justify political arguments already evident in Washington for an expanded BMD system designed to blunt China's deterrent. In the broader context of Chinese grand strategy, hostile regional reactions to the Beijing's nuclear posture would undermine China's painstaking efforts to cultivate perceptions that it will rise peacefully.[39] As such, the PRC may be content to emphasize sufficiency: the minimum, requisite force posture needed to defeat BMD. Such restraint is reinforced by and consistent with China's long-standing minimum deterrent posture as reviewed below.

China's Nuclear Doctrine Revisited

The starting point for projecting the future force structure of China's nuclear deterrent lies in a more fundamental debate: whether the PRC will seek to enhance the quality and/or quantity of its nuclear forces to assure the credibility of its modest nuclear posture, or whether Beijing will reformulate its nuclear doctrine to cope with more demanding strategic requirements. There has been considerable speculation in the U.S. policy community about the prospects of a shift in China's deterrent posture from minimum to limited deterrence for at least a decade.[40] So, too, Chinese analysts and policy-makers have exhibited greater willingness to reconsider and question the basic merits of a minimalist posture (explored further below). Yet, there is sufficient empirical evidence—at least in terms of what is known about the current force structure—that minimum deterrence remains the bedrock of Beijing's nuclear doctrine.[41]

Reaffirming the continuity in Chinese nuclear doctrine, one Chinese analyst expressed considerable confidence that Beijing will not abandon its cherished tradition of minimalism on the nuclear front.[42] Most recently, the commander of the 2nd Artillery Corps, General Jing Zhiyuan, assured Secretary of Defense Donald Rumsfeld during his visit to Jing's headquarters that China remains committed to its "no first use" policy.[43] A RAND study argues persuasively that Beijing has only recently begun to attain credibility in its minimum deterrent posture.[44] If true, then China has a long way to go before it can establish a more robust posture connoting the capacity to use nuclear weapons for war-fighting purposes.

One reasonable baseline for analysis, then, is to assume that China would hew closely to its minimum deterrent posture well into the next decade.[45] To establish credible minimum deterrence, three overriding factors loom large in China's calculus. First, the ability of its nuclear forces to survive an all-out preemptive first strike, and then to penetrate America's missile shield would be a critical benchmark. Second, sufficiency would require China to build up enough to defeat BMD but not enough to trigger competitive responses from the United States. Third, comfort with minimum sufficiency would require China to maintain high levels of ambiguity surrounding its retaliatory capabilities. Beijing counts on the uncertainty in the minds of adversaries about the possibility of even a few nuclear weapons to survive a first strike to generate deterrence. Willingness to rely on the psychological effects of ambiguity has been a persistent hallmark of Chinese nuclear doctrine.

How Much Is Enough?

Against the backdrop of China's well established preference for minimum deterrence, what are the types of force structures that Beijing would consider viable? And, what factors related to missile defense might tend to favor reliance on its nascent ballistic-missile submarine (SSBN) fleet? An important intervening variable is Beijing's calculations concerning the proper force mix and trade-offs between its DF-31s and its sea-based JL-2 submarine-launched ballistic-missiles (SLBMs). Each leg of the dyad presents distinct advantages and disadvantages that will surely influence the PRC's cost-and-benefit analysis.

In terms of survivability, both land- and sea-based options enhance China's ability to escape a disarming first strike. The mobility of the DF-31s would maximize the geographic depth that China enjoys, while the next-generation Type 094 SSBN currently under development would impose additional targeting, tracking, and other intelligence challenges on the adversary.[46] Ideally, an interactively survivable nuclear dyad would greatly increase the versatility of China's nuclear forces. Adding relatively cheap countermeasures to the warheads of each nuclear leg or mounting multiple warheads would further enhance China's ability to defeat the BMD.[47] Modest quantitative increases combined with qualitative advances would largely ameliorate the survivability concern.[48]

Some factors unique to an undersea strategic force (at least in theory) magnify the relative importance of SSBNs vis-à-vis missile defense. A

ballistic-missile submarine distinguishes itself even from a road- or rail-
mobile ICBM by its stealth and unlimited mobility and endurance, which
generate virtually infinite possibilities in terms of launch locations. According to Jing-dong Yuan, "Missile defense would make submarines more attractive as a means of increasing missile survivability and for launching from
locations and depressed trajectories where missile defenses have limited coverage."[49] Such advantages would severely strain the ability of a missile defense
system to gather cuing data, to track, and to engage a launch. Indeed, for at
least the next two decades, missile defense as currently conceived will have
no answer to a capable SSBN patrolling the open ocean.[50] The survivability of SSBNs would also reduce temptations for Beijing to adopt land-based
postures and policies that undermine crisis stability and escalation control,
including increased dispersion and decentralized command and control.

However, the persuasiveness of abstract operational benefits of an
undersea strategic force will not likely convince the Chinese leadership to
lean decisively in favor of SSBNs over ICBMs. Foremost in the thinking of
any political leadership is command and control of its nuclear arsenal. It is
unclear whether Beijing would be willing to delegate operational control of a
nuclear-armed submarine to a tactical commander. Practical considerations,
such as technical feasibility and steep financial costs, could impose burdens
that the PRC may be unwilling to carry. The enormous technological, scientific, and engineering challenges of building an SSBN are already well documented.[51] The very troubled history of the first-generation Xia-class SSBN
is a testament to the tremendous hurdles that the Chinese had to overcome
to master a craft involving extraordinarily high barriers to entry. In terms
of costs, the price tags of modern U.S. SSBNs provide a rough sense of the
financial liabilities that Beijing confronts. The average per unit cost of an
Ohio-class SSBN, measured over ten years from 1981 to 1991, was an estimated $1.2 billion in 1994 dollar terms.[52] Relying on similar estimates of U.S.
expenditures on SSBNs and SSNs, Chinese observers have also commented
on the prohibitive costs of nuclear-powered submarines.[53] Land basing, then,
still appears to have significant financial advantages.

Finally, the attractiveness of SLBMs also depends in part on whether
futuristic concepts for sea-based boost-phase missile defenses can be translated into reality. In reference to potential effects that such a capability might
have on Russia's undersea strategic forces, one study notes, "a sea-based
boost-phase system would potentially threaten Russia's submarine-launched
deterrent, *assuming a capability existed to estimate the general location of the
submarine* (emphasis added)."[54] However, the prospects for such a develop-

ment remain distant as this program is still in the conceptual stages. According to one report, even a primitive prototype of a sea-based boost-phase missile-defense system is not expected until 2015 at the earliest.[55] Given the long timelines involved, speculation concerning how China might respond to a distant capability is probably not currently a useful exercise.[56]

In theory, a relatively modest number of survivable ICBMs and SSBNs should reduce the probability that "bean counting" would prompt U.S. responses that could be conducive to competition. In other words, Beijing will likely favor configurations that demonstrate restraint in order to maintain a stable deterrent relationship with Washington. Incremental expansions would also restore Chinese confidence in the uncertainty principle of its nuclear doctrine. However, accurately measuring China's quantitative ceiling of ICBMs and SLBMs that would prevent countervailing U.S. responses is a delicate affair. According to one analysis based on numerous interviews with Chinese strategists, even a moderate response to BMD would likely involve as much as a tenfold jump in the number of China's strategic missiles or warheads.[57] Such a dramatic increase would likely raise concerns in Washington, even if the United States enjoyed commanding quantitative and qualitative advantages over China's nuclear arsenal.[58] While a classic arms race resembling the Cold War would not ensue as a result of such a shift in the nuclear balance, it is unlikely that U.S. defense planners would respond passively to the expected orders of magnitude increases in the Chinese nuclear inventory.[59]

Several scenarios are conceivable as the PRC meets the BMD challenge. If Beijing is willing to engage in transparency measures (hitherto absent in its current posture) to reassure Washington, then the two sides might be able to avoid the types of overt rivalry that characterized the Cold War. Alternatively, a significant PRC response in securing a credible second strike might be sufficient to demonstrate the futility of BMD in negating China's deterrent. In other words, Beijing could make good its promises to counter missile defense. It is possible that China would pursue both options—a buildup combined with enhanced openness about its nuclear doctrine and force structure—to preclude costly competition with the United States.

In any event, the potential role of the PRC's undersea strategic forces would only be one among many factors in Beijing's calculus as it considers a range of options to defeat BMD. At present, the expected number of Chinese SSBNs remains a subject of contention. The available literature has provided disparate estimates concerning the number of SSBNs that the Chinese plan to, or will be able to, build. One report carefully hedges its prediction that a dozen JL-2 SLBMs would be available by 2005 with a caveat that the missiles' operational status would depend on the uncertain production schedule of the Type 094.[60] A more conservative assessment of China's strategic forces postulates that the first ballistic-missile submarine will not be in service before 2010.[61] Similarly, the U.S. intelligence community and the Pentagon believe that both the JL-2 ballistic missiles and the strategic nuclear submarine will not enter service until the end of the decade.[62] In contrast, two U.S. analysts cite sources predicting the availability of two to three strategic submarines by 2010.[63] Another analyst projects five to six vessels over the next five years.[64] Jane's speculates that China will ultimately build four to six Type 094 submarines.[65] Another study cites both Chinese and Russian sources that place the final numbers of SSBNs at twelve.[66] The degree of uncertainty over the operational status of the Type 094 was on full public display in Taiwan as politicians openly disputed the veracity of the National Security Bureau's intelligence report, which claimed that the Type 094 had completed sea trials and would be in service in the near future.[67] Simply put, the future size of the fleet is still anybody's guess.

Operational Implications

How might China respond specifically in the operational realm to an effective missile defense system? Recently, speculation concerning the logic of a bastion strategy for China has emerged among U.S. analysts.[68] China could seek to replicate the Soviet Union's experience by exploiting the geographical features of the mainland coastline to its advantage.[69] Beijing could concentrate its SSBNs within the protective confines of the Bohai and Yellow Seas.[70] Nuclear attack submarines, shore-based fighter aircraft, and surface combatants could be poised as "palace guards" to quickly respond against hostile forces seeking to hold China's SSBNs at risk. As an alternative to the bastion strategy, the strategic submarines could operate more freely along China's long coastline under the protective cover of naval and land-based aviation forces on the mainland. One analyst speculates that China could deploy its SSBNs to the South China Sea, enabling the submarines to slip into deeper waters.[71] More ambitiously, China could deploy its submarines out to the Pacific in forays reminiscent of the U.S.-Soviet undersea competition during the Cold War.

Each of these options accrues certain benefits and incurs different types of costs. On the one hand, the bastion approach provides sanctuaries within which high-value SSBNs can operate. In theory, sea- and shore-based assets would be able to identify and hold at bay hostile forces operating near or in the Bohai/Yellow Sea. Moreover, the shallowness and the complex acoustic environment of littoral waters would pose serious challenges to high-speed American hunter-killer submarines designed for Cold War-era open ocean operations. On the other hand, a bastion strategy would 1) constrain patrol patterns; 2) forego the inherent stealth and mobility of an SSBN; and 3) limit targeting options (assuming that the JL-2's expected range is eight thousand kilometers). In other words, the confined operational space and shallowness of the Bohai/Yellow Sea area could create equally unfavorable conditions for a Chinese SSBN. If the Soviet experiences were any guide, China would have to build a large multidimensional conventional force to protect the SSBNs within the bastion and to break out of it should hostile forces seek to bottle up and hunt down the undersea strategic forces. The main risk is that an overinvestment in protecting its SSBN forces could detract from Beijing's broader maritime priorities, including nearer-term contingencies related to Taiwan.[72]

The more expansive options from coastal to open ocean patrols increase Chinese options in several ways. Recent studies have postulated that China has already embarked on an ambitious plan to create "contested zones" along its maritime periphery.[73] Premised on the concept of sea denial, Beijing would arrange a formidable power-projection force capable of exercising local superiority roughly within the first island chain stretching from the Japanese archipelago to the northern Philippines. Under this scenario, China might be confident enough to permit SSBN patrols along China's long coastline, particularly in the Bohai, Yellow, East China, and South China Seas, as well as the Taiwan Strait. Given that China confronts several deterrent relationships in Asia, including India, one analysis argues that the presence of SSBNs in the South China Sea would help shore up its deterrent on the southern flank.[74] Forward patrols would also force the United States to devote more of its hunter-killers to shadow and track Chinese submarines in different subtheaters of Asian waters, thereby serving to tie down American SSNs that might otherwise be available for a Taiwan or another contingency.

In the late 1980s, some U.S. analysts speculated that the Soviets might reverse its retreat into the bastion areas and patrol closer to American shores. Observers believed that Soviet concerns about the Reagan administration's Strategic Defense Initiative could trigger such a breakout.[75] As noted above, the depressed trajectory of SLBMs reduces vulnerabilities to midcourse missile defenses and significantly stresses the response times of any BMD system. These operational advantages may have been behind the speculations about a potential Soviet reorientation. Furthermore, assuming that China can develop very capable and quiet submarines, Chinese patrols in the Pacific would pose the greatest challenges to U.S. defenders seeking to keep track of and to trail lurking SSBNs. It is therefore possible that China might be tempted to employ open ocean patrols to impose additional stress on U.S. missile defense systems, not to mention antisubmarine warfare (ASW) forces.

On the other hand, some real operational risks would restrain Chinese SSBN patrol patterns beyond coastal waters. Of greatest concern, projecting submarine forces beyond the mainland littoral would increase exposure to U.S. and allied ASW.[76] Throughout the Cold War, the United States developed extensive and highly effective undersea detection networks—most notably the Sound Surveillance System (SOSUS)—to track the location of Soviet submarines. In the Pacific theater, U.S. submarines aided by SOSUS monitored every movement of Soviet SSBNs in waters off the Kamchatka Peninsula. In the 1980s, American and Japanese naval forces jointly perfected the art of ASW and cooperated closely to bottle up Soviet forces operating in the seas of Okhostk and Japan. These "legacy" systems and well-developed tactics could be effortlessly applied to Chinese SSBNs. For instance, the intrusion of a Han-class SSN into Japanese territorial waters and the Maritime Self-Defense Forces' (MSDF) subsequent tracking of the vessel demonstrated Tokyo's relatively high levels of readiness in ASW operations. Remarking upon the incident, a former chief of staff of the MSDF boasted that Chinese submarines seeking to slip into deeper waters of the Pacific via the Ryukyu island chain, north and south of Taiwan, or the Bashi (Luzon) Strait would not be able to escape U.S. and Japanese detection.[77]

Given such potent risks, China would probably avoid blue-water patrols especially during the initial stages of deployment, when training, tactical skills, and doctrine are still immature.[78] Additionally, Beijing would not likely opt for forward patrols until a larger fleet (assuming that the PRC is willing or able to pay for such an expensive project) eases attrition concerns. Politically, patrols in the Pacific could prove highly provocative to the United States and would almost certainly stimulate competitive responses. Compared against the collapse of Russian deterrent patrols in the Pacific theater since the end of the Cold War, China's entry into blue waters would likely be perceived as a dramatic change in the threat environment.

The more modest patrol option in the South China Sea also poses problems. Large portions of this body of water are relatively shallow. The principal target for an SSBN in the South China Sea would presumably be India, and could be viewed as a diversion from primary deterrent missions related to the United States. Unless the range of the JL-2 is sufficient to reach the continental United Sates from that location, operating further from American shores may be deemed counterproductive.

Until China builds a sizable number of vessels to permit secondary roles for its SSBN fleet, Beijing is not likely to squander away its precious few assets. These constraining factors suggest that if China chooses to expand submarine deployment patterns, it will probably be sequential and incremental. Beijing would likely favor protection over effectiveness during the early phases of SSBN deployment and would thus rely on some type of bastion strategy. Over time, if sufficient numbers of SSBNs are constructed and the vessels are operationally capable of extended patrols far beyond the Chinese coastline, then China might be willing to relax its protectiveness and permit more forward patrols.

The assessment above suggests that most cost-benefit analyses at the operational level are not directly tied to China's concerns about BMD. Any meaningful offense-defense racing is a very distant proposition at which point Beijing may possess alternative countermeasures to defeat missile defense.[79] Even if the PRC is tempted in the near term to undermine the effectiveness of U.S. BMD with open ocean patrols, significant operational risks to the emerging fleet would militate against power projection into the Pacific. Most importantly, assessments about patrol options require a better appreciation for the SSBN fleet's place within China's broader maritime strategy.

Future Sources of Doctrinal Change

The above analysis outlines how a restrained Chinese nuclear posture could lead to a relatively stable offense-defense dynamic between Beijing and Washington over the next decade. Nevertheless, it is worth exploring how China's willingness to retain its minimum deterrence posture could come under significant pressure in the future. Identifying such sources of change may help both sides to avoid crossing red lines that might fuel temptations to engage in nuclear competition.

First, China's ongoing refusal to acknowledge the utility of an adversary's nuclear first-strike option, which is central to the concept of minimum deterrence, depends in part on whether the United States wants to be submitted to the logic of assured (but minimal) retaliation vis-à-vis China. There is evidence that some U.S. strategists have dismissed such a mutual vulnerability, asserting that the United States should direct its BMD specifically to negate China's deterrent.[80] Reflecting such an attitude, the current U.S. National Security Council Advisor has previously argued that should Beijing continue to exhibit hostile intent toward Washington, particularly with regard to Taiwan, then the United States "may simply have no choice" but build defenses against China.[81] If Washington overtly seeks to deny China a retaliatory option, then Beijing will almost certainly respond with a larger and faster buildup. The consequences of such an offense-defense arms race would be unwelcome, especially for the United States, because the far lower costs of penetrating missile defenses than improving them would favor China's strategic position.

Second, China's more leisurely approach to its nuclear posture could come under strain with the emergence of strategic technical surprises. As noted above, the expected performance of the exo-atmospheric, hit-to-kill, ground-based missile defense system currently deployed to defend the U.S. homeland will not severely shake China's deterrent calculus. It is conceivable (although highly improbable in the near term) that the advent of space-based lasers and other advanced boost-phase capabilities could radically reshape China's outlook.[82] The track record of the missile defense program to date suggests that such radical breakthroughs are highly unlikely over the next decade. But, should such a technological contest emerge, then SSBNs might emerge as one among many operationally useful answers to BMD. As mentioned above, cheaper countermeasures, alternative delivery systems, and quantitative increases would also provide a more diverse and credible counter to advanced missile defenses.[83]

Third, the reconnaissance-precision strike complex that the United States boasts could alter China's exclusively retaliatory posture. In July 2005, Major General Zhu Chenghu caused a sensation when he declared to the foreign press that, "If the Americans draw their missiles and position-guided ammunition onto the target zone on China's territory, I think we will have to respond with nuclear weapons." He argued that if China faced the prospect of defeat in a conventional conflict over Taiwan, then Beijing would have no choice but to conduct a preemptive nuclear strike against American cities. Similarly, in a candid assessment of how Chinese calculations might change, Shen Dingli argues that precision conventional strikes against China's nuclear forces during a Taiwan contingency could force Beijing to abandon its no-first-use pledge. He asserts that, "If China's conventional forces are devastated, and if Taiwan takes the opportunity to declare de jure independence, it is inconceivable that China would allow its nuclear weapons to be destroyed by a precision attack with conventional munitions, rather than use them as true means of deterrence."[84] In other words, if the effects of America's conventional attacks are indistinguishable from a disarming nuclear strike, then China's no-first-use policy would quite sensibly become untenable.[85] Shen's conclusion seems consistent with China's long-standing aversion to nuclear blackmail.

In sum, the future state of overall Sino-U.S. relations, technological change, and calculations about a Taiwan contingency could all interact to lift China's restraint. This could in turn lead to more competitive interactions, including elevating the significance of the SSBN program.

Conclusion

Despite the apparent theoretical and political character of Chinese objections to BMD, there is genuine merit to Beijing's concerns stemming in part from deeply embedded fears of nuclear coercion. As such, China will almost certainly respond to missile defenses with qualitative and quantitative solutions to shore up the credibility of its modest second-strike deterrent. In particular, a survivable ballistic-missile submarine would bolster, if not secure, Chinese confidence in the offense-dominant nuclear regime. At the same time, Beijing will likely modernize and build up its nuclear forces with restraint, not least because the technological realities confronting missile defense planners suggest that many of the triggering points for a major Chinese expansion lie far in the future.

The analysis above also underscores how little China watchers know about the Chinese nuclear program. This basic methodological challenge limits any attempt to discern how the PRC will respond specifically to missile defense. To further complicate matters, the potential impact that missile defense will have on decisions concerning the future of the SSBN fleet is less direct and not immediately apparent. Conversely, one would be hard pressed to directly link China's behavior related to its undersea strategic forces to developments in U.S. BMD, at least at this point. Whether missile defense will compel the PRC to adopt a bastion strategy or a much higher tempo of SSBN patrols in the Pacific remains unknowable. There are simply too many intervening variables that obscure the correlations between the two.

Broader internal and external factors are more likely to determine the future course of China's SSBN strategy. Domestic debates and decisions about nuclear doctrine are key arbiters of Beijing's undersea strategic posture. Such discourse is in turn subject to broader strategic/political considerations and other internal determinants, including technological feasibility, resource availability, bureaucratic/interservice politics, and confidence among Chinese leaders to decentralize command and control. The way in which the broader Sino-U.S. relationship evolves will also determine Chinese thinking about nuclear doctrine and associated force structures. If bilateral relations deteriorate significantly and irreparably, then a fundamental reassessment of China's nuclear posture could very well become necessary.

On the other hand, fears that an expanded arsenal would unnecessarily alarm Beijing's neighbors and the United States and risk triggering balancing behavior would tend to restrain decisions about a more expansive doctrine. As Paul Godwin notes, "whereas limited deterrence may be attractive to analysts engaged in abstract assessments of nuclear doctrine and strategy, the potential political costs could be viewed as outweighing whatever increases in confidence this nuclear posture may prove."[86] For instance, regional hostilities resulting from the PRC's nuclear buildup would severely set back China's ongoing efforts to promote the concept of its peaceful rise.

Politics, then, will trump the effects of emerging offense-defense interactions in military technology. In a cautionary tale about the dangers of technological determinism, Stephen Cimbala states, "deterrence and stability are politically driven concepts, and states that are determined to have a war will find ways to do so, regardless of the shifting sands of technology competition."[87] Conversely, two countries determined not to fight each other will almost certainly negate the political spillover effects of a technological race. In other words, the broader state of Sino-U.S. relations will dictate how each responds to the technical-military developments of the other. While mutual ambivalence continues to characterize bilateral ties, as long as Washington and Beijing refuse a Cold War-style rivalry, radical shifts in China's nuclear posture are not likely. Political calculations on both sides of the Pacific, then, will determine the doctrines that in turn shape the future strategy for China's undersea strategic forces.

Notes

1. Ann Scott Tyson, "U.S. Missile Defense Being Expanded, General Says," *Washington Post*, July 22, 2005, 10.

2. In May 2001, Assistant Secretary of State for East Asian and Pacific Affairs James Kelly reassured the Chinese leadership about U.S. intentions over missile defense. In his departure statement, Kelly explained, "I stressed that our plans for a missile defense system would not be a threat to China. Rather, our approaches are intended

to defend against threats or attacks from rogue states as well as from accidental and unauthorized launches." For the full text of Kelly's statement, see http://hongkong .usconsulate.gov/uscn/state/2001/051601.htm.

3. According to the MDA's full transcript, Obering states, "We are not desiring to go against a Chinese threat, but we need to, in our development program, to address the Chinese capabilities, because that's prudent, because often times technologies that are developed by one country find their way into other nations, so we need to be cognizant of that . . . and so we are not developing a missile defense for the Chinese, but we need to be cognizant of that, and keep track of their development program."

4. For an early assessment of China's responses to BMD during this period, see Michael McDevitt, "Beijing's Bind," *Washington Quarterly* 23, no. 3 (Summer 2000): 177–86.

5. See Shen Dingli, "China's Evaluation of the Adjustment to U.S. Security Policy Since September 11, 2001," *Defense and Security Analysis* 19, no. 4 (December 2003): 321.

6. For an estimate of China's nuclear forces based strictly on publicly available U.S. intelligence sources, see Jeffrey Lewis, "The Ambiguous Arsenal," *Bulletin of Atomic Scientists* 61, no. 3 (May/June 2005): 52–59. The author argues that the modest force structure strongly suggests that China remains tied to the philosophy of maintaining a "minimum means of reprisal" for its deterrent posture. The rest of the ICBM arsenal is deployed in hardened silos, which are presumably identifiable through national technical means.

7. Gen. Eugene Habiger (ret.), former head of the U.S. Strategic Command, asserted that "several tens of hours" would be required for the Chinese to prepare missile launches. Eugene Habiger, "Problems and Prospects of New Alaska Missile Interceptor Site," Presentation at the Carnegie Endowment for International Peace, February 20, 2004.

8. Memories of nuclear blackmail (*he ezha*) during the Cold War remain an integral part of the leadership's collective psyche. As such, a return to such vulnerability is deemed unacceptable. For a sense of China's historical perspective on *he ezha* (核讹诈), see You Guangrong, Ge Hanyi, and Zhou Ying (游光荣、葛含益、周莺), "Liangdan Yixing de Yenzhi ji Qidui Xinshiqi Wuqi Zhuangbei Jianshe de Qishi (两弹一星的研制及其对新时期　武器装备建设的启示)," *Zhongguo Junshi Kexue* (中国军事科学) 16, no. 6 (2003): 28.

9. The survivability of the DF-31s will depend on whether the PRC permits active patrols. It is possible for China to choose a more "recessed" posture. Consistent with its current low levels of readiness, the missiles and the transporters could be stored separately and readied for mating and deployment in the event of a crisis.

10. Assuming that China possesses small, lightweight warheads, the DF-31 could be armed with multiple reentry vehicles. A modified version, the DF-31A with ten-to-fourteen-thousand-kilometer range, will reportedly enter service within the decade.

11. It is important to note that the DF-31 was originally designed to replace the DF-4s in order to modernize its deterrent against the Soviet Union, and, possibly, India. The range and basing locations appear to validate China's initial intent. Moreover, the DF-31s are at most capable of reaching Hawaii, Alaska, and perhaps portions of the U.S. West Coast. In this context, it is not at all clear whether the DF-31 substantially changes the Sino-U.S. deterrent relationship.

12. The International Institute for Strategic Studies (IISS), *The Military Balance 2004–2005*, (London: Oxford University Press, October 2004), 170. IISS began reporting the operational status of the DF-31s in its October 2001 issue of the *Military Balance*. The Stockholm International Peace Research Institute (SIPRI) draws on the IISS report in its analysis of China's nuclear forces. See, SIPRI, *SIPRI Yearbook 2005: Armaments, Disarmament and International Security* (London: Oxford University Press, 2005), 592.

13. Duncan Lennox, ed. *Jane's Strategic Weapon Systems* (Surrey, U.K.: Jane's Information Group, January 2006), 21. Another Jane's database reports a lower figure of eight to twelve DF-31s in service. See Jane's Sentinel, *Security Assessment: China and Northeast Asia*, (Surrey, U.K.: Jane's Information Group, 2005), 96.

14. Department of Defense, *Annual Report to Congress: The Military Power of the People's Republic of China* (Washington D.C., Department of Defense, July 2005), 28.

15. Lowell Jacoby, *Current and Projected National Security Threats to the United States*, Statement for the Record, Senate Select Intelligence Committee, February 16, 2005, 11.

16. Liu Xuecheng, "Missile Control and Missile Defense: A Chinese Perspective," workshop paper presented at the Institute of International Studies, Fudan University, Shanghai, July 16–18, 2004, 6.

17. For a fairly typical Chinese interpretation of Japan's motives for pursuing missile defense, see Li Wensheng and Zhang Huiying, [李文盛, 张慧英], "Toutian Xianjing: Toushi Riben Fan Dandao Daodan Xitong Jihua [偷天陷阱 透视日本反弹道导弹系统计划]," *Bingqi Zhishi* [兵器知识] 10, no. 192 (October 2003): 8–12.

18. Kori Urayama, "China Debates Missile Defence," *Survival* 46, no. 2 (Summer 2004): 126.

19. One Chinese analysis calculates that Taiwan's point defenses, such as the Patriot PAC-2 batteries, can at most intercept forty incoming ballistic missiles. The report confidently asserts that Taiwan would be unable to cope with the waves of Chinese attacks involving hundreds of ballistic missiles. Zheng Zhiren [郑治仁], "Taiwan Fan Dandao Daodan Fangyu Xitong, [台湾反弹道导弹防御系统]," *Bingqi Zhishi* 10, no. 216 (October 2005): 57.

20. For an in-depth analysis of the shift in China's diplomatic posture, see Brad Roberts, *China and Ballistic Missile: 1955 to 2002 and Beyond* (Alexandria, Va.: Institute for Defense Analyses, September 2003), 32–34.

21. Some U.S. analysts have concluded that missile defense has no other real purpose except to blunt China's deterrent. For a polemical study on this perspective, see James J. Hentz, "The Paradox of Instability and Stability: United States 'Primacy,'

China, and the National Missile Defense Debate," *Defense and Security Analysis* 19, no. 3 (September 2003): 293–99.

22. Tian Jingmei, "The Bush Administration's Nuclear Strategy and Its Implications for China's Security," Working Paper, Project on Peace and Cooperation in the Asia-Pacific Region, Center for International Security and Cooperation, Stanford University, March 2003, 15.

23. David M. Finkelstein, "National Missile Defense and China's Current Security Perceptions," in *China and Missile Defense: Managing U.S.-PRC Strategic Relations*, ed. Alan D. Romberg and Michael McDevitt (Washington, D.C.: The Henry L. Stimson Center, 2003), 41.

24. Li Bin, Zhou Baogen, and Liu Zhiwei, "China Will Have to Respond," *Bulletin of Atomic Scientists* 57, no. 6 (November/December 2001): 25–28.

25. Li Bin, "The Effects of NMD on Chinese Strategy," *Jane's Intelligence Review*, March 7, 2001.

26. "The Impact of Missile Defence in Asia: The Dilemmas of Transition," *Strategic Comments* 10, Issue 6, International Institute for Strategic Studies (August 1, 2004).

27. Julian Pamore, "U.S. Ballistic Missile Defense and China," *Defense and Security Analysis* 19, no. 4 (December 2003): 373.

28. Ambassador Sha Zukang, the former Director-General of the Foreign Ministry's Department of Arms Control, underscored China's predicament. He observed that the Bush administration (in contrast to its predecessor) provided no technical information of its BMD system to the Chinese side. Transcript of Ambassador Sha Zukang's Briefing on Missile Defense Issue, Beijing, March 14, 2001 at http://www.fmprc.gov.cn/eng/wjb/zzjg/jks/cjjk/2622/t15417.htm#.

29. For an excellent analysis of the Bush administration's approach to missile defense, see Steven A. Hildreth, *Missile Defense: The Current Debate* (Washington, D.C.: Congressional Research Service, July 19, 2005).

30. During this period (when the operational status of the DF-31s was still largely in doubt) many observers believed that even the limited National Missile Defense system envisioned by the Clinton administration would have required a corresponding expansion of China's force structure. It was argued that in the absence of a buildup the few remaining Chinese ICBMs that managed to survive a disarming first strike would have been neutralized by the U.S. BMD.

31. For a scathing critique of the current missile defense plan, see Lisbeth Gronlund, "Fire, Aim, Ready," *The Bulletin of Atomic Scientists* 61, no. 5 (September/October 2005): 67–68.

32. See Missile Defense Agency New Release, "Missile Defense Flight Test Successfully Completed," December 13, 2005 at http://www.mda.mil. By contrast, theater-level, sea-based missile defenses, designed to intercept short- to intermediate-range ballistic missiles, have enjoyed far more successes. Since early 2002, five of six tests of the Standard Missile 3 resulted in the interception of the target.

33. Steven A. Hildreth, *Missile Defense: The Current Debate*, 14.

34. For example, premised on the "test as you fly, fly as you test" standard, MDA deployed eight ground-based interceptors in Alaska and California in September 2004 despite doubts about their actual effectiveness. Presumably, improved interceptors will replace these early versions as they become available.

35. For an analysis of how capabilities-based planning impacts the BMD acquisition strategy, see David C. Isby and Timothy Bigss, "Enabling Defense Transformation: Network-Centric Warfare and Ballistic Missile Defense," *Comparative Strategy* 22, Issue 4 (October 2003): 325–34.

36. For instance, an article cites U.S. official and independent reports on the technical difficulties of the proposed BMD. Zhong Jianye [钟建业], "Shijie Daodan Fangyu zai 2003-nian [世界导弹防御在2003年]," *Bingqi Zhishi* 3, no. 197 (March 2004): 42. One analyst describes the test record of the ground-based missile defense system as a "great failure." But the author is convinced that the United States will press ahead regardless of the difficulties that the program has been experiencing. Le Mengwen [李梦汶], "Lingren Youyu: GMD de Shibai [令人忧郁 GMD的失败]," *Bingqi Zhishi* 2, no. 208 (February 2005): 16–20. Two Chinese observers question the operational capability of what they consider hastily deployed BMDs in 2004. They state, "In reality, America's first phase of BMD deployment embodies far greater political purpose than military meaning while its military meaning far exceeds its technical purpose." Li Wensheng and Sun Shihong [李文盛 孙世红], "2004 Jieduan Toushi Meiguo Xinban Daodan Fangyu Xitong [2004 阶段 透视美国新版导弹防御系统]," *Bingqi Zhishi* 1, no. 207 (January 2005): 29.

37. Eric A. McVadon, "Chinese Reaction to New U.S. Initiatives on Missile Defense," in *China's Growing Military Power: Perspectives on Security, Ballistic Missiles, and Conventional Capabilities*, ed. Andrew Scobell and Larry M. Wortzel (Carlisle Barracks, Pa.: Strategic Studies, September 2002), 177. This study was based on extensive interviews of Chinese scholars, strategists, and military officers in late 2001.

38. Brad Roberts, "China and Ballistic Missile Defense," 29.

39. The "peaceful rise" hypothesis rests on several assumptions and projections. First, China needs a stable external environment to develop its economy. Second, Beijing faces severe internal problems that will distract it from hegemonic ambitions. Third, China's rise to a "middle rung of advanced nations" will take twenty-five to thirty-five years, by which time the country will be fully integrated into the international system. Finally, China's military growth is proportionate to the vastness of the country in terms of both geography and population. See Zheng Bijian, "China's 'Peaceful Rise' to Great-Power Status," *Foreign Affairs* 84, no. 5 (September/October 2005): 18–24. Zheng, the architect of the peaceful-rise theory, is a close advisor to Chinese President Hu Jintao.

40. For the most widely cited work on this issue, see Alastair Iain Johnston, "China's New 'Old Thinking': The Concept of Limited Deterrence," *International Security* 20, no. 3 (Winter 1995/96).

41. Even assuming that the Chinese have deployed up to two brigades of DF-31s, Beijing would still lack the necessary quantity of missiles to substantially change

the strategic deterrence equation vis-à-vis the United States. China's enhanced second-strike capabilities would still likely be confined to countervalue (city busting) targets. It is doubtful that a handful of mobile ICBMs would enable Beijing to credibly conduct counterforce strikes in a bid to engage in escalation dominance. A far larger force, one that lies much farther in the future, would be required for such a fundamental doctrinal shift.

42. For a compelling argument on the durability of China's minimum deterrence posture, see Sun Xiangli, "Analysis of China's Nuclear Strategy," *China Security* 1 (Autumn 2005): 23–27.

43. Demetri Sevastopulo, "China Rejects Rumsfeld Spending Claim," *Financial Times*, October 19, 2005.

44. Bates Gill, James Mulvenon, and Mark Stokes, "The Chinese Second Artillery Corps: Transition to Credible Deterrence," in *The People's Liberation Army as an Organization: Reference Volume v 1.0*, ed. James C. Mulvenon and Andrew N. D. Yang (Washington, D.C.: RAND, 2001), 557.

45. This assumption does not imply any permanence to China's strategic nuclear posture. Should circumstances (such as a radical reordering of the international security environment) warrant, China would certainly harness the necessary political will and resources to depart from minimum deterrence.

46. The ability of the ICBMs to fully exploit China's strategic depth would depend on whether the country's road networks are extensive enough and robust enough to support the mass of the DF-31.

47. For an analysis of the possible ranges of Chinese BMD countermeasures, see Andrew S. Erickson, "Chinese BMD Countermeasures: Breaching America's Great Wall in Space?" in *China's Nuclear Force Modernization*, ed. Lyle J. Goldstein with Andrew Erickson (Newport, R.I.: Naval War College, 2005), 77–88. For a Chinese overview of ballistic missile decoy technologies, see Li Wensheng [李文盛], "Manhua Zhanlue Dandao Daodan Youer Jishu [漫话战略弹道导弹诱饵技术]," *Bingqi Zhishi* 2, no. 208 (February 2005): 28–31.

48. Paul Godwin calls this qualitative and quantitative mix as "assured minimum deterrence." His assessment dovetails with conclusions drawn by Gill, Mulvenon, and Stokes (cited above) that the second-generation strategic weaponry would finally (after decades of "incredible" deterrence) endow China with a credible retaliatory capability. Paul H. B. Godwin, "Potential Chinese Responses to U.S. Ballistic Missile Defense," in *China and Missile Defense: Managing U.S.-PRC Strategic Relations*, ed. Alan D. Romberg and Michael McDevitt (Washington, D.C.: The Henry L. Stimson Center, 2003), 66–67.

49. Jing-dong Yuan, "Chinese Responses to U.S. Missile Defenses," *Nonproliferation Review* 10, no. 1 (Spring 2003): 89.

50. To illustrate the SSBN challenge, consider the Global Protection Against Limited Strikes (GPALS) missile defense program introduced in the early 1990s. A key component of GPALS involved the now-abandoned Brilliant Pebbles (BP), the most futuristic space-based concept that emerged in the 1980s and survived into the early

1990s. Even such an advanced capability (assuming that it was technically feasible and one that was far more ambitious than those being considered today) would have been hard pressed to deal with SLBMs. A longtime advocate of BP, Gregory Canavan, acknowledges that a salvo launch from a Typhoon-class SSBN near U.S. shores would severely stress GPALS. See Gregory H. Canavan, *Missile Defense for the 21st Century* (Washington, D.C.: Heritage Foundation, 2003), 48. This asymmetry in capability suggests that, for the time being, the only effective response to a capable Chinese SSBN is the employment of traditional antisubmarine warfare assets, particularly hunter-killer nuclear attack submarines (SSNs).

51. John Wilson Lewis and Xue Litai, *China's Strategic Seapower: The Politics of Force Modernization in the Nuclear Age* (Stanford, Calif.: Stanford University Press, 1994).

52. This study acknowledges cost differentials between two very different economies, including calculations of purchasing power parity. But the figures are suggestive. Ted Nicholas and Rita Rossi, *U.S. Weapons Systems Costs, 1994* (Fountain Valley, Calif.: Data Search Associates, April 1994), 6–10. This figure does not include the costs of research, development, training, and education, or the price of SLBMs prior to and during construction of each SSBN. A more recent (although not entirely comparable) program, the new *Virginia*-class SSN is also instructive of the escalating costs of big-ticket defense items for a modern military. The average unit cost is estimated at $2.5 billion. Ted Nicholas and Rita Rossi, *U.S. Weapons Systems Costs, 1994*, 6–9.

53. According to an anonymous PLA naval officer interviewed for a report, the cost of a nuclear submarine is simply too high for China. He observes, "the price of one nuclear submarine can buy several, even more than ten, conventional submarines. . . . As a developing country, our nation's military budget is still quite low, and thus the size of the navy's nuclear submarine fleet can only be maintained at a basic scale (jiben gueimo [基本规模])." See "Gangtie Shayu (钢铁鲨鱼)," *Sanlian Shenhuo Zhoukan* (三联生活周刊) 20 (May 19, 2003): 29–30.

54. Hans Binnendijk and George Stewart, "Toward Missile Defense from the Sea," in *Contemporary Nuclear Debates: Missile Defense, Arms Control, and Arms Races in the Twenty-first Century*, ed. Alexander T. J. Lennon (Washington, D.C.: MIT Press, 2002), 56.

55. Evan S. Medeiros, *Ballistic Missile Defense and Northeast Asian Security* (Monterey, Calif.: Monterey Institute of International Studies, 2001), 4. For an in-depth critique of the viability of sea-based boost-phase missile defense, see Charles V. Pena, "From the Sea: National Missile Defense Is Neither Cheap Nor Easy," *Foreign Policy Brief*, no. 60, CATO Institute, September 6, 2000.

56. It is important to note that space-based capabilities are probably a mid-century proposition. By that time, a whole range of technological measures and countermeasures could be available to render this speculative exercise moot.

57. See Joanne Tompkins, "How U.S. Strategic Policy Is Changing China's Nuclear Plans," *Arms Control Today* (January/February 2003): 15. The ten-fold increase seems to be a reasonable estimate. The U.S. intelligence community projects Chi-

na's ICBMs to expand to seventy to one hundred by 2015. According to Michael McDevitt, China's nuclear forces will grow to those numbers regardless of U.S. missile defense plans. Michael McDevitt, "Missile Defense and U.S. Policy Options toward Beijing," 94. Depending on variations in the force mix, the expansion may not necessarily be "visible" in terms of the quantity of platforms. For instance, Beijing could add multiple warheads to its existing DF-5 ICBMs while holding down the numbers of DF-31s and JL-2s.

58. For instance, Washington's unwillingness to cut deeper into its nuclear arsenal in part reflects a fear that China may seek to "race to parity."

59. Despite U.S. nuclear superiority over China, Washington remains acutely aware of the PRC's nuclear modernization program and has provided explicit policy guidelines to put the Chinese deterrent at risk. See excerpts of the 2002 Nuclear Posture Review at http://www.globalsecurity.org/wmd/library/policy/dod/npr.htm. Indeed, America's evolving nuclear posture suggests that defense planners are looking to attain "absolute security" in its deterrent relations with Russia and China. According to a RAND study, major technological advances combined with the anticipated force structure of the U.S. nuclear arsenal suggest that the United States will be increasingly capable of executing a "war winning" strategy premised on devastatingly effective preemptive nuclear strikes to disarm the major powers. The report states: "What the planned force appears best suited to provide beyond the needs of traditional deterrence is a *preemptive counterforce capability against Russia and China*. Otherwise the numbers and the operating procedure simply do not add up." Glenn C. Buchan, David Matonick, Calvin Shipbaugh, and Richard Mesic, *Future Roles of U.S. Nuclear Forces: Implications for U.S. Strategy* (Santa Monica, Calif.: RAND, 2003), 92. In this broader context of U.S. nuclear strategy (and assuming that these analysts are right), it is hardly conceivable that U.S. defense planners would stand idly by as China builds up its arsenal.

60. Mark A. Stokes, "Chinese Ballistic Missile Forces in the Age of Global Missile Defense: Challenges and Responses," in *China's Growing Military Power: Perspectives on Security, Ballistic Missiles, and Conventional Capabilities*, ed. Andrew Scobell and Larry M. Wortzel (Carlisle Barracks, Pa.: Strategic Studies, September 2002), 144. Japan's *Yomiuri Shimbun* was the first to report an apparent successful test of the JL-2 in waters near Qingdao in June 2005. It remains unclear whether the missile was launched from the trial Golf-class submarine or the 094-type SSBN.

61. CFR Independent Task Force, *Chinese Military Power* (New York: Council on Foreign Relations, 2003), 52

62. According to the Director of the Defense Intelligence Agency, Lt. Gen. Michael D. Maples, "the 8,000+ kilometer range JL-2 . . . likely will be ready for deployment later this decade." See Michael D. Maples, *Current and Projected National Security Threats to the United States*, Statement for the Record, Senate Armed Services Committee, February 28, 2006, 11. The Pentagon's 2004 report on Chinese military states, "the JL-2 . . . will be deployed on a new ballistic missile submarine by decade's end." See Department of Defense, *Annual Report on the Military Power of the People's Republic of China*, (Washington, D.C.: Department of Defense, 2004), 37. The 2005 issue estimates that the JL-2 will be operational during the 2008–10 timeframe. See

Department of Defense, *Annual Report to Congress*, 28. According to a 1999 secret report titled *A Primer on the Future Threat, The Decades Ahead: 1999–2020*, the DIA estimated that China will have one new SSBN by 2020. Excerpted in Rowan Scarborough, *Rumsfeld's War: The Untold Story of America's Anti-Terrorist Commander* (New York: Regnery, 2004), 194–223.

63. Lyle Goldstein and William Murray, "China Emerges as a Maritime Power," *Jane's Intelligence Review* (October 2004): 35.

64. Richard Fisher, Jr., "Developing US-Chinese Nuclear Naval Competition in Asia," International Assessment and Strategy Center website, January 16, 2005 at http://www.strategycenter.net/research/pubID.60/pub_detail.asp.

65. Duncan Lennox, *Jane's Strategic Weapon Systems* (Surrey, U.K.: Jane's Information Group, July 2005), 38.

66. Lyle Goldstein and William Murray, "Undersea Dragons: China's Maturing Submarine Force," *International Security* 28, no. 4 (Spring 2004): 173.

67. Rich Chang, "Lawmakers Argue over Chinese Sub Intelligence Report," *Taipei Times*, October 14, 2005, 2.

68. Lyle Goldstein and William Murray, "China Emerges as a Maritime Power," 35. For other studies on the logic of a Chinese SSBN bastion sanctuary, see, for example, Kanwa Editorial Department, "Chinese Navy's Submarine Development Strategy," *Kanwa Defense Review* (July 1, 2005): 44–46, FBIS-CHI, CPP20050801000242. A Japanese analyst speculated that China is propping up North Korea for fear that a collapse scenario would harm Chinese SSBN deployment options in the Bohai Sea, which is flanked by the DPRK. See Junichi Abe, "Why China Does Not Want to See the Unification of the Korean Peninsula," *Sekai Shuho* (February 8, 2005): 54–55, FBIS, JPP20050203000035.

69. One Chinese analyst argues that geography is a major determinant of how countries design their SSBNs and associated deployment options. A long coastline directly facing the ocean and quick access to deep waters just off the shoreline are the ideal operational conditions for an SSBN. In an implicit reference to China, he observes that a country, whose long coastal waters are part of the continental shelf, may need to deploy submarines more than two hundred kilometers out to sea to find the necessary diving depth. He concludes that such geographic constraints would force the country to develop smaller SSBNs to operate in shallower sea lanes and harbors. See Wu Xie [吴谐], "Zhanlue Heqianting Sheji Fangan Jianxi [战略核潜艇设计方案简析]," *Bingqi Zhishi* 4, no. 198 (April 2004): 53.

70. It is worth noting that the Xia-class SSBN is based at the Jianggezhuang Submarine Base, fifteen miles east of Qingdao on the Yellow Sea. For satellite imagery of the Xia at Jianggezhuang, see Thomas B. Cochran, Matthew G. McKinzie, Robert S. Norris, Laura S. Harrison, and Hans M. Kristensen, "China's Nuclear Forces: The World's First Look at China's Underground Facilities for Nuclear Warheads," *Imaging Notes*, Winter 2006 at http://www.imagingnotes.com/go/page4a.php?menu_id=23. There is speculation that the Type 094 could be homeported at this facility, a location that might favor a bastion strategy.

71. Richard Fisher, Jr., "Developing US-Chinese Nuclear Naval Competition in Asia," International Assessment and Strategy Center, http://www.strategycenter.net/research/pubID.60/pub_detail.asp.

72. Chinese defense planners have devoted their attention (almost exclusively) to a Taiwan contingency since the 1995–96 missile crises. In this broader strategic context of a more urgent security challenge, it seems unlikely that Beijing would place SSBN protection ahead of another expected confrontation over Taiwan. At the same time, however, it is important to acknowledge that the maritime capabilities developed to protect SSBNs in a Bohai/Yellow Sea bastion might serve complimentary roles in a Taiwan Strait crisis or war. Further, an SSBN fleet could very well play a more direct role in a Taiwan scenario should Chinese nuclear deterrence and/or coercion enter the equation. For an abstract, generic analysis of how nuclear weapons can deter great power intervention on behalf of a client state, see Chang Ying (长缨), "Qiantan Heweishe de Liangge Zuoyong (浅谈核威慑的两个作用)," *Bingqi Zhishi* 4, no. 198 (April 2004): 51–52. Some U.S. analysts have speculated that an assured second-strike capability underwritten by a more survivable arsenal could embolden China to engage in nuclear brinkmanship, including a "demonstration shot" in-theater to dissuade U.S. and allied intervention in the strait. Intriguingly, one article describes China's SSBN as an "assassins mace" (shashoujian [杀手锏]) that can be employed to deter American and Japanese intervention in a cross-strait conflict. Gao Xintao (高新涛), Zhongguo Haijun Qianting Zhanlue (中国海军潜艇战略)," *Guang Jiao Jing* (广角镜) (January 16–February 15, 2005): 69.

73. Toshi Yoshihara and James Holmes, "Command of the Sea with Chinese Characteristics," *Orbis* 49, no. 4, (Fall 2005): 677–94.

74. Christopher McConnaughy, "China's Undersea Nuclear Deterrent: Will the U.S. Navy Be Ready?" in *China's Nuclear Force Modernization*, ed. Lyle J. Goldstein with Andrew Erickson (Newport, R.I.: Naval War College, 2005), 44.

75. Bryan Ranft and Geoffrey Till, *The Sea in Soviet Strategy*, 2nd ed. (Annapolis, Md.: Naval Institute Press, 1989), 194.

76. The Chinese are quite aware of the ASW challenge. The permanent homeporting of *Los Angeles*-class SSNs at Guam has not gone unnoticed in China. For an in-depth Chinese analysis of Guam's importance to America's security posture in Asia, see 李文盛 [Li Wensheng], "聚焦关岛" ["Focusing Guam"], *Bingqi Zhishi* 9, no. 203 (September 2004): 15–19. One Chinese author argues that the PLA Navy must acquire its own ASW platforms to respond to such a shift in U.S. naval posture in the Pacific. See Tai Feng (台风), "Does China Need Anti-Submarine Patrol Aircraft? (中国需要反潜艇巡逻机吗)" *Jianzai Wuqi* (舰戴武器) (March 1, 2005): 70–75.

77. Oga Ryohei, "What the PRC Submarine Force Is Aiming For," *Sekai no Kansen* (July 1, 2005): 96–101.

78. A Chinese analysis argues that SSBN open ocean patrols would not occur until the PLA Navy develops a more balanced force structure that included aircraft carriers. Strategic nuclear submarines would then be able to operate in blue waters under

the protective cover of carrier-based aviation units. "Heqianting yu Zhongguo Hai-jun," *Jianchuan Zhishi*, no. 306 (March 2005): 13.

79. For instance, the Chinese have devoted substantial energy into developing long-range (possibly nuclear-capable) cruise missiles that can be fired from surface combatants, manned or unmanned aircraft, or nuclear attack submarines. Given the long timelines involved to produce robust missile defenses, any of these developments are possible for the Chinese.

80. Robert A. Manning, Ronald Montaperto, and Brad Roberts, *China, Nuclear Weapons, and Arms Control* (New York: Council on Foreign Relations, 2000), 47.

81. Stephen J. Hadley, "A Call to Deploy," *The Washington Quarterly* 23, no. 3 (Summer 2000): 26.

82. For a range of potential technological breakthroughs in the future, see Stephen F. Cimbala, "Nuclear Weapons in the Twentieth Century: From Simplicity to Complexity," *Defense and Security Analysis* 21, no. 3 (September 2005): 279.

83. Some analysts have speculated that China might be able to develop and deploy crude but effective missile defenses against counterforce strikes to enhance Beijing's confidence in the survivability of its deterrent.

84. Shen Dingli, "Nuclear Deterrence in the 21st Century," *China Security* 1 (Autumn 2005): 13.

85. For an American analysis of this point, see James Mulvenon, "Missile Defenses and the Taiwan Scenario," in *China and Missile Defense: Managing U.S.-PRC Strategic Relations*, ed. Alan D. Romberg and Michael McDevitt (Washington, D.C.: The Henry L. Stimson Center, 2003), 58–60. The author postulates a thought-provoking scenario in which Taiwan unilaterally conducts offensive, conventional precision strikes against the mainland during a cross-strait conflict. Unable to determine the real source of these attacks, worst-case thinking could lead Beijing to mistakenly conclude that Washington was exercising its preemptive option to disarm Chinese nuclear forces. At this point in the crisis, the PRC would face the same type of decision-making crossroad that Zhu and Shen identified above.

86. Paul Godwin, "Potential Chinese Responses to U.S. Ballistic Missile Defense," 71.

87. Stephen Cimbala, "Nuclear Weapons in the Twenty-first Century," 280.

Michael McDevitt

Sea Denial with Chinese Characteristics

Introduction

RESEARCH SUGGESTS THAT THE LEADERSHIP of the People's Liberation Army (PLA) has no doubts about the sort of naval and air force they need to accomplish their national geostrategic objectives over the next two decades. In fact, the PLA has been uncharacteristically open about the importance of its naval and air forces, and therefore by implication its maritime strategy.

U.S. strategists and senior commanders also appear to be quite well informed regarding where the PLA navy seems to be headed. Ever since the 1995–96 PLA missile tests near Taiwan, and the subsequent dispatch of two aircraft carrier battlegroups to the region, the U.S. military has recognized that war with China over Taiwan was a real possibility and, as a result, has been paying close attention to PLA modernization.

The comprehensive and generally well-balanced July 2005 and 2006 Defense Department Reports to the Congress on the topic of PLA modernization are the most recent public manifestation of this focus. The 2005 report made clear that the PRC is making a substantial investment in submarines, both conventional and nuclear-powered. Since 2000, twenty-one new submarines, two of them nuclear, have been commissioned by the PLAN.[1] The objective of this chapter is to provide a context for these developments and to suggest how all of the PRC's maritime-oriented modernization efforts—

especially its submarine force—will contribute to an effective PLAN maritime strategy.

The Defense Department reports, and other public manifestations of military strategy such as the 2001 and 2006 Quadrennial Defense Reviews, are very clear evidence that ongoing PLA modernization, especially its branches with projection potential—the navy, air force and 2nd Artillery—are being watched very closely because they could pose a threat to the region and to the long-standing U.S. military mission of maintaining stability.

Grand Strategy Provides the Context

Any discussion of the PRC's maritime strategy must be informed by an understanding of long-term PRC strategic goals or ambitions. In his recent book on China's grand strategy, Avery Goldstein argues that Beijing has adopted a strategy focused on a "peaceful rise," or more recently, "peaceful development," that is intended to cover China's period of strategic transition—that is, the period between today and the time that China has finally risen—whenever that might be. If Goldstein is correct, then it is also possible to argue that the maritime component of China's national military strategy is also one that is intended to cover the decades-long transition to "fully developed" status. Not surprisingly, no one can predict how Chinese grand strategy might change once the leaders of the Chinese Communist Party determine that it has reached its fully developed stage as a well-rounded great power. Beijing's great power ambitions are not spelled out in any systematic way in any kind of official PRC document such as a national strategy. They have to be derived from a variety of official, semi-official, and academic sources.[2]

That being the case, it is an interesting exercise to attempt to divine how Beijing would like the security dimension of this future world to be at the end of its period of transition. The points below reflect this author's interpretation.

- Recognition and acknowledgement by other Asian nations as Asia's leading power

- Diminution, if not elimination, of the U.S. bilateral alliance architecture in East Asia with Beijing's "New Concept of Security" becoming the organizing principle for East Asian security

- Continued access to global markets for Chinese goods

- Unimpeded access to energy, especially from the Middle East
- Political and military stability on its periphery
- A clear, agreed-upon path to peaceful reunification with Taiwan, if not already achieved
- Neither Japan nor India will become an avowed strategic rival
- Either peaceful coexistence between the two Koreas, or a reunited Korea that assumes a grand strategy of strategic independence
- Continued strategic partnership with Russia
- An end to the U.S. presence in Japan and Central Asia
- A secure second-nuclear-strike capability that is relatively immune to U.S. missile defense capability

Clearly a number of these aims have direct implications for the capabilities that the PLA Navy must possess if these goals are to be achieved.

PLA Aspirations circa 2025

Moving from these geostrategic aspirations to a focus on where the PLA wants to go is an easier task. However, the exact size, the precise organization, and the operational capabilities of the PLA in the distant future are impossible at this point to detail with precision. The PLA is still not a very transparent military when compared to western militaries that are required to rationalize virtually all aspects of their goals and ambitions before congresses or parliaments that represent the public. But the PLA has helped to inform outside students of its intent in a number of ways:

- A series of ever-more-informative defense white papers (the fourth, and most recent, was published in December 2004)
- Publishing a tremendous amount of open-source Chinese-language material related broadly to military modernization
- A willingness to allow both active duty and retired PLA officers to participate in sustained track-II discussions with a small number of U.S. research institutions regarding modernization of the PLA

As a result, it is possible to speak with a bit more assurance about where the PLA wants to be in the next few years. For example, research by Dr. David Finkelstein at the Center for Naval Analyses suggests that by 2025:

- The PLA[3] will certainly be a more professional force in the corporate and institutional sense, and a more operationally capable and sustainable military force in the war-fighting sense than it is today.
- The PLA will still likely be a force tooled for sustainable regional force projection; not global force projection.
- The PLA will still probably be a large organization in terms of numbers. It will be larger than it needs to be or would prefer to be—with most units of uneven quality in terms of equipment and qualified personnel, but with a relatively small core of highly trained and well-equipped units that will make it one of the premier regional military forces in Asia.[4]
- The PLA will be able to coordinate joint operations beyond the littoral of Asia. Although today's PLA is only in the early stages on its road toward joint operations, recent Chinese training activities are now actively exploring how to increase the character of joint operations within its forces and activities. While this does not extend to the entire force, nonetheless the premier units which were once merely going through the motions, or simply trying to get forces to operate in the same area, are now mixing it up much more.
- The PLA will almost certainly have enhanced capabilities to utilize outer space for C4ISR functions—certainly for new architectures to enable new command and control relationships, and probably for enhanced battle space awareness.
- The leadership of the PLA will aspire to have a force capable enough to fight and defeat other regional militaries, and a military that is credible enough to deter outside military intervention in conflicts with regional adversaries.[5]

Realities of the PLA's Intellectual Investment in Modernization

What exactly has the PLA done to realize these ambitions? Overall, research indicates that the PLA is "a learning organization" that has a voracious appetite for information on Western war-fighting and transformational concepts.

In 1999, after years of study and experimentation, the entire body of the PLA's official doctrinal literature focused on the operational (campaign) and tactical levels of warfare was reissued. Doctrine dating from the mid-1980s was retired and new operations manuals and regulations were published.

Informed by lessons learned from the Gulf War and other Western local wars, such as the United Kingdom's Falklands campaign, and dictated by a shift of China's main strategic direction away from the land borders to the north and out to the sea off the Chinese littoral, the PLA is now engaged in attempting to retool its war-fighting concepts. The new PLA doctrine is shifting this massive defense establishment from its previous orientation toward ground-force-centric, positional, defensive, combined-arms operations to offensive mobile joint service operations that that will take place in maritime, air, and space arenas.

The Essence of the New Operational Guidance

The most important construct at the operational level of war to come out of the new doctrinal guidance is what is known in the PLA as "the campaign basic guiding concept" that calls for "integrated operations and key point strikes." This guidance will inform China's maritime strategy.

Integrated operations speaks to the need to integrate: (1) all services (joint operations to include reserves and militia), (2) fighting in all battle-space dimensions (to include the electromagnetic spectrum), (3) all campaign phases to focus on the main operational objective, (4) the newest PLA capabilities to focus on the most important enemy targets, (5) all modes of operations (simultaneous offensive and defensive operations, and front and rear operations), and (6) both mobile and static operations.

Key-point strikes is the operational expression of integrated operations. It calls for the concentration of the PLA's most powerful capabilities to destroy or degrade the enemy's best capabilities in order to (1) level the technological playing field at the inception of hostilities, and (2) disrupt the enemy's campaign before it can achieve operational momentum. The PLA's approach rests upon the correct selection of enemy vital targets and key-point application of force against those targets.

In a change from past doctrine, in which the focus was on concentration of one's own forces (mass) against weak enemy sectors, the new doctrine calls for the PLA to concentrate its best *capabilities* against the vital capabilities that most enable the enemy to prosecute its campaign. In other words, concentrate on what the United States would term centers of gravity. There is no question that in a Taiwan scenario, or in any other conflict scenario that matches the United States against China, the United States would depend upon naval power operating in the vast western Pacific to be a main factor in any U.S. application of force. In short, U.S. maritime striking power is one of America's military centers of gravity. As a related point, the PLA has also decided that an enemy's operational center of gravity includes C4ISR architectures, its most lethal weapons systems, and its operational sustainment capabilities.[6]

In sum, emerging PLA doctrine has shifted from a long-standing emphasis of ground-centric "campaigns of annihilation" (a traditional PLA expression) that focused on force-on-force attrition, to campaigns of paralysis in which offensive and preemptive strikes at the operational level of war deny the technologically superior enemy the ability to conduct its campaign. This has obvious implications for how the PLA thinks about war in the maritime domain, suggesting the need to attack and defeat enemy naval forces before they can reach a position to attack China or its forces.

PRC Geostrategic Realities

China has done a good job over the last fifteen years of securing its land frontiers by resolving territorial disputes with Russia, Vietnam, Kazakhstan, Kyrgyzstan, and India; and by negotiating strategic partnerships with most of these countries. However, the strategic outlook off its eastern seaboard and maritime approaches is replete with problems and vulnerabilities. This is not a new issue for China. Weakness along the maritime frontier has historic resonance for Beijing. The Chinese are still smarting from the Century of Humiliation when they suffered significant losses of sovereignty from Western nations (including Japan) that came from the sea.

The reality that Beijing faces is that the vast majority of China's outstanding sovereignty and unresolved strategic issues are maritime in nature:

- Taiwan is an island. It is the U.S. military that effectively keeps the Taiwan Strait a moat rather than a highway.

- Territorial dispute with Japan—over islands and seabed resources—has become even more serious, and are maritime in nature.

- Territorial issues remain with respect to the Spratly Islands and the South China Sea.

- China's economic center of gravity is on its east coast—quite vulnerable to attack from the sea.

- Trade largely depends upon maritime commerce. Most of China's oil comes by sea. Most of its exports reach markets by way of the sea.

- Beijing's primary military competitor and the one country that can thwart Chinese ambitions is a maritime power that controls China's littoral—the United States, which is also closely allied with a historic antagonist (Japan), which also has an excellent navy and a formidable maritime tradition.

Beijing understands that control of the western Pacific by the United States is currently the greatest potential spoiler to any ambition to resolve by force or intimidation these outstanding strategic issues.

It is not surprising, therefore, that the latest Chinese Defense White Paper (December 2004) breaks with the tradition of land-force dominance and clearly states that the PLA Navy, PLA Air Force, and its ballistic-missile force—the 2nd Artillery—are to receive priority in funding. Further, it explicitly lays out its ambitions for the navy, air force, and 2nd Artillery: "While continuing to attach importance to the building of the Army, the PLA gives priority to the building of the Navy, Air Force and Second Artillery force to seek balanced development of the combat force structure, *in order to strengthen the capabilities for winning both command of the sea and command of the air, and conducting strategic counter strikes*" (emphasis added).[7]

Finally, it is useful to note that all the service chiefs (army, navy, air force, and 2nd Artillery) are now part of the Central Military Commission, the highest level of military authority. This means that the navy's perspectives are being heard at the highest levels of military decision making.

The Central Reality of War over Taiwan

Because of America's five-decade-long commitment to the defense of Taiwan, U.S. defense officials recognize the implications of emphasizing naval and air power by the PLA, and how this increased emphasis would supplement the PLA's already massive missile buildup opposite Taiwan. It is Taiwan that makes the overall Sino-United States relationship unique, very different from any other bilateral relationship that Washington is party to. On many different levels—political, economic, trade, academic, and personal—the Sino-United States relationship is normal, sometimes difficult, sometimes cordial, but overall, mutually productive and central to the peaceful development of Asia and the economic health of the world. At the same time, the black cloud of war, because of Taiwan, is so real that the respective militaries of both countries are actively planning, exercising, and war gaming with the aim of defeating one another.

So long as Beijing insists on keeping the use of force against Taiwan as a central element of its declaratory policy toward Taiwan—keeping its finger on the trigger so to speak—the possibility of conflict cannot be ruled out. As a result, another military dynamic comes into play: long-range planning that informs military and naval modernization and future concept development in both Beijing and Washington.

This has already set in motion a long-term capability competition between an improving PLA and a U.S. military dedicated to being able to sustain regional stability, by maintaining a force capable of frustrating PLA force projection goals. A capabilities competition is defined as an effort by the United States to maintain its current advantages on the Asian littoral by continuing to improve as the PLA improves. As the latest 2006 *Quadrennial Defense Review* (QDR) implies, while the PLA continues to improve, so too does its American counterpart. Both militaries are rising on the same tide. The U.S. response is characterized as both shaping and dissuading.[8]

Some Thoughts on the Roles of the PLA in Commanding the Sea

A good way to speculate about how the maritime component of China's national strategy might be translated into PLAN force structure is to consider what sort of capabilities the PLA will need in order to achieve the stated PLA White Paper objectives of command of the sea. What would PLA forces capable of commanding of the sea look like? One alternative would be a replay of the Imperial Japanese Navy. This example is conceptual shorthand, a way to characterize a truly blue-water navy able to operate independently on the high seas, equipped with balanced capabilities that could actively contest the U.S. Navy for regional maritime dominance.

Such a navy would require aircraft carriers for power projection, a realistic air defense capability, an amphibious force for the Taiwan scenario, an effective ASW capability against U.S. Navy and Japanese submarines, and perhaps, a significant sea-based ballistic-missile force.

Wholehearted adoption of this option by China is unlikely for three reasons. First, it has no real counters to a modern submarine force, something the U.S. and Japan both possess. The ASW problem will be too difficult for the PLAN to overcome for many years, if ever. U.S. attack submarines are simply too fast and too hard for the PLA to detect—its surface fleet could easily be sunk by submarines.

Second, the cost and effort associated with taking militarily significant numbers of tactical aircraft to sea will be prohibitively expensive and time consuming. A small carrier or two like that of Thailand, Italy, or Spain, or even of India for prestige value should not be ruled out. After all, China is the only member of the UN Permanent Five without one. However, a genuinely capable aircraft carrier (CV) force like that of the U.S. Navy does not appear likely, because of the submarine problem mentioned above. The asymmetric advantage the United States and its allies possess in submarines is likely to dissuade the PLAN from attempting a blue-water carrier force that has a substantial military capability.

Third, the reaction of the rest of Asia, especially Japan, to an avowedly power projection PLA Navy would be counterproductive to China's broader strategic objectives of not creating powerful enemies in the region, especially since such a naval force would not be essential to satisfying the PRC's strategic objectives. In this context, diesel submarines are much preferable to nuclear submarines. They are quieter, very hard to find, and create the image of being defensive in nature. They fit within the template in East Asian naval developments that has seen South Korea, Singapore, and Malaysia join Japan, Taiwan, and Australia as nations with conventional submarines.

The more likely option, and the one I believe that the PLA is pursuing, is a variant of the Soviet Union's sea denial strategy of the 1980s—updated, of course, with Chinese characteristics. This is a capability that will satisfy the vast majority of PRC strategic requirements on Beijing's maritime frontier, and is within the PRC's ability to execute.

It will focus on sea control within the first island chain (which includes both the East China Sea and the South China Sea), and sea denial beyond Taiwan in the open ocean approaches to China. It will be a joint force—composed of navy, air force, and ballistic-missile capabilities:

- Land-based air power mated with air-launched cruise missiles. PLA naval aviation and the PLAAF are working on these tactics.
- Offensive use of submarines against U.S. Navy surface forces. A word on conventional versus nuclear-powered submarines: if the PLA had the capability to build acoustically competitive nuclear submarines at a reasonable cost I would expect them to do so. But Beijing currently does not, and therefore the focus on modern conventional submarines, which don't come with the built-in vulnerability of being noisy, makes good sense for the PLAN in the near term. Over the long term, it is reasonable to expect the PLAN to try to master modern

quieting techniques, since the vast distances in the Pacific combined with the logistic limitations of conventional submarines makes nuclear-powered submarines a better weapons system option.

- Land-based conventionally tipped ballistic missiles with maneuverable reentry vehicle (MaRV) warheads that can hit ships at sea. This would be a Chinese "assassin's mace" sort of a capability—something impossible to deal with today, and very difficult under any circumstances if one is forced to defeat it by shooting down ballistic missiles. Such a capability is dependent on Beijing's ability to put together the appropriate space-based surveillance, command, and targeting architecture necessary to make this work.

Beijing must also be able to preserve this architecture, or network, from U.S. disruption. Regardless of whether or not they can make maneuvering ballistic missiles work, they absolutely require an open ocean surveillance capability that can locate approaching naval forces in order to cue relatively slow moving conventional submarines and land-based aircraft. This is the long pole in the tent for the PLA. Without a reliable surveillance capability, PLA ambitions of gaining sea control and denying the approaches to China will remain just that—ambitions.

- This PLAN is also going to require some sort of amphibious capability so long as Taiwan's status remains an unsettled issue, but this capability need not be able to project land power over vast distances. Taiwan is only one hundred miles away from the mainland, and it is hard to imagine that the PRC would actually be interested in trying to invade another country—Japan for example—from the sea.
- Like Imperial Japan, China could also depend upon offshore islands to extend its defenses in the South China Sea—using the Paracels, for example.

Taking Strategic Nuclear Weapons to Sea

While a sea-based nuclear deterrent is not an essential prerequisite for command of the sea, it could form an essential part of a broader maritime strategy. To do so, however, would require the PLAN to overcome its acoustic disadvantage vis-à-vis the U.S. submarine force. It is well known that the PLA has a voracious appetite for any information related to the employment of modern weapons systems.

The combination of close contacts for the past decade with the Russian navy and the growing body of unclassified studies on Cold War naval operations must have made it abundantly clear to PLA planners that unless PLAN SSBNs could operate undetected by U.S. forces, it would be foolish to make substantial investments in a sea-based leg of their nuclear retaliatory capability. SSBNs would be vulnerable if operating on the high seas, and be a resource sump if it was necessary to create a Soviet-like bastion defense to protect them. This is especially true given the vastness of the Chinese mainland, where the 2nd Artillery's new solid-fuel road-mobile systems are far more survivable.

What could be a far more attractive option for the PLAN would be SSNs armed with nuclear-tipped cruise missiles. Not only would these systems circumvent U.S. ballistic-missile defenses, but even if loaded on noisy SSNs operating in the eastern Pacific they would become a magnet for U.S. ASW forces, and create serious resource allocation problems. One need only recall the tremendous national effort involved in keeping track of Soviet submarines operating off the east and west Coasts of the United States during the Cold War. In this case, as Chinese quieting technology improved, the problem would become increasingly difficult for U.S. forces.

What About the PLAN Surface Force?

The absence of discussion above regarding the PLAN's growing destroyer and frigate force is not meant to suggest that these ships have no overall role, despite the fact that their contribution to denying the approaches to China to the U.S. Navy would be marginal. These are the warships that today, and in the future, will continue to be valued symbols of China as a great power, operating and exercising around the world. Showing the flag is an important peacetime mission. They also have the capability to perform escort roles and would have some functions in a Taiwan scenario operating against the Taiwanese navy. However, in a conflict against the U.S. Navy the poor antiaircraft and antisubmarine defenses of these ships would make them very vulnerable to U.S. tactical air or U.S. and allied submarines. The PLA has spent considerable time studying the United Kingdom's 1982 Falklands campaign. The sinking of the Argentine cruiser *Belgrano* is a dramatic illustration of surface ship vulnerability to submarine attack.[9]

Concluding Thoughts

As a continental power only recently coming to grips with defending itself from a serious attack from the sea, Beijing has apparently made a series of sensible decisions regarding how best to solve its outstanding strategic issues, all of which are maritime in nature.

By electing to mimic the Soviet approach, Beijing has opted for a maritime strategy that is at once affordable, militarily practical, and comprehensive. It is comprehensive in the sense that its combined naval, air force, and strategic missile force is well suited to dealing with the long list of Beijing's outstanding strategic issues that are maritime in nature. Not only is this approach to strategy sensible from an operational perspective, it is also on its face inherently defensive, which fits perfectly with Beijing's putative grand strategy of peaceful development.

It would be a mistake, however, not to recognize that while being sensible, it also embodies some serious technical challenges that Beijing must overcome. Effective and timely open ocean surveillance is an essential prerequisite, as it has been for any continental power faced with a foe approaching from the sea. In today's terms that means the PLA will increasingly become dependent on space-based surveillance and communications—becoming over time a mirror image of the United States.

It also means that it must master the difficult feat of being able to hit moving ships with ballistic missiles. This is not a trivial problem, and is one that is dependent on reliable real-time surveillance and communications. If Beijing can actually accomplish this, it can present the United States with two incredibly difficult war-fighting challenges—hunting down very quiet submarines, and somehow negating the ship-killing potential of ballistic missiles.

Of course, nothing in the approach that Beijing is pursuing prejudices its future options, once risen, on deciding that that the PRC should create a genuine power projection navy. As conceptual shorthand, this is the Imperial Japanese Navy model. This is unlikely for a very long time, because the United States holds a decided asymmetric advantage in the form of its nuclear submarine force. Until, and unless, Beijing gets very good at finding submarines, U.S. submarines can hold at risk every warship the PLAN sends to sea.

Finally, let me offer a word about resources available to execute the PRC's maritime strategy. The recently released DoD report makes clear that the resources for modernization should be available to the PLA. The report forecasts respective national GDPs in the year 2025. According to the DoD report, China's GDP forecast is $6.4 trillion, Japan's $6.3 trillion (slips to third place), and the United States' is $22.3 trillion. So while the PRC may have the second largest economy in the world in 2025, the U.S. economy will likely still be almost four times as large.[10]

What this suggests is that the United States will also have the resources to be easily able to stay militarily ahead of the PRC should it elect, or be required, to do so. Economically there is no reason why the United States should not be able to continue to play its stabilizing role in East Asia for the foreseeable future, so long as Washington believes it is in the national interest of the United States to do so. The key is that, in terms of capability, as the PLA gets better so too must the United States improve. We must "rise on the same tide" to preserve today's advantages.

Notes

1. Ronald O'Rourke, "China Naval Modernization: Implications for U.S. Navy Capabilities—Background Issues for Congress," CRS Report for Congress, November 18, 2005, CRS-7. CRS website. Order Code RL33153, www.crs.gov.

2. Avery Goldstein, "China's Grand Strategy and U.S. Foreign Policy," an essay based on his book *Rising to the Challenge: China Grand Strategy and International Security* (Stanford, Calif.: Stanford University Press, 2005). Essay distributed by FPRI e-notes September 27, 2005, www.fpri.org. Apparently, PRC leadership thought that talking about China's rise could be construed as to too threatening to the region, so over the last eighteen months the current term of art preferred by Beijing is peaceful development. The important point is that Beijing is very sensitive to anything that could alarm its neighbors and perhaps trigger bandwagoning with the United States against China.

3. The PRC's armed forces are composed of three components: the active and reserve units of the PLA, the Peoples Armed Police, and the militia. According to China's 2004 Defense White Paper, the active PLA will number 2.3 million personnel, while the militia accounts for another 10 million. "PLA" refers to the entire armed forces of China: the ground forces, navy, air force, and strategic rocket forces (also known as the 2nd Artillery).

4. The sociopolitical challenge to the government in Beijing associated with the demobilization of massive numbers of soldiers is a regime stability issue that is handled with great care. Since 1985 the PLA has downsized by cutting more than 1.5 million troops. Another 200,000-person reduction is underway. The economic burdens on local governments of placing demobilized troops and their families back into the civilian sector is likely the greatest factor that inhibits the PLA from scaling down to a much leaner military—one that can be evenly trained and equipped for excellence across the board.

5. The characteristics of "PLA 2025" cited above are derived from long-term analysis of the PLA's ongoing and impressive reform and modernization efforts, a careful reading of Chinese professional military literature, the statements of key Chinese civilian and military leaders, and a subjective sense of the future geostrategic environment that Chinese military and civilian strategists foresee for the PRC in the next two decades. Dr. David Finkelstein has led this work with great distinction for the past five years.

6. This entire section drawn from David M. Finkelstein, with Kenneth Allen, Dean Cheng, and Maryanne Kivlehan, *Evolving Operational Concepts of the Chinese Peoples Liberation Army and Navy: A Preliminary Exploration*, (Alexandria, Va.: CNA Corporation, October 2002).

7. PRC Defense White Paper, December 2004, Information Office of the State Council of the PRC, December 2004, Beijing, english.people.com.cn/whitepaper/defense2004.

8. *Quadrennial Defense Review* Report, U.S. Department of Defense, February 6, 2006, 29–32, 38–39. In addition, on page 47 the QDR is rather specific regarding changes in the U.S. Navy's posture in the Pacific. "The fleet will have greater presence in the Pacific Ocean, consistent with the global shift of trade and transport. Accordingly, the Navy plans to adjust its force posture and basing to provide at least six operationally available and sustainable carriers and 60% of its submarines in the Pacific to support engagement, presence and deterrence."

9. LTC Wu Jianchu, "Joint Operations—the Basic Form of Combat on High-Tech Terms," *Junshi Kexue* no. 4, 1995. Zhou Xiaoyu, Peng Xiwen, and An Weiping, *New Discussion on Joint Campaigns* (Beijing: National Defense University Publishing House, January 2000), 21–22.

10. Department of Defense, "Annual Report to Congress: The Military Power of the People's Republic of China 2005," The Office of the Secretary of Defense, July 2005, Executive Summary, www.defenselink.mil/news/july2005/d20050719china.pdf.

Thomas G. Mahnken

China's New Nuclear Fleet and the U.S. Navy

FOR THE FORESEEABLE FUTURE, two challenges will dominate U.S. national security planning. The first is the so-called global war on terrorism, a protracted war against jihadist terrorist groups and their supporters.[1] The second is the long-term geostrategic competition with China.[2] These challenges will determine the size and shape of the U.S. armed forces over coming decades.[3] Although each service has a significant role to play in meeting each challenge, the war against jihadist terrorists will involve the Army and Marine Corps more heavily than the Navy and Air Force, whereas the competition with China will involve naval and air forces more heavily than ground forces.

To say that the United States is involved in a long-term geostrategic competition with China is not to prejudge its outcome. History contains examples of rising powers coming to blows with dominant powers, as Germany did twice with Great Britain during the twentieth century. But history also contains instances when competitions between emerging and established powers ending amicably, as when Great Britain accommodated the rise of the United States in the late nineteenth and early twentieth centuries.

The U.S.-Soviet competition represents an intermediate case. Although the superpowers managed to avoid direct conflict for four decades, the Cold

War was far from bloodless. It spawned conflicts that cost the United States alone more than one hundred thousand dead. And indeed, on a number of occasions, it led to direct combat between the United States and the Soviet Union. Between 1950 and 1959, for example, the Air Force and Navy lost at least sixteen aircraft with 164 crewmen killed on reconnaissance missions along the Soviet periphery.[4]

The long-term competition with China could produce conflict. A war across the Taiwan Strait, which could itself take any number of forms, is the most likely, but hardly the only, such contingency.[5] Moreover, as China grows in stature, it will cast its shadow over other relationships—diplomatic, economic, and military—that the United States has in Asia. In recent years Beijing has assiduously cultivated ties with states as diverse as South Korea, Russia, and Venezuela. The U.S.-Chinese competition could also influence other conflicts, such as a war on the Korean Peninsula.

This chapter argues that because we are in a competition with China, we need to understand the character of that competition and develop a strategy to compete effectively over the long term. We need to diagnose the state of the competition, identifying trends, asymmetries, and potential discontinuities. We need to identify the strengths and weaknesses of the Chinese navy, and of the U.S. Navy. We need to determine our objectives for the competition and develop a strategy to achieve them. Specifically, we need to bolster areas of U.S. competitive advantage, identify opportunities to shape Chinese resource allocation, and attempt to change the nature of the competition.

This chapter explores one facet of the U.S.-Chinese competition: that which is concerned with China's nuclear submarine modernization. It begins by assessing the state of our understanding of Chinese naval developments. It then offers a comparison of the U.S. and Chinese submarine forces. It discusses U.S. strategic objectives and how China's nuclear submarine modernization affects them. It concludes with a series of strategic options for the U.S. Navy to compete more effectively.

Understanding the Chinese Navy

China's military modernization poses a significant challenge to the U.S. intelligence community. Though an important topic, it is but one of a number of areas that is vying for the community's limited resources. Moreover, monitoring military force modernization requires technical collection systems that are expensive and may have limited utility for the other main challenge that we face—the war with jihadist terrorist networks. During the Cold

War, for example, the U.S. intelligence community developed an extensive imagery and signals intelligence infrastructure designed to monitor Soviet military developments.[6] Today, however, there is a general perception that the U.S. intelligence community is relatively overinvested in technical collection and underinvested in clandestine human intelligence.

To the extent that the Chinese military is actively exploring new ways of war, it poses an even greater challenge to U.S. intelligence organizations. Intelligence agencies are more inclined to monitor the development of established weapons than to search for new military systems. They also tend to pay more attention to technology and doctrine that have been demonstrated in war than to those that have not seen combat. In other words, they experience more difficulty detecting new or unique systems. Finally, intelligence organizations more readily detect foreign developments that mirror those of their own armed forces than those that differ substantially from them.[7]

There is much that we do not know about the Chinese military. For example, in recent years U.S. analysts reportedly missed more than a dozen significant Chinese military developments.[8] As the Defense Department admitted several years ago in a report to Congress on the China-Taiwan military balance:

> First, we need to know more about how the authorities in the PRC and Taiwan view their military and political situation—in order to identify the most important conflict scenarios and hence the capabilities central to them; in order to assess whether the balance of forces adequately deters Chinese attack and reassures Taiwan; and in order to understand how both sides' calculations of priority, risk, and military capability would shape the course and outcome of a conflict. We are unlikely to be able to replicate their precise views on this military balance, but we probably can learn much more about both sides' ideas about statecraft, their approaches to the use of force, their perceived vulnerabilities, and their preferred operational methods, as well as about the political and military organizations that produce military assessments and plans. Second, as might be predicted, we are less knowledgeable about things that are less visible or tangible—training, logistics, doctrine, command and control, special operations, mine warfare—than we are about airplanes and surface ships. Third, although we can identify emerging methods of warfare that appear likely to be increasingly important in the future—particularly missiles and information warfare— we cannot confidently assess how each side's capabilities will develop or the interaction of measures and countermeasures that these emerging military competitions will generate.[9]

Submarines are by nature stealthy, their operations difficult to monitor. Although it is impossible to discuss definitively the extent of U.S. knowledge of Chinese submarine operations in an open forum, it is safe to conclude that our understanding of Chinese submarine technology, doctrine, and operations is far from complete. It appears, for example, that the existence of the Yuan class of diesel submarines (SSK) came as a surprise to many analysts.[10]

Given the gaps in our understanding of the Chinese navy, there is an understandable tendency to seek analogies, either to the U.S.-Soviet competition or China's past. Although such analogies may be useful and are at times necessary, they should be treated with great care.

First, the U.S.-Chinese competition is different from the U.S.-Soviet competition during the Cold War. The United States enters this competition in a much stronger position than it possessed during even the early phases of the Cold War. The United States is today the most powerful nation in the world, both militarily and economically. It dominates not only the traditional metrics of power, but also culture. On the other hand, it is unlikely that the U.S.-Chinese competition will ever dominate the U.S. national security agenda the way the U.S.-Soviet competition did. For the foreseeable future, the rise of China will have to compete with the worldwide struggle with jihadist terrorists as well as threats in Southwest and Northeast Asia. Moreover, China's goals are significantly different from those of the Soviet Union. As a result, the U.S.-Chinese competition is likely to evolve in ways far different from the U.S.-Soviet competition during the Cold War.

Second, there is a danger of mindlessly applying the U.S. Navy's experience of competing with the Soviet navy during the Cold War to the current situation. To state the obvious, China has a culture and society far different from that of the Soviet Union. Similarly, the Chinese armed forces in general, and the People's Liberation Army Navy (PLAN) in particular, have historical traditions far different from those of the Soviet armed forces.

Third, although China continues to import a wide variety of naval hardware from Russia, including Project 636 Kilo-class SSKs, it would be a mistake to assume that China will employ those submarines the way Russia does or the Soviet Union did. Studies of the diffusion of military ideas and technology show that militaries rarely, if ever, adopt foreign doctrine wholesale.[11] Rather, their political objectives, strategy, operational art, military traditions, organizational culture, and professional competence all conspire to produce unique approaches.

Fourth, analogies from China's past may misinform as well as inform. The PLAN is currently undergoing a period of growth and improvement.

Extrapolations from the past are, if anything, likely to understate the pace of improvement of the Chinese submarine force. To the extent that past performance creates expectations about future capabilities, analysts will tend to underestimate the capabilities of the Chinese military.

China's military modernization may best resemble that of Japan in the 1920s and 1930s. During the early part of that period, analysts accurately reported the Japanese military's substantial material and doctrinal weaknesses. However, estimates of Japanese military capability failed to keep pace with Japanese military modernization, which accelerated in the second half of the 1930s. As a result, in key respects U.S. intelligence underestimated Japanese military power on the eve of World War II in the Pacific.[12]

Weighing the Balance

Several considerations shape China's nuclear submarine modernization. First, China's development of nuclear-powered submarines, like its nuclear-weapon, long-range missile, and manned-space programs, serves as an expression of national power and prestige. The possession of nuclear-powered attack submarines (SSNs) and nuclear-powered ballistic-missile submarines (SSBNs) puts China in the same league as the United States, Russia, Britain, and France. Nuclear submarines not only bolster China's image as a great power, but also provide concrete evidence of Beijing's technological proficiency. In this respect, China's nuclear submarine fleet is aimed as much at China's regional neighbors as it is the United States.

Yet China's nuclear submarine force is more than just a showpiece. It is also the result of resource allocation decisions the Chinese political and military leadership has made over the course of years and decades. It is axiomatic that no nation's resources are unlimited. The decision to build nuclear-powered submarines is also a decision to forego other weapons, whether diesel submarines or aircraft carriers or intercontinental ballistic missiles. In other words, the Chinese leadership clearly attaches substantial value to the possession of nuclear submarines.

Finally, and most concretely, China's submarine force is a military instrument. It is a means to achieve the Chinese leadership's aims in peace and war.

Weighing the balance between the PLAN and the U.S. Navy, let alone the Chinese nuclear submarine force and the U.S. Navy, is a difficult undertaking. To state the obvious, China and the United States are vastly different countries, with vastly different histories and geography that have created vastly different navies. Even a cursory look reveals asymmetries in the missions of the two navies and the structure and purpose of their submarine forces.

Power projection is the *sine qua non* of the U.S. Navy. Its ships, submarines, and aircraft are designed for prolonged operations far from America's shores. Over decades it has built both the technology and the supporting infrastructure for expeditionary operations. Just as importantly, it has built an organizational culture that emphasizes the independent exercise of command.

The main mission of the PLAN, by contrast, is sea denial. It is designed for operations close to China's coast, though it has conducted more blue-water operations in recent years. Whereas the U.S. Navy is designed for combat far from the United States but close to enemy shores, the PLAN is built to fight close to friendly shores. In promoting officers and selecting leaders, the Chinese prize loyalty and reliability over independence and initiative.

The U.S. and Chinese submarine forces are quite different. First and foremost, the U.S. submarine force is composed entirely of nuclear-powered boats.[13] This is an expression of the United States' insular geography and the U.S. Navy's power-projection strategy. By contrast, nuclear submarines comprise only 7 percent of the Chinese submarine fleet.[14] It is likely that percentage will decrease, at least in the short term, as China acquires Project 636 Kilo diesel submarines from Russia and builds Song- and Yuan-class diesels indigenously.

The U.S. Navy currently possesses fifty-four SSNs and sixteen SSBNs. The Chinese submarine force is composed of five SSNs, sixty-one SSKs, and one SSBN.[15] In constructing its submarine force, the U.S. Navy has traditionally emphasized quality over quantity. The Chinese, by contrast, have kept a number of obsolescent submarines, including thirty-five Romeo-class SSKs, in its inventory. Whereas a large portion of the U.S. strategic nuclear arsenal is deployed at sea, submarine-launched ballistic missiles account for only 14 percent of China's intermediate-range and intercontinental ballistic missiles.

Submarines serve a number of purposes for the United States. According to the U.S. Navy, the primary mission of the U.S. attack submarine force is antisubmarine warfare (ASW). U.S. attack submarines also collect intelligence, deliver Special Operations Forces, conduct antisurface warfare (ASUW) and launch strikes against land targets.[16] The United States looks to SSBNs to house a significant portion of the U.S. nuclear deterrent. In the future, it will also deliver conventionally armed ballistic missiles.[17] Finally, the

U.S. Navy is converting four *Ohio*-class SSBNs into nuclear-powered cruise-missile submarines (SSGNs), which will have the ability both to launch 154 Tactical Tomahawk Land-Attack Missiles and to deliver Navy Sea, Air, and Land (SEAL) special operations forces.[18]

Whereas U.S. attack submarines are designed primarily for ASW, Chinese attack submarines possess little ASW capability. The primary mission of China's attack submarine fleet is ASUW. The extent to which the Chinese submarine force has conducted intelligence collection is unclear. The incursion of a Han-class submarine into Japanese territorial waters near Tarama Island in November 2004, however—as detailed in Peter Dutton's contribution to this volume—suggests that this may also be a mission. The PLAN has heretofore lacked the means to launch strikes on land targets, though China's acquisition of the Klub family of submarine-launched weapons, which includes both antiship and land-attack cruise missiles, could change this.

A diagnostic net technical assessment of U.S. and Chinese submarines is beyond the scope of this chapter. Such an assessment would include a comparison of their acoustic signatures, as well as the capabilities of their sensors and weapon systems. To the extent that U.S. submarines are able to detect Chinese nuclear submarines while remaining undetected, for example, they will enjoy a significant advantage.

Assessments of the effectiveness of the Chinese submarine force vary. Michael O'Hanlon, for example, estimates that "in an extreme case" Chinese submarines would be able to sink "a ship or two" in a war across the Taiwan Strait.[19] Lyle Goldstein and William Murray, by contrast, argue that the Chinese submarine force could be significantly more effective.[20] Michael A. Glosny contends, based upon a series of simulations, that in the event of a future Chinese submarine blockade of Taiwan, "the PLAN's small fleet of submarines would inflict an amount of total damage that seems unlikely to be militarily decisive by historical standards."[21]

Such a span of opinion is hardly surprising. First, it is difficult to judge the effectiveness of the PLAN in general and the Chinese submarine force in particular based on existing information. As noted above, because the Chinese submarine force is undergoing significant change, past performance is unlikely to offer a guide to present or future effectiveness. More generally, there is little available data on the effectiveness of modern submarines in ASW and ASUW. The U.S. Navy and the PLAN conduct naval exercises that include submarine operations, but that is not the same thing as war. And whereas conflicts over the past several decades have included submarines, primarily in a land-attack role, since World War II there has been just one case of a submarine sinking a surface ship (the British SSN *Conqueror's* sinking of the Argentine cruiser *General Belgrano* during the 1982 Falklands War) and no cases of a submarine sinking another submarine.

Several discontinuities are possible over the next several decades. First, the PLAN might adopt new roles and missions. The combination of China's expanding interests and Beijing's increasing dependence on oil imports could lead China to adopt a blue-water naval strategy. Indeed, the long endurance afforded by nuclear propulsion would make SSNs an ideal element of a blue-water force. Even if the PLAN did not seek a blue-water capability, the acquisition of increasing numbers of SSNs would give it the ability to contest U.S. naval forces farther from China's shores.

Second, the development of new technology could alter the character of undersea warfare. One such technological area involves unmanned systems. Unmanned aerial vehicles and unmanned combat air vehicles have already changed the character of warfare; the deployment of significant numbers of unmanned undersea vehicles for reconnaissance, surveillance, and strike could have a similarly profound impact on undersea warfare. Other developments that could affect undersea warfare could include major changes in submarine quieting or detection.

The potential for such discontinuities should not be dismissed, particularly over the next two to three decades. Rather, it is important to be on the lookout for indicators of such developments. It would be worthwhile, for example, to track the portion of the Chinese submarine force that is composed of nuclear submarines as an indicator of a shift toward a blue-water capability.

A comparison of the U.S. and Chinese nuclear submarine forces is useful for illuminating the asymmetry between the two sides. It is of limited utility, however, for assessing the implications of China's nuclear submarine force for the U.S. Navy. China's SSN fleet is one element of its attack submarine force. Attack submarines are one means of conducting ASUW; others include China's cruise-missile-armed surface combatants and aircraft. China's ASUW force is, in turn, but one element of China's antiaccess force. A more comprehensive assessment would diagnose trends in U.S. power-projection capabilities relative to China's antiaccess capability.

Similarly, China's SSBN force is one means of delivering nuclear weapons over long range. A more comprehensive assessment of the U.S.-Chinese nuclear balance would also include both sides' ICBMs and nuclear-capable bombers.

Implications for the U.S. Navy

Any discussion of the implications of China's nuclear submarine modernization for the U.S. Navy should begin with a discussion of U.S. objectives. The *National Defense Strategy of the United States of America* lists four strategic objectives: (1) securing the United States from direct attack, (2) securing strategic access and retaining global freedom of action, (3) strengthening alliances and partnerships, and (4) establishing favorable security conditions. It argues that the United States should accomplish these objectives by assuring allies and friends, dissuading potential adversaries, deterring aggression and countering coercion, and defeating adversaries.[22]

China's nuclear submarine buildup affects our ability to achieve a number of these objectives. First, China's SSBN force provides the ability to strike the United States with nuclear weapons. Second, China's nuclear submarines will contribute to Beijing's ability to deny the United States access to the seas on China's periphery. Third, this force has the ability to alter regional balances. Finally, it contributes to an image of China as a great power and a major competitor of the United States.

The United States could adopt several strategies to compete with China in undersea warfare. First, it could choose to bolster areas of current U.S. advantage. During the Cold War, the United States developed a comparative advantage over the Soviet Union in ASW. That capability has languished since the end of the Cold War. The U.S. could, however, reinforce its ASW capability, with particular focus on the need to track Chinese submarines.[23]

The design of quiet submarines is another area of Cold War advantage that has diminished in recent years.

Finally, the United States could more effectively use its technological superiority in the competition with China. There is a widespread presumption that the U.S. lead in advanced technology gives us the ability to do things that other militaries cannot. This is a presumption that should be nurtured. During the 1980s, for example, the United States inaugurated a strategic deception campaign associated with the Strategic Defense Initiative as a way to make the Soviets believe that U.S. ballistic-missile defense capabilities were more formidable than they in fact were.[24] The program was originally designed to block the Soviet Union from gathering accurate information about the U.S. strategic defense program. As it evolved, it sought to force the Soviets into spending fortunes building their own system and countering that of the United States.[25]

Second, the United States could attempt to influence China's resource allocation in ways that favor the United States. One approach would be to force the Chinese down paths that are difficult, expensive, and result in low payoff.

Seen from this perspective, it is unclear whether China's investment in nuclear-powered attack submarines should be a greater concern than other options to perform the same mission. As noted above, the main advantage that nuclear submarines have over diesel submarines is their endurance. Should China opt for a blue-water naval posture, such endurance would be a significant attribute. On the other hand, nuclear-powered submarines are considerably more expensive than diesel submarines. They are also likely noisier than advanced diesel submarines such as Project 636 Kilo-class SSKs.

As the experience of the Cold War demonstrates, building a force of quiet nuclear submarines is a daunting challenge. Although the Soviet Union was able to produce large numbers of nuclear submarines, it had great difficulty producing quiet nuclear submarines, ones that could avoid detection by U.S. attack submarines. Moreover, the Soviet Union's ability to build quiet submarines depended upon Moscow's access to technology from the United States and its allies. By contrast, the United States had a significant lead both in submarine quieting and submarine detection.[26]

There would appear to be few objections to China expanding its SSBN fleet. Such an undertaking is likely to be expensive and offer China little to no advantage in the competition with the United States.

A final strategy would be to attempt to change the nature of the competition in such a way as to render China's investment in submarines obsolete. Beginning in the second half of the 1970s, the United States pursued a strategy for developing low-observable aircraft in order to render obsolete the Soviet Union's substantial investment in strategic air defense. The ability to penetrate Soviet airspace in the face of such formidable defenses represented an area of considerable advantage for the United States. As Secretary of Defense Caspar Weinberger put it in 1987, "Low observable technologies promise to increase further the competitive advantage of our bomber force, to such a degree as to make obsolete much of the Soviets' air defense infrastructure." In his view, the ability of the United States to penetrate Soviet air space had already forced the Soviets to invest the equivalent of over $120 billion in strategic air defense.[27] The continuing development of stealth rendered the Soviet Union vulnerable and forced the Soviets to divert funds from offensive arms to defensive arms.

Concluding Thoughts

This essay has been suggestive rather than definitive. Such an approach is appropriate, considering that we are in a decades-long competition with China.

Still, much more research and analysis is needed. First, we need a much better understanding of the Chinese military in general and the Chinese submarine force in particular. As the chapters in this volume show, much is available through public sources. Much more, however, can be done to analyze these and other Chinese writings on military affairs.

Second, we need to develop strategies to compete effectively with China. Our resources, though substantial, are not unlimited. We must therefore use them wisely if we are to achieve our objectives over the long term.

Notes

1. David J. Kilcullen, "Countering Global Insurgency," *Journal of Strategic Studies* 28, no. 4 (August 2005).

2. Andrew W. Marshall first coined the term "long-term competition" during the Cold War. See A. W. Marshall, *Long-Term Competition with the Soviets: A Framework for Strategic Analysis*, R-862-PR (Santa Monica, Calif.: RAND Corporation, 1972). It is in this sense that I use the term throughout this paper.

3. The former tracks with the 2006 *Quadrennial Defense Review*'s "defeating terrorist networks," "defending the homeland in depth," and "preventing the acquisition of weapons of mass destruction," while the latter is a subset of "shaping the choices of countries at strategic crossroads." See *Quadrennial Defense Review Report* (Washington, D.C.: Department of Defense, 2006).

4. William E. Burrows, *By Any Means Necessary: America's Secret Air War in the Cold War* (New York: Farrar, Straus and Giroux, 2001).

5. For discussions of this contingency from different viewpoints, see Michael O'Hanlon, "Why China Cannot Conquer Taiwan," *International Security* 25, no. 2 (Fall 2000): 51–86; Lyle Goldstein and William Murray, "Undersea Dragons: China's Maturing Submarine Force," *International Security* 28, no. 4 (Spring 2004): 161–96; Michael A. Glosny, "Strangulation from the Sea? A PRC Submarine Blockade of Taiwan," *International Security* 28, no. 4 (Spring 2004): 125–60.

6. Clarence E. Smith, "CIA's Analysis of Soviet Science and Technology" in *Watching the Bear: Essays on CIA's Analysis of the Soviet Union* (Washington, D.C.: Center for the Study of Intelligence, 2003), chapter 4.

7. Thomas G. Mahnken, *Uncovering Ways of War: U.S. Intelligence and Foreign Military Innovation* (Ithaca, NY: Cornell University Press, 2002), 4.

8. Bill Gertz, "Analysts Missed Chinese Buildup," *The Washington Times*, June 9, 2005, www.washingtontimes.com.

9. "Report to Congress Pursuant to Public Law 106-113," at http://www.defenselink
.mil/pubs/twstrait_12182000.doc, accessed October 21, 2005.

10. Bill Gertz, "Chinese Produce New Type of Sub," *The Washington Times* (July 16, 2004): 1.

11. See, for example, the essays in Emily O. Goldman and Leslie C. Eliason, eds., *The Diffusion of Military Technology and Ideas* (Stanford, Calif.: Stanford University Press, 2003).

12. Mahnken, *Uncovering Ways of War*, chapter 3.

13. Adm. Arleigh Burke made the decision that all future U.S. submarines would be nuclear in September 1955, six months after the first cruise of the USS *Nautilus*, the world's first nuclear submarine.

14. International Institute for Strategic Studies, *The Military Balance 2004–2005* (London: IISS, 2005), 272.

15. It also includes an SSG and an SS that are used for tests.

16. U.S. Navy Fact File, "Attack Submarines—SSN," at http://www.chinfo.navy.mil/navpalib/factfile/ships/ship-ssn.html, accessed October 10, 2005.

17. 2006 *QDR*, 50.

18. "SSGN—A Transformational Force for the U.S. Navy," at http://www.chinfo.navy .mil/navpalib/cno/n87/usw/issue_13/ssgn.htm, accessed October 24, 2005.

19. O'Hanlon, "Why China Cannot Conquer Taiwan," 78–79.

20. Goldstein and Murray, "Undersea Dragons," passim.

21. Glosny, "Strangulation from the Sea," 139.

22. *National Defense Strategy of the United States of America* (Washington, D.C.: Department of Defense 2005), 6–8.

23. Owen R. Coté, Jr., *The Third Battle: Innovation in the U.S. Navy's Silent Cold War Struggle with Soviet Submarines*, Newport Paper 16 (Newport, R.I.: Naval War College Press, 2003).

24. General Accounting Office, *Ballistic Missile Defense: Records Indicate Deception Program Did Not Affect 1984 Test Results* (Washington, D.C.: GAO, July 1994), 3.

25. Tim Weiner, "Lies and Rigged 'Star Wars' Test Fooled the Kremlin, and Congress," *New York Times*, August 18, 1993, www.nytimes.com.

26. Coté, *The Third Battle, passim*.

27. Caspar W. Weinberger, *Annual Report to the Congress, Fiscal Year 1988* (Washington, D.C.: GPO, January 12, 1987).

Acronyms

AA/AD	antiaccess/area denial
AAW	antiair warfare
ABM	antiballistic missile
AECL	Atomic Energy of Canada
AESA	Astilleros Españoles S.A.
AEW	airborne early warning
AIP	air-independent propulsion
AMS	Academy of Military Sciences
ARCI	acoustic rapid COTS insertion
ARG	amphibious ready group
ASCM	antiship cruise missiles
ASEAN	Association of Southeast Asian Nations
ASUW	antisurface ship warfare
ASW	antisubmarine warfare
AWACS	airborne warning and control system
BMD	ballistic-missile defense
BP	Brilliant Pebbles
C_3	command, control, and communications
C_3I	command, control, communications, and intelligence
C_4	command, control, communications, and computers
C_4ISR	command, control, communications, computers, intelligence, surveillance, and reconnaissance
CADDS	computer aided drafting and design systems

CANDU	Canada Deuterium Uranium (Reactor)
CCP	Chinese Communist Party
CIAE	China Institute of Atomic Energy
CMC	Central Military Commission
CNA	Center for Naval Analyses
CNNC	China National Nuclear Corporation
CNO	Chief of Naval Operations
CONMAROPS	Concept of Maritime Operations
COSTIND	Commission of Science, Technology, and Industry for National Defense
COTS	commercial off-the-shelf
CSG	aircraft carrier strike groups
CSIC	China Shipbuilding Industry Corporation
CTOL	conventional-takeoff-and-landing
CV	aircraft carrier
CVBG	carrier battle group
DPG	defense planning guidance
ECS	East China Sea
EEZ	exclusive economic zone
ELF	extremely low frequency
Ensa	Equipos Nucleares
FBIS	Foreign Broadcast Information Service
FBM	fleet ballistic missile
FOFA	Follow-On Forces Attack
FON	freedom of navigation
FYP	Yibin Fuel Plant
GIUK	Greenland-Iceland-United Kingdom Gap
GPALS	Global Protection Against Limited Strikes
GSD	General Staff Department
GWOT	global war on terrorism
HF	high frequency
HTGR	high-temperature gas-cooled reactor
I&C	instruments and control equipment
IAE	Institute of Atomic Energy
IAEA	International Atomic Energy Agency
ICBM	intercontinental-range ballistic missile

ICJ	International Court of Justice
IFEP	integrated full-electric propulsion
IGB	inner-German Border
INET	Institute of Nuclear Energy Technology
ISR	intelligence, surveillance, and reconnaissance
ITER	International Thermonuclear Experimental Reactor
IUSS	integrated undersea surveillance systems
JMSDF	Japanese Maritime Self-Defense Force
KMT	Kuomintang
LACM	land attack cruise missile
LF	low frequency
LIC	low intensity conflicts
LNG	liquefied natural gas
LST	landing ship tank
MaRV	maneuvering reentry vehicles
MDA	Missile Defense Agency
MIRV	multiple independently targeted reentry vehicles
MIT	Massachusetts Institute of Technology
MMA	multimission maritime aircraft
MNI	Ministry of Nuclear Industry
MPA	maritime patrol aircraft
MR	military region
MRBM	medium-range ballistic missiles
MRV	multiple reentry vehicle
MSK	minimum shift key
MSDF	*See* JMSDF
NCAPS	naval control and protection of shipping
NCW	network-centric warfare
NDIC	National Defense Industrial Commission
NDIO	National Defense Industry Office
NDU	National Defense University
NFU	no first use
NIE	National Intelligence Estimate
NMD	national missile defense
NNSA	National Nuclear Safety Administration
NWC	U.S. Naval War College

NWDC	Navy Warfare Development Command
ONI	Office of Naval Intelligence
OSD	Office of the Secretary of Defense
PHWR	pressurized heavy-water reactors
PLA	People's Liberation Army
PLAAF	People's Liberation Army Air Force
PLAN	People's Liberation Army Navy
PLANAF	People's Liberation Army Navy Air Force
PRC	People's Republic of China
PWR	pressurized water reactor
QDR	*Quadrennial Defense Review*
QFD	quality function deployment
ROC	Republic of China
ROKN	Republic of Korea Navy
RRS	Reactor Research Section
SAC	Strategic Air Command
SAG	surface action group
SAM	surface-to-air missile
SCS	South China Sea
SEAL	sea, air, and land
SESCO	secure underwater communications system
SG	steam generator
SHAPE	Supreme Headquarters Allied Powers Europe
SINS	ship's inertial navigation system
SIPRI	Stockholm International Peace Research Institute
SLBM	submarine-launched ballistic missile
SLOC	sea lines of communication
SLV	space-launch vehicle
SNERDI	Shanghai Nuclear Engineering, Research, & Design Institute
SOF	Special Operations Force
SOSUS	sound surveillance system
SRBM	short-range ballistic missiles
SS	nonnuclear submarine
SSBN	nuclear-powered ballistic-missile submarine
SSGN	nuclear-powered cruise missile submarine

SSK	diesel-electric submarine
SSN	nuclear-powered attack submarine
SSRN	radar picket submarine
TACAMO	Take Charge and Move Out
TAO	Taiwan area of operations
UAV	unmanned aerial vehicle
UNCLOS	United Nations Convention on the Law of the Sea
USN	United States Navy
UUV	unmanned underwater vehicle
VLF	very low frequency
VSTOL	vertical-and-short-takeoff-and-landing

About the Contributors

PROF. BERNARD D. COLE is professor of international history at the National War College in Washington, D.C. He previously served thirty years as a surface warfare officer in the Navy, all in the Pacific. He commanded USS *Rathburne* (FF 1057) and Destroyer Squadron 35, served as a naval gunfire liaison officer in Vietnam, surface operations officer for CTF 70/77, plans officer for Commander-in-Chief Pacific Fleet, and as special assistant to the Chief of Naval Operations for Expeditionary Warfare. Dr. Cole's first book, *Gunboats and Marines: The U.S. Navy in China,* was published by the University of Delaware Press; *The Great Wall at Sea: China's Navy Enters the 21st Century,* was published in October 2001 by the Naval Institute Press; *Oil for the Lamps of China: Beijing's 21st Century Search for Energy,* was published by the NDU Press in November 2003; and *An Island Adrift: Taiwan's Security Dilemma,* was published in 2006. Dr. Cole earned an A.B. in history from the University of North Carolina, an M.P.A. in national security affairs from the University of Washington, and a Ph.D. in history from Auburn University.

CDR. PETER DUTTON, JAGC, USN, is the Howard S. Levie Chair of Operational Law in the Joint Military Operations Department at the Naval War College, where he is responsible for all international and operational law instruction in the joint military operations curriculum. Commander Dutton also teaches law of the sea and national security law at Roger Williams University in Bristol, Rhode Island. He began his Navy service as a naval flight officer in 1985, flying various electronic warfare aircraft until 1990, when he was selected for transition from aviation into the Judge Advocate General's Corps. As a Navy JAG, Commander Dutton served in various positions with the operating forces, including as the legal advisor to commander, Carrier Group Six (*John F. Kennedy* Battle Group). Commander Dutton received his juris doctor degree from the College of William and Mary in 1993. He received a master's in national security and strategic studies, with honors, from the Naval War College in 1999, and his bachelor's degree, cum laude, from Boston University in 1982.

RICHARD D. FISHER, JR., is International Assessment and Strategy Center vice president and director of the center's Project on Asian Security and Democracy. Fisher has written extensively on the PRC military and the Asian military balance and their implications for Asia and the United States. Fisher has worked as Asian studies director at the Heritage Foundation and as a consultant on PLA issues for the congressionally chartered U.S. China Security & Economic Review Commission. He has testified before the Senate Foreign Relations Committee, the House International Relations Committee, the House Armed Services Committee, and the U.S. China Security Commission on the modernization of China's military. Fisher has been editor of the Jamestown Foundation's *China Brief* and writes regularly in a variety of news and defense periodicals. He has undertaken field research in China, Taiwan, Russia, India, and Pakistan. Fisher studied at Georgetown University and at Eisenhower College, where he received his B.A. with honors.

EDWARD FRANCIS is a research associate with Defense Group Inc.'s Center for Intelligence Research and Analysis. He received a B.A. from Middlebury College, majoring in Chinese and political science. He speaks Mandarin Chinese.

DR. PAUL H. B. GODWIN retired as professor of international affairs at the National War College, Washington, D.C., in the summer of 1998. In the fall of 1987, he was a visiting professor at the Chinese National Defense University. His teaching and research specialties focus on Chinese defense and security policies. Professor Godwin's recent publications include "China as Regional Hegemon?" in Jim Rolfe, ed., *The Asia-Pacific Region in Transition* (Honolulu: Asia-Pacific Center for Security Studies, 2004); "Decisionmaking Under Stress: The Unintentional Bombing of China's Belgrade Embassy and the EP-3 Collision," in Andrew Scobell and Larry M. Wortzel, eds.,

Chinese National Security Decisionmaking Under Stress (Carlisle, Pa.: U.S. Army War College, Strategic Studies Institute, 2005). He graduated from Dartmouth College with a degree in international relations and received his doctorate in political science from the University of Minnesota. Professor Godwin resides in Chico, California, and is now a consultant and serves as a Senior Fellow at the Foreign Policy Research Institute, Philadelphia.

GARTH HEKLER is a research associate with Defense Group Inc.'s Center for Intelligence Research and Analysis. He specializes in security issues related to China and Southeast Asia. Hekler previously held a position in the U.S. Department of Commerce Office of the Chinese Economic Area, where he covered a broad range of trade issues, including trade in services, basic industries, and energy policy. He received an M.A. in China and Southeast Asian studies from the Johns Hopkins School of Advanced International Studies and a B.A. in anthropology from the University of Buffalo. He speaks both Mandarin Chinese and Vietnamese.

CAPT. ROBERT G. LOEWENTHAL, USN (RET.), was a graduate of the U.S. Naval Academy. After a year in the surface Navy, he reported to Submarine School. He has served in both diesel- and nuclear-powered submarines and commanded the USS *George Bancroft* (SSBN 643) (Gold) for three years, making five deterrent patrols. He also commanded the USS *Hunley* (AS 31), a submarine tender, and the Trident Submarine Base at Kings Bay, Georgia, in each instance for two years. Captain Lowenthal held the Vice Admiral Charles Lockwood Chair of Submarine Warfare at the U.S. Naval War College for three years and taught in the Joint Military Operations Department. After retirement from the Navy, Captain Loewenthal was the program manager for research and development at EG&G Corporation, Mechanical Components Group, for eight years. He is survived by his wife JoAnn, who lives in Jamestown, Rhode Island.

PROF. THOMAS G. MAHNKEN is a professor in the Strategy and Policy Department of the Naval War College. He is currently serving as Deputy Assistant Secretary of Defense for Policy Planning. Prof. Mahnken is the author of *Uncovering Ways of War: U.S. Intelligence and Foreign Military Innovation, 1918–1941*, coauthor of *The Limits of Transformation: Officer Attitudes toward the Emerging Revolution in Military Affairs* and a volume of the *Gulf War Air Power Survey*, coeditor of *Paradoxes of Strategic Intelligence: Essays in Honor of Michael I. Handel* and *The Information Revolution in*

Military Affairs in Asia, and has written numerous articles on U.S. national security policy, intelligence assessment, and arms proliferation. He is also the editor of The *Journal of Strategic Studies*. Before joining the strategy and policy faculty, he served in the Defense Department's Office of Net Assessment. A Naval Special Warfare-qualified Navy Reserve intelligence officer, he is a combat veteran of Operation Iraqi Freedom and served in Bahrain during Operation Enduring Freedom and with British forces in Kosovo. During the 2005–06 academic year he served as a Visiting Fellow at the Philip Merrill Center for Strategic Studies at Johns Hopkins SAIS. Professor Mahnken has an M.A. and a Ph.D. from Johns Hopkins SAIS.

LT. CHRISTOPHER J. MCCONNAUGHAY enlisted in the Navy in 1987. In 1994 he was selected for the Navy's Enlisted Commissioning Program and graduated from the University of Illinois Urbana-Champaign as an ensign in the USN with a B.A. in atmospheric science. In 2003, he completed a master of arts in national security and strategic studies from the Naval War College. Research he undertook at NWC was subsequently published in Newport Paper 22 *China's Nuclear Force Modernization* (2005). Lieutenant McConnaughay made five deterrent patrols on the USS *West Virginia* (SSBN 736) (BLUE). He is currently Chief, Submarine-Launched Ballistic-Missile Quality Assurance at United States Strategic Command Joint Functional Component Command for Space and Global Strike.

REAR ADM. MICHAEL MCDEVITT, USN (RET.), is a vice president and director of the Center for Strategic Studies, a division of the CNA Corporation (CNAC)—a not-for-profit research center in Washington, D.C. During his thirty-four-year Navy career Admiral McDevitt held four at-sea commands, including an aircraft carrier battlegroup. He received a bachelor of arts degree in U.S. history from the University of Southern California and a master's degree in American diplomatic history from Georgetown University. He is also a graduate of the National War College in Washington, D.C. He was the director of the East Asia Policy office for the Secretary of Defense during the first Bush administration. He also served for two years as the director for Strategy, War Plans and Policy (J-5) for U.S. CINCPAC and as the commandant of the National War College in Washington, D.C. Admiral McDevitt is an active participant in conferences and workshops regarding security issues in East Asia and has had a number of papers published in edited volumes on this subject.

REAR ADM. ERIC MCVADON, USN (RET.), concluded his thirty-five years of naval service as the U.S. defense and naval attaché at the American Embassy in Beijing 1990–92. A consultant on Asian security affairs, he works extensively with the U.S. policy and intelligence communities and the Department of Defense, directly and indirectly. Among his many other responsibilities, he is an Adjunct Fellow with the International Security Program of the Center for Strategic and International Studies and a nonresident fellow at the Atlantic Council of the United States. His naval experience included extensive experience in air antisubmarine warfare and politico-military affairs, including service as the NATO and U.S. sub-unified commander in Iceland. Admiral McVadon, a designated naval aviator, is a 1958 graduate of Tulane University and has a master's degree in international affairs from George Washington University. He is a distinguished graduate of the Naval Postgraduate School, Naval War College (Command & Staff), and National War College. He and his wife, Marshall, both from Baton Rouge, Louisiana, live and work in Great Falls, Virginia.

CAPT. JAMES H. PATTON, JR., USN (RET.), is an honor graduate of the U.S. Naval Academy and received a master's of science degree in ocean engineering from the University of Rhode Island. He served on two SSBNs and five SSNs, commanding USS *Pargo* (SSN650), and was the deputy commander and the chief staff officer of Submarine Development Squadron 12. Following retirement from the Navy in 1985, Captain Patton founded Submarine Tactics and Technology, Inc. For three years he was the technical consultant to Paramount Pictures for the script and production of the movie *Hunt for Red October*. Captain Patton has published papers in *Aerospace & Defense Science, Air Power Journal, Comparative Strategy, Defense Science, Jane's International Defense Review, Naval Engineers Journal*, USNI *Proceedings, Naval War College Review*, the Army War College journal *Parameters, Sea Technology, Strategic Review*, and *Submarine Review* of the Naval Submarine League.

CMDCM (SS/AW) SHAWN A. CAPPELLANO-SARVER enlisted in the Navy in January 1981. He has served on USS *George Washington Carver* (SSBN 656), USS *Philadelphia* (SSN 690), USS *Richard B. Russell* (SSN 687), USS *Cheyenne* (SSN 773), and USS *Memphis* (SSN 691). Master Chief Cappellano-Sarver earned a bachelor of science in business from University of the State of New York in 1996. In 2005 he was selected as one of the first four command master chiefs to ever attend the Naval War College, graduating in March 2006 with a master's of art in strategic studies and national defense. He is qualified in submarines and aviation warfare and is currently serving as a command master chief in Carrier Air Wing 5, Naval Air Facility Atsugi, Japan.

CAPT. PETER M. SWARTZ, USN (RET.), is a senior analyst at the Center for Strategic Studies (CSS) of the CNA Corporation (CNAC). While serving on active duty he was Special Assistant to Chairman of the Joint Chiefs of Staff Gen. Colin Powell during the first Gulf War, and director of Defense Operations at the U.S. Mission to NATO in Brussels during the Warsaw Pact collapse. Throughout the early and mid-1980s he was a principal author of and spokesman for the Reagan administration's "Maritime Strategy." As a junior officer, he served two tours in Vietnam as an advisor with the Vietnamese navy. He holds a B.A. with honors in international relations from Brown University, an M.A. in international affairs from the Johns Hopkins Nitze School of Advanced International Studies (SAIS), and an M.Phil. in political science from Columbia University. He has authored numerous journal articles and lectured at several military and civilian colleges and universities in the United States and in Europe.

PROF. TOSHI YOSHIHARA is a professor in the Strategy and Policy Department at the U.S. Naval War College. He is also a senior research fellow at the Institute for Foreign Policy Analysis (IFPA) in Cambridge, Massachusetts. Dr. Yoshihara recently served as a visiting professor in the Department of Strategy at the Air War College in Montgomery, Alabama. His research interests include U.S. alliances in the Asia-Pacific region, China's military modernization, security dynamics on the Korean Peninsula, Japan's defense policy, and China-Taiwan relations. Dr. Yoshihara's current research agenda focuses on the influence of geopolitics in Asia, China's long-term maritime strategy, the geostrategic dimensions of Korean unification, and Taiwan's civil-military relations. He recently coauthored several articles on various aspects of Chinese maritime strategy in *Comparative Strategy*, *The Naval War College Review*, *Issues and Studies*, and *Orbis*. He is a coauthor of a monograph titled *Alliance Diversification and the Future of the U.S.-Korean Security Relationship* (May 2004). He has published articles in *Survival*, *The Washington Quarterly*, *Orbis*, *Issues and Studies*, and the *Naval War College Review*. Dr. Yoshihara holds a Ph.D. in international relations from the Fletcher School of Law and Diplomacy, Tufts University, and an M.A. in international relations from Johns Hopkins SAIS.

The Editors

PROF. ANDREW S. ERICKSON is assistant professor in the Strategic Research Department at the U.S. Naval War College. Erickson recently completed his Ph.D. dissertation at Princeton on Chinese aerospace development. Erickson previously worked for Science Applications International Corporation (SAIC) as a Chinese translator and technical analyst. He has also worked at the U.S. Embassy in Beijing, the U.S. Consulate in Hong Kong, the U.S. Senate, and the White House. He is proficient in Mandarin Chinese and Japanese and has traveled extensively in Asia. Erickson graduated magna cum laude from Amherst College with a B.A. in history and political science and received an M.A. from Princeton in international relations and comparative politics. His research, which focuses on East Asian defense, foreign policy, and technology issues, has been published in *Comparative Strategy*, *Chinese Military Update*, *Space Policy*, *Naval War College Review*, *Undersea Warfare*, and *Journal of Strategic Studies*.

PROF. LYLE J. GOLDSTEIN is an associate professor in the Strategic Research Department of the U.S. Naval War College in Newport, Rhode Island. He teaches and writes about issues in East Asian security, focusing on energy, naval, and nuclear issues. Recent research has been published in such journals as *China Quarterly*, *Jane's Intelligence Review*, *Joint Force Quarterly*, *Journal of Contemporary China*, *Journal of Strategic Studies*, *International Security*, and IISS *Survival*. His first book, which draws heavily on China's nuclear history to examine proliferation crises in historical perspective, was published by Stanford University Press in 2005. He is proficient in both Chinese and Russian and has a Ph.D. in political science from Princeton University and an M.A. from Johns Hopkins SAIS. He has also worked in the Office of the Secretary of Defense.

PROF. WILLIAM S. MURRAY is an associate research professor in the Research and Analysis Division of the Naval War College's War Game Department. He received a B.S. in electrical engineering from SUNY Buffalo in 1983 and a master of arts degree from the Naval War College in 1994. A retired submariner, he has conducted SSN deployments in both the Atlantic and Pacific oceans and qualified to command nuclear-powered submarines. Professor Murray has published articles in *International Security*, the U.S. Army War College *Parameters*, *Comparative Strategy*, USNI *Proceedings*, *Jane's Intelligence Review*, and *Undersea Warfare*.

PROF. ANDREW R. WILSON is professor of strategy and policy at the United States Naval War College and received his Ph.D. in history and East Asian languages from Harvard University. He is the author of numerous articles on Chinese military history, Chinese sea power, Sun Tzu's *Art of War*, as well as the Chinese diaspora. He is also the author or editor of two books on the Chinese overseas, *Ambition and Identity: Chinese Merchant-Elites in Colonial Manila, 1885–1916* and *The Chinese in the Caribbean*. Recently he has been involved in editing a multivolume history of the China War, 1937–45; a conference volume titled *War and Virtual War*; and is completing a new translation of Sun Tzu's *Art of War*.

Index